To the Student

This text was created to provide you with a high-quality educational resource. As a publisher specializing in college texts for business and economics, our goal is to provide you with learning materials that will serve you well in your college studies and throughout your career.

The educational process involves learning, retention, and the application of concepts and principles. You can accelerate your learning efforts by utilizing the supplements accompanying this text:

- *Study Guide for Chapters 1–14*
- *Study Guide for Chapters 15–28*
- *Working Papers for Chapters 1–14*
- *Working Papers for Chapters 15–28*
- *Three manual Practice Sets:* *Dominion Lighting Company*
  The Aspen Mountain Camping Equipment Company
  Kelly Company
- *Dominion and Aspen Practice Sets also available in computerized form*
- *Electronic Spreadsheet Program for Chapters 1–14 and 15–28 by Wanlass*
- *It's Your Business by Saftner and Cranor*
- *It's Your Business, Too, by Saftner and Cranor*
- *Visible Accounting Cycle by Wanlass*
- *Principles of Accounting SCOREBUILDER, Volume I, by Baldwin*
- *Principles of Accounting SCOREBUILDER, Volume II, by Baldwin and Pattison*

These learning aids are designed to improve your performance and the course by highlighting key points in the text and providing you with assistance in mastering basic concepts.

Check your local bookstore, or ask the manager to place an order for you today.

We at Irwin sincerely hope that this text package will assist you in reaching your goals both now and in the future.

Volume I
Fourth Edition

Accounting Principles

Volume I
Fourth Edition
Accounting Principles

Hermanson ▪ Edwards ▪ Salmonson

Roger H. Hermanson, Ph.D., CPA

Regents' Professor of Accounting
Ernst & Whinney Professor
School of Accountancy
Georgia State University

James Don Edwards, Ph.D., CPA

J. M. Tull Professor of Accounting
J. M. Tull School of Accounting
University of Georgia

R. F. Salmonson, Ph.D., CPA

Professor Emeritus of Accounting
Michigan State University

EDUCATION POLICY & DEVELOPMENT

AMERICAN
BANKERS
ASSOCIATION

1120 Connecticut Avenue, N.W.
Washington, D.C. 20036

DOW JONES-IRWIN
Homewood, Illinois 60430

Cover photo: *David Bentley*

© RICHARD D. IRWIN, INC., 1980, 1983, 1986, 1987, and 1989

Editor: *Tony Frankos*
Project editor: *Karen Smith*
Production manager: *Ann Cassady*
Cover designer: *Tara L. Bazata/Jeanne M. Oswald*
Compositor: *Better Graphics, Inc.*
Typeface: *11/12 Times Roman*
Printer: *Von Hoffmann Press, Inc.*

ISBN 1-55623-392-2 (ABA edition)

Printed in the United States of America

1 2 3 4 5 6 7 8 9 0 VH 7 6 5 4 3 2 1 0

Preface

This fourth edition of *Accounting Principles* reflects a substantial revision from the previous edition. Numerous reviewer comments resulted in improvements in almost every chapter. The important topic of ethics has been added throughout the text because of its recent emphasis in business.

This text is for use in introductory accounting courses, whether conducted in colleges and universities or in business settings. We recognize that people taking the first-year accounting course seek various careers. Some may choose accounting as a profession, while others will select a different career. All who study from this text will find the ability to use and interpret accounting information valuable in both their professional and personal lives.

Accounting Principles covers both financial and managerial accounting topics and serves as a foundation for subsequent courses in accounting and business. We assume that students using this text have a limited understanding of business concepts. Thus, whenever new terms and concepts are introduced, they are defined, illustrated, and fully explained.

■ NEW FEATURES IN THIS EDITION

- In the Introduction, a discussion of ethics in the accounting profession and a business decision problem involving ethics were added.
- In Chapter 1, a statement of owner's equity was added to show the connection between the income statement and the balance sheet.
- A new diagram showing normal balances appears in Chapter 2.
- Chapter 3 reflects minor changes in illustrations and adjustments involving interest expense and interest revenue.
- A section showing ledger account balances after closing, an Appendix to Chapter 4 in the previous edition, was moved into the chapter.
- A new microcomputer appendix was added to Chapter 6. This appendix, written by personnel from a big-eight accounting firm, discusses the many uses of microcomputers in accounting practice.
- In Chapter 7, illustrations of a purchase requisition and a purchase order were added to strengthen the coverage of internal control. Also, a business decision problem involving kiting was added.
- Chapter 8 underwent substantial revision. Account titles for entries involving uncollectible accounts were changed, accounting procedures for notes receivable discounted were simplified, and accounting for credit card charges was improved.

- In Chapter 9, an illustration showing the use of the LIFO perpetual method and a new business decision problem involving ethics as applied to inventories were added.
- Several new illustrations and a new ethics business decision problem involving the use of depreciation methods were added to Chapter 10.
- Chapter 12 on payroll accounting has been expanded to include a thorough discussion of current liabilities, including clearly determinable, estimated, and contingent liabilities. End-of-chapter material on current liabilities is also new.
- International accounting—an important topic in accounting today—is now covered in an Appendix to Chapter 13. We believe that this coverage is the most complete of any introductory text. This Appendix will assist in meeting the accreditation standards of the American Assembly of Collegiate Schools of Business regarding internationalizing the curriculum.
- Chapter 16 includes three new items: a discussion and illustration of the effect of discontinued operations, a statement of changes in stockholders' equity, and an ethics business decision problem.
- In the Appendix to Chapter 17, the coverage of future value was expanded. Some interesting exercises concerning present and future values of cash flows to and from a state lottery were added to further illustrate the concepts.
- The order of Chapters 19 and 20 was reversed. Chapter 19 covers financial statement analysis, and Chapter 20 covers the new important statement of cash flows. An illustration of "cash flow per share" (not for publication in the financial statements) was added to Chapter 19. Chapter 20 was revised to include the direct method of calculating cash flows from operating activities. The procedures for completing the work sheet under the indirect method were simplified. These changes in Chapter 20 substantially enhance its teachability and completely conform to the terminology used in *FASB Statement No. 95*. Appendix C at the end of the text shows the consolidated cash flow statements for Eli Lilly and Company using the indirect method.
- Coverage of job order and process costing (Chapter 22 in the previous edition) was divided into two chapters (Chapters 22 and 23). Manufacturing overhead costs have been assigned to production on a machine-hour basis to a greater extent to conform to modern practice.
- A new Appendix was added to Chapter 23 illustrating the FIFO method for process costing. Some reviewers prefer this method to the average cost method used in the chapter.
- The chapter on short-term decision making (Chapter 26), now precedes the chapter on budgeting (formerly Chapter 25, now Chapter 27). The short-term decision-making chapter includes a new section on distribution cost analysis and a new Appendix on allocating service center costs to operating departments. The chapter on budgeting contains a short discussion on the effects of zero base budgeting and just-in-time inventory policy on budgeting.
- The chapters on managerial accounting were further modernized in this edition and received high praise from reviewers.
- Coverage of federal income taxes and inflation accounting have been

moved to appendixes at the end of the text. This accommodates instructors who omit these topics.

- A new Appendix D contains the codes of ethics of both the American Institute of Certified Public Accountants and the National Association of Accountants. Reading this appendix will help students understand the high standards of behavior expected of accountants. News reports on matters such as the insider trading scandal on Wall Street and the defense industry scandal underscore the importance of communicating ethical considerations to students.

■ SPECIAL FEATURES THAT ENHANCE READABILITY

- Introductions have been improved. We continue to work at making the introductions both interesting reading and helpful previews to the chapters. Students discover in the first paragraph of each chapter what the chapter contains and how the contents fit into the accounting process. The introductions give the text continuity and demonstrate the relationship between accounting concepts.

- Each chapter has a section entitled "Understanding the Learning Objectives." These overviews enable students to determine how well they have accomplished the learning objectives listed at the beginning of the chapter. In 1974, we were the first authors to include learning objectives in an accounting text. Because of their usefulness as a learning aid, we now rely on them throughout the teaching package. In this edition, they now appear as marginal notes throughout the chapter. In the supplements, they are included in the Examination Booklet, the Instructor's Resource Guide, the Computerized Test Bank, and the Student Study Guide.

- Improvements in the text's organization reflect feedback from adopters, suggestions by reviewers, and a serious study of the learning process itself by the authors and editors. New material is introduced only after the stage has been set by transitional paragraphs between topic headings. Transitions provide students with the reasons for proceeding to the new material, and they explain the progression of topics within the chapter.

- Without business experience, students sometimes lack a frame of reference for relating to accounting concepts and business transactions. In this edition we sought to involve students in more real-life business applications as we introduced and explained the material.

- A "Business Situation for Discussion" for each chapter is located in the Student Study Guide. These situations, taken from articles in current business periodicals such as *The Wall Street Journal, Business Week,* and *Management Accounting,* either relate to material covered in that chapter or present other useful information. These real-world examples demonstrate the business relevance of accounting.

- We retained and revised our popular "Business Decision Problems" at the end of each chapter. These problems give students an opportunity to apply their newly learned accounting concepts to management situations in the business world. Several of these problems now deal with ethics.

- Numerous illustrations adapted from *Accounting Trends & Techniques* show the frequency of use in business of various accounting techniques. Scattered throughout the text, these illustrations give students real-world data to consider while learning about various accounting techniques.
- Special attention was paid to improve the book's teaching effectiveness. Specifically:

  1. Key terms are set in a second color for emphasis.
  2. End-of-chapter glossaries list the page number where the new term was first introduced and defined.
  3. A description of each exercise and problem is located beside it in the left-hand margin.
  4. The use of learning objectives has been extended throughout each chapter and in the supplements.
  5. Four comprehensive problems are included. One comprehensive review problem at the end of Chapter 4 and another at the end of Chapter 6 serve as "mini-practice sets" to test all material covered to that point. Two comprehensive budgeting problems are included at the end of the budgeting chapter (Chapter 27).

■ LEARNING AIDS FOR THE STUDENT—SUPPLEMENTARY MATERIAL

Study Guides. Two comprehensive study guides were developed in cooperation with Professor Gayle Rayburn, Memphis State University. Included for each chapter are learning objectives, a reference outline, a chapter review, a different demonstration problem and solution than is shown in the text, matching and true-false questions, completion questions and exercises, multiple-choice questions, a business situation for discussion, and solutions to all exercises and questions.

Working Papers. Two sets of working papers (one for each half of the text) are available for completing assigned problems and business decision problems. In many instances, the working papers are partially filled in to reduce the "pencil pushing" required to solve the problems, yet are not so complete as to reduce the learning impact. The format and spacing used in the working papers are similar to the Instructor's Solutions Manual and to the transparencies.

Check Figures. A list of check figures gives key amounts for the A and B Series Problems and the Business Decision Problems in the text.

Manual Practice Sets. Three manual practice sets are available. Practice Set I, revised by Brenda Hartman of North Harris County College, Texas, illustrates special journals and includes a work sheet for a retailing company. Practice Set II, revised by Professors Sondra Laemmle and Rebecca Phillips of the University of Louisville, illustrates the use of business papers for a retailing company. Practice Set III, revised by Herbert A. O'Keefe, Georgia Southern College, illustrates the accounting system used by a manufacturing company. Practice Sets I and II may be used any time after Chapter 8 has been covered, and Practice Set III may be used any time after Chapter 21.

Computer Supplements. The following computer supplements are available:

Computerized Versions of Practice Sets I and II. Some students benefit from first working a practice set manually to test their accounting knowledge, then working the computerized version to see how much time and effort is saved.

Tutorial to Accompany Principles of Accounting. This computerized tutorial presents the problems in the Study Guide in an electronic format, with correction and reinforcement provided. The student selects a chapter for study and determines the number and type of questions to review. Explanations and calculations are provided as needed. It is available for use with the IBM PC.

The Visible Accounting Cycle—General Ledger Software by John Wanlass. Available for use with the IBM PC, this program helps students understand financial statements by showing a visible audit trail. Students learn to convert a manual accounting system to a computer system while working with a service company. Based on source documents, students account for merchandising transactions and process them. A concise manual contains examples and problems. The program can be used for any transaction-based problem, not just the ones in the manual.

Electronic Spreadsheet Program (ESP) by John Wanlass. For use with the IBM PC and Lotus 1-2-3, these spreadsheet exercises are built around problems in the text.

It's Your Business by Donald V. Saftner and Rosalind Cranor. This 12-month General Ledger practice set takes the student through the accounting process from journalizing to statement preparation and statement analysis. Each month of the practice set introduces new concepts and procedures and integrates them with the concepts presented in previous months, so they all lead to a better understanding of the accounting process. The practice set may be used with problems from the text or to computerize manual practice sets. It is available for use with the IBM PC. *It's Your Business, Too,* an essentially similar computerized practice set by Saftner and Cranor, is an available alternative.

■ SPECIAL FEATURES THAT MAKE THIS EDITION MORE TEACHABLE

- We provide instructors with a vast amount of resource material within the text: one of the largest selections of end-of-chapter exercises and problems available; two comprehensive review problems (after Chapters 4 and 6) that allow students to review all major concepts; two comprehensive budgeting problems at the end of chapter 27; from one to three business decision problems per chapter (some emphasizing ethics); and financial statements of Eli Lilly and Company that can be used throughout the course to illustrate financial reporting.
- All end-of-chapter problem materials have been thoroughly revised. Approximately two new exercises were added in each chapter.

- Demonstration problems and their solutions are included for each chapter. A demonstration problem and solution, different from those in the text, appear in each chapter of the Study Guide. These problems show students how to work the type of problems they will complete as homework.
- In Chapter 5, we present two variations of the closing process: merchandise-related expense accounts are treated first as closing entries, then as adjusting entries. Instructors seem to be evenly split on their "favorite" procedure and can choose which method(s) to teach.

Teaching Aids for the Instructor—Supplementary Material

A complete package of supplemental teaching aids contains all you need to efficiently and effectively teach the course.

Instructor's Resource Guide and Teaching Transparencies.   This supplement, developed for a previous edition, is helpful both to new instructors of accounting and to new adopters of our test. The instructor's guide now contains sample syllabi for both quarter- and semester-basis courses. Revised for this edition, each chapter contains (1) a summary of major concepts that can serve as a handy lecture organizer; (2) learning objectives from the text repeated for the instructor's convenience; (3) an outline of the chapter; and (4) detailed lecture notes that also refer to specific and end-of-chapter problem materials illustrating the concepts. Any of these formats can serve as effective teaching tools, depending on the instructor's personal preference. Also included are (5) teaching transparency masters for each chapter. (The actual teaching transparencies are available free from the publisher.) Each chapter concludes with (6) a summary of the estimated time, level of difficulty, and content of each exercise and problem, useful in deciding which items to cover in class or to assign as homework.

Solutions Manual.   The solutions manual contains detailed answers to the exercises, questions, problems (Series A and B), comprehensive review problems, and business decision problems for each chapter. The use of large type and paper matched to the students' Working Papers facilitates grading.

Transparencies.   Acetate transparencies of solutions to all exercises and all problems (now including business decision problems) have been increased in size and clarity and are available free to adopters. These transparencies, while useful in many situations, are especially helpful when covering problems involving work sheets and in large classroom situations. The use of new large and bold type enhances student viewing.

Examination Material

In this fourth edition, we provide adopters with four different formats of examination material. Instructors need only select the exam format that best fits their personal needs and resources and then request a copy from their local BPI/RDI sales representative. Any and all exams are available free upon adoption and by request.

Pre-Printed Achievement Tests.   Three series of "class-tested" achievement tests—A, B, and C—have been prepared and printed, and are available in bulk to adopters. Each series consists of six one-hour exams and two two-hour final exams. In each series, three of the one-hour exams and a final exam cover Chapters 1–14; the other three one-hour exams and a final exam cover Chapters 15–28. All questions are multiple choice for ease in grading.

Examination Book. This test bank, expanded and revised significantly in this edition, contains over 2,000 questions and problems to choose from in preparing examinations. The exam book contains true-false questions, multiple-choice questions, and short problems for each chapter. These questions and problems are classified by the learning objectives to which they relate. The multiple-choice questions may also be used to freshen up the Achievement Tests, while the short problems may be used to supplement or replace these questions for those instructors who object to the sole use of multiple-choice questions.

CompuTest. For instructors who have microcomputers, this form of exam preparation is convenient and effective. CompuTest is a microcomputer version of the Examination Book; it is available for use on the IBM PC, Apple II +, and Apple IIe. CompuTest can be used to prepare examinations by selecting questions and problems in a variety of ways. Instructors may even add their own exam material to the test bank. CompuTest itself has been substantially improved, is menu-driven, and has a well-documented instruction manual.

TeleTest. TeleTest is an in-house testing service that will prepare your exams. TeleTest has its own bank of examination questions and problems (taken from the Examination Book). To use TeleTest, all the instructor needs to do is call the Irwin 800 number, ask for TeleTest, and give the required information to RDI's TeleTest service representative. Or the instructor can mail in the required information. Either way, within 72 working hours of receiving the required information, the instructor will be mailed a copy of the exam and an answer key.

■ SPECIAL FEATURES OF THIS EDITION THAT HELP STUDENTS LEARN ACCOUNTING

Students often come into accounting principles courses feeling anxious about learning the material. Recognizing that apprehension, we studied ways to make learning easier and came up with some helpful ideas on how to make this edition work even better for students. Our "study of learning" resulted in the following improvements in *Accounting Principles*, fourth edition. Specifically we:

- Organized ideas for improved flow of material. The improved introductions preview the chapter material, letting students know exactly where they have been and where they are going. Transitional paragraphs are used to improve the flow and continuity of material. Carefully worded and designed headings are strategically placed in the chapters as signposts. Every chapter ends with a reference to what the next chapter covers and how it relates to the chapter just covered.
- Included examples to associate concepts with experience. Through-

out the text we used examples taken from everyday life to relate an accounting concept being introduced or discussed to students' experiences.

- Use an informal style and the active voice. Our research showed that for an accounting principles text today, an informal writing style and the active voice are more effective for learning than the formal style and passive voice. In this edition, we make more use of the pronoun *you,* to involve students with the text material.
- Added several new graphics. Learning is enhanced when a picture reinforces a verbal understanding of new material. Wherever possible, we have added graphic illustrations to help explain accounting concepts to students. For example, in Chapter 10, we have illustrated the four challenges in recording the life history of a depreciable asset.

We are indebted to many individuals for reviewing the manuscript of the fourth edition. In addition to those listed on the acknowledgments page, we are especially indebted to colleagues and students at our respective universities for their helpful suggestions.

Roger H. Hermanson
James Don Edwards
R. F. Salmonson

Note to the Student

Professor Gayle Rayburn of Memphis State University has participated with the authors in revising the comprehensive two-volume student Study Guide to assist you in understanding the material in this text. Students who used the study guide in the previous edition found it to be extremely helpful in maximizing their understanding and class performance. Each chapter of the Study Guide is keyed to a chapter of the text and provides learning objectives, a reference outline, a detailed chapter review, a demonstration problem and answer, matching questions concerning important new terms and concepts, completion questions and exercises, and true-false and multiple-choice questions. Answers to all exercises and questions are included in the Study Guide to provide you with immediate feedback on your responses. Explanations are also given for the answers to many of the true-false and multiple-choice questions. This student Study Guide, published by Richard D. Irwin, Inc., is available through your college bookstore. If it is not in stock, please ask your bookstore manager to order a copy for you.

R.H.H.
J.D.E.
R.F.S.

Acknowledgments

Many instructors and students have made comments and suggestions that have helped us significantly in the preparation of this and all previous editions of this book. In particular, we thank the following faculty who provided helpful suggestions for the fourth edition: Charles D. Bailey, *Florida State University;* Dixon Cooper, *Austin College;* Rosalind Cranor, *Virginia Polytechnic Institute and State University;* Irwin Fine, *Austin Community College;* Kimberly Galligan, *Touche Ross, Milwaukee;* Daniel Galvin, *Diablo Valley Community College;* Ellsworth C. "Bud" Granger, Jr., *Mankato State University;* James Hansen, *North Dakota State University;* Brenda Hartman, *North Harris County College;* Jean Marie Hudson, *Lamar University;* Sondra Laemmle, *University of Louisville;* Terry J. Nunley, *University of North Carolina at Charlotte;* Rebecca L. Phillips, *University of Louisville;* Sharon L. Robinson, *Frostburg State University;* and Pearl Sandelman, *DeAnza College.*

We also wish to acknowledge the assistance of our colleagues and students at our respective universities who have provided many helpful suggestions for improvement in the text and supplements. Our families also provided needed support and showed great patience during the revision process.

Special thanks to George T. Martin and members of the American Bankers Association for their helpful comments.

We would be remiss not to express a special thanks to the production staff at Irwin who gave so much of themselves for this book. Of particular importance are Loretta Scholten, Karen Smith, and Debby Jones, without whom it would have been impossible to complete this project.

R.H.H.
J.D.E.
R.F.S.

Contents

Volume I
Fourth Edition
Accounting Principles

PART

1

Accounting:
The Language of Business

Introduction: The Accounting Environment

After studying this introduction, you should be able to:

1. Define accounting.
2. Describe the functions performed by accountants.
3. Describe employment opportunities in accounting.
4. Differentiate between financial and managerial accounting.
5. Identify the five organizations that have a role in the development of financial accounting standards.
6. Define and use correctly the new terms in the glossary.

Of all the business knowledge you have learned or will learn, the study of accounting will probably be the most useful. Your financial and economic decisions as a student and consumer involve accounting information; and when you file income tax returns, accounting information will help determine your taxes payable. Understanding the discipline of accounting will also influence many of your future professional decisions. You cannot escape the effects of accounting information on your personal and professional life.

Accounting information is used by every profit-seeking business organization that has economic resources such as money, machinery, and buildings. While accounting has been called the *language of business*, it also serves as the language that provides financial information about not-for-profit organizations such as governments, churches, charities, fraternities, and hospitals. This text concentrates on the use of accounting as it relates to the business firm.

The accounting system used by a profit-seeking business may be viewed as an information system designed to provide relevant financial information on the resources of a business and the effects of the use of these resources. Information is relevant if it has some bearing on a decision to be made. This relevant information is presented in financial statements.[1] In preparing these statements, accountants consider the types of users of the information, such as owners and creditors, and the kinds of decisions they make that require financial information.

As a background for studying accounting, this Introduction will define accounting and list the functions performed by accountants. You will learn about the employment opportunities in accounting and be able to differentiate between financial and managerial accounting. Accounting information must conform to certain standards. You will be introduced to the five prominent organizations contributing to these standards. As you continue your study of accounting in the chapters of this text, accounting as the language of business will also become your language as you realize you are constantly exposed to accounting information in your everyday life.

■ ACCOUNTING DEFINED

Objective 1:
Define accounting.

The American Accounting Association—one of the prominent accounting authorities discussed later in this Introduction—defines **accounting** as **"the process of identifying, measuring, and communicating economic information to permit informed judgments and decisions by the users of the information."**[2] This information is primarily financial and generally stated in money terms. Accounting, then, is a measurement and communication process used to report on the activity of profit-seeking business organizations and not-for-profit organizations.

Accounting is often confused with bookkeeping. Bookkeeping is a mechanical process that records the routine economic activities of a business. Accounting includes bookkeeping but goes well beyond it in scope. Accountants analyze and interpret financial information, prepare financial statements, conduct audits, design accounting systems, prepare special business and financial studies, prepare forecasts and budgets, and provide tax services.

Specifically, the accounting process (also called the *accounting cycle*) consists of the following groups of functions (see Illustration 0.1):

Objective 2:
Describe the
functions
performed by
accountants.

1. Accountants **observe** many events and **identify** and **measure** in financial terms (dollars) those events considered evidence of economic activity. (These three functions are often collectively referred to as *analyze*.) The purchase and sale of goods and services are examples of economic activities.

---

[1] When first studying any discipline, new terms are encountered. Usually these terms are set in boldface color and defined at their first occurrence. However, sometimes it is more feasible not to define a term at its first occurrence. This is true with the term *financial statements*. It is defined later in the Introduction and set in boldface color. The boldface color terms are also listed and defined at the end of this Introduction, or in the case of the chapters, at the end of the chapter. After the definition of the term in the term list, a page number is given in parentheses indicating where the term is discussed in the chapter.

[2] American Accounting Association, *A Statement of Basic Accounting Theory* (Evanston, Ill., 1966), p. 1.

Illustration 0.1

Accounting Functions Performed by Accountants

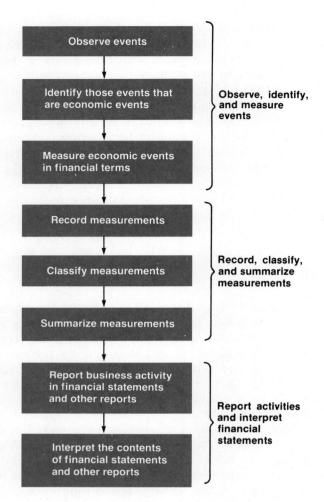

2. Next, the economic events are **recorded, classified** into meaningful groups, and **summarized** for conciseness.
3. Accountants **report** on business activity by preparing financial statements and special reports. Often accountants are asked to **interpret** these statements and reports for various groups such as management and creditors. Interpretation may involve determining how the business is performing compared to prior years and other similar businesses.

■ EMPLOYMENT OPPORTUNITIES IN ACCOUNTING

Objective 3: Describe employment opportunities in accounting.

Accounting is an old profession. Records of business transactions have been prepared for centuries. However, only during the last half-century has accounting been accepted as a profession with the same importance as the medical and legal professions. Today, in the United States, well over a million people are employed as accountants, and several million are employed in accounting-related positions. Typically, accountants are employed in public accounting, management (industrial) accounting, and governmental or other not-for-profit accounting.

Public Accounting

The **public accounting** profession offers accounting and related services for a fee to companies, other organizations, and the general public. An accountant may become a **certified public accountant (CPA)**. A CPA is an accountant who has passed an examination prepared and graded by the American Institute of Certified Public Accountants (AICPA) and has met certain other requirements, including being licensed by the state. These requirements vary by state, but states typically require a CPA to have completed certain courses in accounting, worked a certain number of years in public accounting, and lived in that state a certain length of time before taking the examination. When all requirements are met, the accountant may be licensed by the state to practice as an independent professional.

The public accounting profession in the United States is made up of the "Big-Eight" international CPA firms, several national firms, many regional firms, and numerous local firms. The "Big-Eight" firms include: Arthur Andersen & Co.; Arthur Young & Co.; Coopers & Lybrand; Deloitte, Haskins & Sells; Ernst & Whinney; Peat Marwick Main & Co.; Price Waterhouse & Co.; and Touche Ross & Co. Generally, these public accounting firms provide auditing, tax, and management advisory (or consulting) services.

Auditing.   When a business seeks a loan or attempts to have its securities traded on a stock exchange, the business usually is required to provide statements about its financial affairs. Users of a company's statements are more assured that the statements are presented fairly when the company has been audited by a CPA. For this reason, companies hire CPA firms to conduct an examination (**independent audit**) of their accounting and related records. **Independent auditors** of the CPA firm check some of the company's records by contacting external sources; for example, the accountant may contact a bank to verify the cash balances of the client. After completing a company audit, independent auditors are able to give an **independent auditor's opinion or report** as to whether or not the company's financial statements fairly (equitably) report the economic performance and condition of the business. As you will learn in the section "Management (or Industrial) Accounting," auditors **within** a business also conduct audits, but these audits are not independent audits.

Tax Services.   CPAs often provide expert advice on tax planning and on the preparation of federal, state, and local tax returns. The objective in preparing tax returns is to use legal means to minimize the amount of taxes paid. Since almost every major business decision has a tax impact, clients also need tax planning so they will know the tax effects of each financial decision.

Management Advisory (or Consulting) Services.   Providing management advisory services is the fastest growing area of service for most large CPA firms and for many smaller CPA firms. Management frequently identifies projects for which it decides to retain the services of a CPA. For example, management may seek help in selecting new computer hardware and software. Also, the auditing services provided by CPAs often result in suggestions to clients on how to improve their operations. For example, CPAs might suggest improvements in the design and installation of an accounting system, the electronic processing of accounting data, inventory control, budgeting, or financial planning. In addition, a relatively new area of service provided by CPAs is financial planning, often for the executives of audit clients. These executives are usually so busy with company matters that they frequently neglect their own personal financial affairs.

Management (or Industrial) Accounting

In contrast to public accountants who provide accounting services for many clients, **management accountants** provide accounting services for a single business. Some companies employ only one management accountant, while other companies employ many. In a company with many management accountants, the executive officer in charge of the accounting activity is often called a **controller.**

Management accountants may or may not be CPAs. If these accountants pass an examination prepared and graded by the Institute of Certified Management Accountants (ICMA), an affiliate of the National Association of Accountants, and meet certain other requirements, they become **Certified Management Accountants (CMAs).** The National Association of Accountants is an organization primarily consisting of management accountants employed in private industry.

Management accountants may specialize in one particular job or task. For example, some may specialize in measuring and controlling costs, others in budgeting—the development of plans relating to future operations. Many management accountants become specialists in the design and installation of computerized accounting systems; others are **internal auditors** employed to conduct **internal audits** to see that the policies and procedures established by the business are followed in its divisions and departments. This last group of management accountants may earn the designation of **certified internal auditor (CIA).** The CIA certificate is granted by the Institute of Internal Auditors (IIA) after the accountant has successfully completed an examination prepared and graded by the Institute and has met certain other requirements.

Governmental and Other Not-for-Profit Accounting

Many accountants, including CPAs, are employed in **governmental or other not-for-profit accounting.** These accountants have essentially the same educational background and training as accountants in public and management (or industrial) accounting.

Governmental accountants are employed by government agencies at the federal, state, and local levels. Often these accountants perform accounting duties relating to the control of tax revenues and expenditures. Government agencies that regulate business activity—such as a state public service commission that regulates public utilities (e.g., telephone company, electric company, etc.)—usually employ governmental accountants who can review and evaluate the utilities' financial statements and rate increase requests. FBI agents who have training as accountants find their accounting background useful in investigating criminals involved in illegal business activities, such as drugs or gambling.

Not-for-profit organizations such as churches, charities, fraternities, and universities need the services of accountants to record and account for funds received and disbursed. Universities and colleges hire accountants (CPAs, CMAs, and CIAs who usually have a Ph.D. degree) to teach accounting to students and conduct research on accounting issues.

■ FINANCIAL ACCOUNTING VERSUS MANAGERIAL ACCOUNTING

Objective 4:
Differentiate between
financial and mana-
gerial accounting.

An accounting information system provides data to help the decision-making process of individuals outside the business as well as inside the business. The decision-making individuals **outside** the business **are affected in some way by the performance of the business,** while the decision-making individuals **inside** the business **are responsible for the performance of the business.** For this reason, accounting is often divided into two categories: financial accounting and managerial accounting. This section discusses the distinction between financial and managerial accounting. Note, however, that financial accounting information is used in both financial accounting and managerial accounting.

Financial Accounting

Financial accounting information is intended primarily for external use, while managerial accounting information is intended for internal use. Stockholders and creditors are examples of people outside a company who want and need financial accounting information. These outside people make decisions on matters pertaining to the entire company, such as whether to extend credit to a company or to invest in a company. Consequently, financial accounting information relates to the company as a whole, while managerial accounting information focuses on the parts or segments of the company.

There are several different groups of external users of accounting information. Each group has different interests in the company and wants answers to different questions. The groups and some of their possible questions are:

1. **Owners and prospective owners.**   Has the company had satisfactory income on its total investment? Should an investment be made in this company? Should the present investment be increased, decreased, or retained at the same level? Can the company install costly pollution control equipment and still remain profitable?
2. **Creditors and lenders.**   Should a loan be granted to the company? Will the company be able to pay its debts as they become due?
3. **Employees and their unions.**   Does the company have the ability to pay increased wages? Is the company financially able to provide permanent employment?

4. **Customers.** Does the company offer useful products at fair prices? Will the company survive long enough to honor its product warranties?
5. **Governmental units.** Is the local public utility charging a fair rate for its services?
6. **General public.** Is the company providing useful products and gainful employment for citizens without causing serious environmental problems?

General-purpose financial statements provide most of the information needed by external users of financial accounting. These **financial statements** are formal reports providing information on a company's financial position (solvency), cash inflows and outflows, and the results of operations (profitability). Many companies publish these statements in an annual report. The **annual report** (see Appendix C at the end of the text) also contains the independent auditor's opinion as to the fairness of the financial statements, as well as information about the company's activities, products, and plans.

Financial accounting information is historical in nature, reporting on what has happened in the past. To facilitate comparisons between companies, this information must conform to certain standards or methods of presentation called **generally accepted accounting principles (GAAP).** These generally accepted accounting principles for business or governmental organizations have been developed through accounting practice or have been established by an authoritative organization. You will learn about five of these authoritative organizations in the next major section of the chapter.

Managerial Accounting

Managerial accounting information is intended for internal use; it provides special information for the managers of a company. The kind of information used by managers may range from broad, long-range planning data to detailed explanations of why actual costs varied from cost estimates.

Managerial accounting information should:

1. Relate to the part of the company that the manager oversees. For example, a production manager will want information on costs of production but not on advertising.
2. Involve planning for the future. For instance, a budget may be prepared that shows financial plans for the coming year.
3. Meet two tests: the accounting information must be useful (relevant) and must not cost more to gather than it is worth.

The purpose of managerial accounting is to generate information that a manager can use to make sound internal decisions. Internal management decisions can be classified into four major types:

1. **Financial decisions**—deciding what amounts of capital (funds) are needed to run the business and whether these funds are to be secured from owners or creditors. **Capital** used in this sense means **money** to

be used by the company to purchase resources such as machinery and buildings and to pay expenses of conducting the business.

2. **Resource allocation decisions**—deciding how the total capital of a company is to be invested, such as the amount to be invested in machinery.

3. **Production decisions**—deciding what products are to be produced, by what means, and when.

4. **Marketing decisions**—setting selling prices and advertising budgets; determining the location of a company's markets and how they are to be reached.

Managerial accounting is discussed at length in the later chapters of the text.

■ DEVELOPMENT OF FINANCIAL ACCOUNTING STANDARDS

Objective 5:
Identify the five organizations that have a role in the development of financial accounting standards.

The five organizations most influential in the establishment of generally accepted accounting principles (GAAP) for business or governmental organizations are the American Institute of Certified Public Accountants, the Financial Accounting Standards Board, the Governmental Accounting Standards Board, the Securities and Exchange Commission, and the American Accounting Association. Each organization has contributed in a different way to the development of GAAP.

American Institute of Certified Public Accountants (AICPA)

The **American Institute of Certified Public Accountants (AICPA)** is a professional organization of CPAs, many of whom are in public accounting practice. This organization has been the dominant organization in the development of accounting standards over the past half-century. In a 20-year period ending in 1959, the AICPA Committee on Accounting Procedure issued 51 *Accounting Research Bulletins* recommending certain principles or practices. From 1959 through 1973, the committee's successor, the **Accounting Principles Board (APB)**, issued 31 numbered *Opinions* that CPAs generally are required to follow. Through its monthly magazine, the *Journal of Accountancy,* its research division, and its other divisions and committees, the AICPA continues to influence the development of accounting standards and practices.

Financial Accounting Standards Board (FASB)

The **Accounting Principles Board (APB)** was replaced in 1973 by an independent, seven-member, full-time **Financial Accounting Standards Board (FASB)**. The FASB has issued numerous *Statements of Financial Accounting Standards* and interpretations of those standards. The FASB is widely accepted as the major influence *in the private sector* in the development of new financial accounting standards.

Governmental Accounting Standards Board (GASB)

The **Governmental Accounting Standards Board (GASB)** was established in 1984 with a full-time chairman and four part-time members. The GASB has issued several statements on accounting and financial reporting in the governmental area. This organization is widely accepted as the major influence in the **private sector** in the development of new governmental accounting concepts and standards. The GASB also has the authority to issue interpretations of these standards.

Securities and Exchange Commission (SEC)

Created under the Securities and Exchange Act of 1934, the **Securities and Exchange Commission (SEC)** administers a number of important acts dealing with the interstate sale of securities (stocks and bonds). The SEC has the authority to prescribe accounting and reporting practices for companies under its jurisdiction. This includes virtually every major U.S. business corporation. But rather than exercise this power, the SEC has adopted a policy of working closely with the accounting profession, especially the FASB, in the development of accounting standards. The SEC indicates to the FASB the accounting topics it believes should be addressed.

American Accounting Association (AAA)

Consisting largely of accounting educators, the **American Accounting Association (AAA)** has sought to encourage research and study at a theoretical level into the concepts, standards, and principles of accounting. One of its quarterly magazines, *The Accounting Review,* carries many articles reporting on accounting research. A new quarterly journal, *Accounting Horizons,* reports on more practical matters directly related to accounting practice. A third journal, *Issues in Accounting Education,* contains articles relating to accounting education matters. Students may join the AAA as associate members.

■ ETHICAL BEHAVIOR OF ACCOUNTANTS

Several accounting organizations have formulated codes of ethics that govern the behavior of their members. For instance, both the American Institute of Certified Public Accountants and the National Association of Accountants have formulated such codes. We have included the codes of ethics of these two organizations in Appendix D at the end of the text. By examining these codes, you will gain some understanding of the expectations that exist regarding the ethical behavior of accountants. Some business firms have also developed codes of ethics for their employees to follow.

But there is more to ethical behavior than merely making sure you are not violating a code of ethics. Most of us sense what is right and wrong. Yet many of us are tempted at times by the "get rich quick" opportunities that arise. You can read in the newspaper almost any day about public officials and business leaders who did not "do the right thing" when greed ruled over their sense of right and wrong. Slogans that seem to describe this type of behavior throughout history are: "Get yours while the getting is good"; "Do unto others before they do unto you"; and "You have only done wrong if you get caught." More appropriate slogans might be: "If it seems too good to be true, it usually is"; "There are no free lunches"; and the golden rule, "Do unto others as you would have them do unto you."

An accountant's most valuable asset is his or her reputation. Those who take the *high road* of ethical behavior are praised, honored, and sought out for their advice and other services. They also like themselves and what they represent. Occasionally, accountants do take the *low road* and suffer the consequences. They sometimes find their name in print in *The Wall Street Journal* in an unfavorable light, are scorned by their former friends and colleagues, and occasionally are removed from the profession. Fortunately, the accounting profession has many leaders who have taken the high road, gained the respect of friends and colleagues, and become role models for all of us to follow.

In certain chapters in the text, where appropriate, we have included some business decision problems designated as involving ethics. We think you will benefit from being exposed to the *situational ethics* contained in these problems.

■ *UNDERSTANDING THE LEARNING OBJECTIVES: INTRODUCTION*

1. Define accounting.

    - Accounting is the process of identifying, measuring, and communicating economic information to permit informed judgments and decisions by users of the information.

2. Describe the functions performed by accountants.

    - Accountants observe many events and identify and measure in financial terms (dollars) those events considered evidence of economic activity.
    - The economic events are recorded, classified into meaningful groups, and summarized for conciseness.
    - Accountants report on business activity by preparing financial statements and special reports. And accountants are often asked to interpret these statements and reports for various groups such as management and creditors.

3. Describe employment opportunities in accounting.

    - An accountant may be employed in public accounting and specialize in auditing, tax, or management advisory (or consulting) services.
    - Management accountants are employed by a single company and may specialize in measuring and controlling costs, budgeting, computerized accounting systems, internal auditing, or some other function.

- Other accountants are employed in government agencies or other not-for-profit organizations such as churches, charities, fraternities, and universities.
- Universities and colleges hire accountants (CPAs, CMAs, and CIAs who usually have a Ph.D. degree) to teach accounting to students and conduct research on accounting issues.

4. Differentiate between financial and managerial accounting.

- Financial accounting information is intended primarily for external use; it provides information for groups such as owners and prospective owners, creditors and lenders, employees and their unions, customers, governmental units, and the general public.
- Managerial accounting information is intended for internal use; it provides special information for the managers of the company.

5. Identify the five organizations that have a role in the development of financial accounting standards.

- American Institute of Certified Public Accountants (AICPA)—made up of persons holding the CPA certificate. The Accounting Principles Board (APB) was under the AICPA.
- Financial Accounting Standards Board (FASB)—issues FASB statements, which are the *rules* of financial accounting.
- Governmental Accounting Standards Board (GASB)—issues GASB statements, which are the *rules* of governmental accounting.
- Securities and Exchange Commission (SEC)—a government agency that has legislative authority over financial accounting standards. To date, the SEC has allowed the private sector to set the standards.
- American Accounting Association (AAA)—an organization consisting largely of accountants who teach and engage in research.

6. Define and use correctly the new terms in the glossary.

NEW TERMS USED IN THIS INTRODUCTION

Accounting   "The process of identifying, measuring, and communicating economic information to permit informed judgments and decisions by the users of the information" (3).

Accounting Principles Board (APB)   An organization created in 1959 by the AICPA and empowered to speak for it on matters of accounting principle; replaced in 1973 by the Financial Accounting Standards Board (9).

American Accounting Association (AAA)   A professional organization of accountants, many of whom are college or university professors of accounting (10).

American Institute of Certified Public Accountants (AICPA)   A professional organization of certified public accountants, many of whom are in public accounting practice (9).

Annual report   A pamphlet or document of varying length containing audited financial statements and other information about a company, distributed annually to its owners (8).

Audit (independent)   Performed by independent auditors to determine whether the financial statements of a business fairly reflect the economic performance and condition of the business (5).

Audit (internal)   Performed by accounting employees of a company to determine if company policies and procedures are being followed (6).

Certified internal auditor (CIA)   An accountant who has passed an examination prepared and graded by the Institute of Internal Auditors and who has met certain other requirements (6).

Certified Management Accountants (CMA)
Awarded to accountants who pass an examination prepared and graded by the Institute of Certified Management Accountants (ICMA) and meet certain other requirements (6).

Certified public accountant (CPA) An accountant who has passed an examination prepared and graded by the American Institute of Certified Public Accountants (AICPA) and has met certain other requirements, such as work experience in accounting and specified courses in accounting. The accountant is then awarded a CPA certificate and may be licensed by the state to practice as an independent professional (5).

Controller The executive officer in charge of a company's accounting activity (6).

Financial accounting Relates to the process of supplying financial information to parties external to the reporting entity (7).

Financial Accounting Standards Board (FASB) The major influence in the private sector in the development of new financial accounting standards (9).

Financial statements Formal reports providing information on a company's financial position (solvency), cash inflows and outflows, and the results of operations (profitability) (8).

Generally accepted accounting principles (GAAP) Accounting standards and principles that have been developed through accounting practice or have been established by an authoritative organization (8).

Governmental Accounting Standards Board (GASB) Issues statements on accounting and financial reporting in the governmental area (10).

Governmental or other not-for-profit accounting Governmental accountants are employed by government agencies at the federal, state, and local levels.

Other not-for-profit accountants record and account for receipts and disbursements for churches, charities, fraternities, and universities. Accountants in the academic segment of the accounting profession teach accounting to students and conduct research on accounting issues (6).

Independent audit See Audit (independent).

Independent auditors Certified public accountants who perform audits to determine whether the financial statements of businesses fairly reflect the economic performance and condition of these businesses (5).

Independent auditor's opinion or report The formal written statement by a certified public accountant that states whether or not the client's financial statements fairly reflect the economic performance and condition of the business (5).

Internal audit See Audit (internal).

Internal auditors Private accountants employed to see that the policies and procedures established by the business are followed in its divisions and departments (6).

Management (or industrial) accountants Provide accounting services for a single business (6).

Managerial accounting Relates to the process of supplying financial information for internal management use (8).

Public accounting Offers accounting and related services for a fee to companies, other organizations, and the general public (5).

Securities and Exchange Commission (SEC) A governmental agency created by Congress to administer acts dealing with interstate sales of securities and having the authority to prescribe the accounting and reporting practices of firms under its jurisdiction (10).

QUESTIONS

1. Define accounting. What does the term *relevant* mean when speaking of accounting information? Give an example of relevant information.

2. What is the relationship between *(a)* accounting as an information system and *(b)* economic resources?

3. What is a CPA? What are some of the services usually provided by a CPA?

4. What is the role of the accountant in private industry? What are some of the services provided by the management accountant?

5. Describe the basic difference between financial accounting and managerial accounting.

6. Name five organizations that have played or are playing an important role in the development of accounting standards. Describe each briefly.

7. What guides the ethical behavior of accountants?

BUSINESS DECISION PROBLEM (ETHICS)

Determine ethical behavior

Beth Stone is an accounting major at State University. She has a 3.8 grade point average and is a member of Beta Alpha Psi, the national accounting honor society. She has decided to pursue a career in public accounting and has had her "heart set" on being employed by CPA Firm A after graduation because it has many clients in the high-tech industry. In a conversation with the head recruiter from Firm A, Beth was told that the firm had overhired the year before and probably would be unable to make her an offer at this time. Beth decided to interview with many other CPA firms and finally accepted a position with Firm B at a salary of $30,000 plus overtime. Although she had wanted to audit companies in the high-tech industry, Firm B has few clients in that industry. Firm B does have clients in the health care industry, which is Beth's second favorite industry.

Two months after Beth had accepted the offer from Firm B and before she had started working, she received an urgent call from the recruiter at Firm A. He was unaware that she had already accepted another offer and said the firm had recently experienced some unplanned turnover in its staff. As a result, he was in a position to make her an offer of $31,000 plus overtime. He could also guarantee that she would be able to specialize in the high-tech industry and would be working on interesting jobs with some talented people.

Required: a. What are Beth's options?
                b. What should Beth do?

1

Accounting and Its Use in Business Decisions

LEARNING OBJECTIVES

After studying this chapter, you should be able to:

1. Identify and describe the three basic forms of business organizations.
2. Distinguish among the three types of business activities performed by business organizations.
3. Describe the content and purposes of the income statement, statement of owner's equity, and balance sheet.
4. State the basic accounting equation and describe its relationship to the balance sheet.
5. Analyze business transactions and determine their effects on items in the financial statements.
6. Prepare an income statement, a statement of owner's equity, and a balance sheet.
7. Define and use correctly the new terms in the glossary.

The Introduction to this text provided a background for your study of accounting. You now know how to define accounting and know the functions performed by accountants. After reading about the employment opportunities in accounting, you may have already chosen a field of accounting employment to pursue as a career. Even if you do not become an accountant, accounting information will be useful throughout your lifetime.

Now you are ready to learn about the forms of business organizations and the types of business activities they perform. Three of the financial statements used by these businesses are presented. Then you will learn about the accounting process (or accounting cycle) used to prepare those financial statements. In this accounting process, financial data—such as your daily personal purchases from businesses—are analyzed, recorded, classified, summarized, and finally reported in the financial statements of those businesses. Hopefully, as you study this chapter, you will recognize the unique, systematic nature of accounting—the language of business.

■ FORMS OF BUSINESS ORGANIZATIONS

Objective 1:
Identify and describe
the three basic forms
of business
organizations.

Accountants frequently refer to a business organization as an **accounting entity** or a **business entity.** A business entity is any business organization, such as a hardware store or grocery store, that exists as an economic unit. For accounting purposes, each business organization has an existence separate from its owner(s), creditors, employees, customers, and other businesses. This separate existence of the business organization is known as the **business entity concept.** Thus, in the accounting records of the business entity, the activities of each business should be kept separate from other businesses and the personal financial activities of the owner(s).

If, for example, you own two businesses, a physical fitness center and a horse stable, each would be considered as an independent economic business unit. You would normally keep separate accounting records for each business. Only by treating your physical fitness center and horse stable as two separate business entities could you determine that your physical fitness center is unprofitable because you are not charging enough for the use of your exercise equipment. Also, you cannot include the car you drive only for personal use as a business activity of your physical fitness center or your horse stable. However, the use of your truck to pick up feed for your horse stable is a business activity of your horse stable.

As you will see in the discussion that follows on the three forms of business organizations—single proprietorships, partnerships, and corporations—the business entity concept applies to all forms of businesses. Thus, for accounting purposes, all three business forms are separate from other business entities and from their owners. However, for legal purposes, only corporations are separate from their owners; single proprietorships and partnerships are **not** legally separate from their owners.

Single Proprietorship

A single proprietorship is an unincorporated business owned by an individual and often managed by that same individual. Single proprietors include physicians, lawyers, electricians, and other people who are ''in business for themselves.'' Many small service-type businesses and retail establishments are single proprietorships. No legal formalities are necessary to organize such businesses, and usually only a limited investment is required to begin operations.

In a single proprietorship, the owner is held solely responsible for all debts of the business. For accounting purposes, however, the business is a separate entity. Thus, the financial activities of the business, such as the receipt of fees from selling services to the public, are kept separate from the personal financial activities of the owner. For example, the owner's personal house or car payment should not be entered in the financial records of the business.

Partnership

A **partnership** is an unincorporated business owned by two or more persons associated as partners. The business is often managed by those same persons. Many small retail establishments and professional practices, such as dentists, physicians, attorneys, and many CPA firms, are organized as partnerships. Partnerships are thoroughly discussed and illustrated in Chapter 14.

Partnerships are created by a verbal or written agreement. A written agreement is preferred because it provides a permanent record of the terms of the partnership. Included in the agreement are such terms as the initial investment of each partner, the duties of each partner, the means of dividing profits or losses between the partners each year, and the settlement to be made upon the death or withdrawal of a partner. Each partner may be held liable for all the debts of the partnership and for the actions of each partner within the scope of the business. However, as with the single proprietorship, for accounting purposes, the partnership is a separate business entity.

Corporation

A **corporation** is a business incorporated under the laws of 1 of the 50 states and owned by a few persons or by thousands of persons. Almost all large businesses are corporations, and many small businesses also are incorporated. Corporations are discussed thoroughly in Chapters 15 and 16.

The corporation is unique in that it is a legal business entity. The owners of the corporation are called **stockholders or shareholders.** They buy shares of stock, which are units of ownership, in the corporation. Should the corporation fail, the owners would lose only the amount they paid for their stock. The personal assets of the owners are protected from the creditors of the corporation.

The stockholders do not directly manage the corporation; they elect a board of directors to represent their interests. The board of directors selects the officers, such as the president and vice presidents, who manage the corporation for the stockholders.

Accounting is necessary for all three forms of business organizations, and generally accepted accounting principles (GAAP) are applicable to each. Since the single proprietorship is the simplest form of business, it will be used in the beginning chapters of this text to illustrate the basic accounting principles and concepts.

■ TYPES OF BUSINESS ACTIVITIES PERFORMED BY BUSINESS ORGANIZATIONS

Objective 2: Distinguish among the three types of business activities performed by business organizations.

The forms of business entities discussed in the previous section are classified according to the type of ownership of the business entity. Single proprietors have one owner, partnerships have two or more owners, and corporations usually have many owners. We can also group business entities by the type of business activities they perform—service companies, merchandising companies, and manufacturing companies.

1. **Service companies.** **Service companies** perform services for a fee. This group includes companies such as accounting firms, law firms, repair shops, dry cleaning establishments, and many others. Accounting for service companies is illustrated in the early chapters of this text.

2. **Merchandising companies. Merchandising companies** purchase goods that are ready for sale and then sell them to customers. Merchandising companies include such companies as auto dealerships, clothing stores, and supermarkets. Accounting for merchandising companies is first illustrated in Chapter 5.

3. **Manufacturing companies.** **Manufacturing companies** buy materials, convert them into products, and then sell the products to other companies or to final customers. Examples of manufacturing companies are steel mills, auto manufacturers, and clothing manufacturers. Manufacturing companies are discussed in the last part of the text, since these businesses are more complex and require more detailed accounting records.

All these companies produce financial statements as the final end product of their accounting process. As you learned in the Introduction, these financial statements provide relevant financial information both to those inside the company—management—and those outside the company—creditors, stockholders, and other interested parties. In the next section, you will learn about three common financial statements: the income statement, the statement of owner's equity, and the balance sheet.

■ FINANCIAL STATEMENTS OF BUSINESS ORGANIZATIONS

Objective 3:
Describe the content and purposes of the income statement, statement of owner's equity, and balance sheet.

Business entities may have many objectives and goals (for example, one of your objectives in owning a physical fitness center may be to improve *your* physical fitness). However, the two primary objectives of every business are profitability and solvency. **Profitability** is the ability to generate income. Unless a business can produce satisfactory income and pay its debts as they become due, other objectives a business may have will never be realized simply because the business will not survive. **Solvency** is the ability to pay debts as they become due.

The financial statement that reflects a company's profitability is the **income statement.** The **statement of owner's equity** shows the change in owner's equity between the beginning of a period (e.g., a month) and the end of that period. The **balance sheet** reflects a company's solvency. If you have seen financial statements of actual companies, you will recall that they generally contain the same main headings and elements as we describe in the next section.

A fourth financial statement, the statement of cash flows, is thoroughly discussed and illustrated in Chapter 20. We only mention it now so that you will know it exists. The **statement of cash flows** shows the cash inflows and outflows for a company over a period of time. This statement has three sections—cash flows from operating activities, cash flows from investing activities, and cash flows from financing activities.

The Income Statement

The income statement, sometimes called an *earnings statement,* reports the profitability of a business organization for a stated period of time. In accounting, profitability is measured for a period of time, such as a month or year, by comparing the revenues generated with the expenses incurred to produce these revenues. Revenues are the inflows of assets (such as cash) resulting from the sale of products or the rendering of services to customers. Expenses are the costs incurred to produce revenues. Expenses are measured by the assets surrendered or consumed in servicing customers. If the revenues of a period exceed the expenses of the same period, net income results. Net income is often referred to as the *earnings* of the company. If expenses exceed revenues, the business has a net loss, and it has operated unprofitably.

Illustration 1.1 shows the income statement of Brent Company, a pool service company, for December 1991. Remember that an income statement is for a specified period of time.

Brent's income statement for the month ended December 31, 1991, shows that the revenues generated by serving customers for December totaled $5,700. Expenses for the month amounted to $3,600. As a result of these business activities, Brent's net income for the month of December was $2,100. The net income amount is determined by subtracting the company's expenses of $3,600 from its revenues of $5,700.

The Statement of Owner's Equity

The purpose of the statement of owner's equity is to connect the income statement and the balance sheet. The statement of owner's equity shows the changes that occurred in the owner's capital balance between two balance sheet dates. For instance, the statement of owner's equity in Illustration 1.2 shows the changes that occurred in the William Brent, Capital account between December 1, 1991, and December 31, 1991. The heading of the statement indicates that it is for a period of time, which is similar to the income statement.

Illustration 1.2 shows that the owner's beginning capital balance was $30,000. Then, net income of $2,100, as determined on the income statement (Illustration 1.1), is added to arrive at the ending owner's capital balance of $32,100. This ending balance is then carried to the balance sheet (Illustration 1.3). If there had been a net loss, it would have been deducted from the owner's beginning capital balance on the statement of owner's equity.

There could have been other changes that would affect the owner's capital balance. Any additional owner investments during the period would increase the balance. Any withdrawals (drawings) of cash or other assets by the owner to use for personal reasons would decrease the balance.

Illustration 1.1

Income Statement

BRENT COMPANY
Income Sheet
For the Month Ended December 31, 1991

Revenues:

Service revenue		$5,700

Expenses:

Wages expense	$2,600	
Rent expense	400	
Gas and oil expense	600	
Total expenses		3,600
Net income		$2,100

Illustration 1.2

Statement of Owner's Equity

BRENT COMPANY
Statement of Owner's Equity
For the Month Ended December 31, 1991

William Brent, capital, December 1	$30,000
Add: Net income for December	2,100
William Brent, capital, December 31	$32,100

Illustration 1.3   *Balance Sheet*

BRENT COMPANY
Balance Sheet
December 31, 1991

Assets		Liabilities and Owner's Equity*	
Cash	$15,500	Liabilities:	
Accounts receivable	700	Accounts payable . . . . $ 600	
Truck	6,000	Notes payable 6,000	
Cleaning equipment	14,000	Total liabilities	$ 6,600
Office equipment	2,500	Owner's equity:	
		William Brent, capital	32,100
Total assets	$38,700	Total liabilities and owner's equity . . .	$38,700

* The liabilities and owner's equity portion of the balance sheet may be shown directly beneath the assets instead of to the right of them as shown in the illustration. When liabilities and owner's equity are placed under the assets, it is called the *vertical format* or *report form.* The vertical format is as acceptable as the *horizontal format* (or account form) used above. For an example of the vertical format, see the solution to the demonstration problem, page 38.

When these additional changes are present, the format of the statement is as follows:

COMPANY NAME
Statement of Owner's Equity
For the Month Ended (Date)

Owner's capital, beginning balance		$xx,xxx
Add: Net income for the period	$xx,xxx	
Additional owner investments	xx,xxx	xx,xxx
Total		$xx,xxx
Deduct: Owner drawings for the period		x,xxx
Owner's capital, ending balance		$xx,xxx

Owner's **withdrawals** (drawings) are the taking of cash or other assets out of the business by the owner for personal use. Withdrawals of cash for personal use are recorded as a reduction in cash and a decrease in owner's equity. Also, withdrawals can occur as a result of the business paying a personal bill for the owner. However, personal bills should not be included in determining the entity's income for a period.

An example of such a withdrawal would occur if William Brent took $50 from the Brent Company's cash register to pay his home utility bill. Mr. Brent has every right to the money, but the bill does not relate to the business. This transaction would be recorded as a decrease in cash and a decrease in owner's capital. Even though the transaction summary would show this transaction reducing the owner's capital account balance, the withdrawal would not appear on the income statement of the business. (See the solution to the Demonstration Problem at the end of the chapter for an example of an owner's withdrawal transaction.) A withdrawal by the owner is considered a distribution of assets to the owner.

The effect of a cash withdrawal by the owner is to reduce cash and owner's equity by the amount paid out. Then the income is no longer retained by the business. Being able to withdraw assets from the business for personal use is one of the main reasons why people operate businesses.

The statement of owner's equity is further illustrated in Chapter 4. Our purpose here was only to show that the income statement, statement of owner's equity, and balance sheet articulate with (or are related to) each other.

The Balance Sheet

The **balance sheet,** sometimes called the *statement of financial position,* lists the company's assets, liabilities, and owner's equity (including dollar amounts) **as of a specific moment in time.** Notice how the heading of the balance sheet differs from the headings on the income statement and statement of owner's equity. A balance sheet is like a still photograph; it captures the financial position of a company at a particular **point** in time. The other two statements are for a **period** of time. As you study about the assets, liabilities, and owner's equity contained in a balance sheet, you will understand why this financial statement provides information about the solvency of the business.

Assets are things of value owned by the business. They are also called the **resources** of the business. Assets have value because they can be used or exchanged to produce the services or products of the business. For example, in your horse stable, if you own the land and the stable (building) where horses are boarded, the land and stable are two assets of that business. Cash is also an asset because things such as the feed for your horses can be bought for cash and used in the business. Assets possess service potential or utility to their owner that can be measured and expressed in money terms.

Liabilities are the **debts** owed by a business. Typically, debts must be paid by certain dates. Many liabilities are incurred by purchasing an item on credit, such as the feed for your horses, and promising to pay for it later, or by going to the bank and borrowing money to pay for a new truck to pick up your horse feed. Purchasing horse feed on credit and borrowing from the bank to pay for your truck will result in liabilities on your company's balance sheet.

Owner's equity is the share of the business that the proprietor (owner) owns outright; that is, owner's equity is equal to assets minus liabilities. Owner's equity, then, consists of the owner's investment in the business plus profits made from the business (assuming the business is profitable) that are not withdrawn from the business by the owner.

To illustrate the relationship between assets, liabilities, and owner's equity, assume, for example, that you decided to purchase a new truck to pick up feed for your horse stable. The truck cost $10,000. You have $3,000 for a down payment. You borrow $7,000 from your banker. On your balance sheet, you now have an asset (truck) of $10,000, a liability (bank loan) of $7,000, and owner's equity of $3,000. In other words, your balance sheet shows that what you **own** minus what you **owe** is your **owner's equity.**

All financial statements have headings that include the (1) name of the organization, (2) title of the statement, and (3) date of, or period covered by, the statement. These three headings are shown in the balance sheet of Brent Company given in Illustration 1.3. Brent's assets on December 31, 1991, amount to $38,700. These assets consist of cash, accounts receivable (amounts due from customers for services already provided), and various types of equipment. Brent's liabilities consist of accounts payable (amounts owed to suppliers for goods or services purchased on credit) and notes payable (amounts owed to parties who loan the company money after the owner signs a written agreement for the company to repay each loan).[1] Brent's owner's equity is $32,100. On Brent's balance sheet, owner's equity is shown as "William Brent, capital" and can be calculated as the difference between assets of $38,700 and liabilities of $6,600.

---

[1] Most notes bear interest, but in this chapter we assume that all notes bear no interest. Interest is an amount paid by the borrower to the lender (in addition to the amount of the loan) for use of the money over time.

The balance sheet of Brent Company shows the financial position of the company on December 31, 1991. The William Brent, capital ending balance is as calculated in the statement of owner's equity.

The financial statements of Brent Company are the end products of the accounting process, which is explained in the next section. These financial statements give a picture of the profitability and solvency of the company. The accounting process details how this picture was made.

■ THE FINANCIAL ACCOUNTING PROCESS

Objective 4:
State the basic accounting equation and describe its relationship to the balance sheet.

In this section, we explain first the accounting equation, which is the framework for the entire accounting process. Then, you will learn how to recognize a business transaction and understand the underlying assumptions that accountants use to record business transactions. Next, you will see how Brent Company records transactions affecting its balance sheet and income statement. Accounting—the language of business—is now also becoming your language.

The Accounting Equation

In the balance sheet presented in Illustration 1.3, the total assets of Brent Company were equal to its total liabilities and owner's equity. This equality shows that the assets of a business are equal to its equities; that is,

$$Assets = Equities$$

Assets have been defined as the things of value owned by the business, or the economic resources of the business. We can further define the economic resources as all desired things, except those available in unlimited quantity without cost or effort, that are owned by a business and can be measured.

Equities are all claims to, or interests in, assets. For example, assume that you purchased a new $14,000 company automobile for your physical fitness business by investing $9,400 in your own business and borrowing $4,600 from a bank in the name of the business. Your equity in the automobile is $9,400, and the bank's equity is $4,600. The $4,600 can be further described as a liability because the company owes the bank $4,600.

The basic accounting equation shows the relationship between assets, liabilities, and owner's equity as:

$$Assets\ (A) = Liabilities\ (L) + Owner's\ Equity\ (OE)$$

Returning to the Brent Company's balance sheet in Illustration 1.3, we enter in the amounts of its assets, liabilities, and owner's equity:

$$\begin{array}{ccccc} A & = & L & + & OE \\ \$38,700 & = & \$6,600 & + & \$32,100 \end{array}$$

The basic accounting equation must always be in balance. The left-hand side of the equation shows the assets (things of value owned by the business); the right-hand side of the equation shows who provided the funds to acquire the assets. These funds are provided either by **creditors** or **owners.** In the case of Brent, creditors provided $6,600 of the funds, and the owner provided $32,100. So in accounting terminology, the right-hand side of the equation shows the equities, made up of the liabilities plus owner's equity. (Liabilities can be viewed as creditor's equity.) Equities are interests in, or claims on, assets. The creditor's interest in the assets is $6,600, the amount of liabilities; the owner's interest is $32,100, the amount of owner's equity.

As a business engages in economic activity, the **dollar amounts** and the **composition** of its assets, liabilities, and owner's equity **change. But the equality of the accounting equation always holds.**

Analysis of Transactions

Objective 5:
Analyze business transactions and determine their effects on items in the financial statements.

When you buy feed for the horses in your horse stable business, an economic exchange takes place. In exchange for the feed, you may give cash or the promise to pay for the feed later. An economic exchange also occurs when you provide a service—such as boarding horses—and receive cash. These exchanges of goods and services are called transactions.

Transactions provide much of the raw data used in the accounting process for two reasons. First, an exchange is an observable event providing evidence of business activity. For example, an exchange of cash for merchandise is a business event. Second, an exchange takes place at an agreed price, and this price provides an objective measure of the economic activity that has occurred. For example, the objective measure of the exchange may be $5,000. These two factors—evidence and measurement—make possible the recording of a transaction.

The evidence of the transaction is usually backed by a source document. A source document is any written or printed evidence of a business transaction that describes the essential facts of that transaction. Examples of source documents are receipts for cash paid or received, checks written or received, bills sent to customers for services performed or bills received from suppliers for items purchased, cash register tapes, sales tickets, and notes given or received. The source document you received when you bought the feed for your horses was probably in the form of a sales invoice or receipt. We handle source documents constantly in our everyday life. Each source document initiates the process of recording a transaction.

Generally, in recording business transactions, accountants rely on five underlying assumptions or concepts. The business entity concept was introduced earlier in the chapter. We mention the business entity concept again because it is basic to understanding the accounting process.

1. **Business entity concept.**   Data gathered in an accounting system are assumed to relate to a specific business unit or entity. The business entity concept assumes that each business has an existence separate from its owners, creditors, employees, customers, other interested parties, and other businesses.

2. **Money measurement concept.**   Economic activity is initially recorded and reported in terms of a **common monetary unit of mea-**

sure—the dollar in the United States. This form of measurement is referred to as **money measurement.**

3. **Exchange-price (or cost) concept (principle).**   Most of the amounts entered in an accounting system are the objective money prices determined in the exchange process. The result is that most assets are recorded at their acquisition cost measured in terms of money paid. **Cost** is the sacrifice made or the resources given up, measured in money terms, to acquire some desired thing, such as a new truck (asset).

4. **Going-concern (continuity) concept.**   Unless strong evidence exists to the contrary, the accountant assumes that the business entity will continue operations into the indefinite future. This assumption is referred to as the **continuity or going-concern** assumption. Assuming that the entity will continue indefinitely allows the accountant to value assets at cost on the balance sheet since they are to be used rather than sold. Market values of these assets would only be relevant if they were for sale.

5. **Periodicity (time periods) concept.**   According to the **periodicity (time periods)** concept or assumption, an entity's life can be subdivided into time periods (such as months or years) for purposes of reporting its economic activities.

Now that you understand business transactions and the five basic accounting assumptions, you are ready to follow step by step some actual business transactions. The transactions of Brent Company are used as examples. These transactions are grouped into the transactions affecting only the balance sheet and those affecting the income statement and/or the balance sheet. Then, a summary of the transactions is given.

Transactions Affecting Only the Balance Sheet.   The transactions that follow affect the assets, liabilities, and owner's equity on the balance sheet. The business transactions occurred during the month of November 1991.

1a. Owner Invested Cash.   When Brent Company was organized on November 1, 1991, the owner invested $30,000 cash in the business. This transaction increased assets (cash) of the company by $30,000 and increased owner's equity by $30,000. Consequently, the transaction yields the following basic accounting equation:

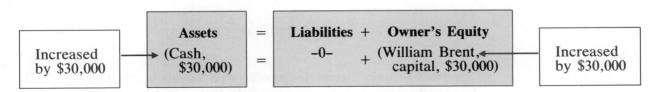

| Increased by $30,000 | **Assets** (Cash, $30,000) | = = | **Liabilities +** -0- + | **Owner's Equity** (William Brent, capital, $30,000) | Increased by $30,000 |

2a. Borrowed Money.   The company borrowed $6,000 from Mrs. Brent's father; a note was signed bearing no interest. After including the effects of this second transaction, the basic equation is:

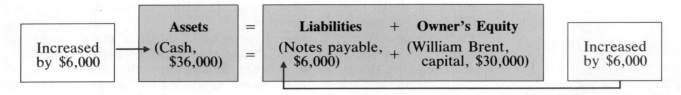

3a. *Purchased Equipment for Cash*. Brent bought (by paying cash) a truck for $6,000, cleaning equipment for $14,000, and office equipment for $1,500. Equipment items are assets because they are used to earn revenues in the future. **Note that this transaction does not change the totals in the basic equation but only changes the composition of the assets.** Cash was decreased, and the truck, cleaning equipment, and office equipment (assets) were increased by the total amount of the cash decrease. Three assets were received, and one asset of equal value was given up. The accounting equation now is:

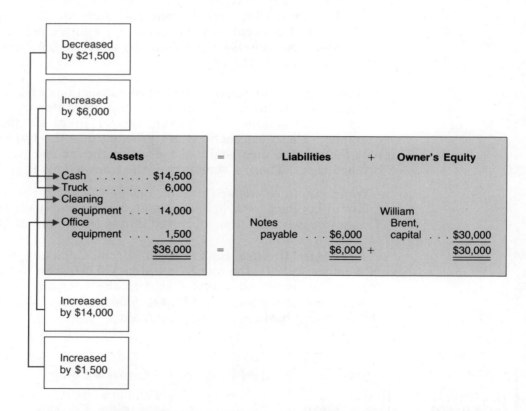

4a. *Purchased Equipment on Account (for Credit)*. Brent purchased $1,000 of office equipment on account, agreeing to pay within 10 days after receiving the bill. (To purchase an item "on account" means to buy it on credit.) This transaction increased assets in the form of office equipment and liabilities in the form of accounts payable by $1,000. As stated earlier, accounts payable are amounts owed to suppliers for items purchased on credit. The increase in the assets and the liabilities of $1,000 is shown as follows:

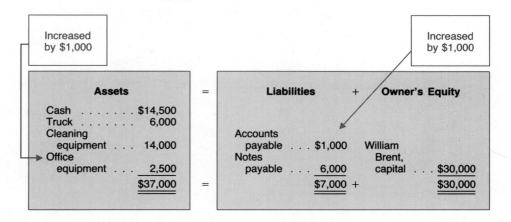

5a. Paid an Account Payable.   Eight days after receiving the bill, Brent paid $1,000 for the office equipment purchased on account (transaction 4a). This transaction reduced cash by $1,000 and reduced the debt owed to the equipment supplier—shown as an account payable—by $1,000. Thus, the assets and liabilities both are reduced by $1,000, and the equation again balances as follows:

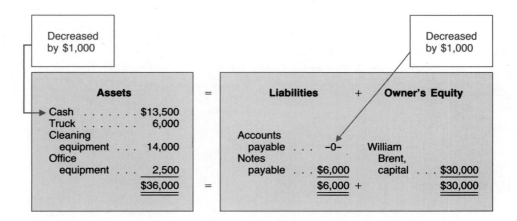

Illustration 1.4 shows a summary of transactions prepared in accounting equation form for the month of November. A **summary of transactions** is a teaching tool used to show the effects of transactions on the balance sheet. Note that the owner's equity has remained at $30,000. This amount will change as the business begins to earn revenues or incur expenses. You can see how the totals at the bottom of Illustration 1.4 tie into the balance sheet shown in Illustration 1.5. The balance sheet in Illustration 1.5 is dated November 30, 1991. These totals become the beginning balances for the month of December 1991.

Illustration 1.4 *Summary of Transactions*

BRENT COMPANY
Summary of Transactions
Month of November 1991

Trans-action	Explanation	Assets					=	Liabilities		+	Owner's Equity
		Cash	Accounts Receivable	Truck	Cleaning Equipment	Office Equipment		Accounts Payable	Notes Payable		William Brent, Capital
	Beginning balances	$ –0–	$ –0–	$ –0–	$ –0–	$ –0– =		$ –0–	$ –0–		$ –0–
1a	Owner invested cash	+30,000									+30,000
		$30,000				=					$30,000
2a	Borrowed money . .	+6,000							+6,000		
		$36,000				=			$6,000 +		$30,000
3a	Purchased equipment for cash . .	–21,500		+6,000	+14,000	+1,500					
		$14,500		$6,000	$14,000	$1,500 =			$6,000 +		$30,000
4a	Purchased equipment on account					+1,000		+1,000			
		$14,500		$6,000	$14,000	$2,500 =		$1,000	$6,000 +		$30,000
5a	Paid on account payable	–1,000						–1,000			
	End of month balances	$13,500	$ –0–	$6,000	$14,000	$2,500 =		$ –0–	$6,000 +		$30,000

Illustration 1.5 *Balance Sheet*

BRENT COMPANY
Balance Sheet
November 30, 1991

Assets		Liabilities and Owner's Equity	
Cash	$13,500	Liabilities:	
Truck	6,000	Notes payable	$6,000
Cleaning equipment	14,000	Total liabilities	$ 6,000
Office equipment	2,500	Owner's equity:	
		William Brent, capital	30,000
Total assets	$36,000	Total liabilities and owner's equity	$36,000

Thus far, all transactions have consisted of exchanges or acquisitions of assets either by borrowing or by owner investment. This procedure was used so that you could focus on the accounting equation as it relates to the balance sheet. However, a business is not formed only to **hold present assets; a business seeks to use its assets to generate greater amounts of assets.** A business increases its assets by providing goods or services to customers.

The results of these activities are shown in the income statement. The section that follows carries on the transactions of Brent Company as it begins its business of earning revenues and incurring expenses.

Transactions Affecting the Income Statement and/or Balance Sheet. To survive, a business must be profitable. This means that the revenues earned by providing goods and services to customers must exceed the expenses incurred.

In December 1991, Brent Company began selling services and incurring expenses. The explanations of transactions that follow will allow you to participate in this process and learn the necessary accounting procedures.

1b. Earned Service Revenue and Received Cash. As its first transaction in December, Brent performed cleaning services for a large motel chain and received $4,800 cash. This transaction increased the cash balance by $4,800. Owner's capital also increased by $4,800, and the accounting equation is again in balance.

The $4,800 is a revenue earned by the business and, as such, increases owner's equity because the owner prospers when the business earns profits. Likewise, the owner would sustain the losses if the business fails.

The effects of this $4,800 transaction on the financial status of Brent are:

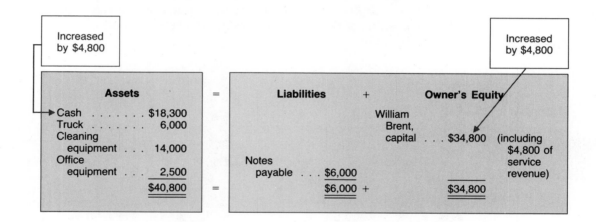

2b. Service Revenue Earned on Account (for Credit). Brent performed services for a customer who agreed to pay $900 at a later date. The company granted credit rather than requiring the customer to pay cash immediately. This is called earning revenue *on account*. The transaction consists of an exchange of services for a promise by the customer to pay later. This transaction is similar to the preceding transaction in that owner's equity is increased because revenues have been earned. But the transaction differs because cash has not been received. Instead, another asset, called an *account receivable,* has been received. As noted earlier, an account receivable is the amount due from a customer for goods or services already provided. The company has a legal right to collect from the customer in the future. In accounting, such claims are recognized as assets. The accounting equation, including this $900 item, is as follows:

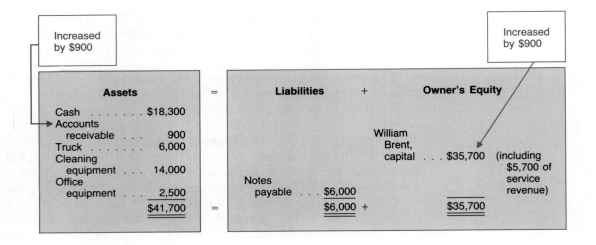

3b. Collected Cash on Accounts Receivable. Brent collected $200 on account from the customer in transaction 2b. The remaining $700 will be received later. This transaction affects only the balance sheet and consists of giving up a claim on a customer in exchange for cash. The effects of the transaction are to increase cash by $200 and to decrease accounts receivable by $200. **Note that this transaction consists solely of a change in the composition of the assets.** The revenue was recorded when the services were performed.

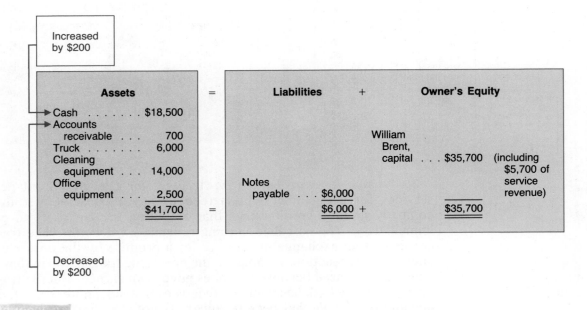

4b. Paid Wages. Brent paid employees $2,600 in wages, which is an exchange of cash for employee services. Typically, employees are paid for their services after their work is performed. Wages are costs incurred by the company to produce revenues and are considered an expense. Thus, the accountant treats the transaction as a decrease in an asset (cash) and a decrease in owner's equity because an expense has been incurred. Expense transactions reduce net income. Since net income becomes a part of the owner's capital balance, expense transactions reduce the owner's capital.

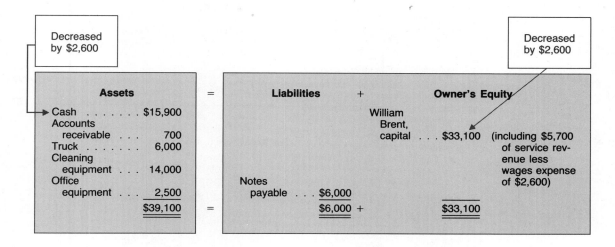

5b. Paid Rent.   In December, Brent paid $400 cash for office space rental. This transaction causes a decrease in cash of $400 and a decrease in the owner's equity of $400 because of the incurrence of rent expense.

Transaction 5b has the following effects on the amounts in the accounting equation:

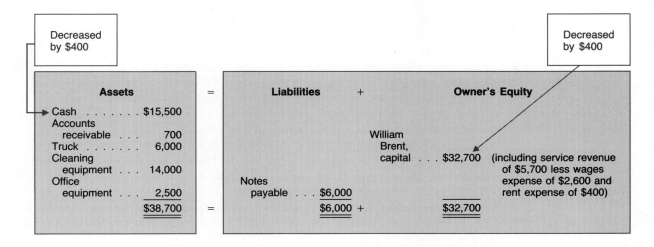

Paying cash for other expenses, such as advertising, gas and oil, and miscellaneous, would be recorded in the same way as transactions 4b and 5b.

6b. Received Bill for Gas and Oil Used. At the end of the month, Brent received a $600 bill for gasoline, oil, and other supplies consumed during the month. This transaction involves an increase in accounts payable (a liability) because the bill has not yet been paid and a decrease in owner's equity because an expense has been incurred. Brent's accounting equation now reads:

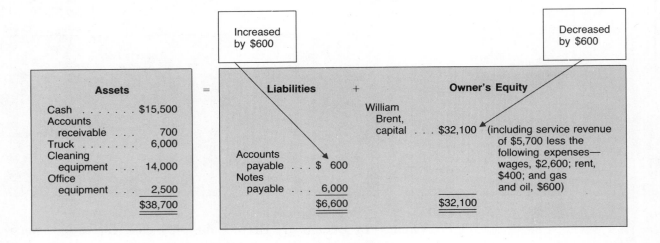

Summary of Balance Sheet and Income Statement Transactions. The effects of all the preceding transactions on the assets, liabilities, and owner's equity of Brent Company in its second month of operations are summarized in Illustration 1.6. The beginning balances are those shown as ending balances in Illustration 1.4. The summary shows subtotals after each transaction; these subtotals are optional and may be omitted. Note how the accounting equation remains in balance after each transaction and at the end of the month.

Objective 6: Prepare an income statement, a statement of owner's equity, and a balance sheet.

The totals shown at the bottom of Illustration 1.6 are the amounts reported in the balance sheet in Illustration 1.7. Illustration 1.8 shows the revenue and expense items listed in the Owner's Equity column of the transactions summary. Brent's capital account on the balance sheet consists of his $30,000 investment plus the $2,100 earned during the month of December. A statement of owner's equity could also be prepared (see Illustration 1.2 on page 20).

Remember that if the amount of revenues exceeds the amount of expenses, the business has net income. The net income is an addition to the owner's capital balance. Later chapters will show that revenues and expenses affect the owner's capital only at the end of an accounting period. The procedure shown here is a shortcut used to explain why the accounting equation remains in balance.

Illustration 1.6 *Summary of Transactions*

BRENT COMPANY
Summary of Transactions
Month of December 1991

Trans-action	Explanation	Cash	Accounts Receiv-able	Truck	Cleaning Equip-ment	Office Equip-ment	=	Accounts Payable	Notes Payable	+	William Brent, Capital
	Beginning balances (Illustration 1.4) .	$13,500	$-0-	$6,000	$14,000	$2,500	=	$-0-	$6,000	+	$30,000
1b.	Earned service revenue and received cash . .	+4,800									+4,800 (service revenue)
		$18,300		$6,000	$14,000	$2,500	=		$6,000	+	$34,800
2b.	Earned service revenue on account		+900								+900 (service revenue)
		$18,300	$900	$6,000	$14,000	$2,500	=		$6,000	+	$35,700
3b.	Collected cash on account . . .	+200	−200								
		$18,500	$700	$6,000	$14,000	$2,500	=		$6,000	+	$35,700
4b.	Paid wages	−2,600									−2,600 (wages expense)
		$15,900	$700	$6,000	$14,000	$2,500	=		$6,000	+	$33,100
5b.	Paid rent	−400									−400 (rent expense)
		$15,500	$700	$6,000	$14,000	$2,500	=		$6,000	+	$32,700
6b.	Received bill for gas and oil used . . .							+600			−600 (gas and oil expense)
	End of month balances	$15,500	$700	$6,000	$14,000	$2,500	=	$600	$6,000	+	$32,100
			$38,700				=	$6,600		+	$32,100

Illustration 1.7 *Balance Sheet*

BRENT COMPANY
Balance Sheet
December 31, 1991

Assets		Liabilities and Owner's Equity	
Cash	$15,500	Liabilities:	
Accounts receivable . .	700	Accounts payable . . . . $ 600	
Truck	6,000	Notes payable 6,000	
Cleaning equipment . .	14,000	Total liabilities . . . . $ 6,600	
Office equipment	2,500	Owner's equity:	
		William Brent, capital . . 32,100	
Total assets	$38,700	Total liabilities and owner's equity $38,700	

Illustration 1.8 *Income Statement*

BRENT COMPANY
Income Statement
For the Month Ended December 31, 1991

Revenues:		
Service revenue		$5,700
Expenses:		
Wages expense	$2,600	
Rent expense	400	
Gas and oil expense . .	600	
Total expenses		3,600
Net income		$2,100

Illustration 1.9 shows the effects of expenses, revenues, owner's withdrawals (drawings), and owner investments on owner's equity.

Illustration 1.9

Changes in owner's equity

Owner's Equity	
Decreases:	**Increases:**
Expenses	Revenues
Withdrawals by owner	Investments by owner

Chapter 1 has introduced two important ingredients of the accounting process—the accounting equation and the business transaction. In Chapter 2, you will learn about debits and credits and how they are used in recording transactions.

■ UNDERSTANDING THE LEARNING OBJECTIVES: CHAPTER 1

1. Identify and describe the three basic forms of business organizations.
   - A single proprietorship is an unincorporated business owned by an individual and often managed by that same individual.
   - A partnership is an unincorporated business owned by two or more persons associated as partners and is often managed by those same persons.
   - A corporation is a business incorporated under the laws of 1 of the 50 states and owned by a few persons or by thousands.

2. Distinguish among the three types of business activities performed by business organizations.
   - Service companies perform services for a fee.
   - Merchandising companies purchase goods that are ready for sale and then sell them to customers.
   - Manufacturing companies buy materials, convert them into products, and then sell the products to other companies or to final customers.

3. Describe the content and purposes of the income statement, statement of owner's equity, and balance sheet.
   - The income statement reports the profitability of a business organization for a stated period of time.
   - The statement of owner's equity explains the changes that occurred in the owner's capital balance between two balance sheet dates.
   - The balance sheet lists the assets, liabilities, and owner's equity (including dollar amounts) of a business organization at a specific moment in time.

4. State the basic accounting equation and describe its relationship to the balance sheet.

- The accounting equation is: Assets = Liabilities + Owner's Equity.
- The left-hand side of the equation represents the left-hand side of the balance sheet and shows things of value owned by the business.
- The right-hand side of the equation represents the right-hand side of the balance sheet and shows who provided the funds to acquire the things of value (assets).

5. Analyze business transactions and determine their effects on items in the financial statements.

- Some transactions only affect balance sheet items: assets (such as cash, accounts receivable, and equipment), liabilities (such as accounts payable and notes payable), and owner's equity (owner's capital account). Other transactions affect both balance sheet items and income statement items (revenues and expenses).
- Illustration 1.6 shows the effects of business transactions on the accounting equation.

6. Prepare an income statement, a statement of owner's equity, and a balance sheet.

- The income statement is shown in Illustrations 1.1 and 1.8.
- The statement of owner's equity is shown in Illustration 1.2.
- The balance sheet is shown in Illustrations 1.3 and 1.7.

7. Define and use correctly the new terms in the glossary.

NEW TERMS INTRODUCED IN CHAPTER 1

Accounting equation Assets = Liabilities + Owner's equity (23).

Accounts payable Amounts owed to suppliers for goods or services purchased on credit (22).

Accounts receivable Amounts due from customers for services already provided (22).

Assets Things of value owned by the business. Examples include money, machines, and buildings. Assets possess service potential or utility to their owner that can be measured and expressed in money terms (22).

Balance sheet Financial statement that lists the company's assets, liabilities, and owner's equity (including dollar amounts) as of a specific moment in time. Also called a *statement of financial position* (21).

Business entity concept Each business organization has an existence separate from its owner(s), creditors, employees, customers, and other businesses (16).

Continuity or going concern The assumption by the accountant that unless strong evidence exists to the contrary, a business entity will continue operations into the indefinite future (25).

Corporation Business incorporated under the laws of 1 of the 50 states and owned by a few persons or by thousands of persons (17).

Cost Sacrifice made or the resources given up, measured in money terms, to acquire some desired thing, such as a new truck—an asset (25).

Equities Broadly speaking, all claims to, or interests in, assets; includes liabilities and owner's equity (23).

Expenses Costs incurred to produce revenues (19).

Going concern See Continuity.

Income statement Financial statement that shows the revenues and expenses and reports the profitability of a business organization for a stated period of time. Sometimes called an *earnings statement* (19).

Liabilities   Debts owed by a business—or creditors' equity. Examples include notes payable and accounts payable (22).

Manufacturing companies   Companies that buy materials, convert them into products, and then sell the products to other companies or to final customers (18).

Merchandising companies   Companies that purchase goods that are ready for sale and then sell them to customers (18).

Money measurement   Recording and reporting economic activity in terms of a common monetary unit of measure such as the dollar (25).

Net income   Amount by which the revenues of a period exceed the expenses of the same period (19).

Net loss   Amount by which the expenses of a period exceed the revenues of the same period (19).

Notes payable   Amounts owed to parties who loan the company money after the owner signs a written agreement (a note) for the company to repay each loan (22).

Owner's equity   That share of the business that the proprietor (owner) owns outright; that is, owner's equity is equal to assets minus liabilities (22).

Partnership   An unincorporated business owned by two or more persons associated as partners (17).

Profitability   Ability to generate income. The income statement reflects a company's profitability (18).

Revenues   Inflow of assets (such as cash) resulting from the sale of products or the rendering of services to customers (19).

Service companies   Companies that perform services (such as accounting firms, law firms, repair shops, or dry cleaning establishments) for a fee (18).

Single proprietorship   An unincorporated business owned by an individual and often managed by that same individual (16).

Solvency   Ability to pay debts as they become due. The balance sheet reflects a company's solvency (18).

Source document   Any written or printed evidence of a business transaction that describes the essential facts of that transaction, such as receipts for cash paid or received (24).

Statement of cash flows   Shows cash inflows and outflows for a company over a period of time (18).

Statement of owner's equity   Financial statement that shows the changes that occurred in the owner's capital account between two balance sheet dates (19).

Stockholders or shareholders   Owners of the corporation; they buy shares of stock, which are units of ownership, in the corporation (17).

Summary of transactions   Teaching tool used in chapter to show effects of transactions on balance sheet items (27).

Transactions   Exchanges of goods and services. Transactions affect the assets, liabilities, owner's equity, revenues, and expenses of an entity (24).

Withdrawals   Cash or other assets taken out of the business by the owner for personal use (21).

DEMONSTRATION PROBLEM

On June 1, 1991, Joanna Willis formed the Briarcliff Riding Stable. The following transactions occurred during June:

June 1 The owner invested $10,000 cash in the business.
      4 A horse stable and riding equipment were rented (and paid for) for June at a cost of $1,200.
      8 Horse feed for June was purchased on credit, $800.
     20 Miscellaneous expenses of $600 for June were paid (to the suppliers of various items and services).
     24 The owner withdrew $500 cash.
     29 The company purchased land costing $40,000 from a relative of the owner by signing a note. The note is due to be repaid in five years with no interest.
     30 Salaries of $700 for June were paid.

June 30   Riding and lesson fees were billed in the amount of $2,400 to a riding club, whose members used the stable facilities. (This bill is due July 10.)

30   Fees of $3,000 for June were billed to the riding club, whose members were boarding their horses at the stable. (This amount is due on July 10.)

Required: a.   Prepare a summary of the above transactions similar to Illustration 1.6. Include money columns for Cash, Accounts Receivable, Land, Accounts Payable, Notes Payable, and Joanna Willis, Capital. Determine balances after each transaction to show that the basic equation is in balance.

b.   Prepare an income statement for June 1991.

c.   Prepare a statement of owner's equity for June 1991.

d.   Prepare a balance sheet as of June 30, 1991.

Solution to demonstration problem

a.

BRIARCLIFF RIDING STABLE
Summary of Transactions
Month of June 1991

Date	Explanation	Cash	Accounts Receivable	Land		Accounts Payable	Notes Payable		Joanna Willis, Capital	
		Assets			=	**Liabilities**		+	**Owner's Equity**	
	Beginning balances	$ –0–	$–0–	$–0–		$–0–	$–0–		$ –0–	
June 1	Owner investment	10,000			=				10,000	
		$10,000							$10,000	
4	Rent expense	–1,200							–1,200	(rent expense)
		$ 8,800			=				$ 8,800	
8	Feed expense					+800			–800	(feed expense)
		$ 8,800			=	$800		+	$ 8,000	
20	Miscellaneous expenses	–600							–600	(miscellaneous expense)
		$ 8,200			=	$800		+	$ 7,400	
24	Owner withdrawal	–500							–500	(drawings)
		$ 7,700			=	$800		+	$ 6,900	
29	Purchased land by borrowing			+40,000			+40,000			
		$ 7,700		$40,000	=	$800	$40,000	+	$ 6,900	
30	Salaries paid	–700							–700	(salaries expense)
		$ 7,000		$40,000	=	$800	$40,000	+	$ 6,200	
30	Riding and lesson fees revenue billed		+2,400						+2,400	(riding and lesson fees revenue)
		$ 7,000	$2,400	$40,000	=	$800	$40,000	+	$ 8,600	
30	Boarding fees revenue		+3,000						+3,000	(horse boarding fees revenue)
	End of month balances	$ 7,000	$5,400	$40,000	=	$800	$40,000	+	$11,600	

b.

BRIARCLIFF RIDING STABLE
Income Statement
For the Month Ended June 30, 1991

Revenues:

Horse boarding fees revenue	$3,000	
Riding and lesson fees revenue	2,400	
Total revenues		$5,400

Expenses:

Rent expense	$1,200	
Feed expense	800	
Salaries expense	700	
Miscellaneous expense	600	
Total expenses		3,300
Net income		$2,100

c.

BRIARCLIFF RIDING STABLE
Statement of Owner's Equity
For the Month Ended June 30, 1991

Joanna Wills, capital, June 1	$ –0–
Add: Owner investment in June	10,000
Net income for June	2,100
Total	$12,100
Deduct: Owner drawings for June	500
Joanna Wills, capital, June 30	$11,600

d.

BRIARCLIFF RIDING STABLE
Balance Sheet
June 30, 1991

Assets

Cash	$ 7,000
Accounts receivable	5,400
Land	40,000
Total assets	$52,400

Liabilities and Owner's Equity

Liabilities:

Accounts payable	$ 800
Notes payable	40,000
Total liabilities	$40,800

Owner's equity:

Joanna Willis, capital	11,600
Total liabilities and owner's equity	$52,400

QUESTIONS

1. Identify and briefly describe the three forms of business organizations.

2. Identify and briefly describe the three types of businesses (according to functions performed).

3. What is an income statement? This statement provides information on what aspect of a business?

4. What are revenues?

5. Define expenses. How are expenses measured?

6. Describe the purpose and content of the statement of owner's equity.

7. What is a balance sheet? This statement provides information on what aspect of a business?

8. Define asset, liability, and owner's equity.

9. How do liabilities and owner's equity differ? In what respects are they similar?

10. What is the basic accounting equation?

11. What is a transaction? What use does the accountant make of transactions? Why?

12. What is the business entity assumption?

EXERCISES

E-1
Analyze transactions

Baxter Company, engaged in a service business, completed the following selected transactions during July 1991:

a. Purchased office equipment on account.
b. Paid an account payable.
c. Earned service revenue on account.
d. The company borrowed cash from a relative of the owner; a note was signed bearing no interest.
e. Paid July wages to employees.
f. Received cash on account from a charge customer.
g. Received gas and oil bill for July.
h. Purchased truck for cash.

Using a tabular form similar to Illustration 1.6, indicate the effect of each transaction on the accounting equation using (+) for increase and (−) for decrease. You will need columns for Cash, Accounts Receivable, Truck, Office Equipment, Accounts Payable, Notes Payable, and Baxter, Capital. No dollar amounts are needed, and you need not fill in the Explanation column.

E-2
Determine effect of transactions on owner's equity

Indicate the immediate amount of change (if any) in the owner's equity balance based on each of the following transactions:

a. The owner invested $45,000 cash in the business.
b. Land costing $10,000 was purchased by paying cash.
c. The company performed services for a customer who agreed to pay $20,000 in one month.
d. Paid wages for the month, $12,200.
e. Paid $7,500 on an account payable.

E-3
Give examples of transactions

Give examples of transactions that would have the following effects on the elements in a firm's accounting system:

a. Increase cash; decrease some other asset.
b. Decrease cash; increase some other asset.
c. Increase an asset; increase a liability.
d. Increase an expense; decrease an asset.
e. Increase an asset other than cash; increase revenue.
f. Decrease an asset; decrease a liability.

E-4
Compute revenue

Assume that owner's capital increased because of net income by $118,000 from June 30, 1991, to June 30, 1992. Assume expenses for the year were $240,000. Compute the revenue for the year.

E-5
Compute owner's equity

On December 31, 1991, P Company had assets of $920,000, liabilities of $520,000, and owner's equity of $400,000. During 1992, the company earned revenues of $260,000 and incurred expenses of $204,000. Compute the owner's equity amount as of December 31, 1992.

E-6
Analyze transactions

For each of the following transactions, identify the type of accounts affected:

a.   Purchased a truck for cash, $15,000.
b.   Purchased land for $65,000; payment to be made next month.
c.   Paid $1,600 cash for the current month's utilities.
d.   Paid for the land purchased in (b).

E-7
Identify transactions that increase expenses

Which of the following transactions result in an increase in an expense?

a.   Cash of $76,000 was paid to employees for services received during the month.
b.   Cash of $5,000 was paid for some advertising services during the month.
c.   Paid $9,000 on a loan payable.
d.   Paid $400 cash in a payment of an account payable.
e.   The owner withdrew $1,300 cash.

E-8
Determine total assets at beginning of year and owner's equity at end of year

At the start of the year, a company had liabilities of $216,000 and owner's equity of $720,000. Net income for the year was $300,000, and $90,000 cash was withdrawn by the owner. Compute total assets at the beginning of the year and owner's equity at the end of the year.

E-9
Compute net income and prepare a statement of owner's equity

From the following selected data for Cook Company, compute net income for 1991:

Revenue from services rendered on account $300,000
Revenue from services rendered for cash 60,000
Cash collected from customers on account 168,000
Bill Cook, capital, January 1, 1991 324,000
Expenses incurred on account 200,000
Expenses incurred for cash 80,000
Cash withdrawn by owner 24,000
Additional cash invested by owner 40,000
Bill Cook, capital, December 31, 1991 420,000

Why would you not use all of the above items in your answer? Verify the ending balance in the owner's capital account by preparing a statement of owner's equity.

E-10
Determine owner's equity and net income

The information given below appears in the financial records of Stoffer Company at the end of 1991.

Cash $15,000
Accounts payable 10,000
Accounts receivable 20,000
Truck 12,000
Notes payable 5,000
Office equipment 16,000
John Stoffer, capital . . . . .   ?

Required: a.   Calculate the amount of owner's capital at the end of the year.
b.   If (1) the owner's capital balance at the beginning of the year was $20,000 and (2) the owner made an additional cash investment of $25,000 during the year and withdrew $50,000 for personal use, how much was net income for the year?

E-11
Calculate missing amounts

In each of the independent situations given below, find the missing amount.

	(1)	(2)	(3)
Beginning balances:			
Assets	$100,000	$200,000	$300,000
Liabilities	60,000	120,000	160,000
Ending balances:			
Assets	150,000	240,000	280,000
Liabilities	90,000	130,000	170,000
During year:			
Net income	?	60,000	20,000
Additional owner investments	10,000	40,000	?
Cash drawings by owner	15,000	?	60,000

PROBLEMS, SERIES A

P1-1-A
Prepare income statement, statement of owner's equity, and balance sheet

Analysis of the summary of transactions for Strike Bowling Lanes for January 1991 revealed the following ending balances:

Balances, January 31, 1991:
Cash	$ 70,000
Land	300,000
Accounts Payable	28,000
Notes Payable	60,000
John Lucia, Capital	282,000

The owner's capital balance at the beginning of the month was $263,800. A breakdown of the owner's capital balance showed the following revenues and expenses for the month:

Bowling revenue	$52,000
Rent expense for building and equipment . .	22,000
Advertising expense	1,600
Wages expense	8,000
Utilities expense	2,200

Required:
a. Prepare an income statement for January 1991.
b. Prepare a statement of owner's equity for January 1991.
c. Prepare a balance sheet as of January 31, 1991.

P1-2-A
Prepare summary of transactions and balance sheet

Dillard Company engaged in the following transactions in January 1991, its first month of operations:

1. The owner, Kelly Dillard, invested $200,000 cash in the business.
2. The company borrowed $80,000 from Kelly's brother-in-law; a note was signed bearing no interest.
3. The following assets were purchased for cash: truck, $32,000; cleaning equipment, $16,000; and office equipment, $20,000.
4. Office equipment was purchased on account, $24,000.
5. The account payable in (4) was paid, $24,000.

Required:
a. Prepare a summary of the above transactions (see Illustration 1.4). Include money columns for Cash, Truck, Cleaning Equipment, Office Equipment, Accounts Payable, Notes Payable, and Kelly Dillard, Capital. Determine new balances after each transaction.
b. Prepare a balance sheet as of January 31, 1991.

P1-3-A

Prepare summary of transactions, income statement, and balance sheet

Drew Carter Company completed the following transactions in July 1991:

1. The company was organized and received $78,000 cash investment from the owner.
2. The company bought equipment for cash at a cost of $59,670.
3. The company performed services for a customer who agreed to pay $7,800 in one week.
4. The company received $7,800 from transaction (3).
5. Equipment that cost $3,900 was acquired on account.
6. A partial payment of $2,340 was made on the liability incurred in transaction (5).
7. Employee wages for the month were paid, $4,680.

Required:

a. Prepare a summary of the above transactions (see Illustration 1.6). Include money columns for Cash, Accounts Receivable, Equipment, Accounts Payable, and Drew Carter, Capital. Determine balances after each transaction.
b. Prepare an income statement for July 1991.
c. Prepare a balance sheet as of July 31, 1991.

P1-4-A

Prepare income statement, statement of owner's equity, and balance sheet

Following is a list of balances for Mathews Company. The revenues and expenses are for December 1991. The asset and liability balances are as of December 31, 1991. Edward Mathews' equity balance on December 1, 1991, was $64,900.

Office Equipment	$12,000	Cash	$41,800
Wages Expense	11,600	Gas and Oil Expense	1,700
Accounts Payable	3,400	Notes Payable	12,400
Service Revenue	23,200	Accounts Receivable	9,600
Truck	23,600	Rent Expense	1,600

The owner withdrew $2,000 cash during the month.

Required:

a. Prepare an income statement for December 1991.
b. Prepare a statement of owner's equity for December 1991.
c. Prepare a balance sheet as of December 31, 1991.

P1-5-A

Prepare summary of transactions, income statement, statement of owner's equity, and balance sheet

The transactions shown below are for Nancy Hobbs Company for June 1991. This was the first month of operation of the business.

1. The owner invested cash, $84,000.
2. The company borrowed $14,000 from a relative of the owner; a note was signed bearing no interest.
3. Purchased office equipment for cash, $16,800.
4. Performed services for a customer and received cash, $11,200.
5. Paid wages, $5,600.
6. Paid rent, $1,400.
7. Received bill for gas and oil used, $980.
8. Made a $7,000 payment on notes payable.

Required:

a. Prepare a summary of the above transactions (see Illustration 1.6). Include money columns for Cash, Office Equipment, Accounts Payable, Notes Payable, and Nancy Hobbs, Capital. Determine new balances after each transaction.
b. Prepare an income statement for June 1991.
c. Prepare a statement of owner's equity for June 1991.
d. Prepare a balance sheet as of June 30, 1991.

P1-6-A

Prepare summary of transactions, income statement, statement of owner's equity, and balance sheet

The following selected transactions are data for the Sara Patterson Company, a parking ramp business, for May 1991. The business was formed in April 1991.

May 1 Paid May rent on the parking structure, $42,000.
8 Cash was received for parking services, $102,900. (Actually, cash would be received daily throughout the month, but we assume it was all received on May 8 to simplify the problem.)
17 Received cash from additional investment by owner, $21,000.
19 Paid advertising expenses for May, $3,360.

May 30 Purchased motorized sweeper to clean parking structure, $25,200. Payment will be made next month.
31 Paid wages for May, $22,680.

Required: a. Prepare a summary of the above transactions (see Illustration 1.6, except it is not necessary to include subtotals after each transaction). Include money columns for Cash, Equipment, Accounts Payable, and Sara Patterson, Capital. Beginning balances were Cash, $84,000, and Sara Patterson, Capital, $84,000.
b. Prepare an income statement for May 1991.
c. Prepare a statement of owner's equity for May 1991.
d. Prepare a balance sheet as of May 31, 1991.

P1-7-A
Prepare summary of transactions, income statement, statement of owner's equity, and balance sheet (beginning balances in the accounts)

The balance sheet of Andy Roebuck Company as of September 30, 1991, was as follows:

ANDY ROEBUCK COMPANY
Balance Sheet
September 30, 1991

Assets

Cash	$272,000
Accounts receivable	24,000
Total assets	$296,000

Liabilities and Owner's Equity

Liabilities:

Accounts payable	$ 72,000

Owner's equity:

Andy Roebuck, capital	224,000
Total liabilities and owner's equity . .	$296,000

The company engaged in the following transactions in October 1991:

Oct. 1 The account payable owed as of September 30 ($72,000) was paid.
2 The company paid rent for October, $25,600.
7 The company received cash from a customer for services performed, $5,600.
10 The company collected $20,000 on account receivable.
14 Cash received from a customer for services, $8,800.
15 Revenue earned but not yet collected from a customer was $4,000.
16 The company paid wages of $4,000 for October 1–15.
19 The company paid advertising expenses of $1,600 for October.
21 Cash received from a customer for services performed, $12,000.
24 The company incurred miscellaneous expenses of $1,120 for various items and services provided by a supplier. The bill will be paid November 10.
31 Cash received from a customer for services performed, $11,200.
31 The company paid wages of $4,000 for October 16–31.
31 A customer was sent a bill for $28,800 for services provided in October.

Required: a. Prepare a summary of the above transactions (see Illustration 1.6) using column headings for items given in the above balance sheet. Enter the balances shown in the September 30, 1991, balance sheet as beginning balances in the summary of transactions. Determine balances after each transaction.
b. Prepare an income statement for October 1991.
c. Prepare a statement of owner's equity for October 1991.
d. Prepare a balance sheet as of October 31, 1991.

PROBLEMS, SERIES B

P1-1-B
Prepare income statement, statement of owner's equity, and balance sheet

Analysis of the summary of transactions for Midnight Drive-in Theater for July 1991 disclosed the following ending balances:

Balances, July 31:

Cash	$ 80,000
Land	200,000
Accounts Payable	28,000
Notes Payable	40,000
Ron Mott, Capital	212,000

The owner's capital balance at the beginning of the month was $180,400. A breakdown of the owner's capital balance revealed the following revenues and expenses for the month:

Ticket revenue	$62,000
Equipment rent expense	10,000
Film rent expense	18,000
Advertising expense	1,400
Wages expense	8,400
Utilities expense	3,400
Commission revenue received from concessionaires (percentage of concessionaire sales is paid to Midnight Drive-In)	10,800

Required:
a. Prepare an income statement for July 1991.
b. Prepare a statement of owner's equity for July 1991.
c. Prepare a balance sheet as of July 31, 1991.

P1-2-B
Prepare summary of transactions and balance sheet

Vince Ross Company began operations on March 1, 1991. During March, the company engaged in the following transactions:

1. Vince Ross invested $450,000 in the business.
2. Vince's father loaned $225,000 to the company; a note was signed bearing no interest.
3. The following assets were purchased for cash: truck, $54,000; cleaning equipment, $90,000; and office equipment, $112,500.
4. Office equipment was purchased on account, $67,500.
5. The account payable in (4) was paid, $67,500.

Required:
a. Prepare a summary of the above transactions (see Illustration 1.4). Include money columns for Cash, Truck, Cleaning Equipment, Office Equipment, Accounts Payable, Notes Payable, and Vince Ross, Capital. Determine new balances after each transaction.
b. Prepare a balance sheet as of March 31, 1991.

P1-3-B
Prepare summary of transactions, income statement, and balance sheet

Martin Taylor Company, which provides financial advisory services, completed the following transactions during October 1991:

1. Received $180,000 cash investment from the owner.
2. The company borrowed $24,000 from a friend of the owner; a note was signed bearing no interest.
3. The company bought $150,000 of computer equipment for cash.
4. Cash was received from a customer for services performed, $11,400.
5. Services were performed for a customer who agreed to pay within a month, $9,000.
6. Employee wages were paid, $9,900.
7. The customer in transaction (5) made a partial payment of $2,400 on the amount owed the company.

Required:
a. Prepare a summary of the above transactions (see Illustration 1.6). Include money columns for Cash, Accounts Receivable, Equipment, Notes Payable, and Martin Taylor, Capital. Determine balances after each transaction.

b. Prepare an income statement for October 1991.

c. Prepare a balance sheet as of October 31, 1991.

P1-4-B

Prepare income statement, statement of owner's equity, and balance sheet

The following balances are for Williams Company. All revenues and expenses are for September 1991. All asset and liability balances are as of September 30, 1991. The owner's equity balance is as of September 1, 1991.

Cash	$33,000
Service Revenue	24,000
Accounts Payable	4,320
Accounts Receivable	6,240
Cleaning Equipment	28,800
Office Equipment	7,200
Gas and Oil Expense	1,680
Advertising Expense	720
Wages Expense	11,520
Marcie Williams, Capital, September 1, 1991	60,576
Truck	14,400
Notes Payable	19,200
Rent Expense	1,440
Miscellaneous Expense	96

The owner withdrew $3,000 cash during the month.

Required:

a. Prepare an income statement for September 1991.

b. Prepare a statement of owner's equity for September 1991.

c. Prepare a balance sheet as of September 30, 1991.

P1-5-B

Prepare summary of transactions, income statement, statement of owner's equity, and balance sheet

The transactions appearing below are those of John Jacobs Company for April 1991. This was the first month of operation of the business.

1. Owner invested cash, $300,000.
2. Purchased cleaning equipment on account, $90,000.
3. Earned service revenue on account, $72,000.
4. Collected cash on account $24,000.
5. Paid wages, $18,000.
6. Paid rent, $12,000.
7. Received bill for advertising for April, $3,600.
8. Paid an account payable, $90,000.

Required:

a. Prepare a summary of the above transactions (see Illustration 1.6). Include money columns for Cash, Accounts Receivable, Cleaning Equipment, Accounts Payable, and John Jacobs, Capital. Determine new balances after each transaction.

b. Prepare an income statement for April 1991.

c. Prepare a statement of owner's equity for April 1991.

d. Prepare a balance sheet as of April 30, 1991.

P1-6-B

Prepare summary of transactions, income statement, statement of owner's equity, and balance sheet

Following are the transactions for August 1991 of Sunrise Theater, a theater owned by Robert Foster. The business was formed in July 1991.

Aug. 2 Paid current month's rent of building, $16,800.

15 Cash withdrawal by owner was $1,600.

24 Received month's advertising bill, $6,080.

27 Miscellaneous expenses were paid to the supplier of various items and services, $2,240.

31 Paid rental on films shown during month, $16,000.

31 Received $19,840 cash as concession revenue from the operator of various concessions who sold candy, popcorn, and similar items in the theater during August.

31 Cash ticket revenue for August was $37,280. (Actually cash would be received daily throughout the month, but we assume it was all received on August 31 to simplify the problem.)

31 Paid payroll for the month, $20,640.

Required:
a. Prepare a summary of the above transactions (see Illustration 1.6, except it is not necessary to include subtotals after each transaction). Include money columns for Cash, Equipment, Accounts Payable, and Robert Foster, Capital. Beginning balances were Cash, $30,000, Equipment, $34,000, and Robert Foster, Capital, $64,000.
b. Prepare an income statement for August 1991.
c. Prepare a statement of owner's equity for August 1991.
d. Prepare a balance sheet as of August 31, 1991.

P1-7-B
Prepare summary of transactions, income statement, statement of owner's equity, and balance sheet (beginning balances in the accounts)

The balance sheet of Marianne Mills Company as of April 30, 1991, was as follows:

MARIANNE MILLS COMPANY
Balance Sheet
April 30, 1991

Assets

Cash	$ 56,000
Accounts receivable	160,000
Land	600,000
Total assets	$816,000

Liabilities and Owner's Equity

Liabilities:

Accounts payable	$144,000

Owner's equity:

Marianne Mills, capital	672,000
Total liabilities and owner's equity	$816,000

The summarized transactions for May 1991 were as follows:

1. The owner invested an additional $200,000 cash in the business.
2. Collected $120,000 on account receivable.
3. Paid $104,000 on account payable.
4. Sold land costing $200,000 for $200,000 cash.
5. Decorating services were rendered to a major department store on account, $380,000.
6. Paid payroll for the month, $220,000.
7. The owner withdrew $24,000 cash.

Required:
a. Prepare a summary of the above transactions (see Illustration 1.6) using column headings for items given in the above balance sheet. Enter the balances shown in the April 30, 1991, balance sheet as beginning balances in the summary of transactions. Determine balances after each transaction.
b. Prepare an income statement for May 1991.
c. Prepare a statement of owner's equity for May 1991.
d. Prepare a balance sheet as of May 31, 1991.

BUSINESS DECISION PROBLEM 1-1

Identify information needed to make decision

On graduation from high school, Jeff Prichett went to work for a builder of houses and small apartment buildings. During the next six years, Jeff earned a reputation as an excellent employee—hardworking, dedicated, and dependable—in the light construction industry. He could handle almost any job requiring carpentry, electrical, or plumbing skills.

Jeff then decided to go into business for himself under the name of Jeff's Fix-It Shop. He invested cash, some power tools, and a used truck in his business. He completed many repair and remodeling jobs for both homeowners and apartment owners. The demand for his services was so large that he had more than he could handle. He operated out of his garage, which he had converted into a shop, adding several new pieces of power woodworking equipment.

Now two years after going into business for himself, Jeff is faced with a decision of whether to continue in his own business or to accept a position as construction supervisor for a home builder. He has been offered an annual salary of $100,000 and a package of "fringe benefits" (medical and hospitalization insurance, pension contribution, vacation and sick pay, and life insurance) worth approximately $20,000 per year. The offer is attractive to Jeff. But he dislikes giving up his business since he has thoroughly enjoyed "being his own boss," even though it has led to an average workweek well in excess of the standard 40-hour week.

Required: Suppose Jeff comes to you for asistance in gathering the information needed to help him make a decision. He brings along the accounting records that have been maintained for his business by an experienced accountant. Using logic and your own life experiences, indicate the nature of the information Jeff needs if he is to make an informed decision. Pay particular attention to the information likely to be found in the accounting records for his business that would be useful. Does the accounting information available enter directly into the decision? Explain.

BUSINESS DECISION PROBLEM 1-2

Prepare income statement and balance sheet; judge profitability of company

Analysis of the transactions of Starlight Drive-In Theater, owned by Tom Summers, for June 1991 discloses the following:

Ticket revenue	$142,000
Rent expense for premises and equipment	18,000
Film rental expense paid	35,600
Revenue received from operators of candy and popcorn concessions	20,000
Advertising expense	16,800
Wages and salaries expense	31,200
Utilities expenses	10,000

The accountant calculated the asset and liability amounts as of June 30 to include the following:

Cash	$200,000
Land	32,000
Accounts payable	41,600

The balance in the Tom Summers, Capital account on June 1 was $140,000.

Required:
a. Prepare an income statement for June 1991.
b. Prepare a balance sheet as of June 30, 1991.
c. Did June seem to be a profitable month for this company?

Processing Accounting Information

2

Recording Business Transactions

LEARNING OBJECTIVES

After studying this chapter, you should be able to:

1. Use the account as the basic classifying and storage unit for information.
2. Express the effects of business transactions in terms of debits and credits to six different types of accounts.
3. Record the effects of business transactions in a journal.
4. Post journal entries to the accounts in the ledger.
5. Prepare a trial balance to test the equality of debits and credits in the journalizing and posting process.
6. Define and use correctly the new terms in the glossary.

In Chapter 1, you learned that the three forms of business organizations—single proprietorships, partnerships, and corporations—perform three types of business activities—service, merchandising, and manufacturing. Three common financial statements produced by these business organizations are the income statement, the statement of owner's equity, and the balance sheet. These statements are the end products of the financial accounting process (or cycle), which has as its foundation the accounting equation.

The raw data of accounting are the business transactions. The transactions in Chapter 1 were recorded as increases or decreases in accounting equation items. However, as you probably noticed when working through the sample transactions given in Chapter 1, listing all business transactions as increases or decreases in the columns provided in the summary of transactions would become most cumbersome in actual practice. Most businesses, even small ones, enter into many transactions every day. Chapter 2 teaches you how business transactions are actually recorded in the accounting process.

To understand the dual procedure of recording business transactions with debits and credits, you begin by using the T-account, which classifies and summarizes the measurements of business activity. Then you learn about the ledger—a collection of accounts. You will follow a company through its various business transactions using these new tools. The need for a journal is explained, and soon you will be "journalizing." The recording of transactions must be checked for the equality of debits and credits. The trial balance is used to do this.

■ THE ACCOUNT

Objective 1:
Use the account as the basic classifying and storage unit for information.

A business may engage in thousands of transactions during a period of time. The data in these transactions must be classified and summarized before becoming useful information. Making the accountant's task somewhat easier is the fact that most business transactions are repetitive in nature and can be classified into groups having common characteristics. For example, a company may have thousands of receipts or payments of cash. As a result, a part of every cash transaction can be recorded and summarized in a single place called an *account*.

An **account** is an element in an accounting system that is used to classify and summarize money measurements of business activity of a similar nature. An account is set up whenever it is necessary to provide useful information about a particular business item. Thus, every business has a **Cash account** in its accounting system because knowledge of the amount of cash owned is useful information.

Accountants may differ on the account title (or name) they give for the same item. For example, one accountant might name an account Notes Payable and another might call it Loans Payable. Both account titles refer to the amounts borrowed by the company. The account title should be logical to help the accountant group similar transactions into the same account. Once an account is given a title, that same title must be used throughout the accounting records.

Accounts may take on a variety of formats. Some accounts are printed, and entries are written in by hand; others are on magnetic tape, and "invisible" entries are encoded by a computer. Every account format must provide for increases and decreases in the item for which the account was established. Then the account balance (the difference between the increases and decreases) can be determined.

The number of accounts in a company's accounting system depends on the information needed by those interested in the business. **The main requirement is that each account provide useful information.** Thus, one account may be set up for all cash rather than having a separate account for each form of cash (coins on hand, dollars on hand, and deposits in banks). The amount of cash is useful information; the form of cash is not.

The T-Account

To understand how the increases and decreases in an account are recorded, texts use the **T-account,** which derives its name from the fact that it looks like the letter T. The title (name) of the item accounted for, such as cash, is written across the top of the T. Increases are recorded on one side of the vertical line of the T, and decreases on the other side, depending on the type of account. A T-account appears as follows:

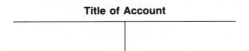

Title of Account

In Chapter 1, you saw that each business transaction affects at least two items. For example, if you—an owner—invest cash in your business, your assets increase and your owner's equity increases. This was illustrated in the summary of transactions schedule given in Chapter 1, Illustration 1.4. Using debits and credits and the double-entry procedure, we explain in the following sections how accountants record the increases and decreases caused by business transactions.

Debits and Credits

Objective 2:
Express the effects of business transactions in terms of debits and credits to six different types of accounts.

The accountant uses the term **debit (or charge)** instead of saying "place an entry on the left side of the T-account" and **credit** for "place an entry on the right side of the T-account." Debit (abbreviated Dr.) simply means left side; credit (abbreviated Cr.) means right side. A debit entry is an entry on the left side of an account, while a credit entry is an entry on the right side of an account. **Thus, for any account, the left side is the debit side, and the right side is the credit side, as shown below:**

Any Account

Left, or debit, side	Right, or credit, side

A synonym for **debit** an account is charge an account.

Double-Entry Procedure

Once a business event is recognized as a business transaction, it is analyzed to determine its increase or decrease effect on the assets, liabilities, owner's equity, revenues, or expenses of the business. These increase or decrease effects are then translated into debits and credits.

In each business transaction that is recorded, the total dollar amount of debits must equal the total dollar amount of credits. This means that when one account (or accounts) is debited for $100, another account (or accounts) must be credited for a total of $100. The accounting requirement that each transaction must be recorded by an entry that has equal debits and credits is called the **double-entry procedure,** or *duality*. This double-entry procedure keeps the accounting equation in balance.

The dual recording process produces two sets of accounts—those with debit balances and those with credit balances. When the totals of these two groups of accounts are equal, the accountant has some assurance that the arithmetic part of the transaction recording process has been properly carried out. You are now ready to learn how to actually record business transactions in T-accounts using debits and credits.

Recording Changes in Assets, Liabilities, and Owner's Equity.   In Chapter 1, you learned that the basic accounting equation is:

$$\text{Assets} = \text{Liabilities} + \text{Owner's Equity}$$

When you begin to record transactions into the T-accounts of the accounting equation, think first of the equal sign. Then, remember that assets, which are on the left of the equal sign, are increased on the left side of the T-accounts. Liabilities and owner's equity, which are on the right of the equal sign, are increased on the right side of the T-accounts. You already know that the left side of the T-account is the debit side and the right side is the credit side. So you should be able to fill in the rest of the rules for increases and decreases by deduction as follows:

Assets		=	Liabilities		+	Owner's Equity	
Debit for increases	Credit for decreases		Debit for decreases	Credit for increases		Debit for decreases	Credit for increases

To summarize:

1. Assets are **increased** by debits on the left side of the T-account and **decreased** by credits on the right side of the T-account.
2. Liabilities and owner's equity are **decreased** by debits on the left side of the T-account and **increased** by credits on the right side of the T-account.

Applying these two rules keeps the accounting equation in balance. And now we will apply the debit and credit rules for assets, liabilities, and owner's equity to actual business transactions.

Assume that John Stevens invested $10,000 in his company. The company records the receipt of $10,000 as follows:

(Dr.)	Cash	(Cr.)	(Dr.)	John Stevens, Capital	(Cr.)
(1)	10,000			(1)	10,000

The transaction involves an increase in the asset, cash, which is recorded on the left side of the Cash account, and an increase in owner's equity, which is recorded on the right side of the John Stevens, Capital account.

Assume John Stevens went to the bank and borrowed $5,000 on a note. As explained in Chapter 1, a **note** is a written promise to pay to another party (in this case the bank) the amount owed either when demanded or at a certain specified date. The transaction is recorded as follows:

(Dr.)	Cash	(Cr.)	(Dr.)	Notes Payable—Bank	(Cr.)
(1)	10,000			(2)	5,000
(2)	5,000				

Note that liabilities, in this case Notes Payable—Bank, are increased by an entry on the right (credit) side of the account.

Recording Changes in Revenues and Expenses. In Chapter 1, we recorded the revenues and expenses directly in the owner's capital account. However, in actual practice this is not recommended because of the volume of revenue and expense transactions. Since the amounts of revenues and expenses are needed to prepare the income statement, a separate account should be kept for each revenue and expense. Expense accounts are treated as if they were subclassifications of the debit side of the owner's capital account, and revenue accounts as if they were subclassifications of the credit side. The recording rules for revenues and expenses are:

1. Increases in revenues are recorded on the right (credit) side of the T-account and decreases on the left (debit) side. This is because revenues increase owner's equity, and, as you learned earlier, increases in owner's equity are recorded on the right side.
2. Increases in expenses are recorded on the left (debit) side of the T-account and decreases on the right (credit) side. This is because expenses decrease owner's equity, and decreases in owner's equity are recorded on the left side.

To illustrate these rules, assume a company received $800 cash from a customer for services rendered. The Cash account, an asset, is increased on the left (debit) side of the T-account; and the Service Revenue account, an increase in owner's equity, is increased on the right (credit) side.

(Dr.)	Cash	(Cr.)	(Dr.)	Service Revenue	(Cr.)
(1)	10,000			(3)	800
(2)	5,000				
(3)	800				

Assume a company paid $600 wages to employees. The Cash account, an asset, is decreased on the right (credit) side of the T-account; and the Wages Expense account, a decrease in owner's equity, is increased on the left (debit) side.[1]

(Dr.)	Cash	(Cr.)		(Dr.)	Wages Expense	(Cr.)
(1)	10,000	(4)	600	(4)	600	
(2)	5,000					
(3)	800					

Recording Withdrawals by the Owner. Owner withdrawals are a distribution of assets to the owner. Just as an owner investment increases owner's equity, owner withdrawals reduce it. Since owner withdrawals reduce the owner's equity in the business, they have the same effect on owner's equity as an expense.

Owner withdrawals could be shown directly as a reduction of the owner's capital account balance by entering the amount on the left (debit) side of that account. But a clearer record of withdrawals is available if a separate

---

[1] Certain deductions are normally taken out of employees' pay for social security taxes, federal and state withholding, and so on. Those deductions will be ignored until the topic of payroll is covered in more detail (Chapter 12).

drawing account is used to record all amounts withdrawn. A drawing account acts like a subclassification of the owner's capital account, as are revenues and expenses. Withdrawals are shown as debits to the owner's drawing account. The drawing account is increased by debits and decreased by credits.

A withdrawal of $100 cash by John Stevens would be shown as follows:

(Dr.)	Cash		(Cr.)	(Dr.)	John Stevens, Drawing	(Cr.)
(1)	10,000	(4)	600	(5)	100	
(2)	5,000	(5)	100			
(3)	800					

There comes a time when a business owner looks at the company accounts with all the debits and credits and asks, "Where am I financially— ahead or behind?" The only way the owner can determine this is to balance the accounts. The next section explains how to balance an account.

Determining the Balance of an Account

The balance of any T-account is obtained by totaling the debits to the account, totaling the credits to the account, and subtracting the smaller sum from the larger. If the sum of the debits exceeds the sum of the credits, the account has a **debit balance.** For example, the Cash account shown below uses the information from the preceding transactions. The account has a debit balance of $15,100, computed as total debits of $15,800 less total credits of $700.

(Dr.)	Cash		(Cr.)
(1)	10,000	(4)	600
(2)	5,000	(5)	100
(3)	800		
	15,800		700
Dr. bal.	15,100		

If, on the other hand, the sum of the credits exceeds the sum of the debits, the account will have a **credit balance.** For instance, assume that a company has an Accounts Payable account with a total of $10,000 in debits and $13,000 in credits. The account will have a credit balance of $3,000, as shown in the following T-account:

(Dr.)	Accounts Payable	(Cr.)
	10,000	7,000
		6,000
	10,000	13,000
	Cr. bal.	3,000

Normal Balances.   Since asset, expense, and drawing accounts are increased by debits, they **normally** have debit (or left-side) balances. Conversely, liability, owner's equity, and revenue accounts are increased by credits and **normally** have credit (or right-side) balances.

The normal balances of the six types of accounts we have used are given in the following diagram:

Types of Accounts	Normal Balances	
	Debit	Credit
Assets	X	
Liabilities		X
Owner's equity:		
Capital		X
Drawing	X	
Revenues		X
Expenses	X	

Rules of Debit and Credit Summarized

At this point you are ready for a summary of the rules of debit and credit. At first, it may be necessary to memorize these rules. Later, as you proceed in your study of accounting, the rules will become automatic, and you no longer will ask yourself, "Is this increase or decrease a debit or credit?"

As we stated earlier, asset accounts are increased on the debit side, while liabilities and owner's equity accounts are increased on the credit side. When the account balances are totaled, they will conform to the following two independent equations:

$$\text{Assets} = \text{Liabilities} + \text{Owner's Equity}$$

$$\text{Debits} = \text{Credits}$$

The arrangement of these two formulas gives the first three rules of debit and credit:

1. Increases in asset accounts are debits; decreases are credits.
2. Decreases in liability accounts are debits; increases are credits.
3. Decreases in owner's equity accounts are debits; increases are credits.

The debit and credit rules for expense and revenue accounts follow logically if you remember that expenses are decreases in owner's equity and revenues are increases in owner's equity. Since owner's equity accounts decrease on the debit side, expense accounts increase on the debit side; and since owner's equity accounts increase on the credit side, revenue accounts increase on the credit side. Debit and credit rules 4 and 5 are:

4. Decreases in revenue accounts are debits; increases are credits.
5. Increases in expense accounts are debits; decreases are credits.

These five rules of debit and credit are shown in Illustration 2.1. Note the treatment of expense accounts as if they were subclassifications of the debit side of the owner's capital account and of revenue accounts as if they were subclassifications of the credit side of the owner's capital account. Also note that assets, which are seemingly "good" things, and expenses, which

Illustration 2.1 *Rules of Debit and Credit*

Assets = Liabilities + Owner's Equity					
Asset Accounts =		**Liability Accounts** +		**Owner's Equity Account(s)**	
Debit*	Credit	Debit	Credit*	Debit	Credit*
+ Debit for increase	− Credit for decrease	− Debit for decrease	+ Credit for increase	− Debit for decrease	+ Credit for increase

Debits	**Credits**
1. Increase assets.	1. Decrease assets.
2. Decrease liabilities.	2. Increase liabilities.
3. Decrease owner's equity.	3. Increase owner's equity.
4. Decrease revenues.	4. Increase revenues.
5. Increase expenses.	5. Decrease expenses.

Expense Accounts and Owner's Drawing Account		Revenue Accounts	
Debit*	Credit	Debit	Credit*
+ Debit for increase	− Credit for decrease	− Debit for decrease	+ Credit for increase

* Normal balance.

are seemingly "bad" things, both increase on the debit side, and that liability and revenue accounts both increase on the credit side. This reinforces the fact that in accounting, *debit* and *credit* are neutral terms and do not connote value judgments.

■ THE LEDGER

A ledger (general ledger) is the complete collection of all the accounts of a company. Accounts are classified into two general groups: (1) **balance sheet accounts** (assets, liabilities, and owner's equity) and (2) **income statement accounts** (revenues and expenses). Balance sheet accounts are also called real accounts because they are **not** subclassifications or subdivisions of any other account. Income statement accounts are also called nominal accounts because they are merely subclassifications of the owner's equity accounts. *Nominal* literally means "in name only." Nominal accounts temporarily contain the revenue and expense information that eventually becomes part of the balance of a real account, owner's capital. The ledger may be in loose-leaf form, in a bound volume, or in a computer memory.

A complete listing of account titles and account numbers of all the accounts in the ledger is known as the chart of accounts. The chart of accounts is comparable to a table of contents. Each account typically has an identification number as well as a title to help locate accounts when recording data. For example, asset accounts might be numbered 100–199; liability accounts, 200–299; owner's equity accounts and drawing account, 300–399; revenue accounts, 400–499; and expense accounts, 500–599. Other numbering systems may be used. For instance, sometimes the accounts are numbered in sequence starting with 1, 2, and so on. **The important idea is that some numbering system typically is used.** The groups of accounts usually appear in the following order in the ledger—assets, liabilities, owner's equity, owner's drawing, revenues, and expenses. Individual accounts are arranged in numerical sequence in the ledger.

Now that you understand how to record debits and credits in an account and how all accounts together form a ledger, you are ready to study the accounting process in operation. To illustrate the accounting process, we use Rapid Delivery Company, owned by John Turner, as our example.

■ THE ACCOUNTING PROCESS IN OPERATION

John Turner owns a small delivery service company, Rapid Delivery Company. The accounting process used by John Turner is similar to that of any small company. The ledger accounts used in this chapter for Rapid Delivery Company are as follows:

	Account No.	Account Title	Description
Assets	100	Cash	Bank deposits and cash on hand.
	101	Accounts Receivable	Amounts owed to the company by customers.
	102	Supplies on Hand	Items such as paper, envelopes, writing materials, rope, and other materials used in performing services for customers or in doing administrative and clerical office work.
	103	Prepaid Insurance	Insurance policy premium paid in advance of the periods for which the insurance coverage applies.
	104	Prepaid Rent	Rent paid in advance of the periods for which the rent payment applies.
	110	Delivery Trucks	Trucks used to perform delivery services for customers.
Liabilities	200	Accounts Payable	Amounts owed to creditors for items purchased from them.
	201	Unearned Delivery Fees	Amounts received from customers before the services have been performed for the customers.
Owner's equity	300	John Turner, Capital	The owner's equity or interest in the business.
	301	John Turner, Drawing	The amount of withdrawals made by the owner this accounting period.
Revenues	400	Delivery Service Revenue	Amounts earned by performing delivery services for customers.
Expenses	500	Advertising Expense	The cost of advertising incurred in the current period.
	501	Gas and Oil Expense	The cost of gas and oil used in trucks in the current period.
	502	Salaries Expense	The amount of salaries incurred in the current period.
	503	Utilities Expense	The cost of utilities incurred in the current period.

Other accounts to be used for Rapid Delivery Company will be introduced in the next chapter.

Transaction 1: Rapid Delivery Company was formed on November 28, 1991, when the owner, John Turner, invested $50,000 in the business. The two accounts affected were:

(Dr.)	Cash	(Cr.)	(Dr.)	John Turner, Capital	(Cr.)
50,000					50,000

Cash is increased (debited) and John Turner, Capital is increased (credited) by $50,000. No other transactions occurred in November. The company prepares financial statements at the end of each month. The company's balance sheet at November 30, 1991, is shown in Illustration 2.2.

Illustration 2.2

Balance Sheet

RAPID DELIVERY COMPANY
Balance Sheet
November 30, 1991

Assets		Liabilities and Owner's Equity	
Cash	$50,000	Owner's equity:	
		John Turner, capital	$50,000
Total assets	$50,000	Total liabilities and owner's equity	$50,000

The balance sheet reflects ledger account balances as of the close of business on November 30, 1991. These closing balances are the opening balances on December 1, 1991, and are shown as such in the ledger accounts.

Now assume that in December 1991, Rapid Delivery Company engages in the transactions given below. The proper recording of each transaction is shown in T-account form, and a brief explanation is given.

Transaction 2: Dec. 1 Paid cash for four delivery trucks, $40,000.

(Dr.)	Delivery Trucks	(Cr.)	
1991 Dec. 1	40,000		One asset, delivery trucks, is increased (debited); and another asset, cash, is decreased (credited) by $40,000.

(Dr.)	Cash	(Cr.)	
1991 Nov. 30 Beg. bal.	50,000	1991 Dec. 1 40,000	

Transaction 3:   Dec. 1   Purchased $2,400 of insurance on the trucks to cover a one-year period from this date. Payment will be made in January.

(Dr.)	**Prepaid Insurance**	(Cr.)
1991		
Dec. 1	2,400	

(Dr.)	**Accounts Payable**	(Cr.)
		1991
		Dec. 1 2,400

An asset, prepaid insurance, is increased (debited); and a liability, accounts payable, is increased (credited) by $2,400. The debit is to Prepaid Insurance (indicating the insurance was paid in advance) rather than Insurance Expense because the policy covers more than the current accounting period of December (insurance policies are usually paid one year in advance). As you will see in Chapter 3, prepaid items are expensed as they are used. If this insurance policy was only written for the month of December, the entire $2,400 debit would have been to Insurance Expense.

Transaction 4:   Dec. 1   Rented a building and paid $1,200 to cover a three-month period from this date.

(Dr.)	**Prepaid Rent**	(Cr.)
1991		
Dec. 1	1,200	

(Dr.)	**Cash**	(Cr.)
1991		1991
Nov. 30		Dec. 1 40,000
Beg. bal.	50,000	1 1,200

An asset, prepaid rent, is increased (debited); and another asset, cash, is decreased (credited) by $1,200. The debt is to Prepaid Rent rather than Rent Expense because the payment covers more than the current month. If the payment had just been for December, the debit would have been to Rent Expense.

Transaction 5:   Dec. 4   Purchased $1,400 of supplies on account to be used over the next several months.

(Dr.)	**Supplies on Hand**	(Cr.)
1991		
Dec. 4	1,400	

(Dr.)	**Accounts Payable**	(Cr.)
		1991
		Dec. 1 2,400
		4 1,400

An asset, supplies on hand, is increased (debited); and a liability, accounts payable, is increased (credited) by $1,400. The debit is to Supplies on Hand rather than Supplies Expense because the supplies are to be used over several accounting periods.

In each of the preceding three entries, an asset was debited rather than an expense. The reason given was that the expenditure applies to (or benefits) more than just the current accounting period. Whenever an item such as insurance, rent, or supplies will not be fully used up in the period in which purchased, an asset should be debited.

Sometimes prepaid expenses such as insurance, rent, and supplies are bought and will be fully used up within the current accounting period. For example, the company may buy supplies during the first part of the month that it intends to fully consume during that month. If supplies will be fully consumed during the period of purchase, it is best to debit Supplies Expense rather than Supplies on Hand at time of purchase. This same advice applies to insurance and rent. If insurance is purchased that will be fully consumed during the current period, Insurance Expense rather than Prepaid Insurance should be debited at time of purchase. If rent is paid that applies only to the current period, Rent Expense rather than Prepaid Rent should be debited at time of purchase. As illustrated in the next chapter, following this advice simplifies the procedures at the end of the accounting period.

Transaction 6: Dec. 7 Received $4,500 from a customer in payment for future delivery services.

(Dr.)		Cash		(Cr.)
1991		1991		
Nov. 30		Dec. 1	40,000	
Beg. bal.	50,000	1	1,200	
Dec. 7	4,500			

(Dr.)	Unearned Delivery Fees		(Cr.)
		1991	
		Dec. 7	4,500

An asset, cash, is increased (debited); and a liability, unearned delivery revenue, is increased (credited) by $4,500. The credit is to Unearned Delivery Fees rather than Delivery Service Revenue because the $4,500 applies to more than just the current accounting period. Unearned Delivery Fees is a liability because if the services are never performed, the $4,500 will have to be refunded. If the payment had been for services to be provided in December, the credit would have been to Delivery Service Revenue.

Transaction 7: Dec. 15 Performed delivery service for a customer for cash, $5,000.

(Dr.)		Cash		(Cr.)
1991		1991		
Nov. 30		Dec. 1	40,000	
Beg. bal.	50,000	1	1,200	
Dec. 7	4,500			
15	5,000			

(Dr.)	Delivery Service Revenue		(Cr.)
		1991	
		Dec. 15	5,000

An asset, cash, is increased (debited); and a revenue, delivery service revenue, is increased (credited) by $5,000.

Transaction 8: *Dec. 17 Paid the $1,400 account payable resulting from the transaction of December 4.*

(Dr.)	Accounts Payable		(Cr.)
1991		1991	
Dec. 17	1,400	Dec. 1	2,400
		4	1,400

(Dr.)	Cash		(Cr.)
1991		1991	
Nov. 30		Dec. 1	40,000
Beg. bal.	50,000	1	1,200
Dec. 7	4,500	17	1,400
15	5,000		

A liability, accounts payable, is decreased (debited); and an asset, cash, is decreased (credited) by $1,400.

Transaction 9: *Dec. 20 Billed a customer for delivery services performed, $5,700.*

(Dr.)	Accounts Receivable		(Cr.)
1991			
Dec. 20	5,700		

(Dr.)	Delivery Service Revenue		(Cr.)
		1991	
		Dec. 15	5,000
		20	5,700

An asset, accounts receivable, is increased (debited); and a revenue, delivery service revenue, is increased (credited) by $5,700.

Transaction 10: *Dec. 24 Received a bill for advertising that appeared in a local newspaper in December, $50.*

(Dr.)	Advertising Expense		(Cr.)
1991			
Dec. 24	50		

(Dr.)	Accounts Payable		(Cr.)
1991		1991	
Dec. 17	1,400	Dec. 1	2,400
		4	1,400
		24	50

An expense, advertising expense, is increased (debited); and a liability, accounts payable, is increased (credited) by $50. The reason for debiting an expense rather than an asset is because the cost all pertains to the current accounting period, the month of December. Otherwise Prepaid Advertising (an asset) would have been debited.

Transaction 11:   Dec. 26   Received $500 on accounts receivable from a customer.

(Dr.)		Cash		(Cr.)
1991		1991		
Nov. 30		Dec. 1	40,000	
Beg. bal.	50,000	1	1,200	
Dec. 7	4,500	17	1,400	
15	5,000			
26	500			

(Dr.)	Accounts Receivable		(Cr.)
1991		1991	
Dec. 20	5,700	Dec. 26	500

One asset, cash, is increased (debited); and another asset, accounts receivable, is decreased (credited) by $500.

Transaction 12:   Dec. 28   Paid salaries of $3,600 to truck drivers for the first four weeks of December. (Payroll and other deductions are to be ignored since they have not yet been discussed.)

(Dr.)	Salaries Expense	(Cr.)
1991		
Dec. 28	3,600	

(Dr.)		Cash		(Cr.)
1991		1991		
Nov. 30		Dec. 1	40,000	
Beg. bal.	50,000	1	1,200	
Dec. 7	4,500	17	1,400	
15	5,000	28	3,600	
26	500			

An expense, salaries expense, is increased (debited); and an asset, cash, is decreased (credited) by $3,600.

Transaction 13:   Dec. 29   Received and paid the utilities bill for December, $150.

(Dr.)	Utilities Expense	(Cr.)
1991		
Dec. 29	150	

(Dr.)		Cash		(Cr.)
1991		1991		
Nov. 30		Dec. 1	40,000	
Beg. bal.	50,000	1	1,200	
Dec. 7	4,500	17	1,400	
15	5,000	28	3,600	
26	500	29	150	

An expense, utilities expense, is increased (debited); and an asset, cash, is decreased (credited) by $150.

Transaction 14:   Dec. 30   Received a bill for gas and oil used in the trucks for December, $680.

(Dr.)	Gas and Oil Expense		(Cr.)
1991			
Dec. 30	680		

An expense, gas and oil expense, is increased (debited); and a liability, accounts payable, is increased (credited) by $680.

(Dr.)	Accounts Payable			(Cr.)
1991		1991		
Dec. 17	1,400	Dec. 1	2,400	
		4	1,400	
		24	50	
		30	680	

Transaction 15:   Dec. 31   John Turner withdrew $3,000 cash to pay personal living expenses.

(Dr.)	John Turner, Drawing		(Cr.)
1991			
Dec. 31	3,000		

The owner's drawing account is increased (debited); and an asset, cash, is decreased (credited) by $3,000.

(Dr.)	Cash			(Cr.)
1991		1991		
Nov. 30		Dec. 1	40,000	
Beg. bal.	50,000	1	1,200	
Dec. 7	4,500	17	1,400	
15	5,000	28	3,600	
26	500	29	150	
		31	3,000	

The T-accounts used in the above transactions are shown only for purposes of analysis. In actual practice, the transactions given above would have been first entered in a journal (which is explained in the next section) and then posted to the ledger.

■ THE JOURNAL

Objective 3:
Record the effects of business transactions in a journal.

So far in Chapter 2, transactions have been recorded directly in the accounts. Each ledger (general ledger) account shows only the increases and decreases in that account. Thus, all of the effects of a single business transaction would not appear in any one account. For example, the Cash account contains only data on changes in cash and does not show how the cash was generated or what it was spent on. To have a permanent record of an entire transaction, the accountant uses a book or record known as a *journal.* A **journal** is a chronological (arranged in order of time) record of business transactions. A journal entry is the recording of a business transaction in the journal. A **journal entry** shows all of the effects of a business transaction as expressed in terms of debit(s) and credit(s) and may include an explanation of the transaction. **A transaction is entered in a journal before it is entered in ledger accounts.** Because each transaction is initially recorded in a journal rather than directly in the ledger, a journal is called a **book of original entry.**

The General Journal

A business generally has more than one journal. Chapter 6 describes several special journals. In this chapter, we use the basic form of journal, which is the general journal. As shown in Illustration 2.3 for Rapid Delivery Company, a general journal contains the following columns:

1. **Date column.**   The first column on each journal page is for the date. For the first journal entry on a page, the year, the month, and the day (number) are entered here. For all other journal entries on a page, only the day of the month is shown, until the month changes.
2. **Account Titles and Explanation column.**   The first line of an entry shows the account debited. The second line shows the account credited. Notice that the account title for the credit is indented to the right. For instance, in Illustration 2.3, the debit to the Cash account is shown first and the credit to the John Turner, Capital account is shown next. Any necessary explanation of a transaction appears on the line(s) below the credit entry and is indented halfway between the accounts debited and credited. A journal entry explanation should be complete enough to fully describe the transaction and prove the entry's accuracy, and yet be concise. If a journal entry is self-explanatory, the explanation may be omitted.
3. **Posting Reference column.**   This column shows the account number of the account that has been debited or credited. For instance, in Illustration 2.3, the number 100 in the first entry means that the Cash account number is 100. No number appears in this column until the information is posted to the appropriate ledger account. Posting is discussed later in the chapter.

Illustration 2.3   *General Journal (after posting)*

RAPID DELIVERY COMPANY
GENERAL JOURNAL   *Page 1*

Date		Account Titles and Explanation	Post. Ref.	Debit	Credit
1991 Nov.	28	Cash	100	50000	
		John Turner, Capital	300		50000
		The owner invested $50,000 cash in the business.			

Illustration 2.4 *General Journal—Extended Illustration*

RAPID DELIVERY COMPANY
GENERAL JOURNAL

Page 1

Date		Account Titles and Explanation	Post. Ref.	Debit	Credit
1991 Dec.	1	Delivery Trucks		4 0 0 0 0	
		Cash			4 0 0 0 0
		To record the purchase of four delivery trucks.			
	1	Prepaid Insurance		2 4 0 0	
		Accounts Payable			2 4 0 0
		Purchased truck insurance to cover a one-year period.			
	1	Prepaid Rent		1 2 0 0	
		Cash			1 2 0 0
		Paid three months' rent on a building.			
	4	Supplies on Hand		1 4 0 0	
		Accounts Payable			1 4 0 0
		To record the purchase of supplies for future use.			
	7	Cash		4 5 0 0	
		Unearned Delivery Fees			4 5 0 0
		To record the receipt of cash from a customer in payment for future delivery services.			
	15	Cash		5 0 0 0	
		Delivery Service Revenue			5 0 0 0
		To record the receipt of cash for performing delivery services for a customer.			
	17	Accounts Payable		1 4 0 0	
		Cash			1 4 0 0
		Paid the account payable arising from the purchase of supplies on December 4.			
	20	Accounts Receivable		5 7 0 0	
		Delivery Service Revenue			5 7 0 0
		To record the performance of delivery services on account for which a customer was billed.			

Illustration 2.4   *(concluded)*

		GENERAL JOURNAL					Page 2
Date		**Account Titles and Explanation**	**Post. Ref.**	**Debit**		**Credit**	
1991 Dec.	24	Advertising Expense		5 0			
		Accounts Payable				5 0	
		Received a bill for advertising for the month of December.					
	26	Cash		5 0 0			
		Accounts Receivable				5 0 0	
		Received $500 from a customer on accounts receivable.					
	28	Salaries Expense		3 6 0 0			
		Cash				3 6 0 0	
		Paid truck driver salaries for the first four weeks of December.					
	29	Utilities Expense		1 5 0			
		Cash				1 5 0	
		Paid the utilities bill for December.					
	30	Gas and Oil Expense		6 8 0			
		Accounts Payable				6 8 0	
		Received a bill for gas and oil used in the trucks in December.					
	31	John Turner, Drawing		3 0 0 0			
		Cash				3 0 0 0	
		The owner withdrew $3,000 to pay personal expenses.					

4. **Debit column.**   The amount of the debit is placed in this column on the same line as the title of the account debited.
5. **Credit column.**   The amount of the credit is placed in this column on the same line as the title of the account credited.

Illustration 2.4 shows how the December transactions of Rapid Delivery Company presented on pages 59–64 would be journalized. As shown in Illustration 2.4, a line is skipped between each journal entry to show where one journal entry ends and another begins. This is standard practice among accountants. Note that dollar signs are not used in journals or ledgers. When amounts are in even dollar amounts, the cents column may be left blank, or zeros or a dash may be used. When lined accounting work papers are used, commas or a period are not needed to record an amount. When using unlined paper, both commas and a period should be used.

Journalizing

Journalizing is the process of entering a transaction in a journal (in this chapter, the general journal). Business information comes from a variety of source documents, such as invoices, cash register tapes, time cards, and checks. The information appearing on these documents must be analyzed to determine the specific accounts affected and the dollar amounts of the changes. Then the proper journal entry must be recorded.

Posting

Objective 4:
Post journal entries to the accounts in the ledger.

A journal entry is like a set of instructions. The carrying out of these instructions is known as *posting*. **Posting** is recording in the ledger the information contained in the journal. A journal entry directs the entry of a certain dollar amount as a debit in a specific ledger account and directs the entry of a certain dollar amount as a credit in a specific ledger account. First, let's use a new situation to illustrate the posting process—Sandra Jenks Company. In Illustration 2.5, the first journal entry directs that $10,000 be posted in the ledger as a debit to the Cash account and as a credit to the Sandra Jenks, Capital account. Later, you will be shown how Rapid Delivery Company journal entries are posted.

The debit is posted in the ledger Cash account by entering the date, a short explanation (optional), the page number of the journal from which posted, and the $10,000 in the Debit column. Then the account number (100) to which the debit is posted is entered in the Posting Reference column of the general journal. The credit is posted in a similar manner but as a credit to Account No. 300. The arrows in the illustration show how these amounts have been posted to the correct accounts.

Illustration 2.5 also shows the three-column balance type of account. In contrast to the two-sided T-account format shown so far, the three-column format has columns for debit, credit, and balance. One advantage of this form is that the balance of the account is shown after each item has been posted. In addition, in this chapter, we indicate whether each balance is a debit or a credit. In subsequent chapters and in practice, the nature of the balance is not indicated since it is understood. Also, notice that an explanation is given for each item in the ledger accounts. Often these explanations are omitted because each item can be traced back to the general journal for the explanation.

Posting is always from the journal to the ledger accounts. Postings may be made (1) at the time the transaction is journalized; (2) at the end of the day, week, or month; or (3) as each journal page is filled.

Cross-Indexing (Referencing)

Since it is frequently necessary for accountants to check and trace the origin of their transactions, they provide for cross-indexing. **Cross-indexing** is the placing of (1) the account number of the ledger account in the journal and (2) the journal page number in the ledger account. As shown in Illustration 2.5, the account number of the ledger account to which the posting was made is placed in the Posting Reference column of the general journal. Note the arrow from Account No. 100 in the ledger to the 100 in the Posting Reference column beside the first debit in the general journal. The number

Illustration 2.5   *General Journal and General Ledger; Posting and Cross-Indexing*

SANDRA JENKS COMPANY
GENERAL JOURNAL

Page 1

Date	Account Titles and Explanation	Post. Ref.	Debit	Credit
1991 Jan. 1	Cash	100	1 0 0 0 0	
	Sandra Jenks, Capital	300		1 0 0 0 0
	The owner invested $10,000 cash in the business.			
5	Cash	100	5 0 0 0	
	Notes Payable—Bank	201		5 0 0 0
	Borrowed $5,000 from the bank on a note.			

GENERAL LEDGER

Cash

Account No. 100

Date	Explanation	Post. Ref.	Debit	Credit	Balance
1991 Jan. 1	Owner investment	G1	1 0 0 0 0		1 0 0 0 0 Dr.
5	Bank loan	G1	5 0 0 0		1 5 0 0 0 Dr.

Notes Payable—Bank

Account No. 201

Date	Explanation	Post. Ref.	Debit	Credit	Balance
1991 Jan. 5	Borrowed cash	G1		5 0 0 0	5 0 0 0 Cr.

Sandra Jenks, Capital

Account No. 300

Date	Explanation	Post. Ref.	Debit	Credit	Balance
1991 Jan. 1	Cash from owner	G1		1 0 0 0 0	1 0 0 0 0 Cr.

of the journal page **from** which the entry was posted is placed in the Posting Reference column of the ledger account. Note the arrow from page 1 in the general journal to G1 in the Posting Reference column of the ledger. The date of the transaction is also shown in the ledger. Note the arrows from the date in the general journal to the dates in the ledger.

Cross-indexing aids the tracing of any recorded transaction, either from general journal to ledger or from ledger to general journal. Cross-reference numbers normally are not placed in the Posting Reference column of the general journal until the entry is posted. If this practice is followed, the cross-reference numbers indicate the entry has been posted.

An understanding of the posting and cross-indexing process can be obtained by tracing the entries from the general journal to the ledger. The ledger accounts need not contain explanations of all the entries, since any needed explanations can be obtained from the general journal.

Posting and Cross-Indexing—An Illustration

Illustration 2.6 presents the general ledger accounts of Rapid Delivery Company after the journal entries on pages 66–67 have been posted. Each ledger account would appear on a separate page in the ledger. You should trace at least a few of the postings from the general journal to the general ledger to make sure you know how to post journal entries.

Compound Journal Entries

All the journal entries illustrated so far have involved one debit and one credit; these journal entries are called *simple journal entries*. Many business transactions, however, affect more than two accounts. The journal entry for these transactions will involve more than one debit and/or credit; such journal entries are called compound journal entries.

As an illustration of a compound journal entry, assume that on July 1, 1992, John Turner purchased $8,000 of machinery from the Myers Company, paying $2,000 cash with the balance due on December 31, 1993. The journal entry for Turner would be shown in the general journal as follows:

	Debit	Credit
1992		
July 1 Machinery	8,000	
Cash		2,000
Accounts Payable		6,000
Machinery purchased from Myers Company.		

Summary of Functions and Advantages of a Journal

The functions and advantages of using a journal are summarized below.

> The journal—
> 1. Records each transaction in chronological order.
> 2. Shows the analysis of each transaction in terms of debit and credit.
> 3. Supplies an explanation of each transaction when necessary.
> 4. Serves as a source for future reference to accounting transactions.
> 5. Removes lengthy explanations from the accounts.
> 6. Makes possible posting to the ledger at convenient times.
> 7. Assists in maintaining the ledger in balance.
> 8. Aids in tracing errors.

Illustration 2.6 *General Ledger—Extended Illustration*

RAPID DELIVERY COMPANY
GENERAL LEDGER

Cash
Account No. 100

Date		Explanation	Post. Ref.	Debit	Credit	Balance
1991 Dec.	1	Beginning balance*				5 0 0 0 0 Dr.
	1	Delivery trucks	G1		4 0 0 0 0	1 0 0 0 0 Dr.
	1	Prepaid rent	G1		1 2 0 0	8 8 0 0 Dr.
	7	Unearned delivery service revenue	G1	4 5 0 0		1 3 3 0 0 Dr.
	15	Delivery service revenue	G1	5 0 0 0		1 8 3 0 0 Dr.
	17	Paid account payable	G1		1 4 0 0	1 6 9 0 0 Dr.
	26	Collected account receivable	G2	5 0 0		1 7 4 0 0 Dr.
	28	Salaries	G2		3 6 0 0	1 3 8 0 0 Dr.
	29	Utilities	G2		1 5 0	1 3 6 5 0 Dr.
	31	Owner withdrawal	G2		3 0 0 0	1 0 6 5 0 Dr.

Accounts Receivable
Account No. 101

Date		Explanation	Post. Ref.	Debit	Credit	Balance
1991 Dec.	20	Delivery service revenue	G1	5 7 0 0		5 7 0 0 Dr.
	26	Collections	G2		5 0 0	5 2 0 0 Dr.

Supplies on Hand
Account No. 102

Date		Explanation	Post. Ref.	Debit	Credit	Balance
1991 Dec.	4	Purchased on account	G1	1 4 0 0		1 4 0 0 Dr.

Prepaid Insurance
Account No. 103

Date		Explanation	Post. Ref.	Debit	Credit	Balance
1991 Dec.	1	One-year policy on trucks	G1	2 4 0 0		2 4 0 0 Dr.

* Beginning balances result from carrying forward a balance from a preceding page for this account. The Cash account, for example, is likely to use page after page over a period of time since so many transactions involve cash. This particular beginning balance came from John Turner's investment in November.

Illustration 2.6 *(continued)*

GENERAL LEDGER *(continued)*

Prepaid Rent

Account No. 104

Date		Explanation	Post. Ref.	Debit	Credit	Balance
1991 Dec.	1	Three-month payment	G1	1 2 0 0		1 2 0 0 Dr.

Delivery Trucks

Account No. 110

Date		Explanation	Post. Ref.	Debit	Credit	Balance
1991 Dec.	1	Paid cash	G1	4 0 0 0 0		4 0 0 0 0 Dr.

Accounts Payable

Account No. 200

Date		Explanation	Post. Ref.	Debit	Credit	Balance
1991 Dec.	1	Insurance	G1		2 4 0 0	2 4 0 0 Cr.
	4	Supplies	G1		1 4 0 0	3 8 0 0 Cr.
	17	Paid for supplies	G1	1 4 0 0		2 4 0 0 Cr.
	24	Advertising	G2		5 0	2 4 5 0 Cr.
	30	Gas and oil	G2		6 8 0	3 1 3 0 Cr.

Unearned Delivery Fees

Account No. 201

Date		Explanation	Post. Ref.	Debit	Credit	Balance
1991 Dec.	7	Received cash	G1		4 5 0 0	4 5 0 0 Cr.

John Turner, Capital

Account No. 300

Date		Explanation	Post. Ref.	Debit	Credit	Balance
1991 Dec.	1	Beginning balance				5 0 0 0 0 Cr.

Illustration 2.6 *(concluded)*

GENERAL LEDGER *(concluded)*

John Turner, Drawing   *Account No. 301*

Date		Explanation	Post. Ref.	Debit	Credit	Balance
1991 Dec.	31	Cash	G2	3 0 0 0		3 0 0 0 Dr.

Delivery Service Revenue   *Account No. 400*

Date		Explanation	Post. Ref.	Debit	Credit	Balance
1991 Dec.	15	Cash	G1		5 0 0 0	5 0 0 0 Cr.
	20	On account	G1		5 7 0 0	1 0 7 0 0 Cr.

Advertising Expense   *Account No. 500*

Date		Explanation	Post. Ref.	Debit	Credit	Balance
1991 Dec.	24	On account	G2	5 0		5 0 Dr.

Gas and Oil Expense   *Account No. 501*

Date		Explanation	Post. Ref.	Debit	Credit	Balance
1991 Dec.	30	On account	G2	6 8 0		6 8 0 Dr.

Salaries Expense   *Account No. 502*

Date		Explanation	Post. Ref.	Debit	Credit	Balance
1991 Dec.	28	Cash paid	G2	3 6 0 0		3 6 0 0 Dr.

Utilities Expense   *Account No. 503*

Date		Explanation	Post. Ref.	Debit	Credit	Balance
1991 Dec.	29	Cash paid	G2	1 5 0		1 5 0 Dr.

■ THE TRIAL BALANCE

Objective 5:
Prepare a trial balance to test the equality of debits and credits in the journalizing and posting process.

Periodically, accountants use a trial balance to test the equality of their debits and credits. A **trial balance** is a listing of the ledger accounts and their debit or credit balances to determine that debits equal credits in the recording process. The accounts appear in the same order as in the general ledger and in the chart of accounts. Thus, they appear in the following order—assets, liabilities, owner's equity, revenues, expenses. Within assets, the most liquid (closest to becoming cash) asset appears first and the least liquid appears last. Among liabilities, those with the shortest "maturities" appear first. The trial balance for Rapid Delivery Company is shown in Illustration 2.7. Note the listing of the account titles on the left (account numbers could be included if desired), the column for debit balances, the column for credit balances, and the equality of the two totals.

When the trial balance does not balance, the first thing to do is to retotal the two columns. If this step does not locate the error, divide the difference in the totals by 2 and then by 9. If the difference is divisible by 2, you may have transferred a debit-balanced account to the trial balance as a credit, or a credit-balanced account as a debit. So if the difference is divisible by 2, look for an amount in the trial balance that is equal to one half of the difference. Thus, if the difference is $800, look for an account with a balance of $400 and see if it is in the wrong column.

If the difference is divisible by 9, you may have made a transposition error in transferring a balance to the trial balance or a slide error. A transposition error occurs when two numbers in an amount are reversed (e.g., writing 753 as 573 or 110 as 101). A slide error occurs when the decimal point is placed incorrectly (e.g., $1,500 recorded as $15.00). Thus,

Illustration 2.7

Trial Balance

RAPID DELIVERY SERVICE Trial Balance December 31, 1991	Debits	Credits
Cash	$10,650	
Accounts Receivable	5,200	
Supplies on Hand	1,400	
Prepaid Insurance	2,400	
Prepaid Rent	1,200	
Delivery Trucks	40,000	
Accounts Payable		$ 3,130
Unearned Delivery Fees		4,500
John Turner, Capital, December 1		50,000
John Turner, Drawing	3,000	
Delivery Service Revenue		10,700
Advertising Expense	50	
Gas and Oil Expense	680	
Salaries Expense	3,600	
Utilities Expense	150	
	$68,330	$68,330

when a difference is divisible by 9, compare the trial balance amounts with the ledger account balances to see if you made a transposition or slide error in transferring the amounts.

If none of these steps locates the error, the error may be due to one of the following causes:

1. Failing to post part of a journal entry.
2. Posting a debit as a credit, or vice versa.
3. Incorrectly determining the balance of an account.
4. Omitting an account from the trial balance.
5. Making a transposition or slide error in the accounts or the journal.

Generally, you should work backward through the steps taken to prepare the trial balance. Assuming you have already retotaled the columns and traced the amounts appearing in the trial balance back to the ledger account balances, the remaining steps are as follows. Verify the balance of each ledger account, verify postings to the ledger, verify journal entries, and then review the transactions.

The equality of the two totals in the trial balance does not necessarily mean that the accounting has been error-free. Serious errors may have been made, such as failure to record a transaction, or posting a debit or credit to the wrong account. For instance, if a transaction involving payment of a $100 account payable is never recorded, the trial balance totals will still balance, but at an amount which is $100 too high. Both cash and accounts payable would be overstated by $100.

A trial balance may be prepared at any time—at the end of a day, a week, a month, a quarter, or a year. Typically, a trial balance is prepared prior to the preparation of financial statements. Dollar signs may be used but are not required.

What you have learned in this chapter is basic to your study of accounting. The entire process of accounting is based on the double-entry principle. In Chapter 3, you will learn that not all business transactions are "cut and dried." Sometimes adjustments are needed.

■ UNDERSTANDING THE LEARNING OBJECTIVES: CHAPTER 2

1. Use the account as the basic classifying and storage unit for information.

   - An account is a storage unit used to classify and summarize money measurements of business activity of a similar nature.
   - An account is set up whenever it is necessary to provide useful information about a particular business item to some party having a valid interest in the business.

2. Express the effects of business transactions in terms of debits and credits to six different types of accounts.

   - A T-account resembles the letter T.

- Debits are entries on the left-hand side of a T-account.
- Credits are entries on the right-hand side of a T-account.
- Asset, expense, and drawings accounts are increased by debits.
- Liability, owner's capital, and revenue accounts are increased by credits.

3. Record the effects of business transactions in a journal.

- A journal contains a chronological record of the transactions of a business.
- An example of a general journal is shown in Illustration 2.3.
- Journalizing is the process of entering a transaction in a journal.

4. Post journal entries to the accounts in the ledger.

- Posting is the process of transferring information recorded in the journal to the proper place in the ledger.
- Cross-indexing is the placing of the account number of the ledger account in the journal and the placing of the journal page number in the ledger account.
- An example of cross-indexing appears in Illustration 2.5.

5. Prepare a trial balance to test the equality of debits and credits in the journalizing and posting process.

- A trial balance is a listing of the ledger accounts and their debit or credit balances.
- If the trial balance does not balance, the accountant should work backward to discover the error.
- A trial balance is shown in Illustration 2.7.

6. Define and use correctly the new terms in the glossary.

NEW TERMS INTRODUCED IN CHAPTER 2

Account   An element in an accounting system that is used to classify and summarize money measurements of business activity of a similar nature. The three-column account is normally used. It contains columns for debit, credit, and balance (51).

Charge   Means the same as the word *debit* (52).

Chart of accounts   The complete listing of the titles and account numbers of all of the accounts in the ledger; somewhat comparable to a table of contents (57).

Compound journal entry   A journal entry with more than one debit and/or credit (70).

Credit   The right side of any account; when used as a verb, to enter a dollar amount on the right side of an account; credits increase liability, owner's equity, and revenue accounts and decrease asset, expense, and owner's drawing accounts (52).

Credit balance   The balance in an account when the sum of the credits to the account exceeds the sum of the debits to that account (55).

Cross-indexing   The placing of the account number of the ledger account in the journal and the placing of the journal page number in the ledger account (68).

Debit   The left side of any account; when used as a verb, to enter a dollar amount on the left side of an account; debits increase asset, expense, and owner's drawing accounts and decrease liability, owner's equity, and revenue accounts (52).

Debit balance   The balance in an account when the sum of the debits to the account exceeds the sum of the credits to that account (55).

Double-entry procedure   The accounting requirement that each transaction must be recorded by an entry that has equal debits and credits (52).

Journal   A chronological (arranged in order of time) record of business transactions; the simplest form of journal is the two-column general journal (64).

Journal entry   Shows all of the effects of a business transaction as expressed in terms of debit(s) and credit(s) and may include an explanation of the transaction (65).

Journalizing   A step in the accounting recording process that consists of entering a transaction in a journal (68).

Ledger   The complete collection of all of the accounts of a company; often referred to as the *general ledger* (57).

Nominal accounts   Income statement accounts (revenues and expenses) (57).

Note   A written promise to pay to another party the amount owed either when demanded or at a certain specified date (53).

Posting   Recording in the ledger the information contained in the journal (68).

Real accounts   Balance sheet accounts (assets, liabilities, and owner's equity) (57).

T-account   An account resembling the letter T, which is used for illustrative purposes only. Debits are entered on the left side of the account, and credits are entered on the right side of the account (51).

Trial balance   A listing of the ledger accounts and their debit or credit balances to determine that debits equal credits in the recording process (74).

DEMONSTRATION PROBLEM

Briarcliff Riding Stable, owned by Joanna Willis, had the following balance sheet on June 30, 1991:

BRIARCLIFF RIDING STABLE
Balance Sheet
June 30, 1991

Assets

Cash	$ 7,000
Accounts receivable	5,400
Land	40,000
Total assets	$52,400

Liabilities and Owner's Equity

Liabilities:	
Accounts payable	$ 800
Loan payable	40,000
Total liabilities	$40,800
Owner's equity:	
Joanna Willis, capital	11,600
Total liabilities and owner's equity	$52,400

Transactions for July 1991 were as follows:

July 1   The owner invested additional cash of $25,000.
    1   Paid for a prefabricated building constructed on the land at a cost of $24,000.
    8   Paid an account payable of $800.
  10   Collected an account receivable of $5,400.
  12   Horse feed to be used in July was purchased on credit for $1,100.
  24   A miscellaneous expense of $800 for July was paid.
  28   The owner withdrew $700 cash.
  31   Salaries of $1,600 for the month were paid.
  31   Riding and lesson fees for July were billed to a riding club in the amount of $3,600. Payment is due on August 10.
  31   Boarding fees for July were billed to the riding club in the amount of $4,500. This amount is due August 10.

Required: a.   Prepare the journal entries to record the transactions for July 1991.

b.   Post the journal entries to the ledger accounts after entering the beginning balances in those accounts. Insert cross-indexing references in the general journal and ledger. Use the following chart of accounts:

Account No.	Account Title
100	Cash
101	Accounts Receivable
112	Land
114	Building
200	Accounts Payable
205	Loan Payable
300	Joanna Willis, Capital
301	Joanna Willis, Drawing
400	Horse Boarding Fees Revenue
401	Riding and Lesson Fees Revenue
501	Feed Expense
502	Salaries Expense
510	Miscellaneous Expense

c.   Prepare a trial balance.

Solution to demonstration problem

a.

BRIARCLIFF RIDING STABLE
GENERAL JOURNAL   *Page 1*

Date		Account Titles and Explanation	Post. Ref.	Debit	Credit
1991 July	1	Cash	100	2 5 0 0 0	
		Joanna Willis, Capital	300		2 5 0 0 0
		Additional cash was invested by owner.			
	1	Building	114	2 4 0 0 0	
		Cash	100		2 4 0 0 0
		Paid for a building.			
	8	Accounts Payable	200	8 0 0	
		Cash	100		8 0 0
		Paid an account payable.			
	10	Cash	100	5 4 0 0	
		Accounts Receivable	101		5 4 0 0
		Collected an account receivable.			
	12	Feed Expense	501	1 1 0 0	
		Accounts Payable	200		1 1 0 0
		Purchased feed on credit.			
	24	Miscellaneous Expense	510	8 0 0	
		Cash	100		8 0 0
		Paid a miscellaneous expense.			
	28	Joanna Willis, Drawing	301	7 0 0	
		Cash	100		7 0 0
		Owner withdrew cash.			
	31	Salaries Expense	502	1 6 0 0	
		Cash	100		1 6 0 0
		Paid salaries for July.			
	31	Accounts Receivable	101	3 6 0 0	
		Riding and Lesson Fees Revenue	401		3 6 0 0
		Billed riding and lesson fees for July.			
	31	Accounts Receivable	101	4 5 0 0	
		Horse Boarding Fees Revenue	400		4 5 0 0
		Billed boarding fees for July.			

b.

BRIARCLIFF RIDING STABLE
GENERAL LEDGER

Cash   *Account No. 100*

Date		Explanation	Post. Ref.	Debit	Credit	Balance
1991 June	30	Balance				7 0 0 0 Dr.
July	1	Owner investment	G1	2 5 0 0 0		3 2 0 0 0 Dr.
	1	Building	G1		2 4 0 0 0	8 0 0 0 Dr.
	8	Accounts payable	G1		8 0 0	7 2 0 0 Dr.
	10	Accounts receivable	G1	5 4 0 0		1 2 6 0 0 Dr.
	24	Miscellaneous expense	G1		8 0 0	1 1 8 0 0 Dr.
	28	Owner withdrawal	G1		7 0 0	1 1 1 0 0 Dr.
	31	Salaries expense	G1		1 6 0 0	9 5 0 0 Dr.

Accounts Receivable   *Account No. 101*

Date		Explanation	Post. Ref.	Debit	Credit	Balance
1991 June	30	Balance				5 4 0 0 Dr.
July	10	Cash	G1		5 4 0 0	– 0 –
	31	Riding and lesson fees	G1	3 6 0 0		3 6 0 0 Dr.
	31	Horse boarding fees	G1	4 5 0 0		8 1 0 0 Dr.

Land   *Account No. 112*

Date		Explanation	Post. Ref.	Debit	Credit	Balance
1991 June	30	Balance				4 0 0 0 0 Dr.

Building   *Account No. 114*

Date		Explanation	Post. Ref.	Debit	Credit	Balance
1991 July	1	Cash	G1	2 4 0 0 0		2 4 0 0 0 Dr.

GENERAL LEDGER *(continued)*

Accounts Payable — Account No. 200

Date		Explanation	Post. Ref.	Debit	Credit	Balance
1991 June	30	Balance				800 Cr.
July	8	Cash	G1	800		-0-
	12	Feed expense	G1		1100	1100 Cr.

Loan Payable — Account No. 205

Date		Explanation	Post. Ref.	Debit	Credit	Balance
1991 June	30	Balance				40000 Cr.

Joanna Willis, Capital — Account No. 300

Date		Explanation	Post. Ref.	Debit	Credit	Balance
1991 June	30	Balance				11600 Cr.
July	1	Cash	G1		25000	36600 Cr.

Joanna Willis, Drawing — Account No. 301

Date		Explanation	Post. Ref.	Debit	Credit	Balance
1991 July	28	Cash	G1	700		700 Dr.

Horse Boarding Fees Revenue — Account No. 400

Date		Explanation	Post. Ref.	Debit	Credit	Balance
1991 July	31	Accounts receivable	G1		4500	4500 Cr.

Riding and Lesson Fees Revenue — Account No. 401

Date		Explanation	Post. Ref.	Debit	Credit	Balance
1991 July	31	Accounts receivable	G1		3600	3600 Cr.

GENERAL LEDGER *(concluded)*

Feed Expense   *Account No. 501*

Date		Explanation	Post. Ref.	Debit	Credit	Balance
1991 July	12	Accounts payable	G1	1 1 0 0		1 1 0 0 Dr.

Salaries Expense   *Account No. 502*

Date		Explanation	Post. Ref.	Debit	Credit	Balance
1991 July	31	Cash	G1	1 6 0 0		1 6 0 0 Dr.

Miscellaneous Expense   *Account No. 510*

Date		Explanation	Post. Ref.	Debit	Credit	Balance
1991 July	24	Cash	G1	8 0 0		8 0 0 Dr.

c.

BRIARCLIFF RIDING STABLE
Trial Balance
July 31, 1991

	Debits	Credits
Cash	$ 9,500	
Accounts Receivable	8,100	
Land	40,000	
Building	24,000	
Accounts Payable		$ 1,100
Loan Payable		40,000
Joanna Willis, Capital		36,600
Joanna Willis, Drawing	700	
Horse Boarding Fees Revenue		4,500
Riding and Lesson Fees Revenue		3,600
Feed Expense	1,100	
Salaries Expense	1,600	
Miscellaneous Expense	800	
	$85,800	$85,800

QUESTIONS

1. Define debit and credit. Name the types of accounts that are:

   a. Increased by debits.
   b. Decreased by debits.
   c. Increased by credits.
   d. Decreased by credits.

      Do you think this system makes sense? Can you conceive of other possible methods for recording changes in accounts?

2. Why are expense and revenue accounts used when all revenues and expenses could be shown directly in the owner's equity account?

3. What is the purpose of the owner's drawing account and how is it increased?

4. Are the following possibilities conceivable in an entry involving only one debit and one credit? Why?

   a. Increase a liability and increase an expense.
   b. Increase an asset and decrease a liability.
   c. Increase a revenue and decrease an expense.
   d. Decrease an asset and increase another asset.
   e. Decrease an asset and increase a liability.
   f. Decrease a revenue and decrease an asset.
   g. Decrease a liability and increase a revenue.

5. Describe a ledger and a chart of accounts. How do these two compare with a book and its table of contents?

6. Describe the nature and purposes of the general journal. What does "journalizing" mean? Give an example of a compound entry in the general journal.

7. Describe the act of posting. What difficulties could arise if no cross-indexing existed between the general journal and the ledger accounts?

8. Which of the following cash payments would involve the immediate recording of an expense? Why?

   a. Paid an account payable.
   b. Paid for land to use as a future plant site.
   c. Paid the current month's rent.
   d. Paid salaries for the last half of the current month.

9. What types of accounts appear in the trial balance? What are the purposes of the trial balance?

10. You have found that the total of the Debits column of the trial balance of Landers Company is $200,000, while the total of the Credits column is $180,000. What are some of the possible causes of this difference? If the difference between the columns is divisible by 9, what types of errors are possible?

11. Store equipment was purchased for $1,500. Instead of debiting the Store Equipment account, the debit was made to Delivery Equipment. Of what help will the trial balance be in locating this error? Why?

12. A student remembered that the side toward the window in the classroom was the debit side of an account. The student took an examination in a room where the windows were on the other side of the room and became confused and consistently reversed debits and credits. Would the student's trial balance have equal debit and credit totals? If there were no existing balances in any of the accounts to begin with, would the error prevent the student from preparing correct financial statements? Why or why not?

EXERCISES

E-1
Indicate rules of debit and credit

Below is a diagram of the various types of accounts. Indicate where pluses (+) or minuses (−) should be inserted to indicate what effect debits and credits have on each account.

Asset Accounts		=	Liability Accounts		+	Owner's Equity Accounts	
Debit	Credit		Debit	Credit		Debit	Credit

	Expense Accounts and Owner's Drawing Account		Revenue Accounts	
	Debit	Credit	Debit	Credit

E-2
Record transactions in T-accounts

Using T-accounts, show how the following transactions would be recorded:

a. Cash of $65,000 was invested in a business by its owner, Pete Wilkens.
b. Wages for the period were paid to employees, $7,000.
c. Services were performed for a customer on account, $13,000.
d. The customer in (c) paid $500 on the account receivable.

E-3
Prepare journal entries

Give the journal entry required for each of the following transactions:

a. Larry Hoeflin invested $85,000 cash in his business.
b. A $52,000 loan was arranged with a bank. The bank increased the company's checking account by $52,000 after the owner signed a written promise to return the $52,000 in 30 days.
c. Cash was received for services performed for a customer, $1,360.
d. Services were performed for a customer on account, $2,120.
e. The customer in (d) paid the account.

E-4
Prepare journal entries

Prepare journal entries to record each of the following transactions for Joe Fennell Company. Use the letter of the transaction in place of the date. Include an explanation for each entry.

a. The owner invested $320,000 cash in the business.
b. Purchased delivery equipment on account, $200,000.
c. Earned (but did not yet receive) delivery fee revenue, $4,000.
d. Collected the account receivable for the delivery fees, $4,000.
e. Paid the account payable for the delivery equipment purchased, $200,000.
f. Paid for utilities used during the month, $2,000.
g. Paid salaries for the month, $6,000.
h. Incurred $1,600 gas and oil expenses but did not yet pay for them.
i. Purchased more delivery equipment for cash, $40,000.
j. Performed delivery services for a retail store on account, $20,000.

E-5
Record transactions in T-accounts

Using the data in Exercise E-4, record the transactions directly in T-accounts. Write the letter of the transaction in the T-account before the dollar amount. Determine a balance for each account.

E-6
Prepare a trial balance

Using your answer for Exercise E-5, prepare a trial balance. Assume the date of the trial balance is March 31, 1991.

E-7
Prepare simple and
compound journal
entries

Becker Company purchased land for $200,000 cash and a building for $700,000 cash. Show how this transaction can be recorded in two separate simple journal entries or in one compound journal entry. Which is correct?

E-8
Prepare journal
entries

Give the journal entry (without dollar amounts) for a transaction that would involve each of the following combinations of types of accounts:

a.   An asset and a liability.
b.   An expense and an asset.
c.   A liability and an expense.
d.   Owner's equity and an asset.
e.   Two asset accounts.
f.   An asset and a revenue.

E-9
Determine trial
balance errors

Jeff Dennis owns and manages a bowling center called Tri-Angle Lanes. He also maintains his own accounting records and was about to prepare financial statements for the year 1991. When he prepared the trial balance from the ledger accounts, the total of the Debits column was $2,486,700, and the total of the Credits column was $2,474,700. What are the possible reasons why the totals of the debits and credits are out of balance?

E-10
Determine source of
trial balance error

Joe Wells was trying to finish his homework assignment quickly so he could go out on a date. The trial balance totals were $432,000 (Dr.) and $436,860 (Cr.) causing a difference of $4,860. How would you go about finding the cause(s) of the difference?

PROBLEMS, SERIES A

P2-1-A
Record transactions
in T-accounts

Larson Company engaged in the following transactions in May 1991:

May   1   The owner, Sam Larson, invested $80,000 cash in the business.
      2   Purchased cleaning equipment on account, $20,000.
      3   Paid cash for a building, $50,000.
      5   Paid $900 to rent a truck for a three-month period.
    10   Performed cleaning services for a customer on account, $9,000.
    15   Paid for the cleaning equipment purchased on May 2.
    22   Performed cleaning services for a customer for cash, $4,400.
    27   Received bill and paid for cleaning supplies used this month, $3,200.
    31   Paid salaries for the month, $1,600.
    31   The owner withdrew $800 for personal living expenses.

Required: Record the transactions directly into T-accounts. Determine the ending balance in each account.

P2-2-A
Prepare journal
entries

Presented below are the transactions of Floyd Realty Company for March 1991.

1.   The owner, Donna Floyd, invested $120,000 cash.
2.   Paid $10,800 as the rent for March on an office building.
3.   Billed a client for commissions revenue for March, $96,000.
4.   Paid $1,200 for office supplies received and used in March.
5.   Borrowed $30,000 from the bank on a note.
6.   Collected $72,000 cash on an account receivable.
7.   Received a bill for $3,600 for advertising appearing in the local newspaper in March.
8.   Paid cash for gas and oil consumed in March, $2,550.

9. Paid $96,000 to employees for wages earned in March.
10. The owner withdrew $3,000 cash.

Required: Prepare general journal entries for the above transactions.

P2-3-A
Prepare trial balance

The following is a list of accounts and their balances for Woods Company as of December 31, 1991:

Jack Woods, Drawing	$ 2,800	Cash	$11,200
Accounts Payable	3,360	Rent Expense	5,600
Salaries Expense	42,000	Miscellaneous Expense	2,100
Furniture and Equipment	16,800	Supplies on Hand	3,500
Accounts Receivable	6,440	Prepaid Insurance	5,320
Jack Woods, Capital	19,180	Unearned Service Fees	8,820
Service Revenue	64,400		

Required: Prepare a trial balance as of December 31, 1991. Arrange the accounts in the order in which they would appear in the ledger. Assume the accounts have normal balances.

P2-4-A
Prepare journal entries, post to ledger accounts, and prepare trial balance

The transactions for October 1991 for Overland Freight Company are given below.

Oct. 1 The owner, Randy Cooper, invested cash, $41,600.
 3 Borrowed $13,000 from the bank on a note.
 4 Purchased a truck for $24,180 cash.
 6 Delivery services were performed for a customer who promised to pay later, $9,360.
 7 Employee services received and paid for, $3,640.
 10 Partial collection was made for the services performed on October 6, $2,080.
 14 Office supplies were purchased for $1,300 on account. They will be paid for and used next month.
 17 A bill for $1,400 was received for gas and oil used to date.
 25 Delivery services were performed for a customer who paid immediately, $11,700.
 31 Wages paid were $3,900.
 31 The owner withdrew $1,040 for personal use.

Required: a. Prepare journal entries to record the transactions. Assume all entries are entered on page 10 of the general journal.
b. Open three-column ledger accounts and post the entries. Number the accounts starting with 1, 2, 3, and so on.
c. Prepare a trial balance as of October 31, 1991.

P2-5-A
Prepare journal entries, post to ledger accounts, and prepare trial balance

The transactions given below are for Appliance Repair Company for July 1991.

July 2 The owner, Bob Sears, invested $40,000 cash in the business.
 3 The company paid rent for July, $2,000.
 5 A truck was purchased for $12,000 cash.
 9 A bill for $2,000 for advertising for July was received and paid.
 14 Cash of $5,600 was received for appliance repair services performed for a condominium complex.
 15 Wages of $1,600 for the first half of July were paid.
 20 The company performed appliance repair services on account for a company, $1,600.
 22 Office furniture was acquired for $3,200 on account.
 25 The owner withdrew $1,200 cash for personal use.
 30 Cash of $9,000 was received for appliance repair service performed for a company.
 31 Wages of $1,600 for the second half of July were paid.

Required: a. Prepare journal entries to record the transactions. Assume all entries are entered on page 40 of the general journal.
b. Open three-column ledger accounts and post the entries. Number the accounts 100, 101, 102, and so on.
c. Prepare a trial balance as of July 31, 1991.

P2-6-A
Open ledger accounts, journalize transactions, post journal entries, and prepare trial balance; ledger accounts have beginning balances

Green Lawn Care Company, owned by Gene Harper, was formed several years ago. The company's trial balance at the end of the first 11 months of its current fiscal year is presented below.

GREEN LAWN CARE COMPANY
Trial Balance
June 30, 1991

Account No.	Account Title	Debits	Credits
101	Cash	$ 196,640	
102	Accounts Receivable	209,600	
110	Land	254,120	
201	Accounts Payable		$ 89,600
301	Gene Harper, Capital		342,760
302	Gene Harper, Drawing	88,000	
400	Lawn Care Revenue		720,000
410	Shrubbery Care Revenue		269,360
510	Salaries Expense	175,600	
520	Chemical Supplies Expense	198,400	
530	Advertising Expense	48,800	
540	Truck Operating Expense	58,400	
550	Office Rent Expense	88,000	
560	Office Supplies Expense	3,200	
570	Telephone and Utilities Expense	6,160	
580	Customer Entertainment Expense	6,800	
590	Truck Rent Expense	88,000	
		$1,421,720	$1,421,720

Transactions for July 1991 were as follows:

July 2 Paid office rent for July, $8,000.
     5 Paid the account payable of $89,600.
     8 Paid advertising for July, $3,200.
    10 Purchased a small tract of land for cash, $2,800.
    13 Purchased on account $640 of office supplies for use in July.
    15 Collected cash from a large homeowners' association on account, $204,800.
    20 Paid for customer entertainment in July, $200.
    26 Paid for gasoline used in the trucks in July, $720.
    28 Billed homeowners' association for services performed in July; lawn care, $126,000, and shrubbery care, $86,000.
    30 Paid for July chemical supplies, $52,800.
    31 Paid truck rent expense for July, $8,000.
    31 Paid July salaries, $40,800.
    31 The owner withdrew $8,000 cash.

Required: a. Open three-column ledger accounts for each of the accounts in the trial balance. Place the word *balance* in the explanation space, enter the date July 1, 1991, on the same line, and enter the proper beginning balance in each account.
b. Prepare general journal entries for the transactions.
c. Post the journal entries to the general ledger accounts.
d. Prepare a trial balance as of July 31, 1991.

P2-7-A
Prepare corrected trial balance

Casey Jones prepared a trial balance for Cross Company that did not balance. The trial balance she prepared was as follows:

CROSS COMPANY
Trial Balance
December 31, 1991

	Debits	Credits
Cash	$ 48,000	
Accounts Receivable	30,600	
Equipment	120,000	
Accounts Payable		$ 18,000
J. Cross, Capital		120,000
J. Cross, Drawing	12,000	
Service Revenue		324,000
Advertising Expense	900	
Salaries Expense	132,000	
Rent Expense	48,000	
Utilities Expense	33,600	
	$425,100	$462,000

In trying to find out why the trial balance did not balance, Casey discovered the following errors:

1. Cash was understated (too low) by $6,000 because of an error in addition in determining the balance of that account in the ledger.
2. A credit of $3,600 to Accounts Receivable in the journal was not posted to the ledger at all.
3. A debit of $12,000 for a withdrawal by the owner was posted as a credit to the owner's capital account.
4. The balance of $9,000 in the Advertising Expense account was entered as $900 in the trial balance.
5. Miscellaneous Expense, with a balance of $2,400, was omitted from the trial balance.

Required:

Prepare a corrected trial balance for Cross Company as of December 31, 1991. Hint: Some errors may not cause the trial balance to be out of balance, but all errors should be corrected.

PROBLEMS, SERIES B

P2-1-B
Record transactions in T-accounts

Lacy Company engaged in the following transactions in June 1991:

June 1   The owner, Bill Lacy, invested $180,000 cash in the business.
      4   Paid cash for a delivery truck, $60,000.
      7   Rented a building and paid $1,800 to cover a three-month period from this date.
     12   Performed delivery services for a customer on account, $7,500.
     17   Received and paid bill for gas and oil, $1,260.
     22   Performed delivery services for a customer for cash, $4,200.
     26   Received the utilities bill for June, $225.
     30   Paid salaries of $3,600.
     30   The owner withdrew $1,500 for personal living expenses.

Required:

Record the transactions directly into T-accounts. Determine the ending balance in each account.

P2-2-B
Prepare journal entries

Jefferson Cleaners entered into the following transactions in August 1991:

Aug. 2   The owner, Dale Jefferson, invested $540,000 cash in the business.
3   Paid rent for August on a building and laundry equipment, $9,450.
4   Purchased and paid for a delivery truck, $72,000.
6   Cash received for laundry services performed for a large motel chain, $81,000.
13   Laundry services were performed on account for a large industrial company, $72,000.
15   Received and paid a bill for $1,773 for gasoline and oil used in operations.
23   Cash collected from a customer on account, $67,500.
31   Paid $24,300 to employees for wages earned during August.
31   Received the electric and gas bill for August, $1,395.

Required: Prepare general journal entries for the above transactions.

P2-3-B
Prepare trial balance

The following is a list of accounts and their balances for Phillips Company as of December 31, 1991:

Skip Phillips, Drawing	$13,200	Skip Phillips, Capital	$62,260
Accounts Payable	22,000	Rent Expense	7,920
Supplies Expense	2,640	Delivery Equipment	70,400
Office Equipment	19,800	Delivery Service Revenue	81,400
Notes Payable	33,880	Salaries Expense	35,200
Accounts Receivable	32,780	Prepaid Insurance	3,960
Utilities Expense	5,280	Salaries Payable	6,600
Cash	14,960		

Required: Prepare a trial balance as of December 31, 1991. Arrange the accounts in the order in which they would appear in the ledger. Assume the accounts have normal balances.

P2-4-B
Prepare journal entries, post to ledger accounts, and prepare trial balance

The transactions listed below are those of Grant Company for April 1991.

Apr. 1   The owner, Kathy Grant, invested $180,000 cash in the business.
3   Rent was paid for April, $1,200.
6   Delivery equipment was purchased and paid for, $21,000.
7   Office equipment was purchased on account from Benton Company for $14,200.
14   Wages were paid, $4,200.
15   $8,700 was received from a customer for services performed.
18   An invoice was received from Bill's Gas Station for $150 for gas and oil used.
23   Borrowed $15,000 from the bank on a note.
29   Purchased delivery equipment for $27,600 on account.
30   Wages of $5,400 were paid.

Required: a.   Prepare journal entries to record the transactions. Assume all entries are entered on page 20 of the general journal.
b.   Open three-column ledger accounts and post the entries. Number the accounts 100, 101, 102, and so on.
c.   Prepare a trial balance as of April 30, 1991.

P2-5-B
Prepare journal entries, post to ledger accounts, and prepare trial balance

The transactions given below are for Aerobic Company for April 1991.

Apr. 1   The owner, Betty Allen, invested $300,000 cash in the business.
5   The company borrowed $150,000 from its bank and issued its note payable to the bank.
9   Paid $120,000 cash for land and $285,000 cash for a building located on the land.
14   Purchased $48,000 of exercise equipment on account.
17   Paid $3,600 cash for supplies to be used in April.
25   Sales of services to a customer on account were $30,000.
30   Sales of services to a customer for cash were $6,000.
30   Paid salaries for April, $6,000.

Required: a.   Prepare journal entries to record the transactions. Assume all entries are entered on page 30 of the general ledger.

b. Open three-column ledger accounts and post the entries. Number the accounts 10, 11, 12, and so on.

c. Prepare a trial balance as of April 30, 1991.

P2-6-B
Open ledger accounts, journalize transactions, post journal entries, and prepare trial balance; ledger accounts have beginning balances

The trial balance of Tennis Company at the end of the first 11 months of its fiscal year is given below.

TENNIS COMPANY
Trial Balance
May 31, 1991

Account No.	Account Title	Debits	Credits
100	Cash	$129,888	
102	Accounts Receivable	130,800	
121	Land	48,000	
210	Accounts Payable		$ 30,000
220	Notes Payable		24,000
310	Debra Lewis, Capital		170,880
320	Debra Lewis, Drawing	26,400	
400	Tennis Lesson Revenue		324,000
510	Tennis Professionals' Salaries Expense	79,200	
520	Advertising Expense	33,600	
530	Lesson Supplies Expense	3,600	
540	Equipment Repairs Expense	2,400	
550	Office Salaries Expense	26,400	
560	Building Rent Expense	52,800	
570	Utilities Expense	3,360	
580	Entertainment Expense	1,392	
590	Equipment Rent Expense	10,560	
600	Miscellaneous Expense	480	
		$548,880	$548,880

Transactions for June 1991 were as follows:

June 1   Paid building rent for June, $4,800.
     2   Paid an accounts payable, $9,160.
     5   Purchased a small tract of land for cash, $3,600.
     7   Gave tennis lessons to members of a large tennis organization on account, $5,200.
    10   Paid the note payable of $24,000.
    13   Received cash from a customer on account, $5,600.
    19   Received a bill for equipment repairs, $360.
    24   Paid the June telephone bill, $132, and the June electric bill, $156.
    28   Received a bill for June advertising, $2,640.
    30   Gave tennis lessons to members of a tennis club for cash, $7,200.
    30   Paid office salaries, $2,400, and tennis professionals' salaries, $7,200.
    30   Gave tennis lessons to members of a tennis club on account, $8,800.
    30   Costs paid in entertaining persons who subsequently became members, $408.
    30   Paid equipment rent expenses for June, $960.
    30   The owner withdrew $2,400 cash.

Required: a. Open three-column ledger accounts for each of the accounts in the trial balance. Place the word *Balance* in the explanation space, enter the date June 1, 1991, on the same line, and enter the proper beginning balance in each account.

b. Prepare general journal entries for the transactions.

c. Post the journal entries to the general ledger accounts.

d. Prepare a trial balance as of June 30, 1991.

P2-7-B
*Prepare corrected
trial balance*

Charlie Perdomo, the owner of Misty Sprinkler Company, prepared the following trial balance from the ledger, which did not balance.

MISTY SPRINKLER COMPANY
Trial Balance
December 31, 1991

	Debits	Credits
Cash	$ 44,400	
Accounts Receivable	30,600	
Furniture and Equipment	90,000	
Office Fixtures	36,000	
Accounts Payable		$ 16,800
Charlie Perdomo, Capital		180,000
Charlie Perdomo, Drawing	21,600	
Service Revenue		270,000
Salaries Expense	210,000	
Rent Expense	30,000	
Miscellaneous Expense	5,400	
	$468,000	$466,800

In trying to find out why the trial balance did not balance, Charlie examined the accounting records carefully. In searching back through the accounting records, Charlie found that the following errors had been made:

1. One entire entry was never posted. It included a debit to Cash and a credit to Accounts Receivable for $3,600.
2. In computing the balance of the Accounts Payable account, a credit of $2,400 was omitted from the computation.
3. In preparing the trial balance, the capital account balance was miscopied as $180,000. The ledger account has the balance at its correct amount of $182,400.
4. One debit of $1,800 to the Charlie Perdomo, Drawing account was incorrectly posted as a credit to that account.
5. Office fixtures of $6,000 were debited to Furniture and Equipment when purchased.

Required: Prepare a corrected trial balance for Misty Sprinkler Company as of December 31, 1991. Hint: Some errors may not cause the trial balance to be out of balance, but all errors should be corrected.

BUSINESS DECISION PROBLEM

*Prepare journal
entries, post to
T-accounts, and
judge profitability*

Phillip Grant lost his job as a carpenter with a contractor when a recession hit the construction industry. Phillip had been making $100,000 per year. He decided to form his own company and do home repairs.

The following is a summary of the transactions of the business during the first three months of operations in 1991:

> Jan. 15   Phillip invested $40,000 in the business.
> Feb. 10   Owner withdrew $4,000 for living expenses.
> 25   Received payment of $8,800 for remodeling a basement into a recreation room. The homeowner purchased all of the building materials.

Mar. 5   Paid cash for an advertisement that appeared in the local newspaper, $220.

18   Owner withdrew $3,600 for personal living expenses.

Apr. 10   Received $12,800 for converting a room over a garage into an office for a college professor. The professor purchased all of the materials for the job.

Jan. 15–Apr. 15   Paid gas and oil expenses for automobile, $1,400.

Jan. 15–Apr. 15   Miscellaneous business expenses were paid, $900.

Jan. 15–Apr. 15   The owner withdrew an additional $17,080 to pay various personal expenses.

Required: a.   Prepare journal entries for the above transactions.

b.   Post the journal entries to T-accounts.

c.   How is Phillip doing in this new venture?

3 Adjusting the Accounts

After studying this chapter, you should be able to:

1. Identify the reasons why adjusting entries must be made.
2. Describe the basic characteristics of the accrual basis and the cash basis of accounting.
3. Identify the classes and types of adjusting entries.
4. Prepare adjusting entries.
5. Define and use correctly the new terms in the glossary.

Chapters 1 and 2 introduced the accounting process (or cycle) of analyzing, classifying, and summarizing business transactions into accounts. You learned how these transactions are entered in journals and ledgers. The trial balance was shown as a way to test the equality of debits and credits in the journalizing and posting process. The purpose of the entire accounting process is to produce accurate financial statements. At this point in your study of accounting, you are concentrating on three financial statements—the income statement, the statement of owner's equity, and the balance sheet.

As you learned in Chapter 1 when you first began to analyze business transactions, the evidence of the transaction is usually a source document. A source document is any written or printed evidence of a business transaction that describes the essential facts of that transaction; for example, receipts for cash paid or received, checks written or received, bills sent to customers, or bills received from suppliers. You should be familiar with some or all of these source documents by now. The journal entries made in Chapter 2 were triggered by the giving, receiving, or creating of a source document. Source documents are used to prepare journal entries during an accounting period.

The journal entries we will discuss in this chapter are called *adjusting entries*. Adjusting entries are triggered by the arrival of the end of the accounting period rather than the giving, receiving, or creating of a source document. The purpose of adjusting entries is to bring the accounts to their proper balances before financial statements are prepared. In this chapter, you will learn about the classes and types of adjusting entries and how to record them.

■ THE NEED FOR ADJUSTING ENTRIES

Objective 1:
Identify the reasons
why adjusting entries
must be made.

The income statement of a business reports all revenues earned and all expenses incurred to generate those revenues during a given period. If the income statement does not report all revenues and expenses, it is incomplete, inaccurate, and possibly misleading. Similarly, a balance sheet that does not report all of an entity's assets, liabilities, and owner's equities at a specific point in time may be misleading. Each adjusting entry has a dual purpose: (1) to make the income statement report the proper revenue or expense and (2) to make the balance sheet report the proper asset or liability. Thus, every adjusting entry affects one income statement account and one balance sheet account.

Since those interested in the activities of a business need timely information, financial statements must be prepared periodically. To prepare such statements, the accountant arbitrarily divides an entity's life into time periods. These time periods are usually equal in length and are called *accounting periods*. An **accounting period** may be one month, one quarter, or one year. An accounting period of one year is called an **accounting year,** or fiscal year. A **fiscal year** is any 12 consecutive months, and it may or may not coincide with the **calendar year,** which ends on December 31. Illustration 3.1 shows the fiscal year endings of a survey of 600 companies. More than half of the companies have a fiscal year that coincides with the calendar year. Companies in certain industries tend to have a fiscal year that differs from the calendar year. For instance, to avoid the Christmas holidays, many retail stores end their fiscal year on January 31.

Illustration 3.1

Summary—Fiscal
Year Endings by
Month

	1986	1985	1984	1983
January	23	24	25	25
February	15	16	12	12
March	11	12	13	13
April	5	5	6	6
May	16	14	13	13
June	43	43	40	37
July	14	16	16	17
August	18	20	20	23
September	36	39	39	39
October	23	26	28	25
November	15	11	14	13
Subtotal	219	226	226	223
December	381	374	374	377
Total companies	600	600	600	600

Source: American Institute of Certified Public Accountants, *Accounting Trends & Techniques* (New York: AICPA, 1987), p. 34.

Periodic reporting necessitates the preparation of adjusting entries. **Adjusting entries** are journal entries made at the end of an accounting period to bring about a proper **matching** of revenues and expenses. Adjusting entries reflect economic activity that has taken place but has not yet been properly recorded. Why hasn't this activity already been recorded by the end of the period? The reason is that either (1) it is more convenient and economical to wait until the end of the period to record the activity, or (2) no source documents concerning that activity have yet come to the accountant's attention.

Most adjusting entries are the result of **continuous events,** such as the using up of insurance coverage that had been prepaid. The amounts in the ledger accounts must be brought to their proper balances before financial statements are prepared. That is, **adjusting entries convert the amounts that are actually in the ledger accounts to the amounts that should be in the ledger accounts for proper financial reporting.** To make this conversion, accountants analyze the accounts and determine which accounts need adjustment. For example, assume a three-year insurance policy costing $600 was purchased at the beginning of the year and debited to Prepaid Insurance. At year-end, it is obvious that $200 of the cost should be removed from the asset and recorded as an expense. Failure to do so misstates assets and net income on the financial statements.

The need for adjusting entries is based on the matching principle. The **matching principle** requires that expenses incurred in producing revenues be deducted from the revenues they generated during the accounting period. This matching of expenses and revenues is necessary for the income statement to present an accurate picture of the profitability of a business.

Benefits from many assets such as prepaid expenses (e.g., prepaid insurance and prepaid rent) are being received **continuously** by a company. Thus, the expense relating to these items could also be recognized **continuously** as time elapses. An entry could be made frequently, even daily, to record the expense incurred. But typically, the entry is not made until financial statements are to be prepared. Therefore, if monthly financial statements are prepared, monthly adjusting entries are required. By custom, and in some instances by law, businesses report to their owners at least annually. Accordingly, adjusting entries will be required at least once a year. Remember, however, that the entry transferring an amount from an asset account to an expense account should transfer only the cost of the portion of the asset that has expired.

Cash versus Accrual Basis Accounting

*Objective 2:
Describe the basic
characteristics of the
accrual basis and the
cash basis of
accounting.*

Some relatively small businesses and professional persons, such as physicians, lawyers, and accountants, may account for their revenues and expenses on a cash basis. The **cash basis of accounting** recognizes revenues when cash is received and recognizes expenses when cash is paid out. For example, under the cash basis, services rendered to clients in 1991 for which cash was collected in 1992 would be treated as 1992 revenues. Similarly, under the cash basis, expenses incurred in 1991 for which cash was disbursed in 1992 would be treated as 1992 expenses. Because the cash basis does not match "efforts" and "accomplishments" in terms of expenses incurred and revenues earned, the cash basis of accounting is generally considered unacceptable. Companies using the cash basis may not have to prepare any adjusting entries. The cash basis is acceptable only under those circumstances that approximate the results obtained under the accrual basis of accounting. Under certain circumstances, the cash basis may be used for income tax purposes.

Throughout the text we use the accrual basis of accounting. The **accrual basis of accounting** recognizes revenues when sales are made or services are performed, regardless of when cash is received. Expenses are recognized as incurred, whether or not cash has been paid out. For instance, when services are performed for a customer on account, the revenue is recorded at that time even though cash has not been received. Later, when the cash is received, no revenue is recorded because it has already been recorded. Under the accrual basis, adjusting entries are used to bring the accounts up to date for economic activity that has taken place but has not yet been recorded. Accurate financial statements can then be prepared.

An example of economic activity that would require an adjusting entry is the purchase and gradual use of office supplies. When office supplies are purchased, they are recorded in an asset account, Office Supplies on Hand. Even though office supplies are used during the accounting period, the accountant usually waits until the end of the accounting period to record their consumption. The cost and nuisance of making an entry every time a small amount of office supplies is used outweighs the benefits of having precisely accurate account balances during the period. Instead, an adjusting entry is made at the end of the period to bring the accounts to their proper balances before financial statements are prepared.

■ CLASSES AND TYPES OF ADJUSTING ENTRIES

Objective 3:
Identify the classes and types of adjusting entries.

Adjusting entries can be grouped into two broad classes: deferred (meaning to postpone or delay) items and accrued (meaning to grow or accumulate) items. **Deferred items** consist of adjusting entries involving data previously recorded in accounts. These entries involve the transfer of data already recorded in asset and liability accounts to expense and revenue accounts. **Accrued items** consist of adjusting entries relating to activity on which no data have been previously recorded in the accounts. These entries involve the initial, or first, recording of assets and liabilities and the related revenues and expenses (see Illustration 3.2).

Deferred items require two types of adjusting entries: asset/expense adjustments and liability/revenue adjustments. For example, prepaid insurance and prepaid rent are shown as assets until they are used up; then they become expenses. Also, if a company receives cash for a service it has not yet rendered, this is recorded as an unearned revenue (liability); however, as the company renders the service, the unearned revenue becomes earned revenue.

Illustration 3.2

Two Classes and Four Types of Adjusting Entries

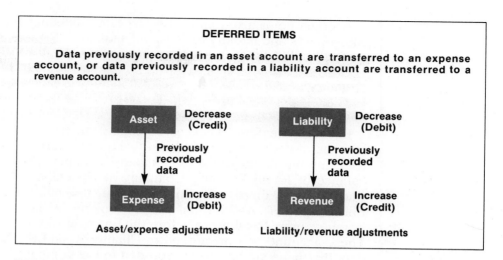

DEFERRED ITEMS

Data previously recorded in an asset account are transferred to an expense account, or data previously recorded in a liability account are transferred to a revenue account.

Asset — Decrease (Credit)

Previously recorded data

Expense — Increase (Debit)

Asset/expense adjustments

Liability — Decrease (Debit)

Previously recorded data

Revenue — Increase (Credit)

Liability/revenue adjustments

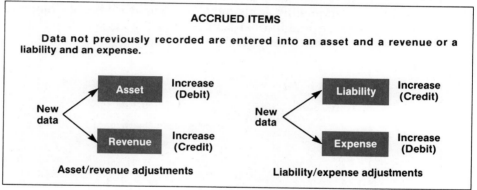

ACCRUED ITEMS

Data not previously recorded are entered into an asset and a revenue or a liability and an expense.

New data

Asset — Increase (Debit)

Revenue — Increase (Credit)

Asset/revenue adjustments

New data

Liability — Increase (Credit)

Expense — Increase (Debit)

Liability/expense adjustments

Illustration 3.3

Trial Balance

RAPID DELIVERY COMPANY
Trial Balance
December 31, 1991

	Debits	Credits
Cash	$10,650	
Accounts Receivable	5,200	
Supplies on Hand	1,400	
Prepaid Insurance	2,400	
Prepaid Rent	1,200	
Delivery Trucks	40,000	
Accounts Payable		$ 3,130
Unearned Delivery Fees		4,500
John Turner, Capital, December 1		50,000
John Turner, Drawing	3,000	
Delivery Service Revenue		10,700
Advertising Expense	50	
Gas and Oil Expense	680	
Salaries Expense	3,600	
Utilities Expense	150	
	$68,330	$68,330

Accrued items also require two types of adjusting entries: asset/revenue adjustments and liability/expense adjustments. For example, if a company performs a service for a customer but has not yet billed the customer, this is recorded as an asset in the form of a receivable and as revenue because the company expects to be paid. Also, if a company owes its employees wages that have not yet been paid, this is recorded as a liability and expense because the company has incurred an expense that must soon be paid.

Each of the four types of adjusting entries—asset/expense, liability/revenue, asset/revenue, and liability/expense—are illustrated in this chapter using the Rapid Delivery Company example from Chapter 2. The trial balance of Rapid Delivery Company at December 31, 1991, is shown in Illustration 3.3 on page 97; this is the same trial balance shown in Chapter 2, Illustration 2.7. As you can see by looking at the trial balance, several accounts must be adjusted before the financial statements can be prepared. These accounts are mentioned in Chapter 2, and the adjustments involve data that have already been recorded in the company's accounts.

In making adjustments for Rapid Delivery Company, we will need to add several additional accounts to the company's chart of accounts shown in Chapter 2 on page 58. These are:

Type of Account	Account No.	Account Title	Description
Contra asset*	110A	Accumulated Depreciation— Delivery Trucks	The total depreciation cost taken on delivery trucks. The balance of this account is deducted from Delivery trucks on the balance sheet.
Liability	202	Salaries Payable	The amount of salaries earned by employees but not yet paid by the company.
Expenses	504	Insurance Expense	The cost of insurance incurred in the current period.
	505	Rent Expense	The cost of rent incurred in the current period.
	506	Supplies Expense	The cost of supplies used in the current period.
	507	Depreciation Expense— Delivery Trucks	The cost of the portion of delivery trucks used up during the current period.

* A contra asset is deducted from an asset account on the balance sheet.

You are now ready to make the actual adjustments for deferred items. If you find the process confusing, go back and restudy the beginning of this chapter so you clearly understand the purpose of adjusting entries.

■ ADJUSTMENTS FOR DEFERRED ITEMS

Objective 4: Prepare adjusting entries.

This section discusses the two types of adjustments for deferred items: asset/expense adjustments and liability/revenue adjustments. In the asset/expense group, you will learn how to prepare adjusting entries for prepaid expenses and depreciation; in the liability/revenue group, you will learn how to prepare adjusting entries for unearned revenues.

Asset/Expense Adjustments—Prepaid Expenses and Depreciation

Rapid Delivery Company must make several asset/expense adjustments for prepaid expenses. A **prepaid expense** is an asset awaiting assignment to expense, such as prepaid insurance, prepaid rent, and supplies on hand. As you will see, the nature of these three adjustments is the same.

Prepaid Insurance.   When an insurance policy premium is paid in advance, the purchase creates the asset, **prepaid insurance.** For accounting purposes, this advance payment is an asset because insurance coverage will be received in the future. With the passage of time, however, the asset gradually expires, and the portion that has expired becomes an expense. To illustrate this point, recall that in Chapter 2, Rapid Delivery Company purchased on account an insurance policy on its delivery trucks for the period December 1, 1991, to December 1, 1992. The journal entry made on December 1, 1991, to record the purchase of the policy was:

```
1991
Dec.  1   Prepaid Insurance . . . . . . . . . . . . . . . . . . . . . .   2,400
              Accounts Payable  . . . . . . . . . . . . . . . . . . .           2,400
          Purchased truck insurance to cover a one-year
          period.
```

The two accounts that relate to insurance are Prepaid Insurance (an asset) and Insurance Expense (an expense). After posting the above entry, the Prepaid Insurance account has a $2,400 debit balance on December 1, 1991, the day the 12-month policy goes into effect. The Insurance Expense account has a zero balance on December 1, 1991, because no time has elapsed to use any of the policy's benefits.

(Dr.)	Prepaid Insurance	(Cr.)	(Dr.)	Insurance Expense	(Cr.)
1991 Dec. 1 Bal.	2,400		1991 Dec. 1 Bal.	-0-	

By December 31, part of the period covered by the policy has expired. Therefore, part of the **service potential** (or benefits that can be obtained from the asset) has expired. The asset will now provide fewer future services or benefits than when it was acquired. The future services that an asset can render make the asset a "thing of value" to the business. We must recognize this reduction of the asset's ability to provide future services by treating the cost of the services received from the asset as an expense. In the case of Rapid Delivery Company, the service received was one month of insurance coverage. Since the policy provides the same services for every month of its one-year life, we assign an equal amount ($200) of cost to each month. Thus, 1/12 of the annual premium is charged to Insurance Expense on December 31. The adjusting journal entry is as follows:

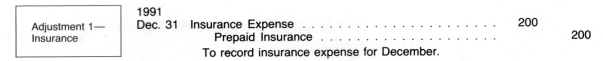

Adjustment 1—
Insurance

1991
Dec. 31   Insurance Expense   200
               Prepaid Insurance   200
          To record insurance expense for December.

In T-account format, the accounts appear as follows after posting the two journal entries above:

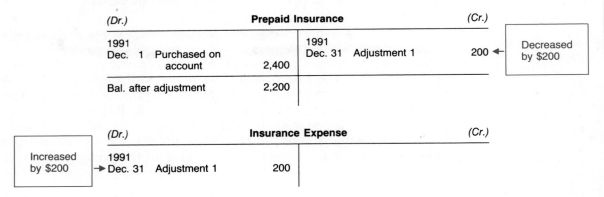

(Dr.)	Prepaid Insurance	(Cr.)
1991 Dec. 1 Purchased on account 2,400	1991 Dec. 31 Adjustment 1 200	← Decreased by $200
Bal. after adjustment 2,200		

(Dr.)	Insurance Expense	(Cr.)
Increased by $200 → 1991 Dec. 31 Adjustment 1 200		

In actual practice, accountants do not use T-accounts. Instead they use three-column ledger forms that have the advantage of showing a balance after each transaction. After posting the two entries above, the three-column ledger accounts appear as follows:

Prepaid Insurance   *Account No. 103*

Date	Explanation	Post. Ref.	Debit	Credit	Balance
1991 Dec. 1	Purchased on account	G1*	2 4 0 0		2 4 0 0 Dr.
31	Adjustment	G3*		2 0 0	2 2 0 0 Dr.

Insurance Expense   *Account No. 504*

Date	Explanation	Post. Ref.	Debit	Credit	Balance
1991 Dec. 31	Adjustment	G3*	2 0 0		2 0 0 Dr.

* Note: These posting references are assumed.

Before the above adjusting entry was made, the entire $2,400 insurance payment made on December 1, 1991, was a prepaid expense for 12 months of insurance protection. As explained earlier, a prepaid expense is an asset awaiting assignment to expense. So on December 31, 1991, one month of protection had passed, and an adjusting entry transferred $200 of the $2,400 ($2,400/12 = $200) to insurance expense. On the income statement for the year ended December 31, 1991, one month of insurance expense, $200, is reported as one of the expenses incurred in generating that year's revenues. The remaining amount of the prepaid insurance, $2,200, is reported on the balance sheet as an asset. The $2,200 prepaid insurance represents the cost of 11 months of insurance protection that remains as a future benefit.

Prepaid Rent.   Prepaid rent is another example of the gradual using up of a previously recorded asset. When rent is paid in advance to cover more than one accounting period, on the date it is paid the prepayment is debited to the Prepaid Rent account (an asset account). Benefits resulting from this expenditure are yet to be received. Thus, the expenditure creates an asset.

The measurement of rent expense is similar to insurance expense and is usually quite simple. Generally, the rental contract specifies the amount of rent per unit of time. If the prepayment covers a three-month rental, one third of this rental is charged to each month. The same amount is charged to each month even though there are varying numbers of days in some months.

For example, in Chapter 2, Rapid Delivery Company paid $1,200 rent in advance on December 1, 1991, to cover a three-month period beginning on that date. The journal entry made at that time was:

```
1991
Dec.  1   Prepaid Rent . . . . . . . . . . . . . . . . . . . . . . . . . .   1,200
              Cash . . . . . . . . . . . . . . . . . . . . . . . . . . . .           1,200
          Paid three months' rent on a building.
```

The two accounts relating to rent are Prepaid Rent (an asset) and Rent Expense. After this entry has been posted, the Prepaid Rent account has a $1,200 balance, and the Rent Expense account has a zero balance because no part of the rent period has yet elapsed.

(Dr.)	**Prepaid Rent**	(Cr.)	(Dr.)	**Rent Expense**	(Cr.)
1991 Dec. 1 Bal. Cash paid 1,200			1991 Dec. 1 Bal. –0–		

On December 31, 1991, an adjusting entry must be prepared. Since one third of the period covered by the prepaid rent (one of three months) has elapsed, one third of the $1,200 of prepaid rent is charged to expense. The required adjusting entry is as follows:

Adjustment 2—
Rent

```
1991
Dec. 31   Rent Expense . . . . . . . . . . . . . . . . . . . . . . . .   400
              Prepaid Rent . . . . . . . . . . . . . . . . . . . . . . .           400
          To record rent expense for December.
```

The T-accounts appear as follows after posting this adjusting entry:

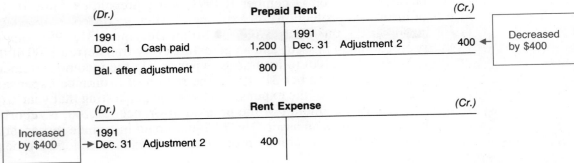

(Dr.)	Prepaid Rent		(Cr.)
1991		1991	
Dec. 1 Cash paid 1,200		Dec. 31 Adjustment 2 400 ←	Decreased by $400
Bal. after adjustment 800			

(Dr.)	Rent Expense	(Cr.)
Increased by $400	1991 → Dec. 31 Adjustment 2 400	

The $400 rent expense appears in the income statement for the year ended December 31, 1991. The remaining $800 of prepaid rent is reported as an asset in the balance sheet for December 31, 1991. Thus, the adjusting entries have accomplished their purpose of maintaining the accuracy of the financial statements.

Supplies on Hand. Almost every business uses supplies in its operations. Supplies may be classified simply as supplies (to include all types of supplies), or more specifically as office supplies (paper, stationery, carbon paper, pencils), selling supplies (gummed tape, string, paper bags or cartons, wrapping paper), or, possibly, cleaning supplies (soap, disinfectants). Supplies are frequently bought in bulk and are an asset until they are used. This asset may be called **supplies on hand** or **supplies inventory.** Even though this term is a prepaid expense, it does not use "prepaid" in its title.

On December 4, 1991, Rapid Delivery Company purchased supplies for $1,400 and recorded the transaction as follows:

```
1991
Dec.  4  Supplies on Hand . . . . . . . . . . . . . . . . . . . . . . .  1,400
            Cash . . . . . . . . . . . . . . . . . . . . . . . . . . .          1,400
         To record the purchase of supplies for future use.
```

The two accounts relating to supplies are Supplies on Hand (an asset) and Supplies Expense. After this entry has been posted, the Supplies on Hand account shows a debit balance of $1,400, and the Supplies Expense account has a zero balance as shown:

(Dr.)	Supplies on Hand	(Cr.)	(Dr.)	Supplies Expense	(Cr.)
1991			1991		
Dec. 4			Dec. 4		
Bal. Cash paid 1,400			Bal. –0–		

An actual physical inventory (a count of the supplies on hand) at the end of the month showed that only $900 of supplies were on hand at that time. Thus, $500 of supplies must have been used in December. An adjusting journal entry is required to bring the two accounts pertaining to supplies to their proper balances. The adjusting entry recognizes the reduction in the asset (Supplies on Hand) and the recording of an expense (Supplies Expense) by transferring $500 from the asset to the expense. From the information given, the asset balance should be $900 and the expense balance, $500. So the following adjusting entry is made:

	1991			
Adjustment 3— Supplies	Dec. 31	Supplies Expense	500	
		Supplies on Hand		500
		To record supplies used during December.		

The T-accounts, after posting this adjusting entry, appear as follows:

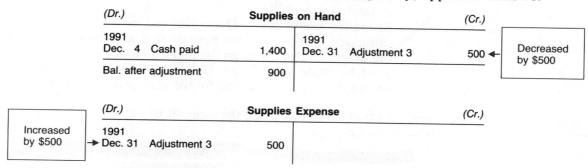

| (Dr.) | Supplies on Hand | | | (Cr.) |

1991			1991		
Dec. 4	Cash paid	1,400	Dec. 31	Adjustment 3	500 ← Decreased by $500
Bal. after adjustment		900			

| (Dr.) | Supplies Expense | | (Cr.) |

Increased by $500

1991		
→ Dec. 31	Adjustment 3	500

The entry to record the use of supplies could be made when the supplies are issued from the storeroom. But such careful accounting for small items each time they are issued is usually too costly a procedure.

Adjusting entries for supplies on hand, like for any other prepaid expense, are made before financial statements are prepared. Supplies expense appears in the income statement. Supplies on hand is reported as an asset in the balance sheet.

Sometimes prepaid expenses such as insurance, rent, and supplies are bought knowing that they will be fully used up within one accounting period (usually one month or one year). If so, at the time of purchase, accountants usually debit an expense rather than an asset. This procedure avoids having to make an adjusting entry at the end of the accounting period. Also, accountants sometimes debit an expense even though the asset will benefit more than the current period. Then, at the end of the accounting period, the adjusting entry must transfer some of the cost from the expense to the asset. For instance, assume that on January 1, rent of $1,200 is paid to cover a three-year period and is debited to Rent Expense. At the end of the year, $800 must be transferred from Rent Expense to Prepaid Rent. To simplify our approach, we will consistently debit the asset account when the asset will benefit more than the current accounting period.

Depreciation.   Just as prepaid insurance and prepaid rent indicate a gradual using up of a previously recorded asset, so does depreciation. However, the overall period of time involved in using up a depreciable asset (such as a building) is much longer and less definite than for prepaid expenses. A prepaid expense generally involves a fairly small amount of money; depreciable assets usually involve large sums of money.

A **depreciable asset** is a manufactured asset such as a building, machine, vehicle, or piece of equipment that provides service to a business. Since these assets are gradually used up over time, depreciation expense is recorded. **Depreciation expense** is the amount of asset cost assigned as an expense to a particular time period. The process of recording depreciation expense is called **depreciation accounting.**

The three factors involved in computing depreciation expense are:

1. **Asset cost.** The asset cost is the amount that a company paid to purchase the depreciable asset.
2. **Estimated salvage value.** The estimated salvage value (scrap value) is the amount that the asset can probably be sold for at the end of its estimated useful life.
3. **Estimated useful life.** The estimated useful life of an asset is the estimated number of time periods that a company can make use of the asset. Useful life is an estimate, not an exact measurement, that must be made in advance. Unfortunately, individuals are unable to see 10 to 15 years into the future with precise accuracy.

The equation for determining the amount of depreciation expense for each time period is:

$$\text{Depreciation expense for each time period} = \frac{\text{Asset cost} - \text{Estimated salvage value}}{\text{Estimated number of time periods in asset's useful life}}$$

Accountants use different methods for recording depreciation. The method illustrated here is known as the **straight-line method.** Other depreciation methods are discussed in Chapter 10. Straight-line depreciation assigns the same amount of depreciation expense to each accounting period over the life of the asset. The **depreciation formula (straight-line)** to compute straight-line depreciation for a one-year period is:

$$\text{Annual depreciation} = \frac{\text{Asset cost} - \text{Estimated salvage value}}{\text{Estimated number of years of useful life}}$$

To illustrate the use of this formula, recall that on December 1, Rapid Delivery Company purchased four trucks at a cost of $40,000. The journal entry made at that time was:

```
1991
Dec.  1  Delivery Trucks . . . . . . . . . . . . . . . . . . . . . . . . .  40,000
            Cash . . . . . . . . . . . . . . . . . . . . . . . . . . . . . .            40,000
              To record the purchase of four delivery trucks.
```

The estimated salvage value for each truck was $1,000, so total salvage value for all four trucks was estimated at $4,000. The useful life of each truck was estimated to be four years. Using the straight-line depreciation formula, annual depreciation on the trucks is calculated as follows:

$$\text{Annual depreciation} = \frac{\$40,000 - \$4,000}{4 \text{ years}} = \$9,000$$

The amount of depreciation expense for one month would be $\frac{1}{12}$ of the annual amount. Thus, depreciation expense for December is $9,000 ÷ 12 = $750.

The difference between an asset's cost and its estimated salvage value is sometimes referred to as an asset's **depreciable amount.** The depreciable amount must be allocated as an expense to the various periods in the asset's useful life to satisfy the matching principle.

The amount of depreciation for a period is debited to a depreciation expense account and credited to an accumulated depreciation account. The depreciation on the delivery trucks for December is $750 and is recorded as follows:

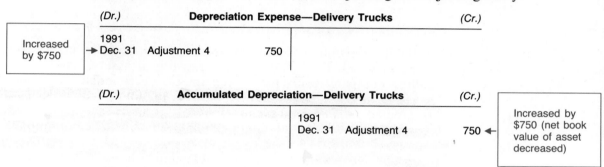

Adjustment 4— Depreciation	1991		
	Dec. 31 Depreciation Expense—Delivery Trucks	750	
	Accumulated Depreciation—Delivery Trucks		750
	To record depreciation expense for December.		

The T-accounts appear as follows after posting the adjusting entry:

Increased by $750	*(Dr.)* **Depreciation Expense—Delivery Trucks** *(Cr.)*
	1991
	→ Dec. 31 Adjustment 4 750

(Dr.) **Accumulated Depreciation—Delivery Trucks** *(Cr.)*	Increased by $750 (net book value of asset decreased)
1991	
Dec. 31 Adjustment 4 750 ←	

Depreciation expense is reported in the income statement. Accumulated depreciation is reported in the balance sheet as a deduction from the related asset.

The **accumulated depreciation account** is a contra asset account that shows the total of all depreciation recorded on the asset up through the balance sheet date. A **contra asset account** is a deduction from the asset to which it relates in the balance sheet. The purpose of a contra asset account is to reduce the original cost of the asset down to its remaining undepreciated cost or book value. The **undepreciated cost of the asset** is the debit balance in the asset account (original cost) minus the credit balance in the accumulated depreciation contra account. Accountants also refer to an asset's cost less accumulated depreciation as the **book value** (or net book value) of the asset. Thus, book value is the cost not yet allocated to an expense. In the above example, the book value of the delivery equipment after the first month is:

Cost	$40,000
Less: Accumulated depreciation	750
Book value (or cost not yet allocated as an expense)	$39,250

Depreciation is credited to an accumulated depreciation account instead of directly to the asset because recorded amounts of depreciation are estimates. No one is sure that the estimates are correct. To provide more complete balance sheet information to users of the financial statements, both original acquisition cost and accumulated depreciation are shown. For example, on the December 31, 1991, balance sheet, the accumulated depreciation is shown as a deduction from the asset delivery trucks:

Assets

Delivery trucks	$40,000
Less: Accumulated depreciation—delivery trucks	750
	$39,250

As you may expect, the accumulated depreciation account balance increases each period by the amount of depreciation expense recorded until it finally reaches an amount equal to the original cost of the asset less estimated salvage value.

Liability/Revenue Adjustments—Unearned Revenues

A liability/revenue adjustment involving unearned revenues covers situations in which the customer has transferred assets, usually cash, to the selling company prior to the receipt of merchandise or services. When assets are received before being earned, a liability called **unearned revenue** is created. Such receipts are debited to the asset account, Cash, and credited to a liability account. The liability account credited may be called Unearned Fees, Revenue Received in Advance, Advances by Customers, or some similar title. The seller is obligated either to provide the services or return the customer's money. By performing the services, revenue is earned, and the liability is canceled.

Advance payments are received for many items, such as delivery services, tickets, and magazine or newspaper subscriptions. While only advance receipt of delivery fees is illustrated and discussed, the other items are treated similarly.

Unearned Delivery Fees. On December 7, Rapid Delivery Company received $4,500 from a customer in payment for future delivery services. The journal entry was recorded as follows:

1991				
Dec.	7	Cash	4,500	
		Unearned Delivery Fees		4,500
		To record the receipt of cash from a customer in payment for future delivery services.		

The two T-accounts relating to delivery fees are Unearned Delivery Fees (a liability) and Delivery Service Revenue. These accounts appear as follows on December 31, 1991 (before adjustment):

(Dr.)	**Unearned Delivery Fees**	(Cr.)
	1991	
	Dec. 7 Cash received	
	in advance 4,500	

(Dr.)	Delivery Service Revenue	(Cr.)
	1991 Dec. 15 Cash 20 On account	5,000 5,700
	Bal. before adjustment	10,700*

* The $10,700 balance came from transactions discussed in Chapter 2.

The balance in the Unearned Delivery Fees liability account, established when the cash was received by the company, will be converted into revenue as the delivery services are performed. Before the financial statements are prepared, it will be necessary to make an adjusting entry to transfer the amount of the services performed by the company from a liability account to a revenue account. If we assume that one third of the $4,500 in the Unearned Delivery Fees account has been earned by December 31, then $1,500 will be transferred to the Delivery Service Revenue account as follows:

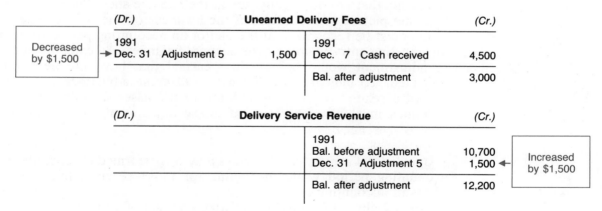

Adjustment 5—
Previously
unearned
revenue

1991		
Dec. 31 Unearned Delivery Fees	1,500	
Delivery Service Revenue		1,500
To transfer a portion of delivery fees from the liability account to the revenue account.		

The T-accounts would appear as follows after the adjusting entry has been posted:

Decreased
by $1,500

(Dr.)	Unearned Delivery Fees	(Cr.)
1991 Dec. 31 Adjustment 5 1,500	1991 Dec. 7 Cash received	4,500
	Bal. after adjustment	3,000

(Dr.)	Delivery Service Revenue	(Cr.)
	1991 Bal. before adjustment Dec. 31 Adjustment 5	10,700 1,500
	Bal. after adjustment	12,200

Increased
by $1,500

The delivery service revenue is reported in the income statement for 1991. The $3,000 balance in the Unearned Delivery Fees account is reported as a liability in the balance sheet. In 1992, the $3,000 will be earned and transferred to a revenue account.

If the services are not performed, the money would have to be refunded to the delivery service customers. For instance, if the company for some reason could not perform the remaining $3,000 of delivery services, the money would have to be refunded and the following entry made:

Unearned Delivery Fees	3,000	
Cash		3,000
To record the refund of unearned delivery fees.		

Thus, the company is obligated to either perform the services or to refund the fees. This fact may serve to strengthen your understanding that unearned delivery fees and similar items are liabilities.

The adjusting entries for deferred items are made on data already recorded in a company's asset and liability accounts. Adjusting entries on accrued items, which you will learn about in the next section, are made for business data not yet recorded in the accounting records. We will continue using Rapid Delivery Company for our example transactions.

■ ADJUSTMENTS FOR ACCRUED ITEMS

Accrued items require two types of adjusting entries: asset/revenue adjustments and liability/expense adjustments. The first group—asset/revenue adjustments—involves accrued assets; the second group—liability/expense adjustments—involves accrued liabilities.

Asset/Revenue Adjustments—Accrued Assets

Accrued assets are assets that exist at the end of an accounting period but have not yet been recorded. These assets represent rights to receive future payments that are not legally due at the balance sheet date. To present an accurate picture of the affairs of the business on the balance sheet, these rights must be recognized at the end of an accounting period by preparing an adjusting entry to correct the account balances. An example of this type of adjustment would be revenues earned that have not been billed or collected. To indicate the dual nature of these adjustments, accountants record a related revenue in addition to the asset recorded. Because the revenues must also be recorded, these adjustments may also be called **accrued revenues.**

Unbilled Delivery Fees.   Services may be performed for customers in one accounting period while the billing for those services takes place in a different accounting period.

Rapid Delivery Company performed $1,000 of delivery services on account for a client in the last few days of December. Because it takes time to do the paper work, the client will be billed for the services in January. The necessary adjusting journal entry at December 31, 1991, is:

	1991		
Adjustment 6— Unbilled revenues	Dec. 31 Accounts Receivable (or Delivery Fees Receivable) . . .	1,000	
	Delivery Service Revenue		1,000
	To record unbilled delivery services performed in December.		

After posting the adjusting entry, the T-accounts will appear as follows:

(Dr.)	Accounts Receivable		(Cr.)
1991			
Previous bal.	5,200*		
Dec. 31 Adjustment 6	1,000		
Bal. after adjustment	6,200		

Increased by $1,000

* This previous balance came from transactions discussed in Chapter 2.

(Dr.)	Delivery Service Revenue		(Cr.)
	1991		
	Bal. before adjustment	10,700	
	Dec. 31 Adjustment 5— previously unearned revenue	1,500	
	31 Adjustment 6	1,000	
	Bal. after adjustment	13,200	

Increased by $1,000

The delivery service revenue appears in the income statement, and the asset, accounts receivable, appears in the balance sheet.

Another example of an asset/revenue adjustment is when a company earns interest on a note receivable or on a bank account. The debit would be to Interest Receivable, and the credit would be to Interest Revenue. This topic of interest is covered thoroughly in Chapter 8.

Liability/Expense Adjustments—Accrued Liabilities

Accrued liabilities are liabilities that exist at the end of an accounting period but have not yet been recorded. They represent obligations to make payments not legally due at the balance sheet date, such as employee salaries. At the end of the accounting period, these obligations are recognized by preparing an adjusting entry including both a liability and an expense. For this reason, they may also be called **accrued expenses.**

Salaries. The recording of the payment of employee salaries usually involves a debit to an expense account and a credit to Cash. Unless salaries are paid on the last day of the accounting period for a pay period ending on that date, an adjusting entry is required to record any salaries incurred but not yet paid.

Rapid Delivery Company paid $3,600 of salaries on Friday, December 28, 1991, to cover the first four weeks of December. The entry made at that time was:

```
1991
Dec. 28  Salaries Expense  . . . . . . . . . . . . . . . . . . . . . . .  3,600
               Cash  . . . . . . . . . . . . . . . . . . . . . . . . . . . . .         3,600
         Paid truck driver salaries for the first four weeks of
         December.
```

Assuming the last day of December 1991 falls on a Monday, the above expense account does not show salaries earned by employees for the last day of the month. Nor does the account show the employer's obligation to pay these salaries. The accounts pertaining to salaries appear as follows before adjustment:

(Dr.)	Salaries Expense	(Cr.)	(Dr.)	Salaries Payable	(Cr.)
1991 Dec. 28 3,600				1991 Dec. 28 Bal. –0–	

If salaries are $3,600 for four weeks, they are $900 per week. For a five-day workweek, daily salaries are $180. The following adjusting entry is needed on December 31:

Adjustment 7—
Accrued
salaries

Dec. 31   Salaries Expense   180
              Salaries Payable   180
              To accrue one day's salaries that were earned
              but are unpaid.

The two T-accounts involved appear as follows after adjustment:

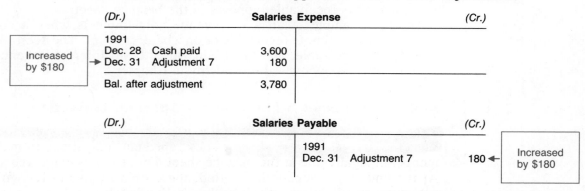

(Dr.)	Salaries Expense		(Cr.)
1991			
Dec. 28 Cash paid	3,600		
Dec. 31 Adjustment 7	180		
Bal. after adjustment	3,780		

Increased
by $180

(Dr.)	Salaries Payable		(Cr.)
		1991	
		Dec. 31 Adjustment 7	180

Increased
by $180

The debit in the adjusting journal entry brings the month's salaries expense up to its correct $3,780 amount for income statement purposes. The credit to Salaries Payable records the $180 salary liability to employees. Salaries payable is shown as a liability in the balance sheet.

Another example of a liability/expense adjustment is when a company incurs interest on a note payable. The debit would be to Interest Expense, and the credit would be to Interest Payable. Examples of this adjustment are given in Chapter 8.

■ EFFECTS OF FAILING TO PREPARE ADJUSTING ENTRIES

Failure to prepare proper adjusting entries causes net income and the balance sheet to be in error. Illustration 3.4 shows the effect on net income and balance sheet items of failing to record each of the major types of adjusting entries.

Illustration 3.4

Effects of Failure to Recognize Adjustments

Failure to Recognize	Effect on Net Income	Effect on Balance Sheet Items
1. Consumption of the benefits of an asset (prepaid expense).	Overstates net income	Overstates assets Overstates owner's capital
2. Earning of previously unearned revenues.	Understates net income	Overstates liabilities Understates owner's capital
3. Accrual of assets.	Understates net income	Understates assets Understates owner's capital
4. Accrual of liabilities.	Overstates net income	Understates liabilities Overstates owner's capital

Using Rapid Delivery Company as an example, this chapter has discussed and illustrated many of the typical entries that companies must make at the end of an accounting period. Other types of adjusting entries such as those involving interest expense and interest revenue were not discussed in this chapter but will be covered in later chapters.

In the first three chapters of this text, you have learned several of the steps of the accounting process. To help you understand them, some of these steps have been presented out of the actual order an accountant would use. These steps as a group are usually referred to as the *accounting process* (or cycle). Chapter 4 will organize these steps as actually performed by accountants and will complete the accounting cycle.

■ UNDERSTANDING THE LEARNING OBJECTIVES: CHAPTER 3

1. Identify the reasons why adjusting entries must be made.
   - Adjusting entries are needed to convert the amounts that are actually in the accounts to the amounts that should be in the accounts for proper periodic financial reporting.
   - Many business events such as the using up of prepaid insurance coverage are known as *continuous events*. Continuous events are usually recorded periodically in adjusting entries before financial statements are prepared.

2. Describe the basic characteristics of the accrual basis and the cash basis of accounting.
   - Under the cash basis of accounting, expenses and revenues usually are not recorded until cash is paid out or received.
   - Under the accrual basis of accounting, revenues are recognized

when sales are made or services are performed, regardless of when cash is received; and expenses are recognized as incurred, whether or not cash has been paid out.

■ The accrual basis is more generally accepted than the cash basis because it provides a better matching of revenues and expenses.

3. Identify the classes and types of adjusting entries.

■ Deferred items consist of adjusting entries involving data previously recorded in accounts. Adjusting entries in this class normally involve moving data from asset and liability accounts to expense and revenue accounts. The two types of adjustments within this deferred items class are asset/expense adjustments and liability/revenue adjustments.

■ Accrued items consist of adjusting entries relating to activity on which no data have been previously recorded in the accounts. These entries involve the initial, or first, recording of assets and liabilities and the related revenues and expenses. The two types of adjustments within this accrued items class are asset/revenue adjustments and liability/expense adjustments.

4. Prepare adjusting entries.

■ Entries for deferred items and accrued items are illustrated in the chapter.

5. Define and use correctly the new items in the glossary.

NEW TERMS INTRODUCED IN CHAPTER 3

Accounting period A time period normally of one month, one quarter, or one year into which an entity's life is arbitrarily divided for financial reporting purposes (94).

Accounting year (fiscal year) An accounting period of one year. The accounting year may or may not coincide with the calendar year (94).

Accrual basis of accounting Recognizes revenues when sales are made or services are performed, regardless of when cash is received. Recognizes expenses as incurred, whether or not cash has been paid out (96).

Accrued assets and liabilities Assets and liabilities that exist at the end of an accounting period but have not yet been recorded; they represent rights to receive, or obligations to make, payments that are not legally due at the balance sheet date. Examples are accrued fees receivable and salaries payable (108, 109).

Accrued items See Accrued assets and liabilities.

Accrued revenues and expenses Other names for accrued assets and liabilities.

Accumulated depreciation account A contra asset account that shows the total of all depreciation recorded on the asset up through the balance sheet date (105).

Adjusting entries Journal entries made at the end of an accounting period to bring about a proper matching of revenues and expenses; reflect economic activity that has taken place but has not yet been recorded. Adjusting entries are made to bring the accounts to their proper balances before financial statements are prepared (95).

Book value For depreciable assets, book value equals cost less accumulated depreciation (105).

Calendar year The normal year, which ends on December 31 (94).

Cash basis of accounting Recognizes revenues when cash is received and recognizes expenses when cash is paid out (95).

Contra asset account An account shown as a deduction from the asset to which it relates in the balance sheet; used to reduce the original cost of the asset down to its undepreciated cost or book value (105).

Deferred items   Adjusting entries involving data previously recorded in the accounts. Data are transferred from asset and liability accounts to expense and revenue accounts. Examples are prepaid expenses, depreciation, and unearned revenues (96).

Depreciable amount   The difference between an asset's cost and its estimated salvage value (105).

Depreciable asset   A building, machine, vehicle, or equipment on which depreciation expense is recorded (103).

Depreciation accounting   The process of recording depreciation expense (104).

Depreciation expense   The amount of asset cost assigned as an expense to a particular time period (103).

Depreciation formula (straight-line)

$$\text{Annual depreciation} = \frac{\text{Asset cost} - \text{Estimated salvage value}}{\text{Estimated number of years of useful life}} \quad (104).$$

Fiscal year   An accounting year of 12 consecutive months that may or may not coincide with the calendar year. For example, a company may have an accounting or fiscal year that runs from April 1 of one year to March 31 of the next (94).

Matching principle   An accounting principle requiring that expenses incurred in producing revenues be deducted from the revenues they generated during the accounting period (95).

Prepaid expense   An asset that is awaiting assignment to expense. An example is prepaid insurance. Assets such as cash and accounts receivable are not prepaid expenses (99).

Salvage value (scrap value)   The amount that an asset can probably be sold for at the end of its estimated useful life (104).

Service potential   The benefits that can be obtained from assets. The future services that assets can render make assets "things of value" to a business (99).

Unearned revenue   Assets received from customers before services are performed for them. Since the revenue has not been earned, it is a liability, often called *revenue received in advance* or *advances by customers* (106).

Useful life   The estimated number of time periods that a company can make use of the asset (104).

DEMONSTRATION PROBLEM

The trial balance of Korman Company for December 31, 1991, includes, among other items, the following account balances:

	Debits	Credits
Office Supplies on Hand	$ 6,000	
Prepaid Rent	25,200	
Buildings	200,000	
Accumulated Depreciation—Buildings		$33,250
Salaries Expense	124,000	
Unearned Delivery Fees		4,000

Additional data:

1. Part of the supplies represented by the $6,000 balance of the Office Supplies on Hand account have beeen consumed. An inventory count of the supplies actually on hand at December 31 totaled to $2,400.
2. On May 1 of the current year, a rental payment of $25,200 was made for 12 months of rent; it was debited to Prepaid Rent.
3. The annual depreciation for the buildings is based on the cost shown in the Buildings account less an estimated salvage value of $10,000. The estimated useful lives of the buildings are 40 years each.
4. The salaries expense of $124,000 does not include $6,000 of unpaid salaries earned since the last payday.
5. One fourth of the unearned delivery fees have been earned by December 31.
6. Delivery services of $600 were performed for a customer, but a bill has not yet been sent.

Required: a. Prepare the adjusting journal entries for December 31, assuming adjusting entries are prepared only at year-end.

b. Based on the adjusted balance shown in the Accumulated Depreciation—Building account, how many years has Korman Company owned the building?

Solution to demonstration problem

a.

KORMAN COMPANY
GENERAL JOURNAL

Date		Account Titles and Explanation	Post. Ref.	Debit	Credit
1991 Dec.	31	Office Supplies Expense		3 6 0 0	
		Office Supplies on Hand			3 6 0 0
		To record office supplies expense ($6,000 − $2,400).			
	31	Rent Expense		1 6 8 0 0	
		Prepaid Rent			1 6 8 0 0
		To record rent expense ($25,200 × 8/12).			
	31	Depreciation Expense—Buildings		4 7 5 0	
		Accumulated Depreciation—Buildings			4 7 5 0
		To record depreciation [($200,000 − 10,000) ÷ 40 years].			
	31	Salaries Expense		6 0 0 0	
		Salaries Payable			6 0 0 0
		To record accrued salaries.			
	31	Unearned Delivery Fees		1 0 0 0	
		Delivery Service Revenue			1 0 0 0
		To record delivery fees earned.			
	31	Accounts Receivable		6 0 0	
		Delivery Service Revenue			6 0 0
		To record delivery fees earned.			

b. Eight years; computed as:

$$\frac{\text{Total accumulated depreciation}}{\text{Annual depreciation expense}} = \frac{\$33,250 + \$4,750}{\$4,750} = 8$$

QUESTIONS

1. Why are adjusting entries necessary? Why not treat every cash disbursement as an expense and every cash receipt as revenue when the cash changes hands?

2. "Adjusting entries would not be necessary if the cash basis of accounting were followed (assuming no mistakes were made in recording cash transactions as they occurred). Under the cash basis,

receipts that are of a revenue nature are considered revenue when received and expenditures that are of an expense nature are considered expenses when paid. It is the use of the accrual basis of accounting, where an effort is made to match expenses incurred against the revenues they create, that makes adjusting entries necessary." Do you agree with this statement? Why?

3. Why don't accountants keep all the accounts at their proper balances continuously throughout the period so that adjusting entries would not have to be made before financial statements are prepared?

4. Identify the two major classes of adjusting entries and the types of adjusting entries that are included in each.

5. Give an example of an adjusting journal entry for each of the following:
   a. Increase an expense and decrease an asset.
   b. Increase a revenue and decrease a liability.
   c. Increase both an asset and a revenue.
   d. Increase both an expense and a liability.

6. You notice that the Supplies on Hand account has a debit balance of $14,800 at the end of the accounting period. How would you determine the extent to which this account needs adjustment?

7. Some assets are converted into expenses as they expire, and some liabilities become revenues as they are earned. Give examples of asset and liability accounts for which the statement is true. Give examples of asset and liability accounts for which the statement does not apply.

8. Give the depreciation formula for straight-line depreciation.

9. What does the term *accrued liability* mean?

10. What is meant by the term *service potential*?

11. When assets are received before they are earned, what type of an account is credited? As the amounts are earned where must the data be transferred?

EXERCISES

E-1
Prepare and post adjusting entry for insurance

a. A one-year insurance policy was purchased on, and provided coverage from, October 1, 1991, for $14,400. The following entry was made at that time:

```
1991
Oct. 1  Prepaid Insurance . . . . . . . . . . . . . . . . . . . . . 14,400
            Cash . . . . . . . . . . . . . . . . . . . . . . . . . .        14,400
        To record the purchase of insurance to cover
        a one-year period.
```

The company prepares financial statements once a year at year-end. What adjusting entry is necessary on December 31?
b. Show how the T-accounts for Prepaid Insurance and Insurance Expense would appear after the entries are posted.

E-2
Prepare adjusting entry for rent

Assume that rent of $28,800 was paid on September 1, 1991, to cover a one-year period from that date. Prepaid Rent was debited. If financial statements are prepared only on December 31 of each year, what adjusting entry is necessary on December 31, 1991, to bring the accounts involved to their proper balances?

E-3
Prepare entries for purchase of supplies and adjustment at year-end

Office supplies were purchased for cash on December 2, 1991, for $2,780. The supplies were to be used over the next several months. A physical inventory showed that $980 of the supplies were on hand on December 31, 1991. Show the entry for the purchase. What adjusting entry would be necessary at December 31 assuming that financial statements are prepared at that time?

E-4
Prepare adjusting entry for depreciation

Assume that a company acquires a building on January 1, 1991, at a cost of $1,000,000. The building has an estimated useful life of 40 years and an estimated salvage value of $200,000. What adjusting entry is needed on December 31, 1991, to record the depreciation for the entire year 1991?

E-5
Determine salvage value of building

A building is being depreciated by an amount of $50,000 per year. You know it had an original cost of $560,000 and was expected to last 10 years. What is the estimated salvage value?

E-6
Prepare entries for receipt of subscription fees and adjustment at year-end

On September 1, 1991, Beardon Company received a total of $360,000 as payment in advance for a number of one-year subscriptions to a monthly magazine. By the end of the year, one third of the magazines paid for in advance had been delivered. Give the entries to record the receipt of the subscription fees and to adjust the accounts on December 31, assuming annual financial statements are prepared at year-end.

E-7
Prepare entries for receipt of ticket fees, adjustment for earning revenue, and refund of fees

On April 15, 1991, Blakely Theater sold $180,000 of tickets for the summer musicals to be performed (one per month) during the months of June, July, and August. On July 15, 1991, Blakely Theater discovered that the group that was to perform the July and August musicals could not do so. It was too late to find another group qualified to perform the musicals. A decision was made to refund the remaining unearned ticket revenue to its ticket holders, and this was done on July 20. Show the appropriate journal entries to be made on April 15, June 30, and July 20. Blakely has a June 30th year-end.

E-8
Prepare adjusting entry for accrued legal services

Johnson and Wells, a law firm, performed legal services in late December 1991 for clients. The $51,000 of services will be billed to the clients in January 1992. Give the adjusting entry that is necessary on December 31, 1991, if financial statements are prepared at the end of each month.

E-9
Prepare adjusting entry for accrued salaries

Bailey Company incurs salaries at the rate of $2,000 per day. The last payday in January is Friday, January 27. Salaries for Monday and Tuesday of the next week have not been recorded or paid as of January 31. Financial statements are prepared monthly. Give the necessary adjusting entry on January 31.

E-10
Determine effect on net income from failing to record adjusting entries

State the income statement and balance sheet effects that each of the following would have for 1991:

a. No adjustment was made for accrued salaries of $7,200 as of December 31, 1991.

b. The collection of $6,400 for services not yet performed as of December 31, 1991, was credited to a revenue account and not adjusted. The services are performed in 1992.

E-11
Show the effects of failing to recognize indicated adjustments

In the following box, indicate the effects of failing to recognize each of the indicated adjustments by writing "O" for overstated and "U" for understated.

			Effect on Balance Sheet Items		
	Failure to Recognize	Effect on Net Income	Assets	Liabilities	Owner's Equity
1.	Depreciation on a building.				
2.	Consumption of supplies on hand.				
3.	The earning of ticket revenue received in advance.				
4.	The earning of interest on a bank account.				
5.	Salaries incurred but unpaid.				

PROBLEMS, SERIES A

P3-1-A
Prepare adjusting entries

The trial balance of Taylor Company at December 31, 1991, includes, among other items, the following account balances:

	Debits
Prepaid Insurance	$90,000
Prepaid Rent	80,000
Supplies on Hand	20,000

Examination of the records shows that annual adjustments should be made for the following items:

1. Of the prepaid insurance in the trial balance, $36,000 is for coverage during the months after December 31 of the current year.
2. The balance in the Prepaid Rent account is for a 12-month period that started October 1 of the current year.
3. Supplies on hand at the end of the year are $5,000.

Required: Prepare the annual adjusting journal entries at December 31, 1991.

P3-2-A
Prepare and post adjusting entries

Sellers Company acquired a new truck on January 1, 1991. The truck has a cost of $48,000, an estimated useful life of three years, and an estimated salvage value of $3,000.

Required:
a. Prepare annual adjusting journal entries for the end of 1991, 1992, and 1993 to record depreciation on the truck.
b. Using T-accounts, show how the entries made in *(a)* would appear.

P3-3-A
Prepare and post adjusting entries; show balance sheet and income statement data

The following data for Drake Company are:

	Account Title	Trial Balance	Information for Adjustments
Item 1:	Office Building	$1,870,000	The useful life is 50 years. Salvage value is estimated at $110,000. The amount shown for Accumulated Depreciation—Office Building resulted from credits to that account made in adjusting entries for previous years.
	Accumulated Depreciation —Office Building	352,000	
Item 2:	Salaries Expense	224,400	Salaries earned by employees since the last payday are $6,000. These have not been recorded.
Item 3:	Office Supplies on Hand . . .	13,200	At the end of the period, office supplies on hand are $4,400.

Required: For each of the above items:

a. Prepare the annual adjusting journal entry, dating it December 31, 1991.
b. Set up T-accounts for each of the accounts, enter balances before adjustment, post the adjusting entries made in part *(a),* and determine balances after adjustment.
c. Show the data that would appear in the balance sheet.
d. Show the data for the year that would appear in the income statement.

P3-4-A
*Prepare and post
adjusting entries*

Mize Company has the following account balances included in its trial balance for December 31, 1991:

	Debits	Credits
Accounts Receivable	$150,000	
Supplies on Hand	7,740	
Prepaid Rent	14,400	
Service Revenue		$522,000
Salaries Expense	246,000	

Additional data:

1. The amount of supplies on hand on December 31 is $540.
2. The balance in the Prepaid Rent account is for a one-year period, beginning October 1 of the current year.
3. Since the last payday, the employees of the company earned additional salaries of $12,180.
4. Services performed in December that will not be billed until January amount to $36,000.

Required: a. Prepare the annual adjusting journal entries for December 31. The adjusting entries are made on page 22 of the general journal.
   b. Open three-column ledger accounts for each of the accounts involved, enter the balances as shown in the trial balance, post the adjusting journal entries, and show ending balances.

P3-5-A
*Prepare and post
adjusting entries*

Faldo Delivery Company has the following account balances included in its trial balance for December 31, 1991:

	Debits	Credits
Accounts Receivable	$ 44,000	
Prepaid Insurance	9,600	
Supplies on Hand	5,200	
Building	200,000	
Accumulated Depreciation—Building		$ 16,000
Unearned Delivery Fees		4,000 (deposit)
Delivery Service Revenue		128,000

Additional data:

1. The balance in the Prepaid Insurance account is for a four-year period beginning January 1, 1991.
2. At December 31, 1991, supplies on hand totaled $1,600.
3. The building was acquired on January 1, 1989, and had an expected useful life of 20 years, with a salvage value of $40,000.
4. $3,000 of the unearned delivery fees in the trial balance have now been earned.
5. Delivery services were performed on account for a customer on December 31, $2,400. No bill has been sent to the customer, and no journal entry has been made.

Required: a. Prepare the annual adjusting entries for December 31. The adjusting entries are made on page 10 of the general journal.
   b. Open three-column ledger accounts for each of the accounts involved, enter the balances as shown in the trial balance, post the adjusting entries, and show ending balances.

P3-6-A
Prepare adjusting entries

Dorothy Bean Company adjusts and closes its books each December 31. Given below are a number of the company's account balances prior to adjustment on December 31, 1991:

	Debits	Credits
Prepaid Insurance	$ 30,000	
Supplies on Hand	12,900	
Building	510,000	
Accumulated Depreciation—Building		$204,000
Unearned Delivery Fees		10,800
Service Revenue		555,000
Salaries Expense	138,000	

Additional data:

1. The Prepaid Insurance account balance represents the remaining cost of a four-year insurance policy dated June 30, 1989, having a total premium of $48,000.
2. The physical inventory of the supply stockroom indicates that the supplies on hand on December 31 total $4,500.
3. The building was originally acquired on January 1, 1974, with an estimated useful life of 40 years and a salvage value of $30,000.
4. Salaries earned since the last payday, but unpaid as of December 31, amount to $15,000.
5. Of the delivery fees received in advance, $2,700 has been earned by year-end.

Required: Prepare the adjusting entries indicated by the additional data.

PROBLEMS, SERIES B

P3-1-B
Prepare adjusting entries

The trial balance of Billy Simpson Company as of December 31, 1991, includes, among other items, the following account balances:

	Debits	Credits
Prepaid Rent	$ 48,000	
Prepaid Insurance	24,000	
Buildings	400,000	
Accumulated Depreciation—Buildings		$128,000
Salaries Expense	220,000	

Additional data:

1. The debit balance in the Prepaid Insurance account is the advance premium for one year from September 1 of the current year.
2. The buildings have an estimated useful life of 25 years and an estimated salvage value of $80,000.
3. Salaries incurred but not paid at December 31 are $17,600.
4. The debit balance in Prepaid Rent is for a one-year period that started March 1 of the current year.

Required: Prepare the annual adjusting journal entries for December 31, 1991.

P3-2-B
Prepare and post adjusting entries

Pate Company bought a new machine on January 1, 1991, at a cost of $28,000. The machine had an estimated life of three years and an estimated salvage value of $2,800.

Required:
a. Prepare annual adjusting journal entries for the end of 1991, 1992, and 1993 to record depreciation on the machine.
b. Using T-accounts, show how the entries made in *(a)* would appear.

P3-3-B
Prepare and post adjusting entries; show balance sheet and income statement data

The following data for Bauer Company are:

Account Title	Trial Balance	Information for Adjustments
Item 1: Equipment	$540,000	Depreciation is based on a five-year life and a $60,000 estimated salvage value. The amount shown for Accumulated Depreciation—Equipment resulted from credits to that account made in adjusting entries for previous years.
Accumulated Depreciation —Equipment	192,000	
Item 2: Salaries Expense	264,000	Unpaid salaries incurred amount to $12,000. The $12,000 is not included in the amount shown in the trial balance.
Item 3: Prepaid Insurance	107,400	Of the prepaid insurance in the trial balance, only $32,400 is for additional protection after December 31.

Required:

For each of the above items:

a. Prepare the annual adjusting journal entry, dating it December 31, 1991.
b. Set up T-accounts for each of the accounts adjusted, enter balances before adjustment, post the adjusting entries made in part *(a),* and determine balances after adjustment.
c. Show the data that would appear in the balance sheet.
d. Show the data for the year that would appear in the income statement.

P3-4-B
Prepare and post adjusting entries

Stafford Company has the following account balances included in its trial balance for December 31, 1991:

	Debits	Credits
Supplies on Hand	$ 13,920	
Prepaid Insurance	19,200	
Buildings	336,000	
Accumulated Depreciation—Buildings		$78,000

Additional data:

1. The amount of the supplies on hand on December 31 is $2,400.
2. The balance in the Prepaid Insurance account is for a two-year policy, beginning June 1 of the current year.
3. Depreciation for the buildings is based on an estimated salvage value of $36,000 and an estimated useful life of 50 years.

Required:

a. Prepare the annual adjusting journal entries for December 31. The adjusting entries are made on page 27 of the general journal.
b. Open three-column ledger accounts for each of the accounts involved, enter the balances as shown in the trial balance, post the adjusting entries, and show ending balances.

P3-5-B
Prepare and post adjusting entries

Nichols Laundry Company has the following account balances included in its trial balance for December 31, 1991:

	Debits	Credits
Accounts Receivable	$78,000	
Prepaid Rent	3,600	
Equipment	45,000	
Unearned Laundry Fees		$ 9,000
Laundry Service Revenue		144,000
Salaries Expense	63,000	

Additional data:

1. The balance in the Prepaid Rent account is for a one-year period beginning July 1, 1991.
2. The equipment was purchased on July 1, 1991, and is expected to have a useful life of six years, with a salvage value of $9,000.
3. Of the $9,000 unearned laundry service fees in the trial balance, $6,000 has been earned by December 31.
4. Laundry services of $144 were performed on account for a customer on December 30. No bill has been sent to the customer, and no journal entry has been made.
5. Salaries incurred but not paid at year-end are $1,500.

Required: a. Prepare the annual adjusting entries for December 31. The adjusting entries are made on page 16 of the general journal.

b. Open three-column ledger accounts for each of the accounts involved, enter the balances as shown in the trial balance, post adjusting journal entries, and show ending balances.

P3–6–B
Prepare adjusting entries

Sanders Company occupies rented quarters on the main street of the city. To get this location, it was necessary for the company to rent a store larger than needed, so a portion of the area is subleased (rented) to Dudley's Restaurant.

The following partial trial balance was taken from the company's ledger as of the close of business on December 31, 1991. It is necessary to study the partial trial balance to determine how certain transactions were originally recorded. Then you will be able to determine the necessary annual adjusting entries.

SANDERS COMPANY
Partial Trial Balance
December 31, 1991

	Debits	Credits
Cash	$120,000	
Prepaid Rent	4,000	
Prepaid Insurance	10,800	
Supplies on Hand	2,000	
Store Equipment	140,000	
Accumulated Depreciation—Store Equipment		$ 12,000
Service Revenue		900,000
Store Salaries Expense	147,000	
Rent Revenue		22,000

Additional data:

1. The salaries of the store clerks amount to $540 per day and were paid through Thursday, December 27. December 31 is a Monday. Saturday is a workday, and the store is closed on Sundays.
2. The equipment had a cost of $140,000, an estimated useful life of 20 years, and an estimated salvage value of $20,000.
3. The store carries one combined annual insurance policy that was taken out on August 1. The policy was new this year and costs $10,800 per year.
4. Supplies on hand on December 31, 1991, amount to $920.
5. The prepaid rent applies to December 1991 and January 1992.
6. Services of $16,000 were performed in December and will be billed to customers in January.

Required: Prepare the adjusting entries required by the data presented above.

BUSINESS DECISION PROBLEM

Prepare report giving appraisal of offer to sell a business, correct computation of net income, determine book value of assets

A friend of yours, Daisy Casper, is quite excited over the opportunity she has to purchase the land, building, equipment, and several other assets of Jackson Bowling Lanes for $750,000. Daisy tells you that the owner (who is moving because of poor health) reports that the business had net income of $150,000 in 1991 (last year). Daisy believes that annual net income of $150,000 on an investment of $750,000 is a really good deal. But, before completing the deal, she asks you to look it over. You agree to look it over and discover the following:

1. The owner has computed his annual income for 1991 as the sum of his cash withdrawals plus the increase in the Cash account: Withdrawals of $90,000 + Increase in Cash account of $60,000 = $150,000 income.
2. As buyer of the business, Daisy will take over responsibility for repayment of a $600,000 loan owed to a relative of the previous owner. The land, building, and equipment were acquired seven years ago at a cost of $60,000, $1,600,000, and $640,000, respectively. The building has a useful life of 40 years and an estimated salvage value of $160,000. The equipment has an estimated useful life of eight years and an estimated salvage value of $64,000.
3. An analysis of the Cash account shows the following for 1991:

Revenues received		$840,000
Cash paid out in 1991 for:		
Wages paid to employees in 1991	$516,000	
Utilities paid for 1991	36,000	
Advertising expenses paid	30,000	
Supplies purchased and used in 1991	48,000	
Payment on loan	60,000	
Owner withdrawals	90,000	780,000
Increase in cash balance for the year		$ 60,000

4. You also find that the December utility bill of $6,000 and an advertising bill for December of $9,000 have not been paid.

Required: Prepare a written report for Daisy giving your appraisal of the offer to sell Jackson Bowling Lanes. Comment on the owner's method of computing the annual net income of the business.

4

Completing the Accounting Cycle: Work Sheet, Closing Entries, and Classified Balance Sheet

---

LEARNING OBJECTIVES

After studying this chapter, you should be able to:

1. Prepare a work sheet for a service company.
2. Prepare an income statement, statement of owner's equity, and balance sheet using information contained in a work sheet.
3. Prepare adjusting and closing entries using information contained in the work sheet.
4. Prepare a classified balance sheet.
5. Prepare reversing entries (Appendix).
6. Define and use correctly the new terms in the glossary.

This chapter organizes the accounting process you learned in Chapters 1 through 3 into what accountants call the **accounting cycle.** The accounting cycle is a series of steps that accountants perform during the accounting period to analyze, record, classify, summarize, and report useful financial information for the purpose of preparing financial statements. For ease of teaching, the order in which we previously discussed the accounting steps was different from the order in which they are actually performed. Chapter 4 presents the accounting cycle steps in the exact order accountants follow to prepare financial statements. In the beginning of the chapter, the order of the eight accounting steps is correctly listed and their relationship to each other is shown in a diagram.

As you study the accounting cycle, you will see two new steps—the work sheet and closing entries. These new steps are discussed in this chapter. In addition, a classified balance sheet is presented. This balance sheet format more closely resembles actual company balance sheets that you may have seen. (Appendix C at the end of the text contains a classified balance sheet and other financial statements of Eli Lilly and Company.) The chapter Appendix presents an optional step in the accounting cycle—preparing reversing entries. This chapter continues using the Rapid Delivery Company example given in Chapters 2 and 3. After completing this chapter, you will have cleared the first hurdle in your study of accounting—understanding how an accountant begins with documents as evidence of transactions of a business entity and ends with financial statements showing the profitability and solvency of that entity.

■ THE ACCOUNTING CYCLE SUMMARIZED

Before you can visualize all of the steps in the accounting cycle, you must first be able to recognize a business transaction, which is a measurable event that affects the financial situation of a business. For example, the fact that a pot of coffee was spilled in the business office or that the owner broke her leg while skiing may briefly interrupt the operation of the business, but these events are not measurable in terms that will affect the solvency and profitability of the business.

Business transactions can be events involving the exchanges of goods for cash between the business and an external party, such as the sale of a book, or they can be events such as paying wages to employees. These events have one fundamental criterion: They must have caused a measurable change in the amounts in the accounting equation, Assets = Liabilities + Owner's Equity. Business events are evidenced by **source documents** such as sales tickets, checks, and so on. Source documents are important because they are the ultimate proof of business transactions.

After you have determined that an event is a measurable business transaction and have adequate source proof of this transaction, you must mentally analyze the transaction in terms of increasing and decreasing the elements of the accounting equation. You learned how to do this in Chapter 1. Other steps in the accounting cycle were performed in Chapters 2 and 3. The steps in the accounting cycle and the chapter(s) in which they are discussed are listed below:

Performed during accounting period

1. Analyze transactions by examining source documents (Chapters 1 and 2).
2. Journalize transactions in the journal (Chapter 2).
3. Post journal entries to the accounts in the ledger (Chapter 2).

<table>
<tr><td>

Performed at end of accounting period

</td><td>

4. Take a trial balance of the accounts (Chapter 2) and complete the work sheet (Chapter 4).
5. Prepare financial statements (Chapter 4).
6. Journalize and post adjusting entries (Chapters 3 and 4).
7. Journalize and post closing entries (Chapter 4).
8. Take a post-closing trial balance (Chapter 4).

</td></tr>
</table>

As indicated in the list of accounting cycle steps, the first three steps are performed during the accounting period. The last five steps are performed at the end of the accounting period. Illustration 4.1 is a diagram showing the steps in the accounting cycle. The next section explains how to use the work sheet to make the completion of the accounting cycle easier.

Illustration 4.1

Steps in the Accounting Cycle

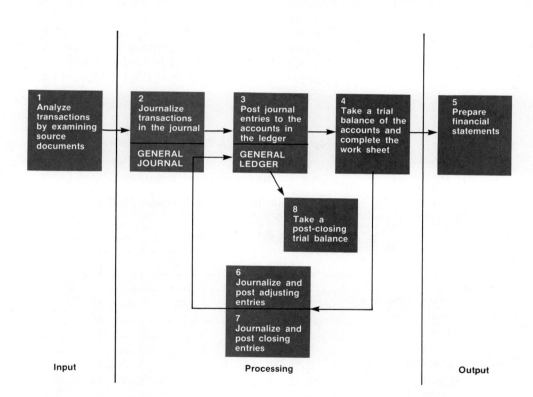

■ **THE WORK SHEET**

*Objective 1:
Prepare a work sheet
for a service
company.*

The **work sheet** is a columnar sheet of paper on which accountants have summarized information needed to make the adjusting and closing entries and to prepare the financial statements. A work sheet is only a tool used by accountants and is not part of the formal accounting records. Therefore, work sheets may vary in format and are usually prepared in pencil so that errors can be easily corrected. Work sheets may be used each time financial statements are prepared—that is, monthly, quarterly, or at the end of the accounting year.

This chapter illustrates a 10-column work sheet that includes sets of columns for a trial balance (unadjusted), adjustments, adjusted trial balance, income statement, and balance sheet. Each set of columns has a debit and a credit column. Illustration 4.2 shows a work sheet for Rapid Delivery Company with only the Trial Balance columns filled in, using the facts presented in Chapters 2 and 3.

The steps in preparing the work sheet are listed below. These steps are described more fully in the sections that follow.

1. Enter the titles and balances of ledger accounts in the Trial Balance columns.
2. Enter adjustments in the Adjustments columns.
3. Enter adjusted account balances in the Adjusted Trial Balance columns.
4. Extend adjusted balances of revenue and expense accounts from the Adjusted Trial Balance columns to the Income Statement columns.
5. Extend adjusted balances of asset, liability, and owner's equity accounts from the Adjusted Trial Balance columns to the Balance Sheet columns.

Illustration 4.2   *Partially Completed Work Sheet—Trial Balance Columns*

RAPID DELIVERY COMPANY
Work Sheet
For the Month Ended December 31, 1991

Acct. No.	Account Titles	Trial Balance Debit	Trial Balance Credit	Adjustments Debit	Adjustments Credit	Adjusted Trial Balance Debit	Adjusted Trial Balance Credit	Income Statement Debit	Income Statement Credit	Balance Sheet Debit	Balance Sheet Credit
100	Cash	10,650									
101	Accounts Receivable	5,200									
102	Supplies on Hand	1,400									
103	Prepaid Insurance	2,400									
104	Prepaid Rent	1,200									
110	Delivery Trucks	40,000									
200	Accounts Payable		3,130								
201	Unearned Delivery Fees		4,500								
300	John Turner, Capital, 12/1/91		50,000								
301	John Turner, Drawing	3,000									
400	Delivery Service Revenue		10,700								
500	Advertising Expense	50									
501	Gas and Oil Expense	680									
502	Salaries Expense	3,600									
503	Utilities Expense	150									
		68,330	68,330								

■ The Trial Balance Columns

Instead of preparing a separate trial balance as was done in Chapter 2, the trial balance can be entered in the work sheet. As shown in Illustration 4.2, numbers and titles of ledger accounts are entered in the left-hand portion of the work sheet. Usually only those accounts with balances as of the end of the accounting period are listed. (Alternatively, all of the account titles in the chart of accounts could be listed, even those with zero balances.) The balances of the ledger accounts are entered in the Trial Balance columns of the work sheet, and the columns are totaled. If the debit and credit column totals are not equal, an error exists and must be found and corrected before proceeding with the work sheet.

The Adjustments Columns

As you learned in Chapter 3, adjustments are required to bring the accounts up to date prior to preparing the income statement, statement of owner's equity (introduced in Chapter 1), and balance sheet. The adjustments discussed in Chapter 3 are entered in the work sheet in the Adjustments columns (Illustration 4.3). The debits and credits of the entries are cross-referenced by placing a key number or letter to the left of each amount (we have used numbers). This key number facilitates the actual journalizing of the adjusting entries later without having to "rethink" the adjustments to record them. For example, the adjustment debiting Insurance Expense and crediting Prepaid Insurance is identified by the number *(1)*. Note that in the Account Titles column, the Insurance Expense account title is written below the trial balance totals because it did not have a balance prior to the adjustment.

Brief explanations are sometimes provided at the bottom of the work sheet for the keyed entries. Although these explanations are optional, they provide valuable information for other people who may review the work sheet at a later date. The explanations will not be repeated in subsequent illustrations in this chapter.

The adjustments for Rapid Delivery Company (explained in Chapter 3) are as follows:

- Entry *(1)* records the expiration of $200 of prepaid insurance in the month of December.
- Entry *(2)* records the expiration of $400 of prepaid rent in the month of December.
- Entry *(3)* records the using up of $500 of supplies during the month. This amount was determined by taking a physical inventory of supplies, which came to $900, and deducting that amount from the balance in the Supplies on Hand account.
- Entry *(4)* records $750 depreciation expense on the delivery truck for the month. The truck was acquired at the beginning of December.
- Entry *(5)* records the earning of $1,500 of the $4,500 in the Unearned Delivery Fees account.

Illustration 4.3

Partially Completed Work Sheet—Adjustments Columns

RAPID DELIVERY COMPANY
Work Sheet
For the Month Ended December 31, 1991

Acct. No.	Account Titles	Trial Balance Debit	Trial Balance Credit	Adjustments Debit	Adjustments Credit
100	Cash	10,650			
101	Accounts Receivable	5,200		(6) 1,000	
102	Supplies on Hand	1,400			(3) 500
103	Prepaid Insurance	2,400			(1) 200
104	Prepaid Rent	1,200			(2) 400
110	Delivery Trucks	40,000			
200	Accounts Payable		3,130		
201	Unearned Delivery Fees		4,500	(5) 1,500	
300	John Turner, Capital, 12/1/91		50,000		
301	John Turner, Drawing	3,000			
400	Delivery Service Revenue		10,700		(5) 1,500
					(6) 1,000
500	Advertising Expense	50			
501	Gas and Oil Expense	680			
502	Salaries Expense	3,600		(7) 180	
503	Utilities Expense	150			
		68,330	68,330		
504	Insurance Expense			(1) 200	
505	Rent Expense			(2) 400	
506	Supplies Expense			(3) 500	
507	Depreciation Expense— Delivery Trucks			(4) 750	
110A	Accumulated Depreciation— Delivery Trucks				(4) 750
202	Salaries Payable				(7) 180
				4,530	4,530

Adjustments explanations:

(1) To record insurance expense for December ($2,400 ÷ 12) = $200.

(2) To record rent expense for December ($1,200 ÷ 3) = $400.

(3) To record supplies used during December ($1,400 − $900) = $500.

(4) To record depreciation expense for December ($40,000 − $4,000)/4 = $9,000 per year; ($9,000 ÷ 12) = $750.

(5) To transfer a portion of delivery fees from the liability account to the revenue account ($4,500 × ⅓) = $1,500.

(6) To record unbilled delivery services performed in December (amount given).

(7) To accrue one day's salaries which were earned but are unpaid (amount given).

- Entry *(6)* records $1,000 of unbilled delivery services performed in December.
- Entry *(7)* records the $180 accrual of salaries expense at the end of the month.

Discovering all of the adjusting entries that should be made is often a difficult task for the accountant. The following steps should aid in this task:

1. Examine adjusting entries made at the end of the preceding accounting period. The same types of entries often are necessary period after period.
2. Examine the account titles appearing in the trial balance. For example, if an account is titled Delivery Trucks, an entry for depreciation must be made.
3. Examine various business papers (such as bills for services received or rendered) to discover other assets, liabilities, revenues, and expenses that have not yet been recorded.
4. Ask the owner or other personnel specific questions regarding adjustments that may be necessary. For example, "Were there any services performed during the month that have not yet been billed?"

After all adjusting entries have been entered in the Adjustments columns, the two columns are totaled. The totals of the two columns should be equal if all debits and credits have been entered properly.

The Adjusted Trial Balance Columns

After adjustments have been entered, the adjusted balance of each account is computed and entered in the Adjusted Trial Balance columns (see Illustration 4.4). For example, Supplies on Hand (Account No. 102) had an unadjusted balance of $1,400. Adjusting entry *(3)* credited the account for $500, leaving a debit balance of $900. This amount is shown as a debit in the Adjusted Trial Balance columns.

All accounts having balances are extended to the Adjusted Trial Balance columns. Note carefully how the rules of debit and credit apply in determining whether an adjustment increases or decreases the account balance. For example, Salaries Expense (Account No. 502) has a $3,600 debit balance in the Trial Balance columns. This account is **increased** by a $180 debit adjustment, giving a $3,780 debit balance in the Adjusted Trial Balance columns.

Note also that some account balances remain the same because no adjustments have affected them. For example, the balance in Accounts Payable (Account No. 200) does not change. These account balances are simply extended to the Adjusted Trial Balance columns in the work sheet.

The Adjusted Trial Balance debit and credit columns are totaled, and the totals must be equal before taking the next step in completing the work sheet. If the Trial Balance columns and the Adjustments columns both balance but the Adjusted Trial Balance columns do not, the most probable cause is a math error or an error in extension. The Adjusted Trial Balance columns are not essential, but they make the next step of sorting the amounts to the Income Statement and Balance Sheet columns much easier.

Illustration 4.4 *Partially Completed Work Sheet—Adjusted Trial Balance Columns*

RAPID DELIVERY COMPANY
Work Sheet
For the Month Ended December 31, 1991

Acct. No.	Account Titles	Trial Balance		Adjustments		Adjusted Trial Balance	
		Debit	Credit	Debit	Credit	Debit	Credit
100	Cash	10,650				10,650	
101	Accounts Receivable	5,200		(6) 1,000		6,200	
102	Supplies on Hand	1,400			(3) 500	900	
103	Prepaid Insurance	2,400			(1) 200	2,200	
104	Prepaid Rent	1,200			(2) 400	800	
110	Delivery Trucks	40,000				40,000	
200	Accounts Payable		3,130				3,130
201	Unearned Delivery Fees		4,500	(5) 1,500			3,000
300	John Turner, Capital, 12/1/91		50,000				50,000
301	John Turner, Drawing	3,000				3,000	
400	Delivery Service Revenue		10,700		{(5) 1,500 / (6) 1,000		13,200
500	Advertising Expense	50				50	
501	Gas and Oil Expense	680				680	
502	Salaries Expense	3,600		(7) 180		3,780	
503	Utilities Expense	150				150	
		68,330	68,330				
504	Insurance Expense			(1) 200		200	
505	Rent Expense			(2) 400		400	
506	Supplies Expense			(3) 500		500	
507	Depreciation Expense— Delivery Trucks			(4) 750		750	
110A	Accumulated Depreciation— Delivery Trucks				(4) 750		750
202	Salaries Payable				(7) 180		180
				4,530	4,530	70,260	70,260

The Income Statement Columns

All revenue and expense account balances in the Adjusted Trial Balance columns are extended to the Income Statement columns (see Illustration 4.5). Since revenues carry credit balances, they are extended to the credit column; expenses are extended to the debit column. Each column is then subtotaled. For Rapid Delivery Company, total expenses are $6,510 and total revenues are $13,200. Thus, net income for the period is $6,690 ($13,200 − $6,510). This $6,690 amount is entered in the debit column to make the two column totals balance. A net loss would be recorded in the

Illustration 4.5   *Partially Completed Work Sheet—Income Statement Columns*

RAPID DELIVERY COMPANY
Work Sheet
For the Month Ended December 31, 1991

Acct. No.	Account Titles	Trial Balance Debit	Trial Balance Credit	Adjustments Debit	Adjustments Credit	Adjusted Trial Balance Debit	Adjusted Trial Balance Credit	Income Statement Debit	Income Statement Credit
100	Cash	10,650				10,650			
101	Accounts Receivable	5,200		(6) 1,000		6,200			
102	Supplies on Hand	1,400			(3) 500	900			
103	Prepaid Insurance	2,400			(1) 200	2,200			
104	Prepaid Rent	1,200			(2) 400	800			
110	Delivery Trucks	40,000				40,000			
200	Accounts Payable		3,130				3,130		
201	Unearned Delivery Fees		4,500	(5) 1,500			3,000		
300	John Turner, Capital, 12/1/91		50,000				50,000		
301	John Turner, Drawing	3,000				3,000			
400	Delivery Service Revenue		10,700		{(5) 1,500 {(6) 1,000		13,200		13,200
500	Advertising Expense	50				50		50	
501	Gas and Oil Expense	680				680		680	
502	Salaries Expense	3,600		(7) 180		3,780		3,780	
503	Utilities Expense	150				150		150	
		68,330	68,330						
504	Insurance Expense			(1) 200		200		200	
505	Rent Expense			(2) 400		400		400	
506	Supplies Expense			(3) 500		500		500	
507	Depreciation Expense— Delivery Trucks			(4) 750		750		750	
110A	Accumulated Depreciation— Delivery Trucks				(4) 750		750		
202	Salaries Payable				(7) 180		180		
				4,530	4,530	70,260	70,260	6,510	13,200
	Net income							6,690	
								13,200	13,200

opposite manner: expenses (debits) would have been larger than revenues (credits), so a net loss would be entered in the credit column to make the columns balance.

The Balance Sheet Columns

Assets, liabilities, and owner's equity accounts listed in the Adjusted Trial Balance columns are extended to the Balance Sheet columns—assets as debits, and liabilities and owner's equity amounts as credits (see Illustration

Illustration 4.6 Completed Work Sheet—Balance Sheet Columns

RAPID DELIVERY COMPANY
Work Sheet
For the Month Ended December 31, 1991

Acct. No.	Account Titles	Trial Balance Debit	Trial Balance Credit	Adjustments Debit	Adjustments Credit	Adjusted Trial Balance Debit	Adjusted Trial Balance Credit	Income Statement Debit	Income Statement Credit	Balance Sheet Debit	Balance Sheet Credit
100	Cash	10,650				10,650				10,650	
101	Accounts Receivable	5,200		(6) 1,000		6,200				6,200	
102	Supplies on Hand	1,400			(3) 500	900				900	
103	Prepaid Insurance	2,400			(1) 200	2,200				2,200	
104	Prepaid Rent	1,200			(2) 400	800				800	
110	Delivery Trucks	40,000				40,000				40,000	
200	Accounts Payable		3,130				3,130				3,130
201	Unearned Delivery Fees		4,500	(5) 1,500			3,000				3,000
300	John Turner, Capital, 12/1/91		50,000				50,000				50,000
301	John Turner, Drawing	3,000				3,000				3,000	
400	Delivery Service Revenue		10,700		(5) 1,500 / (6) 1,000		13,200		13,200		
500	Advertising Expense	50				50		50			
501	Gas and Oil Expense	680				680		680			
502	Salaries Expense	3,600		(7) 180		3,780		3,780			
503	Utilities Expense	150				150		150			
		68,330	68,330								
504	Insurance Expense			(1) 200		200		200			
505	Rent Expense			(2) 400		400		400			
506	Supplies Expense			(3) 500		500		500			
507	Depreciation Expense—Delivery Trucks			(4) 750		750		750			
110A	Accumulated Depreciation—Delivery Trucks				(4) 750		750				750
202	Salaries Payable				(7) 180		180				180
				4,530	4,530	70,260	70,260	6,510	13,200	63,750	57,060
	Net income							6,690			6,690
								13,200	13,200	63,750	63,750

132

4.6).[1] Note that the beginning, rather than the ending, balance of John Turner's capital account is carried to the credit column because closing entries have not yet been prepared and posted.

Note also that the net income that was determined in the Income Statement columns appears again in the Balance Sheet columns. The net income amount was shown as a debit in the Income Statement columns in order to balance those columns. **Net income is shown as a credit in the Balance Sheet columns** because it increases owner's equity or capital, and increases in owner's equity are accounted for as credits. With the inclusion of the net income amount, the Balance Sheet columns balance.

If the Balance Sheet column totals do not agree on the first attempt, work backward through the process used in preparing the work sheet. Specifically, the following steps should be taken until the error is discovered:

1. Retotal the two Balance Sheet columns to see if an error in addition was made. If the column totals do not agree, check to see if some balance sheet item was not extended or was extended incorrectly from the Adjusted Trial Balance columns.
2. Retotal the Income Statement columns and determine whether the correct amount of net income or net loss for the period was entered in the appropriate columns in the Income Statement and Balance Sheet columns.
3. Retotal the Adjusted Trial Balance columns. If the totals agree, check to see that each item was transferred to the correct Income Statement or Balance Sheet column. If the totals do not agree, make sure that each adjustment was properly added to or subtracted from the related amount in the Trial Balance column.
4. Retotal the Adjustments columns.
5. Retotal the Trial Balance columns. If the totals do not agree, review the ledger accounts to find the error.

■ PREPARING FINANCIAL STATEMENTS FROM THE WORK SHEET

Objective 2:
Prepare an income statement, statement of owner's equity, and balance sheet using information contained in a work sheet.

When the work sheet has been completed, all the information needed to prepare the income statement, statement of owner's equity, and balance sheet is readily available. Now the information only needs to be recast into the appropriate financial statement format.

Income Statement

Information needed to prepare the income statement can be taken from the Income Statement columns in the work sheet. The income statement in Illustration 4.7 is based on the information in the Income Statement columns in Illustration 4.6.

---

[1] Accountants sometimes work straight down from the first account appearing on the work sheet and continue down, sorting each item to the appropriate column of the work sheet. This procedure typically results in sorting the balance sheet accounts before the income statement accounts.

Illustration 4.7

Income Statement

RAPID DELIVERY COMPANY
Income Statement
For the Month Ended December 31, 1991

Revenues:		
Delivery service revenue		$13,200
Expenses:		
Advertising expense	$ 50	
Gas and oil expense	680	
Salaries expense	3,780	
Utilities expense	150	
Insurance expense	200	
Rent expense	400	
Supplies expense	500	
Depreciation expense—delivery trucks	750	
Total expenses		6,510
Net income		$ 6,690

Statement of Owner's Equity

The **statement of owner's equity** (also called *statement of owner's capital*) is a financial statement that summarizes the transactions affecting the owner's capital account balance. This statement was introduced in Chapter 1. Information needed to prepare this financial statement is taken from the Balance Sheet columns in the work sheet (Illustration 4.6). Such a statement (Illustration 4.8) is prepared by showing the beginning capital account balance (Account No. 300), adding additional owner investments, adding net income (or deducting net loss), and then subtracting the owner's withdrawals (Account No. 301). The ending capital balance is then carried forward to the balance sheet. **The statement of owner's equity helps to relate income statement information to balance sheet information** and indicates how net income, shown on the income statement, relates to the amount of owner's capital, shown on the balance sheet under owner's equity.

Illustration 4.8

Statement of Owner's Equity

RAPID DELIVERY COMPANY
Statement of Owner's Equity
For the Month Ended December 31, 1991

John Turner, capital, December 1, 1991	$50,000
Add: Net income for December	6,690
Total	$56,690
Deduct: Owner drawings for December	3,000
John Turner, capital, December 31, 1991	$53,690

Illustration 4.9

Balance Sheet

RAPID DELIVERY COMPANY
Balance Sheet
December 31, 1991

Assets

Cash		$10,650
Accounts receivable		6,200
Supplies on hand		900
Prepaid insurance		2,200
Prepaid rent		800
Delivery trucks	$40,000	
Less: Accumulated depreciation	750	39,250
Total assets		$60,000

Liabilities and Owner's Equity

Liabilities:

Accounts payable	$ 3,130
Unearned delivery fees	3,000
Salaries payable	180
Total liabilities	$ 6,310

Owner's equity:

John Turner, capital	53,690
Total liabilities and owner's equity	$60,000

Balance Sheet

The balance sheet is completed from the information in the Balance Sheet columns of the work sheet (Illustration 4.6). The beginning balance shown for owner's capital must be revised to include net income less owner's withdrawals for December. The correct amount for ending owner's equity is shown on the statement of owner's equity. The balance sheet for Rapid Delivery Company is shown in Illustration 4.9.

■ JOURNALIZING ADJUSTING ENTRIES

Objective 3:
Prepare adjusting
and closing entries
using information
contained in the
work sheet.

Now that the financial statements have been completed from the work sheet, the adjusting entries entered in the Adjustments columns must be entered in the general journal and posted to the appropriate ledger accounts. The process of preparing these adjusting entries is the same as we used in Chapter 3, except the work sheet is now the source for making the entries. **The preparation of a work sheet does not eliminate the need to journalize and post adjusting entries because the work sheet is only an accounting tool and is not part of the formal accounting records.**

Each adjusting entry can be identified through the numerical notations in the Adjustments columns and the adjustments explanations at the bottom of the work sheet, and each entry is shown with its appropriate debit(s) and credit(s). The adjusting entries for Rapid Delivery Company as they would appear in the general journal are:

RAPID DELIVERY COMPANY
GENERAL JOURNAL
Page 3

Date		Account Titles and Explanation	Post. Ref.	Debit	Credit
1991		**Adjusting Entries**			
Dec.	31	Insurance Expense	504	2 0 0	
		Prepaid Insurance	103		2 0 0
		To record insurance expense for December.			
	31	Rent Expense	505	4 0 0	
		Prepaid Rent	104		4 0 0
		To record rent expense for December.			
	31	Supplies Expense	506	5 0 0	
		Supplies on Hand	102		5 0 0
		To record supplies used during December.			
	31	Depreciation Expense—Delivery Trucks	507	7 5 0	
		Accumulated Depreciation—Delivery Trucks	110A		7 5 0
		To record depreciation expense for December.			
	31	Unearned Delivery Fees	201	1 5 0 0	
		Delivery Service Revenue	400		1 5 0 0
		To transfer a portion of delivery fees from the liability account to the revenue account.			
	31	Accounts Receivable	101	1 0 0 0	
		Delivery Service Revenue	400		1 0 0 0
		To record unbilled delivery services performed in December.			
	31	Salaries Expense	502	1 8 0	
		Salaries Payable	202		1 8 0
		To accrue one day's salaries that were earned but are unpaid.			

■ THE CLOSING PROCESS

From Chapter 3, you learned that (1) revenue and expense accounts are **nominal (temporary) accounts** since they are merely subclassifications of a **real (permanent) account**, Owner's Equity; and (2) financial statements are prepared for certain accounting periods. The **closing process** is (1) the act of transferring the balances in the revenue and expense accounts to a clearing account called *Income Summary* and then to owner's capital, and (2) the act of transferring the balance in the owner's drawing account to the owner's capital account. The closing process reduces revenue, expense, and owner's drawing account balances to zero so they will be ready to receive data for the next accounting period. The closing process may be performed monthly or annually.

The **Income Summary account** is a clearing account used only at the end of an accounting period to summarize revenues and expenses for the period. After all revenue and expense account balances have been transferred to Income Summary, the balance in the Income Summary account represents the net income or net loss for the period. The balance in the Income Summary account is then closed, or transferred, to the owner's capital account, resulting in a zero balance in Income Summary.

The owner's drawing account is also closed at the end of the accounting period. This account shows the amount of cash or goods that the owner took out of the business during the current period. Accountants close the owner's drawing account directly to the owner's capital account and not to Income Summary because drawings have no effect on income or loss for the period.

The process of closing is often referred to as *closing the books*. Remember, though, that only revenue, expense, and drawing accounts are closed—not asset, liability, or owner's equity accounts.

There are four basic steps in the closing process:

1. **Closing the revenue account(s)**—the balances in the revenue accounts are transferred to a clearing account called *Income Summary*.
2. **Closing the expense account(s)**—the balances in the expense accounts are transferred to a clearing account called *Income Summary*.
3. **Closing the Income Summary account**—the balance of the Income Summary account is transferred to the owner's capital account.
4. **Closing the owner's drawing account**—the balance of the owner's drawing account is transferred to the owner's capital account.

An explanation of each these steps follows, using the closing process for Rapid Delivery Company as an example.

Step 1: Closing the Revenue Account(s)

Revenues appear in the Income Statement credit column of the work sheet. The only revenue appearing in the Income Statement credit column for Rapid Delivery Company is delivery service revenue of $13,200 (Illustration 4.6). Since revenue accounts have credit balances, they must be debited for an equal amount to bring them to a zero balance. When Delivery Service Revenue is debited, Income Summary (Account No. 600) is credited. This entry is made in the general journal to close the Delivery Service Revenue account. The account numbers in the Posting Reference column are entered when the journal entry has been posted to the ledger. This same statement is true for the other closing journal entries illustrated.

RAPID DELIVERY COMPANY
GENERAL JOURNAL   *Page 4*

Date		Account Titles and Explanation	Post. Ref.	Debit	Credit
1991		**Closing Entries**			
Dec.	31	Delivery Service Revenue	400	1 3 2 0 0	
		Income Summary	600		1 3 2 0 0
		To close the revenue account in the Income Statement credit			
		column to Income Summary.			

After closing, the Delivery Service Revenue account (in T-account format) appears as shown below. Note that the account now has a zero balance.

	Delivery Service Revenue	*Account No. 400*
Decreased by $13,200 →	1991	Bal. before closing 13,200
	Dec. 31 To close to Income Summary 13,200	
		Bal. after closing –0–

The Income Summary account was credited for $13,200 as a result of the above entry. The Income Summary account will be shown later.

Step 2: Closing the Expense Account(s)

Expenses appear in the Income Statement debit column of the work sheet. There are eight expenses for Rapid Delivery Company appearing in the Income Statement debit column (Illustration 4.6). As shown by the column subtotal, they add up to $6,510. Since expense accounts have debit balances, **each one** must be credited to bring it to a zero balance. The debit in the closing entry is made to the Income Summary account for $6,510. The following entry is made to close the expense accounts:

RAPID DELIVERY COMPANY
GENERAL JOURNAL   *Page 4*

Date	Account Titles and Explanation	Post. Ref.	Debit	Credit
1991 Dec. 31	Income Summary	600	6 5 1 0	
	Advertising Expense	500		5 0
	Gas and Oil Expense	501		6 8 0
	Salaries Expense	502		3 7 8 0
	Utilities Expense	503		1 5 0
	Insurance Expense	504		2 0 0
	Rent Expense	505		4 0 0
	Supplies Expense	506		5 0 0
	Depreciation Expense—Delivery Trucks	507		7 5 0
	To close the expense accounts appearing in the Income			
	Statement debit column to Income Summary.			

The debit of $6,510 to the Income Summary account agrees with the Income Statement debit column subtotal in the work sheet. The comparison with the work sheet can serve as a check to make certain that all revenue and expense items are listed and have been closed; had the debit in the above entry been for a different amount than the column subtotal, there would be an error in the closing entry for expenses.

The expense accounts appear as shown below after they have been closed. Note that each account has a zero balance after closing.

Advertising Expense   *Account No. 500*

Bal. before closing	50	1991 Dec. 31 To close to Income Summary	50 ← Decreased by $50
Bal. after closing	–0–		

Gas and Oil Expense   *Account No. 501*

Bal. before closing	680	1991 Dec. 31 To close to Income Summary	680 ← Decreased by $680
Bal. after closing	–0–		

Salaries Expense   *Account No. 502*

Bal. before closing	3,780	1991 Dec. 31 To close to Income Summary	3,780 ← Decreased by $3,780
Bal. after closing	–0–		

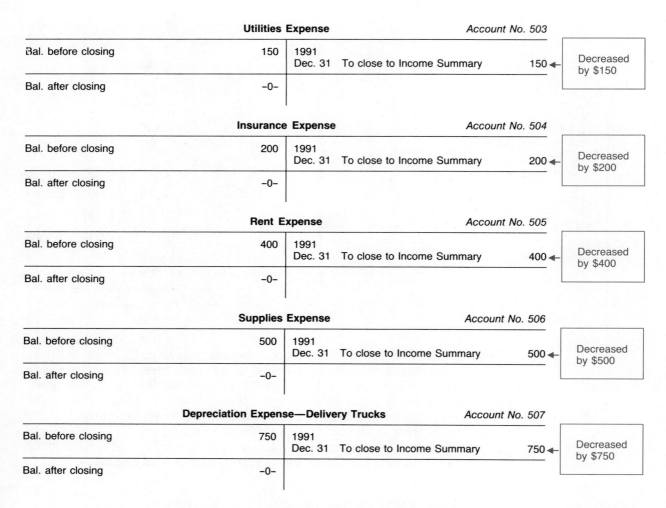

The expense accounts could be closed before closing the revenue accounts. The end result is the same either way.

Step 3: Closing the Income Summary Account

After the revenues and expenses have been closed, the total amounts that formerly were carried in those accounts now are carried in the Income Summary account.

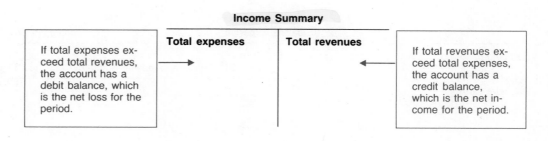

For Rapid Delivery Company, the Income Summary account appears as follows:

Income Summary   *Account No. 600*

1991			1991		
Dec. 31	From closing the expense accounts	6,510	Dec. 31	From closing the revenue account	13,200
				Bal. before closing this account (net income)	6,690

The credit balance of $6,690 is the net income for December.

Now the Income Summary account needs to be closed to the owner's capital account. The journal entry to do this is:

RAPID DELIVERY COMPANY
GENERAL JOURNAL

Page 4

Date	Account Titles and Explanation	Post. Ref.	Debit	Credit
1991 Dec. 31	Income Summary	600	6 6 9 0	
	John Turner, Capital	300		6 6 9 0
	To close the Income Summary account to the owner's capital			
	account.			

The Income Summary and John Turner, Capital accounts will appear as follows after the Income Summary account is closed:

Income Summary   *Account No. 600*

1991			1991		
Dec. 31	From closing the expense accounts	6,510	Dec. 31	From closing the revenue account	13,200
Dec. 31	To close this account to owner's capital	6,690		Bal. before closing this account (net income)	6,690
				Bal. after closing	–0–

Decreased by $6,690

John Turner, Capital   *Account No. 300*

	Bal. before closing process	50,000
	1991	
	Dec. 31 From Income Summary	6,690
	Bal. after closing	56,690

Increased by $6,690

Step 4: Closing the Owner's Drawing Account

The last closing entry that must be made is to close the owner's drawing account. This account has a debit balance before closing. To close the account, the owner's drawing account is credited and the owner's capital account is debited. Notice that the drawing account is not closed to Income Summary. The drawing account is not an expense and does not enter into income determination.

For Rapid Delivery Company, the journal entry to close the owner's drawing account is:

RAPID DELIVERY COMPANY
GENERAL JOURNAL   *Page 4*

Date	Account Titles and Explanation	Post. Ref.	Debit	Credit
1991 Dec. 31	John Turner, Capital	300	3 0 0 0	
	John Turner, Drawing	301		3 0 0 0
	To close the owner's drawing account to the owner's capital			
	account.			

The owner's drawing and owner's capital accounts as they appear after this closing entry has been posted are:

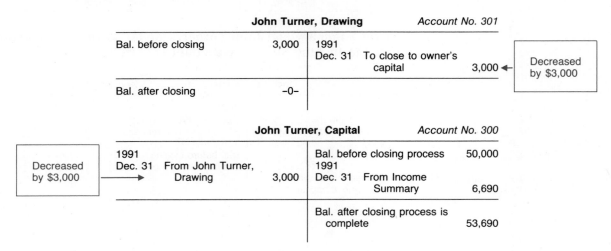

			John Turner, Drawing		*Account No. 301*
Bal. before closing	3,000		1991		
			Dec. 31 To close to owner's capital	3,000	← Decreased by $3,000
Bal. after closing	–0–				

				John Turner, Capital		*Account No. 300*
Decreased by $3,000 →	1991 Dec. 31 From John Turner, Drawing	3,000		Bal. before closing process	50,000	
				1991 Dec. 31 From Income Summary	6,690	
				Bal. after closing process is complete	53,690	

Closing Process Summarized

The closing process is the transferring of revenue and expense account balances to a clearing account called *Income Summary* and then transferring from Income Summary to owner's capital the amount of net income or net loss for the period. Closing also includes the elimination of the balance in the owner's drawing account by transferring that amount to owner's capital. A summary of the process used to close Rapid Delivery Company accounts shown on the work sheet in Illustration 4.6 is as follows:

1. The only revenue account appearing in the Income Summary credit column (revenues) was debited, and the Income Summary account was credited for the amount of revenue earned for the period, $13,200. Note that the credit to Income Summary is equal to the subtotal of the Income Statement credit column of the work sheet. This will be true no matter how many revenue accounts are closed.
2. Each expense account appearing in the Income Statement debit column (expenses) was credited for its balance, and the Income Summary account was debited for the total amount of expenses incurred for the period, $6,510. Note that the debit to Income Summary is equal to the subtotal of the Income Statement debit column of the work sheet.
3. The balance of the Income Summary account, $6,690, was closed to the owner's capital account. Since the Income Summary account balance was a credit (net income), it was closed by a debit to the Income Summary account and a credit to owner's capital. If a net loss had occurred, Income Summary would have had a debit balance, and closing would have been through a credit to Income Summary and a debit to owner's capital.
4. The balance in the owner's drawing account was closed to the owner's capital account by debiting the capital account and crediting the drawing account. The balance in the drawing account is found in the Balance Sheet debit column of the work sheet.

In our explanation of the closing process, we have used the T-account format to illustrate the adjusting and closing entries for Rapid Delivery Company. These same adjusting and closing entries shown in three-column ledger accounts are illustrated in the next section.

■ LEDGER ACCOUNTS AFTER CLOSING PROCESS COMPLETED

The ledger accounts for Rapid Delivery Company after the adjusting and closing entries have been posted are shown below. Assume that all adjusting entries were made on page 3 of the general journal and that all closing entries were entered on page 4. The initial December 31 balances in the ledger accounts below are before adjusting and closing entries have been posted. The balances are labeled as a debit or a credit to assist you in understanding the example. Normally, these labels are not included in the ledger since an experienced accountant knows whether each balance is a debit or credit.

RAPID DELIVERY COMPANY
GENERAL LEDGER

Cash — Account No. 100

Date		Explanation	Post. Ref.	Debit	Credit	Balance
1991 Dec.	31	Balance				1 0 6 5 0 Dr.

Accounts Receivable — Account No. 101

Date		Explanation	Post. Ref.	Debit	Credit	Balance
1991 Dec.	31	Balance				5 2 0 0 Dr.
	31	Adjustment	G3	1 0 0 0		6 2 0 0 Dr.

Supplies on Hand — Account No. 102

Date		Explanation	Post. Ref.	Debit	Credit	Balance
1991 Dec.	31	Balance				1 4 0 0 Dr.
	31	Adjustment	G3		5 0 0	9 0 0 Dr.

Prepaid Insurance — Account No. 103

Date		Explanation	Post. Ref.	Debit	Credit	Balance
1991 Dec.	31	Balance				2 4 0 0 Dr.
	31	Adjustment	G3		2 0 0	2 2 0 0 Dr.

Prepaid Rent — Account No. 104

Date		Explanation	Post. Ref.	Debit	Credit	Balance
1991 Dec.	31	Balance				1 2 0 0 Dr.
	31	Adjustment	G3		4 0 0	8 0 0 Dr.

Delivery Trucks — Account No. 110

Date		Explanation	Post. Ref.	Debit	Credit	Balance
1991 Dec.	31	Balance				4 0 0 0 0 Dr.

GENERAL LEDGER *(continued)*

Accumulated Depreciation—Delivery Trucks   *Account No. 110A*

Date		Explanation	Post. Ref.	Debit	Credit	Balance
1991 Dec.	31	Balance				– 0 –
	31	Adjustment	G3		7 5 0	7 5 0 Cr.

Accounts Payable   *Account No. 200*

Date		Explanation	Post. Ref.	Debit	Credit	Balance
1991 Dec.	31	Balance				3 1 3 0 Cr.

Unearned Delivery Fees   *Account No. 201*

Date		Explanation	Post. Ref.	Debit	Credit	Balance
1991 Dec.	31	Balance				4 5 0 0 Cr.
	31	Adjustment	G3	1 5 0 0		3 0 0 0 Cr.

Salaries Payable   *Account No. 202*

Date		Explanation	Post. Ref.	Debit	Credit	Balance
1991 Dec.	31	Balance				– 0 –
	31	Adjustment	G3		1 8 0	1 8 0 Cr.

John Turner, Capital   *Account No. 300*

Date		Explanation	Post. Ref.	Debit	Credit	Balance
1991 Dec.	31	Balance				5 0 0 0 0 Cr.
	31	Net income	G4		6 6 9 0	5 6 6 9 0 Cr.
	31	Drawings	G4	3 0 0 0		5 3 6 9 0 Cr.

GENERAL LEDGER *(continued)*

John Turner, Drawing — Account No. 301

Date		Explanation	Post. Ref.	Debit	Credit	Balance
1991 Dec.	31	Balance				3 0 0 0 Dr.
	31	To close	G4		3 0 0 0	– 0 –

Delivery Service Revenue — Account No. 400

Date		Explanation	Post. Ref.	Debit	Credit	Balance
1991 Dec.	31	Balance				1 0 7 0 0 Cr.
	31	Adjustment	G3		1 5 0 0	1 2 2 0 0 Cr.
	31	Adjustment	G3		1 0 0 0	1 3 2 0 0 Cr.
	31	To close	G4	1 3 2 0 0		– 0 –

Advertising Expense — Account No. 500

Date		Explanation	Post. Ref.	Debit	Credit	Balance
1991 Dec.	31	Balance				5 0 Dr.
	31	To close	G4		5 0	– 0 –

Gas and Oil Expense — Account No. 501

Date		Explanation	Post. Ref.	Debit	Credit	Balance
1991 Dec.	31	Balance				6 8 0 Dr.
	31	To close	G4		6 8 0	– 0 –

Salaries Expense — Account No. 502

Date		Explanation	Post. Ref.	Debit	Credit	Balance
1991 Dec.	31	Balance				3 6 0 0 Dr.
	31	Adjustment	G3	1 8 0		3 7 8 0 Dr.
	31	To close	G4		3 7 8 0	– 0 –

GENERAL LEDGER *(continued)*

Utilities Expense
Account No. 503

Date		Explanation	Post. Ref.	Debit	Credit	Balance
1991 Dec.	31	Balance				1 5 0 Dr.
	31	To close	G4		1 5 0	- 0 -

Insurance Expense
Account No. 504

Date		Explanation	Post. Ref.	Debit	Credit	Balance
1991 Dec.	31	Balance				- 0 -
	31	Adjustment	G3	2 0 0		2 0 0 Dr.
	31	To close	G4		2 0 0	- 0 -

Rent Expense
Account No. 505

Date		Explanation	Post. Ref.	Debit	Credit	Balance
1991 Dec.	31	Balance				- 0 -
	31	Adjustment	G3	4 0 0		4 0 0 Dr.
	31	To close	G4		4 0 0	- 0 -

Supplies Expense
Account No. 506

Date		Explanation	Post. Ref.	Debit	Credit	Balance
1991 Dec.	31	Balance				- 0 -
	31	Adjustment	G3	5 0 0		5 0 0 Dr.
	31	To close	G4		5 0 0	- 0 -

Depreciation Expense—Delivery Trucks
Account No. 507

Date		Explanation	Post. Ref.	Debit	Credit	Balance
1991 Dec.	31	Balance				- 0 -
	31	Adjustment	G3	7 5 0		7 5 0 Dr.
	31	To close	G4		7 5 0	- 0 -

GENERAL LEDGER *(concluded)*

Income Summary   *Account No. 600*

Date		Explanation	Post. Ref.	Debit	Credit	Balance
1991 Dec.	31	Balance				– 0 –
	31	Revenue	G4		1 3 2 0 0	1 3 2 0 0 Cr.
	31	Expenses	G4	6 5 1 0		6 6 9 0 Cr.
	31	To close	G4	6 6 9 0		– 0 –

As each of the expense and revenue accounts is closed, its balance is reduced to zero. The balances formerly in those accounts are transferred to the Income Summary account. Note that the Income Summary account shows clearly the net income for the period—the final amount transferred, or closed, to the John Turner, Capital account. The balance in the John Turner, Capital account of $53,690 is the amount of owner's capital shown in the balance sheet for December 31, 1991.

Post-Closing Trial Balance

After closing has been completed, the only accounts in the ledger that have not been closed are the balance sheet accounts (the permanent, or real, accounts). Since these accounts contain the opening balances for the coming accounting period, they must, of course, be in balance. The preparation of a post-closing trial balance serves as a means of checking the accuracy of the closing process and ensures that the books are in balance at the start of the new accounting period. The post-closing trial balance differs from the

Illustration 4.10

Post-Closing Trial Balance

RAPID DELIVERY COMPANY
Post-Closing Trial Balance
December 31, 1991

Account No.		Debits	Credits
100	Cash	$10,650	
101	Accounts Receivable	6,200	
102	Supplies on Hand	900	
103	Prepaid Insurance	2,200	
104	Prepaid Rent	800	
110	Delivery Trucks	40,000	
110A	Accumulated Depreciation—Delivery Trucks		$ 750
200	Accounts Payable		3,130
201	Unearned Delivery Fees		3,000
202	Salaries Payable		180
300	John Turner, Capital		53,690
		$60,750	$60,750

adjusted trial balance in only two important respects: (1) it excludes all nominal accounts since they have been closed and (2) the capital account has been updated to its proper ending balance.

A **post-closing trial balance** is a trial balance taken after the closing entries have been posted. The only accounts that should be open are assets, liabilities, and owner's capital. Account balances are listed in debit and credit columns and totaled to make sure debits and credits are equal.

A post-closing trial balance for Rapid Delivery Company as of December 31, 1991, is shown in Illustration 4.10. The amounts appearing in the post-closing trial balance are taken from the ledger after the closing entries have been posted. You can verify this by comparing the amounts in Illustration 4.10 with those appearing in the ledger accounts for Rapid Delivery Company, shown on pages 144–48. (This concludes the Rapid Delivery Company illustration, which has been used in Chapters 2, 3, and 4.)

■ THE CLASSIFIED BALANCE SHEET

Objective 4:
Prepare a classified
balance sheet.

The balance sheets presented so far in this text have been unclassified balance sheets. An **unclassified balance sheet** has three major categories: assets, liabilities, and owner's equity. Illustration 4.9 (page 135) shows an unclassified balance sheet. A **classified balance sheet** contains the same three major categories but then subdivides at least some of the three major categories to provide useful information for interpretation and analysis by users of financial statements. For example, assets may be subdivided into many different categories. At this point in the text we will divide assets into (1) current assets and (2) property, plant, and equipment. Liabilities may be classified as either current or long-term. Owner's equity for a single proprietorship cannot be subdivided into classifications.

An example of a classified balance sheet for Jamestown Sports Arena is shown in Illustration 4.11. This new example is used so that we can include items not contained in the Rapid Delivery Company balance sheet of Illustration 4.9. Jamestown Sports Arena rents its facilities for sporting events, concerts, and other activities. This balance sheet is presented in a vertical format (assets appearing above liabilities and owner's equity) rather than the horizontal format (assets on the left and liabilities and owner's equity on the right) which has been used previously in the text. The two formats are equally acceptable.

In this section, the following subdivisions within the three major categories of a classified balance sheet are discussed: current assets; property, plant, and equipment; current liabilities; and long-term liabilities. Owner's equity is no different in a classified balance sheet than in an unclassified balance sheet.

The items listed in the classified balance sheet are discussed in greater detail in the remainder of the text. Our only purpose here is to give a brief description of each item listed.

Illustration 4.11

A Classified Balance Sheet

JAMESTOWN SPORTS ARENA
Balance Sheet
June 30, 1991

Assets

Current assets:			
Cash		$ 40,000	
Accounts receivable		55,000	
Notes receivable		15,000	
Prepaid insurance		2,000	
Total current assets			$112,000
Property, plant, and equipment:			
Land		$114,000	
Building	$300,000		
Less: Accumulated depreciation	100,000	200,000	
Sports equipment	$ 75,000		
Less: Accumulated depreciation	15,000	60,000	
Office equipment	$ 18,000		
Less: Accumulated depreciation	6,000	12,000	
Total property, plant, and equipment			386,000
Total assets			$498,000

Liabilities and Owner's Equity

Current liabilities:		
Accounts payable	$ 25,000	
Notes payable	6,000	
Salaries payable	800	
Unearned rental fees	1,100	
Total current liabilities		$ 32,900
Long-term liabilities:		
Note payable, 15% (due in 1997)		150,000
Total liabilities		$182,900
Owner's equity:		
Andrews, capital		315,100
Total liabilities and owner's equity		$498,000

Current Assets

Current assets are cash and other assets that will be converted to cash or used up by the business in a relatively short period of time, usually a year or less. Common current assets in a service-type business include cash, accounts receivable, notes receivable, and prepaid expenses. Current assets are normally listed in order of liquidity, or how easily they are convertible into cash.

Cash includes deposits in banks available for current operations at the balance sheet date plus cash on hand consisting of currency, undeposited checks, drafts, and money orders. Cash is usually the first current asset to appear on a balance sheet.

Accounts receivable (also called *trade accounts receivable*) are amounts owed to a business by customers (debtors). An account receivable arises when a service is performed or merchandise is sold and cash is not received immediately. Customers normally provide no written evidence of indebtedness on sales invoices or delivery tickets except their signatures.

A **note** is an unconditional written promise to pay a definite sum of money at a certain or determinable date, usually with interest (a charge made for use of the money) at a specified rate. A note is a **note receivable** on the balance sheet of the company to which the note is given. A note receivable arises *(a)* when a sale is made and a note is received from the customer, *(b)* when a customer gives a note for an amount due on an account receivable, or *(c)* when money is loaned and a note is received as evidence. Notes are discussed at length in Chapter 8.

Prepaid expenses include items such as rent, insurance, and supplies that have been paid for but not yet used. If prepaid expenses had not been paid for in advance at the balance sheet date, they would require the disbursement of cash in the following period. Furthermore, prepaid expenses are current assets because they have service potential.

Property, Plant, and Equipment

Property, plant, and equipment are assets acquired for use in a business rather than for resale. The assets classified as property, plant, and equipment also are termed **plant assets** or **fixed assets.** To agree with the order in the heading, items within property, plant, and equipment are usually listed in that order (property first and equipment last) and are called *fixed assets* because they are used for long-term purposes. Several types of property, plant, and equipment are described below.

Land is ground on which the business buildings of the company are located. Land could also be used for outside storage space or a parking lot.

Buildings are structures used to carry on the business. Buildings owned as investments are not included as plant assets.

Machinery is heavy equipment such as a commercial press used in a laundry or a stamping machine used to punch out metal parts.

Sports equipment includes items such as hockey goals, basketball gear, and wrestling mats.

Store equipment, or **store fixtures,** includes items such as showcases, counters, stools, chairs, and cash registers.

Office equipment, or **office fixtures,** includes items such as file cabinets, calculators, typewriters, computers, desks, and chairs.

Delivery equipment includes autos, trucks, and vans used primarily in making deliveries to customers.

Accumulated depreciation is a contra asset account to depreciable assets such as buildings, machinery, and equipment. This account shows the total depreciation taken for each related asset. On the balance sheet, the accumulated depreciation is deducted (as a contra asset) from its related asset.

Current Liabilities

Current liabilities are debts, usually due within one year, the payment of which will require the use of current assets. Current liabilities are listed in order of how soon they must be paid; the sooner a liability must be paid, the earlier it is listed. Examples of current liabilities follow.

Accounts payable are amounts owed by the company to creditors for items or services purchased from them. Accounts payable are generally due in 30 or 60 days and do not bear interest. In the balance sheet, accounts payable are shown in one amount, which is the sum of the individual accounts payable.

Notes payable are unconditional written promises by the company to pay a certain sum of money at a certain or determinable future date. The notes may arise from borrowing money from a bank, from the purchase of assets, or from the giving of a note in settlement of an account payable. Generally, only notes payable due in one year or less are included as current liabilities.

Salaries payable are amounts owed to employees for services rendered, but for which payment has not been made at the balance sheet date. These wages have not been paid at the balance sheet date because they are not due until later.

Unearned revenues (revenues received in advance) result when payment is received for goods or services before revenue has been earned, such as a subscription to a magazine. These unearned revenues represent a liability to perform the agreed services or other contractual requirements or to return the assets received.

Long-Term Liabilities

Long-term liabilities are those debts such as a mortgage payable and bonds payable that are not due for a relatively long period of time, usually more than one year. Maturity dates should be shown in the balance sheet for all long-term liabilities. Normally, the liabilities with the earliest due dates are listed first.

Notes payable with maturity dates at least one year beyond the balance sheet date are also long-term liabilities. Another common long-term liability, bonds payable, is discussed and illustrated in a later chapter.

These first four chapters have concentrated on accounting for service companies. Although the basic accounting principles and the accounting process apply to all companies, accounting for merchandising and manufacturing companies involves some special accounting practices and procedures. In the next chapter, you will learn about accounting as it pertains to merchandising companies.

■ UNDERSTANDING THE LEARNING OBJECTIVES: CHAPTER 4

1. Prepare a work sheet for a service company.

   - The work sheet is a columnar sheet of paper on which accountants have summarized information needed to make the adjusting and closing entries and to prepare the financial statements.
   - Work sheets may vary in format. The work sheet illustrated in the chapter has 10 columns—two each for Trial Balance, Adjustments, Adjusted Trial Balance, Income Statement, and Balance Sheet.

2. Prepare an income statement, statement of owner's equity, and balance sheet, using information contained in a work sheet.

- All of the information needed to prepare the income statement is in the Income Statement columns of the work sheet. Net income for the period is the amount needed to balance the two Income Statement columns in the work sheet.
- The statement of owner's equity starts with the beginning balance in owner's capital, adds net income for the period, and deducts owner's drawings.
- The balance sheet is prepared using the information in the last two columns of the work sheet.

3. Prepare adjusting and closing entries using information contained in the work sheet.

- Adjusting entries were explained in the preceding chapter. They are necessary to bring the accounts to their proper balances before financial statements are prepared.
- Closing entries are necessary to reduce the balances of expense and revenue accounts to zero so they will be ready to receive data for the next accounting period.
- Expense accounts are closed by crediting them and debiting Income Summary.
- Revenue accounts are closed by debiting them and crediting Income Summary.
- If there is net income, the Income Summary account is closed by debiting that account and crediting owner's capital. If a net loss occurs, the Income Summary account is closed by debiting owner's capital and crediting Income Summary.
- The owner's drawing account is closed by crediting that account and debiting owner's capital.

4. Prepare a classified balance sheet.

- A classified balance sheet subdivides the major categories on the balance sheet into subcategories. For instance, assets are subdivided into current assets and property, plant, and equipment. Liabilities are subdivided into current liabilities and long-term liabilities. Owner's equity for a single proprietorship cannot be subdivided into classifications.

5. Prepare reversing entries (Appendix).

- Reversing entries reverse the effects of the adjusting entries to which they relate. Reversing entries are prepared on the first day of the next accounting period following the period in which the adjusting entries were made.
- Adjusting entries that increase assets or liabilities may be reversed, while those that decrease assets or liabilities may not be reversed.

- The purpose of a reversing entry is to simplify the first entry relating to that same item in the next accounting period. Reversing entries are completely optional.

6. Define and use correctly the new terms in the glossary.

- See the new terms introduced following the Appendix to this chapter.

■ APPENDIX: REVERSING ENTRIES

Objective 5:
Prepare reversing
entries.

For certain types of adjusting entries, reversing entries may be prepared as of the first day of the next accounting period. **Reversing entries** are so named because they reverse the effects of the adjusting entry to which they relate. The purpose of a reversing entry is to simplify the first entry relating to that same item in the next accounting period.

Recall that in Chapter 3 an adjusting entry (adjustment 7) was made for Rapid Delivery Company at December 31, 1991, to recognize $180 of salaries payable. This adjusting entry was made to record one day's salaries that had been incurred but had not yet been paid. The company pays salaries every four weeks. Thus, the next payday is Friday, January 25, 1992. Below are illustrated the entries from December 31, 1991, through January 25, 1992, assuming (1) no reversing entry is used and (2) a reversing entry is used.

Whether or not a reversing entry is used, the adjusting entry as of December 31, 1991, is the same. The reversing entry, dated January 1, 1992, shown in the second column below is the exact reverse of the debit and credit used in the adjusting entry. Use of the reversing entry simplifies the entry made on January 25. The accountant does not have to remember that salaries payable of $180 have already been recorded. When the $3,600 payment is made, the entry is simply a debit to Salaries Expense and a credit to Cash for $3,600.

Another reason for using reversing entries is that, when the accounts are maintained on a computer, the computer may have been programmed to debit Salaries Expense and credit Cash every time salaries are paid. The use of a reversing entry on January 1 permits the January 25 entry to be recorded in this manner.

The end result in the accounts is the same whether or not a reversing entry is used. To prove this, the accounts as they would appear are shown on page 156. The beginning balance in Salaries Payable results from the adjusting entry made on December 31, 1991. The adjusting entry from 1991 is not shown since it was the same under either method.

Not all adjusting entries may be reversed on the first day of the next accounting period. Ideal entries for reversal are those relating to situations where cash is going to be paid or received in the following period for an item that accrues and has resulted in an adjusting entry. Examples of such items would include accrued salaries and unbilled revenues. Adjustments for items that will **not** result in a subsequent receipt or payment of cash, such as the adjustment for depreciation, are **not** reversed. **A general rule to follow is that all adjusting journal entries that increase assets or liabilities may be reversed, but those adjusting journal entries that decrease assets or liabilities may not be reversed.** Thus, adjusting entries that involve accruals of assets (accrued receivables) and liabilities (accrued payables) may be reversed.

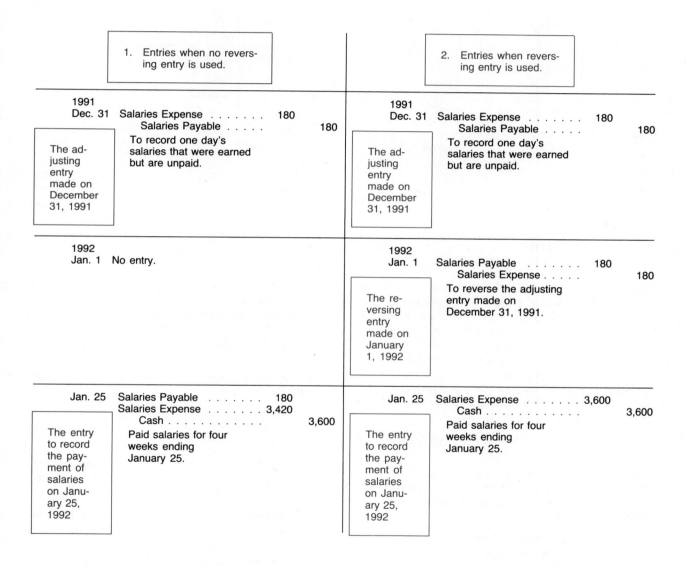

Reversing entries are optional and relate to bookkeeping technique; they have no effect on the financial statements. Students may encounter the use of reversing entries in more advanced accounting courses or in actual practice. An understanding of reversing entries is not essential to understanding the remainder of this text since they will not be used.

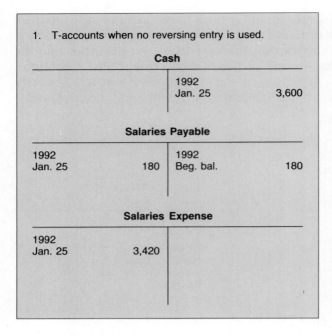

1. T-accounts when no reversing entry is used.

Cash

	1992 Jan. 25	3,600

Salaries Payable

1992 Jan. 25	180	1992 Beg. bal.	180

Salaries Expense

1992 Jan. 25	3,420	

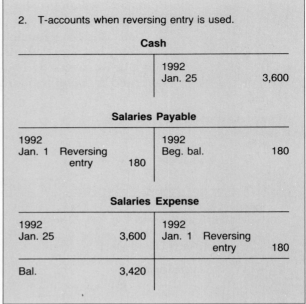

2. T-accounts when reversing entry is used.

Cash

	1992 Jan. 25	3,600

Salaries Payable

1992 Jan. 1 Reversing entry	180	1992 Beg. bal.	180

Salaries Expense

1992 Jan. 25	3,600	1992 Jan. 1 Reversing entry	180
Bal.	3,420		

NEW TERMS INTRODUCED IN CHAPTER 4

Accounting cycle   Series of steps that accountants perform during the accounting period to analyze, record, classify, summarize, and report useful financial information for the purpose of preparing financial statements. The steps include analyzing transactions, journalizing transactions, posting journal entries, taking a trial balance and completing the work sheet, preparing financial statements, journalizing and posting adjusting entries, journalizing and posting closing entries, and taking a post-closing trial balance (123).

Buildings   Structures used to carry on the business (151).

Cash   Includes deposits in banks available for current operations at the balance sheet date, plus cash on hand consisting of currency, undeposited checks, drafts, and money orders (150).

Classified balance sheet   Subdivides the three major balance sheet categories to provide more information for the users of financial statements. Assets may be divided into current assets and property, plant, and equipment; and liabilities may be divided into current liabilities and long-term liabilities (149).

Closing process   The act of transferring the balances in the revenue and expense accounts to a clearing ac- count called *Income Summary* and then to the owner's capital account. The balance in the owner's drawing account is also transferred to the owner's capital account (137).

Current assets   Cash and other assets that will be converted to cash or used up by the business in a relatively short period of time, usually a year or less (150).

Current liabilities   Debts, usually due within one year, the payment of which will require the use of current assets (151).

Income Summary account   A clearing account used only at the end of an accounting period to summarize revenues and expenses for the period (137).

Land   Ground on which the business buildings of the company are located. Land could also be used for out- side storage space or a parking lot (151).

Long-term liabilities   Debts such as mortgage pay- able and bonds payable that are not due for a relatively long period of time, usually more than a year (152).

Machinery   Heavy equipment such as a commercial press used in a laundry or a stamping machine used to punch out metal parts (151).

Post-closing trial balance   A trial balance taken after the closing entries have been posted (149).

Property, plant, and equipment   Assets acquired for use in a business rather than for resale; also called *plant assets* or *fixed assets* (151).

Reversing entries   Reverse the effects of the adjusting entries to which they relate. They are made on the first day of the next accounting period. Their purpose is to make easier the recording of subsequent transactions relating to those same items. Reversing entries may only be used for certain types of adjusting entries—usually those accruals where cash is to be paid or received in the next accounting period (154).

Statement of owner's equity   A financial statement that summarizes the transactions affecting the owner's capital account balance. The statement starts with the beginning capital account balance, adds net income or deducts a net loss, and then subtracts the owner's withdrawals to arrive at the ending capital account balance (134).

Unclassified balance sheet   One showing only three major categories: assets, liabilities, and owner's equity (149).

Work sheet   A columnar sheet of paper on which accountants have summarized information needed to make the adjusting and closing entries and to prepare the financial statements (125).

DEMONSTRATION PROBLEM

The demonstration problem for Chapters 1 and 2 used information for Briarcliff Riding Stable to illustrate certain concepts. This problem illustrates the use of a work sheet for the same company for the month ended July 31, 1991. Financial statements are also prepared. Then the closing process is illustrated. The trial balance for Briarcliff Riding Stable as of July 31, 1991, is as follows:

BRIARCLIFF RIDING STABLE
Trial Balance
July 31, 1991

Account Number		Debits	Credits
100	Cash	$ 9,500	
101	Accounts Receivable	8,100	
110	Land	40,000	
114	Building	24,000	
200	Accounts Payable		$ 1,100
201	Loan Payable (due June 1996)		40,000
300	Joanna Willis, Capital		36,600
301	Joanna Willis, Drawing	700	
400	Horse Boarding Fees Revenue		4,500
401	Riding and Lesson Fees Revenue		3,600
501	Feed Expense	1,100	
502	Salaries Expense	1,600	
510	Miscellaneous Expense	800	
		$85,800	$85,800

Additional data:

1. Depreciation expense for July is $200.
2. Accrued salaries at the end of July are $100.

Required: a.   Prepare a 10-column work sheet for July 1991.
              b.   Prepare an income statement for July 1991.
              c.   Prepare a statement of owner's equity for July 1991.
              d.   Prepare a balance sheet as of July 31, 1991. (Classify the items to the extent possible.)
              e.   Journalize the adjusting entries and show how the Posting Reference column would look after posting.
              f.   Journalize the closing entries and show how the Posting Reference column would look after posting.

Solution to demonstration problem

a.

BRIARCLIFF RIDING STABLE
Work Sheet
For the Month Ended July 31, 1991

Account Titles	Trial Balance Debit	Trial Balance Credit	Adjustments Debit	Adjustments Credit	Adjusted Trial Balance Debit	Adjusted Trial Balance Credit	Income Statement Debit	Income Statement Credit	Balance Sheet Debit	Balance Sheet Credit
Cash	9,500				9,500				9,500	
Accounts Receivable	8,100				8,100				8,100	
Land	40,000				40,000				40,000	
Building	24,000				24,000				24,000	
Accounts Payable		1,100				1,100				1,100
Loan Payable		40,000				40,000				40,000
Joanna Willis, Capital		36,600				36,600				36,600
Joanna Willis, Drawing	700				700				700	
Horse Boarding Fees Revenue		4,500				4,500		4,500		
Riding and Lesson Fees Revenue		3,600				3,600		3,600		
Feed Expense	1,100				1,100		1,100			
Salaries Expense	1,600		(2) 100		1,700		1,700			
Miscellaneous Expense	800				800		800			
	85,800	85,800								
Depreciation Expense—Building			(1) 200		200		200			
Accumulated Depreciation—Building				(1) 200		200				200
Salaries Payable				(2) 100		100				100
			300	300	86,100	86,100	3,800	8,100	82,300	78,000
Net income							4,300			4,300
							8,100	8,100	82,300	82,300

Adjustments:
(1) To record depreciation of building for July.
(2) To record accrued salaries.

b.

BRIARCLIFF RIDING STABLE
Income Statement
For the Month Ended July 31, 1991

Revenues:

Horse boarding fees revenue	$4,500	
Riding and lesson fees revenue	3,600	
Total revenues		$8,100

Expenses:

Feed expense	$1,100	
Salaries expense	1,700	
Miscellaneous expense	800	
Depreciation expense—building	200	
Total expenses		3,800
Net income		$4,300

c.

BRIARCLIFF RIDING STABLE
Statement of Owner's Equity
For the Month Ended July 31, 1991

Joanna Willis, capital, July 1, 1991	$36,600
Add: Net income for July 31, ...	4,300
Total	$40,900
Deduct: Owner drawings for July	700
Joanna Willis, capital, July 31, 1991	$40,200

d.

BRIARCLIFF RIDING STABLE
Balance Sheet
July 31, 1991

Assets

Current assets:

Cash	$ 9,500	
Accounts receivable	8,100	
Total current assets		$17,600

Property, plant, and equipment:

Land		$40,000	
Building	$24,000		
Less: Accumulated depreciation	200	23,800	
Total property, plant, and equipment			63,800
Total assets			$81,400

Liabilities and Owner's Equity

Current liabilities:

Accounts payable	$ 1,100	
Salaries payable	100	
Total current liabilities		$ 1,200

Long-term liabilities:

Loan payable (due June 1996)	40,000
Total liabilities	$41,200

Owner's equity:

Joanna Willis, capital	40,200
Total liabilities and owner's equity	$81,400

e.

BRIARCLIFF RIDING STABLE
GENERAL JOURNAL

Date		Account Titles and Explanation	Post. Ref.	Debit	Credit
1991		**Adjusting Entries**			
July	31	Depreciation Expense—Building	503*	2 0 0	
		Accumulated Depreciation—Building	115*		2 0 0
		To record depreciation for July.			
	31	Salaries Expense	502	1 0 0	
		Salaries Payable	202*		1 0 0
		To record salaries accrued at the end of the period.			

* Assumed account number.

f.

BRIARCLIFF RIDING STABLE
GENERAL JOURNAL

Date		Account Titles and Explanation	Post. Ref.	Debit	Credit
1991		**Closing Entries**			
July	31	Horse Boarding Fees Revenue	400	4 5 0 0	
		Riding and Lesson Fees Revenue	401	3 6 0 0	
		Income Summary	600*		8 1 0 0
		To close accounts in the Income Statement credit column			
		of the work sheet.			
	31	Income Summary	600	3 8 0 0	
		Feed Expense	501		1 1 0 0
		Salaries Expense	502		1 7 0 0
		Miscellaneous Expense	510		8 0 0
		Depreciation Expense—Building	503*		2 0 0
		To close accounts in the Income Statement debit column			
		of the work sheet.			
	31	Income Summary	600*	4 3 0 0	
		Joanna Willis, Capital	300		4 3 0 0
		To close Income Summary account.			
	31	Joanna Willis, Capital	300	7 0 0	
		Joanna Willis, Drawing	301		7 0 0
		To close the owner's drawing account.			

* Assumed account number.

QUESTIONS

1. Why do accountants use work sheets?

2. At what point in the accounting cycle is a work sheet usually prepared?

3. You have taken over a set of accounting books for a small business as a part-time job. At the end of the first accounting period, you have partially completed the work sheet by listing the proper ledger accounts and entering their balances in the Trial Balance columns. You turn to the manager and ask, "Where is the list of additional information I can use in entering the adjusting entries?" The manager indicates there is no such list. In all the text problems you have done, you have always been given this information. How would you obtain the information for this real-life situation? What are the consequences of not making all of the adjustments required at the end of the accounting period?

4. How are the amounts in the Adjusted Trial Balance columns of a work sheet determined?

5. After the Adjusted Trial Balance columns of a work sheet have been totaled, which account balances are extended to the Income Statement columns, and which account balances are extended to the Balance Sheet columns?

6. A company has net income of $2,500 for the year. In which columns of the work sheet does net income appear?

7. Your uncle knows you are taking a course in accounting in college, and he asks you to come over and help him. His new bookkeeper has journalized all of the business transactions for the month and has posted the journal entries to the ledger accounts. The bookkeeper now admits a difficulty in knowing how to proceed in completing the accounting process for the month. Your uncle asks you to tell the bookkeeper what should now be done to complete the process.

8. Describe the format of the statement of owner's equity.

9. Assuming that the closing process has been accomplished properly, which of the following statements is true? Why?

   a. After closing, expense and revenue accounts never have a balance other than zero.
   b. After closing, balance sheet accounts always have a balance other than zero.

10. In what important way do the pre-closing trial balance and the post-closing trial balance differ? Why is the post-closing trial balance prepared?

11. Describe the differences between an unclassified balance sheet and a classified balance sheet.

12. (Based on Appendix)   Describe the nature and purpose of a reversing entry.

EXERCISES

E-1
Determine where items would appear in work sheet

Three of the major column headings on a work sheet are Trial Balance, Income Statement, and Balance Sheet. For each of the following items, determine under which major column heading it would appear and whether it would be a debit or credit. (For example, Cash would appear under the debit side of the Trial Balance and Balance Sheet columns.)

	Trial Balance		Income Statement		Balance Sheet	
	Debit	Credit	Debit	Credit	Debit	Credit
a. Accounts Receivable.						
b. Accounts Payable.						
c. Service Revenue.						
d. Advertising Expense.						
e. T. P. Howse, Capital.						
f. Fees Revenue.						
g. Net income for the month.						
h. Net loss for the month.						

E-2
Find cause of Balance Sheet columns not in balance

Sam Bentley was preparing the work sheet for McDaniel Company. He calculated the net income to be $60,000. When he totaled the Balance Sheet columns, the column totals were debit, $558,000; and credit, $438,000. What was the probable cause of this difference? If this was not the cause, what should he do to find the error?

E-3
Prepare adjusting entries and determine correct net income

The first attempt at preparing the work sheet for Spaulding Company resulted in net income of $300,000 for the current year. Careful examination of the work sheet and supporting data indicated that the following items were ignored:

1.   Accrued salaries were $18,000 at December 31.
2.   Depreciation on equipment acquired on July 1 amounted to $24,000.
3.   The amount of prepaid insurance that had expired by year-end was $6,000.

a.   Based on the above information, what adjusting journal entries should be included to make the work sheet correct? Show them in journal entry form.
b.   What is the correct net income?

E-4
Prepare statement of owner's equity

Stafford Company reported net income of $53,000 for 1991. The John Stafford, Capital account had a beginning balance of $45,000. During the year, the owner withdrew $30,000 for personal living expenses. Prepare a statement of owner's equity for the year ended December 31, 1991.

E-5
Prepare closing entries

After adjustment, selected account balances of King Campground are:

	Debits	Credits
Campsite Rental Revenue		$240,000
Salaries Expense	$84,000	
Depreciation Expense	16,000	
Utilities Expense	52,000	
Redford, Drawing	28,000	
Redford, Capital		160,000

Enter the above balances in T-accounts. Then give the entries required to close the books for the period. Key the postings from the first closing entry with the number *(1)*, the second with the number *(2)*, and so on.

E-6
Prepare closing entries

After preparing and posting adjusting entries, Marburg Company had the following balances in its nominal accounts on December 31, 1991, before closing the books:

Rent Expense	$10,000
Service Revenue	50,000
J. Marburg, Drawing	15,000
J. Marburg, Capital	85,000
Wages Expense	35,000
Interest Revenue	1,000

Prepare journal entries to record the necessary closing entries.

E-7
Post to Income Summary account from Income Statement column totals

The Income Statement column totals on a work sheet prepared on December 31, 1991, are debit, $150,000; and credit, $175,000. In T-account format show how the postings to the Income Summary account would appear as a result of the closing process. Identify what each posting represents.

E-8
Describe how classified balance sheet should be prepared

Restructure the following unclassified balance sheet into a classified balance sheet.

KELLY MODELING AGENCY
Balance Sheet
December 31, 1991

Assets

Cash		$ 18,000
Accounts receivable		27,000
Prepaid insurance		7,200
Land		45,000
Building	$180,000	
Less: Accumulated depreciation	72,000	108,000
Total assets		$205,200

Liabilities and Owner's Equity

Liabilities:

Accounts payable		$ 14,400
Note payable, due 1995		21,600
Total liabilities		$ 36,000

Owner's equity:

J. Kelly, capital		169,200
Total liabilities and owner's equity		$205,200

E-9
Show entries for salaries (1) if no reversing entry used and (2) if reversing entry used (based on Appendix)

Assume that an adjusting entry made on December 31, 1991, was as follows:

1991
Dec. 31 Salaries Expense 3,600
               Salaries Payable   3,600
          To accrue salaries for last four days of December.

Show how the January 3, 1992, payment of $5,400 of salaries would be recorded assuming (1) no reversing entry is used and (2) a reversing entry is used on January 1, 1992 (show this entry also). Then show by the use of T-accounts that the end result is the same whether a reversing entry is used or not.

PROBLEMS, SERIES A

P4-1-A
Prepare work sheet

The trial balance of Fitch Plumbing Company as of December 31, 1991, is as follows:

FITCH PLUMBING COMPANY
Trial Balance
December 31, 1991

	Debits	Credits
Cash	$180,000	
Accounts Receivable	54,400	
Supplies on Hand	8,000	
Prepaid Insurance	7,200	
Land	30,000	
Building	250,000	
Accumulated Depreciation—Building		$ 50,000
Plumbing Tools and Equipment	72,000	
Accumulated Depreciation—Plumbing Tools and Equipment		18,000
Accounts Payable		44,000
D. Fitch, Capital		208,400
D. Fitch, Drawing	80,000	
Plumbing Service Revenue		560,000
Salaries Expense	192,000	
Utilities Expense	6,800	
	$880,400	$880,400

Additional data:

1. Supplies on hand at December 31, 1991, have a cost of $2,400.
2. The balance in the Prepaid Insurance account represents the cost of a two-year insurance policy covering the period from January 1, 1991, through December 31, 1992.
3. Depreciation expense is $5,000 on the building and $3,600 on the equipment.

Required: Prepare a work sheet using the same format as in Illustration 4.6 for Fitch Plumbing Company for the year ended December 31, 1991. Include adjustments explanations on the work sheet.

P4–2–A
Prepare work sheet,
adjusting entries,
and closing entries

The trial balance of Hanson Equipment Rental Company as of December 31, 1991, contains the following account balances:

HANSON EQUIPMENT RENTAL COMPANY
Trial Balance
December 31, 1991

	Debits	Credits
Cash	$ 140,800	
Accounts Receivable	96,800	
Prepaid Rent	15,840	
Prepaid Insurance	7,920	
Equipment	264,000	
Accumulated Depreciation—Equipment		$ 88,000
Accounts Payable		68,200
Pamela Hanson, Capital		306,240
Pamela Hanson, Drawing	52,800	
Rental Service Revenue		770,000
Salaries Expense	550,000	
Travel Expense	77,880	
Miscellaneous Expense	26,400	
	$1,232,440	$1,232,440

Additional data:

1. The prepaid rent was for the period January 1, 1991, to December 31, 1992.
2. The depreciation on the equipment is $17,600 per year.
3. The prepaid insurance was for the period April 1, 1991, to March 31, 1992.
4. Salaries incurred but unpaid total $6,600 at December 31.

Required: Prepare the following:

a. A 10-column work sheet for the year ended December 31, 1991.
b. The adjusting journal entries in the general journal.
c. The closing journal entries in the general journal.

P4–3–A
Prepare and post
closing entries and
prepare income
statement

The following account balances appeared in the Income Statement columns of the work sheet prepared for Reliable TV Repair Company for the year ended December 31, 1991:

	Income Statement	
	Debit	Credit
TV Repair Service Revenue		1,196,800
Advertising Expense	5,100	
Salaries Expense	374,000	
Utilities Expense	6,800	
Insurance Expense	3,400	
Rent Expense	20,400	
Supplies Expense	6,800	
Depreciation Expense—Equipment	15,300	
	431,800	1,196,800
Net income	765,000	
	1,196,800	1,196,800

Required: Assume that on December 31, 1991, the J. M. Thompson, Drawing account had a debit balance of $85,000 and the J. M. Thompson, Capital account had a credit balance of $238,000 before the closing process began.

   a.   Prepare the closing journal entries.
   b.   Using T-accounts show how the accounts appear after all of the closing entries have been posted.
   c.   Prepare an income statement for the year ended December 31, 1991.

P4-4-A
Prepare and post
closing entries

Given below are the amounts appearing in the Adjusted Trial Balance columns of the June 30, 1991, work sheet for Sorg Real Estate Company.

	Adjusted Trial Balance	
	Debit	Credit
Cash	480,000	
Accounts Receivable	58,500	
Office Equipment	210,000	
Accumulated Depreciation—Office Equipment		84,000
Automobiles	330,000	
Accumulated Depreciation—Automobiles		120,000
Accounts Payable		18,000
Donna Sorg, Capital		932,400
Donna Sorg, Drawing	30,000	
Sales Commissions Revenue		780,000
Office Salaries Expense	150,000	
Salespersons' Commissions Expense	540,000	
Automobile Operating Expense	24,000	
Rent Expense	25,500	
Supplies Expense	5,400	
Utilities Expense	12,000	
Depreciation Expense—Office Equipment	21,000	
Depreciation Expense—Automobiles	48,000	
	1,934,400	1,934,400

Required: a.   Based on the above data, prepare closing entries. (Hint: You may wish to mentally determine which of the above items would appear in the Income Statement columns of the work sheet. In preparing the third closing entry, you will also need to determine whether the company had a net income or a net loss for the period.)
   b.   Using T-accounts, show how the accounts appear after all of the closing entries have been posted.

P4-5-A

Prepare work sheet, income statement, statement of owner's equity, classified balance sheet, and closing entries

Baxter Electric Contracting Company has the following trial balance as of December 31, 1991:

BAXTER ELECTRICAL CONTRACTING COMPANY
Trial Balance
December 31, 1991

	Debits	Credits
Cash	$ 544,000	
Accounts Receivable	63,040	
Prepaid Insurance	9,600	
Prepaid Rent—Building	115,200	
Supplies on Hand	10,720	
Equipment	336,000	
Accumulated Depreciation—Equipment		$ 35,200
Accounts Payable		7,600
R. Baxter, Capital		1,104,000
R. Baxter, Drawing	60,000	
Electrician Service Revenue		954,720
Salaries Expense	760,400	
Rent Expense—Truck	156,000	
Advertising Expense	19,760	
Legal and Accounting Expense	18,000	
Miscellaneous Expense	8,800	
	$2,101,520	$2,101,520

Additional data:

1. Insurance expense is $6,800.
2. Supplies on hand are $3,400.
3. Rent expense on the building is $101,200.
4. Depreciation expense on the equipment is $17,600.
5. Salaries incurred but unpaid are $14,000.

Required: Prepare the following:

a. A 10-column work sheet for the year ended December 31, 1991.
b. An income statement.
c. A statement of owner's equity.
d. A classified balance sheet.
e. The December 31, 1991, closing entries.

P4-6-A

Prepare work sheet, income statement, statement of owner's equity, classified balance sheet, adjusting entries, and closing entries

The trial balance for Finley Cleaning Service Company as of December 31, 1991, is as follows:

FINLEY CLEANING SERVICE COMPANY
Trial Balance
December 31, 1991

	Debits	Credits
Cash	$ 116,000	
Accounts Receivable	87,200	
Prepaid Insurance	19,200	
Prepaid Rent	36,000	
Supplies on Hand	46,000	
Office Equipment	40,000	
Accumulated Depreciation— Office Equipment		$ 14,000
Cleaning Equipment	120,000	
Accumulated Depreciation— Cleaning Equipment		35,000
Service Trucks	300,000	
Accumulated Depreciation— Service Trucks		93,752
Accounts Payable		28,000
M. Finley, Capital		236,648
M. Finley, Drawing	120,000	
Cleaning Service Revenue		960,000
Salaries Expense	457,000	
Gas and Oil Expense	14,000	
Utilities Expense	12,000	
	$1,367,400	$1,367,400

Additional data:

1. The balance in the Prepaid Insurance account represents the remaining cost of a five-year insurance policy purchased on January 2, 1990. The account was last adjusted on December 31, 1990.
2. The balance in the Prepaid Rent account represents the amount paid on January 2, 1991, to cover rent for the period from January 2, 1991, through June 30, 1992.
3. Depreciation on the plant assets is office equipment, $4,000; cleaning equipment, $10,000; and service trucks, $37,500.
4. Salaries incurred but unpaid as of December 31, 1991, are $12,400.
5. A physical inventory shows that $8,000 of the supplies are on hand at December 31, 1991.

Required: Prepare the following:

a. A 10-column work sheet for the year ended December 31, 1991.
b. An income statement.
c. A statement of owner's equity.
d. A classified balance sheet.
e. The adjusting journal entries in the general journal.
f. The closing journal entries in the general journal.

P4-7-A

Prepare work sheet, income statement, statement of owner's equity, classified balance sheet, adjusting and closing entries, and post-closing trial balance

D. Herman, CPA, has prepared the following trial balance for December 1991:

D. HERMAN, CPA
Trial Balance
December 31, 1991

	Debits	Credits
Cash	$ 288,000	
Accounts Receivable	57,600	
Supplies on Hand	12,000	
Prepaid Rent	36,720	
Prepaid Insurance	21,840	
Office Equipment	22,800	
Accumulated Depreciation— Office Equipment		$ 8,280
Furniture and Fixtures	87,600	
Accumulated Depreciation— Furniture and Fixtures		24,840
Accounts Payable		3,600
D. Herman, Capital		385,800
D. Herman, Drawing	127,560	
Accounting Service Revenue		600,000
Salaries Expense	296,400	
Utilities Expense	18,000	
Travel Expense	42,000	
Miscellaneous Expense	12,000	
	$1,022,520	$1,022,520

Additional data:

1. Supplies on hand December 31, 1991, are $3,000.
2. $27,600 of the prepaid rent was consumed in 1991.
3. $7,200 of the prepaid insurance expired in 1991.
4. Depreciation expense is office equipment, $2,400; and furniture and fixtures, $9,000.
5. Salaries incurred but unpaid are $13,050.

Required: Prepare the following:

a. A 10-column work sheet for the year ended December 31, 1991.
b. An income statement.
c. A statement of owner's equity.
d. A classified balance sheet.
e. The adjusting and closing entries in the general journal.
f. A post-closing trial balance. Normally the post-closing trial balance would be prepared from the ledger accounts, but use the information in the Balance Sheet columns of the work sheet to prepare it. You will have to use the ending balance in the owner's capital account to prepare the post-closing trial balance.

PROBLEMS, SERIES B

P4-1-B
Prepare work sheet

The trial balance of Ray Tucker Travel Agency as of December 31, 1991, is as follows:

RAY TUCKER TRAVEL AGENCY
Trial Balance
December 31, 1991

	Debits	Credits
Cash	$ 80,000	
Accounts Receivable	20,000	
Supplies on Hand	16,000	
Prepaid Insurance	24,000	
Furniture and Fixtures	56,000	
Accumulated Depreciation—Furniture and Fixtures		$ 8,000
Accounts Payable		8,000
Ray Tucker, Capital		132,000
Ray Tucker, Drawing	32,000	
Travel Service Revenue		180,000
Advertising Expense	4,000	
Salaries Expense	64,000	
Rent Expense	20,000	
Miscellaneous Expense	12,000	
	$328,000	$328,000

Additional data:

1. An inventory shows that $4,000 of the supplies are on hand at the end of the year.
2. The balance in the Prepaid Insurance account represents the cost of a three-year policy from January 1, 1991, through December 31, 1993.
3. The depreciation expense for the year on furniture and fixtures is $4,000.
4. Salaries incurred but unpaid at the end of the year are $4,800.

Required: Prepare a work sheet using the same format as in Illustration 4.6 for Ray Tucker Travel Agency for the year ended December 31, 1991. Include adjustments explanations on the work sheet.

P4-2-B
Prepare work sheet,
adjusting entries,
and closing entries

The trial balance of Jacobs Auto Repair Company for December 31, 1991, appears below:

JACOBS AUTO REPAIR COMPANY
Trial Balance
December 31, 1991

	Debits	Credits
Cash	$ 66,000	
Accounts Receivable	11,200	
Prepaid Rent	19,200	
Equipment	77,200	
Accumulated Depreciation—Equipment		$ 8,800
Accounts Payable		18,000
T. Jacobs, Capital		82,000
T. Jacobs, Drawing	19,200	
Auto Repair Service Revenue		268,000
Salaries Expense	144,200	
Supplies Expense	32,000	
Insurance Expense	7,800	
	$376,800	$376,800

Additional data:

1. The prepaid rent is for the period of July 1, 1991, to June 30, 1992.
2. The depreciation on the equipment is $5,320.
3. Salaries incurred but unpaid as of December 31 are $12,000.

Required: Prepare the following:

a. A 10-column work sheet for the year ended December 31, 1991.
b. The adjusting journal entries in the general journal.
c. The closing journal entries in the general journal.

P4-3-B
Prepare and post
closing entries and
prepare income
statement

The account balances below are for Bill Rogers, Architect, as they appear in the work sheet for the month ended December 31, 1991.

	Income Statement	
	Debit	Credit
Architect Service Revenue		60,000
Salaries Expense	12,000	
Advertising Expense	2,400	
Insurance Expense	300	
Supplies Expense	1,020	
Depreciation Expense—Building	1,500	
Miscellaneous Expense	1,200	
	18,420	60,000
Net income	41,580	
	60,000	60,000

Required: Assume that on December 31, 1991, the Bill Rogers, Drawing account has a debit balance of $24,000 and the Bill Rogers, Capital account has a credit balance of $300,000 before the closing process begins.

a. Prepare the closing journal entries.
b. Using T-accounts, show how the accounts would appear after all of the closing entries have been posted.
c. Prepare an income statement for December 1991.

P4–4–B
***Prepare and post
closing entries***

Given below are the amounts appearing in the Adjusted Trial Balance columns of the December 31, 1991, work sheet for Maxwell Advertising Agency.

	Adjusted Trial Balance	
	Debit	Credit
Cash	84,000	
Accounts Receivable	40,800	
Office Equipment	240,000	
Accumulated Depreciation—Office Equipment		144,000
Accounts Payable		25,920
G. Maxwell, Capital		291,600
G. Maxwell, Drawing	67,200	
Advertising Service Revenue		264,000
Rent Expense	28,800	
Travel Expense	12,000	
Salaries Expense	216,000	
Supplies Expense	3,600	
Insurance Expense	2,880	
Depreciation Expense—Office Equipment	28,800	
Miscellaneous Expense	1,440	
	725,520	725,520

Required:
a. Based on the above data, prepare closing entries. (Hint: You may want to mentally determine which of the above items would appear in the Income Statement columns of the work sheet. In preparing the third closing entry, you will need to determine whether the agency had a net income or a net loss for the period.)
b. Using T-accounts, show how the accounts appear after all of the closing entries have been posted.

P4-5-B

Prepare work sheet, income statement, statement of owner's equity, classified balance sheet, and closing entries

Baird Photography Company has the following trial balance as of December 31, 1991:

BAIRD PHOTOGRAPHY COMPANY
Trial Balance
December 31, 1991

	Debits	Credits
Cash	$182,650	
Accounts Receivable	22,100	
Prepaid Insurance	4,290	
Land	92,950	
Building	143,000	
Accumulated Depreciation—		
Building		$ 42,900
Photography Equipment	72,280	
Accumulated Depreciation—		
Photography Equipment		14,456
Accounts Payable		7,670
G. Baird, Capital		365,274
G. Baird, Drawing	26,000	
Photography Service Revenue		310,570
Salaries Expense	182,000	
Advertising Expense	15,600	
	$740,870	$740,870

Additional data:

1. Depreciation on the building is $2,860 for the year.
2. Depreciation on the photography equipment is $7,228 for the year.
3. Salaries incurred but unpaid are $1,820.
4. Prepaid insurance at year-end is $520.

Required: Prepare the following:

a. A 10-column work sheet for the year ended December 31, 1991.
b. An income statement.
c. A statement of owner's equity.
d. A classified balance sheet.
e. The December 31, 1991, closing entries.

P4-6-B
Prepare work sheet, income statement, statement of owner's equity, classified balance sheet, adjusting entries, and closing entries

The trial balance for Owens Printing Company as of December 31, 1991, is as follows:

OWENS PRINTING COMPANY
Trial Balance
December 31, 1991

	Debits	Credits
Cash	$183,600	
Accounts Receivable	40,500	
Prepaid Insurance	9,000	
Supplies on Hand	6,000	
Furniture	240,000	
Accumulated Depreciation—Furniture		$120,000
Printing Equipment	120,000	
Accumulated Depreciation—Printing Equipment		60,000
Accounts Payable		30,000
J. Owens, Capital		169,200
J. Owens, Drawing	54,000	
Printing Service Revenue		480,000
Salaries Expense	180,000	
Rent Expense	5,400	
Utilities Expense	18,600	
Miscellaneous Expense	2,100	
	$859,200	$859,200

Additional data:

1. Insurance expense for the year is $7,200.
2. A physical inventory shows that supplies costing $1,200 are on hand at December 31, 1991.
3. Depreciation expense on the furniture is $24,000.
4. Depreciation expense on the printing equipment is $7,500.
5. Salaries incurred but unpaid are $18,000.

Required: Prepare the following:

a. A 10-column work sheet for the year ended December 31, 1991.
b. An income statement.
c. A statement of owner's equity.
d. A classified balance sheet.
e. The adjusting journal entries in the general journal.
f. The closing journal entries in the general journal.

P4-7-B

Prepare work sheet, income statement, statement of owner's equity, classified balance sheet, adjusting and closing entries, and post-closing trial balance

Chandler Realty has prepared the following trial balance for December 1991:

CHANDLER REALTY
Trial Balance
December 31, 1991

	Debits	Credits
Cash	$ 80,000	
Prepaid Rent	14,400	
Prepaid Insurance on Automobile	3,840	
Supplies on Hand	1,200	
Office Equipment	12,000	
Accumulated Depreciation— Office Equipment		$ 2,880
Automobile	32,000	
Accumulated Depreciation— Automobile		8,000
Accounts Payable		1,440
Unearned Management Fees		6,240
R. Chandler, Capital		178,320
R. Chandler, Drawing	94,000	
Sales Commissions Revenue		120,000
Management Service Revenue		9,600
Salaries Expense	79,920	
Advertising Expense	1,200	
Automobile Expense	7,120	
Miscellaneous Expense	800	
	$326,480	$326,480

Additional data:

1. Insurance expense on the automobile for the year is $1,920.
2. Rent expense for the year is $9,600.
3. Depreciation expense for office equipment, $1,440; and automobile, $6,400.
4. Salaries incurred but unpaid as of December 31 are $13,320.
5. Supplies on hand on December 31, $400.
6. The unearned management fees were received and recorded on October 1, 1991. The advance payment covered six months' management of an apartment building.

Required: Prepare the following:

a. A 10-column work sheet for the year ended December 31, 1991.
b. An income statement.
c. A statement of owner's equity.
d. A classified balance sheet.
e. The adjusting and closing entries in the general journal.
f. A post-closing trial balance. Normally the post-closing trail balance would be prepared from the ledger accounts, but use the information in the Balance Sheet columns of the work sheet to prepare it. You will have to use the ending balance in the owner's capital account to prepare the post-closing trial balance.

BUSINESS DECISION PROBLEM 4–1

Prepare report on profitability of business

Lisa and Randy Barron met while both were employed in the interior trim and upholstery department of an auto manufacturer. After their marriage, they decided to earn some extra income by doing small jobs involving canvas, vinyl, and upholstered products. Their work was considered excellent. At the urging of their customers, they decided to go into business for themselves, operating out of the basement of the house they owned. To do this, they invested $40,000 cash in their business. They spent $28,000 for a sewing machine (expected life is 10 years) and $4,000 for other miscellaneous tools and equipment (expected life is 5 years). They undertook only custom work, with the customer purchasing the required materials other than miscellaneous supplies. An advance deposit was generally required on all jobs.

The business seemed to be successful from the start, but they felt something was wrong. They worked hard and charged competitive prices. Yet there seemed to be barely enough cash available for withdrawal from the business to cover immediate personal needs. Summarized, the checkbook of the business for 1991, their second year of operation, shows:

Balance, January 1, 1991		$ 6,400
Cash received from customers:		
For work done in 1990	$ 12,000	
For work done in 1991	192,000	
For work to be done in 1992	16,000	220,000
		$226,400
Cash paid out:		
Two-year insurance policy dated January 1, 1991	$ 6,400	
Utilities	16,000	
Supplies	48,000	
Taxes	8,800	
Miscellaneous	24,000	
Owner withdrawals	116,000	219,200
Balance, December 31, 1991		$ 7,200

Considering how much they have worked, the Barrons believe that they should have earned more than the $116,000 of cash flow they withdrew from their business. This is $20,000 less than their combined income when they were employed by the auto manufacturer. They are seriously considering giving up their business and going back to work for the auto manufacturer. They turn to you for advice. You discover the following:

1. Of the supplies purchased in 1991, $8,000 were used on jobs billed to customers in 1991; no supplies were used for any other work.
2. Work completed in 1991 and billed to customers for which cash had not yet been received by year-end amounted to $36,000 (which is considered fully collectible).

Required: Prepare a written report for the Barrons, responding to their belief that their business is not sufficiently profitable. (Hint: Prepare an income statement for 1991 and include it in your report.)

BUSINESS DECISION PROBLEM 4-2

Prepare income statement and statement of owner's equity; determine effect of closing entries on income statement and balance sheet accounts; complete closing process

On December 31, 1991, Alex Brown's bookkeeper quit his job without even notifying Mr. Brown of his net income for 1991. The bookkeeper had taken Mr. Brown's accounting records home with him the previous night and failed to bring them to work on December 31, 1991. But Mr. Brown found the following closing entries on a pad in the bookkeeper's desk:

```
1991
Dec. 31  Service Revenue . . . . . . . . . . . . . . . . . . . . . . 270,000
             Income Summary . . . . . . . . . . . . . . . . . . .            270,000
         To close the revenue account appearing in the
         Income Statement credit column of the work sheet
         to Income Summary.

     31  Income Summary . . . . . . . . . . . . . . . . . . . . . . 112,800
             Rent Expense . . . . . . . . . . . . . . . . . . . . .             12,000
             Salaries Expense . . . . . . . . . . . . . . . . . . .             72,000
             Advertising Expense . . . . . . . . . . . . . . . . .              6,000
             Utilities Expense . . . . . . . . . . . . . . . . . . .            7,200
             Depreciation Expense—Automobiles . . . . . . . .                  6,000
             Depreciation Expense—Office Equipment . . . . .                   1,500
             Insurance Expense . . . . . . . . . . . . . . . . . .              7,560
             Miscellaneous Expense . . . . . . . . . . . . . . .                 540
         To close the expense accounts appearing in the
         Income Statement debit column of the work sheet
         to Income Summary.
```

Mr. Brown knows that his capital account balance was $120,000 on January 1, 1991, and that he withdrew $60,000 for personal use during 1991.

Required: a.   Using the information given above, prepare an income statement and a statement of owner's equity for the year ended December 31, 1991.
b.   What effect do the closing journal entries have on the income statement accounts?
c.   What effect do the closing journal entries have on the balance sheet accounts?
d.   Did the bookkeeper make all of the necessary closing entries? If not, what other entries should be made?

COMPREHENSIVE REVIEW PROBLEM

Problem covers all steps in the accounting cycle covered in Chapters 1–4. Open ledger accounts and enter beginning balances. Journalize transactions and post to ledger accounts. Prepare work sheet, income statement, statement of owner's equity, classified balance sheet, adjusting and closing entries, and post-closing trial balance.

Foster Delivery Service Company has the following chart of accounts:

Account No.	Account Title	Account No.	Account Title
100	Cash	301	M. Foster, Drawing
101	Accounts Receivable	400	Delivery Service Revenue
102	Supplies on Hand	500	Supplies Expense
103	Prepaid Insurance	501	Insurance Expense
104	Prepaid Rent	502	Rent Expense
110	Furniture and Equipment	503	Depreciation Expense— Furniture and Equipment
110A	Accumulated Depreciation— Furniture and Equipment	504	Depreciation Expense—Trucks
111	Trucks	505	Salaries Expense
111A	Accumulated Depreciation—Trucks	506	Utilities Expense
200	Accounts Payable	507	Miscellaneous Expense
201	Salaries Payable	600	Income Summary
300	M. Foster, Capital		

The post-closing trial balance as of May 31, 1991, was as follows:

FOSTER DELIVERY SERVICE COMPANY
Post-Closing Trial Balance
May 31, 1991

	Debits	Credits
Cash	$ 40,000	
Accounts Receivable	60,000	
Supplies on Hand	28,000	
Prepaid Insurance	9,600	
Prepaid Rent	24,000	
Furniture and Equipment	640,000	
Accumulated Depreciation— Furniture and Equipment		$ 72,000
Trucks	160,000	
Accumulated Depreciation—Trucks		60,000
Accounts Payable		48,000
M. Foster, Capital		781,600
	$961,600	$961,600

The transactions for June 1991 were as follows:

June 1 Performed delivery services for customers on account, $80,000.
      3 M. Foster withdrew $20,000 to pay some personal bills.
      4 Purchased a $40,000 truck on account.
      7 Collected $44,000 of the accounts receivable.
      8 Paid $32,000 of the accounts payable.
     11 Purchased $8,000 of supplies on account. The asset account for supplies was debited.
     17 Performed delivery services for cash, $64,000.
     20 Paid the utilities bills for June, $2,400.
     23 Paid miscellaneous expenses for June, $1,200.
     28 Paid salaries of $56,000.

Supplemental data needed to prepare adjusting entries:

1. Depreciation expense on the furniture and equipment for June is $1,600.
2. Depreciation expense on the trucks for June is $800.
3. Salaries incurred but unpaid as of June 30 are $4,000.
4. A physical count showed that there are $24,000 of supplies on hand as of June 30.
5. The prepaid insurance balance of $9,600 applies to a two-year period beginning June 1, 1991.
6. The prepaid rent of $24,000 applies to a one-year period beginning on June 1, 1991.
7. The company performed $24,000 of delivery services for customers as of June 30 that will not be billed to those customers until July.

Required:

a. Open three-column ledger accounts for the accounts listed in the chart of accounts.
b. Enter the May 31, 1991, account balances in the accounts.
c. Journalize the transactions for June 1991 (assume all journal entries appear on page 10 of the general journal).
d. Post the June journal entries and include cross-references.
e. Prepare a 10-column work sheet for the month ended June 30, 1991.
f. Prepare an income statement, a statement of owner's equity, and a classified balance sheet.
g. Prepare and post the adjusting entries (assume they appear on page 11 of the general journal).
h. Prepare and post the closing entries (assume they appear on page 12 of the general journal).
i. Prepare a post-closing trial balance.

5 Merchandising Transactions, Introduction to Inventories, and Classified Income Statement

---

LEARNING OBJECTIVES

After studying this chapter, you should be able to:

1. Record journal entries for sales transactions.
2. Determine cost of goods sold.
3. Record journal entries for purchase transactions under periodic inventory procedure.
4. Describe the freight terms.
5. Prepare a classified income statement.
6. Prepare a work sheet and closing entries for a merchandising company.
7. Define and use correctly the new terms in the glossary.

In the first four chapters, you learned about the accounting process and how it begins with recording business transactions and results in the preparation of financial statements. As you studied the accounting process, you followed step-by-step the business transactions of a service company— Rapid Delivery Company. This company provided a delivery service to customers in return for a fee. Because service companies are the least complicated type of business, they are shown first as examples in the study of accounting. You are now ready to apply the accounting process to a more complex type of business—a merchandising company. The fundamental accounting concepts for service-type businesses also apply to merchandising businesses, but some additional accounts and techniques are needed to account for purchases and sales.

The normal flow of goods from manufacturer to final customer is as follows:

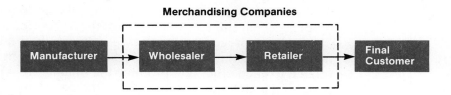

Manufacturers produce goods from raw materials and normally sell them to wholesalers. After performing certain functions, such as packaging or labeling, **wholesalers** normally sell the goods to retailers. **Retailers** sell the goods to final customers. The two middle boxes in the diagram above represent merchandising companies. These companies buy goods in finished form for resale.

In this chapter, you will see a comparison of the income statements of a service company and a merchandising company. Then you will learn how to record merchandise-related transactions. Finally, a work sheet and the closing process for a merchandising company are described.

■ TWO INCOME STATEMENTS COMPARED—SERVICE COMPANY AND MERCHANDISING COMPANY

Illustration 5.1 compares the main divisions of an income statement of a service company with those of a merchandising company. To determine profitability or net income for a service company, total expenses incurred are deducted from revenues earned. A merchandising company is a more complex type of business and, therefore, has a more complex income statement.

As shown in Illustration 5.1, merchandising companies first must deduct from revenues the cost of the goods they sell to customers. Then they

Illustration 5.1

Condensed Income Statement of a Service Company Compared with a Condensed Income Statement of a Merchandising Company

SERVICE COMPANY Income Statement For the Year Ended December 31, 1991		MERCHANDISING COMPANY Income Statement For the Year Ended December 31, 1991	
Service revenues	$13,200	Sales revenues	$262,000
		Cost of goods sold	159,000
		Gross margin	$103,000
Expenses	6,510	Expenses	74,900
Net income	$ 6,690	Net income	$ 28,100

deduct other expenses. The income statement of a merchandising company has three main divisions: (1) sales revenues, (2) cost of goods sold, and (3) expenses. Sales revenues result from the sale of goods by the company; cost of goods sold indicates how much the goods that were sold cost the company; and the expenses are the company's expenses in running the business.

The next two sections of the chapter discuss the first two main divisions of the income statement of a merchandising company. The third division (expenses) is similar to expenses for a service company and has been illustrated in preceding chapters. As you study these chapter sections, keep in mind how the divisions of the merchandising income statement are related to each other and produce the final figure—net income or net loss—which indicates the profitability of the company.

■ SALES REVENUES

*Objective 1:
Record journal entries for sales transactions.*

The sale of goods occurs between two parties. The seller of the goods transfers them to the buyer in exchange for cash or a promise to pay at a later date. This exchange is a relatively simple business transaction.

From the seller's point of view, sales are made to create revenue. As you recall, revenue is the inflow of assets resulting from the rendering of services or the sale of goods to customers. Illustration 5.1 showed a condensed income statement so that major divisions could be emphasized. Now the more complete income statement actually prepared by accountants is described. The merchandising company that we will use to illustrate the income statement is called Hanlon Retail Food Store. This section first explains how to record sales revenues, including the effect of trade discounts. Next, you will learn how to record the two deductions from sales revenues—sales discounts and sales returns and allowances (see Illustration 5.2). The amount that remains is **net sales**. The formula, then, for determining net sales is:

Net sales = Gross sales − (Sales discounts + Sales returns and allowances)

Illustration 5.2

Partial Income Statement of Merchandising Company

HANLON RETAIL FOOD STORE Partial Income Statement For the Year Ended December 31, 1991		
Operating revenues:		
Gross sales		$282,000
Less: Sales discounts	$ 5,000	
Sales returns and allowances	15,000	20,000
Net sales		$262,000

Recording Gross Sales

In a sales transaction, the legal ownership (title) of goods is transferred from the seller to the buyer. The sale is usually accompanied by the physical delivery of goods, and the recording of the sale is based on a business document called an *invoice* (usually called a *sales invoice* by the seller and a *purchase invoice* by the buyer).

An **invoice** is a document, prepared by the seller of merchandise and sent to the buyer, that contains the details of a sale, such as the number of units, unit price, total price billed, terms of sale, and manner of shipment. In a retail company, the invoice is prepared at the point of sale. In a wholesale company, which supplies goods to retailers, the invoice is prepared after the accounting department receives notification from the shipping department that the goods have been shipped to the retailer. Illustration 5.3 shows an invoice prepared by a wholesale company for goods sold to a retail company.

Illustration 5.3

Invoice

BRYAN WHOLESALE CO. **476 Mason Street** **Detroit, Michigan 48823**				**Invoice No.:** 1258 **Date:** Dec. 19, 1991	
Customer's Order No.: 218 **Sold to:** Baier Company **Address:** 2255 Hannon Street Big Rapids, Michigan 48106 **Terms:** Net 30, FOB Destination			**Date Shipped:** Dec. 19, 1991 **Shipped by:** Nagel Trucking Co.		

Description	Item Number	Quantity	Price per Unit	Total Amount
True-tone stereo radios	Model No. 5868–24393	200	$100	$20,000
		Total		$20,000

Using the invoice as the source document, the revenue from the sale is recorded at the time of the sale for the following reasons:

1. **Legal title** to the goods has passed, and the goods are now the responsibility and property of the buyer.
2. The selling price of the goods has been established.
3. The seller's obligation has been completed.
4. The goods have been exchanged for another asset, such as cash or accounts receivable.
5. The costs incurred can be determined.

Each time a sale is made, revenue is produced for the company. This revenue increases a revenue account called *Sales*. As you learned in Chapter 2, revenues are increased by credits. So the Sales account is credited for the amount of the sale.

Usually sales are for cash or on account. When a sale is for cash, the credit to the Sales account is accompanied by a debit to Cash; when a sale is on account, the Sales account credit is accompanied by a debit to Accounts Receivable. For example, a $20,000 sale for cash is recorded as follows:

Cash	20,000	
Sales		20,000
To record the sale of merchandise for cash.		

A $20,000 sale on account is recorded as follows:

Accounts Receivable   20,000
    Sales   20,000
    To record the sale of merchandise on account.

A seller usually quotes the gross invoice price of goods to the buyer, but sometimes a seller quotes a list price of goods along with trade discounts that are available. In this latter situation, the buyer must calculate the gross invoice price. The list price less all trade discounts is the **gross selling price**. The gross selling price is used by the merchandising company to determine the actual selling price to the customer.

Determining Gross Sales Price When There Are Trade Discounts.   Unlike cash discounts (discussed later), which are related to the prompt payment of an invoice, a **trade discount** is a percentage deduction, or discount, from the specified list price or catalog price of merchandise. Trade discounts are used to:

1. Reduce the cost of catalog publication. When list prices are printed in the catalog and separate discount sheets are given to the salespersons whenever prices change, a catalog may be used for a longer period of time.
2. Grant quantity discounts.
3. Allow quotation of different prices to different types of customers, such as retailers and wholesalers.

Trade discounts may be shown on the seller's invoice, but they are not recorded in the seller's accounting records because they are only used to calculate the gross selling price. Nor are trade discounts recorded on the books of the purchaser. To illustrate, assume an invoice contains the following data:

List price, 200 swimsuits at $6 . . . . . . $1,200
Less: Trade discount, 30%   360
Gross invoice price . . . . $ 840

The seller records a sale of $840. The purchaser records a purchase of $840. In other words, **list prices and their trade discounts are not entered on the books of either the seller or the purchaser.**

Sometimes the list price of a product is subject to several trade discounts; this is called a **chain discount**. Chain discounts exist, for example, when a wholesaler receives two trade discounts because of certain services performed, such as packaging and distributing. When more than one discount is given, each discount is applied to the declining balance successively. If a product has a list price of $100 and is subject to trade discounts of 20% and 10%, the actual price paid by the purchaser would be: $100 − 0.2($100) = $80; $80 − 0.1($80) = $72. The same results can be obtained by multiplying the list price by the complements of the trade discounts allowed. The complement of 20% is 80% because 20% + 80% = 100%. The complement of 10% is 90% because 10% + 90% = 100%. Thus, the gross invoice price is $100 × 0.8 × 0.9 = $72.

Recording Deductions from Gross Sales

Two common deductions from gross sales are (1) sales discounts and (2) sales returns and allowances. These deductions are recorded in contra accounts to the Sales account. Contra accounts have normal balances that are opposite the balance of the account they reduce. For example, since the Sales account normally has a credit balance, the Sales Discounts account and Sales Returns and Allowances account will have debit balances. The methods accountants use to record these contra accounts are explained in the paragraphs that follow.

Sales Discounts. Whenever goods are sold on account, terms of payment are clearly specified on the invoice. For example, in Illustration 5.3, the terms of payment are stated as "net 30," which really means "gross 30." "Net 30" is sometimes written as "n/30." This means that no discount may be taken and the $20,000 gross amount of the invoice must be paid on or before 30 days after December 19, 1991 (date of sale)—in other words, on or before January 18, 1992. If the terms had read "n/10/EOM" (EOM means end of month), no discount could be taken, and the invoice would be due on the 10th day of the month following the month of sale—or January 10, 1992, in the case of the invoice in Illustration 5.3. Credit terms vary from industry to industry.

Credit terms in some industries include a cash discount of 1% to 3% to induce early payment of an amount due. A **cash discount** is a deduction from the gross invoice price that can be taken only if the invoice is paid within a specified period of time. A cash discount is called a **sales discount** by the seller and a **purchase discount** by the buyer.

Cash discount terms are often stated as follows:

- 2/10, n/30—means a discount of 2% of the gross invoice price of the merchandise may be deducted if payment is made within 10 days following the invoice date. The **gross** invoice price is due 30 days from the invoice date.
- 2/EOM, n/60—means a 2% discount may be deducted if the invoice is paid by the end of the month. The gross invoice amount is due 60 days from the date of the invoice.
- 2/10/EOM, n/60—means a 2% discount may be deducted if the invoice is paid by the 10th day of the month following the date of sale. The gross invoice amount is due 60 days from the date of the invoice.

Since a cash discount taken by the buyer reduces the amount of cash the seller actually collects from the sale of the goods, the seller must indicate this in the accounting records of the company. The following illustration shows how this is done.

Assume that on July 12, a business sold merchandise for $2,000 on account; terms are 2/10, n/30. A check in payment of the account was received on July 21 (nine days after invoice date) in the amount $1,960. The required journal entries for the seller are:

July 12	Accounts Receivable	2,000	
	Sales		2,000
	To record sale on account; terms 2/10, n/30.	

```
July 21   Cash  . . . . . . . . . . . . . . . . . . . . . . . . . . . . . . . . 1,960
          Sales Discounts . . . . . . . . . . . . . . . . . . . . . . . .     40
              Accounts Receivable  . . . . . . . . . . . . . . . . . . .           2,000
          To record collection on account, less discount.
```

The **Sales Discounts account** is a contra revenue account to the Sales account. In the income statement, this contra account is deducted from gross sales. The Sales Discounts account is used (rather than directly reducing the Sales account) so that the owners can use the sales discounts figure to evaluate the company's sales discount policy. Note that the Sales Discounts account is not an expense incurred in generating revenue. Rather, the purpose of the account is to reduce recorded revenue to the amount actually realized from the sale, which is the net invoice price when the discount is taken.

Sales Returns and Allowances.   Merchandising companies usually allow a customer to return goods that are defective or unsatisfactory for a variety of reasons, such as wrong color, wrong size, wrong style, wrong amounts, or inferior quality. In fact, when the seller's policy is "satisfaction guaranteed," some companies allow customers to return goods simply because the customer does not like the merchandise. A **sales return** is merchandise returned by a buyer and is considered a cancellation of a sale. Sometimes the customer keeps the unsatisfactory goods and is given an allowance off the original price. A **sales allowance** is a deduction from the original invoiced sales price granted to a customer when the customer keeps the merchandise but is dissatisfied.

Both sales returns and sales allowances could, in theory, be recorded as debits to the Sales account because they cancel part of the recorded selling price. However, the amount of sales returns and sales allowances is useful information to owners. The amount of returns and allowances in relation to goods sold can be an indication of the quality of the goods (high-return percentage, low quality) or of pressure applied by salespersons (high-pressure sales, high returns). Thus, sales returns and sales allowances are recorded in a separate Sales Returns and Allowances account. **Sales Returns and Allowances** is a contra revenue account (to Sales) used to record the selling price of merchandise returned by buyers or reductions in selling prices granted. (Some companies use separate accounts for sales returns and for sales allowances, but this text does not.)

Following are two examples illustrating the recording of sales returns in the Sales Returns and Allowances account:

1. Assume that $300 of goods sold on account are returned by a customer. If payment has not yet been received, the required entry is:

```
Sales Returns and Allowances  . . . . . . . . . . . . . . . . . . . . 300
    Accounts Receivable  . . . . . . . . . . . . . . . . . . . . . . .       300
    To record a sales return from a customer.
```

2. Assume the customer has already paid the account, and the seller gives the customer a refund. Now, the credit is to Cash rather than Accounts Receivable. The customer either receives a cash (or check) refund or the customer's account is credited for the amount of the original sale. If a 2% discount was taken by the customer when the

account was paid, only the sales price less the sales discount amount would be returned to the customer. For example, if a customer returns a $300 sale on which a 2% discount was taken, the following entry would be made:

```
Sales Returns and Allowances . . . . . . . . . . . . . . . . . . . . .  300
    Cash . . . . . . . . . . . . . . . . . . . . . . . . . . . . . . . . . . . .       294
        Sales Discounts . . . . . . . . . . . . . . . . . . . . . . . . . .         6
    To record a sales return from a customer who had taken a
    discount and was sent a cash refund.
```

The debit to the Sales Returns and Allowances account is for the full selling price of the purchase. The credit to Sales Discounts reduces the balance of that account.

Now we will illustrate the recording of a sales allowance in the Sales Returns and Allowances account. Assume that a $400 allowance is granted to a customer for damage resulting from improperly packed merchandise. If the customer has not yet paid the account, the required entry would read:

```
Sales Returns and Allowances . . . . . . . . . . . . . . . . . . . . .  400
    Accounts Receivable . . . . . . . . . . . . . . . . . . . . . . . .         400
    To record sales allowance granted for damaged merchandise.
```

If the customer has already paid the account, the credit is to Cash instead of Accounts Receivable. If the customer took a 2% discount when paying the account, only the net amount ($392) would be refunded, and Sales Discounts would be credited for $8. The entry would be:

```
Sales Returns and Allowances . . . . . . . . . . . . . . . . . . . . .  400
    Cash . . . . . . . . . . . . . . . . . . . . . . . . . . . . . . . . . . . .       392
        Sales Discounts . . . . . . . . . . . . . . . . . . . . . . . . . .         8
    To record sales allowances when a customer has paid and taken a 2%
    discount.
```

Reporting Net Sales in the Income Statement

Illustration 5.4 contains a partial income statement showing how sales, sales discounts, and sales returns and allowances would be reported. Many times the income statement published in a company's annual report begins with "Net sales" because the details of this computation are not important to financial statement users outside the company.

Illustration 5.4

Partial Income Statement *

HANLON RETAIL FOOD STORE
Partial Income Statement
For the Year Ended December 31, 1991

Operating revenues:		
Gross sales		$282,000
Less: Sales discounts	$ 5,000	
Sales returns and allowances	15,000	20,000
Net sales		$262,000

* This is the same as Illustration 5.2, repeated here for your convenience.

■ COST OF GOODS SOLD

Objective 2:
Determine cost of
goods sold.

The second main division of an income statement for a merchandising business is cost of goods sold. **Cost of goods sold** is the cost to the seller of the goods sold to customers. For a merchandising company, the cost of goods sold can be relatively large. Since all merchandising companies usually have goods on hand to sell to customers, they have what is called *merchandise inventory*. **Merchandise inventory** (or **inventory**) is the quantity of goods on hand and available for sale at any given time. Cost of goods sold is determined by computing the cost of (1) the beginning inventory, (2) the net cost of goods purchased, and (3) the ending inventory.

Illustration 5.5 gives the cost of goods sold section of the Hanlon Retail Food Store's income statement. The merchandise inventory on January 1, 1991, was $24,000. The net cost of purchases for the year was $166,000. Thus, Hanlon had $190,000 of merchandise available for sale during 1991. On December 31, 1991, the merchandise inventory was $31,000, meaning that this amount was left unsold. Subtracting the unsold amount of inventory, $31,000, from the amount Hanlon had available for sale during the year, $190,000, gives the cost of goods sold for the year of $159,000. Understanding this relationship, as shown on the Hanlon Retail Food Store's partial income statement in Illustration 5.5, gives you the necessary background to study the steps taken by accountants to determine the cost of goods sold as presented in this section. This illustration is repeated at the end of the following discussion.

Two Procedures for Accounting for Inventories

To determine the cost of goods sold, accountants must have accurate merchandise inventory figures. Accountants use two basic methods in determining the amount of merchandising inventory—perpetual inventory procedure and periodic inventory procedure. Perpetual inventory procedure is only mentioned briefly in this chapter. Periodic inventory procedure is used extensively in this chapter.

Perpetual Inventory Procedure.   **Perpetual inventory procedure** is usually used by companies that sell merchandise with a high individual unit value, such as automobiles, furniture, and appliances. For retail companies selling

Illustration 5.5

Determination of
Cost of Goods Sold
for Hanlon Retail
Food Store

Cost of goods sold:			
Merchandise inventory, January 1, 1991			$ 24,000
Purchases		$167,000	
Less: Purchase discounts	$3,000		
Purchase returns and allowances	8,000	11,000	
Net purchases		$156,000	
Add: Transportation-in		10,000	
Net cost of purchases			166,000
Cost of goods available for sale			$190,000
Less: Merchandise inventory, December 31, 1991			31,000
Cost of goods sold			$159,000

goods such as these items, it is a relatively easy task to maintain records of the cost of each unit of purchased merchandise and, in turn, the cost of each unit sold. Since the advent of computerized cash registers and accounting software programs that are designed to keep track of inflows and outflows of each type of inventory item, some retail stores find it economical to use perpetual inventory procedure even for goods of low unit value.

When perpetual inventory procedure is used, inventory records are designed and maintained to provide close control over the actual goods on hand by showing exactly which goods are supposed to be on hand at any particular point in time. The Merchandise Inventory account is debited for each purchase and credited for each sale so that the current balance is shown in the account at all times. At the end of the accounting period, a physical inventory is taken by actually counting the number of units of inventory on hand. This physical count can be compared with the records showing the number of units that should be on hand. Perpetual inventory procedure will be described in more detail in Chapter 9.

Periodic Inventory Procedure.   Merchandising companies that sell merchandise with a low value per unit (such as nuts and bolts, nails, Christmas cards, or pencils) often find that the extra costs of record-keeping under perpetual inventory procedure more than outweigh the benefits. Close control of such items is not necessary nor is it economically wise. These merchandising companies use periodic inventory procedure.

Under **periodic inventory procedure,** the inventory account is not used to record each purchase and sale of merchandise as it is under perpetual inventory procedure. Instead, adjustments are made to the Merchandise Inventory account only at the end of the accounting period to bring it to its proper balance. Also, the company usually does not maintain other records that show the exact number of units that should be on hand. Record-keeping is reduced considerably, but so is the control over inventory items.

No entries are made to the Merchandise Inventory account during the accounting period. Thus, there is no up-to-date account balance against which to check the physical count at the end of the accounting period. Under periodic inventory procedure, no attempt is made to determine the cost of the goods sold at the time of each sale. Instead, the cost of all the goods sold during the accounting period is determined at the **end** of the period. To do this requires the knowledge of these three items:

1. Beginning inventory (cost of goods on hand at the beginning of the period).
2. Net cost of purchases during the period.
3. Ending inventory (cost of unsold goods on hand at the end of the period).

This information would be shown as follows:

Beginning inventory	$ 24,000
Add: Net cost of purchases during the period	140,000
Cost of goods available for sale during the period	$164,000
Deduct: Ending inventory	20,000
Cost of goods sold during the period	$144,000

From the above schedule you see that the company began the accounting period with $24,000 of merchandise and purchased an additional $140,000, making a total of $164,000 of goods that could have been sold during the period. Then, a physical inventory showed that $20,000 remained unsold at the end of the period, which implies that $144,000 was the cost of goods sold during the period. Of course, the $144,000 is not necessarily the precise amount of goods sold during the period because no actual record was made of the cost of the goods sold as they were sold. Periodic inventory procedure basically assumes that everything not on hand at the end of the period has been sold. This method disregards problems such as theft or breakage because there is no up-to-date balance in the Merchandise Inventory account at the end of the accounting period against which the physical count can be compared.

The main emphasis in this chapter will be on periodic inventory procedure. You are now ready for an in-depth discussion of the accounts and journal entries accountants use under periodic inventory procedure.

Purchases of Merchandise

Objective 3: Record journal entries for purchase transactions under periodic inventory procedure.

Under periodic inventory procedure, a merchandising company uses the **Purchases account** to record cost of goods or merchandise bought for resale during the current accounting period. The Purchases account is increased by debits and is listed with the income statement accounts in the chart of accounts.

To illustrate entries affecting the Purchases account, assume that Hanlon Retail Food Store made two purchases of merchandise from Smith Wholesale Company. Hanlon purchased $30,000 of merchandise on credit (on account) on May 4 and on May 21 purchased $20,000 of merchandise for cash. The required journal entries for Hanlon are:

```
May   4   Purchases  . . . . . . . . . . . . . . . . . . . . . . . . . 30,000
              Accounts Payable  . . . . . . . . . . . . . . . . .          30,000
          To record purchase of merchandise on account.

     21   Purchases  . . . . . . . . . . . . . . . . . . . . . . . . . 20,000
              Cash . . . . . . . . . . . . . . . . . . . . . . . . .          20,000
          To record purchase of merchandise for cash.
```

Deductions from Purchases

On the buyer's books, purchase discounts and purchase returns and allowances are deducted from purchases to arrive at net purchases. These items are recorded in contra accounts to the Purchases account.

Purchase Discounts.   Merchandise is often purchased under credit terms that permit the buyer to deduct a stated discount if the invoice is paid within a specified period of time. Assume credit terms for Hanlon's May 4 purchase are 2/10, n/30. If the merchandise is paid for by May 14, a 2% discount may be taken. Thus, only $29,400 must be paid to settle the $30,000 account payable. The entry to record the payment of the invoice on May 14 is:

```
May 14   Accounts Payable . . . . . . . . . . . . . . . . . . . . . . 30,000
            Cash . . . . . . . . . . . . . . . . . . . . . . . . . . . . .        29,400
            Purchase Discounts . . . . . . . . . . . . . . . . . . .              600
         To record payment on account within discount period.
```

The purchase discount is recorded only when the invoice is paid within the discount period and the discount is taken. The **Purchase Discounts account** is a contra account to Purchases that reduces the recorded gross invoice cost of the purchase to the price actually paid. Purchase discounts are reported in the income statement as a deduction from purchases.

Note that the May 4 purchase was recorded at gross invoice price. This method is called the *gross invoice price method*. An alternative is to record purchases at net invoice price. This latter alternative is described in Chapter 7.

Purchase discounts are based on the invoice price of goods. If there are purchase returns or allowances, they must be deducted from the invoice price before calculating purchase discounts. For example, in the transaction above, the invoice price of goods purchased was $30,000. If $2,000 of the goods were returned, the purchase discount would be calculated on $28,000.

Purchase Returns and Allowances. A purchase return occurs when a buyer returns merchandise to a seller. When a buyer receives an allowance (or reduction in the price of goods shipped), a purchase allowance results. Both returns and allowances serve to reduce the buyer's debt to the seller and to reduce the cost of the goods purchased. The buyer may be interested in knowing the amount of returns and allowances as the first step in controlling the costs incurred in returning unsatisfactory merchandise or negotiating purchase allowances. For this reason, purchase returns and allowances are recorded in a separate **Purchase Returns and Allowances account.** If Hanlon returned $350 of merchandise to Smith Wholesale before paying for the goods, the following journal entry would be made:

```
Accounts Payable . . . . . . . . . . . . . . . . . . . . . . . . . . .        350
   Purchase Returns and Allowances . . . . . . . . . . . . . . .               350
   To record return of damaged merchandise to supplier.
```

The entry would have been the same to record a $350 allowance. Only the explanation would change.

If Hanlon had already paid the account, the debit would be to Cash instead of Accounts Payable, since a refund of cash would be received. If the company took a discount at the time it paid the account, then only the net amount would be refunded. For instance, if a 2% discount had been taken, the buyer's journal entry for the return would be:

```
Cash . . . . . . . . . . . . . . . . . . . . . . . . . . . . . . . . . .        343
Purchase Discounts . . . . . . . . . . . . . . . . . . . . . . . . . .            7
   Purchase Returns and Allowances . . . . . . . . . . . . . . .               350
   To record return of damaged merchandise to supplier and record
   receipt of cash.
```

Purchase Returns and Allowances is a contra account to the Purchases account and is shown on the income statement as a deduction from purchases. When both purchase discounts and purchase returns and allowances are deducted from purchases, the result is called **net purchases.**

Transportation Costs

Transportation costs are an important part of cost of goods sold. To understand how to account for transportation costs you must know the meaning of the following terms:

- **FOB shipping point:** The term **FOB shipping point** means "free on board at shipping point"; that is, the buyer incurs all transportation costs after the merchandise is loaded on a railroad car or truck at the point of shipment. Thus, the buyer is responsible for paying the freight charges.
- **FOB destination:** The term **FOB destination** means "free on board at destination"; that is, goods are shipped to their destination without charge to the buyer. Thus, the seller is responsible for paying the freight charges.
- **Passage of title:** **Passage of title** is a legal term used to indicate transfer of legal ownership of goods. Title to the goods passes from seller to buyer at the FOB point. Thus, when goods are shipped FOB shipping point, title passes to the buyer at the shipping point. When goods are shipped FOB destination, title passes at destination.
- **Freight prepaid:** When the **seller** pays the freight at the time of shipment, the term **freight prepaid** is used.
- **Freight collect:** When the **buyer** pays the freight bill on the arrival of the goods, the term **freight collect** is used.

To illustrate the use of these terms, assume that certain goods are shipped FOB shipping point, freight collect. Title passes at the shipping point. The buyer is responsible for paying the $100 freight costs and does so. No entry for freight charges is made on the seller's books. The entry on the buyer's books is:

Transportation-In (or Freight-In)	100	
Cash		100
To record payment of freight bill on goods purchased.		

The **Transportation-In account** is used to record freight costs incurred in the acquisition of merchandise. Transportation-In is an adjunct account in that it is added to net purchases to arrive at **net cost of purchases. An adjunct account** is closely related to another account (Purchases, in this instance), and its balance is added to the balance of the related account in the financial statements. Recall that a contra account is just the opposite of an adjunct account. A contra account, such as accumulated depreciation, is **deducted** from the related account in the financial statements.

If goods are shipped FOB destination, freight prepaid, the seller pays the freight bill and is responsible for it. No separate freight cost is billed to the buyer. No entry for freight is required on the buyer's books. The freight cost undoubtedly was taken into consideration by the seller in setting selling prices. The following entry is required on the seller's books:

Delivery Expense (or Transportation-Out Expense)	100	
Cash		100
To record freight cost on goods sold.		

When the terms are FOB destination, the seller records the freight costs as **delivery expense,** which is a selling expense shown on the income statement with other selling expenses.

FOB terms are especially important at the end of an accounting period. Goods that are in transit at the end of an accounting period belong to either the seller or the buyer and must be included in ending inventory by one of the parties. Goods shipped FOB destination belong to the seller while in transit and should be included in the seller's ending inventory. Goods shipped FOB shipping point belong to the buyer while in transit and should be recorded as a purchase and included in the buyer's ending inventory. For example, assume that goods are shipped by a seller on December 30, 1990, and arrive at their destination on January 5, 1991. If terms are FOB destination, the seller includes the goods in its December 31, 1990, inventory, and neither the seller nor buyer records the exchange transaction until January 5, 1991. If terms are FOB shipping point, the buyer includes the goods in its December 31, 1990, inventory, and the exchange transaction is recorded by both parties as of December 31, 1990.

Sometimes the seller prepays the freight as a convenience to the buyer even though the buyer is responsible for paying it. In such cases, the buyer merely reimburses the seller for the amount of freight paid. For example, assume Wood Company sold merchandise to Loud Company with terms of FOB shipping point. The freight charges of $100 were to be prepaid. The following entries are necessary on the books of the buyer and seller:

Buyer—Loud Company		**Seller—Wood Company**	
Transportation-In	100	Accounts Receivable	100
Accounts Payable	100	Cash	100

Such entries are necessary because Wood paid the freight charges when the company was not required to do so; therefore, Loud Company must reimburse Wood for the charges. If the buyer pays the freight for the seller (e.g., FOB destination, freight collect), the buyer merely deducts the freight paid from the amount owed to the seller. The following entries are necessary on the books of the buyer and seller:

Buyer—Loud Company		**Seller—Wood Company**	
Accounts Payable	100	Delivery Expense	100
Cash	100	Accounts Receivable	100

Merchandise Inventories

As stated earlier, **merchandise inventory** is the cost of goods on hand and available for sale at any given time. For a company to determine the cost of goods sold in any accounting period, inventory information is needed. Cost of goods on hand at the start of the period (beginning inventory), purchases made during the period, and the cost of goods on hand at the close of the period (ending inventory) must be known. Since the ending inventory of the preceding period is the beginning inventory for the current period, the cost of the beginning inventory is already known. Purchases are recorded throughout the period. Therefore, only the cost of the ending inventory need be determined at the end of the period.

Taking a Physical Inventory.   Under periodic inventory procedure, ending inventory cost is determined by taking a physical inventory. Taking a **physical inventory** consists of counting physical units of each type of merchandise on hand. To calculate inventory cost, multiply the number of units of each kind of merchandise by its unit cost. Total costs of the various kinds of merchandise are then totaled to provide the total ending inventory cost.

In taking a physical inventory, care must be exercised to ensure that all goods owned, regardless of where they are located, are counted and included in the inventory. Thus, goods shipped to a potential customer "on approval" should not be recorded as sold. They should be included in the owner's inventory. Similarly, **consigned goods,** which are goods delivered to another party who will attempt to sell the goods for the owner at a commission, should not be recorded as sold. These goods remain the property of the owner (consignor) until sold by the consignee and must be included in the owner's inventory.

Merchandise in transit is merchandise in the hands of a freight company on the date of a physical inventory. Merchandise in transit at the end of the accounting period must be recorded as a purchase and included in the buyer's inventory if passage of title to the buyer has occurred. In general, the goods belong to the party who must bear the transportation charges.

Determining Cost of Goods Sold

When beginning and ending inventories and the various items making up the net cost of purchases are known, cost of goods sold can be determined.

To illustrate, assume the following account balances for Hanlon Retail Food Store as of December 31, 1991:

Merchandise Inventory, January 1, 1991	$ 24,000 Dr.
Purchases	167,000 Dr.
Purchase Discounts	3,000 Cr.
Purchase Returns and Allowances	8,000 Cr.
Transportation-In	10,000 Dr.

By taking a physical inventory, merchandise inventory on December 31, 1991, was determined to be $31,000. Cost of goods sold would be calculated as shown in Illustration 5.6. This computation appears in a section of the income statement directly below the calculation of net sales.

Illustration 5.6

Determination of Cost of Goods Sold for Hanlon Retail Food Store*

Cost of goods sold:			
Merchandise inventory, January 1, 1991			$ 24,000
Purchases		$167,000	
Less: Purchase discounts	$3,000		
Purchase returns and allowances	8,000	11,000	
Net purchases		$156,000	
Add: Transportation-in		10,000	
Net cost of purchases			166,000
Cost of goods available for sale			$190,000
Less: Merchandise inventory, December 31, 1991			31,000
Cost of goods sold			$159,000

* This is the same illustration as Illustration 5.5, repeated here for your convenience.

In Illustration 5.6, beginning inventory ($24,000) plus net cost of purchases ($166,000) is equal to **cost of goods available for sale** ($190,000). Ending inventory cost ($31,000) is deducted from cost of goods available for sale to arrive at cost of goods sold ($159,000). The relationship between these items is shown in the diagram below:

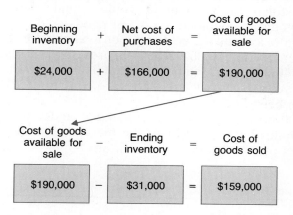

Another way of looking at this relationship is shown in the following diagram:

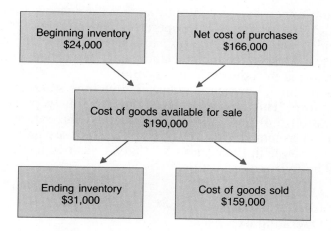

Beginning inventory and net cost of purchases combine to form cost of goods available for sale. The cost of goods available for sale is divided into ending inventory (which is the cost of goods not sold) and cost of goods sold.

To continue the calculation appearing in Illustration 5.6, net cost of purchases ($166,000) is equal to purchases ($167,000), **less** purchase discounts ($3,000) and purchase returns and allowances ($8,000), **plus** transportation-in ($10,000).

As shown in Illustration 5.6, ending inventory cost appears in the income statement as a deduction from cost of goods available for sale to compute cost of goods sold. Ending inventory cost (merchandise inventory) is also reported as a current asset in the end-of-period balance sheet.

Lack of Control under Periodic Inventory Procedure

Periodic inventory procedure is used because of its simplicity and relatively low cost; but, as mentioned earlier, it provides for little control over inventory. Any items not included in the physical count of inventory at the end of the period are assumed to have been sold. Thus, even if the items have been stolen, the accountant would assume they had been sold, and their cost would be included in cost of goods sold.

To illustrate, assume the cost of goods available for sale was $200,000 and ending inventory is $60,000. These figures suggest that the cost of goods sold was $140,000. But assume that $2,000 of goods were actually shoplifted during the year. If such goods had not been stolen, the ending inventory would have been $62,000 and the cost of goods sold only $138,000. Thus, the $140,000 cost of goods sold calculated under periodic inventory procedure includes both the cost of the merchandise delivered to customers and the cost of merchandise stolen (if any).

■ CLASSIFIED INCOME STATEMENT

Objective 5:
Prepare a classified income statement.

In preceding chapters, we illustrated only an unclassified income statement. An **unclassified income statement** has only two categories of items—revenues and expenses. In contrast, a **classified income statement** divides both revenues and expenses into operating and nonoperating items. The statement also separates operating expenses into selling and administrative expenses. A classified income statement, also called a multiple-step income statement, is introduced in this section.

Illustration 5.7 presents a classified income statement for Hanlon Retail Food Store. This statement uses the previously presented data on sales (Illustration 5.4) and cost of goods sold (Illustration 5.6), together with additional assumed data on operating expenses and other expenses and revenues. Note in Illustration 5.7 that a classified income statement has the following four major sections:

1. Operating revenues.
2. Cost of goods sold.
3. Operating expenses.
4. Nonoperating revenues and expenses (other revenues and other expenses).

The classified income statement shows important relationships that help in analyzing how well the company is performing. For example, by deducting cost of goods sold from operating revenues, you can determine by what amount sales revenues exceed the cost of items being sold. If this margin is inadequate, selling prices may need to be increased or the cost of goods sold may need to be decreased. Operating expenses are subdivided into selling and administrative expenses so the statement user can see how much expense is being incurred in selling the product and how much is being incurred in administering the business. Comparisons can be made with other years for the same business and with other businesses. Nonoperating

Illustration 5.7

Classified Income Statement for a Merchandising Company

HANLON RETAIL FOOD STORE
Income Statement
For the Year Ended December 31, 1991

Operating revenues:

Gross sales			$282,000
Less: Sales discounts		$ 5,000	
Sales returns and allowances		15,000	20,000
Net sales			$262,000

Cost of goods sold:

Merchandise inventory, January 1, 1991			$ 24,000	
Purchases		$167,000		
Less: Purchase discounts	$3,000			
Purchase returns and allowances	8,000	11,000		
Net purchases		$156,000		
Add: Transportation-in		10,000		
Net cost of purchases			166,000	
Cost of goods available for sale			$190,000	
Less: Merchandise inventory,				
December 31, 1991			31,000	
Cost of goods sold				159,000
Gross margin				$103,000

Operating expenses:

Selling expenses:			
Sales salaries and commissions expense	$ 26,000		
Salespersons' travel expense	3,000		
Delivery expense	2,000		
Advertising expense	4,000		
Rent expense—store building	2,500		
Supplies expense	1,000		
Utilities expense	1,800		
Depreciation expense—store equipment	700		
Other selling expense	400	$ 41,400	
Administrative expenses:			
Salaries expense, executive	$ 29,000		
Rent expense—administrative building	1,600		
Insurance expense	1,500		
Supplies expense	800		
Depreciation expense—office equipment	1,100		
Other administrative expense	300	34,300	
Total operating expenses			75,700
Income from operations			$ 27,300

Nonoperating revenues and expenses:

Nonoperating revenues:	
Interest revenue	1,400
	$ 28,700
Nonoperating expenses:	
Interest expense	600
Net income	$ 28,100

revenues and expenses appear at the bottom of the income statement because they are less significant in assessing the profitability of the business.

The major headings of the classified income statement shown in Illustration 5.7 are explained in the paragraphs that follow. The terms in some of these headings are already familiar to you.

1. **Operating revenues** are the revenues generated by the major activities of the business—usually the sale of products or services or both.

2. **Cost of goods sold** is the major expense in merchandising companies. The cost of goods sold section of the classified income statement was shown in Illustration 5.6, and the items used in calculating cost of goods sold have already been discussed in this chapter. It is common to highlight the amount by which sales revenues exceed the cost of goods sold in the top part of the income statement. The excess of net sales over cost of goods sold is called **gross margin** or **gross profit.** Gross margin may also be expressed as a percentage rate, computed by dividing gross margin by net sales. In Illustration 5.7, the gross margin rate is approximately 39.3% ($103,000/$262,000). The gross margin rate indicates that out of each sales dollar, approximately 39 cents is available to cover other expenses and produce income. The gross margin rate is watched closely by the owner since a small percentage fluctuation can cause a large dollar change in net income.

3. **Operating expenses** for a merchandising company are those expenses other than cost of goods sold incurred in the normal business functions of a company. Usually, operating expenses are classified as either selling expenses or administrative expenses. **Selling expenses** are expenses incurred in selling and marketing efforts. Examples include salaries and commissions of salespersons, expenses for salespersons' travel, delivery, advertising, rent and utilities on sales building, sales supplies used, and depreciation on delivery equipment used in sales. **Administrative expenses** are expenses incurred in the overall management of a business. Examples include administrative salaries, rent and utilities on administrative building, insurance expense, administrative supplies used, and depreciation on office equipment.

Certain operating expenses may be related partly to the selling function and partly to the administrative function. For example, rent, taxes, and insurance on a building might be incurred for both sales and administrative purposes. Expenses covering both the selling and administrative functions are analyzed and prorated between the two functions in the income statement. For instance, if $1,000 of depreciation expense relates 60% to selling and 40% to administrative based on the square footage or number of employees, $600 would be shown as a selling expense and $400 as an administrative expense.

4. **Nonoperating revenues (other revenues)** are revenues not related to the sale of products or services regularly offered for sale by a business. An example of a nonoperating revenue is interest that a business earns on notes receivable. **Nonoperating expenses (other expenses)** are expenses not related to the acquisition and sale of the products or services regularly offered for sale. An example of a nonoperating expense is interest incurred on money borrowed by the company.

Important Relationships in the Income Statement

The more important relationships in the income statement of a merchandising firm can be summarized in equation form, as follows:

1. **Net sales** = Gross sales − (Sales discounts + Sales returns and allowances).
2. **Net purchases** = Purchases − (Purchase discounts + Purchase returns and allowances).
3. **Net cost of purchases** = Net purchases + Transportation-in.
4. **Cost of goods sold** = Beginning inventory + Net cost of purchases − Ending inventory.
5. **Gross margin** = Net sales − Cost of goods sold.
6. **Income from operations** = Gross margin − Operating (selling and administrative) expenses.
7. **Net income** = Income from operations + Nonoperating revenues − Nonoperating expenses.

Each of these relationships is important because of the way it relates to an overall measure of business profitability. For example, a company may produce a high gross margin on sales. However, because of large sales commissions and delivery expenses, only a very small percentage of the gross margin may ever be realized by the owner as profit. The classifications in the income statement allow a user to focus on the whole picture (net income) as well as on how it was derived (statement relationships).

Future illustrations may vary somewhat in form, but the basic organization of the classified income statement described above will be retained.

■ THE WORK SHEET FOR A MERCHANDISING COMPANY

Objective 6:
Prepare a work sheet and closing entries for a merchandising company.

Illustration 5.8 shows a work sheet for a merchandising company. To keep the illustration simple, a different retail company will be introduced. Lyons Company is a small sporting goods firm owned by Sam Lyons. The illustration for Lyons Company focuses on the merchandise-related accounts. For this reason, selling and administrative expenses have been grouped into two accounts rather than including all actual expense accounts. Also, the fixed assets (land, building, and delivery equipment) are not shown. Except for the merchandise-related accounts, the work sheet for a merchandising company is the same as for a service company. Recall that use of a work sheet assists in the preparation of the adjusting and closing entries. The work sheet also contains all of the information needed for the preparation of the financial statements.

To further simplify this illustration, assume no adjusting entries are necessary at month-end. The trial balance is taken from the ledger accounts at December 31, 1991. The $7,000 merchandise inventory in the trial balance is the beginning inventory. The sales and sales-related accounts and the purchases and purchases-related accounts summarize the merchandising activity for December 1991.

Illustration 5.8 *Work Sheet for a Merchandising Company*

LYONS COMPANY
Work Sheet
For the Month Ended December 31, 1991

Acct. No.	Account Titles	Trial Balance Debit	Trial Balance Credit	Adjustments Debit	Adjustments Credit	Adjusted Trial Balance Debit	Adjusted Trial Balance Credit	Income Statement Debit	Income Statement Credit	Balance Sheet Debit	Balance Sheet Credit
1	Cash	19,663				19,663				19,663	
2	Accounts Receivable	1,880				1,880				1,880	
3	Merchandise Inventory	7,000				7,000		7,000	8,000	8,000	
4	Accounts Payable		700				700				700
5	Sam Lyons, Capital, December 1		25,000				25,000				25,000
6	Sam Lyons, Drawing	2,000				2,000				2,000	
7	Sales		14,600				14,600		14,600		
8	Sales Discounts	44				44		44			
9	Sales Returns and Allowances	20				20		20			
10	Purchases	6,000				6,000		6,000			
11	Purchase Discounts		82				82		82		
12	Purchase Returns and Allowances		100				100		100		
13	Transportation-In	75				75		75			
14	Selling Expenses	2,650				2,650		2,650			
15	Administrative Expenses	1,150				1,150		1,150			
		40,482	40,482			40,482	40,482	16,939	22,782	31,543	25,700
	Net income							5,843			5,843
								22,782	22,782	31,543	31,543

Completing the Work Sheet

Any revenue accounts (Sales) and contra purchases accounts (Purchase Discounts, Purchase Returns and Allowances) that appear in the Adjusted Trial Balance credit columns of the work sheet are carried to the Income Statement credit column. Beginning inventory, contra revenue accounts (Sales Discounts, Sales Returns and Allowances), Purchases, Transportation-In, and expense accounts (Selling Expenses, Administrative Expenses) shown in the Adjusted Trial Balance debit column are carried to the Income Statement debit column.

Note that the amount of ending merchandise inventory, $8,000, is entered in the Income Statement credit column to reduce cost of goods sold and in the Balance Sheet debit column to establish the proper balance in the Merchandise Inventory account. The reason both beginning and ending inventories are brought to the Income Statement columns is because both are used to calculate cost of goods sold in the income statement. Net income or net loss for the period will balance the Income Statement columns as it did in previous work sheets. Net income/loss is carried to the Balance Sheet credit/debit column. For Lyons Company, the net income is $5,843 for the month of December.

All other assets (Cash and Accounts Receivable) and the owner's drawing account balance are carried to the Balance Sheet debit column. The liability (Accounts Payable) and owner's capital are carried to the Balance Sheet credit column.

Financial Statements for a Merchandising Company

Once the work sheet has been completed, the financial statements are prepared. Next, any adjusting and closing entries are entered in the journal and posted to the ledger. This process clears the accounting records for the next accounting period.

Income Statement.   The income statement in Illustration 5.9 is prepared from the work sheet in Illustration 5.8. The focus in this income statement is on the determination of the cost of goods sold. That is why other expenses are shown in summary form.

Statement of Owner's Equity.   The statement of owner's equity, as you recall, is a financial statement that summarizes the transactions affecting the owner's capital account balance. In Illustration 5.10, the statement of owner's equity shows the increase in equity resulting from net income and the decrease in equity resulting from the owner's withdrawals.

Balance Sheet.   The balance sheet, Illustration 5.11, contains the assets, liabilities, and owner's equity items taken from the work sheet. Note that the $8,000 ending inventory is shown as a current asset. The Sam Lyons capital account balance comes from the statement of owner's equity.

Illustration 5.9

Income Statement for a Merchandising Company

LYONS COMPANY
Income Statement
For the Month Ended December 31, 1991

Operating revenues:			
Gross sales			$14,600
Less: Sales discounts		$ 44	
Sales returns and allowances		20	64
Net sales			$14,536
Cost of goods sold:			
Merchandise inventory, December 1, 1991		$ 7,000	
Purchases	$6,000		
Less: Purchase discounts	$ 82		
Purchase returns and allowances	100	182	
Net purchases	$5,818		
Add: Transportation-in	75		
Net cost of purchases		5,893	
Cost of goods available for sale		$12,893	
Less: Merchandise inventory, December 31, 1991		8,000	
Cost of goods sold			4,893
Gross margin			$ 9,643
Operating expenses:			
Selling expenses (summary)		$ 2,650	
Administrative expenses (summary)		1,150	
Total operating expenses			3,800
Net income			$ 5,843

Closing Entries

Recall from Chapter 4 that the closing process normally takes place after the financial statements for the period have been prepared. The closing process closes revenue and expense accounts by transferring their balances to a clearing account called Income Summary and then to owner's capital. The closing process reduces the revenue and expense account balances to zero so that information for each accounting period may be accumulated separately from any previous period.

Closing entries may be prepared directly from the work sheet in Illustration 5.8 using the same procedure as presented in Chapter 4. The closing entries for Lyons Company are as follows:

The first journal entry **debits** all items appearing in the Income Statement credit column of the work sheet and **credits** Income Summary for the total of the column, $22,782.

1st entry	

```
1991
Dec. 31  Merchandise Inventory (ending) . . . . . . . . . . . . . .   8,000
         Sales . . . . . . . . . . . . . . . . . . . . . . . . . .  14,600
         Purchase Discounts . . . . . . . . . . . . . . . . . . .      82
         Purchase Returns and Allowances . . . . . . . . . . . .     100
             Income Summary . . . . . . . . . . . . . . . . . . .            22,782
         To close accounts with a credit balance in the Income
         Statement columns and to establish ending
         merchandise inventory.
```

Illustration 5.10

Statement of Owner's Equity

> **LYONS COMPANY**
> *Statement of Owner's Equity*
> *For the Month Ended December 31, 1991*
>
> Sam Lyons, capital, December 1, 1991 . . . . . . $25,000
> Add: Net income for December   5,843
> Total $30,843
> Deduct: Owner drawings for December   2,000
> Sam Lyons, capital, December 31, 1991 . . . . . $28,843

Illustration 5.11

Balance Sheet for a Merchandising Company

> **LYONS COMPANY**
> *Balance Sheet*
> *December 31, 1991*
>
> **Assets**
> Current assets:
>   Cash $19,663
>   Accounts receivable   1,880
>   Merchandise inventory   8,000
> Total assets $29,543
>
> **Liabilities and Owner's Equity**
> Current liabilities:
>   Accounts payable . . . . $ 700
> Owner's equity:
>   Sam Lyons, capital   28,843
> Total liabilities and owner's equity $29,543

The second entry **credits** all items appearing in the Income Statement debit column and **debits** Income Summary for the total of that column, $16,939.[1]

2nd entry			

Dec. 31	Income Summary	16,939	
	Merchandise Inventory (beginning)		7,000
	Sales Discounts		44
	Sales Returns and Allowances		20
	Purchases		6,000
	Transportation-In		75
	Selling Expenses		2,650
	Administrative Expenses		1,150

To close accounts with a debit balance in the Income Statement columns.

In the third entry, the credit balance in the Income Summary account of $5,843 is closed to the owner's capital account.

---

[1] You may close debit balanced accounts (in the Income Statement) before credit balanced accounts. This practice does not affect the balance of the Income Summary account or the amount of net income.

| 3rd entry |

Dec. 31   Income Summary   5,843
        Sam Lyons, Capital   5,843
        To close the Income Summary account to the owner's
        capital account.

In the fourth entry, the owner's drawing account balance of $2,000 is closed to the owner's capital account by debiting Sam Lyons, Capital and crediting Sam Lyons, Drawing.

| 4th entry |

Dec. 31   Sam Lyons, Capital   2,000
        Sam Lyons, Drawing   2,000
        To close the owner's drawing account to the owner's
        capital account.

Note how the first three closing entries tie into the totals shown in the Income Statement columns of the work sheet in Illustration 5.8. In the first closing journal entry, the credit to the Income Summary account is equal to the total of the Income Statement credit column. In the second entry, the debit to the Income Summary account is equal to the subtotal of the Income Statement debit column. The difference between the totals of the two Income Statement columns ($5,843) represents net income and is the amount of the third closing entry.

The effects of these closing entries are shown in the following T-accounts:

Merchandise Inventory

Bal. before closing	7,000	1991 Dec. 31 To close to Income Summary	7,000
1991 Dec. 31 To establish actual ending inventory balance	8,000		

Sales

1991 Dec. 31 To close to Income Summary	14,600	Bal. before closing	14,600
		Bal. after closing	–0–

Sales Discounts

Bal. before closing	44	1991 Dec. 31 To close to Income Summary	44
Bal. after closing	–0–		

Sales Returns and Allowances

Bal. before closing	20	1991 Dec. 31 To close to Income Summary	20
Bal. after closing	–0–		

Purchases

Bal. before closing	6,000	1991 Dec. 31 To close to Income Summary	6,000
Bal. after closing	–0–		

Purchase Discounts

1991 Dec. 31 To close to Income Summary	82	Bal. before closing	82
		Bal. after closing	–0–

Purchase Returns and Allowances

1991 Dec. 31 To close to Income Summary	100	Bal. before closing	100
		Bal. after closing	–0–

Transportation-In

Bal. before closing	75	1991 Dec. 31 To close to Income Summary	75
Bal. after closing	–0–		

Selling Expenses

Bal. before closing	2,650	1991 Dec. 31 To close to Income Summary	2,650
Bal. after closing	–0–		

Administrative Expenses

Bal. before closing	1,150	1991 Dec. 31 To close to Income Summary	1,150
Bal. after closing	–0–		

Income Summary

1991 Dec. 31 From closing accounts appearing in Income Statement debit column of work sheet	16,939	1991 Dec. 31 From closing accounts appearing in Income Statement credit column of work sheet	22,782
1991 Dec. 31 To close to owner's capital account	5,843	Bal. (net income) before closing this account	5,843
		Bal. after closing	–0–

Sam Lyons, Capital

1991			1991		
Dec. 31.	From closing owner's drawing account	2,000	Dec. 31	Beg. bal.	25,000
				From closing Income Summary account	5,843
				End. bal.	28,843

Sam Lyons, Drawing

			1991		
Bal. before closing		2,000	Dec. 31	To close to owner's capital account	2,000
Bal. after closing		–0–			

After the entries have been posted to the ledger, only the balance sheet accounts have balances. The revenue, expense, and drawing accounts have zero balances.

You should now understand the distinction between accounting for a service company and a merchandising company. The next chapter takes you back to the accounting process (or cycle) and builds on the knowledge you have already acquired as you study accounting systems and special journals.

■ UNDERSTANDING THE LEARNING OBJECTIVES: CHAPTER 5

1. Record journal entries for sales transactions.

   - In a sales transaction, the legal ownership (title) of goods is transferred from the seller to the buyer.
   - An invoice is a document, prepared by the seller and sent to the buyer, that contains the details of a sale, such as the number of units, unit price, total price, terms of sale, and manner of shipment.
   - Usually sales are for cash or on account. When a sale is for cash, the debit is to Cash and the credit is to Sales. When a sale is on account, the debit is to Accounts Receivable, and the credit is to Sales.
   - When there are trade discounts, the gross invoice price (gross selling price) at which the sale is recorded is equal to the list price minus any trade discounts.
   - Two common deductions from gross sales are (1) sales discounts and (2) sales returns and allowances. These deductions are reported in contra accounts to the Sales account. Both the Sales Discounts account and the Sales Returns and Allowances account normally have debit balances. Net sales = Sales − (Sales discounts + Sales returns and allowances).

- Sales discounts arise when the seller offers the buyer a cash discount of 1% to 3% to induce early payment of an amount due.
- Sales returns result from merchandise being returned by a buyer because the goods are considered unsatisfactory or have been damaged. A sales allowance is a deduction from the original invoiced sales price granted to a customer when the customer keeps the merchandise but is dissatisfied.

2. Determine cost of goods sold.

- Cost of goods sold = Beginning inventory + Net cost of purchases − Ending inventory. Net cost of purchases = Purchases − (Purchase discounts + Purchase returns and allowances) + Transportation-in.
- Two methods of accounting for inventory are perpetual inventory procedure and periodic inventory procedure. Under perpetual inventory procedure, the inventory account is continually kept up to date during the accounting period. Under periodic inventory procedure, the inventory account is only brought up to its proper balance at the end of the accounting period.

3. Record journal entries for purchase transactions under periodic inventory procedure.

- Purchases of merchandise are recorded by debiting Purchases and crediting Cash (for cash purchases) or crediting Accounts Payable (for purchases on account).
- Two common deductions from purchases are shown in (1) purchase discounts and (2) purchase returns and allowances. In the general ledger, both of these items normally carry credit balances. From the buyer's side of the transactions, cash discounts are purchase discounts, and merchandise returns and allowances are purchase returns and allowances.

4. Describe the freight terms.

- FOB shipping point means "free on board at shipping point"—the buyer incurs the freight.
- FOB destination means "free on board at destination"—the seller incurs the freight.
- Passage of title is a legal term used to indicate transfer of legal ownership of goods.
- Freight prepaid is when the seller (at least initially) pays the freight at the time of shipment.
- Freight collect is when the buyer (at least initially) pays the freight on the arrival of the goods.

5. Prepare a classified income statement.

- A classified income statement has four major sections—operating revenues, cost of goods sold, operating expenses, and nonoperating revenues and expenses.
- Operating revenues are the revenues generated by the major ac-

tivities of the business—usually the sale of products or services or both.

- Cost of goods sold is the major expense in merchandising companies.
- Operating expenses for a merchandising company are those expenses other than cost of goods sold incurred in the normal business functions of a company. Operating expenses are usually classified as either selling expenses or administrative expenses.
- Nonoperating revenues and expenses are revenues and expenses not related to the sale of products or services regularly offered for sale by a business.

6. Prepare a work sheet and closing entries for a merchandising company.

- Except for the merchandise-related accounts, the work sheet for a merchandising company is the same as for a service company.
- Any revenue accounts and contra purchases accounts that appear in the Adjusted Trial Balance credit column of the work sheet are carried to the Income Statement credit column.
- Beginning inventory, contra revenue accounts, Purchases, Transportation-In, and expense accounts shown in the Adjusted Trial Balance debit column are carried to the Income Statement debit column.
- Ending merchandise inventory is entered in the Income Statement credit column and in the Balance Sheet debit column.
- Closing entries may be prepared directly from the work sheet. The first journal entry debits all items appearing in the Income Statement credit column and credits Income Summary. The second entry credits all items appearing in the Income Statement debit column and debits Income Summary. The third entry debits Income Summary and credits the owner's capital account (assuming positive net income). The fourth entry debits the owner's capital account and credits the owner's drawing account.

7. Define and use correctly the new terms in the glossary.

- See the new terms introduced following the Appendix to this chapter.

■ APPENDIX: ALTERNATIVE CLOSING PROCEDURE

Many of the users of this text prefer the closing process illustrated in the chapter because it is easy to perform. If you are satisfied with that approach, you need not read this appendix. But some users prefer an alternative procedure that they believe communicates more effectively the purposes behind the closing process. Since the end result of both methods is the same, both are correct. The procedure used depends on personal preference.

This appendix illustrates the alternative closing procedure. Under this alternative procedure, the beginning inventory balance and balances in all purchase-related accounts are transferred into the Cost of Goods Sold account in an **adjusting entry.** In a separate **adjusting entry,** the ending inventory is established by debiting Merchandise Inventory and crediting Cost of Goods Sold.

Using the same data from Illustration 5.8, the required adjusting entries for inventory and cost of goods sold under this alternative procedure are as shown below.

The first adjusting entry transfers into the Cost of Goods Sold account the net cost of all the goods available for sale during the year. At this point the Cost of Goods Sold account contains the cost of goods available for sale. The second adjusting entry then removes from the Cost of Goods Sold account the cost of goods unsold at year-end and establishes this amount as the ending inventory.

1991			
Dec. 31	Cost of Goods Sold	12,893	
	Purchase Discounts	82	
	Purchase Returns and Allowances	100	
	Merchandise Inventory (beginning)		7,000
	Purchases		6,000
	Transportation-In		75
	To transfer the beginning inventory and the accounts comprising net purchases to the Cost of Goods Sold account.		
31	Merchandise Inventory (ending)	8,000	
	Cost of Goods Sold		8,000
	To set up ending inventory and reduce Cost of Goods Sold by the cost of goods not sold.		

The result of these two entries is that the Cost of Goods Sold account contains the amount of expense incurred during the year for merchandise delivered to customers. The Cost of Goods Sold account is closed as follows:

1991			
Dec. 31	Income Summary	4,893	
	Cost of Goods Sold		4,893
	To close Cost of Goods Sold to Income Summary.		

This final entry would generally be included in the compound closing entry for all expenses closed at the end of the period rather than being journalized separately. A difference between the two alternatives is that the method in the chapter does not set up a ledger account for Cost of Goods Sold, while this method does.

Illustration 5.12 shows how a work sheet is prepared using this alternative procedure and focuses on the merchandise-related accounts.

Trial Balance Columns. The Trial Balance columns have the same data as shown in Illustration 5.8 in this chapter.

Adjusted Trial Balance Columns. Note that under this method the net balance in Cost of Goods Sold ($4,893) is shown in the Adjusted Trial Balance debit column. Also, the $8,000 ending inventory appears in the same column.

Income Statement Columns. The only purchase-related item that appears in the Income Statement columns is the cost of goods sold ($4,893).

Illustration 5.12 Work Sheet Using Alternative Procedure

LYONS COMPANY
Work Sheet
For the Month Ended December 31, 1991

Acct. No.	Account Titles	Trial Balance Debit	Trial Balance Credit	Adjustments Debit	Adjustments Credit	Adjusted Trial Balance Debit	Adjusted Trial Balance Credit	Income Statement Debit	Income Statement Credit	Balance Sheet Debit	Balance Sheet Credit
1	Cash	19,663				19,663				19,663	
2	Accounts Receivable	1,880				1,880				1,880	
3	Merchandise Inventory, December 1	7,000			(1) 7,000						
4	Accounts Payable		700				700				700
5	Sam Lyons, Capital, December 1		25,000				25,000				25,000
6	Sam Lyons, Drawing	2,000				2,000				2,000	
7	Sales		14,600				14,600		14,600		
8	Sales Discounts	44				44		44			
9	Sales Returns and Allowances	20				20		20			
10	Purchases	6,000			(1) 6,000						
11	Purchase Discounts		82	(1) 82							
12	Purchase Returns and Allowances		100	(1) 100							
13	Transportation-In	75			(1) 75						
14	Selling Expenses	2,650				2,650		2,650			
15	Administrative Expenses	1,150				1,150		1,150			
		40,482	40,482								
	Cost of Goods Sold			(1) 12,893	(2) 8,000	4,893		4,893			
	Merchandise Inventory, December 31*			(2) 8,000		8,000				8,000	
				21,075	21,075	40,300	40,300	8,757	14,600	31,543	25,700
	Net income							5,843			5,843
								14,600	14,600	31,543	31,543

Adjustments:
(1) To transfer the beginning inventory and the accounts comprising net purchases to the Cost of Goods Sold account.
(2) To set up ending inventory and reduce Cost of Goods Sold by the cost of goods not sold.
* If desired, the $8,000 in the Adjustments column and in the Balance Sheet columns may be placed on the same line as the $7,000 beginning inventory figure.

Balance Sheet Columns.   The Balance Sheet columns have the same data as shown in Illustration 5.8 in the chapter.

Closing Entries.   The closing entries under this alternative procedure are as follows:

```
1991
Dec. 31  Sales . . . . . . . . . . . . . . . . . . . . . . . .  14,600
                  Income Summary . . . . . . . . . . . . . . . . .            14,600
             To close accounts with a balance in the Income
             Statement credit column.


      31  Income Summary . . . . . . . . . . . . . . . . . . . .   8,757
                  Sales Discounts . . . . . . . . . . . . . . . .                  44
                  Sales Returns and Allowances . . . . . . . . . .              20
                  Selling Expenses . . . . . . . . . . . . . . . .           2,650
                  Administrative Expenses . . . . . . . . . . . . .          1,150
                  Cost of Goods Sold . . . . . . . . . . . . . . .           4,893
             To close accounts with a balance in the Income
             Statement debit column.


      31  Income Summary . . . . . . . . . . . . . . . . . . . .   5,843
                  Sam Lyons, Capital . . . . . . . . . . . . . . .           5,843
             To close the Income Summary account to the
             owner's capital account.


      31  Sam Lyons, Capital . . . . . . . . . . . . . . . . . .   2,000
                  Sam Lyons, Drawing . . . . . . . . . . . . . . .           2,000
             To close the owner's drawing account to the owner's
             capital account.
```

NEW TERMS INTRODUCED IN CHAPTER 5

Adjunct account   Closely related to another account, and its balance is added to the balance of the related account in the financial statements (192).

Administrative expenses   Expenses incurred in the overall management of a business (198).

Cash discount   A deduction from the gross invoice price that can be taken only if the invoice is paid within a specified period of time: to the seller, it is a sales discount; to the buyer, it is a purchase discount (185).

Chain discount   Occurs when a list price of a product is subject to several trade discounts (184).

Classified income statement   Divides both revenues and expenses into operating and nonoperating items. The statement also separates operating expenses into selling and administrative expenses (196).

Consigned goods   Goods delivered to another party who will attempt to sell the goods for the owner at a commission (194).

Cost of goods available for sale   Equal to beginning inventory plus net cost of purchases (195).

Cost of goods sold   Shows the cost to the seller of the goods sold to customers; under periodic inventory procedure, cost of goods sold is computed as Beginning inventory + Net cost of purchases − Ending inventory (188, 199).

Delivery expense   A selling expense recorded by the seller for freight costs incurred when terms are FOB destination (193).

FOB destination   Means free on board at destination; goods are shipped to their destination without charge to the buyer; the seller is responsible for paying the freight charges (192).

FOB shipping point   Means free on board at shipping point; buyer incurs all transportation costs after the merchandise is loaded on a railroad car or truck at the point of shipment (192).

Freight collect   Terms that require the buyer to pay the freight bill on the arrival of the goods (192).

Freight prepaid   Terms that indicate the seller has paid the freight bill at the time of shipment (192).

Gross margin or **gross profit**   Net sales − Cost of goods sold; identifies the number of dollars available to cover expenses; may be expressed as a percentage rate (198, 199).

Gross selling price   The list price less all trade discounts (184).

Income from operations   Gross margin − Operating (selling and administrative) expenses (199).

Inventory   See Merchandise inventory.

Invoice   A document, prepared by the seller of merchandise and sent to the buyer, that contains the details of a sale, such as the number of units, unit price, total price billed, terms of sale, and manner of shipment; a purchase invoice from the buyer's point of view and a sales invoice from the seller's point of view (183).

Manufacturers   Companies that produce goods from raw materials and normally sell them to wholesalers (181).

Merchandise in transit   Merchandise in the hands of a freight company on the date of a physical inventory (194).

Merchandise inventory   The quantity of goods on hand and available for sale at any given time (188).

Net cost of purchases   Net purchases + Transportation-in (192, 199).

Net income   Net income from operations + Nonoperating revenues − Nonoperating expenses (199).

Net purchases   Purchases − (Purchase discounts + Purchase returns and allowances) (191, 199).

Net sales   Gross sales − (Sales discounts + Sales returns and allowances) (182, 199).

Nonoperating   expenses   Expenses incurred by a business that are not related to the acquisition and sale of the products or services regularly offered for sale (198).

Nonoperating revenues (other revenues)   Revenues not related to the sale of products or services regularly offered for sale by a business (198).

Operating expenses   Those expenses other than cost of goods sold incurred in the normal business functions of a company (198).

Operating revenues   Those revenues generated by the major activities of the business (198).

Passage of title   A legal term used to indicate transfer of legal ownership of goods (192).

Periodic inventory procedure   A method of accounting for merchandise acquired for sale to customers wherein the cost of merchandise sold and the cost of merchandise on hand are determined only at the end of the accounting period by taking a physical inventory (189).

Perpetual inventory procedure   A method of accounting for merchandise acquired for sale to customers wherein the Merchandise Inventory account is debited for each purchase and credited for each sale so that the current balance is shown in the account at all times (188).

Physical inventory   Consists of counting physical units of each type of merchandise on hand (194).

Purchase discount   See Cash discount.

Purchase Discounts account   A contra account to Purchases that reduces the recorded gross invoice cost of the purchase to the price actually paid (191).

Purchase Returns and Allowances account   An account used under periodic inventory procedure to record the cost of merchandise returned to a seller and to record reductions in selling prices granted by a seller because merchandise was not satisfactory to a buyer; viewed as a reduction in the recorded cost of purchases (191).

Purchases account   An account used under periodic inventory procedure to record the cost of goods or merchandise bought for resale during the current accounting period (190).

Retailers   Companies that sell goods to final consumers (181).

Sales allowance   A deduction from the original invoice sales price granted to a customer when the customer keeps the merchandise but is dissatisfied for any of a number of reasons, including inferior quality or damage or deterioration in transit (186).

Sales discount   See Cash discount.

Sales Discounts account   A contra revenue account to Sales and is shown as a deduction from gross sales in the income statement (186).

Sales return   From the seller's point of view, merchandise returned by a buyer for any of a variety of reasons; to the buyer, a purchase return (186).

Sales Returns and Allowances account   A contra revenue account to Sales used to record the selling price of merchandise returned by buyers or reductions in selling prices granted (186).

Selling expenses   Expenses incurred in the selling and marketing efforts (198).

Trade discount   A percentage deduction, or discount, from the specified list price or catalog price of merchandise to arrive at the gross invoice price; granted to particular categories of customers (e.g., retailers and wholesalers). Also see Chain discount (184).

Transportation-In account   An account used under periodic inventory procedure to record freight costs in-

curred in the acquisition of merchandise; a part of cost of goods sold (192).

Unclassified income statement   Shows only major categories for revenues and expenses (196).

Wholesalers   Companies that normally sell goods to retailers for resale (181).

DEMONSTRATION PROBLEM 5-1

The following transactions occurred between Companies A and B during June 1991:

June 10   Company A purchased merchandise from Company B, $40,000; terms 2/10/EOM, n/60, FOB destination.
　　11   Company B paid freight of $600.
　　14   Company A received an allowance of $2,000 from the gross invoice price because of damaged goods.
　　23   Company A returned $4,000 of goods purchased because they were not the quality ordered.
　　30   Company B received payment in full from Company A.

Required:　a.   Journalize the transactions for Company A.
　　　　　b.   Journalize the transactions for Company B.

Solution to demonstration problem 5-1

GENERAL JOURNAL

Date		Account Titles and Explanation	Post. Ref.	Debit	Credit
a.		**Company A**			
1991 June	10	Purchases		4 0 0 0 0	
		Accounts Payable			4 0 0 0 0
		Purchased merchandise from Company B; terms 2/10/EOM, n/60.			
	14	Accounts Payable		2 0 0 0	
		Purchase Returns and Allowances			2 0 0 0
		Received an allowance from Company B for damaged goods.			
	23	Accounts Payable		4 0 0 0	
		Purchase Returns and Allowances			4 0 0 0
		Returned merchandise to Company B because of improper quality.			
	30	Accounts Payable ($40,000 − $2,000 − $4,000)		3 4 0 0 0	
		Purchase Discounts ($34,000 × 0.02)			6 8 0
		Cash ($34,000 − $680)			3 3 3 2 0
		Paid the amount due to Company B.			

Solution to demonstration problem 5–1 *(concluded)*

<table>
<tr><th colspan="7">GENERAL JOURNAL (concluded)</th></tr>
<tr><th colspan="2">Date</th><th>Account Titles and Explanation</th><th>Post. Ref.</th><th>Debit</th><th>Credit</th></tr>
<tr><td>b.</td><td></td><td align="center">Company B</td><td></td><td></td><td></td></tr>
<tr><td>1991
June</td><td>10</td><td>Accounts Receivable</td><td></td><td>4 0 0 0 0</td><td></td></tr>
<tr><td></td><td></td><td>Sales</td><td></td><td></td><td>4 0 0 0 0</td></tr>
<tr><td></td><td></td><td>Sold merchandise to Company A; terms 2/10/EOM, n/60.</td><td></td><td></td><td></td></tr>
<tr><td></td><td></td><td></td><td></td><td></td><td></td></tr>
<tr><td></td><td>11</td><td>Delivery Expense</td><td></td><td>6 0 0</td><td></td></tr>
<tr><td></td><td></td><td>Cash</td><td></td><td></td><td>6 0 0</td></tr>
<tr><td></td><td></td><td>Paid freight on sale of merchandise shipped FOB destination.</td><td></td><td></td><td></td></tr>
<tr><td></td><td></td><td></td><td></td><td></td><td></td></tr>
<tr><td></td><td>14</td><td>Sales Returns and Allowances</td><td></td><td>2 0 0 0</td><td></td></tr>
<tr><td></td><td></td><td>Accounts Receivable</td><td></td><td></td><td>2 0 0 0</td></tr>
<tr><td></td><td></td><td>Granted an allowance to Company A for damaged goods.</td><td></td><td></td><td></td></tr>
<tr><td></td><td></td><td></td><td></td><td></td><td></td></tr>
<tr><td></td><td>23</td><td>Sales Returns and Allowances</td><td></td><td>4 0 0 0</td><td></td></tr>
<tr><td></td><td></td><td>Accounts Receivable</td><td></td><td></td><td>4 0 0 0</td></tr>
<tr><td></td><td></td><td>Merchandise returned from Company A due to improper quality.</td><td></td><td></td><td></td></tr>
<tr><td></td><td></td><td></td><td></td><td></td><td></td></tr>
<tr><td></td><td>30</td><td>Cash ($34,000 − $680)</td><td></td><td>3 3 3 2 0</td><td></td></tr>
<tr><td></td><td></td><td>Sales Discounts ($34,000 × 0.02)</td><td></td><td>6 8 0</td><td></td></tr>
<tr><td></td><td></td><td>Accounts Receivable ($40,000 − $2,000 − $4,000)</td><td></td><td></td><td>3 4 0 0 0</td></tr>
<tr><td></td><td></td><td>Received the amount due from Company A.</td><td></td><td></td><td></td></tr>
</table>

DEMONSTRATION PROBLEM 5–2

CAMP'S MUSIC STORE
Trial Balance
July 31, 1991

	Debits	Credits
Cash	$ 34,780	
Accounts Receivable	4,600	
Merchandise Inventory, August 1, 1990	31,400	
Prepaid Fire Insurance	720	
Prepaid Rent	4,800	
Office Equipment	12,000	
Accumulated Depreciation—Office Equipment		$ 4,500
Accounts Payable		8,000
Clay Camp, Capital		22,000
Clay Camp, Drawing	20,000	
Sales		300,000
Sales Returns and Allowances	1,000	
Purchases	194,000	
Purchase Returns and Allowances		1,400
Transportation-In	5,200	
Advertising Expense	1,000	
Supplies Expense	1,800	
Salaries Expense	23,200	
Utilities Expense	1,400	
	$335,900	$335,900

Clay Camp has prepared the above trial balance for Camp's Music Store. The following information will be used to prepare the work sheet.

1. A 12-month fire insurance policy was purchased for $720 on April 1, 1991, the date on which insurance coverage began.
2. On February 1, 1991, Camp paid $4,800 for the next 12 months' rent. The payment was recorded in the Prepaid Rent account.
3. Depreciation expense on the office equipment is $1,500.
4. Merchandise inventory at July 31, 1991, was $26,400.

Required:
a. Prepare a 10-column work sheet for Camp's Music Store for the fiscal year ended July 31, 1991.
b. Prepare a classified income statement for the fiscal year ended July 31, 1991. Do not separate operating expenses into selling and administrative categories.
c. Prepare a statement of owner's equity for the fiscal year ended July 31, 1991.
d. Prepare a classified balance sheet as of July 31, 1991.
e. Prepare closing entries.

Solution to demonstration problem 5–2

a. See the work sheet on the following page.

CAMP'S MUSIC STORE
Work Sheet
For the Year Ended July 31, 1991

Account Titles	Trial Balance		Adjustments		Adjusted Trial Balance		Income Statement		Balance Sheet	
	Debit	Credit	Debit	Credit	Debit	Credit	Debit	Credit	Debit	Credit
Cash	34,780				34,780				34,780	
Accounts Receivable	4,600				4,600				4,600	
Merchandise Inventory	31,400				31,400		31,400	26,400	26,400	
Prepaid Fire Insurance	720			(1) 240	480				480	
Prepaid Rent	4,800			(2) 2,400	2,400				2,400	
Office Equipment	12,000				12,000				12,000	
Accumulated Depreciation—Office Equipment		4,500		(3) 1,500		6,000				6,000
Accounts Payable		8,000				8,000				8,000
Clay Camp, Capital		22,000				22,000				22,000
Clay Camp, Drawing	20,000				20,000				20,000	
Sales		300,000				300,000		300,000		
Sales Returns and Allowances	1,000				1,000		1,000			
Purchases	194,000				194,000		194,000			
Purchase Returns and Allowances		1,400				1,400		1,400		
Transportation-In	5,200				5,200		5,200			
Advertising Expense	1,000				1,000		1,000			
Supplies Expense	1,800				1,800		1,800			
Salaries Expense	23,200				23,200		23,200			
Utilities Expense	1,400				1,400		1,400			
	335,900	335,900								
Fire Insurance Expense			(1) 240		240		240			
Rent Expense			(2) 2,400		2,400		2,400			
Depreciation Expense—Office Equipment			(3) 1,500		1,500		1,500			
			4,140	4,140	337,400	337,400	263,140	327,800	100,660	36,000
Net income							64,660			64,660
							327,800	327,800	100,660	100,660

Adjustments:
(1) Expiration of prepaid fire insurance ($720 × 4/12).
(2) Expiration of prepaid rent ($4,800 × 6/12).
(3) Depreciation expense on office equipment for the fiscal year ended July 31, 1991.

b.

CAMP'S MUSIC STORE
Income Statement
For the Year Ended July 31, 1991

Operating revenues:		
Gross sales		$300,000
Less: Sales returns and allowances		1,000
Net sales		$299,000
Cost of goods sold:		
Merchandise inventory, August 1, 1990	$ 31,400	
Purchases	$194,000	
Less: Purchase returns and allowances	1,400	
Net purchases	$192,600	
Add: Transportation-in	5,200	
Net cost of purchases	197,800	
Cost of goods available for sale	$229,200	
Less: Merchandise inventory, July 31, 1991	26,400	
Cost of goods sold		202,800
Gross margin		$ 96,200
Operating expenses:		
Advertising expense	$ 1,000	
Supplies expense	1,800	
Salaries expense	23,200	
Utilities expense	1,400	
Fire insurance expense	240	
Rent expense	2,400	
Depreciation expense—office equipment	1,500	
Total operating expenses		31,540
Net income		$ 64,660

c.

CAMP'S MUSIC STORE
Statement of Owner's Equity
For the Year Ended July 31, 1991

Clay Camp, capital, August 1, 1990	$22,000
Add: Net income for the year	64,660
Total	$86,660
Deduct: Owner drawings for the year	20,000
Clay Camp, capital, July 31, 1991	$66,660

d.

CAMP'S MUSIC STORE
Balance Sheet
July 31, 1991

Assets

Current assets:

Cash	$34,780	
Accounts receivable	4,600	
Merchandise inventory	26,400	
Prepaid fire insurance	480	
Prepaid rent	2,400	
Total current assets		$68,660

Property, plant, and equipment:

Office equipment	$12,000	
Less: Accumulated depreciation	6,000	
Total property, plant, and equipment		6,000
Total assets		$74,660

Liabilities and Owner's Equity

Liabilities:

Accounts payable	$ 8,000

Owner's equity:

Clay Camp, capital	66,660
Total liabilities and owner's equity	$74,660

e. Closing entries:

1991
July 31	Merchandise Inventory		26,400	
	Sales		300,000	
	Purchase Returns and Allowances		1,400	
	Income Summary			327,800
	To close accounts with credit balances in the Income Statement column and to set up the ending merchandise inventory.			
31	Income Summary		263,140	
	Merchandise Inventory			31,400
	Sales Returns and Allowances			1,000
	Purchases			194,000
	Transportation-In			5,200
	Advertising Expense			1,000
	Supplies Expense			1,800
	Salaries Expense			23,200
	Utilities Expense			1,400
	Fire Insurance Expense			240
	Rent Expense			2,400
	Depreciation Expense—Office Equipment			1,500
	To close accounts with debit balances in the Income Statement column.			
31	Income Summary		64,660	
	Clay Camp, Capital			64,660
	To close the Income Summary account to the owner's capital account.			

```
31  Clay Camp, Capital . . . . . . . . . . . . . . . . . . . .  20,000
        Clay Camp, Drawing  . . . . . . . . . . . . . . . .           20,000
        To close drawing account.
```

QUESTIONS

1. What account titles are likely to appear in the ledger of a merchandising company that do not appear in the ledger of a service enterprise?

2. What entry is made to record a sale of merchandise on account?

3. Describe trade discounts and chain discounts.

4. Sales discounts and sales returns and allowances are deducted from sales on the income statement to arrive at net sales. Why not deduct these directly from the Sales account by debiting sales each time a sales discount, return, or allowance occurs?

5. What are the two basic procedures for accounting for inventory? How do these two procedures differ?

6. What useful purpose does the Purchases account serve?

7. What do the letters FOB stand for? When terms are *FOB destination,* who incurs the cost of freight?

8. What type of an expense is delivery expense? Where is it reported in the income statement?

9. Periodic inventory procedure is said to afford little control over inventory. Explain why.

10. How does the accountant arrive at the total dollar amount of the inventory after taking a physical inventory?

11. How is cost of goods sold determined under periodic inventory procedure?

12. If the cost of goods available for sale and the cost of the ending inventory are known, what other amount appearing on the income statement can be calculated?

13. What are the major sections in a classified income statement for a merchandising company, and in what order do they appear?

14. What is gross margin? Why might management be interested in the percentage of gross margin to net sales?

EXERCISES

E-1
Apply rules of debit and credit for merchandise-related accounts

In the following table, indicate how each account shown is increased and decreased (debit or credit), and indicate the normal balance (debit or credit).

Title of Account	Increased by (debit or credit)	Decreased by (debit or credit)	Normal Balance (debit or credit)
Merchandise Inventory			
Sales			
Sales Returns and Allowances			
Sales Discounts			
Accounts Receivable			
Purchases			
Purchase Returns and Allowances			
Purchase Discounts			
Accounts Payable			
Transportation-In			

E-2
Prepare entries for merchandise purchase/sale, return, and allowance on both buyer's and seller's books

a. Dixon Company purchased $35,000 of merchandise from Smith Company on account. Before paying its account, Dixon Company returned damaged merchandise with an invoice price of $7,300. Assuming use of periodic inventory procedure, prepare entries on both companies' books to record both the purchase/sale and the return.

b. Show how any of the required entries would change assuming that Smith Company granted an allowance of $2,100 on the damaged goods instead of giving permission to return the merchandise.

E-3
Determine end of discount period and prepare entry to record payment

What is the last payment date on which the cash discount can be taken on goods sold on March 5 for $64,000; terms 3/10/EOM, n/60? Assume that the bill is paid on this date and prepare the correct entry on both the buyer's and seller's books to record the payment.

E-4
Calculate effect of trade and cash discounts on payment

You have purchased merchandise with a list price of $24,000. Because you are a wholesaler, you are granted trade discounts of 30%, 20%, and 10%. The cash discount terms are 2/EOM, n/60. How much will you remit if you pay the invoice by the end of the month of purchase? How much will you remit if you do not pay the invoice until the following month?

E-5
Calculate gross invoice price and final payment

Wilson Company sold merchandise with a list price of $10,000 on July 1, 1991. For each of the independent assumptions below, calculate (1) the gross invoice price that would be used to record the sale and (2) the amount that the buyer would have to pay when paying the invoice.

	Trade Discount Granted	Credit Terms	Date Paid
a.	30%, 20%	2/10, n/30	July 10
b.	40%, 10%	2/EOM, n/60	August 10
c.	30%, 10%, 5%	3/10/EOM, n/60	August 10
d.	40%	1/10, n/30	July 12

E-6
Determine cash discount available and amount of cash paid

Grant Company purchased goods at a gross invoice price of $1,000 on August 1, 1991. Discount terms of 2/10, n/30 were available. For each of the following independent situations, determine (1) the cash discount available on the final payment and (2) the amount of cash paid if payment is made within the discount period.

	Transportation Terms	Freight Paid (by)	Purchase Allowance Granted
a.	FOB shipping point	$100 (buyer)	$200
b.	FOB destination	50 (seller)	100
c.	FOB shipping point	75 (seller)	300
d.	FOB destination	80 (buyer)	50

E-7
Determine cost of goods sold

Krueger Company uses periodic inventory procedure. Determine the cost of goods sold for the company assuming purchases during the period were $24,000, transportation-in was $180, purchase returns and allowances were $600, beginning inventory was $15,000, purchase discounts were $1,200, and ending inventory was $7,800.

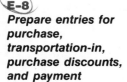
Prepare entries for purchase, transportation-in, purchase discounts, and payment

Bosco Company purchased goods for $17,500 on June 14 under the following terms: 3/10, n/30; FOB shipping point, freight collect. The bill for the freight amounted to $500.

a.   Assume that the invoice was paid within the discount period, and prepare all entries required on Bosco Company's books.

b.   Assume that the invoice was paid on July 11. Prepare the entry to record the payment made on that date.

E-9
Prepare partial work sheet using merchandise-related accounts

Given the balances shown in the partial trial balance, indicate how the balances would be treated in the work sheet. The ending inventory is $64. (The amounts are unusually small for ease in rewriting the numbers.)

Account Titles	Trial Balance		Adjustments		Adjusted Trial Balance		Income Statement		Balance Sheet	
	Debit	Credit	Debit	Credit	Debit	Credit	Debit	Credit	Debit	Credit
Merchandise Inventory	80									
Sales		560								
Sales Discounts	12									
Sales Returns and Allowances	32									
Purchases	400									
Purchase Discounts		8								
Purchase Returns and Allowances		16								
Transportation-In	24									

E-10
Prepare and post closing entries using T-accounts

Using the data in Exercise E-9:

a.   Prepare closing entries for the accounts shown above. Do not close the Income Summary account.

b.   Show in T-account format how the accounts would appear after this portion of the closing process has been completed.

E-11
Supply missing terms in formulas showing income statement relationships

In each of the following equations supply the missing term(s):

a.   Net sales = Gross sales − (_____ _____ + Sales returns and allowances).

b.   Cost of goods sold = Beginning inventory + Net cost of purchases − _____ _____.

c.   Gross margin = _____ _____ − Cost of goods sold.

d.   Income from operations = _____ _____ − Operating expenses.

e.   Net income = Income from operations + _____ _____ − _____ _____.

E-12
Supply missing amounts in the income statement

In each case below use the information provided to calculate the missing information.

	Case 1	Case 2	Case 3
Gross sales	$400,000	$?	$?
Sales discounts	?	16,000	12,000
Sales returns and allowances	12,000	28,000	20,000
Net sales	380,000	756,000	?
Merchandise inventory, January 1	160,000	?	240,000
Purchases	240,000	480,000	?
Purchase discounts	4,800	8,400	8,000
Purchase returns and allowances	15,200	19,600	20,000
Net purchases	220,000	?	420,000
Transportation-in	16,000	24,000	20,000
Net cost of purchases	236,000	476,000	?
Cost of goods available for sale	?	676,000	680,000
Merchandise inventory, December 31 . . .	?	240,000	280,000
Cost of goods sold	200,000	?	400,000
Gross margin	?	320,000	200,000

PROBLEMS, SERIES A

P5-1-A
Journalize merchandise transactions for two different companies

a. Ling Sporting Goods Company engaged in the following transactions in April 1991:

Apr. 1   Sold merchandise on account for $96,000; terms 2/10, n/30, FOB destination.
     5   $14,400 of the goods sold on account on April 1 were returned for full credit. Payment for these goods had not yet been received.
     8   A sales allowance of $1,920 was granted on the merchandise sold on April 1 because the merchandise was damaged in shipment.
    10   Payment was received for the net amount due from the sale of April 1.

b. Bently Stereo Company engaged in the following transactions in July 1991:

July 2   Purchased stereo merchandise on account at a cost of $14,400; terms 2/10, n/30, FOB destination.
    15   Sold merchandise for $21,600; terms 2/10, n/30, FOB destination.
    16   Paid freight costs on the merchandise sold, $720.
    20   Bently Stereo Company was granted an allowance of $960 on the purchase of July 2 because of damaged merchandise.
    31   Paid the amount due on the purchase of July 2.

Required: Prepare journal entries to record the transactions.

P5-2-A
Journalize merchandise transactions on both buyer's and seller's books

Taylor Musical Instrument Company and Reynolds Company engaged in the following transactions with each other during July 1991:

July 2   Taylor Musical Instrument Company purchased merchandise on account with a list price of $16,000 from Reynolds Company. The terms were 3/EOM, n/60, FOB shipping point, freight collect. Trade discounts of 15%, 10%, and 5% were granted by Reynolds Company.
    5   The buyer paid the freight bill on the purchase of July 2, $368.
    6   The buyer returned damaged merchandise with an invoice price of $930 to the seller and received full credit.

On the last day of the discount period, the buyer paid the seller for the merchandise.

Required: Prepare all the necessary journal entries for the buyer and the seller.

P5–3–A
Journalize merchandise transactions on both buyer's and seller's books

Carcello Ski Shop and Gentry Company entered into the following transactions with each other during March 1991:

Mar. 1 Carcello Ski Shop purchased merchandise on account from Gentry Company, at a list price of $24,000. Trade discounts of 30%, 25%, and 5% were granted. Terms were 2/EOM, n/60, FOB shipping point.
    4 The buyer paid the freight of $496.
  25 The seller granted the buyer an allowance of $2,400 against the amount due because of damaged merchandise.
  31 The buyer paid the amount due.

Required: Journalize all the entries on the books of both the buyer and seller.

P5–4–A
Prepare and post journal entries, and prepare trial balance and classified income statement

The data for June 1991 given below are for Pate Company's first month of operations:

June 1 Pate Company was organized, and the owner, Sam Pate, invested $315,000 cash, $105,000 of merchandise inventory, and a $90,000 plot of land.
    4 Merchandise was purchased for cash, $135,000; FOB shipping point.
    9 Cash of $3,150 was paid to a trucking company for delivery of the merchandise purchased June 4.
  13 The company sold merchandise on account, $90,000; terms 2/10, n/30.
  15 The company sold merchandise on account, $72,000; terms 2/10, n/30.
  16 Of the merchandise sold May 13, $9,900 was returned for credit.
  20 Salaries for services received were paid as follows: to office employees, $9,900; to salespersons, $26,100.
  22 The company collected the amount of $80,100 due on the accounts receivable arising from the sale of June 13.
  24 The company purchased merchandise on account at a cost of $108,000; terms 2/10, n/30, FOB shipping point.
  26 The company returned $18,000 of the merchandise purchased June 24 to the vendor for credit.
  27 A trucking company was paid $2,250 for delivery to Pate Company of the goods purchased June 24.
  29 The company sold merchandise on account, $120,000; terms 2/10, n/30.
  30 Sold merchandise for cash, $54,000.
  30 Payment was received for the sale of June 15.
  30 Paid store rent for June, $13,500.
  30 Paid the amount due on the purchase of June 24.

Additional data:

The inventory on hand at the close of business June 30 was $210,000 at cost.

Required:
a. Prepare journal entries for the transactions.
b. Post the journal entries to the proper ledger accounts.
c. Prepare a trial balance as of June 30, 1991.
d. Prepare a classified income statement for the month ended June 30, 1991.

P5–5–A

Prepare work sheet, classified income statement, statement of owner's equity, classified balance sheet, and closing entries

The following data are for Essex Lumber Company:

ESSEX LUMBER COMPANY
Trial Balance
December 31, 1991

	Debits	Credits
Cash	$ 42,384	
Accounts Receivable	95,712	
Merchandise Inventory	171,120	
Sales Supplies on Hand	3,216	
Prepaid Fire Insurance	2,880	
Prepaid Rent	34,560	
Store Equipment	52,800	
Accumulated Depreciation—Store Equipment		$ 10,560
Accounts Payable		61,680
J. Essex, Capital		251,784
Sales		673,416
Sales Returns and Allowances	3,096	
Purchases	300,504	
Purchase Returns and Allowances		2,424
Transportation-In	4,704	
Sales Salaries Expense	83,040	
Advertising Expense	46,800	
General Office Expense	5,928	
Office Salaries Expense	48,480	
Officers' Salaries Expense	96,000	
Legal and Auditing Expense	6,000	
Telephone Expense	2,880	
Interest Revenue		600
Interest Expense	360	
	$1,000,464	$1,000,464

Additional data as of December 31, 1991:

1. Prepaid fire insurance expired, $2,040.
2. Sales supplies consumed, $2,196.
3. Prepaid rent expired during the year, $30,360.
4. Depreciation expense on store equipment, $5,280.
5. Accrued sales salaries, $2,400.
6. Accrued office salaries, $1,800.
7. Merchandise inventory on hand, $210,000.

Required: Prepare the following:

a. A work sheet for the year ended December 31, 1991.
b. A classified income statement. The only selling expenses are sales salaries, advertising, sales supplies, and depreciation—store equipment.
c. A statement of owner's equity.
d. A classified balance sheet.
e. The December 31, 1991, closing entries.

P5-6-A
Prepare and post journal entries, prepare work sheet, classified income statement, classified balance sheet, and closing entries

Texas Western Wear Company is a wholesaler of western wear clothing. The company sells its merchandise to retailers. The company entered into the following transactions in May 1991:

May 1   Texas Western Wear Company was organized as a single proprietorship. Mark Hall invested the following assets in the business: $308,000 cash, $112,000 merchandise, and $70,000 land.

1   Paid rent on administrative offices for May, $16,800.

5   The company purchased merchandise from Andco Company on account, $126,000; terms 2/10, n/30. Freight terms were FOB shipping point.

8   Cash of $5,600 was paid to a trucking company for delivery of the merchandise purchased May 5.

14   The company sold merchandise on account, $210,000; terms 2/10, n/30.

15   Paid Andco Company the amount due on the purchase of May 5.

16   Of the merchandise sold May 14, $9,240 was returned for credit.

19   Salaries for services received were paid for May as follows: office employees, $11,200; salespersons, $22,400.

24   The company collected the amount due on $84,000 of the accounts receivable arising from the sale of May 14.

25   The company purchased merchandise on account from Hill Company, $100,800; terms 2/10, n/30. Freight terms were FOB shipping point.

27   Of the merchandise purchased May 25, $16,800 was returned to the vendor.

28   A trucking company was paid $1,400 for delivery to Texas Western Wear Company of the goods purchased May 25.

29   The company sold merchandise on open account, $10,080; terms 2/10, n/30.

30   Cash sales were $49,392.

30   Cash of $67,200 was received from the sale of May 14.

31   Paid Hill Company for the merchandise purchased on May 25, taking into consideration the merchandise returned on May 27.

Additional data:

The inventory on hand at the close of business on May 31 is $199,360.

Required: From the data given for Texas Western Wear Company:

a.   Prepare journal entries for the transactions.
b.   Post the journal entries to the proper ledger accounts.
c.   Prepare a work sheet. (There were no adjusting journal entries.)
d.   Prepare a classified income statement for the month ended May 31, 1991.
e.   Prepare a classified balance sheet as of May 31, 1991.
f.   Prepare and post the necessary closing entries.

PROBLEMS, SERIES B

P5-1-B
Journalize merchandise transactions for two different companies

a.   Ward Carpet Company engaged in the following transactions in August 1991:

Aug. 2   Sold merchandise on account for $60,000; terms 2/10, n/30, FOB destination.

18   Received payment for the sale of August 2.

20   A total of $2,000 of the merchandise sold on August 2 was returned, and a full refund was made because it was the wrong merchandise.

28   An allowance of $3,200 was granted on the sale of August 2 because some merchandise was found to be damaged. $3,200 cash was returned to the customer.

b.   Albers Furniture Company engaged in the following transactions in August 1991:

Aug.   4   Purchased merchandise on account at a cost of $28,000; terms 2/10, n/30, FOB shipping point.
       6   Paid freight of $400 on the purchase of August 4.
      10   Sold goods for $20,000; terms 2/10, n/30.
      12   Returned $4,800 of the merchandise purchased on August 4.
      14   Paid the amount due on the purchase of August 4.

Required: Prepare journal entries for the transactions.

P5-2-B
Journalize merchandise transactions on both buyer's and seller's books

Jordan Auto Parts Company and Alcott Company engaged in the following transactions with each other during August 1991:

Aug. 15   Jordan Auto Parts Company purchased merchandise on account with a list price of $120,000 from Alcott Company. Trade discounts of 20% and 10% were allowed. Terms were 2/10, n/30, FOB destination, freight prepaid.
      16   The seller paid the freight charges, $1,500.
      17   The buyer requested an allowance of $2,820 against the amount due because the goods were damaged in transit.
      20   The seller granted the allowance requested on August 17.

The buyer paid the amount due on the last day of the discount period.

Required: Record all of the entries required on the books of both the buyer and the seller.

P5-3-B
Journalize merchandise transactions on both buyer's and seller's books

Kean Hardware Store and Stacy Company engaged in the following transactions with each other during 1991:

Aug.   1   Kean Hardware Store purchased merchandise on account with a list price of $9,000 from Stacy Company. Trade discounts of 30% and 10% were allowed. Terms were 2/10/EOM, n/60, FOB destination, freight prepaid.
       1   The seller paid the freight, $60.
       8   The buyer returned merchandise with an invoice price of $470 because it was the wrong type of merchandise.
Sept. 9   The buyer paid the balance due.

Required: Journalize all the entries on the books of both the buyer and seller.

P5-4-B
Prepare and post journal entries, and prepare trial balance and classified income statement

Miller Company engaged in the following transactions in June 1991, the company's first month of operations:

June   1   The owner, Paul Miller, invested $80,000 cash and $30,000 of merchandise inventory in the business.
       3   Merchandise was purchased on account, $40,000; terms 2/10, n/30, FOB shipping point.
       4   Paid freight on the June 3 purchase, $1,100.
       7   Merchandise was purchased on account, $20,000; terms 2/10, n/30, FOB destination.
      10   Sold merchandise on account, $48,000; terms 2/10, n/30, FOB shipping point.
      11   Returned $6,000 of the merchandise purchased on June 3.
      12   Paid the amount due on the purchase of June 3.
      13   Sold merchandise on account, $50,000; terms 2/10, n/30, FOB destination.
      14   Paid freight on sale of June 13, $3,000.
      20   Paid the amount due on the purchase of June 7.
      21   $10,000 of the goods sold on June 13 were returned for credit.
      22   Received the amount due on sale of June 13.
      25   Received the amount due on sale of June 10.
      29   Paid rent for the administration building for June, $4,000.
      30   Paid sales salaries of $12,000 for June.
      30   Purchased merchandise on account, $10,000; terms 2/10, n/30, FOB shipping point.

Additional data:

The inventory on hand on June 30 was $60,000.

Required:
a. Prepare journal entries for the transactions.
b. Post the journal entries to the proper ledger accounts.
c. Prepare a trial balance as of June 30, 1991.
d. Prepare a classified income statement for the month ended June 30, 1991.

P5-5-B
Prepare work sheet, classified income statement, statement of owner's equity, classified balance sheet, and closing entries

The following data are for Read Lamp Company:

READ LAMP COMPANY
Trial Balance
December 31, 1991

	Debits	Credits
Cash	$ 114,400	
Accounts Receivable	96,600	
Prepaid Insurance	5,800	
Merchandise Inventory, January 1, 1991	83,200	
Land	120,000	
Store Building	220,000	
Accumulated Depreciation—Store Building		$ 66,000
Store fixtures	111,200	
Accumulated Depreciation—Store Fixtures		22,240
Accounts Payable		75,800
R. Read, Capital		440,360
Sales		1,103,000
Sales Discounts	7,400	
Sales Returns and Allowances	4,000	
Purchases	625,800	
Purchase Discounts		5,200
Purchase Returns and Allowances		2,800
Transportation-In	14,600	
Sales Salaries Expense	128,000	
Advertising Expense	24,000	
Delivery Expense	9,200	
Office Salaries Expense	148,000	
Interest Revenue		800
Interest Expense	4,000	
	$1,716,200	$1,716,200

Additional data:

1. Depreciation expense on the store building is $4,400.
2. Depreciation expense on the store fixtures is $11,120.
3. Accrued sales salaries are $2,800.
4. Insurance expired in 1991 is $5,000.
5. Cost of merchandise inventory on hand December 31, 1991, is $111,000.

Required: Prepare the following:

a. A work sheet for the year ended December 31, 1991.
b. A classified income statement. The only administrative expenses are office salaries and insurance.
c. A statement of owner's equity.
d. A classified balance sheet.
e. The required closing entries.

P5-6-B
Prepare and post journal entries; prepare work sheet, classified income statement, and closing entries

Rizzo Cabinet Company was organized May 1, 1991, and engaged in the following transactions:

May	1	Ron Rizzo invested $600,000 in his new business.
	1	Purchased merchandise on account from Robertson Company, $31,200; terms n/60, FOB shipping point.
	3	Sold merchandise for cash, $19,200.
	6	Paid transportation charges on May 1 purchase, $960 cash.
	7	Returned $2,400 of merchandise to Robertson Company due to improper size.
	10	Requested and received an allowance of $1,200 from Robertson Company for improper quality of certain items.
	14	Sold merchandise on account to Lewis Company, $12,000; terms 2/20, n/30.
	16	Issued cash refund for return of merchandise relating to sale made on May 3, $120.
	18	Purchased merchandise on account from White Company invoiced at $19,200; terms 2/15, n/30, FOB shipping point.
	18	Received a bill for freight charges of $600 from Ace Trucking Company on the purchase from White Company.
	19	Lewis Company returned $240 of merchandise purchased on May 14.
	24	Returned $1,920 of defective merchandise to White Company. Received full credit.
	28	Lewis Company remitted balance due on sale of May 14.
	31	Paid White Company for the purchase of May 18 after adjusting for transaction of May 24.
	31	Paid miscellaneous selling expenses of $4,800.
	31	Paid miscellaneous administrative expenses of $7,200.

Additional data:

The May 31st inventory is $38,400.

Required: From the data for Rizzo Cabinet Company:

a. Journalize the transactions. Round all amounts to the nearest dollar.
b. Post the entries to the proper ledger accounts.
c. Prepare a work sheet as of May 31, 1991. (There were no adjusting journal entries.)
d. Prepare a classified income statement as of May 31, 1991.
e. Prepare and post the required closing entries.

BUSINESS DECISION PROBLEM

Prepare income statement and balance sheet for merchandising company

Tom Baker taught physical education classes at Brooke High School for 20 years. In 1990, Tom's uncle died and left Tom $300,000. Tom quit his teaching job in December 1990 and opened a hardware store in January 1991. On January 2, 1991, Tom deposited $180,000 in a checking account opened in the store's name, Baker's Hardware Store. During the first week of January, Tom rented a building and paid the first year's rent of $14,400 in advance. Also during that week, he purchased the following assets for cash:

Delivery truck	$30,000
Store equipment	15,000
Office equipment	9,000

During the remainder of the first six months of 1991, Tom received cash of $210,000 from customers and disbursed cash of $156,000 for merchandise purchases and $45,000 for operating expenses.

Tom never took an accounting course, but he was familiar with the term **net income.** He decided to compute his net income for the first six months of 1991 and prepared the following schedule:

Cash receipts		$210,000
Cash disbursements:		
Delivery truck . . . . $ 30,000		
Store equipment 15,000		
Office equipment 9,000		
Prepaid rent 14,400		
Merchandise purchases 156,000		
Operating expenses 45,000	269,400	
Net loss	$ 59,400	

Assume that the depreciation amounts for the six-month period are as follows:

Delivery truck	$3,000
Store equipment	750
Office equipment	525

Also assume that you obtained the following information:

1. Baker owes $24,000 to creditors for merchandise purchases.
2. Customers owe Baker $30,000 on June 30, 1991, for goods purchased.
3. Merchandise costing $48,000 is on hand at the end of the six months.

Required: a. Do you agree with Tom Baker's statement that his hardware store suffered a net loss of $59,400 for the six months ended June 30, 1991? If not, show how you would determine the net income (or net loss).

b. Is it possible to prepare a balance sheet on June 30, 1991, or does Mr. Baker have to wait until December 31, 1991, to prepare a balance sheet? If a balance sheet can be prepared on June 30, 1991, prepare one.

6 Accounting Systems and Special Journals

LEARNING OBJECTIVES

After studying this chapter, you should be able to:

1. Describe the relationship between subsidiary accounts in subsidiary ledgers and control accounts in the general ledger.

2. Describe the relationship between special journals and the general journal.

3. Record transactions in special journals.

4. Post special journals.

5. Describe computer applications in accounting (Appendix 6-A).

6. Describe basic computer concepts (Appendix 6-B).

7. Define and use correctly the new terms in the glossary.

In Chapters 1 through 5, you learned how to produce financial statements by processing the raw data of business transactions through the steps of the accounting cycle. The process of analyzing, recording, classifying, summarizing, and reporting business transactions is the same for all businesses. However, the speed and efficiency of the processing depends on which accounting system is used.

For example, assume you decide to drive home after your accounting class. You can either go home the "long way" by using the side roads or "make time" by using the superhighway. Whichever route you take, your destination is going to be the same—home. The process of going home is the same whether you take the side roads or the superhighway—you are driving your car. However, the system you use to get to your destination— the side roads or the superhighway—is different. You probably decide to take the superhighway because it is faster. The same is true of processing accounting information. The accounting process also can be accomplished faster and more efficiently by using one particular accounting system rather than any other accounting system. This chapter identifies various accounting systems and describes their features.

So far in this text you have used the manual accounting system with one journal and one ledger. Now you will be introduced to two additions to that manual system—subsidiary ledgers and special journals. Then you will proceed to a discussion of other systems used in accounting, ending with the computerized accounting system. This chapter makes it possible for you to process business transactions in a more efficient and time-saving manner.

■ THE PROCESSING OF DATA—MANUAL SYSTEM

The masses of raw data generated by even a small business are not useful until processed. Businesses must routinely process these data in an orderly and efficient manner to accomplish the following:

1. Results of operations (income statement) and financial position (balance sheet) of the firm are determined and reported on a timely basis.
2. Bills are paid when due.
3. Proper quantities and items of inventory are sent to customers.
4. Other aspects of business, such as sending invoices to customers and ordering merchandise, are conducted in an orderly and purposeful manner.
5. Reports required by the government or regulatory agencies are prepared efficiently.

Businesses accomplish this orderly and efficient processing of accounting data by using the accounting system that best fits their needs. The basic accounting system is the manual system with one journal and one ledger. This basic system is generally used by very small businesses. Given an unlimited amount of time, all business transactions can be processed through this manual system. However, as a business grows, its number of business transactions also grows, and the company looks for ways to speed up the accounting process by streamlining its accounting system.

An accounting system can be defined as a set of records (journals, ledgers, work sheets, trial balances, and reports) plus the procedures and equipment regularly used to process business transactions. To be effective, accounting systems should:

1. Provide for the efficient processing of data at the least possible cost. (The cost of the system should be less than the value of the benefits received.)
2. Ensure a high degree of accuracy.
3. Provide for internal control to prevent theft or fraud.
4. Provide for the growth of a business.

In this chapter, you will learn first how a business begins to enlarge its accounting system by using control accounts in the general ledger and adding subsidiary ledgers that are periodically totaled to these control accounts. Then you will learn about other journals (called special journals) that can be used along with the general journal.

■ CONTROL ACCOUNTS AND SUBSIDIARY LEDGERS

Objective 1:
Describe the relationship between subsidiary accounts in subsidiary ledgers and control accounts in the general ledger.

To efficiently process information, a business must adapt its accounting system to the type and quantity of information it needs. When a business has only a few customers and suppliers, a separate account can be set up for each customer and supplier in the general ledger. However, when a business has many customers and suppliers, a control account for accounts receivable and a control account for accounts payable are established in the general ledger. Also, subsidiary ledgers for receivables and payables are added to the accounting system to show the balances for individual customers and suppliers.

A **control account** is an account in the general ledger that shows the total balance of all the subsidiary accounts related to it. An example of a control account is the general ledger **Accounts Receivable** control account, which summarizes all of the amounts owed to the company. Since this is a summary account, it would be impossible to send out customer statements based on the summary data provided in this account.

Subsidiary ledger accounts show the details supporting the related general ledger control account balance. The subsidiary accounts for **receivables** may be used to send out customer statements. The subsidiary accounts for **payables** may be used to determine the amount payable to each supplier. The accounts are normally alphabetized by the name of the customer or supplier. The sum of the balances in the subsidiary accounts in a subsidiary ledger should agree with the balance in the related general ledger control account when the financial statements are prepared.

A **subsidiary ledger**, then, is a group of related accounts showing the details of the balance of a general ledger control account. Subsidiary ledgers are separated from the general ledger to relieve the general ledger of a mass of detail and thereby shorten the general ledger trial balance. Also, having separate ledgers promotes a division of labor.

In T-account form, the relationship between a control account and subsidiary accounts is as follows:

Control account in the general ledger	Subsidiary accounts in the accounts receivable subsidiary ledger	
Accounts Receivable	**Customer A**	**Customer C**
1991 May 31 Bal. 1,000	1991 May 31 Bal. 100	1991 May 31 Bal. 400
	Customer B	**Customer D**
	1991 May 31 Bal. 200	1991 May 31 Bal. 300

Note that the sum of all balances in the subsidiary accounts ($100 + $200 + $400 + $300) on May 31, 1991, is equal to the balance on that same date in the control account ($1,000).

When a transaction occurs that affects a control account, some account(s) in the subsidiary ledger will also be affected. Since a transaction is entered in the journal before it is entered in the ledger accounts, the journal entry must indicate which of the subsidiary ledger accounts is affected. Posting will be made to both the control account (indicated by the account number) and the subsidiary ledger account (indicated by the √). For example, if a $400 sale is made on July 10 to Debbi Kahan on account, the journal entry would be:

July 10	Accounts Receivable—D. Kahan	111/√	400	
	Sales	301		400
	To record sale of merchandise on account.			

The amount of the sale ($400) would be posted as a debit to both the Accounts Receivable control account (111) in the general ledger and D. Kahan's account in the subsidiary ledger (indicated by the √) and as a credit to the Sales account (301) in the general ledger.

Detailed subsidiary ledgers may exist for other accounts in the general ledger in addition to the Accounts Receivable account. Some examples of accounts that frequently have detailed subsidiary ledgers are:

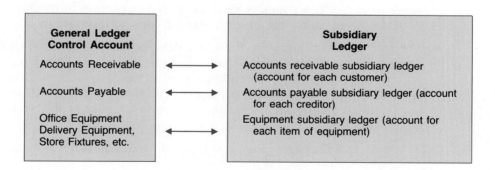

The number of subsidiary ledgers maintained by a company varies according to the company's information requirements. Control accounts and subsidiary ledgers are generally set up whenever a company has many transactions in a given account and detailed information is needed about these transactions on a continuing basis. This chapter focuses on the use of accounts receivable subsidiary ledgers and accounts payable subsidiary ledgers.

In the next section, you will learn about special journals. You should remember that control accounts and subsidiary ledgers may be used even if special journals are not used. Both subsidiary ledgers and special journals are likely to be used when a company has numerous transactions that are similar.

■ SPECIAL JOURNALS

Objective 2:
Describe the rela-
tionship between
special journals and
the general journal.

Until now, only one book of original entry, the general journal, has been used to record transactions. As the transactions of a company increase, the first step in altering the manual accounting system is usually to use special journals along with the original general journal. Each **special journal** records one particular type of transaction, such as sales on account, cash receipts, purchases on account, or cash disbursements.

The following advantages are obtained from the use of special journals:

1. **Time is saved in journalizing.** Only one line is used for each transaction; usually a full description is not necessary. The amount of writing is reduced because it is not necessary to repeat the account titles printed at the top of the special column or columns.
2. **Time is saved in posting.** Many amounts are posted as column totals rather than individually.
3. **Detail is eliminated from the general ledger.** Column totals are posted to the general ledger, and the detail is left in the special journals.
4. **Division of labor is promoted.** Several persons can work simultaneously on the accounting records. This specialization and division of labor pinpoints responsibility and allows for more rapid location of errors.
5. **Management analysis is aided.** The journals themselves can be useful to management in analyzing classes of transactions, such as credit sales, because all similar transactions are in one place.

Special journals, then, are designed to systematize the original recording of major recurring types of transactions. The number and format of the special journals actually used in a company depend primarily on the nature of the company's business transactions. The special journals illustrated in this chapter are the sales, cash receipts, purchases, and cash disbursements journals:

- The **sales journal** is used to record all sales of merchandise on account (on credit).
- The **cash receipts journal** is used to record all inflows of cash into the business.
- The **purchases journal** is used to record all purchases of merchandise on account (on credit). Merchandise refers to items of inventory that are available for sale to customers.
- The **cash disbursements journal** is used to record all payments (or outflows) of cash by the business.

The **general journal** is not eliminated by the use of special journals but is used to record all transactions that cannot be entered in one of the special journals. All five of these journals are books of original entry. If a transaction is recorded in any one of the journals, that transaction will be posted and become part of the accounting records. Therefore, a transaction that is recorded in a special journal should **not** be recorded in the general journal because this would record the transaction twice.

Since the journals are posted to ledger accounts, the Posting Reference column in the ledger should indicate the source of the posting. The following abbreviations are used for the five journals:

Journal	Transaction	Abbreviation
Special journals Sales journal	Merchandise sold on account	S
Cash receipts journal	Cash receipts from all sources	CR
Purchases journal	Merchandise purchased on account	P
Cash disbursements journal . .	Cash payments for all purposes	CD
General journal	Any transactions that are not included in the special journals are recorded in the general journal	G

You will learn how to use each of the four special journals in the sections that follow. As you study these journals, you will realize how effective they are in accelerating the recording process.

Sales Journal

Objective 3: Record transactions in special journals.

Sales are normally made either for cash or on credit. The sales journal is used only for sales on account; cash sales would be recorded in the cash receipts journal. The simplest form of sales journal has only one money column (labeled Accounts Receivable Dr. and Sales Cr.) because every sale on account is journalized by this same debit and credit. The headings in this form of sales journal might appear as follows:

Date	Customer	Invoice No.	Accounts Receivable Dr. Sales Cr.	
			Amount	√

Variations in the sales journal will depend on the information needs of the business. For example, a separate Sales Cr. column could be used for each department in a company. If this is done, a separate column will be needed for Accounts Receivable Dr. because the debit will always be to Accounts Receivable regardless of which department sold the goods. The headings in a sales journal with separate columns for each department might appear as follows:

Accounts Receivable Dr.		Date	Customer	Invoice No.	Sales Cr.		
Amount	√				Dept. A	Dept. B	Dept. C

In either format, the customer's name is necessary to know which subsidiary ledger account is affected by the sales transaction. The invoice number simply provides documentation that a sale actually occurred. The

Illustration 6.1   *Sales Journal*

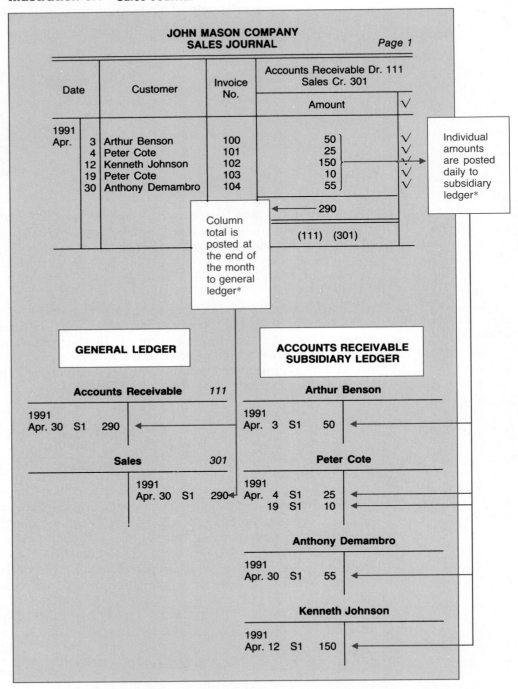

* Subsidiary ledger accounts are posted daily to keep up-to-date balances in the subsidiary ledger. The general ledger accounts will usually be posted at end-of-month or end-of-page (whichever comes first) because the balances in the control accounts are not really necessary until the end of the period for financial statement purposes.

column with the check mark is similar to a Posting Reference column; a check mark is placed in that column when the amount of the sale is posted to the customer's subsidiary ledger account. No Posting Reference column is needed because the column heading indicates to which account and in what manner (debit or credit) the column total will be posted.

Illustration 6.1 shows a sales journal with only one money column for John Mason Company, a retail clothing store. In Illustration 6.1, five credit sales transactions occurred in April.

Objective 4:
Post special journals.

Posting the Sales Journal. Individual amounts in the money column are posted daily to each individual customer's account in the subsidiary ledger. Posting is done daily to show the amount currently due from the customer. As each individual amount is posted, a check mark, $\checkmark$, is placed in the column headed $\checkmark$ opposite the amount to show that it has been posted. At the end of the month, the total of the money column, $290, is posted in the general ledger as a debit to the Accounts Receivable control account and as a credit to the Sales account. The posting reference of S1 (sales journal, page 1) is entered in the Accounts Receivable control account and the Sales account. The account numbers, 111 for Accounts Receivable and 301 for Sales, are written in the sales journal under the total of the money column to show that $290 was posted to those accounts.

When the posting of accounts receivable has been completed, the Accounts Receivable control account in the general ledger will show a balance of $290. This $290 is equal to the sum of the balances in the Accounts Receivable subsidiary ledger accounts, assuming no previous balances were in the control account or the subsidiary accounts. Since the composition of subsidiary ledger accounts is constantly changing, these accounts are usually not numbered but are kept in alphabetical order.

Some companies do not use a formal sales journal for sales on account. Instead, the amount of each sales invoice is entered directly in the subsidiary ledger account of the customer. The sales invoices for a month are arranged in numerical order and fastened together. At the end of the month, all of the sales invoices for the month are totaled, and an entry is made debiting the Accounts Receivable control account and crediting Sales for the total amount. This procedure eliminates the need for separate recording of each credit sale in a sales journal.

Cash Receipts Journal

The cash receipts journal is used for all transactions involving the receipt of cash by the business. The most frequent types of cash receipts transactions are cash sales and collections on accounts receivable. Therefore, separate credit columns appear for those items in the cash receipts journal shown in Illustration 6.2. Notice that three of the transactions recorded in the cash receipts journal were collections of accounts receivables that were recorded in the sales journal.

Many other types of transactions may result in the receipt of cash by the business, but these transactions involve various accounts as the credits. Since the **other accounts** (miscellaneous accounts) do not occur with enough

Illustration 6.2 Cash Receipts Journal

JOHN MASON COMPANY
CASH RECEIPTS JOURNAL
Page 5

101 Cash Dr.	302 Sales Discounts Dr.	Date	Description	301 Sales Cr.	111 Accounts Receivable Cr. — Amount	Other Accounts Cr. — Account Title	Other Accounts Cr. — Acct. No.	Other Accounts Cr. — Amount
		1991 Apr.						
5,000		1	Cash sales	5,000				
49	1	6	Arthur Benson—Invoice No. 100		50			
8,000		7	Cash sales	8,000				
6,000		10	Sold land at cost to Wells Corporation			Land	138	6,000
7,000		14	Cash sales	7,000				
25		19	Peter Cote—Invoice No. 101		25			
147	3	20	Kenneth Johnson—Invoice No. 102		150			
9,000		25	Cash sales	9,000				
200		26	Cash received from sale of scrap			Miscellaneous Revenue	303	200
35,421	4			29,000	225			6,200
(101)	(302)			(301)	(111)			(X)

Individual amounts in Accounts Receivable Cr. column are posted daily to subsidiary ledger accounts. Individual amounts in the Other Accounts Cr. column are posted daily to general ledger accounts.

Total is not posted because it relates to more than one general ledger account

Totals are posted at the end of the month to general ledger accounts

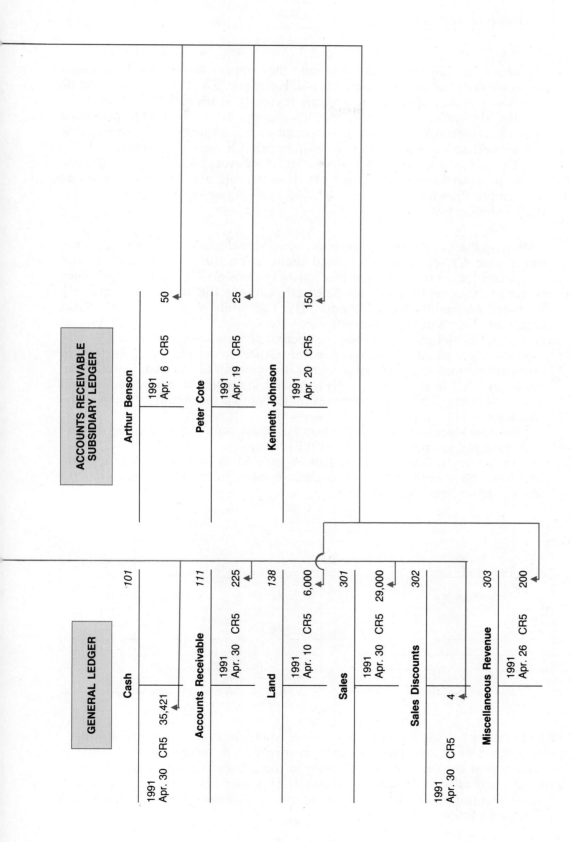

frequency to warrant special columns, they appear in the **Other Accounts Cr.** column of the cash receipts journal. However, if after several months or periods, a certain transaction appears regularly in the Other Accounts Cr. column, the format of the cash receipts journal may be revised to provide a special column for that type of transaction. For example, a company that has several rental properties may wish to provide a column for Rent Revenue Cr. in the cash receipts journal. An Other Accounts Dr. column could be included to handle transactions such as the sale of a machine (discussed in Chapter 10) where there is a debit to at least one other account besides the Cash account.

Posting the Cash Receipts Journal.   Individual amounts in the Accounts Receivable Cr. column are posted daily to customers' accounts in the subsidiary ledger to keep customer balances current. The items in the Other Accounts Cr. column are also posted daily to the individual accounts indicated (Accounts Nos. 138 and 303). The totals of the Cash Dr., Sales Discounts Dr., Sales Cr., and Accounts Receivable Cr. columns are posted at the end of the month to their respective general ledger accounts.

Since the amounts appearing in the Other Accounts Cr. column will normally pertain to different accounts, the column total is not posted, and the letter "X" in parentheses (X) is placed immediately below the column total. This letter "X" in parentheses indicates that the amount shown as the column total is not posted to any account.

The ledger accounts in Illustration 6.2 show only the postings from the cash receipts journal of John Mason Company.

The Accounts Receivable control account in the general ledger appears as follows after both the sales and cash receipts journals in Illustrations 6.1 and 6.2 have been posted:

Accounts Receivable						*Account No. 111*
Date	Explanation	Post. Ref.	Debit	Credit	Balance	
1991 Apr. 30		S1	2 9 0		2 9 0 Dr.	
30		CR5		2 2 5	6 5 Dr.	

Illustration 6.3 shows the subsidiary accounts at the same point in time.

A **schedule of accounts receivable** is prepared at the end of the period to ensure that the total of the balances in the accounts receivable subsidiary ledger agrees with the control account. This schedule is merely a listing of open account balances. An example of this schedule for the John Mason Company follows:

JOHN MASON COMPANY
Schedule of Accounts Receivable
April 30, 1991

Peter Cote	$10
Anthony Demambro	55
Balance in the control account	$65

Illustration 6.3 *Accounts Receivable Subsidiary Ledger*

JOHN MASON COMPANY
SUBSIDIARY ACCOUNTS RECEIVABLE LEDGER
Arthur Benson

Date	Explanation	Post. Ref.	Debit	Credit	Balance
1991 Apr. 3		S1	50		50 Dr.
6		CR5		50	-0-

Peter Cote

Date	Explanation	Post. Ref.	Debit	Credit	Balance
1991 Apr. 4		S1	25		25 Dr.
19		S1	10		35 Dr.
19		CR5		25	10 Dr.

Anthony Demambro

Date	Explanation	Post. Ref.	Debit	Credit	Balance
1991 Apr. 30		S1	55		55 Dr.

Kenneth Johnson

Date	Explanation	Post. Ref.	Debit	Credit	Balance
1991 Apr. 12		S1	150		150 Dr.
20		CR5		150	-0-

Combined Sales and Cash Receipts Journal

The sales and cash receipts journals may be combined into one journal. A combined sales and cash receipts journal is illustrated in Demonstration Problem 6–1 at the end of the chapter. In considering whether or not to combine these journals, posting and journalizing convenience is only one consideration. Remember that having separate sales and cash receipts journals allows more people to work with the data in the journals at the same time.

Purchases Journal

The purchases journal is used to record all purchases of merchandise made on account. A number of formats can be used for the purchases journal. One common format has only one money column headed Purchases Dr. and Accounts Payable Cr. The headings in a purchases journal with one money column might be as follows:

Date	Creditor	Terms	Invoice No.	Purchases Dr. Accounts Payable Cr.	
				Amount	√

Note that the above purchases journal has a "Terms" column. The sales journal discussed in the previous section did not have a Terms column because a company's terms are generally the same for each customer, and the terms are already known to the company. However, in the purchases journal, a Terms column is used because various creditors often differ in the terms they offer a company. The terms offered on purchased merchandise must be known so that companies can pay for the merchandise within the discount period.

Companies often have several departments for which purchases are made. When the company wants to keep the purchases of each department separate, a purchases journal could provide a separate column for the purchases of each department. The headings in such a purchases journal might appear as follows:

Purchases Dr.			Date	Creditor	Terms	Invoice No.	Accounts Payable Cr.	
Dept. A	Dept. B	Dept. C					Amount	√

Illustration 6.4 shows a purchases journal having one money column. In Illustration 6.4, John Mason Company made eight purchases of merchandise on account during the month. Each purchase results in a debit to Purchases and a credit to Accounts Payable.

Posting the Purchases Journal. Individual amounts in the money column are posted daily to the accounts payable subsidiary ledger so that the subsidiary accounts will be current at all times. The money column total is posted to the general ledger Purchases account as a debit and to the general ledger Accounts Payable control account as a credit at the end of the month.

Cash Disbursements Journal

The cash disbursements journal is used to record all transactions that involve the payment of cash. To have an acceptable level of control over cash disbursements, most companies pay all bills by check. Therefore, the cash disbursements journal (see Illustration 6.5) contains a column in which to record the number of the check written for each disbursement.

Payments on accounts payable constitute a major type of cash disbursement transaction. These accounts payable were initially recorded in the purchases journal when the purchases on account were made. Therefore, a separate column entitled Accounts Payable Dr. is provided. Many payments on account involve a purchase discount, so a separate column is provided for discounts (Purchase Discounts Cr.). John Mason Company frequently purchases numerous supplies by writing a check, so the journal has a separate column for Supplies Expense (Supplies Expense Dr.). As with other special journals, companies adapt the cash disbursements journal to their individual needs. For instance, an Other Accounts Cr. column could be added to record transactions such as the purchase of land by paying cash and giving a note, since an additional account besides Cash is credited.

Posting the Cash Disbursements Journal. As shown in Illustration 6.5, individual items in the Accounts Payable Dr. column are posted daily to accounts in the accounts payable subsidiary ledger. Individual items in the Other Accounts Dr. column are posted daily to the appropriate accounts in the general ledger. The column totals for Accounts Payable Dr., Supplies Expense Dr., Cash Cr., and Purchase Discounts Cr. are posted at the end of the month to accounts in the general ledger. The total of the Other Accounts Dr. column is not posted. The only amounts shown in the accounts in Illustration 6.5 are those from the posting of the cash disbursements journal to make it easier to trace the postings.

The general ledger Accounts Payable control account appears as follows after both the purchases and cash disbursements journals have been posted:

			Accounts Payable							Account No. 201	
Date		Explanation	Post. Ref.	Debit		Credit			Balance		
1991 Apr.	30		P10			2 4 1 0 0			2 4 1 0 0	Cr.	
	30		CD7	1 8 3 0 0					5 8 0 0	Cr.	

Illustration 6.4 *Purchases Journal*

JOHN MASON COMPANY
PURCHASES JOURNAL

Page 10

Date		Creditor	Terms	Invoice No.	Purchases Dr. 401 Accounts Payable Cr. 201	
					Amount	√
1991						
Apr.	1	Smith Corporation	2/10, n/30	862	200	√
	7	Lasky Company	1/15, n/60	121	100	√
	12	Booth Corporation	2/10, n/60	561	5,000	√
	15	Gooch Corporation	2/10, n/30	1042	3,000	√
	21	Wyngarden Company	3/15, n/60	633	10,000	√
	26	Mertz Company	2/10, n/30	734	300	√
	30	Nelson Company	2/10, n/30	287	4,000	√
	30	Booth Corporation	2/20, n/60	568	1,500	√
					24,100	
					(401)(201)	

Individual amounts are posted daily to subsidiary ledger accounts

Total is posted at end of month to general ledger accounts

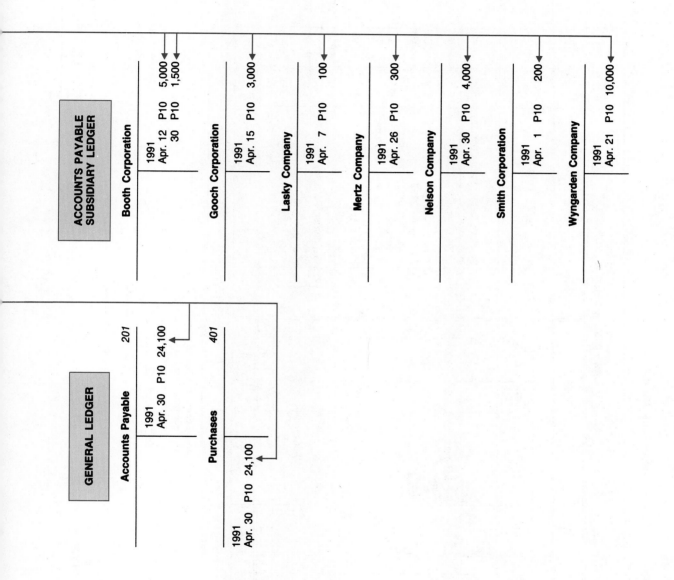

ACCOUNTS PAYABLE
SUBSIDIARY LEDGER

Booth Corporation

1991			
Apr. 12	P10	5,000
30	P10	1,500

Gooch Corporation

1991		
Apr. 15	P10	3,000

Lasky Company

1991		
Apr. 7	P10	100

Mertz Company

1991		
Apr. 26	P10	300

Nelson Company

1991		
Apr. 30	P10	4,000

Smith Corporation

1991		
Apr. 1	P10	200

Wyngarden Company

1991		
Apr. 21	P10	10,000

GENERAL LEDGER

Accounts Payable   *201*

1991		
Apr. 30	P10	24,100

Purchases   *401*

1991		
Apr. 30	P10	24,100

Illustration 6.5   Cash Disbursements Journal

JOHN MASON COMPANY
CASH DISBURSEMENTS JOURNAL

Page 7

Date	Description	Check No.	Accounts Payable Dr. (201) ✓	Amount	Supplies Expense Dr. (422)	Other Accounts Dr. — Account Title	Acct. No.	Amount	✓	Cash Cr. (101)	Purchase Discounts Cr. (402)
1991 Apr. 2	Brooklyn Square Paint Company	524			42					42	
3	Insurance policy to cover May 1 1991—April 30, 1992	525				Prepaid Insurance	123	1,200	✓	1,200	
4	Furniture—office	526				Furniture and Equipment	140	500	✓	500	
4	Rent for April 1991	527				Rent Expense	423	200	✓	200	
8	Smith Corporation—Invoice No. 862	528	✓	200						196	4
14	Allan Park Stationery Company	529			10					10	
18	Lasky Company—Invoice No. 121	530	✓	100						99	1
21	Booth Corporation—Invoice No. 561	531	✓	5,000						4,900	100
27	Wyngarden Company—Invoice No. 633	532	✓	10,000						9,700	300
28	Gooch Corporation—Invoice No. 1042	533	✓	3,000						3,000	
				18,300	52			1,900		19,847	405
				(201)	(422)			(X)		(101)	(402)

Individual amounts in the Accounts Payable Dr. column are posted daily to accounts payable subsidiary ledger accounts.

Individual amounts in the Other Accounts Dr. column are posted daily to indicated general ledger accounts.

Total is not posted because it pertains to several accounts

Totals are posted at the end of the month to general ledger accounts

246

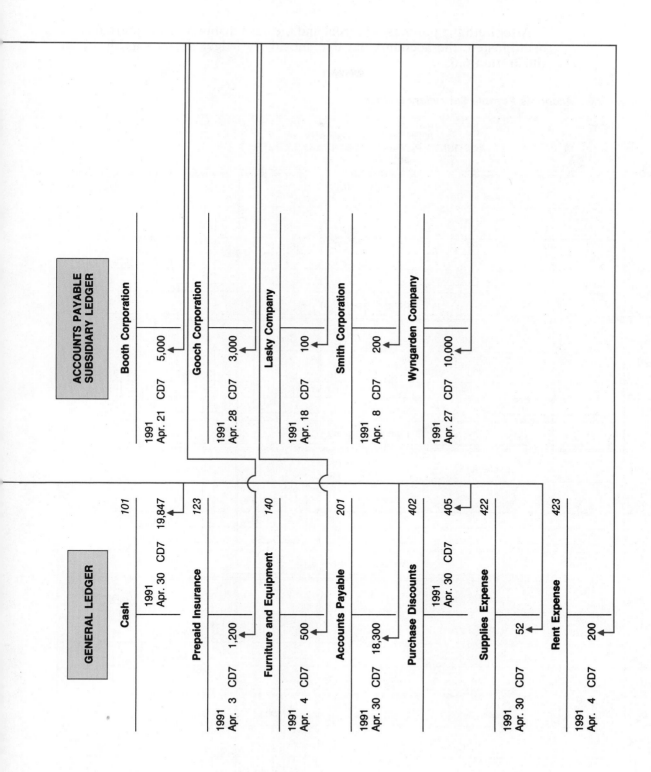

After both the purchases journal and the cash disbursements journal have been posted, the accounts payable subsidiary ledger appears as shown in Illustration 6.6.

Illustration 6.6   *Accounts Payable Subsidiary Ledger*

JOHN MASON COMPANY
ACCOUNTS PAYABLE SUBSIDIARY LEDGER
Booth Corporation

Date	Explanation	Post. Ref.	Debit	Credit	Balance
1991 Apr. 12		P10		5000	5000 Cr.
21		CD7	5000		-0-
30		P10		1500	1500 Cr.

Gooch Corporation

Date	Explanation	Post. Ref.	Debit	Credit	Balance
1991 Apr. 15		P10		3000	3000 Cr.
28		CD7	3000		-0-

Lasky Company

Date	Explanation	Post. Ref.	Debit	Credit	Balance
1991 Apr. 7		P10		100	100 Cr.
18		CD7	100		-0-

Mertz Company

Date	Explanation	Post. Ref.	Debit	Credit	Balance
1991 Apr. 26		P10		300	300 Cr.

Nelson Company

Date	Explanation	Post. Ref.	Debit	Credit	Balance
1991 Apr. 30		P10		4000	4000 Cr.

Illustration 6.6   (concluded)

ACCOUNTS RECEIVABLE SUBSIDIARY LEDGER (concluded)
Smith Corporation

Date		Explanation	Post. Ref.	Debit	Credit	Balance
1991 Apr.	1		P10		2 0 0	2 0 0 Cr.
	8		CD7	2 0 0		– 0 –

Wyngarden Company

Date		Explanation	Post. Ref.	Debit	Credit	Balance
1991 Apr.	21		P10		1 0 0 0 0	1 0 0 0 0 Cr.
	27		CD7	1 0 0 0 0		– 0 –

A **schedule of accounts payable** is prepared at the end of the period to make certain that the total of the balances in the accounts payable subsidiary ledger agrees with the balance in the Accounts Payable control account. The schedule for the John Mason Company appears below.

JOHN MASON COMPANY
Schedule of Accounts Payable
April 30, 1991

Booth Corporation	$1,500
Mertz Company	300
Nelson Company	4,000
Balance in the control account	$5,800

Combined Purchases and Cash Disbursements Journal

The purchases and the cash disbursements journals could be combined into one journal. A combined purchases and cash disbursements journal is illustrated in Demonstration Problem 6–2 at the end of the chapter. But use of a combined journal limits the number of persons who can work with the data in the journals at any one time.

General Ledger Illustrated

After all four special journals for John Mason Company have been posted, the general ledger appears as shown in Illustration 6.7.

Illustration 6.7 *General Ledger*

JOHN MASON COMPANY
GENERAL LEDGER
Cash   *Account No. 101*

Date		Explanation	Post. Ref.	Debit	Credit	Balance
1991 Apr.	1	Beginning balance (assumed)				1 0 0 0 0 Dr.
	30		CR5	3 5 4 2 1		4 5 4 2 1 Dr.
	30		CD7		1 9 8 4 7	2 5 5 7 4 Dr.

Accounts Receivable   *Account No. 111*

Date		Explanation	Post. Ref.	Debit	Credit	Balance
1991 Apr.	30		S1	2 9 0		2 9 0 Dr.
	30		CR5		2 2 5	6 5 Dr.

Prepaid Insurance   *Account No. 123*

Date		Explanation	Post. Ref.	Debit	Credit	Balance
1991 Apr.	3		CD7	1 2 0 0		1 2 0 0 Dr.

Land   *Account No. 138*

Date		Explanation	Post. Ref.	Debit	Credit	Balance
1991 Apr.	1	Beginning balance (assumed)				1 8 0 0 0 Dr.
	10		CR5		6 0 0 0	1 2 0 0 0 Dr.

Furniture and Equipment   *Account No. 140*

Date		Explanation	Post. Ref.	Debit	Credit	Balance
1991 Apr.	4		CD7	5 0 0		5 0 0 Dr.

Illustration 6.7   *(continued)*

GENERAL LEDGER *(continued)*
Accounts Payable

Account No. 201

Date		Explanation	Post. Ref.	Debit	Credit	Balance
1991 Apr.	30		P10		2 4 1 0 0	2 4 1 0 0 Cr.
	30		CD7	1 8 3 0 0		5 8 0 0 Cr.

John Mason, Capital

Account No. 250

Date		Explanation	Post. Ref.	Debit	Credit	Balance
1991 Apr.	1	Beginning balance (assumed)				2 8 0 0 0 Cr.

Sales

Account No. 301

Date		Explanation	Post. Ref.	Debit	Credit	Balance
1991 Apr.	30		S1		2 9 0	2 9 0 Cr.
	30		CR5		2 9 0 0 0	2 9 2 9 0 Cr.

Sales Discounts

Account No. 302

Date		Explanation	Post. Ref.	Debit	Credit	Balance
1991 Apr.	30		CR5	4		4 Dr.

Miscellaneous Revenue

Account No. 303

Date		Explanation	Post. Ref.	Debit	Credit	Balance
1991 Apr.	26		CR5		2 0 0	2 0 0 Cr.

Purchases

Account No. 401

Date		Explanation	Post. Ref.	Debit	Credit	Balance
1991 Apr.	30		P10	2 4 1 0 0		2 4 1 0 0 Dr.

Illustration 6.7 *(concluded)*

GENERAL LEDGER *(concluded)*
Purchase Discounts   *Account No. 402*

Date		Explanation	Post. Ref.	Debit	Credit	Balance
1991 Apr.	30		CD7		4 0 5	4 0 5 Cr.

Supplies Expense   *Account No. 422*

Date		Explanation	Post. Ref.	Debit	Credit	Balance
1991 Apr.	30		CD7	5 2		5 2 Dr.

Rent Expense   *Account No. 423*

Date		Explanation	Post. Ref.	Debit	Credit	Balance
1991 Apr.	4		CD7	2 0 0		2 0 0 Dr.

General Journal

As mentioned earlier in the chapter, each transaction that does not belong in a special journal is entered in the general journal. For example, the general journal could be used to record the receipt of a note from a customer in settlement of an account receivable. A note would allow the company to begin earning interest on the amount due. An example of such an entry would be as follows (all account numbers are assumed):

Notes Receivable	114	2,000	
Accounts Receivable—A. Smith	111/√		2,000
To record the receipt of a 60-day, 12% note from Alex Smith in settlement of his account receivable.			

The √ shows that the entry has been posted to the subsidiary ledger account.

Other types of transactions that would be recorded in the general journal include the purchase of equipment or some other asset by giving a note, the payment of an account payable by giving a note, sales returns and allowances, and purchase returns and allowances. For instance, the entry to record a sales allowance of $100 granted to John Burke for damaged merchandise is:

Sales Returns and Allowances	303	100	
Accounts Receivable—J. Burke	111/√		100
To record a sales allowance of $100 to John Burke for damaged merchandise.			

All adjusting and closing entries are made in the general journal. For instance, the general journal would be used to record an adjusting entry for depreciation expense of $1,500 on an office building as follows:

Depreciation Expense—Office Building	424	1,500	
Accumulated Depreciation—Office Building	141		1,500
To record depreciation expense.			

■ ALTERNATIVE METHODS OF PROCESSING DATA

The variety of equipment used in an accounting system is extensive, ranging from the hand-posted special journals of a manual system to large computers. Regardless of which accounting system a company selects, all companies use the basic steps of the accounting cycle to process their data, and the end result—financial statements—is the same. The selection a company makes of one system over another depends on the company's individual situation, such as the volume of transactions, types of transactions, need for speed, resources of the company, and other cost-benefit considerations. In this section, you will learn about some of the alternative accounting systems available to companies.

Manual System

So far in this text, you have used the manual system. This system is typical of the system used by some of today's smaller businesses in which the accounting function is handled by an accountant and possibly one or two clerks. In the manual system, all accounting entries are recorded by hand, and journals are summarized and posted to the general ledger. Textbooks use the manual system to teach accounting because all other systems are based on it. In this chapter, you learned about the advantages of adding subsidiary ledgers and special journals to the manual system. In the following paragraphs, you will see how companies save time and effort either by adding special equipment to the manual system or by substituting an electronic system.

Bookkeeping Machine System

Bookkeeping machines were once very common, but in recent years they are being replaced by computers. The bookkeeping machine was used for recording recurring transactions. These machines posted transactions to the general ledger and subsidiary ledger accounts and computed new balances. Much time was saved by using these machines for such recurring transactions as sales on account. Many small businesses first upgraded their accounting systems from manual systems to bookkeeping machines and then to computers.

Microcomputers and Minicomputers

In this age of fast-developing computer technology with the continued lowering of computer prices, many small and medium-size businesses are turning to computers and off-the-shelf software to maintain their accounting records. Large businesses may use mainframe computers (described later), while small businesses might use minicomputers and/or microcomputers. **Microcomputers** are smaller than minicomputers and accommodate one person, whereas **minicomputers** are designed for use by several persons. The distinction between microcomputers and minicomputers is more one of price rather than quality or capacity.

Microcomputers cost from a few hundred dollars to about $10,000. Minicomputers generally cost between $10,000 and $100,000. Microcomputers can fit on top of a desk; minicomputers are larger—about the size of a six-foot refrigerator. Minicomputers may be used in divisions of large companies; these computers can have several terminals connected to them. Microcomputers are used for word processing, graphics, database management, and preparing spreadsheets for planning and decision making as well as for processing business transactions. Microcomputers can be networked (linked) into a system as powerful as a minicomputer. Many business executives have microcomputers on their desks and use them daily. As the price of computers continues to drop, more businesses will use computer systems. Appendix 6-A at the end of this chapter describes in more detail the use of the microcomputer in accounting.

Service Bureaus

Some businesses still find it economical to send certain data (e.g., payroll, inventory, and accounts receivable) to a local service bureau for processing. A **service bureau** is a large computer facility that takes data from a client, enters the data into its computer, produces required statements or reports, and returns this output to the client. Client personnel do not have to interact with the computer. Service bureaus can usually meet the specific output requirements of a business if some advance planning is done.

Time-Sharing Terminals

Significant advances have been made in the field of computer time sharing. **Time sharing** occurs when several users utilize the same host computer to process data. In a time-sharing arrangement, client personnel interact with a computer through a remote terminal located in the client's building. The users literally share time on the computer through remote terminals connected by telephone lines or radio waves to the host computer. The host computer can be called up by the company employee operating the remote terminal. Typical applications of time sharing enable clients to process large amounts of transactions data (e.g., printing and summarizing sales invoices, updating inventory records, and updating accounts receivable and accounts payable records).

Mainframe In-House Computer

Many business firms purchase their own mainframe computer to process data. The cost of these computers can be several hundred thousand dollars. Where the volume of transactions is very large, the decision to purchase a large computer is often justified. Terminals may exist throughout the company for employees to use to communicate with the mainframe computer. Appendix 6-B contains more information about basic concepts regarding computers.

In the next chapter, you will learn the general principles of internal control and how to control cash. Cash is one of a company's most important assets; however, it is also the company's most mobile asset. As you study the subject of controlling cash, you will realize that to be successful a company must have competent and trustworthy employees.

■ *UNDERSTANDING THE LEARNING OBJECTIVES: CHAPTER 6*

1. Describe the relationship between subsidiary accounts in subsidiary ledgers and control accounts in the general ledger.

   ■ A control account is an account, such as accounts receivable, in the general ledger that shows the total balance of all the subsidiary accounts related to it.

   ■ Subsidiary ledger accounts, such as individual customer accounts, show the details supporting the related general ledger account balance.

2. Describe the relationship between special journals and the general journal.

   ■ Each special journal records one particular type of transaction, such as sales on account, cash receipts, purchases on account, or cash disbursements.

   ■ The general journal is used to record all transactions that cannot be entered in one of the special journals.

3. Record transactions in special journals.

   ■ The dollar amounts of journal entries are entered in columns established in the special journals. Each of the special journals has its unique sets of columns.

4. Post special journals.

   ■ For certain columns in the special journals, only the column total is posted to the general ledger.

- For some columns in the special journals, the column total is posted to the general ledger, and the individual amounts in the column are posted to subsidiary ledger accounts.
- For a few columns in the special journals, the column total is not posted, but the individual amounts in the column are posted to general ledger accounts.

5. Describe computer applications in accounting (Appendix 6-A).

- Numerous accounting system packages for microcomputers are currently available on the market. These packages allow companies to gather information and produce financial statements much more efficiently than with manual systems.
- The modules normally include: general ledger, accounts receivable, accounts payable, inventory management, payroll, and invoicing.
- Another type of computer program is the electronic spreadsheet. Spreadsheets are ideal for creating large schedules and performing great volumes of calculations.
- Database management software is used to develop integrated accounting systems and to help solve problems by accessing needed data from the database files.
- Microcomputers are used increasingly in audit, tax, and management consulting activities of public accounting firms.
- Future applications of the computer in public accounting will involve the use of "expert systems" and artificial intelligence.

6. Describe basic computer concepts (Appendix 6-B).

- The storage unit is the computer's internal memory system.
- The arithmetic unit of a computer performs simple computations and comparisons.
- The control unit of a computer interprets the program, assigns storage space, and alters the sequence of operations if so instructed by the program.
- Peripheral equipment can be attached to the computer and be used mainly for input and output of information.

7. Define and use correctly the new terms in the glossary.

- See the new terms introduced following the Appendixes to this chapter.

■ APPENDIX 6-A: THE USE OF THE MICROCOMPUTER IN ACCOUNTING*

Objective 5:
Describe computer applications in accounting.

The use of the microcomputer in American business has greatly increased in recent years due to decreasing computer prices and significant technological advances in both computer hardware and software. Microcomputers now frequently cost under $5,000 and have as much power as computers that would have cost millions of dollars and filled several large

---

* Written by Gary Fayard, Partner in the Atlanta Office of Ernst & Whinney, and Dana R. Hermanson, Senior Accountant in the Atlanta Office of Ernst & Whinney.

rooms only a short time ago. The microcomputer is especially useful in the accounting field because of the great need for fast and accurate information processing when dealing with large volumes of financial data. To further your understanding of the microcomputer and its use in accounting, we will discuss the following topics: computerized accounting systems, computer spreadsheets, database management systems, and the use of microcomputers in public accounting.

■ COMPUTERIZED ACCOUNTING SYSTEMS

Numerous accounting system packages for microcomputers are currently available on the market, and most of them cost from just under $100 to $2,500. These packages are designed for use by small businesses, and they can provide many advantages over manual accounting systems. Companies can greatly reduce the clerical work performed by their accounting staff and can also substantially reduce clerical errors in the financial data by changing from a manual to a computerized accounting system. Computerized systems also allow companies to gather information and produce reports much more efficiently than is possible with manual systems. The proper implementation of one of these accounting system packages can result in a company having a computerized accounting system that is both more efficient and less expensive than a manual system.

Now that we understand the potential advantages of using an accounting system package, let us examine the typical characteristics of a package on the market today. One basic characteristic of all effective systems is that some type of control exists over who can use the computer to make journal entries. Many packages have a password that must be used to get into the accounting system, while other packages are protected by physically locking up the terminals when they are not being used by authorized personnel. The importance of this control cannot be overstated.

Another common characteristic of most accounting packages today is that they are menu driven. This means that the program user selects an option listed on the screen to access the part of the accounting system that he or she wishes to use. For example, when the user first turns on the computer and enters the proper password, a screen similar to this may appear:

```
                XYZ Company

    1> General Ledger
    2> Accounts Receivable
    3> Accounts Payable
    4> Inventory Management
    5> Payroll
    6> Invoicing
    7> End Session
```

If the user wanted to access the Accounts Payable section of the program, he or she would type a "3" into the computer and hit "ENTER." The user would then have access to the Accounts Payable section, and another menu would appear that would provide the user with several options within that section. The menu system is designed to make accounting packages much more "user friendly."

The final characteristic to be discussed is the typical organization or format of a computerized accounting package. Most packages are divided into the modules shown on the screen above—General Ledger, Accounts Receivable, Accounts Payable, Inventory Management, Payroll, and Invoicing. Let us now briefly discuss the function of each module.

The General Ledger module contains all of a company's accounts and their balances. General journal entries are made in this section, and these entries include all entries not made in one of the other system modules. For example, an entry relating to accounts receivable would be made in the Accounts Receivable module; however, an entry to record the borrowing of cash from a bank does not fit into any of the specific modules and would be made in the General Ledger module as a general journal entry. Adjusting entries would also be entered in the General Ledger module. One other function performed in the General Ledger module is the printing of a company's financial statements. Most accounting packages will automatically make all the necessary closing entries before printing out the financial statements.

The Accounts Receivable module is used to record sales on credit to various customers and amounts received from customers. This module serves as the accounts receivable subsidiary ledger, and the Accounts Receivable control account in the General Ledger module is usually automatically updated when entries are made to the Accounts Receivable module.

The Accounts Payable module is used to record credit purchases of merchandise from various vendors as well as payments made to those vendors. This module also acts as the subsidiary ledger for Accounts Payable, and the control account is usually automatically updated when entries are made in the Accounts Payable module.

The Inventory Management module is designed to keep the perpetual inventory, and all purchases and sales of inventory are reflected in this module. The Inventory Management module interfaces with the Accounts Receivable and Accounts Payable modules to keep track of the receivables and payables resulting from sales and purchases.

The Payroll module is used to record all of the payroll entries. The totals from the Payroll module are often automatically posted to the appropriate General Ledger accounts, although this automatic posting is not always available.

The Invoicing module is simply used to print the sales invoices that are sent to customers. Sometimes this Invoicing module is combined with the Accounts Receivable module.

■ COMPUTER SPREADSHEETS

Another type of computer program that has become extremely popular during the last decade is the electronic spreadsheet. Two of the most popular spreadsheet programs are LOTUS© 1-2-3© and SuperCalc3©. These programs have numerous applications in business and specifically in accounting. Spreadsheets are ideal for creating large schedules and performing great volumes of calculations. Their specific uses in accounting range from performing depreciation calculations to creating trial balances and other schedules. Other specific uses of spreadsheets will be discussed in the section on the use of the microcomputer in public accounting.

Let us now examine the basics of the electronic spreadsheet. An electronic spreadsheet is simply a large blank "page" on the computer screen that is made up of rows and columns. The spreadsheet is so large that only a very small percentage of the sheet can be seen on the screen at one time. The blocks created by the intersection of the rows and columns are called cells, and each cell can hold a word, a number, or the product of a mathematical formula. This is what a typical blank spreadsheet looks like:

```
        A    B    C    D    E    F    G

   1

   2    ▨  (Cursor)

   3

   4              □  (Cell C4)

   5

   6

   7

   8

   9

  10

A2> (Type appears here)

(Cursor location)
```

The cursor indicates the cell on the screen in which information can be entered at a given time. For example, on the above screen, the user can now enter a word, number, or formula into cell A2. Note that the information will appear at the bottom (on some programs, at the top) of the screen next to the cursor location until the user presses the ENTER key to transfer the information to its cell. The user can move the cursor around the screen by pressing different cursor control keys.

By going through the following example you can gain a better understanding of how the electronic spreadsheet actually works. Assume you are an accountant in Burke Company and wish to create an income statement for 1990 and a projected income statement for 1991 like those shown below:

	A	B	C	D
1	▨	BURKE CO.		
2		INCOME STATEMENT	PROJECTED	
3		YEAR ENDED 12/31/90	12/31/91	
4				
5	Sales	1,000,000	1,100,000	
6	Cost of Sales	600,000	660,000	
7	Gross Profit	400,000	440,000	
8	Other Expenses	100,000	110,000	
9	Net Income	300,000	330,000	
10				

A1>

The first step in creating these statements is to set up the proper headings. In cell B1 we would enter BURKE CO by moving the cursor to B1, typing in the words BURKE CO, and pressing the ENTER key to transfer the words to cell B1. Likewise, the appropriate headings would be entered into cells B2, B3, C2, and C3. The second step is to enter the income statement items in column A, and these would be placed in cells A5 through A9 in the same way that the other headings were entered.

Now that all of the headings and titles have been entered, let us begin to enter the financial figures into the 1990 Income Statement. Cell B5 will contain the Sales figure of $1,000,000, and B6 will hold the $600,000 Cost of Goods Sold figure. These numbers will be entered in the same manner that the headings and titles were entered. Cell B7 will not hold a specific word or number; however, it will contain the result of a mathematical formula (B5 − B6). By moving the cursor to B7, typing +B5 − B6, and pressing the ENTER key, the result of this formula is entered into B7. Finally, $100,000 will be entered in cell B8. The result of +B7 − B8 will be entered in cell B9.

The final step in constructing this spreadsheet is to complete cells C5 through C9, which will show the projected Income Statement figures for 1991. If we assume that Sales, Cost of Goods Sold, and Other Expenses will increase by 10% from 1990 to 1991, then we can enter the following formulas for cells C5, C6, and C8. Cell C5 will contain the number resulting from the formula +B5*1.1. Cells C6 and C8 will show the results of +B6*1.1 and +B8*1.1, respectively. Finally, C7 and C9 will hold the results of +C5 − C6 and +C7 − C8, respectively. Our spreadsheet is now complete, as it presents the 1990 Income Statement for Burke Company as well as a projected Income Statement for 1991.

We have only used a few of the columns and rows available in a typical spreadsheet. Most spreadsheets contain many columns and rows. For instance, LOTUS 1-2-3 contains 256 columns and 8,192 rows.

While the Income Statement just constructed is a simple example of spreadsheet use, it is important to note several more advanced functions that spreadsheets can perform. First, when showing a current schedule and projections of that schedule far into the future, the user can play "what if" games by changing various numbers or formulas in the spreadsheet, and the program will recalculate all of the schedules based on the changes made. Second, many spreadsheet programs allow the user to construct various types of graphs showing the data contained in spreadsheet schedules. Finally, the schedules that appear on the user's computer screen can be printed out on paper for use by other people.

The computerized spreadsheet is a powerful tool, but the potential for inefficient use of spreadsheets is great. To promote better use of spreadsheets, Ernst & Whinney has developed the following tips for its staff:

1. Spend time on planning. Planning how to design, organize, and construct your spreadsheet can ensure that the spreadsheet meets your requirements. This reduces errors and makes the spreadsheet easier to use.
2. Keep the overall design simple. Spreadsheet design should aim at producing clear and concise analyses. Quality is more important than quantity.
3. Organize the spreadsheet to make it easy to understand. Separate data input areas from reports. Include instructions and a table of contents to make the spreadsheet understandable to other people.
4. Use simple formulas to make your printed output more understandable and to make errors easier to detect.
5. Use validation tests to alert you if errors occur.
6. Test the spreadsheet before use. Always check spreadsheet calculations before using the results.
7. Use graphics to highlight patterns or trends in your data and to make your spreadsheets more interesting and understandable.
8. Document the spreadsheet. Both users and reviewers need adequate documentation of spreadsheet logic and design. Proper headings and descriptions, as well as other documentation, are important for a well-designed spreadsheet.
9. Use the "protect" command to safeguard the spreadsheet and identify where data should be entered.
10. Make regular backups. Maintain up-to-date copies of spreadsheet files to avoid losing important data and development work.

■ DATABASE MANAGEMENT SYSTEMS

In many accounting systems, various applications of the same data have been developed independently. As a result, although inventory, purchasing, sales, and production all use part numbers to identify inventory items, that piece of information would have to be stored in each file for each application. The same data stored in separate files could vary as far as accuracy and timeliness are concerned. This can result in inefficiencies (data redundancy) and inaccuracies (data inconsistency). A database management system helps solve these problems by storing related data together independent of the application. Many of today's modern accounting systems have integrated applications through the use of a database management system. This means in the above example that the inventory part number is stored in only one file but is used by all the applications.

Database management software is frequently used on microcomputers. Two of the most popular microcomputer database management systems are dBASE III© and rBASE©. These systems can be used to develop integrated accounting systems and are useful for many single applications. With database software, you can easily enter data into a microcomputer and then analyze, sort, and print the information using English-like commands. The advantage of using the database management system for a single application over writing the application in a programming language (i.e., BASIC, PASCAL) is that the database management system takes care of data file access for you.

Let us look at an example of a database application. The database file can be any organized collection of related information, such as monthly sales information. The information is kept in records, with each record consisting of a series of fields. A field is the part of a record that holds a particular item of information. An example of a record might be all information related to a salesperson. The fields in the record might include the salesperson's name, address, and ZIP code.

Suppose you are a sales manager and you need to maintain information relative to your salespersons, your customers, and your company's products. You could use a database management system to help you keep up with this information. In this case, you would probably have three database files—one for salespersons, one for customers, and one for products—however, all of this information would be interrelated to the database management system. The salespersons are related to the customers, the customers to the products, and so on. Once this information has been defined to the database management system you can use English-like commands to help answer such questions as: What products have been sold? Who are the customers? What are the amounts of sales by salespersons? You would also be able to print a customer list sorted by ZIP code, alphabetical order, or salesperson.

■ USE OF MICROCOMPUTERS IN PUBLIC ACCOUNTING

Microcomputers are having far-reaching effects in all areas of accounting. The following discussion explains some of the uses of microcomputers in public accounting.

Auditing

Auditing involves performing an examination of the financial statements of a company to enable the certified public accountant to express an opinion on the financial statements. The examination of the financial statements involves many different types of tests. Many times statistical sampling techniques are used to test the details of account balances. The microcomputer is very useful in helping both to plan and select the sample and to evaluate the results of the sample.

A typical example of microcomputer-based statistical sampling is the selection of random numbers for a test of cash disbursements. You enter the sequences of the checks written during the year, and the statistical sampling package will select a random sample of the checks to be tested. After the test is completed, the results of the test are entered to determine the statistical results of the test.

The microcomputer has had a tremendous impact on the auditing profession in the areas of analytical review and trial balance/financial statement preparation. Microcomputer packages are available that enable the auditor to enter the client's general ledger information and post adjusting journal entries. These packages will print analytical review information, such as percentage changes in expense accounts as compared with the prior year. Also, such packages are useful in calculating financial ratios. They will also consolidate the financial statements of several related companies and print consolidated financial statements. Another benefit of some of these packages is that they will print the financial information in a way to facilitate income tax return preparation.

Other uses of the microcomputer in auditing are calculations of present/future values, amortization schedules for debt, depreciation schedules for fixed assets, and flowcharting of accounting systems.

Computer spreadsheets are used extensively both for their ease of use and the capability to quickly change and recalculate computations. Use of a computer spreadsheet to calculate the income tax provision is a typical example. The calculation of the income tax provision can be a complicated computation and is subject to change if adjustments to the financial statements are made as a result of the audit. The use of a computer spreadsheet allows the auditor to quickly reflect the adjusted amounts and recalculate the income tax provision.

Tax

The microcomputer has also had a dramatic impact on the tax practice of public accounting firms. Microcomputers are used to prepare tax returns and are used extensively in income and estate tax planning. Specialized tax programs and computer spreadsheets are both used to perform tax planning. Use of the microcomputer allows the tax professional to ask "what if" questions and quickly see the results of different tax strategies.

Another important use of the microcomputer is in the area of tax research. Through the use of a modem, research databases can be accessed over phone lines. These databases have current tax law, tax cases, and revenue rulings that can be quickly searched and the information found can be downloaded to the microcomputer for review and printing.

Management Consulting Services

Management consultants, as the name implies, work with clients in a variety of areas. These areas include advising on acquisitions of computer hardware and software, implementing accounting systems, analyzing staffing needs, reviewing manufacturing procedures and cost systems, and performing financial modeling tasks.

Financial modeling is the process of taking historical financial information and projecting the results based on various scenarios. Financial modeling can be performed by use of a computer spreadsheet; however, most large, complicated models are performed by use of microcomputer financial modeling packages.

The following are examples of the uses of financial modeling.

1. A manufacturer needs help in overcoming a seasonal cash shortage. Because of the nature of the business, the company annually builds up large inventories, which result in dramatic increases in payables. Using a financial model, the company is able to anticipate its cash requirements and avert an annual cash crisis.

2. A manufacturer wants to expand its business by acquiring the manufacturing capabilities of existing companies. Using a financial model, the company can develop a series of projections of the anticipated results of various acquisitions and the impact on the company's debt service and borrowing capabilities.

3. A privately held company has plans to go public. A key ingredient to a successful public offering is a well-conceived business plan that allows underwriters to make an objective initial assessment of the company's current situation and future potential. A financial model can be used to prepare projections of the company's financial statements. These projected financial statements would be included in the business plan to allow the underwriters to assess the company's future potential.

■ YOUR FUTURE AND THE MICROCOMPUTER

The microcomputer is now firmly established as a valuable tool in the accounting field. As computer technology continues to progress, accountants will find more and more ways in which to use these powerful machines.

Future applications of the computer in public accounting will involve the use of "expert systems" and artificial intelligence. Expert systems are software programs designed to duplicate the decisions of an "expert," given certain facts and circumstances. For instance, the program might be able to predict whether or not a client is a going concern with the same success rate as an expert on this topic could. These programs are extremely expensive and time consuming to develop.

Artificial intelligence is a much broader concept than expert systems. The field of artificial intelligence is devoted to making the computer think like a human being by being able to interact with humans and adapt to unstructured situations. In the distant future we may have computers that think and respond like humans.

Your success as an accountant in the future may depend greatly on your ability to use microcomputers efficiently. We hope this appendix has alerted you to the need for an understanding of the uses of the microcomputer in accounting.

■ APPENDIX 6-B: THE COMPUTER—BASIC CONCEPTS

■ THE COMPUTER

Objective 6:
Describe basic
computer concepts.

The search for greater speed, accuracy, and storage capacity in an accounting system has presented a persistent challenge to both the accounting profession and the designers of information systems. This challenge has been met over the years through the increasing use of more sophisticated devices. The most recent sophisticated device has been the computer. The computer has permitted human participation in the processing of data to be limited to the preparation of the input (transaction) data and the program, or set of instructions, telling the computer how to process the data. If properly programmed, the computer is capable of journalizing and posting transactions with great speed and a high degree of accuracy.

The distinguishing features of a computer are its abilities to accept instructions on the processing of transaction data, store these instructions, and execute them any number of times precisely in the desired sequence. The computer uses elementary logic to alter the sequence of instructions by observing the outcome of a numeric or alphabetic comparison. For example, the computer can be instructed to test whether the cash balance is zero before each transaction and to continue processing cash disbursements only if the balance is greater than zero. Use of such techniques allows the computer to perform functions that are most time consuming when performed manually.

The advantages of a computerized accounting system are many. Computers remain exceedingly accurate at high calculating speeds. Since sets of operating instructions can be given to the computer at the outset, human effort is conserved. The performance of repetitive tasks, routine numerical decision making, and certain types of logical decision making can be taken over by the computer. The time will come when almost every business uses a computerized system of accounting.

■ COMPUTER COMPONENTS

The computer consists of three basic components—storage unit, arithmetic unit, and control unit.

The **storage unit** (sometimes called core storage) of a computer is its internal memory system; it records and retains data until they are required by and transferred to other areas of the computer. This unit is the most expensive component of the computer. To determine the optimum size of the storage unit, speed and cost factors must be considered. Generally, the greater the speed and storage required, the greater the cost. Storage space can be added to the computer by utilizing peripheral devices such as disks, drums, or tape units for temporary external storage.

The **arithmetic unit** of a computer performs simple computations and comparisons. Mathematical operations such as addition, subtraction, multiplication, and division are handled through the arithmetic unit. This unit is also the logic unit of the computer.

The **control unit** of a computer is the unit that interprets the **program** (the set of **instructions** submitted to the computer that specifies the operations to be performed and the correct sequence), assigns storage space, and alters the sequence of operations if so instructed by the program. If the unit encounters a situation for which no explicit instructions are given, it will instruct the computer to halt operations. The computer operator can then find and correct the problem situation and restart the processing by means of a console. The **console** allows the operator to exercise control over the computer when necessary.

Peripheral equipment can be attached to the computer and be used mainly to feed unprocessed information into the computer and receive the output of processed information. Examples of peripheral equipment are tape drives, card readers, and printers. The manner in which this peripheral equipment is connected and controlled varies from computer to computer.

Illustration 6.8 shows a schematic design of a simple computer system. The control unit controls operation of the system. The peripheral equipment is not part of the computer but is used to transmit data into and out of the computer as directed by the control unit. The control unit sends the data to the storage unit until there is time available to process the data. At that time, the data are recalled from storage and transferred to the arithmetic unit, where the required arithmetic operations are performed. On completion, processed data are sent by the control unit either to the peripheral equipment or, if there is more processing to be done using the data, back to storage. The peripheral equipment will display the processed output in a predefined format.

Illustration 6.8

Main Elements of a Computer

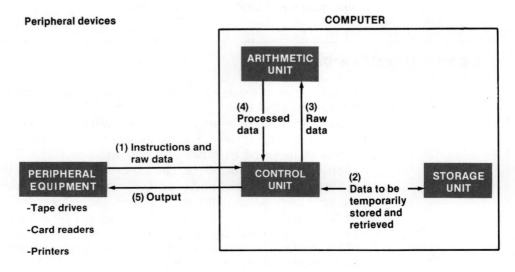

■ APPLICATIONS OF ELECTRONIC DATA PROCESSING TO ACCOUNTING

Early electronic data processing applications in accounting were in the areas of payroll, accounts receivable, accounts payable, and inventory. Now programs exist for all phases of accounting, including manufacturing operations and total integration of other accounting programs with the general ledger. Nearly all applications of data processing, and particularly those that involve the accounting process, have made considerable use of files.

A **file** is a grouping of records arranged in some order. For example, the accounts receivable subsidiary ledger is a file. The records are the individual customer accounts.

Files also exist for accounts payable and inventory. Recently, an effort has been made to create one large database for a company that would include all of the data in these files in addition to other information regarding company operations and the current status of resources. The database can be used for many purposes, including accounting functions. Developments in the hardware and software areas will have a significant impact on how accounting tasks will be performed in the future.

NEW TERMS INTRODUCED IN CHAPTER 6

Arithmetic unit   A central component of a computer; it performs simple computations and comparisons (265).

Cash disbursements journal   A special journal used to record all payments (or outflows) of cash by the business (234).

Cash receipts journal   A special journal used to record all transactions involving the inflows of cash into the business (234).

Console   The component of an electronic computer system that enables an operator to communicate manually with the system and start, stop, or alter operations (266).

Control account   An account in the general ledger that shows the total balance of all the subsidiary accounts related to it (232).

Control unit   The unit of a computer that interprets the program, assigns storage space, and alters the sequence of operations if so instructed by the program (266).

File   A grouping of records arranged in some order (267).

General journal   A general-purpose journal used to record all transactions that cannot be entered in one of the special journals (234).

Instructions   Coded information that causes the computer's control unit to perform specified operations (266).

Microcomputers   Small computers that can be used to maintain the accounting records for a small business; designed for use by one person (254).

Minicomputers   Medium-size computers that can be used to maintain the accounting records for a small or medium-size business; designed for use by several persons (254).

Other accounts   Miscellaneous accounts (237).

Peripheral equipment   Can be attached to a computer and be used mainly to feed unprocessed information into the computer and receive the output of processed information (266).

Program   The set of instructions submitted to the computer that specifies the operations to be performed and the correct sequence (266).

Purchases journal   A special journal used to record all purchases of merchandise on account (on credit) (234).

Sales journal   A special journal used to record all sales of merchandise on account (on credit) (234).

Schedule of accounts payable   Prepared at the end of the period to make certain that the total of the balances in the accounts payable subsidiary ledger agrees with the balance in the Accounts Payable control account (249).

Schedule of accounts receivable   Prepared at the end of the period to ensure that the total of the balances in the accounts receivable subsidiary ledger agrees with the control account (240).

Service bureau   A large computer facility that takes data from a client, enters the data into its computer, produces required statements or reports, and returns this output to the client (254).

Special journal   Used to record one particular type of transaction, such as sales on account, cash receipts, purchases on account, or cash disbursements (234).

Storage unit   A computer's internal memory system; it records and retains data until they are required by and transferred to other areas of the computer (265).

Subsidiary ledger   A group of related accounts showing the details of the balance of a general ledger control account (232).

Subsidiary ledger accounts   Accounts in a subsidiary ledger that show the details supporting the related general ledger control account balance (232).

Time sharing   A system whereby several users utilize the same host computer to process data (254).

DEMONSTRATION PROBLEM 6-1

The chapter mentioned, but did not illustrate, that the sales journal and cash receipts journal could be combined.

Required: Using the data in Illustrations 6.1 and 6.2, prepare a combined sales and cash receipts journal for John Mason Company. Show all the posting marks as they would be made.

DEMONSTRATION PROBLEM 6-2

The chapter mentioned, but did not illustrate, that the purchases journal and the cash disbursements journal could be combined.

Required: Using the data in Illustrations 6.4 and 6.5, prepare a combined purchases and cash disbursements journal for John Mason Company. Show all the posting marks as they would be made.

Solution to demonstration problem 6-1

JOHN MASON COMPANY
COMBINED SALES AND CASH RECEIPTS JOURNAL

101 Cash Dr.	302 Sales Discounts Dr.	111 Accounts Receivable Dr. Amount	✓	Date	Description	Invoice No.	301 Sales Cr.	111 Accounts Receivable Cr. Amount	✓	Other Accounts Cr. Account Title	Acct. No.	Amount	✓
				1991 Apr.									
5,000				1	Cash sales		5,000						
		50	✓	3	Arthur Benson	100	50						
		25	✓	4	Peter Cote	101	25						
49	1			6	Arthur Benson	100		50	✓				
8,000				7	Cash sales		8,000						
6,000				10	Sold land at cost to Wells Corporation					Land	138	6,000	✓
		150	✓	12	Kenneth Johnson	102	150						
7,000				14	Cash sales		7,000						
		10	✓	19	Peter Cote	103	10						
25				19	Peter Cote	101		25	✓				
147	3			20	Kenneth Johnson	102		150	✓				
9,000				25	Cash sales		9,000						
200				26	Cash received from sale of scrap					Miscellaneous Revenue	303	200	✓
		55	✓	30	Anthony Demambro	104	55						
35,421	4	290					29,290	225				6,200	
(101)	(302)	(111)					(301)	(111)				(X)	

269

Solution to demonstration problem 6-2

JOHN MASON COMPANY
COMBINED PURCHASES AND CASH DISBURSEMENTS JOURNAL

401 Purchases Dr.	201 Accounts Payable Dr. Amount	✓	422 Supplies Expense Dr.	Other Accounts Dr. Account Title	Acct. No.	Amount	✓	Date	Terms	Invoice No.	Description	Check No.	101 Cash Cr.	402 Purchase Discounts Cr.	201 Accounts Payable Cr. Amount	✓
								1991								
200								Apr. 1	2/10, n/30	862	Smith Corporation				200	✓
								2			Brooklyn Square					
			42								Paint Company	542	42			
				Prepaid Insurance	123	1,200	✓	3			Insurance policy to	525	1,200			
											cover May 1, 1991—					
											April 30, 1992					
				Furniture and Equipment	140	500	✓	4			Furniture—office	526	500			
				Rent Expense	423	200	✓	4			Rent for April 1991	527	200			
100								7	1/15, n/60	121	Lasky Company				100	✓
	200	✓						8			Smith Corporation—					
											Invoice No. 862	528	196	4		
5,000								12	2/10, n/60	561	Booth Corporation				5,000	✓
								14			Allan Park Sta-					
			10								tionery Company	529	10			
3,000								15	2/10, n/30	1042	Gooch Corporation				3,000	✓
	100	✓						18			Lasky Company—					
											Invoice No. 121	530	99	1		
10,000								21	3/15, n/60	633	Wyngarden Company				10,000	✓
	5,000	✓						21			Booth Corporation—					
											Invoice No. 561	531	4,900	100		
300								26	2/10, n/30	734	Mertz Company				300	✓
	10,000	✓						27			Wyngarden Company—					
											Invoice No. 633	532	9,700	300		
	3,000	✓						28			Gooch Corporation—					
											Invoice No. 1042	533	3,000			
4,000								30	2/10, n/30	287	Nelson Company				4,000	✓
1,500								30	2/10, n/60	568	Booth Company				1,500	✓
24,100	18,300		52			1,900							19,847	405	24,100	
(401)	(201)		(422)			(X)							(101)	(402)	(201)	

QUESTIONS

1. The processing of data is usually costly. Why bother with this task?

2. Is the balance of a control account equal to the total of its subsidiary accounts at all times? Explain.

3. In a manual system, the subsidiary accounts receivable and accounts payable accounts usually do not have account numbers. Why?

4. What is the definition of a special journal?

5. Describe the purpose of each of the following journals by giving the types of entries that would be recorded in each: sales, purchases, cash receipts, cash disbursements, and general.

6. Why might a sales journal or a purchases journal have more than one money column?

7. Why are some column totals in special journals posted while others are not?

8. Why does the purchases journal have a Terms column while the sales journal does not?

9. How can you tell whether a special journal has been completely posted? Describe the posting marks.

10. What is the purpose of preparing a schedule of accounts receivable and a schedule of accounts payable?

11. Of what use is the general journal when special journals are used?

12. Identify the alternative methods of processing data. What factors should a company consider in deciding which alternative to select?

EXERCISES

E-1
Prepare T-accounts to show Accounts Receivable and subsidiary accounts

The correct accounts receivable subsidiary ledger account balances for a company are as follows at the end of an accounting period:

Langley $1,200
Gibson 1,600
Golden 2,400
Martin 2,000

Using T-accounts, show how these accounts would appear and what the balance on this same date would be in the control account in the general ledger. If the balance in the control account is $8,000, what should be done?

E-2
Design sales journal for company with three selling departments

You are employed by a company that has three selling departments. You are asked to design a sales journal that will provide a departmental breakdown of credit sales. Give the column headings that you would use and describe how postings would be made.

E-3
Post data from cash receipts journal to T-accounts

The column totals of a cash receipts journal are as follows:

Cash Dr. $59,100
Sales Discounts Dr. 300
Sales Cr. 30,000
Accounts Receivable Cr. 15,000
Other accounts Cr. (sold land at cost
  for $13,500 and sold scrap for $900) 14,400

Using T-accounts, post the amounts that appear in the cash receipts journal. How would the individual amounts in the Accounts Receivable Cr. column be posted? How would the information in the Other Accounts Cr. column be posted?

E–4

Match transactions with journals in which they would be recorded

Match each transaction in column A with the appropriate journal in column B in which it would be recorded. Assume each of the journals listed is used as a book of original entry and is designed as illustrated in the chapter.

Column A	Column B
1. Purchased merchandise on account.	a. Sales journal.
2. Recorded depreciation expense.	b. Cash receipts journal.
3. Sold merchandise on account.	c. Purchases journal.
4. Sold merchandise for cash.	d. Cash disbursements journal.
5. Collected cash on account.	e. General journal.
6. Gave a note to a trade creditor.	
7. Received cash for services performed.	
8. Granted a sales allowance to a customer.	
9. Paid rent for the month.	
10. Received notice of a purchase allowance from a trade creditor.	
11. Paid a trade creditor.	
12. Recorded closing entries at the end of the period.	

E–5

Determine postings to general ledger

Which of the following amounts would be posted to the general ledger?

a. The Cash Cr. column total in the cash disbursements journal.
b. The Other Accounts Dr. column total in the cash disbursements journal.
c. The individual items in the purchases journal.
d. The individual items in the sales journal.
e. The column total in the sales journal.

E–6

Answer multiple-choice questions

For each of the following questions select the one best answer.

1. Select the **true** statement regarding control accounts and subsidiary accounts.
   a. A control account must equal the total of the related subsidiary accounts at all times during the accounting period.
   b. The only subsidiary accounts are those for accounts receivable and accounts payable.
   c. Both control and subsidiary accounts appear in the general ledger.
   d. In a given company there are fewer control accounts than there are subsidiary accounts.
2. The sales journal is:
   a. Used only to record sales on credit.
   b. Used to record all sales.
   c. Used only to record cash sales.
   d. None of the above.
3. The cash receipts journal:
   a. Cannot be used to record cash sales.
   b. Is used to record amounts received on accounts receivable.
   c. Cannot be used to record the sale of a plant asset for cash.
   d. Usually has only one money column.
4. The cash disbursements journal:
   a. Cannot be used to record purchases on account.
   b. Is used only to record the payment of accounts payable.
   c. Cannot be used to record the purchase of a plant asset for cash.
   d. Usually has only one money column.
5. Which of the following statements is **true?**
   a. The end result (financial statements) is different depending on which method of processing is used.

b. One method of processing data is the best for all companies.
c. Microcomputers can be used to maintain the accounting records of a small company.
d. The purchase of a mainframe in-house computer is almost never justified.

E-7
Indicate how special journal columns should be posted

Using the following legend, indicate how the data in each special journal column should be posted:

1—Do not post the individual amounts in the column, but post the column total to general ledger account(s) at the end of the accounting period.
2—Post the individual amounts in the column to subsidiary ledger accounts during the accounting period, and post the column total to general ledger account(s) at the end of the accounting period.
3—Post the individual amounts in the column to general ledger accounts during the accounting period and do not post the column total.

Special journals:
Sales journal:
Accounts Receivable Dr., Sales Cr. 2

Cash receipts journal:
Cash Dr. . . . . ___
Sales Discounts Dr. . . . . ___
Sales Cr. . . . . ___
Accounts Receivable Cr. . . . . . ___
Other Accounts Cr. . . . . ___

Purchases journal:
Purchases Dr., Accounts Payable Cr. . . . . ___

Cash disbursements journal:
Accounts Payable Dr. . . . . ___
Supplies Expense Dr. . . . . ___
Other Accounts Dr. . . . . ___
Cash Cr. . . . . ___
Purchase Discounts Cr. . . . . . . ___

E-8
Answer multiple-choice questions (based on Appendix 6-A)

Answer the following multiple-choice questions regarding the use of microcomputers in accounting. Select the one best answer.

1. Characteristics of microcomputer accounting system packages include (select the **false** statement):
a. Many packages have a password that must be used to get into the accounting system.
b. These packages are usually menu driven.
c. These packages usually cost in excess of $2,500.
d. Modules in the packages generally include: General Ledger, Accounts Receivable, Accounts Payable, Inventory Management, Payroll, and Invoicing.

2. All but which one of the following is a characteristic of computer spreadsheets?
a. The user can play "what if" games by changing various numbers or formulas in the spreadsheet, and the program will recalculate all of the schedules automatically.
b. Many spreadsheet programs allow the user to construct various types of graphs showing the data contained in the spreadsheet schedules.
c. The schedules that appear on the user's computer screen can be printed out on paper for use by other people.
d. Because the spreadsheet packages are so well designed, it is virtually impossible to use them inefficiently.

3. A database management system (select the **true** statement):
a. Stores related data together independent of any one application.
b. Enables one item of information to be stored in only one file but to be used by all the applications.
c. Uses English-like commands.
d. All of the above.

4. Which of the following statements is **false?**
   a. Artificial intelligence is a much narrower concept than is expert systems.
   b. The microcomputer is helpful in selecting statistical samples and in evaluating the results.
   c. Microcomputers are used to prepare tax returns and are used extensively in income and estate tax planning.
   d. Complicated financial modeling can be performed on microcomputers.

E-9
Answer matching question regarding computer terminology (based on Appendix 6-B)

Match each description in column A with the appropriate term in column B.

Column A	Column B
1. A computer's internal memory system.	a. Program.
2. Equipment that is attached to the computer.	b. Arithmetic unit.
3. A part of the computer that interprets the program.	c. Service bureau.
4. Any grouping of similar items of data arranged in some identifiable order.	d. Peripheral equipment.
5. A part of a computer that does the computing.	e. Microcomputer.
6. A set of instructions submitted to a computer that specifies the operations to be performed and their correct sequence.	f. File.
7. A large computer facility that rents out time for data processing.	g. Storage unit.
8. A small computer that can be used to maintain the accounting records for a small company.	h. Control unit.

PROBLEMS, SERIES A

P6-1-A
Record transactions in sales and purchases journals; post to T-accounts in general and subsidiary ledgers

a. Beck Clothing Store sold goods on account to the following persons on the dates indicated:

Date	Customer	Invoice No.	Amount
1991			
June 1	John James	200	$2,700
4	David Jones	201	1,800
12	Joseph Branch	202	3,600
18	Bob Blake	203	5,400
29	Craig Jacobi	204	4,500

The general ledger account numbers are:

Accounts Receivable 101
Sales 300

Required: Record the transactions on page 1 of a sales journal. Then, using T-account format, post the data to accounts in the general ledger and accounts receivable subsidiary ledger.

b. Reetz Book Store purchased merchandise from the following companies on the dates indicated:

Date		Customer	Terms	Invoice No.	Amount
1991					
July	3	Able Company	2/10, n/30	240	$18,000
	5	Crane Company	1/15, n/30	360	9,000
	14	Greer Company	2/20, n/30	142	36,000
	22	Rextex Corporation	2/20, n/60	58	45,000
	30	Zeetex Corporation	2/10, n/30	410	63,000

The general ledger account numbers are:

Accounts Payable 201
Purchases 410

Required: Record the transactions on page 10 of a purchases journal. Using T-account format, post the data to accounts in the general ledger and accounts payable subsidiary ledger.

P6-2-A
Journalize transactions in appropriate journals; post to accounts in general ledger and subsidiary ledger; prepare schedule of accounts receivable

On August 31, 1991, the Accounts Receivable control account on the books of Ace Wholesale Furniture Store was equal to the total of the accounts in the accounts receivable subsidiary ledger. The balances were as follows: Accounts Receivable control account (Account No. 120), $360,000; Battle Corporation, $144,000; East Corporation, $96,000; and Ferguson Company, $120,000.

Transactions (ignore the fact that usually the terms to all customers are the same):

Sept. 1   Received $54,880 from Ferguson Company. A discount of $1,120 had been taken.
       2   On this date, merchandise was sold on account for $88,000 to Oliva Company; Invoice No. 501; terms 2/20, n/30.
       4   Cash sales, $200,000.
       7   Received $72,000 on account from Battle Corporation. No discount was taken.
       8   Received $160,000 cash for land sold at its original cost.
      12   Sold merchandise on account to Ferguson Company, $72,000; Invoice No. 502; terms n/30.
      15   Received payment for $40,000 of the merchandise purchased on September 2 by Oliva Company. The discount was taken on this payment.
      18   Sold merchandise on account to Miles Corporation, $272,000; Invoice No. 503; terms n/30.
      21   Cash sales, $456,000.
      23   Allowed $8,000 credit to Miles Corporation for goods returned.
      26   Sold merchandise on account to Newton Company, $80,000; Invoice No. 504; terms 2/20, n/30.
      29   Received $80,000 cash from Miles Corporation to apply against the amount due on Invoice No. 503.
      30   Cash sales were $312,000.

Required: Prepare a sales journal (Illustration 6.1) and cash receipts journal (Illustration 6.2). Also set up a general journal. Then using the above information:

a. Completely journalize the transactions in the appropriate journals.
b. Post only the amounts pertaining to accounts receivable to the subsidiary accounts and to the control account. Prepare additional subsidiary accounts and keep them all in alphabetical order. You will need additional accounts for Miles Corporation, Newton Company, and Oliva Company.
c. Prepare a schedule of accounts receivable at September 30, 1991, and compare it with the balance of the control account at the same date.

P6-3-A

Journalize transactions in appropriate journal; post to general ledger and subsidiary ledger accounts; prepare schedule of accounts payable

On August 31, 1991, the Accounts Payable control account on the books of Ace Wholesale Furniture Store was equal to the total of the accounts in the accounts payable subsidiary ledger. The balances were as follows: Accounts Payable control account (Account No. 220), $432,000; Bond Corporation, $96,000; Helzburg Company, $192,000; and Zales Corporation, $144,000.

Transactions:

Sept. 1 Purchased merchandise on account costing $180,000 from Werling Company; Invoice No. 542; terms 2/10, n/30.

3 Paid Bond Corporation $96,000 with Check No. 451. The original discount of 2% was not taken because the discount period had expired.

4 Paid rent for the month of September, $6,000, with Check No. 452.

5 Paid Helzburg Company $108,000 on account with Check No. 453. No discount was offered.

6 Gave Helzburg Company a $84,000, 30-day, 12% note for the balance due.

7 Purchased merchandise on account costing $96,000 from York Corporation; Invoice No. 982; terms 2/10, n/30.

8 Purchased merchandise on account costing $108,000 from Bond Corporation; Invoice No. 1522; terms 2/10, n/30.

9 Received credit from York Corporation for returning $12,000 of the $96,000 of merchandise purchased.

12 Paid Werling Company the amount due on the purchase of September 1 with Check No. 454.

15 Purchased merchandise on account costing $144,000 from New Point Corporation; Invoice No. 841; terms n/30.

17 Paid Bond Corporation the amount due on the purchase of September 8 with Check No. 455.

20 Purchased merchandise on account costing $156,000 from Bond Corporation; Invoice No. 1566; terms 2/10, n/30.

22 Purchased merchandise on account costing $84,000 from Quarter Company; Invoice No. 1910; terms n/30.

25 Paid $96,000 on account to New Point Corporation on the purchase of September 15 with Check No. 456.

29 Received $36,000 credit from Bond Corporation for returning part of the merchandise purchased on September 20.

30 Purchased merchandise on account having a cost of $60,000 from Jane Company; Invoice No. 2125; terms n/60.

Required: Prepare a purchases journal (Illustration 6.4) and cash disbursements journal (Illustration 6.5, except that the Supplies Expense column should be omitted because it is not used). Also set up a general journal. Then using the above information:

a. Completely journalize each of the transactions in the appropriate journals.

b. Post only the amounts pertaining to accounts payable to the subsidiary accounts and to the control account. Create some additional subsidiary accounts and arrange all subsidiary accounts in alphabetical order. Additional accounts should be created for Jane Company, New Point Corporation, Quarter Company, Werling Company, and York Corporation.

c. Prepare a schedule of accounts payable at September 30, 1991, and compare it with the balance of the control account at the same date.

P6-4-A

Post data from journals to ledger accounts after entering beginning balances in the accounts; prepare trial balance

The post-closing trial balance of Queen Department Store as of November 30, 1991, was as follows:

QUEEN DEPARTMENT STORE
Post-Closing Trial Balance
November 30, 1991

	Debits	Credits
Cash	$ 35,000	
Accounts Receivable	24,000	
Inventory—Men's Clothing	12,000	
Inventory—Women's Clothing	20,000	
Inventory—Shoes	2,000	
Inventory—Cosmetics and Jewelry	8,000	
Inventory—Sporting Goods	11,000	
Inventory—Miscellaneous	2,600	
Office Equipment	10,000	
Accumulated Depreciation—Office Equipment		$ 3,400
Land	6,320	
Buildings	80,000	
Accumulated Depreciation—Buildings		19,400
Accounts Payable		20,200
Notes Payable		2,000
T. Queen, Capital		165,920
	$210,920	$210,920

The company has five major selling departments and several minor ones. Separate general ledger accounts are maintained for sales and purchases for each of the major departments. Sales and purchases for the minor departments are grouped under Sales—Miscellaneous and Purchases—Miscellaneous.

The December transactions were recorded in its five journals: sales journal, cash receipts journal, purchases journal, cash disbursements journal, and general journal. At December 31, 1991, the column totals in the sales journal were as follows:

Accounts Receivable Dr.	Sales— Men's Clothing Cr.	Sales— Women's Clothing Cr.	Sales— Shoes Cr.	Sales— Cosmetics and Jewelry Cr.	Sales— Sporting Goods Cr.	Sales— Miscellaneous Cr.
81,000	20,000	25,000	8,400	8,000	15,600	4,000

The column totals of the cash receipts journal were as follows:

Cash Dr.	Sales Discounts Dr.	Sales— Men's Clothing Cr.	Sales— Women's Clothing Cr.	Sales— Shoes Cr.	Sales— Cosmetics and Jewelry Cr.	Sales— Sporting Goods Cr.	Sales— Miscel- laneous Cr.	Accounts Receivable Cr.	Other Accounts Cr.
140,200	1,120	12,000	16,000	6,600	12,000	6,400	8,000	72,000	8,320

The entries in the Other Accounts Cr. column resulted from the sale of land at cost of $6,320 (December 4) and $2,000 of revenue from the operation of a delivery service for other companies (December 31).

The column totals in the purchases journal were as follows:

Purchases—Men's Clothing Dr.	Purchases—Women's Clothing Dr.	Purchases—Shoes Dr.	Purchases—Cosmetics and Jewelry Dr.	Purchases—Sporting Goods Dr.	Purchases—Miscellaneous Dr.	Accounts Payable Cr.
28,000	38,000	12,000	15,000	27,800	8,000	128,800

The column totals of the cash disbursements journal were as follows:

Accounts Payable Dr.	Supplies Expense Dr.	Other Accounts Dr.	Cash Cr.	Purchase Discounts Cr.
117,000	19,400	15,800	149,400	2,800

The entries in the Other Accounts Dr. column resulted from the payment of $1,920 for a delivery truck (December 7) and $13,880 for the purchase of a garage (December 15).

The general journal includes the following entry during the month:

Dec. 21   Buildings 17,400
            Notes Payable   17,400

Required: Enter the trial balance totals in the ledger accounts and then post information from the journals above. After posting, prepare a trial balance.

P6-5-A
Journalize transactions; post to general ledger accounts; prepare trial balance

Massey Microcomputer Store uses special journals for sales, cash receipts, purchases, and cash disbursements, as well as a general journal. These journals follow the same general design as those illustrated in this chapter. Cash discount terms of 2/10, n/30 are granted on all credit sales.

Transactions:

Aug. 1   Sold Cod, Inc., a $24,000 computer on account; terms 2/10, n/30; Invoice No. WI-A1.
       3   Bought computer merchandise on account from Brad Company; Invoice No. 33-NP, $16,800.
       5   Cash sales, $76,000.
       9   Rent revenue received, $3,200.
      11   Received amount due from Cod, Inc., for sale of August 1. The discount was taken.
      11   Paid for office equipment received today, $9,600 (Check No. 132). The equipment was for the company's own use.
      12   Paid Brad Company for purchase of August 3 (Check No. 133).
      14   Sold a $16,000 computer on account to McGuinn, Inc.; Invoice No. WI-A2.
      15   Sold a $5,600 computer on account to Franks Company; Invoice No. WI-A3.
      15   Bought computer merchandise on account from Brad Company, $7,920; Invoice No. 34-NP; terms n/10.
      17   Bought computer merchandise on account from Brown Company, $12,000; Invoice No. 98-VX; terms 2/10, n/30.
      18   Bought office equipment for $7,600 and gave a 30-day, 12% note in payment. The equipment was for the company's own use.
      19   Received a 90-day, 12% note receivable for an account receivable (Paul McAllister) in the amount of $2,800.
      19   Cash sales of computer software, $14,400.
      20   Collected $6,160 on account from Charles Barfield.
      21   Cash sales of computer software, $8,960.

Aug. 22   Cash sales of computer software, $2,400.
    23   Collected net amount due from McGuinn, Inc., on sale of August 14.
    24   Collected net amount due from Franks Company on sale of August 15.
    25   Paid Brad Company on invoice of August 15 (Check No. 134).
    26   Paid Brown Company on invoice of August 17 (Check No. 135).
    28   Paid delivery expense in cash, $3,200 (Check No. 136).
    28   Paid advertising expense in cash, $6,400 (Check No. 137).
    29   Sold two computers for $29,600 on account to Franks Company; Invoice No. WI-A4; terms 2/10, n/30.
    30   Sold three computers for $39,200 on account to McGuinn, Inc.; Invoice No. WI-A5.
    31   Bought computer merchandise on account from Brad Company, $7,120; Invoice No. 137-NP.

Required: a.   Enter the transactions for August 1991 in the proper journals. All journal pages are to be numbered page 5.

          b.   Post the entries to the general ledger accounts shown below. The Cash account and E. Massey, Capital account each have a beginning balance of $40,000.

          c.   Prepare a trial balance as of the end of the period. General ledger accounts are:

1. Cash.	8. Sales.
2. Accounts Receivable.	9. Sales Discounts.
3. Notes Receivable.	10. Purchases.
4. Office Equipment.	11. Purchase Discounts.
5. Accounts Payable.	12. Delivery Expense.
6. Notes Payable.	13. Advertising Expense.
7. E. Massey, Capital.	14. Rental Revenue.

PROBLEMS, SERIES B

P6-1-B
Record transactions in sales and purchases journals; post to T-accounts in general and subsidiary ledgers

a.   Hayes Stereo Store sold merchandise on account to the following customers on the dates indicated:

Date	Customer	Invoice No.	Amount
1991			
Dec. 2	Susan Moore	300	$ 600
8	Margarett Allen	301	7,200
14	Barbara Malloy	302	5,400
21	Janet Gibson	303	3,600
31	Susan Miller	304	2,700

The general ledger account numbers are:

Accounts Receivable 101
Sales 300

Required: Record the transactions on page 5 of a sales journal. Using T-account format, post the data to accounts in the general ledger and accounts receivable subsidiary ledger.

b. Heather Appliance Store purchased merchandise from the following companies on the dates indicated:

Date	Creditor	Terms	Invoice No.	Amount
1991				
Sept. 2	Baker Company	2/20, n/60	642	$ 90,000
7	Dexter Company	2/10, n/30	441	108,000
15	Hanley Corporation	2/EOM	543	36,000
23	Stanton Company	1/15, n/30	286	81,000
28	Welker Corporation	2/10, n/30	324	135,000

The general ledger account numbers are:

Accounts Payable 201
Purchases 410

Required: Record the transactions on page 20 of a purchases journal. Using T-account format, post the data to accounts in the general ledger and accounts payable subsidiary ledger.

P6-2-B
Journalize transactions in appropriate journal; post to accounts in general and subsidiary ledgers; prepare schedule of accounts receivable

On June 30, 1991, the Accounts Receivable control account balance on the books of Green Wholesale Shoe Company was equal to the total balances of the accounts in the accounts receivable subsidiary ledger. The balances were as follows: Accounts Receivable control account (Account No. 131), $68,720; Billings, Inc., $26,400; Haygood Products, Inc., $12,320; and Johnson Company, $30,000.

Transactions (ignore the fact that usually the terms to all customers are the same):

July   1   Sales of merchandise on account to Johnson Company, $4,800; Invoice No. 306; terms n/30.
       3   Cash sales, $13,800.
       5   Received cash for land sold at its original cost of $20,000.
       5   Received $18,000 cash as partial collection of amount due today from Billings, Inc. No discount was allowed.
       9   Sold merchandise on account to Glasco Company, $3,600; Invoice No. 307; terms 3/10, n/30.
      11   Received $12,073.60 from Haygood Products, Inc. A discount of 2% of the account receivable balance was granted.
      16   Sold merchandise on account to Wilson Company, $4,000; Invoice No. 308; terms n/30.
      18   Sold merchandise on account to Haygood Products, Inc., $7,200; Invoice No. 309; terms n/30.
      20   Allowed Haygood Products, Inc., credit for $1,000 on goods returned to Green on Invoice No. 309.
      22   Sold $4,800 of merchandise to Billings, Inc.; Invoice No. 310; terms n/10.
      23   Received $16,000 cash on balance due today from Johnson Company. No discount was taken.
      25   Sold $6,000 of merchandise on account to Billings, Inc.; Invoice No. 311; terms n/10.
      27   Allowed Billings, Inc., credit of $400 on goods sold July 25 and damaged in transit due to faulty packing by Green Company.
      31   Sold $5,200 of merchandise on account to May Company; Invoice No. 312; terms 2/10, n/30.
      31   Cash sales, $82,400.

Required: Prepare a sales journal (Illustration 6.1) and cash receipts journal (Illustration 6.2). Also set up a general journal. Then using the above information:

a. Completely journalize each of the transactions in the appropriate journal.
b. Post only the amounts pertaining to accounts receivable to the subsidiary accounts and to the control account. Set up some additional subsidiary accounts. Keep all subsidiary accounts in alphabetical order. You will need additional accounts for Glasco Company, May Company, and Wilson Company.
c. Prepare a schedule of accounts receivable at July 31, 1991, and compare it with the balance of the control account at the same date.

P6-3-B
Journalize transactions in appropriate journal; post to general and subsidiary ledger accounts; prepare schedule of accounts payable

On June 30, 1991, the Accounts Payable control account on the books of Green Wholesale Shoe Company was equal to the total of the accounts in the accounts payable subsidiary ledger. The balances were as follows: Accounts Payable control account (Account No. 201), $23,250; Gate Company, $10,575; Jones Corporation, $3,675; and White Company, $9,000.

Transactions:

July 1 Purchased merchandise on account costing $7,500 from Hall Company; Invoice No. 562; terms 2/10, n/30.
 2 Paid Gate Company $7,500 on account with Check No. 101. No discount was available when the purchase was originally made.
 3 Paid rent for July with Check No. 102, $900.
 5 Gave Jones Corporation a 60-day, 12% note for the amount owed.
 6 Purchased merchandise on account costing $3,750 from Gate Company; Invoice No. 261; terms 2/10, n/30.
 9 Paid $7,350 to Hall Company on the July 1 purchase with Check No. 103.
11 Paid $3,000 for a life insurance policy on top executives to cover the period from August 1, 1991, to July 31, 1992. Used Check No. 104.
17 Purchased merchandise on account costing $6,000 from Hall Company; Invoice No. 581; terms 2/10, n/30.
21 Received credit from White Company for $1,500 on merchandise returned to it. No discount was available as of the date of purchase.
23 Purchased merchandise on account costing $2,250 from Andrews Corporation; Invoice No. 1031; terms n/30.
25 Paid $4,500 to White Company with Check No. 105. No discount was allowed as of the date of purchase.
27 Purchased merchandise on account costing $5,250 from Sand Corporation; Invoice No. 328; terms 2/10, n/30.
29 Paid Hall Company $3,000 on the purchase of July 17, Check No. 106.
31 Purchased merchandise on account costing $6,000 from Dodge Company; Invoice No. 168; terms 2/20, n/60.

Required: Prepare a purchases journal (Illustration 6.4) and a cash disbursements journal (Illustration 6.5, except that the Supplies Expense column should be omitted since it is not used). Also set up a general journal. Then using the above information:

a. Completely journalize each of the transactions in the appropriate journal.
b. Post only the amounts pertaining to accounts payable to the subsidiary accounts and to the control account. Arrange all subsidiary accounts in alphabetical order. Additional accounts will be needed for Andrews Corporation, Hall Company, Dodge Company, and Sand Corporation.
c. Prepare a schedule of accounts payable at July 31, 1991, and compare it with the balance of the control account at the same date.

P6–4–B

Post data from journals to ledger accounts after entering beginning balances in the accounts; prepare trial balance

The post-closing trial balance of Discount Department Store as of November 30, 1991, was as follows:

DISCOUNT DEPARTMENT STORE
Post-Closing Trial Balance
November 30, 1991

	Debits	Credits
Cash	$ 17,500	
Accounts Receivable	13,750	
Notes Receivable	1,250	
Inventory—Men's Clothing	3,750	
Inventory—Women's Clothing	4,500	
Inventory—Appliances	3,000	
Inventory—Furniture	7,000	
Inventory—Bargain Basement	1,750	
Inventory—Other Departments	1,250	
Office Equipment	5,000	
Accumulated Depreciation—Office Equipment		$ 2,000
Buildings	70,000	
Accumulated Depreciation—Buildings		13,750
Accounts Payable		10,876
L. Pierce, Capital		102,124
	$128,750	$128,750

The company has five major selling departments and several minor ones. Separate general ledger accounts are maintained for sales and purchases for each of the major departments. Sales and purchases for the minor departments are grouped under Sales—Other Departments and Purchases—Other Departments.

The December transactions were recorded in its five journals: sales journal, cash receipts journal, purchases journal, cash disbursements journal, and general journal. At December 31, 1991, the column totals in the sales journal were as follows:

Accounts Receivable Dr.	Sales—Men's Clothing Cr.	Sales—Women's Clothing Cr.	Sales—Appliances Cr.	Sales—Furniture Cr.	Sales—Bargain Basement Cr.	Sales—Other Departments Cr.
112,750	20,000	22,500	17,500	30,000	15,000	7,750

The column totals of the cash receipts journal were as follows:

Cash Dr.	Sales Discounts Dr.	Sales—Men's Clothing Cr.	Sales—Women's Clothing Cr.	Sales—Appliances Cr.	Sales—Furniture Cr.	Sales—Bargain Basement Cr.	Sales—Other Departments Cr.	Accounts Receivable Cr.	Other Accounts Cr.
166,500	1,538	11,250	12,500	10,000	16,250	6,000	6,750	96,412	8,876

The entries in the Other Accounts Cr. column resulted from the collection of $6,500 of rental revenue (December 8) and $2,376 of miscellaneous revenue from the sale of scrap (December 14).

The column totals in the purchases journal were as follows:

Purchases— Men's Clothing Dr.	Purchases— Women's Clothing Dr.	Purchases— Appliances Dr.	Purchases— Furniture Dr.	Purchases— Bargain Basement Dr.	Purchases— Other Departments Dr.	Accounts Payable Cr.
26,250	27,000	13,750	25,500	18,750	10,874	122,124

The column totals of the cash disbursements journal were:

Accounts Payable Dr.	Supplies Expense Dr.	Other Accounts Dr.	Cash Cr.	Purchase Discounts Cr.
96,500	13,750	11,388	120,888	750

The entries in the Other Accounts Dr. column result from the payment of $638 for ordinary repairs to the buildings (December 15) and $10,750 for the purchase of a small storage building (December 22). These amounts have not been posted.

The general journal includes the following entry at the date indicated:

Dec. 18 Office Equipment   2,000
           Notes Payable   2,000

Required: Enter the trial balance totals in ledger accounts and then post information that is in the journals above. After posting, prepare a trial balance.

P6–5–B
Journalize transactions; post to general ledger accounts; prepare trial balance

Mays Wholesale Food Company uses special journals for sales, cash receipts, purchases, and cash disbursements, as well as a general journal. These journals follow the same general design as those illustrated in this chapter. Cash discount terms of 2/10, n/30 are granted on all credit sales.

Transactions:

Dec. 1 Purchased merchandise on account from Dixon Company, $33,600; Invoice No. C1109; terms 2/10, n/30.
      2 Purchased merchandise on account from Bailey Company, $19,200; Invoice No. 1888Z; terms n/10.
      3 Bought office equipment from Harrell Company, $46,560; Invoice No. 854. Gave a 30-day, 12% note in payment.
      5 Purchased merchandise on account from Abel Company, $26,400; Invoice No. X9784; terms 2/10, n/30.
      6 Cash sales, $34,080.
      7 Collected rent revenue for December, $45,600.
      8 Sold $24,000 of merchandise on account to David, Inc.; Invoice No. 3345.
     10 Sold $33,600 of merchandise on account to Potts Company; Invoice No. 3346.
     11 Sold $38,400 of merchandise on account to Zap Company; Invoice No. 3347.
     12 Paid Dixon Company for purchase of December 1 with Check No. 201.
     12 Paid Bailey Company for purchase of December 2 with Check No. 202.
     14 Paid Abel Company for purchase of December 5 with Check No. 203.
     16 Cash sales, $94,560.
     18 Collected amount due on sale of December 8 to David, Inc.
     20 Collected amount due on sale of December 10 to Potts Company.
     21 Collected amount due on sale of December 11 to Zap Company.
     23 Cash sales, $60,000.
     24 Paid *The Newton News* for advertising expense, $3,600 (Check No. 204).

Dec. 26   Sold $28,800 of merchandise on account to Zap Company; Invoice No. 3348.
  26   Sold $67,200 of merchandise on account to Dee Company; Invoice No. 3349.
  27   Sold $142,560 of merchandise on account to Kote Company; Invoice No. 3350.

Required: a. Enter the transactions for December 1991 in the proper journals. All journals are to be numbered page 40.
   b. Post the entries to the general ledger accounts shown below. The Cash account and M. Mays, Capital account each have a beginning balance of $120,000.
   c. Prepare a trial balance as of the end of the period. General ledger accounts are:

1. Cash.
2. Accounts Receivable.
3. Office Equipment.
4. Accounts Payable.
5. Notes Payable.
6. M. Mays, Capital.
7. Sales.
8. Sales Discounts.
9. Purchases.
10. Purchase Discounts.
11. Advertising Expense.
12. Rental Revenue.

BUSINESS DECISION PROBLEM 6–1

Describe and discuss special journals

Mike Davis, the owner and operator of Mike's Bowling Lanes, has been using a general journal to record all business transactions. The posting task has taken an increasing amount of his time. He asks your assistance in designing special journals that would make the task less time consuming.

His wife is to handle all of the credit purchases, cash disbursements, and adjusting entries in her office at home. Mike or his assistant will record all sales and cash receipts at the bowling lanes.

Sales are classified as follows: Bowling Fees, Equipment, Supplies, Shoe Rental, and Miscellaneous Services. (The adjoining restaurant is owned and operated by another party.) Sales are made for both cash and credit. No sales discounts are offered.

Purchases are made from various suppliers. Periodic inventory procedure is used.

Required: a. Determine which special journals should be used.
   b. Show the column headings that could be used in each of the special journals. Illustrate the use of the special journals by journalizing a sufficient number of assumed transactions for 1991 so that at least one number appears in each of the columns you have designed.
   c. Describe the posting of each of the special journals you have designed.

BUSINESS DECISION PROBLEM 6–2

Describe and discuss special journals

Bill Lewis, the golf professional at the Dogwood Country Club, has been using a general journal to record all business transactions. The volume of business has been increasing, and now Bill seeks your assistance in devising some special journals. He wants his wife to keep track of all receipts, disbursements, and adjusting entries in her office at home. He and his assistant are to record all credit sales and purchases at the golf shop.

Sales are classified as follows: Golf Equipment, Golf Supplies, Apparel, Lessons, Cart Rental, and Miscellaneous Services. Sales are made for both cash and on account. No sales discounts are offered.

Purchases are made from many different suppliers. Items purchased include apparel, golf supplies, and golf equipment. Periodic inventory procedure is used.

Required:
   a. Determine which special journals should be used.
   b. Show the column headings that could be used in each of the special journals. Illustrate the use of each special journal by journalizing enough assumed transactions for 1991 so that at least one number appears in each of the columns you have designed.
   c. Describe the posting of each of the special journals you have designed.

BUSINESS DECISION PROBLEM 6-3

Describe important factors in deciding how to process data

Cite some of the factors that would be important in deciding whether a company should utilize an accounting (bookkeeping) machine, a time-sharing facility, a service bureau, or a computer system installed at the firm.

COMPREHENSIVE REVIEW PROBLEM

Problem reviews concepts covered in Chapters 1–6; enter beginning balances in general ledger accounts; journalize transactions; post journal data to general ledger and subsidiary accounts; prepare work sheet, classified income statement, and classified balance sheet; journalize and post adjusting and closing entries; prepare post-closing trial balance and schedules of accounts receivable and accounts payable

Dana Sportswear Outlet Store sells sporting equipment, clothes, and shoes for use in sports such as tennis, golf, skiing, jogging, racketball, and so on. The company, which has been in business for about five years, is owned and operated by Bill Dana. Most sales are for cash, but some are on credit. Financial statements are prepared at the end of each month. The post-closing trial balance as of November 30, 1991, follows:

DANA SPORTSWEAR OUTLET STORE
Post-Closing Trial Balance
November 30, 1991

Account No.		Debits	Credits
1	Cash	$18,000	
2	Accounts Receivable	5,000	
3	Prepaid Insurance	700	
4	Supplies on Hand	1,200	
5	Merchandise Inventory	25,000	
6	Office Furniture	4,000	
7	Accumulated Depreciation—Office Furniture		$ 1,770
8	Store Equipment	10,000	
9	Accumulated Depreciation—Store Equipment		4,720
10	Accounts Payable		4,500
11	Bill Dana, Capital		52,910
		$63,900	$63,900

The chart of accounts for the Dana Sportswear Outlet Store is as follows:

Account No.	Account Title	Account No.	Account Title
1	Cash	15	Sales Returns and Allowances
2	Accounts Receivable		
3	Prepaid Insurance	16	Miscellaneous Revenue
4	Supplies on Hand	17	Purchases
5	Merchandise Inventory	18	Purchase Discounts
6	Office Furniture	19	Purchase Returns and Allowances
7	Accumulated Depreciation—Office Furniture		
		20	Transportation-In
8	Store Equipment	21	Rent Expense
9	Accumulated Depreciation—Store Equipment	22	Insurance Expense
		23	Supplies Expense
10	Accounts Payable	24	Depreciation Expense—Office Furniture
11	Bill Dana, Capital		
12	Bill Dana, Drawing	25	Depreciation Expense—Store Equipment
13	Sales		
14	Sales Discounts	26	Income Summary

Schedules of accounts receivable and accounts payable prepared at November 30, 1991, are as follows:

DANA SPORTSWEAR OUTLET STORE
Schedule of Accounts Receivable
As of November 30, 1991

Sallie Branscom	$ 800
Cindy Carrel	900
Charles Coleman	750
John Grant	1,100
James Hood	1,000
V. P. Stone	450
	$5,000

DANA SPORTSWEAR OUTLET STORE
Schedule of Accounts Payable
As of November 30, 1991

Athletic Shoe Corporation	$ 900
Rackets, Inc.	1,500
Sports Clothes, Inc.	2,100
	$4,500

The company uses a sales journal, cash receipts journal, purchases journal, cash disbursements journal, and general journal.

Transactions:

Dec. 1 Paid rent for use of the sales building for December, $1,600; Check No. 200.

2 Cash sales were $4,200.

4 Sold merchandise on account to Sallie Branscom, $250; Invoice No. 512; terms 2/10, n/30.

Dec. 5 Received payment on account from the following customers:

Name	Gross Amount	Discount Taken	Net Amount Received
Cindy Carrel	$ 900	$18	$ 882
Charles Coleman . . .	750	15	735
John Grant	1,100	22	1,078
James Hood	1,000	20	980

7 Paid Rackets, Inc., $1,500 on account after deducting a 2% discount; Check No. 201.

8 Paid Sports Clothes, Inc., $2,100 on account after deducting a 2% discount; Check No. 202.

10 Cash sales were $7,200.

12 Granted a sales allowance to Sallie Branscom for $100 because of damaged merchandise.

14 Received payment from Sallie Branscom, $700. No discount was taken.

15 Paid Athletic Shoe Corporation, $900; Check No. 203. No discount was involved.

17 Purchased $2,800 of sports equipment on account from Rackets, Inc.; Invoice No. 210; terms 2/10, n/30, FOB destination.

19 Cash sales were $6,600.

20 Purchased $1,700 of sports clothing on account from Sports Clothes, Inc.; Invoice No. 620; terms n/30, FOB shipping point.

20 Paid freight charge of $60 to Rapid Delivery Company on today's purchase from Sports Clothes, Inc.; Check No. 204.

21 The owner withdrew $1,000 to cover living expenses; Check No. 205.

22 Received payment on account from V. P. Stone, $450. No discount was taken.

23 Purchased $1,000 of sports shoes on account from Athletic Shoe Corporation; Invoice No.125; terms n/30, FOB destination.

24 Sold merchandise on account to John Grant, $850; Invoice No. 513; terms 2/10, n/30.

26 Paid the invoice for the purchase on December 17 after taking the discount; Check No. 206.

26 Sold merchandise to James Hood, $900; Invoice No. 514; terms 2/10, n/30.

27 Cash sales were $4,500.

28 Sold merchandise on account to Janice Thompson, $910; Invoice No. 515; terms 2/10, n/30.

29 Purchased $2,400 of clothing on account from Sports Clothes, Inc.; Invoice No. 1006; terms n/30, FOB shipping point.

29 Paid freight of $40 to Rapid Delivery Company for today's purchase from Sports Clothes, Inc.; Check No. 207.

30 Sold merchandise on account to Jim Westerling, $1,200; Invoice No. 516; terms 2/10, n/30.

31 Received a $200 allowance on the purchase of December 29 because some of the merchandise was damaged.

31 Cash sales were $2,100.

31 Received $100 from the sale of scrap materials located on the premises.

Additional data:

1. Of the prepaid insurance, $150 expired in December.
2. The supplies on hand at December 31 were $900.
3. Depreciation expense on the office furniture for December was $30.
4. Depreciation expense on the store equipment for December was $80.
5. The merchandise inventory on December 31 was $20,000.

Required: a. Enter the beginning balances for December 1991 into the general ledger accounts, the accounts receivable subsidiary ledger accounts, and the accounts payable subsidiary ledger accounts.

b. Journalize in the appropriate journal the transactions given above for December. All special journal pages should be identified as page No. 6.

c. Post the data in the journals to the appropriate general ledger and subsidiary ledger accounts.

d. Prepare a work sheet as of December 31, 1991. Use the additional data given above to prepare the necessary adjustments on the work sheet.

e. Prepare a classified income statement and balance sheet. Rent expense, depreciation expense—store equipment, and supplies expense are the only selling expenses.

f. Journalize in the general journal the adjusting entries and closing entries. The adjusting entries are entered on page 6 of the general journal, and the closing entries are entered on page 7 of the general journal.

g. Post the adjusting entries and closing entries to the general ledger accounts.

h. Prepare a post-closing trial balance.

i. Prepare a schedule of accounts receivable and a schedule of accounts payable at December 31, 1991.

PART

3

Assets and Liabilities

7 Control of Cash

After studying this chapter, you should be able to:

1. Describe the necessity for and features of internal control.
2. Define cash and list the objectives sought by management in handling a company's cash.
3. Identify procedures for controlling cash receipts and disbursements.
4. Prepare a bank reconciliation and make necessary journal entries based on that schedule.
5. Explain why a petty cash fund is used, describe its operations, and make the necessary journal entries.
6. Apply the net price method of handling purchase discounts.
7. Describe the operation of the voucher system and make entries in its special journals—the voucher register and the check register.
8. Define and use correctly the new terms in the glossary.

So far in the text you have studied examples of one-owner businesses. When the owner is also the manager of the business, the owner makes all the important decisions and usually maintains a close watch over the affairs of the business. Often the owner personally signs the checks. However, as the business grows and the need arises for additional employees, including other managers, the owner begins to lose total control and must trust employees to take over some of the affairs of the business. At this point, an owner realizes that precautions must be taken to protect the company's interests. As a result, owners establish internal control measures. This chapter discusses the internal control measures a company takes to protect its assets and to promote the accuracy of its accounting records.

You may think that internal control is used just to prevent theft and fraud. However, there is more to internal control. Company policies must be implemented, especially those policies that require compliance with federal law. Personnel must perform their assigned duties to promote efficiency of operations. Correct accounting records must be maintained so that accurate and reliable information is presented in the accounting reports. In this chapter, you will learn how internal control is established through control of cash receipts and cash disbursements, proper use of the bank checking account, preparation of the bank reconciliation, protection of petty cash funds, and usage of the net price method and the voucher system. The establishment of internal control is enhanced by hiring competent and trustworthy employees, a fact you will appreciate if you ever become a business owner.

■ INTERNAL CONTROL

Objective 1: Describe the necessity for and features of internal control.

The **internal control system** of a company includes its plan of organization and all the procedures and actions taken by the company to:

1. Protect its assets against theft and waste.
2. Ensure compliance with company policies and federal law.
3. Evaluate the performance of all personnel in the company so as to promote efficiency of operations.
4. Ensure accurate and reliable operating data and accounting reports.

As you study the basic procedures and actions comprising an internal control system, you will realize that even the small, one-owner businesses can benefit from the use of some internal control measures. Preventing theft and waste is only a part of internal control. In general terms, the purpose of internal control is to ensure the efficient operations of a business, thus enabling the business to effectively reach its goals. Since additional control procedures are necessary in a computer environment, a discussion of these controls concludes this section on internal control.

Protection of Assets

Assets can be protected by (1) segregation of employee duties, (2) separation of employee functions, (3) rotation of employee job assignments, and (4) use of mechanical devices.

Segregation of Employee Duties.   To accomplish **segregation of duties,** the employee responsible for safeguarding an asset must be someone other than the employee who maintains the accounting records for that asset. Also, responsibility for related transactions should be divided among employees so that one employee's work serves as a check on the work of other employees.

When a company segregates the duties of employees, then collusion between at least two employees is necessary to steal assets and cover up the theft in the accounting records. For example, an employee could not steal cash from a company and have it go undetected unless the cash records could be changed to cover the shortage. Changing the records can only be accomplished if the employee stealing the cash maintains the cash records or is in collusion with the employee who maintains the cash records.

Separate Employee Functions.   When the responsibility for a particular work function is assigned to one employee, that employee is accountable for specific tasks. Then, in the event of a problem, the employee responsible can be quickly identified.

When employees are given specific duties, it is relatively easy to trace lost documents or determine how a particular transaction is recorded. Also, the employee responsible for a given task is the person best able to provide information about that task. In addition, a division of responsibilities gives people a sense of pride and importance that tends to make them want to perform to the best of their ability.

Rotating Employees' Job Assignments.   When the company policy is to rotate job assignments, this policy often discourages employees from engaging in long-term schemes to steal from the company. Employees realize that if they steal from the company, the theft may be discovered by the next employee assigned to that position.

Frequently, companies have the policy that all employees must take an annual vacation. This also discourages theft because many dishonest schemes collapse when the employee does not attend to the job on a daily basis.

Mechanical Devices.   Companies can use mechanical devices to help protect their assets. Devices such as check protectors (machines that perforate the check amount into the check), cash registers, and time clocks make it impossible for employees to alter certain company documents and records.

Compliance with Company Policies and Federal Law

Internal control policies are effective only when the employees of a company follow these policies. To ensure that its internal control policies are carried out, a company must hire competent and trustworthy employees. Thus, the execution of effective internal control begins with the time and effort a company expends in hiring employees. Once the employees are hired, the company must train those employees and clearly communicate to them company policies, such as proper authorization before making a cash disbursement. Frequently, written job descriptions are effective in establishing the responsibilities and duties of employees. The initial training of employees should be such that they know exactly what they are expected to do and how to do it.

In publicly held corporations, the company's internal control system must satisfy the requirements of federal law. In December 1977, the Foreign Corrupt Practices Act (FCPA) was enacted by Congress. Under this law, publicly held corporations are **required** to devise and maintain an effective system of internal control and to keep accurate accounting records. The passage of this law came about partly because of the cover-ups in company accounting records of bribes and kickbacks made to foreign governments or government officials. The FCPA made this specific type of bribery illegal.

Evaluation of Personnel Performance

To evaluate how well company employees are doing their jobs, many companies use an internal auditing staff. **Internal auditing** consists of investigating and evaluating employees' compliance with the company's policies and procedures. Companies hire **internal auditors** to perform these audits; these individuals are trained in company policies and internal auditing duties. For instance, internal auditors might periodically test the effectiveness of controls and procedures involving cash receipts and cash disbursements.

Internal auditors should encourage operating efficiency throughout the company and be constantly alert for breakdowns in the company's system of internal control. In addition, internal auditors make recommendations for the improvement of the company's internal control system when necessary. All companies can benefit from internal auditing; however, internal auditing is especially necessary in large organizations because the owner(s) cannot be personally involved with all aspects of the business.

Accuracy of Accounting Records

Companies should maintain complete and accurate accounting records. The best method to ensure that this is done is to hire and train competent and honest individuals. Periodically, supervisors should evaluate an employee's performance to make sure the employee is following company policies. Inaccurate or inadequate accounting records serve as an invitation to theft by dishonest employees because the theft can be easily concealed.

Almost all accounting transactions are supported by one or more business documents. These source documents are an integral part of the internal control system. For optimal control, source documents should be serially numbered. (Transaction documentation and related aspects of internal control will be presented throughout the text.)

Since source documents serve as documentation of business transactions, from time to time the validity of these documents should be checked. For example, to review a merchandise transaction, the documents used to record the transaction should be checked against the proper accounting records. When the accounting department records a merchandise transaction, it should receive copies of the following four documents:

1. **Purchase requisition.**   A **purchase requisition** (Illustration 7.1) is a written request from an employee inside the company to the purchasing department to purchase certain items.
2. **Purchase order.**   A **purchase order** (Illustration 7.2) is a document sent from the purchasing department to a supplier requesting that merchandise or other items be shipped to the purchaser.

Illustration 7.1

Purchase Requisition

PURCHASE REQUISITION   No. ___2416___

BRYAN WHOLESALE COMPANY

From: _Automotive Supplies Department_   Date: _November 20, 1991_

To: _Purchasing Department_   Suggested
                                              supplier: _Wilkes Radio Company_

Please purchase the following items:

Description	Item Number	Quantity	Estimated Price
True-tone stereo radios	Model No. 5868-24393	200	$50 per unit

Reason for request:

Customer order
Baier Company

To be filled in by purchasing department:

Date ordered _11/21/91_

Purchase order number _N–145_

Approved _R.S.T._

Illustration 7.2

Purchase Order

PURCHASE ORDER   No. ___N–145___

BRYAN WHOLESALE COMPANY
476 Mason Street
Detroit, Michigan   48823

To: _Wilkes Radio Company_
2515 West Peachtree Street   Date: _November 21, 1991_
Atlanta, Georgia   30303   Ship by: _December 20, 1991_
Ship to: _Above address_   FOB terms requested: _Destination_
                                          Discount terms requested: _2/10, n/30_

Please send the following items:

Description	Item Number	Quantity	Price per Unit	Total Amount
True-tone stereo radios	5868-24393	200	$50	$10,000

Ordered by: _Jane Knight_   Please include order number on all
                                        invoices and shipments.

3. **Invoice.** An invoice (Illustration 7.3) is the bill sent from the supplier to the purchaser requesting payment for the merchandise shipped.

Illustration 7.3

Invoice

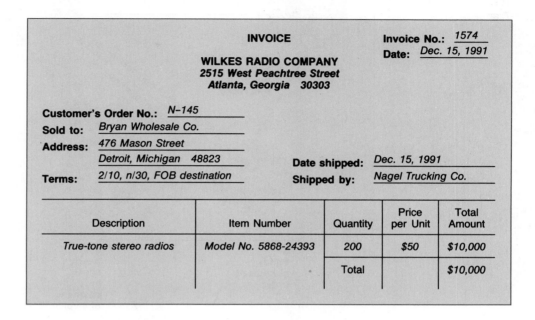

4. **Receiving report.** A receiving report is a document prepared by the receiving department showing the descriptions and quantities of all items received from a supplier in a particular shipment. A copy of the purchase order can serve as a receiving report if the quantity ordered is omitted. Then the receiving department personnel will not know what quantity to expect and probably will count more accurately how many were received.

These four documents together serve as authorization to pay for merchandise and should be checked against the accounting records. In the absence of these documents, a company might fail to pay a legitimate invoice, pay fictitious invoices, or pay an invoice more than once. Proper internal control can be accomplished only by periodically checking the source documents of business transactions with the accounting records of those transactions. Illustration 7.4 shows the flow of documents and goods in a merchandising transaction.

Unfortunately, even if a company implements all of the above features in its internal control system, theft may still occur. If employees are dishonest, they can usually figure out a way to steal from a company, thus circumventing even the most effective internal control system. Therefore, companies should carry adequate casualty insurance on assets. This insurance will reimburse the company for loss of a nonmonetary asset such as specialized equipment. Companies should also have **fidelity bonds** on employees handling cash and other negotiable instruments. These bonds will

Illustration 7.4

Flow of Documents and Goods in a Merchandising Transaction

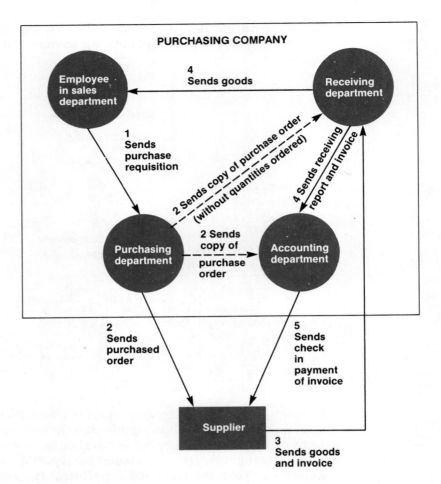

PURCHASING COMPANY

Steps:

1. Employee in sales department sends purchase requisition to purchasing department.
2. Purchasing department sends purchase order to supplier, with copies going to the receiving department (without quantities ordered) and the accounting department.
3. Supplier sends goods and invoice to receiving department, where goods received are checked against purchase order and invoice.
4. Receiving department sends goods to sales department and sends receiving report and invoice to accounting department.
5. Accounting department sends check in payment of invoice to the supplier.

ensure that a company is reimbursed for losses due to theft of cash and other monetary assets. With both casualty insurance on assets and fidelity bonds on employees, a company can recover at least a portion of any loss that occurs.

Internal Control in a Computer Environment

The use of computers to maintain financial records makes it necessary to use the same internal control principles of separation of duties and control over access that are used in a manual accounting system. The exact control steps taken depend on whether you are using larger mainframe and mini-computers or small microcomputers.

Mainframe computers and minicomputers are used in the accounting environments of large corporations. Because of the size and complexity of these computers, specially trained persons are needed to keep these computer systems operating. Systems specialists operate the computer system itself, while programmers develop the programs that direct the computer to perform specific tasks. In a mainframe or minicomputer environment, internal control should include the following:

1. Computer access should be controlled by placing the computer in an easily secured room, and only persons authorized to operate the computer should be allowed to enter the room.
2. Systems specialists who operate the computer should not have programming experience, and programmers should not have access to the computer. This policy prevents a person from making unauthorized changes to certain programs.
3. Some programs, such as ones used to print monthly accounts receivable statements to send to credit customers, should only be run at an authorized time. If programs and data are stored on magnetic tape, the tapes should be stored under lock and key and under the control of a "librarian." The librarian should be independent of the computer systems and programming function.

Internal control for a microcomputer environment is slightly different because smaller businesses often use microcomputers and usually are not able to hire a staff of specialists to run the computer. Thus, the programmers may run the computer. Also, the same microcomputer is often used by several persons.

In a microcomputer environment, the following controls can be useful:

1. The microcomputer should be kept under lock and key, and only persons authorized to use the computer should have a key.
2. Each computer user should have tight control over his or her diskettes on which programs and data are stored. Just as one person maintains custody over a certain set of records in a manual system, in a computer system one person maintains custody over diskettes containing a certain type of information (such as the accounts receivable subsidiary ledger). These diskettes should be locked up at night, and backup copies should be made.

The use of computers in accounting does not lessen the need for internal control. In fact, the access to a computer by an unauthorized person could result in significant theft in a shorter span of time.

Controlling Cash

Objective 2:
Define cash and list the objectives sought by management in handling a company's cash.

In the preceding section, you learned about some of the general principles of internal control. This section focuses specifically on the control of cash. Since cash is the most liquid of all assets, a business cannot survive and prosper if it does not have adequate control over its cash.

In accounting, **cash** includes coins; paper money; certain undeposited negotiable instruments such as checks, bank drafts, and money orders;

amounts in checking and savings accounts; and demand certificates of deposit. A **certificate of deposit** is an interest-bearing deposit in a bank that can be withdrawn at will (demand CD) or at a fixed maturity date (time CD). Cash does not include postage stamps, IOUs, or notes receivable.

In the general ledger, usually two cash accounts are maintained—Cash (bank checking and savings account balances) and Petty Cash. The balances of these two accounts are combined into one amount and reported as "Cash" on the company's balance sheet.

Since many business transactions involve cash, it is a vital factor in the operation of a business. Of all the company's assets, cash is the most easily mishandled either through theft or carelessness. To protect its cash, companies should:

1. Account for all cash transactions accurately so that correct information will be available regarding cash flows and balances.
2. Make certain that enough cash is available to pay bills as they come due.
3. Avoid holding too much idle cash, because excess cash could be invested to generate income such as interest.
4. Prevent loss of cash due to theft or fraud.

The need to control cash is clearly evident. Although you might think first about how to protect cash from the greedy hands of a dishonest employee, as you can see from the list above there is more to controlling cash. Without the proper timing of cash flows and the protection of idle cash, a business cannot survive. This section discusses cash receipts and cash disbursements. Later in the chapter, you will learn about the importance of preparing a bank reconciliation for each bank checking account, as well as controlling the petty cash fund. The net price method and voucher system are also described.

Controlling Cash Receipts

Objective 3:
Identify procedures
for controlling cash
receipts and
disbursements.

When a merchandising company sells its merchandise, it may receive cash immediately or several days or weeks later. The cash that is received immediately *over the counter* is usually recorded and placed in a cash register. The presence of the customer as the sale is *rung up* usually ensures that the correct amount of the sale is entered in the cash register. At the end of each day, the cash in each cash register is reconciled with the cash register tape or computer printout for that register. When cash is received later, it is almost always in the form of checks. A record of the checks received should be prepared as soon as they are received. Some merchandising companies receive all their cash receipts on a delayed basis in the form of payments on accounts receivable (see the cash receipts cycle for merchandise transactions in Illustration 7.5).

Although each business varies its specific procedures for controlling cash receipts, the following basic principles are used:

1. A record of all cash receipts should be prepared as soon as cash is received. Most thefts of cash occur before a record is made of the receipt. Once a record is made, it is easier to trace a theft.

Illustration 7.5

Cash Receipts Cycle for Merchandise Transactions

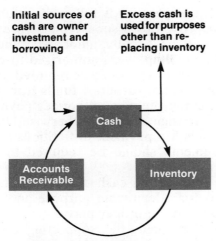

Initial sources of cash are owner investment and borrowing

Excess cash is used for purposes other than replacing inventory

Cash initially comes into the business from owner investment and borrowing. Cash is invested in inventory and other assets. When inventory is sold, cash may be received immediately, or receipt may be delayed and involve accounts receivable. The inventory generally is sold at more than cost so the company can make a profit. Each time the cycle is completed, the amount of cash grows and may be used for purposes other than replacing inventory.

2. All cash receipts should be deposited on the day they are received or on the next business day. Undeposited cash is more susceptible to misappropriation.

3. The employee who handles cash receipts should not also be the employee who records the receipts in the accounting records. This control feature follows the general principle of *segregation of duties* given earlier in the chapter, as does item 4 below.

4. If possible, the employee who receives the cash should not also be the employee to disburse the cash. This control measure is possible in all but the smallest companies.

Controlling Cash Disbursements

Controls are also needed over cash disbursements. Since most of a company's cash is spent by check, many of the internal controls for cash disbursements deal with checks and authorizations for cash payments. The basic principle of segregation of duties is also applied in controlling cash disbursements. Following are some basic control procedures for cash disbursements:

1. All disbursements should be made by check or from petty cash. Proper approval for all disbursements should be obtained, and a permanent record of each disbursement should be created. In many retail stores, refunds for returned merchandise are made from the

cash register. If this practice is followed, refund tickets should be prepared and approved by a supervisor before cash is refunded.

2. All checks should be serially numbered, and access to checks should be limited to employees authorized to write checks.

3. Preferably, two signatures should be required on each check so that one person alone cannot withdraw funds from the bank account.

4. If possible, the employee who authorizes payment of a bill should not be allowed to sign checks. Otherwise, the checks could be written to "friends" in payment of fictitious invoices.

5. Approved documents should be required to support all checks issued.

6. The employee authorizing cash disbursements should be certain that payment is for a legitimate purpose and is made out for the exact amount and to the proper party.

7. When liabilities are paid, the supporting documents should be stamped "paid," and the date and number of the check issued should be indicated. These procedures lessen the chance of paying the same debt more than once.

8. The employee(s) who signs checks should not have access to canceled checks and should not prepare the bank reconciliation. This feature makes it more difficult to conceal a theft.

Illustration 7.6

Some Internal Control Considerations Regarding Cash

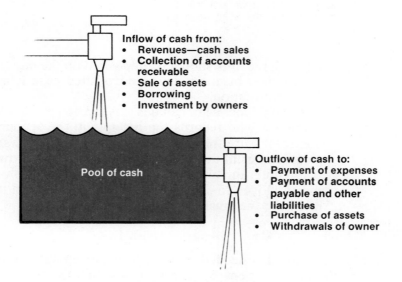

Inflow of cash from:
- Revenues—cash sales
- Collection of accounts receivable
- Sale of assets
- Borrowing
- Investment by owners

Pool of cash

Outflow of cash to:
- Payment of expenses
- Payment of accounts payable and other liabilities
- Purchase of assets
- Withdrawals of owner

Internal Control Considerations

- Are all cash receipts being properly recorded and actually going into the company's pool of cash, or are individuals siphoning off some of these receipts for their own use?
- Is the pool of cash protected from theft? Is the cash on hand managed so as to produce income for the company and yet be available when needed to make legitimate disbursements?
- Is there close control over cash disbursements to ensure that only legitimate disbursements are made in the proper amounts and on a timely basis?

9. The bank reconciliation should be prepared each month, preferably by an employee who has no other cash duties, so that errors and shortages will be quickly discovered.
10. All checks that are prepared incorrectly should be voided. Such checks should be physically marked "void" and retained to prevent their unauthorized use.
11. A voucher system (described later) may be needed in large companies for close control of cash disbursements.
12. Use of the net price method of recording purchases (described later) helps avoid loss of purchase discounts by calling attention to discounts missed.

Illustration 7.6 shows an overview of some of the internal control considerations relating to cash.

Almost without exception, companies use checking accounts to handle their cash transactions. The company deposits its cash receipts in a bank checking account and writes checks to pay its bills. The bank sends the company a statement each month. The company checks this statement against its records to determine if any corrections or adjustments are needed in either the company's balance or the bank's balance. You will learn how to do this later in the chapter when the bank reconciliation is discussed. In the next section, you will learn about the bank checking account. If you have a personal checking account, some of this information will be familiar to you.

■ THE BANK CHECKING ACCOUNT

Banks seek to earn income by providing a variety of services to individuals, businesses, and other entities such as churches or libraries. One of these services is the checking account. A **checking account** is a money balance maintained in the bank that is subject to withdrawal by the depositor, or owner of the money, on demand. To provide depositors with an accurate record of depositor funds received and disbursed, a bank uses the business documents discussed in this section.[1]

The Signature Card

A bank requires a new depositor to complete a **signature card,** which provides the signatures of persons authorized to sign checks drawn on an account. The card is retained at the bank to identify signatures on checks paid by the bank. The bank does not compare every check with this signature card; comparison is usually made only when the depositor disputes the validity of a check paid by the bank.

---

[1] Due to relaxed federal regulations, institutions other than banks—such as savings and loan associations and credit unions—now offer checking account services. All of these institutions function somewhat similarly, but for simplicity's sake only banks will be discussed here.

Deposit Ticket

When a bank deposit is made, the depositor prepares a deposit ticket or slip. A **deposit ticket** is a form that shows the date and the items that make up the deposit (Illustration 7.7). The ticket is often preprinted to show the depositor's name, address, and account number for the account into which the deposit is made. Items comprising the deposit—cash and a list of checks—are entered on the ticket when the deposit is made. After making the deposit, the depositor is given a receipt showing the date and amount deposited.

Illustration 7.7

Deposit Ticket

Check

A **check** is a written order on a bank to pay a specific sum of money to the party designated as the payee by the party issuing the check. Thus, three parties are involved in every check transaction: the **bank,** the **payee** (party to whom the check is made payable), and the **drawer** (depositor). Most checks are serially numbered and preprinted with information about the depositor, such as name, address, and telephone number. Often a business check will have an attached remittance advice. A **remittance advice** informs the payee why the drawer (or maker) of the check is making this payment. Before the check is cashed or deposited, the payee detaches the remittance advice from the check (Illustration 7.8).

Bank Statement

A **bank statement** is a statement issued (usually monthly) by a bank describing the activities in a depositor's checking account during the period. Illustration 7.9 shows a bank statement that includes the following data:

1. Deposits made to the checking account during the period.
2. Checks paid out of the depositor's checking account by the bank during the period. These checks have *cleared* the bank and are *canceled.*

Illustration 7.8

Check with Attached Remittance Advice

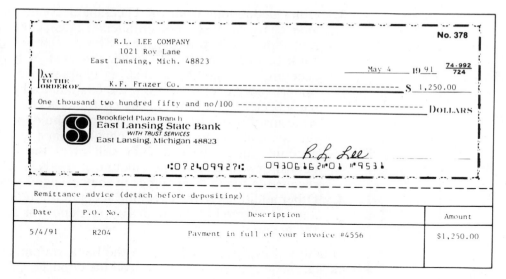

Remittance advice (detach before depositing)

Date	P.O. No.	Description	Amount
5/4/91	R204	Payment in full of your invoice #4556	$1,250.00

Illustration 7.9

Bank Statement

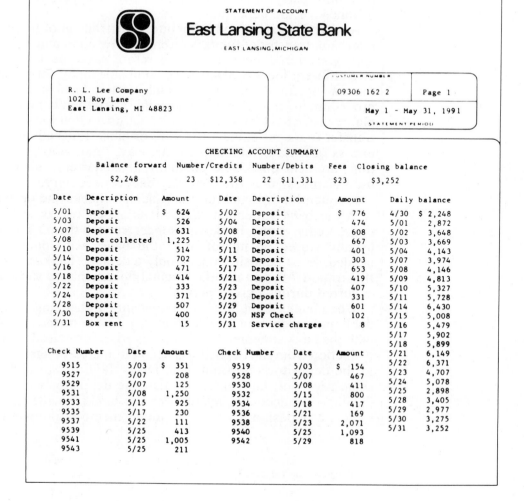

STATEMENT OF ACCOUNT

East Lansing State Bank

EAST LANSING, MICHIGAN

R. L. Lee Company
1021 Roy Lane
East Lansing, MI 48823

CUSTOMER NUMBER

09306 162 2	Page 1

May 1 - May 31, 1991

STATEMENT PERIOD

CHECKING ACCOUNT SUMMARY

	Balance forward	Number/Credits		Number/Debits		Fees	Closing balance
	$2,248	23	$12,358	22	$11,331	$23	$3,252

Date	Description	Amount	Date	Description	Amount		Daily balance
5/01	Deposit	$ 624	5/02	Deposit	$ 776	4/30	$ 2,248
5/03	Deposit	526	5/04	Deposit	474	5/01	2,872
5/07	Deposit	631	5/08	Deposit	608	5/02	3,648
5/08	Note collected	1,225	5/09	Deposit	667	5/03	3,669
5/10	Deposit	514	5/11	Deposit	401	5/04	4,143
5/14	Deposit	702	5/15	Deposit	303	5/07	3,974
5/16	Deposit	471	5/17	Deposit	653	5/08	4,146
5/18	Deposit	414	5/21	Deposit	419	5/09	4,813
5/22	Deposit	333	5/23	Deposit	407	5/10	5,327
5/24	Deposit	371	5/25	Deposit	331	5/11	5,728
5/28	Deposit	507	5/29	Deposit	601	5/14	6,430
5/30	Deposit	400	5/30	NSF Check	102	5/15	5,008
5/31	Box rent	15	5/31	Service charges	8	5/16	5,479
						5/17	5,902
						5/18	5,899

Check Number	Date	Amount	Check Number	Date	Amount		5/21	6,149
9515	5/03	$ 351	9519	5/03	$ 154		5/22	6,371
9527	5/07	208	9528	5/07	467		5/23	4,707
9529	5/07	125	9530	5/08	411		5/24	5,078
9531	5/08	1,250	9532	5/15	800		5/25	2,898
9533	5/15	925	9534	5/18	417		5/28	3,405
9535	5/17	230	9536	5/21	169		5/29	2,977
9537	5/22	111	9538	5/23	2,071		5/30	3,275
9539	5/25	413	9540	5/25	1,093		5/31	3,252
9541	5/25	1,005	9542	5/29	818			
9543	5/25	211						

3. Other deductions from the checking account for items such as service charges, NSF (nonsufficient funds) checks, safe-deposit box rent, and check printing fees. **Service charges** are assessed by the bank on the depositor to cover the cost of handling the checking account, such as check clearing charges. An **NSF check** is a customer's check returned from the customer's bank to the depositor's bank because the funds in the customer's checking account balance were insufficient to cover the check. The depositor's bank deducts the amount of the returned check from the depositor's checking account. Since the customer still owes the depositor money, the depositor will restore the amount of the NSF check to the account receivable for that customer in the company's books.

4. Other additions to the checking account for items such as proceeds of a note collected by the bank for the depositor and interest earned on the account.[2]

In addition to the data shown in the bank statement in Illustration 7.9, bank statements also can show nonroutine deposits made to the depositor's checking account. Such deposits are not made directly by the depositor but by a third party. For example, the bank may have received a wire transfer of funds for the depositor.

A **wire transfer of funds** is an interbank transfer of funds by telephone. An interbank transfer of funds is often used by companies that operate in many widely scattered locations and therefore have checking accounts with several different local banks. These companies may set up special procedures to avoid accumulating too much idle cash in local bank accounts. One such procedure involves the use of special-instruction bank accounts. For example, **transfer bank accounts** may be set up so that local banks automatically transfer to a central bank (by wire or bank draft) all amounts on deposit in excess of a stated amount. In this way, funds not needed for local operations are sent quickly to company headquarters, where the funds can be used or invested as the company deems necessary.

Frequently, the bank returns canceled checks and original deposit tickets with the bank statement. Since it is expensive to sort, handle, and mail these items, some banks no longer return them. These documents are usually stored on microfilm at the bank, with photocopies available if needed. Most depositors need only a detailed bank statement, as shown in Illustration 7.9, and not the original documents to show what transactions occurred during a given period.

When banks debit or credit a depositor's checking account, they prepare debit and credit memoranda (memos). These memos may also be returned with the bank statement. A **debit memo** is a form used by a bank to explain a deduction from the depositor's account; a **credit memo** explains an addition to the depositor's account. The terms *debit memo* and *credit memo* may seem reversed, but remember that the depositor's checking account is a liability—an account payable—of the bank. So, when the bank seeks to reduce a depositor's balance, a debit memo is prepared. To increase the

[2] Effective January 1, 1982, revised federal regulations permit banks to pay interest on a depositor's checking account balance.

Illustration 7.10

Debit Memorandum (top) and Credit Memorandum (bottom)

Debit memo

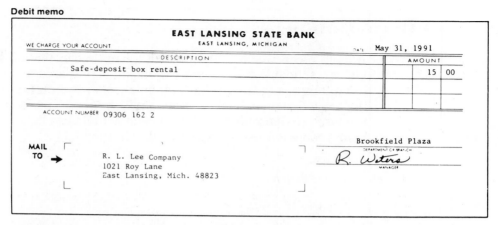

Credit memo

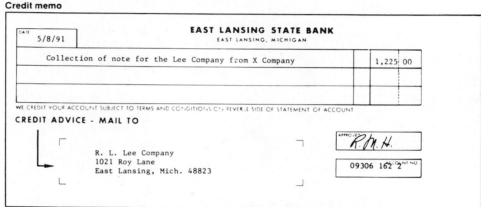

balance, a credit memo is prepared. Illustration 7.10 shows examples of debit and credit memos. Some banks no longer mail these documents to the depositor and rely instead on explanations in the bank statement.

Information that the depositor did not know prior to receiving the bank statement (items 3 and 4 on page 304) requires new journal entries on the company's books. After the entries have been made to record the new information, the balance in the Cash account is the actual cash available to the company. When the depositor has already received notice of NSF checks and other bank charges or credits, the needed journal entries may have been made earlier. In this chapter, we assume no entries have been made for these items unless stated otherwise.

When a company receives its bank statement, it must reconcile the balance shown by the bank with the cash balance shown in the company's books. If you have a personal checking account, you also should check your bank statement with your checkbook. You can use the reconciliation form on the back of the bank statement to list your checks that have not yet been paid by the bank and your deposits not yet shown on the bank statement. Some small businesses may also use this form. However, they may instead prepare a separate bank reconciliation, which you will learn how to prepare in the next section.

■ BANK RECONCILIATION

Objective 4:
Prepare a bank reconciliation and make necessary journal entries based on that schedule.

A **bank reconciliation,** often called a **bank reconciliation statement** or **schedule,** is a schedule the company (depositor) prepares to *reconcile,* or explain, the difference between the cash balance shown on the bank statement and the cash balance on the company's books. The bank reconciliation is prepared to determine the company's actual cash balance. An example of a bank reconciliation is shown in Illustration 7.11.

Illustration 7.11 *Bank Reconciliation*

R. L. LEE COMPANY
Bank Reconciliation
May 31, 1991

Balance per bank statement, May 31, 1991	$3,252	Balance per ledger, May 31, 1991		$1,891
Add: Deposit in transit	452	Add: Note collected (including interest of $25)		1,225
	$3,704			$3,116
Less: Outstanding checks:				
No. 9544 . . . . $322		Less: NSF check	$102	
No. 9545 168		Safe-deposit box rent	15	
No. 9546 223	713	Service charges	8	125
Adjusted balance, May 31, 1991	$2,991	Adjusted balance, May 31, 1991		$2,991

The bank reconciliation is divided into two main sections. One section, on the left in Illustration 7.11, begins with the balance shown on the bank statement. The second section, on the right in Illustration 7.11, begins with the company's balance as shown on the company's books. Adjustments are made to both the *bank* and *book* balances; after these adjustments, both adjusted balances should be the same.

The following steps are used in preparing a bank reconciliation:

1. **Deposits.** The deposits listed on the bank statement are compared with the deposits on the company's books. This can be done by placing check marks in the bank statement and in the company's books by the deposits that agree. Then the deposits in transit are determined. A **deposit in transit** is typically a day's cash receipts recorded in the depositor's books in one period but recorded as a deposit by the bank in the succeeding period. The most common deposit in transit is the deposit of the cash receipts of the last business day of the month. Normally, deposits in transit occur only near the end of the period covered by the bank statement. For example, a deposit made in a bank's night depository on May 31 would be recorded by the company on May 31 and by the bank on June 1. Thus, the deposit will not appear on a bank statement for the month ended May 31. The deposits in transit listed in last month's

bank reconciliation should also be checked against the bank statement. Any deposit made during the month that is missing from the bank statement (unless it involves a deposit made at the end of the period) should be investigated immediately.

2. **Paid checks.**   If canceled checks are returned with the bank statement, first compare them to the bank statement to be sure the amounts on the statement agree with the checks. Then, sort the checks in numerical order. Next, determine which checks are outstanding. **Outstanding checks** are checks issued by a depositor that have not yet been paid by the bank on which they are drawn. The party receiving the check may not deposit it immediately. Once deposited, sometimes it takes several days for checks written to clear the banking system. The outstanding checks are determined by a process of elimination. The check numbers that have cleared the bank are compared with a list of the check numbers issued by the company. Check marks are used in the company's record of checks issued to identify those checks returned by the bank. Checks issued that have not yet been returned by the bank are the outstanding checks. If the bank does not return checks but provides only a listing of the cleared checks on the bank statement, the outstanding checks are determined by comparing this list with the company's record of checks issued.

   Sometimes checks written long ago will still be outstanding. Checks outstanding as of the beginning of the month will appear on the prior month's bank reconciliation. Most of these will have cleared during the current month; those that have not cleared should be listed as still outstanding on the current month's reconciliation.

3. **Bank debit and credit memos.**   Verify all debit and credit memos on the bank statement. Debit memos reflect deductions for such items as service charges, NSF checks, safe-deposit box rent, and notes paid by the bank for the depositor. Credit memos reflect additions for such items as wire transfers of funds from another bank in which the company has funds to the home office bank and notes collected for the depositor by the bank. The bank debit and credit memos should be checked with the depositor's books to see if they have already been recorded. The accountant should make journal entries for any such items not already recorded in the company's books.

4. **Errors.**   List any errors found. A common error is that the depositor records a check in the accounting records at an amount that differs from the actual amount on the check. For example, a $47 check may be recorded at $74. The check will clear the bank at the amount written on the check ($47), but the depositor frequently does not catch the error until the bank statement or canceled checks are reviewed. Any error in the depositor's books will require an adjustment on the depositor's books.

Deposits in transit, outstanding checks, and bank service charges usually account for the difference between the company's Cash account balance and the bank balance. (This is also true for your personal checkbook balance and the bank balance shown on your bank statement.) Remember that **all items shown on the bank reconciliation as adjustments of the book (ledger) balance will require journal entries to adjust the Cash account; items appearing on the bank balance side do not require entries by the depositor.** Any bank errors, of course, should be called to the bank's attention.

To illustrate the preparation of the bank reconciliation shown in Illustration 7.11, assume the following:

1. On May 31, 1991, R. L. Lee Company showed a balance in its Cash account of $1,891. On June 2, Lee received its bank statement for the month ended May 31, which showed an ending balance of $3,252.
2. A matching of debits to the Cash account on the books with deposits on the bank statement showed that the $452 receipts of May 31 are included in Cash but not included as a deposit on the bank statement.
3. An examination of checks issued and checks cleared showed three checks outstanding:

No. 9544	$322
No. 9545	168
No. 9546	223
Total	$713

4. Included with the bank statement was a credit memo for $1,225 (principal of $1,200 + interest of $25) for collection of a note owed to Lee by Shipley Company.
5. Included with the bank statement is a $102 debit memo for an NSF check written by R. Johnson and deposited by Lee.
6. Charges made to Lee's account include $15 for safe-deposit box rent and $8 for service charges.

After reconciling the book and bank balances as shown in Illustration 7.11, Lee Company finds that its actual cash balance is $2,991. The following entries are needed to record information from the bank reconciliation:

Cash	1,225	
Notes Receivable—Shipley Company		1,200
Interest Revenue		25
To record note collected from Shipley Company.		
Bank Service Charge Expense (or Miscellaneous Expense)	23	
Cash		23
To record bank service charges.		
Accounts Receivable—R. Johnson*	102	
Cash		102
To charge NSF check back to customer, R. Johnson.		

* This debit would be posted to the Accounts Receivable control account in the general ledger and to R. Johnson's account in the accounts receivable subsidiary ledger.

The income statement for the period ending May 31, 1991, would include the $23 bank service charge as an expense. The May 31 balance sheet will show $2,991 cash, the actual cash balance.

The corrections could be made in one compound entry as follows:

Cash	1,100	
Bank Service Charge Expense	23	
Accounts Receivable—R. Johnson	102	
Notes Receivable		1,200
Interest Revenue		25

To correct the accounts for needed changes identified in the bank reconciliation.

The deposit in transit and the outstanding checks are already recorded in the depositor's books and will be handled routinely when they reach the bank. Since these items appear on the bank balance side of the reconciliation, they require no entry in the company's books. These items will be processed by the bank in the subsequent period.

When more than one checking account is maintained by a company, each account must be reconciled separately with the balance on the bank statement for that account. The depositor should then also check carefully to see that the bank did not make an error in keeping the transactions of the two accounts separate.

Certified and Cashier's Checks

To make sure a check will not *bounce* and become an NSF check, a payee may demand a certified or cashier's check from the maker. Both certified checks and cashier's checks are liabilities of the bank rather than the depositor. As a result, these checks usually are accepted without question.

- A **certified check** is a check written, or drawn, by a **depositor** and taken to the depositor's bank for certification. The bank will stamp *certified* across the face of the check and insert the name of the bank and the date; the certification will be signed by a bank official. A check is certified only when the depositor's balance is large enough to cover the check. The amount of the check is deducted from the depositor's account at the time the check is certified by the bank.
- A **cashier's check** is a check drawn by a **bank** made out to either the depositor or a third party after deducting the amount of the check from the depositor's account or receiving cash from the depositor.

In this section, you learned that all cash receipts should be deposited in the bank and all cash disbursements should be made by check. However, the next section explains that it is sometimes convenient to have small amounts of cash (petty cash) available for minor expenditures.

■ PETTY CASH FUNDS

*Objective 5:
Explain why a petty cash fund is used, describe its operations, and make the necessary journal entries.*

At times, every business finds it convenient to have small amounts of cash available for immediate payment of items such as delivery charges, postage stamps, taxi fares, supper money for employees working overtime, and other small items. To permit these disbursements to be made in cash and still maintain adequate control over cash, companies frequently establish a **petty cash fund** of a round figure such as $100 or $500.

Usually one individual, called the *petty cash custodian* or *cashier,* is responsible for the operation of the fund, which includes control of the petty cash fund and documenting the disbursements made from the fund. By assigning the responsibility for the fund to one individual, the company has internal control over the cash in the fund. In this section, you will learn how to both establish and operate a petty cash fund.

Establishing the Fund

The petty cash fund is established by writing a check for, say, $100. The amount of a petty cash fund should be large enough to make disbursements for a reasonable period, such as a month.

For example, assume a $100 petty cash fund is to be established. A check in that amount is drawn, payable to the petty cash custodian. The following entry is required:

```
Petty Cash . . . . . . . . . . . . . . . . . . . . . . . . . . . . . . . . . . .      100
    Cash . . . . . . . . . . . . . . . . . . . . . . . . . . . . . . . . . . .               100
        To establish a petty cash fund.
```

The check is cashed, and the money is turned over to the petty cash custodian, who normally places the money in a small box that can be locked. The fund is now ready to be disbursed as needed.

Operating the Fund

One of the conveniences of the petty cash fund is that payments from the fund require no journal entries at the time of payment. Thus, using a petty cash fund avoids the need for making many entries for small amounts. Only when the fund is reimbursed will an entry be made in the journal.

When cash is disbursed from the fund, the petty cash custodian prepares a petty cash voucher, which should be signed by the person receiving the funds. A petty cash voucher (Illustration 7.12) is a document or form that shows the amount of and reason for a petty cash disbursement. A voucher should be prepared for each disbursement from the fund. If an invoice for the expenditure is provided, the invoice should be stapled to the petty cash voucher. The person responsible for petty cash is at all times accountable for having cash and petty cash vouchers equal to the total amount of the fund.

Illustration 7.12

Petty Cash Voucher

PETTY CASH VOUCHER NO. 359			
To Local Cartage, Inc.		Date June 29, 1991	
EXPLANATION	ACCT. NO.	AMOUNT	
Freight on parts	27	2	27
APPROVED BY *a. e. s.*		RECEIVED PAYMENT *Ken Black*	

Replenishing the Fund

The petty cash fund should be replenished at the end of the accounting period, or sooner if it becomes low. The reason for replenishing it at the end of the accounting period is that no record of the fund expenditure is in the accounts until the check is written and a journal entry is made. (The fund is sometimes referred to as an **imprest** fund since it is replenished when it becomes low.) The petty cash vouchers are presented to the person having authority to order that the fund be reimbursed. The vouchers are examined by that person; and if all is in order, a check is drawn to restore the fund to its original amount.

To determine which accounts to debit, the petty cash vouchers are summarized according to the reasons for expenditure. The petty cash vouchers are then stamped or defaced to prevent reuse. The journal entry to record replenishing the fund would debit the various accounts indicated by the summary and credit Cash.

For example, assume the $100 petty cash fund currently has a money balance of $7.40. A summary of the vouchers shows payments of $22.75 for transportation-in, $50.80 for stamps, and $19.05 for an advance to an employee; these payments total $92.60. After the vouchers have been examined and approved, a check is drawn for $92.60 which, when cashed, restores the cash in the fund to its $100 balance. The journal entry to record replenishment is:

Transportation-In	22.75	
Postage Expense	50.80	
Receivable from Employees (or Advances to Employees)	19.05	
Cash		92.60
To replenish petty cash fund.		

At the end of an accounting period, any petty cash disbursements for which the fund has **not** yet been replenished must be recorded. Since the fund has not been replenished, the credit would be to Petty Cash rather than Cash. Failure to make an entry at the end of an accounting period would cause errors in both the income statement and balance sheet. The easiest way to record these disbursements is to replenish the fund. Replenishing the fund at the end of an accounting period is handled exactly as at any other time.

If, after a period of time, the petty cash custodian finds that the petty cash fund is larger than needed, the excess petty cash should be deposited in the company's checking account. **The required entry to record a decrease in the size of the fund debits Cash and credits Petty Cash for the amount returned and deposited.** On the other hand, a petty cash fund may be too small, requiring replenishment every few days. **The entry to record an increase in the size of the fund debits Petty Cash and credits Cash for the amount of the increase.**

To illustrate, the entry to **decrease** the size of the petty cash fund by $400 would be:

Cash	400	
Petty Cash		400
To decrease the size of the petty cash fund by $400.		

The entry to **increase** the size of the petty cash fund by $600 would be:

Petty Cash	600	
Cash		600
To increase the size of the petty cash fund by $600.		

Cash Short and Over

Errors can be made in making change from the petty cash fund. These errors cause the amount of cash in the fund to be more or less than the amount of the fund less the total vouchers. When the fund is restored to its original amount, the credit to Cash is for the difference between the established amount and the actual cash in the fund. Debits are made for all vouchered items. Any discrepancy should be debited or credited to an account called *Cash Short and Over.* The Cash Short and Over account is an expense or a revenue, depending on whether it has a debit or credit balance.

To illustrate, assume in the preceding example that the balance in the fund was only $6.10 instead of $7.40. To restore the fund to $100, a check for $93.90 is needed. Since the petty cash vouchers total only $92.60, the fund is short $1.30. In this case, the entry for replenishment is:

Transportation-In	22.75	
Postage Expense	50.80	
Receivable from Employees	19.05	
Cash Short and Over	1.30	
Cash		93.90
To replenish petty cash fund.		

Entries in the Cash Short and Over account may be entered from other change-making activities. For example, assume that a clerk accidentally shortchanges a customer $1 and that total cash sales for the day are $740.50. At the end of the day, actual cash will be $1 over the sum of the sales tickets or the total of the cash register tape. The journal entry to record the day's cash sales is:

Cash	741.50	
Sales		740.50
Cash Short and Over		1.00
To record cash sales for the day.		

In Chapter 5, you learned how to record the purchases of Hanlon Retail Food Store using the gross invoice price method. In the section that follows, an alternative method—the net price method—is explained. As you will see, the net price method has two advantages over the gross invoice price method.

■ NET PRICE METHOD

Objective 6:
Apply the net price method of handling purchase discounts.

Most well-managed companies take advantage of all the discounts made available to them by their suppliers. Effective internal control over cash disbursements makes certain that these discounts are taken. A company may find it advisable to borrow cash to pay invoices within the discount period.

For example, assume goods are purchased for $10,000 under terms 2/10, n/30. The buyer is unable to pay at the end of 10 days but expects to be able to pay at the end of 30 days. To take the $200 discount offered, the buyer needs a $9,800 loan for 20 days, beginning on the last day of the 10-day discount period. The buyer would benefit if the interest cost of such a loan is less than $200. (Short-term loans and interest computations are discussed in Chapter 8.)

In Chapter 5, purchase discounts were recorded under the gross price method. However, some companies prefer to use the net price method because (1) the accounting theory behind the method is superior and (2) the method strengthens internal control.

Under the **net price method,** a purchase is recorded in Purchases and Accounts Payable *net* of the discount. Thus, the discount is **deducted** from the gross invoice price **before** entering the transaction in the accounts. To illustrate, assume a $1,500 purchase was made on May 14 under terms 2/10, n/30. The invoice was paid on May 24, and the discount taken. The entries comparing the net price method and gross price method are:

		Net		Gross	
May 14	Purchases	1,470		1,500	
	Accounts Payable		1,470		1,500
	Purchased goods under terms 2/10, n/30.				
24	Accounts Payable	1,470		1,500	
	Cash		1,470		1,470
	Purchase Discounts*				30
	Paid account within discount period.				

* This account would not appear in the net price entry.

Theoretically, the net price method is preferred over the gross price method because the goods are recorded at their actual cost. Thus, the cost principle of accounting is applied, and goods are recorded at the total amount of resources given up to acquire them. Also, the liability is shown in the Accounts Payable account at the amount for which it could be settled.

Note that in the above net price example, discounts taken are not shown. But if the invoice had not been paid within 10 days, an entry would have been made to Discounts Lost. For example, assume that the invoice in the above example was paid on May 28 instead of May 24. Then the entries for the payment comparing the net price and gross price methods are:

		Net		Gross	
May 28	Accounts Payable	1,470		1,500	
	Discounts Lost*	30			
	Cash		1,500		1,500
	Paid account after discount had expired.				

* This account would not appear in the gross price entry.

Under the net price method, the only time discounts appear is when they are lost. When discounts of 2% or more are available, good cash management calls for internal control procedures ensuring that all invoices are paid within the discount period. The failure to take a discount highlights a deviation from company policy and directs management's attention to this fact. Calling management's attention to deviations is sometimes called *management by exception*. Losses resulting from inefficiency are contained in the Discounts Lost account, which is usually reported among nonoperating expenses near the bottom of the income statement. Many companies prefer the net price method because it strengthens internal control over cash disbursements.

Companies also use the voucher system to strengthen internal control over cash disbursements. As shown in the next section, the nature of the voucher system is such that it provides a high level of internal control.

■ THE VOUCHER SYSTEM

Objective 7:
Describe the operation of the voucher system and make entries in its special journals—the voucher register and the check register.

Companies often suffer substantial losses from the embezzlement of cash. Frequently, the embezzlement results from the paying of fictitious invoices. Thus, every business must make sure that its cash payments are proper and timely. In small companies, this is often not a problem because the owner usually has personal knowledge of all transactions and personally signs all checks. However, in larger companies, the owners and high-level officers may have no direct part in the payment process. These companies can effectively control cash disbursements by using the voucher system.

The **voucher system** is a set of procedures, special journals, and authorization forms designed to provide control over cash payments. The special journals used are the voucher register and the check register. These journals are defined later in this section.

When a company uses the voucher system, each transaction that involves a cash payment is entered on a voucher (Illustration 7.13) and recorded in the voucher register prior to payment. A **voucher** is a form with spaces provided for data about a liability that must be paid. The data include items such as creditor's name and address, description of the goods or services received, invoice number, terms of payment, due date, amount due, and often shows the ledger accounts and amounts to be debited. The voucher also has spaces for signatures of those approving the liability for payment.

An invoice or other business document is the basis for making a journal entry in the voucher register. The voucher usually forms a *jacket* for the invoice, purchase order, and receiving report. Each voucher should undergo careful examination and receive either approval or disapproval for payment. By the time a voucher is approved for payment, several employees have confirmed that the claim being paid is proper and accurate, thus reducing the chances of embezzlement.

Procedures for Preparing a Voucher

The preparation of a voucher begins with the receipt of an invoice from a supplier or with approved evidence that a liability has been incurred and cash should be disbursed. Then the procedures are as follows:

1. Basic data are entered on the voucher from the invoice.
2. The invoice, voucher, and receiving report are sent to the persons responsible for verifying the correctness of the description of the

Illustration 7.13

A Voucher

ATWELL   SUPPLY   COMPANY
Atwell Plaza
Atwell, Texas 78712

VOUCHER

VOUCHER NO. ___141___
OUR P.O. NO. ___2514___
VENDOR'S INVOICE ___416___
PAID BY CHECK NO. ___587___
DATE PAID ___7/18/91___

Payable To: Gregory Corporation
48 Cadillac Square
Detroit, Michigan 48226

DATE	ACCT. NO.	DESCRIPTION	QUANTITY	UNIT PRICE	TOTAL
July 14	126	X–16 Transistors	100	$2.00	$200.00
		TOTAL			$200.00
		DISCOUNT	2%		4.00
		NET PAYABLE			$196.00

TERMS 2/10, n/30
EXPLANATIONS: *Due date is August 13, 1991*

AUDITED AS TO CORRECTNESS *a.T.*	APPROVED FOR PAYMENT *L J.W.*	ENTERED IN VOUCHER REGISTER *R.E.L.*	DATE ENTERED 7/14/91

goods as to quantity and quality, dollar amounts, and other details. Each person initials the voucher when satisfied as to its correctness.

3. When the voucher and accompanying documents are received by the accounting department, a notation is made on the voucher as to the proper accounts to be debited and credited.

4. After a final review by an authorized person, the proper entry is made in the voucher register, and the voucher is filed in the unpaid voucher file.

The name **voucher system** comes from the fact that **every check issued is authorized by a voucher.** A voucher really can be any written form that serves as a receipt or evidence of authority to act. However, as applied to the voucher system, a voucher is a form that confirms a liability and, as such, serves as the basis for an accounting entry.

In some businesses, the discount and payment terms run from the invoice date. Then, a voucher should be prepared for each invoice (see Illustration 7.13). The voucher should be filed according to the date on which the discount period terminates or payment is due. However, when the discount and payment terms are computed from the end of the month, it is possible to

Illustration 7.14 *A Voucher Register*

Line No.	Voucher Date 1991		Voucher No.	Payee	Explanation	Terms	Date Paid		Check No.	Vouchers Payable Cr. 101
				JACKSON COMPANY **VOUCHER REGISTER**						
1	May	2	223	Hanley Company	Ring binders	2/10, n/30	May	12	1350	980.00
2		4	224	Moore Transport	Transportation, binders	Cash		5	1347	13.00
3		6	225	White Stationery Company	Office supplies	2/10, n/30		12	1351	102.00
4		8	226	Specialty Advertisers	Advertising	Cash		8	1348	1,200.00
5		10	227	Blanch Company	Office equipment and supplies	Cash		10	1349	1,010.00
6										
7		14	228	Swanson Company	Filler paper	2/10, n/30		26	1356	3,920.00
8		16	229	Rizzo Company	Office desk	n/30		25	1355	640.00
9		18	230	Warren Company	Spiral binders	2/10, n/30		28	1357	4,900.00
10		20	231	First National Bank	Mortgage payment			20	1353	154.00
11		22	232	Falconer Company	Books	n/30				10,000.00
12		24	233	Petty cash	Reimbursement			24	1354	132.00
13		26	234	Swanson Company	Discount lost (No. 228)			26	1356	80.00
14		28	235	Celoron Company	Drawing sets	2/20, n/30				9,800.00
15		31	236	Payroll account	Salaries and wages			31	1358	24,000.00
16										56,931.00
										(101)

modify the voucher, reducing the number of vouchers prepared and the entries made in the voucher register. Then, all invoices received from a particular creditor are accumulated and listed on one voucher at the end of the month. One check is written on the due date to pay for all invoices listed on the voucher. These vouchers are filed according to due dates.

Special Journals Used

When a voucher system is used, the voucher register replaces the purchases journal, and the check register replaces the cash disbursements journal. Illustration 7.14 shows a voucher register, and Illustration 7.15 shows a check register for Jackson Company.

Voucher Register.   A **voucher register** is a multicolumn special journal containing a record of all vouchers prepared, listed in order by date and

| | | | | | | Page No.: 15 Month: May 1991 | | | |

Discounts Lost Dr. 122	Purchases Dr. 131	Transportation-In Dr. 144	Salaries and Wages Expense Dr. 158	Office Expense Dr. 175	Advertising Expense Dr. 262	Other Accounts Dr.			
						Account Name	Acct. No.	Amount Dr.	√
	980.00								
		13.00							
				102.00					
					1,200.00				
						Office Equipment	42	1,000.00	√
						Office Supplies	33	10.00	√
	3,920.00								
						Office Equipment	42	640.00	√
	4,860.00	40.00							
						Mortgage Note Payable	151	44.00	√
						Interest Expense	159	110.00	√
	10,000.00								
		31.88		60.12	40.00				
80.00									
	9,800.00								
		24,000.00							
80.00	29,560.00	84.88	24,000.00	162.12	1,240.00			1,804.00	
(122)	(131)	(144)	(158)	(175)	(262)			(X)	

voucher number. A brief explanation of each transaction also may be included. Since each entry in the voucher register includes a credit to a new account, called the *Vouchers Payable account,* a column titled *Vouchers Payable Cr.* is included in the voucher register (see Illustration 7.14). In addition to this credit column, the voucher register has debit columns for the accounts the company most frequently debits when a liability is incurred, as well as a column to enter the other accounts (Other Accounts Dr. column).

At the end of each month, the Vouchers Payable Cr. column total is posted to the general ledger control account, Vouchers Payable. In Illustration 7.14, a voucher is prepared for each invoice. Note that the vouchers are recorded net of purchase discounts allowed. If a discount is missed, another voucher is prepared for the discount lost (see line 13 of Illustration 7.14). (As described below, the voucher system can also be used when purchases are recorded at the gross amount.) The total of each of the specifically titled columns is posted to the account named. The debits in the Other Accounts Dr. column are posted individually to the accounts named, usually on a daily basis. The total of the Other Accounts Dr. column is not posted because it includes amounts affecting more than one account.

Check Register.   A **check register** is a special journal showing all checks issued, listed in order by date and check number. One line is allotted to each check. No check may be issued unless authorized by an approved voucher.

The check register in Illustration 7.15 shows the entry and procedure when a check is issued in payment of a voucher. Note that Check No. 1352 is marked *void*. This notation usually means that a mistake was made in writing the check, and another check had to be prepared.

The net price method was used in Illustration 7.15, so the check register has only one money column. The column total is posted in the general ledger as a debit to Vouchers Payable and a credit to Cash. If the gross price method is used, invoices are entered gross (before discount deductions) in the voucher register, and a Purchase Discounts Cr. column should be included in the check register. Separate columns would be needed for the debit to Vouchers Payable and the credit to Cash, since the dollar amounts posted to these two accounts would differ by the amount of the discount taken (see Demonstration Problem 7-3 for an example).

Illustration 7.15

Check Register

	JACKSON COMPANY CHECK REGISTER			Page No.: *24* Month: *May 1991*

Line No.	Date 1991	Payee	Voucher No.	Check No.	Vouchers Payable Dr., Cash Cr.
1	May 5	Moore Transport	224	1347	13.00
2	8	Specialty Advertisers	226	1348	1,200.00
3	10	Blanch Company	227	1349	1,010.00
4	12	Hanley Company	223	1350	980.00
5	12	White Stationery Company	225	1351	102.00
6	20	VOID		1352	
7	20	First National Bank	231	1353	154.00
8	24	Petty cash	233	1354	132.00
9	25	Rizzo Company	229	1355	640.00
10	26	Swanson Company	228 234	1356	4,000.00
11	28	Warren Company	230	1357	4,900.00
12	31	Payroll account	236	1358	24,000.00
					37,131.00
					(101) (10)

In a voucher system, the voucher register and the check register are the two primary journals from which postings are made to the Vouchers Payable control account in the general ledger.

Procedures for Paying a Voucher

When a voucher is due for payment, it is removed from the unpaid voucher file in the accounting department. A check is prepared for the amount payable. The check, voucher, and supporting documents are then typically sent to the person authorized to sign checks, usually the treasurer (the top financial officer in the company). The treasurer examines the documents. If they are in order, the treasurer initials the voucher to show that final approval has been given and signs the check. The check is mailed to the creditor, usually with a remittance advice attached. The voucher is then returned to the accounting department.

On receipt of the paid voucher, the accounting department makes an entry in the check register showing the date paid, check number, voucher number, and amount paid. The check number and date paid are also inserted in the voucher register and on the voucher itself. The voucher then is filed in the paid voucher file.

Files Maintained in a Voucher System

Two files are maintained in a voucher system—unpaid voucher file and paid voucher file.

The **unpaid voucher file** contains all vouchers that have been prepared and approved as proper liabilities but have not yet been paid. These vouchers are filed according to their due dates. The unpaid voucher file takes the place of the accounts payable subsidiary ledger. The total of the vouchers in the unpaid vouchers file should equal the total of the *open* items (those not paid) in the voucher register and also should equal the balance in the Vouchers Payable control account in the general ledger.

The **paid voucher file** contains all vouchers that have been paid. These vouchers are often filed by voucher number in numerical order, but they can be filed by vendor name. Vouchers become a permanent and convenient reference for anyone who wants to check the details of previous cash disbursements.

Unpaid Vouchers at the End of the Period

At the end of the accounting period, the total of unpaid vouchers is shown in three places. First, they are shown in the voucher register, consisting of the vouchers for which there are no data in the Date Paid and Check No. columns (see Illustration 7.14, lines 11 and 14). Second, the total is shown as the ending balance in the Vouchers Payable account, shown in Illustration 7.16 for Jackson Company. Third, the total is shown in a schedule prepared at the end of the period—the schedule of unpaid vouchers. Illustration 7.17 shows the schedule of unpaid vouchers for Jackson Company.

Illustration 7.16 *Vouchers Payable Account*

					GENERAL LEDGER											
					Vouchers Payable											
Date		Explanation	Post. Ref.	Debit				Credit					Balance			
1991 May	1	Beginning balance												–	0	–
	31	From voucher register						5	6	9	3	1	5	6	9	3	1
	31	From check register		3	7	1	3	1						1	9	8	0	0

Illustration 7.17

Schedule of Unpaid Vouchers

JACKSON COMPANY
Schedule of Unpaid Vouchers
May 31, 1991

Voucher No.	Name	Amount
232	Falconer Company	$10,000
235	Celoron Company	9,800
		$19,800

Now that you have learned how to control a company's most liquid asset, cash, you are ready to study about receivables and payables. You probably already realize that the backbone of our economy is credit. In all probability the car you bought or plan to buy will be financed. Companies are anxious to offer credit to worthy customers and prospective customers. The many offers of credit from oil companies and banks that you will probably receive are evidence of the importance companies place on credit as a method of expanding their business.

■ UNDERSTANDING THE LEARNING OBJECTIVES: CHAPTER 7

1. Describe the necessity for and features of internal control.

   ■ The internal control system of a company includes its plan of organization and all the procedures and actions taken by the company to protect its assets against theft and waste, ensure compliance with company policies and federal law, evaluate the performance of all personnel in the company so as to promote efficiency of operations, and ensure accurate and reliable operating data and accounting records.

- The purpose of internal control is to ensure the efficient operations of a business.

2. Define cash and list the objectives sought by management in handling a company's cash.

   - Cash includes coins; paper money; certain undeposited negotiable instruments such as checks, bank drafts, and money orders; amounts in checking and saving accounts; and demand certificates of deposit.
   - To protect its cash, companies should account for all cash transactions accurately, make certain enough cash is available to pay bills as they come due, avoid holding too much idle cash, and prevent loss of cash due to theft or fraud.

3. Identify procedures for controlling cash receipts and disbursements.

   - Procedures for controlling cash receipts include such basic principles as recording all cash receipts as soon as cash is received, depositing all cash receipts on the day they are received or on the next business day, and preventing the employee who handles cash receipts from also recording the receipts in the accounting records or from disbursing cash.
   - Procedures for controlling cash disbursements include, among others, making all disbursements by check or from petty cash, using checks that are serially numbered, requiring two signatures on each check, and having a different person authorize payment of a bill than the person allowed to sign checks.

4. Prepare a bank reconciliation and make necessary journal entries based on that schedule.

   - A bank reconciliation is prepared to *reconcile,* or explain, the difference between the cash balance shown on the bank statement and the cash balance shown on the company's books.
   - A bank reconciliation is shown in Illustration 7.11.
   - Journal entries are needed for all items that appear in the bank reconciliation as adjustments to the balance per ledger to arrive at the adjusted cash balance.

5. Explain why a petty cash fund is used, describe its operations, and make the necessary journal entries.

   - Companies establish a petty cash fund to permit minor disbursements to be made in cash and still maintain adequate control over cash.
   - When the cash in the petty cash fund becomes low, it should be replenished. A journal entry is necessary to record the replenishment.

6. Apply the net price method of handling purchase discounts.

   - When the net price method is used, a purchase is recorded *net* of the discount.
   - If a discount is missed, the Discounts Lost account is debited. This

procedure focuses management's attention on discounts missed rather than on discounts taken.

7. Describe the operation of the voucher system and make entries in its special journals—the voucher register and the check register.

- The voucher system is a set of procedures, special journals, and authorization forms designed to provide control over cash payments.
- A voucher is a form with spaces provided for data about a liability that must be paid.
- A voucher register is a multicolumn special journal containing a record of all vouchers prepared, listed in order by date and voucher number.
- A check register is a special journal showing all checks issued, listed in order by date and check number.

8. Define and use correctly the new terms in the glossary.

NEW TERMS INTRODUCED IN CHAPTER 7

Bank reconciliation A schedule the company (depositor) prepares to *reconcile,* or explain, the difference between the cash balance shown on the bank statement and the cash balance on the company's books; often called a *bank reconciliation statement* or *schedule* (306).

Bank statement A statement issued (usually monthly) by a bank describing the activities in a depositor's checking account during the period (302).

Cash Includes coins; paper money; certain undeposited negotiable instruments such as checks, bank drafts, and money orders; amounts in checking and savings accounts; and demand certificates of deposit (297).

Cashier's check A check drawn by a bank made out to either the depositor or a third party after deducting the amount of the check from the depositor's account or receiving cash from the depositor (309).

Certificate of deposit An interest-bearing deposit in a bank that can be withdrawn at will (demand CD) or at a fixed maturity date (time CD) (298).

Certified check A check written, or drawn, by a depositor and taken to the depositor's bank for certification. The check is deducted from the depositor's balance immediately and becomes a liability of the bank. Thus, it usually will be accepted without question (309).

Check A written order on a bank to pay a specific sum of money to the party designated as the payee by the party issuing the check (302).

Check register A special journal showing all checks issued, listed in order by date and check number (318).

Checking account A money balance maintained in a bank that is subject to withdrawal by the depositor, or owner of the money, on demand (301).

Credit memo A form used by a bank to explain an addition to the depositor's account (304).

Debit memo A form used by a bank to explain a deduction from the depositor's account (304).

Deposit in transit Typically a day's cash receipts recorded in the depositor's books in one period but recorded as a deposit by the bank in the succeeding period (306).

Deposit ticket A form that shows the date and the items that make up the deposit (302).

Drawer The party (depositor) writing a check (302).

Fidelity bonds Ensure that a company is reimbursed for losses due to theft of cash and other monetary assets (295).

Internal auditing Consists of investigating and evaluating employees' compliance with the company's policies and procedures. Internal auditing is performed by company personnel (293).

Internal auditors   Auditors hired by the company to perform internal audits. These auditors are trained in company policies and in internal auditing duties such as testing effectiveness of controls and procedures involving cash receipts and cash disbursements (293).

Internal control system   Includes a company's plan of organization and all the procedures and actions taken by the company to (1) protect its assets against theft and waste, (2) ensure compliance with company policies and federal law, (3) evaluate the performance of all personnel in the company so as to promote efficiency of operations, and (4) ensure accurate and reliable operating data and accounting reports (291).

Invoice   Bill sent from the supplier to the purchaser requesting payment for the merchandise shipped (295).

Net price method   An accounting procedure in which purchases and accounts payable are initially recorded at net invoice price—gross price less discount offered for prompt payment. Records discounts lost rather than discounts taken (313).

NSF check   A customer's check returned from the customer's bank to the depositor's bank because the funds in the customer's checking account balance were insufficient to cover the check (304).

Outstanding checks   Checks issued by a depositor that have not yet been paid by the bank on which they are drawn (307).

Paid voucher file   A permanent file used in a voucher system where paid vouchers are filed in numerical sequence (319).

Payee   The party to whom a check is made payable (302).

Petty cash fund   A nominal sum of money established as a separate fund from which minor cash disbursements for valid business purposes are made. The cash in the fund plus the vouchers covering disbursements must always equal the balance at which the fund was established and at which it is carried in the Petty Cash account (309).

Petty cash voucher   A document or form that shows the amount of and reason for a petty cash disbursement (310).

Purchase order   A document sent from the purchasing department to a supplier requesting that merchandise or other items be shipped to the purchaser (293).

Purchase requisition   A written request from an employee inside the company to the purchasing department to purchase certain items (293).

Receiving report   A document prepared by the receiving department showing the descriptions and quantities of all items received from a supplier in a particular shipment (295).

Remittance advice   Informs the payee why the drawer (or maker) of the check is making this payment (302).

Segregation of duties   Having the employee responsible for safeguarding an asset be someone other than the employee who maintains the accounting records for that asset (291).

Service charges   Charges assessed by the bank on the depositor to cover the cost of handling the checking account (304).

Signature card   Provides the signatures of persons authorized to sign checks drawn on an account (301).

Transfer bank account   A bank account set up so that local banks automatically transfer to a central bank (by wire or written bank draft) all amounts on deposit in excess of a stated amount (304).

Unpaid voucher file   Contains all vouchers that have been prepared and approved as proper liabilities but have not yet been paid. Serves as an accounts payable subsidiary ledger under a voucher system; unpaid vouchers are filed according to their due dates (319).

Voucher   A form with spaces provided for data about a liability that must be paid. The data include items such as creditor's name and address, description of the goods or services received, invoice number, terms of payment, due date, amount due, and often shows the ledger accounts and amounts to be debited. The voucher also has spaces for signatures of those approving the liability for payment (314).

Voucher register   A multicolumn special journal used in a voucher system; the voucher register contains a record of all vouchers prepared, listed in order by date and voucher number. A brief explanation of each transaction also may be included. In addition to a credit column for Vouchers Payable, a voucher register normally has various columns for debits such as Purchases, Salaries, and Transportation-In (316).

Voucher system   A set of procedures, special journals, and authorization forms designed to provide control over cash payments (314).

Wire transfer of funds   Interbank transfer of funds by telephone (304).

DEMONSTRATION PROBLEM 7-1

You are the manager of a restaurant that has an ice cream parlor as a separate unit. Your accountant comes in once a year to prepare financial statements and the tax return. In the current year, you have a feeling that even though business seems good, net income is going to be lower. You ask the accountant to prepare condensed statements on a monthly basis. All sales are priced to yield an estimated gross margin of 40%. You, your accountant, and several of the accountant's assistants take physical inventories at the end of each of the four months indicated below. The resulting sales, cost of goods sold, and gross margins are:

	March		April		May		June	
	Restaurant	Ice Cream Parlor	Restaurant	Ice Cream Parlor	Restaurant	Ice Cream Parlor	Restaurant	Ice Cream Parlor
Sales	$72,600	$106,000	$78,100	$85,500	$76,200	$78,000	$82,500	$71,000
Cost of goods sold	46,550	63,000	47,600	62,000	45,950	61,500	51,000	62,250
Gross margin	$26,050	$ 43,000	$30,500	$23,500	$30,250	$16,500	$31,500	$ 8,750

Required: What would you suspect after analyzing these reports? What sales control procedures would you recommend to correct the bad situation? All of the points covered in this problem were not specifically covered in the chapter, although the principles were. Use logic, common sense, and knowledge gained elsewhere in coming up with some of the control procedures.

Solution to demonstration problem 7-1

The gross margin percentages are as follows:

	March	April	May	June
Restaurant	35.88%	39.05%	39.70%	38.18%
Ice cream parlor	40.57	27.49	21.15	12.32

Either cash or inventory is being stolen or given away in the ice cream parlor. It may be that cash is being pocketed by the employees or outsiders. Or the employees may be giving extra-large ice cream cones to friends, or eating the ice cream themselves. Several things could be done to improve the sales control procedures:

1. The manager could hire an investigator to come in and watch the employees in action. If cash is being pocketed, the employees could be fired.
2. The prices of ice cream cones could be changed to odd amounts so that employees would not be as able to make change without going to the cash register. Also, the "No Sale" lever could be removed from the cash register.
3. The customers could be encouraged to ask for their cash register receipts by having a monthly drawing (for some prize) by cash register receipt number.
4. The cash register should be placed in a prominent position so that each customer could see the amount recorded for each sale. The customer is not going to be willing to pay 65 cents when the employee rings up 50 cents.
5. The cash register tapes should be inaccessible to the employees. The manager (and possibly assistant manager) should have the only keys to the cash registers.
6. Mention to the employees that you have a control system. The employees do not have to know what the system is.

7. Pay the employees a competitive wage.
8. Require that all sales be rung up immediately after the sale.
9. The manager or assistant manager should reconcile the cash register tapes at the end of each day.

DEMONSTRATION PROBLEM 7-2

The following data pertain to Nunn Company:

1. Balance per bank statement, dated March 31, 1991, is $8,900.
2. Balance of the Cash account on the company's books as of March 31, 1991, is $8,918.
3. The $2,600 deposit of March 31 was not shown on the bank statement.
4. Of the checks recorded as cash disbursements in March, some checks, totaling $2,100, have not yet cleared the bank.
5. Service and collection charges for the month were $20.
6. The bank erroneously charged the Nunn Company account for the $400 check of another company. The check was included with the canceled checks returned with the bank statement.
7. The bank credited the company's account with the $2,000 proceeds of a noninterest-bearing note that it collected for the company.
8. A customer's $150 check marked NSF was returned with the bank statement.
9. As directed, the bank paid and charged to the company's account a $1,015 noninterest-bearing note of Nunn Company. This payment has not been recorded by the company.
10. An examination of the cash receipts and the deposit tickets revealed that the bookkeeper erroneously recorded a customer's check of $263 as $236.
11. The bank credited the company for $40 of interest earned on the company's checking account.

Required: a. Prepare a bank reconciliation as of March 31, 1991.
            b. Prepare the necessary journal entries to adjust the Cash account.

Solution to demonstration problem 7-2

a.

NUNN COMPANY
Bank Reconciliation
March 31, 1991

Balance per bank statement, March 31, 1991		$ 8,900
Add: Deposit in transit	$2,600	
Check charged in error	400	3,000
		$11,900
Less: Outstanding checks		2,100
Adjusted balance, March 31, 1991		$ 9,800
Balance per ledger, March 31, 1991		$ 8,918
Add: Note collected	$2,000	
Interest earned on checking account	40	
Error in recording customer's check	27	2,067
		$10,985
Less: Service and collection charges	$ 20	
NSF check	150	
Nunn Company note charged against account	1,015	1,185
Adjusted balance, March 31, 1991		$ 9,800

b. 1991
March 31 Cash 882
　　　　 Bank Service Charge Expense 20
　　　　 Accounts Receivable 150
　　　　 Notes Payable 1,015
　　　　　　 Notes Receivable 2,000
　　　　　　 Interest Revenue 40
　　　　　　 Accounts Receivable 27
　　　　 To record adjustments to Cash account.

Alternatively:

1991
March 31 Cash 2,067
　　　　　　 Notes Receivable 2,000
　　　　　　 Interest Revenue 40
　　　　　　 Accounts Receivable 27
　　　　 To record additions to Cash account.

　　　　 Bank Service Charge Expense 20
　　　　 Accounts Receivable 150
　　　　 Notes Payable 1,015
　　　　　　 Cash 1,185
　　　　 To record deductions from Cash account.

DEMONSTRATION PROBLEM 7-3

Blankenship Company uses a voucher system to control cash disbursements. Purchases are recorded at gross invoice prices. As of April 30, 1991, two vouchers are unpaid: Voucher No. 404 payable to Akers Company for $850 and Voucher No. 405 payable to Hanson Company for $50.

Blankenship Company engaged in the following transactions affecting vouchers payable:

May 1 Prepared Voucher No. 406 payable to Carol Company for merchandise purchased; price on invoice dated April 30 is $400. Terms are 2/10, n/30, FOB destination.
　　2 Issued Check No. 385 in payment of Voucher No. 405; no discount was offered on this purchase.
　　4 Received a credit memo for $100 for merchandise returned to Akers Company. Purchase was originally recorded in Voucher No. 404. (Record in general journal with notation of return on Voucher No. 404.)
　　5 Prepared Voucher No. 407 payable to Allen Brothers for merchandise with an invoice price of $950 on invoice dated May 3; terms are 2/10, n/30, FOB shipping point, freight prepaid. Supplier paid $50 freight bill and added $50 to the invoice for a total billing of $1,000.
　　6 Prepared Voucher No. 408 payable to API, Inc., for cost incurred to deliver merchandise sold, $120; terms n/10.
　　8 Issued Check No. 386 to pay Voucher No. 404, less return and less a 2% discount.
　　9 Issued Check No. 387 to pay Voucher No. 406.
　　12 Prepared Voucher No. 409 payable to Ames Insurance Company for $300, the three-year premium on an insurance policy. Issued Check No. 388 to pay Voucher No. 409.
　　13 Issued Check No. 389 to pay Voucher No. 407.

May 15   Prepared Voucher No. 410 payable to Cash for $2,000 in salaries for the first half of May. Issued Check No. 390 in payment of Voucher No. 410. Cashed the check and paid employees in cash.

16   Issued Check No. 391 to pay Voucher No. 408.

23   Prepared Voucher No. 411 payable to Manders Company for merchandise with an invoice price of $300 on invoice dated May 22; terms are 2/10, n/30, FOB shipping point, freight collect.

24   Prepare Voucher No. 412 payable to Short-Lines, Inc., for $50 freight on merchandise purchased on May 23.

26   Prepared Voucher No. 413 payable to Bell Telephone Company for $125 for monthly telephone service.

28   Prepared Voucher No. 414 payable to We-Deliver, Inc., for costs incurred to deliver merchandise sold, $80; terms n/30.

31   Prepared Voucher No. 415 payable to Cash for salaries for the last half of May, $2,200. Issued Check No. 392 in payment of Voucher No. 415. Cashed the check and paid employees in cash.

Required:

a. Record the transactions above, using a voucher register, check register, and a general journal.

b. Prepare a Vouchers Payable account and post the portions of the entries that affect this account.

c. Prepare a schedule (list) of unpaid vouchers to prove the accuracy of the balance in the Vouchers Payable account.

Solution to demonstration problem 7-3

a.

BLANKENSHIP COMPANY
VOUCHER REGISTER*

Page 12

Date 1991	Voucher No.	Payee	Terms	Paid Date	Ck. No.	Vouchers Payable Cr.	Purchases Dr.	Transportation-In Dr.	Delivery Expense Dr.	Salaries Expense Dr.	Other Accounts Dr. Account Name	Post. Ref.	Amount Dr.
May 1	406	Carol Company	2/10, n/30	5/9	387	400	400						
5	407	Allen Brothers	2/10, n/30	5/13	389	1,000	950	50					
6	408	API, Inc.	n/10	5/16	391	120			120				
12	409	Ames Insurance Company		5/12	388	300					Unexpired Insurance		300
15	410	Cash		5/15	390	2,000				2,000			
23	411	Manders Company	2/10, n/30			300	300						
24	412	Short-Lines, Inc.				50		50					
26	413	Bell Telephone Company				125					Telephone Expense		125
28	414	We-Deliver, Inc.	n/30			80			80				
31	415	Cash		5/31	392	2,200				2,200			
						6,575	1,650	100	200	4,200			425

BLANKENSHIP COMPANY
CHECK REGISTER

Date 1991		Payee	Voucher No.	Check No.	Vouchers Payable Dr.	Purchase Discounts Cr.	Cash Cr.
May	2	Hanson Company	405	385	50		50
	8	Akers Company	404	386	750	15	735
	9	Carol Company	406	387	400	8	392
	12	Ames Insurance Company	409	388	300		300
	13	Allen Brothers	407	389	1,000	19	981
	15	Cash	410	390	2,000		2,000
	16	API, Inc.	408	391	120		120
	31	Cash	415	392	2,200		2,200
					6,820	42	6,778

BLANKENSHIP COMPANY
GENERAL JOURNAL

Date		Account Titles and Explanation	Post. Ref.	Debit	Credit
1991 May	4	Vouchers Payable		1 0 0	
		Purchase Returns and Allowances			1 0 0
		To record receipt of credit memo for merchandise returned;			
		Voucher No. 404.			

b.

BLANKENSHIP COMPANY
GENERAL LEDGER

Vouchers Payable   *Account No. 201*

Date		Explanation	Post. Ref.	Debit	Credit	Balance
1991 Apr.	30	Beginning balance				9 0 0 Cr.
May	4	Credit memo; Voucher No. 404	J17	1 0 0		8 0 0 Cr.
	31		VR12		6 5 7 5	7 3 7 5 Cr.
	31		CR5	6 8 2 0		5 5 5 Cr.

c.

BLANKENSHIP COMPANY
Schedule of Unpaid Vouchers
May 31, 1991

Voucher No.	Name	Amount
411	Manders Company	$300
412	Short-Lines, Inc.	50
413	Bell Telephone Company	125
414	We-Deliver, Inc.	80
		$555

QUESTIONS

1. Why should a system of internal control be established?

2. Identify some features that if present would strengthen an internal control system.

3. Name several control documents that are used in merchandise transactions.

4. What are the four objectives sought in effective cash management?

5. List four essential features of a system of internal control over cash receipts.

6. The bookkeeper of a given company was stealing cash received from customers in payment of their accounts. To conceal the theft, the bookkeeper made out false credit memos indicating returns and allowances made by or granted to customers. What feature of internal control would have prevented the thefts?

7. List six essential features of a system of internal control over cash disbursements.

8. "The difference between a company's Cash account balance and the balance on its bank statement is usually a matter of timing." Do you agree or disagree? Why?

9. Explain how transfer bank accounts can help bring about effective cash management.

10. Describe the operation of a petty cash fund and cite the advantages from its use. Indicate how control is maintained over petty cash transactions.

11. Explain how the net price method of accounting for purchases can improve internal control.

12. What can be accomplished with a voucher system that is not accomplished through use of a purchases journal and a cash disbursements journal?

13. What should be the relationship between the balance in the Vouchers Payable account, the *open* items in the voucher register, and the total of all vouchers in the unpaid vouchers file?

14. You are the chief accountant of Magnuson Company. An invoice has just been received from Arnott Company in the amount of $2,000, with credit terms of 2/10, n/30. List the procedures you would follow in processing this invoice through the point of filing it in the unpaid vouchers file.

15. Refer to the situation described in Question 14. Assume that the time for payment of the voucher has arrived and the payment is to be made within the discount period. List the actions that would be taken if the company uses the net price method.

16. What would the procedures be if the discount period had elapsed before payment was made in Question 15?

17. List the posting steps that would be used to post the data shown in Illustration 7.14. How many amounts would actually be posted?

EXERCISES

E-1
Answer true-false questions about internal control

State whether each of the following statements about internal control is **true** or **false**:

a. Those employees responsible for safeguarding an asset should maintain the accounting records for that asset.
b. Complete, accurate, and up-to-date accounting records should be maintained.
c. Whenever possible, responsibilities should be assigned and duties subdivided in such a way that only one employee is responsible for a given function.
d. Employees should be assigned to one job and should remain in that job so that skill levels will be as high as possible.
e. The use of check protectors, check registers, and time clocks is recommended.
f. An internal auditing function should not be implemented because it leads the employees to believe that management does not trust them.
g. One of the best protections against theft is to hire honest, competent employees.
h. A foolproof system of internal control can be devised if management puts forth the effort.

E-2
Answer multiple-choice question about internal control

Concerning internal control, which one of the following statements is correct? Explain.

a. Broadly speaking, internal control is only necessary in large organizations.
b. The purposes of internal control are to check the accuracy of accounting data, safeguard assets against theft, promote efficiency of operations, and ensure that management's policies are being followed.
c. Once an internal control system has been established, it should be effective as long as the formal organization remains unchanged.
d. An example of internal control is having one employee count the day's cash receipts and compare the total with the total of the cash register tapes.

E-3
Determine available cash balance from bank statement and Cash account data

The bank statement for McAllister Company at the end of August showed a balance of $102,900. Checks outstanding totaled $31,500, and deposits in transit were $47,925. If these are the only pertinent data available to you, what was the adjusted balance of cash at the end of August?

E-4
Prepare bank reconciliation and specify cash available

From the following data, prepare a bank reconciliation and determine the correct available cash balance for Ward Company as of October 31, 1991.

Balance per bank statement, October 31, 1991	$18,632
Ledger account balance, October 31, 1991	10,784
Proceeds of a note collected by bank not yet entered in ledger (includes $500 of interest)	8,000
Bank charges not yet entered by Ward Company . . .	24
Deposits in transit	2,240
Outstanding checks:	
No. 327	872
No. 328	384
No. 329	520
No. 331	336

E-5
Record necessary journal entry or entries

The following is a bank reconciliation for Ritzman Company as of August 31, 1991.

Balance per bank, August 31, 1991		$3,735
Add: Deposit in transit		2,838
		$6,573
Less: Outstanding checks		3,012
Adjusted balance, August 31, 1991		$3,561
Balance per books, August 31, 1991 . . .		$3,624
Add: Error correction		27*
		$3,651
Less: NSF check	$75	
Service charges	15	90
Adjusted balance, August 31, 1991		$3,561

* The error occurred when the bookkeeper debited Accounts Payable and credited Cash for $96, instead of the correct amount, $69.

Prepare the journal entry or entries needed to adjust or correct the Cash account.

E-6
Determine checks outstanding

On March 1 of the current year, Sheehan Company had outstanding checks of $60,000. During March, the company issued an additional $228,000 of checks. As of March 31, the bank statement showed $192,000 of checks had cleared the bank during the month. What is the amount of outstanding checks on March 31?

E-7
Determine deposits in transit

Little Company's bank statement as of August 31, 1991, shows total deposits into the company's account of $38,505 and a total of 14 separate deposits. On July 31, deposits of $2,025 and $1,575 were in transit. The total cash receipts for August were $49,380, and the company's records show 13 deposits made in August. What is the amount of deposits in transit at August 31?

E-8
Prepare bank reconciliation and necessary journal entry or entries

Gowan Company deposits all cash receipts intact each day and makes all payments by check. On October 31, after all posting was completed, its Cash account had a debit balance of $6,920. The bank statement for the month ended on October 31 showed a balance of $6,380. Other data are:

1. Outstanding checks total $680.
2. October 31 cash receipts of $1,340 were placed in the bank's night depository and do not appear on the bank statement.
3. Bank service charges for October are $24.
4. Check No. 772 for store supplies was entered at $648, but paid by the bank at its actual amount of $504.

Prepare a bank reconciliation for Gowan as of October 31. Also prepare any necessary journal entry or entries.

E-9
Record reimbursement of petty cash fund

On August 31, 1991, Gold Company's petty cash fund contained coins and currency of $174, an IOU from an employee of $20, and vouchers showing expenditures of $80 for postage, $34 for taxi fare, and $92 to entertain a customer. The Petty Cash account shows a balance of $400. The fund is replenished on August 31 because financial statements are to be prepared. What journal entry is required on August 31?

E-10
Record reimbursement of petty cash fund

Use the data in Exercise E-9. What entry would have been required if the amount of coin and currency had been $164.80? Which of the accounts debited would not appear in the income statement?

E-11
Prepare journal entries regarding petty cash

Cheng Company has a $1,800 petty cash fund. The following transactions occurred in December:

Dec. 2   The petty cash fund was increased to $2,700.
      8   Petty Cash Voucher No. 318 for $48.42 of delivery expense was prepared and paid. The fund was not replenished at this time.
     20   The company decided that the fund was too large and reduced it to $2,250.

Prepare any necessary journal entries for the above transactions.

E-12
Record purchases using net price method

Britz Company uses the net price method for handling purchase discounts. Prepare the journal entries necessary to record the following 1991 transactions:

Oct. 6   Purchased $900 of merchandise from Wadkins Company; terms 2/10, n/30.
      7   Purchased $3,000 of merchandise from James Company; terms 2/10, n/30.
     17   Paid the invoice from James Company for the October 7 purchase.
     31   Paid the invoice from Wadkins Company for the October 6 purchase.

E-13
Determine vouchers payable balance; compute current month's vouchers paid

Refer to Illustration 7.14.

a.   Assume that all vouchers written before May 1, 1991, have been paid. By only looking at the voucher register, what is the balance in the Vouchers Payable account on May 31, 1991?
b.   All checks written in May were in payment of May vouchers. By only looking at the voucher register, determine the total dollar amount of vouchers paid in May.
c.   Explain how it is possible to determine the cash paid out in May to pay May's vouchers without looking at the check register.

E-14
Prepare general journal entries to record selected transactions and indicate whether recorded in voucher or check register

Brodie Company uses a voucher system. Recently, the company had the following transactions:

a.   Prepared Voucher No. 801 for purchase of merchandise from Balke Company, $750.
b.   Issued Check No. 723 to pay Voucher No. 801.
c.   Prepared Voucher No. 802 to set up a petty cash fund, $225.
d.   Issued Check No. 724 to pay Voucher No. 802.
e.   Prepared Voucher No. 804 for $30 freight on merchandise in Voucher No. 801.
f.   Prepared Voucher No. 805 to replenish petty cash when it contained cash of $42 and receipts for postage, $99; supplies, $51; and miscellaneous expenses, $30.
g.   Issued Check No. 725 to pay Voucher No. 805.

Prepare entries in general journal form to record the above transactions. Identify the journal or book of original entry in which each transaction would normally appear.

E-15
Describe what amounts and information would appear in a voucher system to record payment for purchase under net price procedure when discount is lost

Assume that Howell Company uses a voucher register and a check register exactly like Illustration 7.14 and Illustration 7.15. On May 1, Howell Company purchased merchandise from Baird Company, $2,000; terms 2/10, n/30. Howell prepared Voucher No. 567 for $1,960. On May 29, Howell paid for the merchandise purchased from Baird Company and missed the discount (Check No. 489).

State what information should be entered in the voucher register and the check register to record the payment of May 29. Assume that the last voucher used was 598.

PROBLEMS, SERIES A

P7-1-A
Prepare bank reconciliation with necessary journal entry or entries

The bank statement for Elder Company showed a balance of $35,105.70 on July 31, 1991. On the same date, the company's Cash account balance was $24,777.90. Returned with the bank statement was a credit memo for $6,150 for proceeds of a note that was collected by the bank for the company. Of that amount, $150 was interest. There were two debit memos—one for service charges of $57 and one for an NSF check of Greer Company for $210. By comparing the canceled checks with the check register, it was found that $14,584.80 of checks were outstanding. The deposit made after banking hours on July 31 of $10,140 was not listed on the bank statement.

Required:
a. Prepare a bank reconciliation for July 31, 1991.
b. Prepare any necessary journal entry or entries to correct the accounts.

P7-2-A
Prepare journal entries to record establishment and reimbursement of petty cash fund

The following transactions pertain to the petty cash fund of Casper Company during 1991:

Nov. 2   A $1,200 check is drawn, cashed, and the cash placed in the care of the assistant office manager to be used as a petty cash fund.

Dec. 17   The fund is replenished. An analysis of the fund shows:

Coins and currency	$393.08
Petty cash vouchers for:	
Delivery expenses	462.60
Transportation-in	296.32
Postage stamps purchased	40.00

31   The end of the accounting period falls on this date. The fund was replenished. The fund's contents on this date consist of:

Coins and currency	$938.80
Petty cash vouchers for:	
Delivery expenses	84.40
Postage stamps purchased	96.80
Employee's IOU	80.00

Required:
Present journal entries to record the above transactions. Use the Cash Short and Over account for any shortage or overage in the fund.

P7-3-A
Prepare journal entries to record establishment, reimbursement, and increase of petty cash fund

The following transactions relate to the petty cash fund of Ballesteros Wrecking Company in 1991:

Apr. 1 The petty cash fund is set up with a $450 cash balance.
  19 Because the money in the fund is down to $93.60, the fund is replenished. Petty cash vouchers are as follows:

    Flowers for hospitalized employee
     (miscellaneous expense) $112.50
    Postage stamps 180.00
    Office supplies 62.28

  30 The cash in the fund is $240.75. The fund is replenished to include petty cash payments in this period's financial statements. The petty cash vouchers are for the following:

    Transportation-in . . . . $ 85.50
    Office supplies 123.75

May 1 The petty cash fund balance is increased to $675.

Required: Prepare the journal entries to record the above transactions.

P7-4-A
Prepare bank reconciliation with necessary journal entry or entries

The following information pertains to Graham Company. The June 30, 1991, bank reconciliation follows:

	Cash Account	Bank Statement
Balance on June 30	$25,524.48	$24,859.08
Add: Deposit not credited by bank		1,256.80
Total		$26,115.88
Deduct: Outstanding checks:		
No. 724 . . . . $ 24.60		
No. 886 . . . . 20.00		
No. 896 . . . . 191.40		
No. 897 . . . . 250.20		
No. 898 . . . . 105.20		591.40
Adjusted cash balance, June 30	$25,524.48	$25,524.48

The July bank statement appears below:

Balance on July 1		$24,859.08
Deposits during July		7,255.92 $32,115.00
Canceled checks returned:		
No. 724 . . . . $ 24.60		
No. 896 . . . . 191.40		
No. 897 . . . . 250.20		
No. 898 . . . . 105.20		
No. 899 . . . . 25.14		
No. 900 . . . . 1,799.40		
No. 902 . . . . 1,262.56		
No. 904 . . . . 58.68	$ 3,717.18	
NSF check of Manley Company	186.64	3,903.82
Bank statement balance, July 31		$28,211.18

The cash receipts deposited in July, including receipts of July 31, amounted to $6,904.40. Checks written in July are listed below:

No. 899 . . . $ 25.14
No. 900 . . . 1,799.40
No. 901 . . .   37.00
No. 902 . . . 1,262.56
No. 903 . . .   79.60
No. 904 . . .   58.68
No. 905 . . . 1,458.00
No. 906 . . .   20.00

The cash balance per the ledger on July 31, 1991, was $27,688.50.

Required: Prepare a bank reconciliation as of July 31, 1991, and any necessary journal entry or entries to correct the accounts.

P7-5-A
Prepare bank reconciliation with necessary journal entry or entries

The following information pertains to Cochran Company as of May 31, 1991:

1. Balance per bank statement as of May 31,1991, was $65,880.
2. Balance per Cochran Company's Cash account at May 31, 1991, was $67,872.
3. A late deposit on May 31 did not appear on the bank statement, $5,700.
4. Outstanding checks as of May 31 totaled $10,152.
5. During May, the bank credited Cochran Company with the proceeds, $9,060, of a note which it had collected for the company. Interest revenue was $60 of the total.
6. Bank service and collection charges for May amounted to $24.
7. Comparison of the canceled checks with the check register revealed that one check in the amount of $1,944 had been recorded in the books at $2,052. The check had been issued in payment of an account payable.
8. A review of the deposit slips with the bank statement showed that a deposit for $3,000 of a company with a similar account number had been credited to the Cochran Company account in error.
9. A $360 check received from a customer, R. Perry, was returned with the bank statement marked NSF.
10. During May, the bank paid an $18,000 note of Cochran Company plus interest of $180 and charged it to the company's account per instructions received. Cochran Company had not recorded the payment of this note.
11. An examination of the cash receipts and the deposit tickets revealed that the bookkeeper erroneously recorded a check from a customer, C. Smith, of $1,944 as $2,592.
12. The bank statement showed a credit to the company's account for interest earned on the account balance in May of $600.

Required: a. Prepare a bank reconciliation as of May 31, 1991.
b. Prepare the journal entry or entries necessary to adjust the accounts as of May 31, 1991.

P7-6-A
Prepare entries in voucher and check registers, using net price method for purchase discounts

Hawkins Company was organized January 1 of the current year, 1991. The company uses a voucher register and a check register with the same column headings as in Illustrations 7.14 and 7.15, except that there are only four voucher register debit columns—Purchases, Transportation-In, Discounts Lost, and Other Accounts. Vouchers are prepared for the net amount of the invoice. For discounts lost, a new voucher is prepared for the amount of the discount.

Transactions:

Jan. 2   Received merchandise from Lind Company with terms of 2/10, n/30. The invoice received was in the amount of $10,400.
3   Paid transportation charges to Moyer Trucking Company on purchase of January 2, $174.

    6 Paid Wilson Display Company $6,600 for billboard advertising for a three-month period beginning February 1, 1991.

  15 Paid Lind Company for the purchase of January 2.

  17 Received merchandise from Bradly Company with terms of 2/10, n/30. The invoice received was for 8,400.

  18 Received merchandise from Casp Company with terms of 2/10, n/30. The invoice received was for $35,500. Paid net amount today to establish a good credit rating.

  23 Received invoice for $3,600 from Office Equipment, Inc., for office equipment recently received. Terms are 2/10, n/30.

  31 The Bradly Company voucher of January 17 was misfiled and had not been paid as of the end of the month. A voucher was prepared for the discount missed.

Required: Enter the above approved transactions for January in these registers and total the registers. Start with Voucher No. 1 and Check No. 1.

P7-7-A
Prepare entries in voucher and check registers, using net price procedure for purchase discounts; confirm balance in Vouchers Payable

Sanders Company uses a voucher register and a check register with the same column headings as in Illustrations 7.14 and 7.15, except that there are only four voucher register debit columns—Purchases, Transportation-In, Discounts Lost, and Other Accounts. The last voucher used was No. 432, and the last check issued was No. A727. As of December 31, 1990, three vouchers were in the unpaid voucher file:

Voucher No. 388, East Company $23,040
Voucher No. 401, Jones Company 44,800
Voucher No. 431, Boxer Company . . . . . <u>13,120</u>
                                         <u>$80,960</u>

The total of the unpaid voucher file agreed with the credit balance in the Vouchers Payable control account.

    The following transactions occurred during January 1991. Vouchers are prepared for the net amount of the invoice. For discounts lost, a new voucher is prepared for the amount of the discount.

Jan. 2 An invoice in the amount of $22,400 was received from Drade Company for office equipment already received. Terms were 2/10, n/30, FOB shipping point.

    3 Paid a $13,000 note that matured this date. Interest on the note was another $56. The payee was Citizens Bank. (Hint: Has a voucher been prepared to authorize this cash payment?)

    4 Received an invoice for $16,000 from Smith Company for merchandise recently received. Terms were 2/10, n/30.

    5 Paid Voucher No. 388 to East Company, $23,040.

    7 Paid $2,240 to Rapid Service Company for transportation for the purchase of office equipment from Drade Company.

  11 Paid Drade Company for the purchase of January 2.

  14 Paid Voucher No. 431 to Boxer Company, $13,120.

  15 Paid $3,520 to Adams Company for advertising services received in January.

  20 Paid Smith Company for the purchase of January 4.

  22 Received an invoice for $48,000 from Smith Company for merchandise; terms, 2/10, n/30.

  31 Received an invoice from Havers Company for $292,800. This amount included $4,800 chargeable to Transportation-In and $288,000 for merchandise, with credit terms, 2/5, n/30. Since the discount period is short, the invoice was paid immediately with a check for $287,040.

Required: Set up a voucher register and a check register, as described, and enter the above transactions. You need not show unpaid vouchers from preceding months in the voucher register. Total the registers at January 31. List the unpaid vouchers at January 31 and compare the total with the balance in the Vouchers Payable control account (Account No. 250) after posting has been completed.

PROBLEMS, SERIES B

P7–1–B
Prepare bank reconciliation with necessary journal entry or entries

The following information pertains to Littler Company:

Balance per bank statement, September 30, 1991 . . . . $146,700
Ledger account balance for cash on September 30, 1991 127,350
Proceeds of a note collected by bank ($100 of which was interest) . . . 9,000
Bank service charges 90
Deposits in transit 8,316
NSF check deposited and returned 756
Outstanding checks 15,462
Bank error—deducted $450 from Littler account for check
  actually written for $4,500.

Required:
a. Prepare a bank reconciliation as of September 30, 1991.
b. Give the necessary journal entry or entries to correct the accounts.

P7–2–B
Prepare journal entries to record establishment and reimbursement of petty cash fund

Transactions involving the petty cash fund of Bell Company during 1991 are as follows:

Mar. 1 Established a petty cash fund of $500, which will be under the control of the assistant office manager.
    31 Fund was replenished on this date. Prior to replenishment, the fund consisted of the following:

Coins and currency $327.70
Petty cash vouchers indicating disbursements for:
  Postage stamps 54.00
  Supper money for office employees working overtime . . . 24.00
  Office supplies 21.80
  Window washing service 40.00
  Flowers for wedding of employee 10.00
  Flowers for hospitalized employee 10.00
  Employee's IOU 10.00

Required: Present journal entries for the above transactions. Use the Cash Short and Over account for any shortage or overage in the fund.

P7–3–B
Prepare journal entries to record establishment, reimbursement, and increase of petty cash fund

Salazar Company has decided to use a petty cash fund. Listed below are transactions involving this fund in 1991:

June 4 Set up a petty cash fund of $225.
    22 When the fund had a cash amount of $31.35, the custodian of the fund was reimbursed for expenditures made, including:

Transportation-in $82.50
Postage 27.00
Office supplies 81.75

    30 The fund was reimbursed so as to include petty cash items in the financial statements prepared for the fiscal year ending on this date. The fund had the following cash and vouchers before reimbursement:

Coins and currency $174.00
Petty cash vouchers for:
  Employee's IOU 15.00
  Postage 27.00
  Office supplies 11.10

July 1 The petty cash fund balance is increased to $300.

Required: Prepare journal entries for all of the above transactions.

P7–4–B
Prepare bank reconciliation with necessary journal entry or entries

The following data pertain to Heath Company:

1. Balance per the bank statement dated June 30, 1991, is $40,760.
2. Balance of the Cash in Bank account on the company books as of June 30, 1991, is $11,980.
3. Outstanding checks as of June 30, 1991, total $19,954.
4. Bank deposit of June 30 for $3,140 was not included in the deposits per the bank statement.
5. The bank had collected proceeds of a note, $30,150 (of which $150 was interest), that it credited to the Heath Company account. The bank charged the company a collection fee of $20 on the above note.
6. The bank erroneously charged Heath Company account for a $14,000 debit memo of another company that has a similar name.
7. Bank service charges for June, exclusive of the collection fee, amounted to $100.
8. Among the canceled checks was one for $690 given in payment of an account. The bookkeeper had recorded the check at $960 in the company records.
9. A check of Crosley, a customer, for $4,154, deposited on June 20, was returned by the bank marked NSF. No entry has been made to reflect the returned check on the company records.
10. A check for $1,780 of Moran, a customer, which had been deposited in the bank, was erroneously recorded by the bookkeeper as $1,960. The check had been received as a payment on the customer's account receivable.

Required: Prepare a bank reconciliation as of June 30, 1991, and any necessary journal entry or entries to correct the accounts.

P7–5–B
Prepare bank reconciliation with necessary journal entry or entries

The bank statement of Boone Company's checking account with the First National Bank shows:

Balance, June 30, 1991		$221,490
Deposits		327,600
		$549,090
Less: Checks deducted	$324,000	
Service charges	90	324,090
Balance, July 31, 1991		$225,000

The following additional data are available:

1. Balance per ledger account as of July 31 was $170,946.
2. A credit memo included with the bank statement indicated the collection of a note by the bank for Boone Company. Proceeds were $18,000, of which $500 was interest.
3. An NSF check in the amount of $8,280 was returned by the bank and included in the total of checks deducted on the bank statement.
4. Deposits in transit as of July 31 totaled $45,000.
5. Checks outstanding as of July 31 were $73,800.
6. The bank added the $38,700 deposit of another company to Boone's account in error.
7. The bank deducted one of Boone's checks as $27,000 instead of the correct amount of $2,700.
8. Deposit of July 21 was recorded by the company as $5,733 and by the bank at the actual amount of $6,057. The receipts for the day were from collections on account.
9. The deposits amount shown on the bank statement includes $900 of interest earned by Boone on its checking account with the bank.

Required:
a. Prepare a bank reconciliation as of July 31, 1991, for Boone Company.
b. Prepare any journal entry or entries needed at July 31, 1991.

P7-6-B
Prepare entries in voucher and check registers, using net price method for purchase discounts

Lyons Company was organized January 1 of the current year, 1991. The company uses a voucher register and a check register with the same column headings as in Illustrations 7.14 and 7.15, except that there are only four voucher register debit columns—Purchases, Transportation-In, Discounts Lost, and Other Accounts. Vouchers are prepared for the net amount of the invoice. For discounts lost, a new voucher is prepared for the amount of the discount.

Transactions:

Jan. 1 Received an invoice from Modern Company in the amount of $2,400 for office equipment. Terms were 2/10, n/30, FOB shipping point.
3 Received an invoice from Bailey Company for merchandise in the amount of $4,200. Terms were 2/10, n/30.
5 Received an invoice from Simpson Company for merchandise in the amount of $3,100. Terms were 2/10, n/30.
7 Paid $360 to Lund Advertising Service for services received in January.
10 Paid $270 of freight charges to James Company for merchandise received from Bailey Company.
14 Paid Simpson Company the amount due.
20 Paid Bailey Company the correct amount due.
31 Paid Thomas Company the net amount of $24,210 for merchandise received today. (Hint: Has the voucher authorizing this payment been prepared?)
31 The Modern Company voucher of January 1 was misfiled and had not been paid as of the end of the month. A voucher was prepared for the discount missed.

Required: Enter the above transactions for January in these registers and total the registers. Start with Voucher No. 1 and Check No. 1.

P7-7-B
Prepare entries in voucher and check registers, using net price method for purchase discounts; prove balance in Vouchers Payable

Mack Company uses a voucher register and a check register with the same column headings as in Illustrations 7.14 and 7.15, except that there are only four voucher register debit columns—Purchases, Transportation-In, Discounts Lost, and Other Accounts. The last voucher number used was 9743, and the last check issued was No. 2096. As of August 31, 1991, three vouchers were in the unpaid voucher file:

Voucher No. 9696, Tims Company . . . . . . $ 3,960
Voucher No. 9741, Jamison Company   7,980
Voucher No. 9742, Kelso Company   3,420
$15,360

The total of the unpaid voucher file agreed with the credit balance in the Vouchers Payable control account.

The following transactions occurred during September 1991. Vouchers are prepared for the net amount of the invoice. For any discounts lost, a new voucher is prepared for the amount of the discount.

Sept. 3 Paid Citizens Bank $3,660 for a note that matured on this date. Of that amount, $160 was interest.
5 Received an invoice for $5,100 from Reese Company for merchandise. Terms were 2/10, n/30.
6 Paid Voucher No. 9696 to Tims Company, $3,960.
10 Received an invoice for $1,764 from Zink Company for merchandise. Terms were 2/10, n/30.
15 Paid Reese Company the amount owed on its invoice of September 5.
17 Paid $780 to Jacklin Company for advertising in September.
30 Paid $53,400 to Arlin Company. This amount included $1,068 chargeable to the Transportation-In account. The balance paid was the net cost of merchandise received today. Terms were 2/10, n/30. (The gross invoice price of the merchandise was $53,400.)
30 Paid Zink Company the amount due on the purchase of September 10.

Required: Enter these transactions in the voucher register and the check register. You need not show unpaid vouchers from preceding months in the voucher register. Total the registers as of September 30. List the unpaid vouchers at September 30 and compare the total with the balance in the Vouchers Payable control account (Account No. 250) after posting has been completed.

BUSINESS DECISION PROBLEM 7–1

Discuss steps to prevent theft

During World War II, a managerial accountant in the United States was called back to active duty with the Army. An acquaintance of the accountant forged papers and assumed the identity of the accountant. He obtained a position in a small company as the only accountant. Eventually he took over (from the manager) the functions of approving bills for payment, preparing and signing checks, and almost all other financial duties. On one weekend, he traveled to some neighboring cities and prepared and mailed invoices made out to the company he worked for. On Monday morning, he returned to work and began receiving, approving, and paying the invoices he had prepared. The following weekend he returned to the neighboring cities and cashed and deposited the checks in bank accounts under his own signature card. After continuing this practice for several months, he withdrew all of the funds and never was heard from again.

Required: Discuss some of the steps that could have been taken to prevent this theft. Remember that this is a small company with limited financial resources.

BUSINESS DECISION PROBLEM 7–2

List procedures that would have prevented theft of cash

Sam Burke was set up in business by his father, who purchased the business of an elderly acquaintance wishing to retire. One of the few changes in personnel made by Sam was to install a college classmate as the office manager-bookkeeper-cashier-sales manager.

During the course of the year, Sam found it necessary to borrow money from the bank (with his father as co-signer) because, although the business seemed profitable, there was a shortage of adequate cash. The investment in inventories and receivables grew substantially during the year. Finally, after a year had elapsed, Sam's father employed a certified public accountant to audit the records of Sam's business. The CPA reported that the office manager-bookkeeper-cashier-sales manager had been stealing funds and had been using a variety of schemes to cover his actions. More specifically, he had:

1. Pocketed cash receipts from sales and understated the cash register readings at the end of the day or altered the copies of the sales tickets retained.
2. Stolen checks mailed to the company in payment of accounts receivable, credited the proper accounts, and then debited fictitious receivables to keep the records in balance.
3. Issued checks to fictitious suppliers and deposited them in accounts bearing these names with himself as signer of checks drawn on these accounts; the books were kept in balance by debiting the Purchases account.
4. Stolen petty cash funds by drawing false vouchers purporting to cover a variety of expenses incurred.
5. Prepared false sales returns vouchers indicating the return of cash sales to cover further thefts of cash receipts.

Required: For each of the above items, indicate at least one feature of a good system of internal control that would have prevented the losses due to dishonesty.

BUSINESS DECISION PROBLEM 7–3*

Describe method used to steal cash; determine amount stolen; prepare correct bank reconciliation; describe internal control procedures that would have prevented such theft

The outstanding checks of Walker Company at November 30, 1991, were:

No. 229	$1,000.00
No. 263	1,089.00
No. 3678	679.00
No. 3679	804.00
No. 3680	1,400.00

During December, checks numbered 3681–3720 were issued, and all of these checks cleared the bank except Nos. 3719 and 3720 for $963.00 and $726.00, respectively. Check Nos. 3678, 3679, and 3680 also cleared the bank.

The bank statement on December 31 showed a balance of $23,944. Service charges amounted to $20, and two checks were returned by the bank, one marked NSF in the amount of $114 and the other marked "No account" in the amount of $2,000.

Mr. Ackerman recently retired as the office manager-cashier-bookkeeper for Walker Company and was replaced by Mr. Miller. Mr. Miller noted the absence of a system of internal control but was momentarily deterred from embezzling for lack of a scheme of concealment. Finally, he hit upon several schemes. The $2,000 check marked "No account" by the bank is the product of one scheme. Mr. Miller took cash receipts and replaced them with a check drawn upon a nonexistent account to make it appear that a customer had given the company a worthless check.

The other scheme was more subtle. Mr. Miller pocketed cash receipts to bring them down to an amount sufficient to prepare the following bank reconciliation:

Balance per bank statement, December 31, 1991		$23,944.00
Add: Deposit in transit		2,837.80
		$26,781.80
Deduct: Outstanding checks:		
No. 3719	$ 963.00	
No. 3720	726.00	1,689.00
Adjusted balance		$25,092.80
Balance, Cash account December 31, 1991		$27,226.80
Deduct:		
Worthless check	$2,000.00	
NSF check	114.00	
Service charges	20.00	2,134.00
Adjusted balance		$25,092.80

Required:

a. State the nature of the second scheme hit on by Mr. Miller. How much in total does it appear he has stolen by use of the two schemes together?

b. Prepare a correct bank reconciliation as of December 31, 1991.

c. Suggest procedures that would have defeated the attempts of Mr. Miller to steal funds and conceal these actions.

---

* Note: This is a challenging problem that was not specifically illustrated in the chapter, but it can be worked by applying the principles discussed in the chapter.

BUSINESS DECISION PROBLEM 7-4

Cite weaknesses in control over petty cash; explain how internal control over petty cash can be improved

Sylvia Gardner recently acquired an importing business from a friend. The business employs 10 salesclerks and 4 office employees. A petty cash fund of $125 has been established. All of the 14 employees are allowed to make disbursements from the fund. Vouchers are not used, and no one keeps a record of the disbursements. The petty cash is kept in a large shoe box in the office.

Required: Discuss the operation of the petty cash fund from an internal control point of view. Indicate the weaknesses that currently exist and suggest how the internal control system can be improved.

BUSINESS DECISION PROBLEM 7-5

Make decisions regarding scheme to cover shortage in checking account

Tom Hanks is a bookkeeper working for the Stanley Company. The company maintains two checking accounts, one where the company is located and another in a distant city where a major customer is located. Tom is a compulsive gambler and had "borrowed" funds from the local bank account by writing a company check to himself (which he never recorded) to cover his gambling losses. When the check was returned by the bank, he destroyed it. At year-end, the local bank account was "short" by $20,000, and Tom wondered how he would hide the shortage from the owner. The owner always asked to see the bank reconciliations at the end of the year and also engaged a local CPA to perform an audit.

Realizing that it takes several days for a check to clear the banking system, Tom wrote a check on the distant bank for $20,000 and deposited the check in the local bank on December 31, 1991, bringing that bank account up to its proper balance. In the cash disbursements journal, Tom dated the check January 1, 1992. The check did not clear the banking system and arrive at the distant bank until January 4, 1992. Tom did not list the check as being outstanding when he prepared the bank reconciliation for the distant bank. He was quite pleased that his scheme seemed to cover the shortage and felt that he surely would win soon and could return the funds.

Required: a.   Will the bank reconciliations appear to be correct?
b.   Do you suppose that others have tried this scheme to cover their shortages?
c.   What could have been done to prevent this situation?
d.   Is it likely that the scheme will be uncovered?

BUSINESS DECISION PROBLEM (ETHICS) 7-6

Discuss ethics of misuse of petty cash funds

The City Club Restaurant is a member-owned entity in Carson City. The manager, John Blue, has managed the restaurant for 20 years and has received only minimal salary increases over that period. He believes he is grossly underpaid in view of the significant inflation that has occurred. A few years ago he began supplementing his income by placing phony "peanut" invoices in the petty cash box, writing a petty cash voucher for the amount of each invoice, withdrawing an amount of cash equal to the amount of each invoice for his personal use, and later approving the vouchers for reimbursement. Through this mechanism, John was able to increase his income by about $12,000 per year, an amount that he considered fair. No one else knows what is happening, and the manager feels fully justified in supplementing his income in this way.

Required: Discuss the ethics of this situation.

8 Receivables and Payables

After studying this chapter, you should be able to:

1. Account for uncollectible accounts receivable.
2. Record credit card sales and collections.
3. Account for notes receivable and payable, including calculation of interest.
4. Record the discounting of a customer's note at a bank.
5. Define and use correctly the new terms in the glossary.

Much of the growth of business in recent years is due to the immense expansion of credit. Businesses have learned that by granting customers the privilege of *charging* their purchases, sales and profits increase. Not only is the use of credit a convenient way to make purchases, but most people could not own high-priced items such as automobiles without credit.

In this chapter, you will study about receivables and payables. For a company, a **receivable** is any sum of money due to be paid to that company from any party for any reason. Similarly, a **payable** describes any sum of money to be paid by that company to any party for any reason.

The receivables you will learn about are primarily receivables arising from the sale of goods and services. Two types of receivables are discussed: accounts receivable, which companies offer for short-term credit with no interest charge; and notes receivable, which companies sometimes extend for both short- and long-term credit with an interest charge. Particular attention is given to accounting for uncollectible accounts receivable.

Companies, like customers, also use credit. To a company, this credit is shown as accounts payable or notes payable. Accounts payable normally result from the purchase of goods or services, do not carry an interest charge, and have already been discussed in earlier chapters. Short-term notes payable carry an interest charge and may arise from those same transactions but can also result from borrowing money from a bank or other institution. Long-term notes payable usually result from borrowing money from a bank or other institution to finance the acquisition of plant assets. As you study this chapter and learn how important credit is to our economy, you will realize that credit in some form will probably always be with us— including our national debt.

■ ACCOUNTS RECEIVABLE

Objective 1:
Account for uncollectible accounts receivable.

In Chapter 3, you learned that revenues and expenses may be recorded on the cash basis or the accrual basis of accounting. The cash basis recognizes revenues when cash is received and expenses when cash is paid out, whereas the accrual basis recognizes revenues when sales are made or services are performed and expenses when they are incurred. Most companies use the accrual basis of accounting since it more properly reflects the actual results of the operations of a business.

Accrual basis accounting generally requires that merchandising companies that extend credit record revenue when a sale is made because at that time the revenue is both earned and realized. The revenue is earned because the seller has completed its part of the sales contract by delivering the goods; the revenue is realized because the company has received the customer's promise to pay in exchange for the goods. This promise to pay by the customer is an account receivable to the seller. Accounts receivable, then, are amounts customers owe a company for goods sold and services rendered on account. Frequently, these receivables resulting from credit sales of goods and services are called **trade receivables.**

When a company sells goods on open account, customers do not sign formal, written promises to pay; rather they agree to abide by the seller's customary credit terms. However, they may sign a sales invoice to acknowledge purchase of goods. Payment terms for open account sales typically run from 30 to 60 days. Interest usually is not charged on amounts owed, except on some past-due amounts.

Unfortunately, customers do not always keep their promises to pay. The use of cash basis and accrual basis accounting differs in that a company using the cash basis does not record sales on account until the cash is received, while a company using the accrual basis records sales on account immediately. So when an uncollectible account occurs, companies using accrual basis accounting must have some provision for recording the uncollectible account as an expense.

Companies use two methods for handling uncollectible accounts: the allowance method, which provides in advance for uncollectible accounts; and the direct write-off method, which recognizes uncollectible accounts as an expense when judged uncollectible. These two methods are discussed in the following two sections. The allowance method is the preferred method to record uncollectible accounts and is discussed in greater detail.

The Allowance Method for Recording Uncollectible Accounts

Regardless of how carefully companies screen customers when giving credit, some accounts will become uncollectible. The matching principle requires that expenses incurred in producing revenues be deducted from the revenues they generated during the accounting period. The allowance method of recording uncollectible accounts adheres to this principle by making a provision for uncollectible accounts expense in advance of the time when the debts are identified as being uncollectible. The entry required has some similarity to the depreciation entry in Chapter 3 because an expense is debited and an allowance (contra asset) is credited. The purpose of the entry is to make the income statement fairly present the proper expense and the balance sheet fairly present the asset. **Uncollectible accounts expense** (also called **bad debts expense**) is an operating expense that a business incurs when it sells on credit. We are inclined to classify uncollectible accounts expense as a selling expense because it results from a sale on credit. Other accountants might classify it as an administrative expense because the credit department has an important role in setting credit terms.

To adhere to the matching principle, the uncollectible accounts expense must be matched against the revenues it generates. Thus, an uncollectible account arising from a sale made in 1991 must be treated as a 1991 expense even though to do so requires the use of estimates. Estimates are necessary because the company cannot determine until 1992 or later which customer accounts existing at year-end 1991 will become uncollectible.

Recording the Uncollectible Account Adjustment.   When uncollectible accounts are estimated, the company makes an adjusting entry at the end of each accounting period. Uncollectible Accounts Expense is debited, thus recording the expense in the proper period. The credit is to an account called *Allowance for Uncollectible Accounts.*

As a contra asset account to the Accounts Receivable account, the **Allowance for Uncollectible Accounts** (also called **Allowance for Doubtful Accounts**) reduces accounts receivable to their net realizable value. **Net realizable value** is the amount expected to be collected from accounts receivable. Since the company does not know which specific accounts will be uncollectible when the uncollectible accounts adjusting entry is made, credits cannot be entered in either the Accounts Receivable control account or the customers' subsidiary ledger accounts. If only one or the other were credited, the Accounts Receivable control account balance would not agree with the total of the balances in the accounts receivable subsidiary ledger. The allowance account lets the company show that a certain amount of the accounts receivable will not be collected without crediting the Accounts Receivable control account.

To illustrate the adjusting entry for uncollectible accounts, assume that a company has $100,000 of accounts receivable and estimates its uncollectible accounts expense for a given year at $4,000. The required year-end adjusting entry is:

```
Dec. 31  Uncollectible Accounts Expense . . . . . . . . . . .   4,000
             Allowance for Uncollectible Accounts  . . . . .          4,000
         To record estimated uncollectible accounts.
```

The debit to Uncollectible Accounts Expense brings about the desired matching of expenses and revenues since uncollectible accounts expense is matched against the revenues of the accounting period. The credit to Allowance for Uncollectible Accounts reduces accounts receivable to their net realizable value. When the books are closed, Uncollectible Accounts Expense is closed to Income Summary. The allowance is reported on the balance sheet as a deduction from accounts receivable as follows:

```
Accounts receivable . . . . . . . . . . . . . . .  $100,000
Less: Allowance for uncollectible accounts  . . . .    4,000    $96,000
```

Now the question is: How is the estimate of uncollectible accounts determined? The next section answers this question.

Estimating Uncollectible Accounts.   Accountants use two basic methods to estimate uncollectible accounts for a period. The first method—percentage-of-sales method—focuses attention on the income statement and the relationship of uncollectible accounts to sales. The second method—percentage-of-receivables method—focuses attention on the balance sheet and the relationship of the allowance for uncollectible accounts to accounts receivable. Either of these two estimation methods is acceptable, and over time the results obtained under both methods are likely to be quite similar. However, some accountants prefer the percentage-of-sales method because it does a better job of matching expenses with revenues.

Percentage-of-Sales Method.   The **percentage-of-sales method** estimates the uncollectible accounts from the credit sales of a given period. In theory, the method is based on a percentage of prior years' actual uncollectible accounts losses to prior years' credit sales. **If cash sales are small or make up a fairly constant percentage of total sales, the calculation can be based on total net sales.** Since at least one of these conditions is usually met, total net sales rather than credit sales are commonly used.

The percentage of uncollectible accounts to last year's sales is reviewed annually to see if it is still valid; if not, the percentage is increased or decreased to reflect the changed condition. For example, in periods of recession, the percentage rate may have to be increased to reflect decreased customer ability to pay. However, if the company adopts a more stringent credit policy, the percentage rate may have to be decreased because fewer uncollectible accounts are expected.

To illustrate, assume that Rankin Company's uncollectible accounts from 1989 sales were 1.1% of total net sales. It does not matter when the accounts were found to be uncollectible; the important point is that they arose from 1989 sales. A similar calculation for 1990 showed an uncollectible account percentage of 0.9%. The average for the two years is 1% [(1.1 + 0.9) ÷ 2]. Rankin does not expect 1991 to differ from the average of the previous two years. Total net sales for 1991 were $500,000; receivables at year-end are $100,000; and the Allowance for Uncollectible Accounts has a zero balance. Rankin would make the following adjusting entry for 1991:

```
Dec. 31   Uncollectible Accounts Expense . . . . . . . . . . .   5,000
              Allowance for Uncollectible Accounts  . . . . .            5,000
          To record estimated uncollectible accounts
          ($500,000 × 0.01).
```

Using T-accounts, Rankin would show:

Uncollectible Accounts Expense		Allowance for Uncollectible Accounts	
Dec. 31 Adjustment 5,000		Bal. before adjustment –0– Dec. 31 Adjustment 5,000	
		Bal. after adjustment 5,000	

Uncollectible Accounts Expense is closed to Income Summary. The accounts receivable less the allowance is reported among current assets in the balance sheet as follows:

Accounts receivable $100,000
Less: Allowance for uncollectible accounts 5,000 $95,000

This information could also be presented in a published balance sheet as:

Accounts receivable (less estimated
  uncollectible accounts, $5,000) . . . . $ 95,000

The Allowance for Uncollectible Accounts account usually has a balance prior to the year-end adjustment. **Under the percentage-of-sales method, any existing balance in the allowance is ignored in calculating the amount of the year-end adjustment.** The expense and addition to the allowance are based on the past average relationship of actual uncollectible accounts to either credit sales or total net sales. In any given year, the average can vary from previous years. Hence, minor balances in the allowance account are ignored.

Assume that in the example above, Rankin's allowance had a $300 credit balance prior to adjustment. The adjusting entry would be the same. But the balance sheet would show $100,000 accounts receivable less a $5,300 allowance for uncollectible accounts, resulting in net receivables of $94,700. Uncollectible Accounts Expense would still appear on the income statement as 1% of total net sales, or $5,000.

Percentage-of-Receivables Method.   The **percentage-of-receivables method** estimates uncollectible accounts by determining the desired size of Allowance for Uncollectible Accounts. The ending balance in Accounts Receivable is multiplied by a rate (or rates) based on past experience regarding uncollectible accounts. In the percentage-of-receivables method, either an overall rate may be used or a different rate may be used for each age category of receivables.

The overall rate of the percentage-of-receivables method is calculated as follows. Using the same information as before, Rankin will make an estimate of uncollectible accounts at the end of 1991. The balance of accounts receivable is $100,000, and the allowance account has no balance. If Rankin estimates that 6% of the receivables will be uncollectible, the adjusting entry is:

Dec. 31	Uncollectible Accounts Expense	6,000	
	Allowance for Uncollectible Accounts		6,000
	To record estimated uncollectible accounts		
	($100,000 × 0.06).		

Using T-accounts, Rankin would show:

Uncollectible Accounts Expense		Allowance for Uncollectible Accounts	
Dec. 31 Adjustment 6,000		Bal. before	
		adjustment –0–	
		Dec. 31	
		Adjustment 6,000	
		Bal. after	
		adjustment 6,000	

If there were a $300 credit balance in the allowance, the entry would be the same as the one just given, except that the amount would be $5,700. The difference in amounts arises because the company wants the allowance to contain a balance equal to 6% of the outstanding receivables when the two accounts are presented on the balance sheet. **Thus, under the percentage-of-receivables method, any balance in the allowance account must be considered when adjusting for uncollectible accounts.**

Using T-accounts, Rankin would show:

Uncollectible Accounts Expense		Allowance for Uncollectible Accounts	
Dec. 31 Adjustment 5,700		Bal. before	
		adjustment 300	
		Dec. 31	
		Adjustment 5,700	
		Bal. after	
		adjustment 6,000	

As another example, suppose that Rankin had a $300 **debit** balance in the allowance account prior to adjustment. Then, a credit of $6,300 would be necessary to get the balance to the required $6,000 credit balance.

Using T-accounts, Rankin would show:

Uncollectible Accounts Expense		Allowance for Uncollectible Accounts	
Dec. 31 Adjustment 6,300		Bal. before adjustment 300	Dec. 31 Adjustment 6,300
			Bal. after adjustment 6,000

No matter what the preadjustment allowance balance is, when Rankin uses the percentage-of-receivables method, the Allowance for Uncollectible Accounts is adjusted so that it has a credit balance of $6,000—which is equal to 6% of its $100,000 in Accounts Receivable.

When the percentage-of-receivables method is calculated by using a **different rate** for each age category of receivables, an aging schedule is

Illustration 8.1

Accounts Receivable Aging Schedule

DARCY COMPANY
Accounts Receivable Aging Schedule
December 31, 1991

Customer	Debit Balance	Not Yet Due	Number of Days Past Due			
			1–30	31–60	61–90	Over 90
X	$ 5,000					$ 5,000
Y	14,000		$ 12,000	$2,000		
Z	400				$200	200
All others	808,600	$560,000	240,000	2,000	600	6,000
	$828,000	$560,000	$252,000	$4,000	$800	$11,200
Estimated uncollectible percentage		1%	5%	10%	25%	50%
Estimated amount uncollectible	$ 24,400	$ 5,600	$ 12,600	$ 400	$200	$ 5,600

used. An **aging schedule** classifies accounts receivable according to their age (how long they have been outstanding) and uses a different uncollectibility percentage rate for each age category. The percentages used are based on past experience. An aging schedule is presented in Illustration 8.1. This schedule shows that the older a receivable is, the more likely it will not be collected.

Classifying accounts receivable according to age gives the company a basis for estimating the total amount of uncollectible accounts. For example, based on prior experience, only 1% of the accounts not yet due (sales made less than 30 days prior to the end of the accounting period) are expected to be uncollectible. At the other extreme, 50% of all accounts over 90 days past due are expected to be uncollectible. For each age category, the accounts receivable are multiplied by the estimated uncollectible percentage to find the estimated amount uncollectible. The sum of the estimated amounts uncollectible for all categories yields the total estimated amount uncollectible and is the desired credit balance in the Allowance for Uncollectible Accounts.

Since the aging schedule is used under the percentage-of-receivables method, the journal entry to record uncollectible accounts is affected by the balance in the allowance prior to adjustment. For example, Illustration 8.1 shows that $24,400 is needed in the allowance. If the allowance currently has a $5,000 credit balance, the adjustment will be for $19,400.

The information contained in an aging schedule may be useful to management for purposes other than estimating uncollectible accounts. Visible information on collection patterns of accounts receivable may suggest the need for changes in credit policies or for added financing. For example, if the age of many customer balances has increased to the 61–90 days past-due category, collection efforts may have to be strengthened, or the company may have to find other sources of cash to pay its debts.

The process of estimating the amount of a company's uncollectible accounts establishes the Allowance for Uncollectible Accounts, which is a contra account to the Accounts Receivable account. As time passes and it becomes evident that certain customer accounts will not be collected, these accounts must be written off. In the next section, you will learn how accountants write off uncollectible accounts.

Write-Off of Receivables.   When a specific customer's account is considered uncollectible, a portion of the allowance account, as well as the specific customer's account, is written off. The Allowance for Uncollectible Accounts is debited. The credit is to the Accounts Receivable control account in the general ledger and to the customer's subsidiary ledger account in the accounts receivable subsidiary ledger. For example, assume Smith's $750 account has been determined to be uncollectible. The entry to write off this account is:

Allowance for Uncollectible Accounts	750	
Accounts Receivable—Smith		750
To write Smith's account off as uncollectible.		

The credit balance that existed in Allowance for Uncollectible Accounts before the above entry was made represented potential uncollectible accounts that had not yet been specifically identified. Debiting the allowance account shows that the particular account of Smith has now been **identified** as uncollectible. Notice that this debit entry in the write-off of receivables **does not involve recording an expense.** The uncollectible accounts expense was recognized in the year of the sale. If Smith's $750 uncollectible account is recorded in Uncollectible Accounts Expense again, it would be ''double counted'' as an expense.

The net realizable value of accounts receivable is not affected by a write-off. For example, suppose that Amos Company has total accounts receivable of $50,000 and an allowance of $3,000 before the above entry; the net realizable value of the accounts receivable is $47,000, as shown below. After posting the above entry, accounts receivable are $49,250, and the allowance is $2,250; net realizable value is still $47,000.

	Before Write-Off	After Write-Off
Accounts receivable	$50,000	$49,250
Allowance for uncollectible accounts	3,000	2,250
Net realizable value	$47,000	$47,000

If the Allowance for Uncollectible Accounts is adjusted only at year-end, it may have a debit balance before adjustment. One reason for this debit balance is that companies do not often carry accounts receivable in their records that are more than one year old. Consequently, by the end of 1991, all accounts from 1990 sales will have either been collected or written off. If the estimates were exact, the allowance resulting from 1990 would have a zero balance. But the allowance may develop a debit balance if estimates were less than actual write-offs. Also, some accounts from 1991 sales probably have been charged off in 1991. Yet no uncollectible accounts adjusting entry has been made for 1991. The result is likely to be a debit balance in the allowance account before the annual adjustment.

After a company has used the allowance method for several years, the balance in the allowance account consists of the net amount of inadequate or excessive estimates of uncollectible accounts of prior years. Errors in estimating preceding years' uncollectibles are corrected by increasing or decreasing the current year's estimate.

Uncollectible Accounts Recovered.   Sometimes accounts considered uncollectible are collected after the account has already been written off. A company usually learns that an account has been written off erroneously when payment, by cash or check, is received. When the payment is received, the original write-off is reversed. The account is reinstated by debiting Accounts Receivable and crediting Allowance for Uncollectible Accounts for the amount received. The debit is posted to both the general ledger account and to the customer's subsidiary ledger account. The amount received is also recorded as a debit to Cash and a credit to Accounts Receivable. The credit is posted to both the general ledger account and to the customer's subsidiary ledger account.

To illustrate, assume that on May 17 a $750 check is received from Smith in payment of the account that was previously written off. The two required journal entries are:

May 17 Accounts Receivable—Smith	750	
Allowance for Uncollectible Accounts		750
To reverse original write-off of Smith's account.		
17 Cash	750	
Accounts Receivable—Smith		750
To record collection of account.		

If only part of a previously written off account is collected, the usual procedure is to reinstate only that portion of the account actually collected, unless evidence indicates that the entire account will be collected.

The Direct Write-Off Method for Recording Uncollectible Accounts

In contrast to the allowance method of writing off uncollectible accounts, the **direct write-off method** directly charges the identified uncollectible accounts receivable to an expense account, Uncollectible Accounts Expense. No adjusting entry is made to record estimated uncollectible accounts. This method is used by some companies with accounts receivable and uncollectible accounts so small that they are immaterial. If these amounts are material (relatively large), the direct write-off method is unacceptable because uncollectible accounts expense might not be matched against the sales that created them.

To illustrate the direct write-off method, assume that a $200 account for Robert Hill is considered uncollectible. Under this method, the journal entry to write off the account is:

Uncollectible Accounts Expense	200	
Accounts Receivable—Robert Hill		200
To write off an uncollectible account.		

Assume that several months later, $125 is received on Robert Hill's account. The required journal entries are:

Accounts Receivable—Robert Hill	125	
Uncollectible Accounts Recoveries		125
To reinstate portion of account written off. (The credit could be to Uncollectible Accounts Expense if the write-off occurred in this accounting period.)		

Cash	125	
Accounts Receivable—Robert Hill		125
To record collection on account.		

Although the direct write-off method is acceptable for income tax purposes, it is usually not acceptable for financial accounting because (1) it does not properly match expenses and revenues, and (2) it overstates accounts receivable in the balance sheet since the allowance account is not used.

Because of the uncollectible accounts that may arise when a company offers customers its credit, many companies now allow customers to use bank or external credit cards. As you will see, this relieves the company of the headaches involved in trying to collect overdue accounts.

Credit Cards

Objective 2:
Record credit card
sales and collections.

Credit cards are either nonbank (American Express and Diners Club) or bank (VISA and MasterCard) charge cards that customers use to charge purchases of goods and services. For some businesses, uncollectible accounts losses and other costs of extending credit are a burden. By paying a service charge of 2% to 8%, businesses can pass these costs on to banks and other credit agencies issuing national credit cards. The banks and credit card agencies then absorb the uncollectible accounts and costs of extending credit and maintaining records.

Usually, banks and credit card agencies issue credit cards to approved credit applicants for an annual fee. When a business agrees to honor these credit cards, the business also agrees to pay the percentage fee charged to the business by the bank or credit agency.

When making a credit card sale, the seller checks the customer's card against a list of canceled cards and calls the credit agency for approval if the sale exceeds a prescribed amount, such as $50. This procedure allows the seller to avoid accepting a lost, stolen, or canceled card. Also, the credit agency is protected from a sale causing the customer to exceed an established credit limit.

The accounting procedures used by the seller for credit card sales differ depending on whether the business accepts a nonbank or a bank credit card. The difference in accounting procedures is shown by the illustrations that follow.

To illustrate the entries for the use of **nonbank** credit cards (such as American Express or Diners Club), assume that a restaurant has Diners Club invoices amounting to $1,400 at the end of a day. The Diners Club charges a 5% service charge. The **Credit Card Expense account** is used to record the credit card agency's service charge. The restaurant makes the following entry:

Accounts Receivable—Diners Club	1,330	
Credit Card Expense	70	
Sales		1,400
To record credit card sales.		

The invoices are mailed to Diners Club. Payment is received from Diners Club some time later. The following entry is made:

Cash	1,330	
Accounts Receivable—Diners Club		1,330
To record remittance from Diners Club.		

To illustrate the accounting entries for the use of **bank** credit cards (such as VISA or MasterCard), assume that a retailer has made sales of $1,000 for which VISA cards were accepted and the VISA service charge is $50 (which is 5% of sales). VISA sales are treated as cash sales because the receipt of cash is certain. The credit card sales invoices are deposited in a checking account maintained in a bank just as checks are deposited in a regular checking account. The entry to record this deposit is:

Cash	950	
Credit Card Expense	50	
Sales		1,000
To record VISA credit card sales.		

So far in this chapter, you learned how to record revenue from accounts receivable by using the accrual basis of accounting and adhering to the matching principle of accounting. Accounts receivable are credit sales made through the seller extending credit. No formal written promises to pay are required. However, many companies have transactions in which written promises to pay (notes) are used to account for sales, purchases, or loans. The remainder of this chapter discusses notes receivable and notes payable.

NOTES RECEIVABLE AND NOTES PAYABLE

Objective 3: Account for notes receivable and payable, including calculation of interest.

In Chapter 4, you learned that a note (also called a **promissory note**) is an unconditional written promise by a borrower (**maker**) to pay a definite sum of money to the lender (**payee**) on demand or on a specific date. On the balance sheet of the lender (payee), a note is a receivable; on the balance sheet of the borrower (maker), a note is a payable. Since the note is usually negotiable, the payee may transfer it to another party, who then receives payment from the maker. An example of a promissory note is shown in Illustration 8.2.

A customer may give a note to a business for an amount due on an account receivable or for the sale of a large item such as a refrigerator.

Illustration 8.2

Promissory Note

```
$ 2,000.00 _____                                      June 1 _____ , 19 90

Sixty days- - - - - - - - - - - - - - - - - - - - - AFTER DATE  We _____ PROMISE TO PAY TO

THE ORDER OF        MOTOR WHEEL CORPORATION

Two Thousand and no/100- - - - - - - - - - - - - - - - - - - - - - - - - DOLLARS

AT Motor Wheel Corporation, Lansing, Michigan

FOR VALUE RECEIVED WITH INTEREST AT THE RATE OF ___10%___ PER ANNUM FROM June 1, 1990

     This note is one of a series of___1___ notes of even date herewith, numbered ___487___ to ___--___ inclusive, and
all of said notes shall become immediately due and payable at the option of the holder hereof on default being made in the payment of any one at maturity.

NO. 487 _____ DUE  July 31, 1990          THE PETERSON COMPANY

                                           John J. Lucia, Treasurer
```

Also, a business may give a note to a supplier in exchange for merchandise to sell or to a bank or an individual for a loan. Thus, a company may have notes receivable or notes payable arising from transactions with customers, suppliers, banks, or individuals.

Companies usually do not establish a subsidiary ledger for notes. Instead, a file is maintained of the actual notes receivable and copies of notes payable.

Interest Calculation

Most promissory notes have an explicit interest charge. **Interest** is the fee charged for use of money through time. To the maker of the note, or borrower, interest is an expense; to the payee of the note, or lender, interest is a revenue. A borrower incurs interest expense; a lender earns interest revenue. For convenience, interest is sometimes calculated on the basis of a 360-day year, and we will do so in this text.

The basic formula for computing interest is:

$$\text{Interest} = \text{Principal} \times \text{Rate} \times \text{Time, or } I = P \times R \times T$$

Principal is the face value of the note. The **rate** is the stated interest rate on the note; interest rates are generally stated on an annual basis. **Time,** which is the amount of time the note is to run, can be expressed in either days or months.

To show how interest is calculated, assume a company borrowed $20,000 from a bank. The note has a principal (face value) of $20,000, an interest rate of 15%, and a life of 90 days. The interest calculation is:

$$\text{Interest} = \$20,000 \times 0.15 \times 90/360$$
$$\text{Interest} = \$750$$

Note that in this calculation the time period is expressed as a fraction of a 360-day year because the interest rate is expressed on an annual basis.

Determination of Maturity Date

The **maturity date** is the date on which a note becomes due and must be paid. The wording used in the note expresses the maturity date and determines when the note is to be paid. Examples of the maturity date wording are:

1. *On demand.* "On demand, I promise to pay. . . ." When the maturity date is "on demand," it is at the option of the holder and cannot be computed. The holder is the payee, or another person who legally acquired the note from the payee.
2. *On a stated date.* "On July 18, 1991, I promise to pay. . . ." When the maturity date is designated, computing the maturity date is not necessary.
3. *At the end of a stated period.*
   a. "One year after date, I promise to pay. . . ." When the maturity is expressed in years, the note matures on the same day of the same month as the date of the note in the year of maturity.
   b. "Four months after date, I promise to pay. . . ." When the maturity is expressed in months, the note will mature on the same date in the month of maturity. For example, one month from July 18, 1991, is August 18, 1991, and two months from July 18, 1991, is September 18, 1991. If a note is issued on the last day of a month and the month of maturity has fewer days than the month of issuance, the note matures on the last day of the month of maturity. A one-month note dated January 31, 1991, matures on February 28, 1991.
   c. "Ninety days after date, I promise to pay. . . ." When the maturity is expressed in days, the exact number of days must be counted. The first day (date of origin) is omitted, and the last day (maturity date) is included in the count. For example, a 90-day note dated October 19, 1991, matures on January 17, 1992, as shown below:

Life of note (days)	90 days
Days remaining in October not counting date of origin of note:	
Days to count in October (31 − 19) . . . 12	
Total days in November . . . 30	
Total days in December . . . 31	73
Maturity date in January	17 days

A note falling due on a Sunday or a holiday is due on the next business day.

Accounting for Notes in Normal Business Transactions

Sometimes a note is received when high-priced merchandise is sold, but often a note results from the conversion of an overdue open account. When a customer does not pay an account receivable when due, the company (creditor) may insist that the customer (debtor) give a note in place of the account. This action allows the customer more time to pay the balance of the account, and the company earns interest on the balance until paid. Also, the company may be able to sell the note to a bank or other financial institution, as you will learn later.

To illustrate the conversion of an open account to a note, assume that Price Company (maker) had purchased $18,000 of merchandise on August 1 from Cooper Company (payee) on open account. The normal credit period has elapsed, and Price cannot pay the bill. Cooper agrees to accept Price's $18,000, 15%, 90-day note dated September 1 to settle Price's open account. Assuming Price paid the note at maturity and both Price and Cooper have a December 31 year-end, the entries on the books of the maker and the books of the payee are:

Price Company, Maker

Aug. 1   Purchases 18,000
           Accounts Payable—Cooper Company   18,000
           To record purchase of merchandise on account.

Sept. 1   Accounts Payable—Cooper Company 18,000
           Notes Payable   18,000
           To record exchange of note to Cooper Company
           for open account.

Nov. 30   Notes Payable 18,000
           Interest Expense   675
           Cash   18,675
           To record payment of note principal and interest.

Cooper Company, Payee

Aug. 1   Accounts Receivable—Price Company 18,000
           Sales   18,000
           To record sale of merchandise on account.

Sept. 1   Notes Receivable 18,000
           Accounts Receivable—Price Company   18,000
           To record exchange of note from Price Company
           for open account.

Nov. 30   Cash 18,675
           Notes Receivable   18,000
           Interest Revenue   675
           To record receipt of Price Company note principal
           and interest.

The $18,675 paid by Price to Cooper is called the *maturity value of the note*. **Maturity value** is the amount that the maker must pay on a note on its maturity date; typically, it includes principal and accrued interest, if any.

Sometimes the maker of a note does not pay the note when it becomes due. In the next section, you will learn how to record a note that has not been paid at maturity.

Dishonored Notes

A **dishonored note** is a note that the maker failed to pay at maturity. Since the note has matured, the holder or payee should remove the note from Notes Receivable and record the amount due in Accounts Receivable. The debit to Accounts Receivable is posted to the general ledger and to the maker's subsidiary ledger account.

At the maturity date of a note, the maker is obligated to pay the principal plus interest. If the interest has not been accrued on the maker's books, the maker of a dishonored note should record interest expense for the life of the note by debiting Interest Expense and crediting Interest Payable. The payee should record the interest earned and remove the note from its Notes Receivable account. To do this, the payee of the note should debit Accounts Receivable for the maturity value of the note and credit Notes Receivable for the note's face value and Interest Revenue for the interest. Thus, the full liability on the note—principal plus interest—is included in the records of both parties.

To illustrate, assume that Price did not pay the note at maturity. The entries on each party's books are:

Cooper Company, Payee

Nov. 30	Accounts Receivable—Price Company	18,675	
	Notes Receivable		18,000
	Interest Revenue		675
	To record dishonor of Price Company note.		

Price Company, Maker

Nov. 30	Interest Expense	675	
	Interest Payable		675
	To record interest on note payable.		

When the maker of a note is unable to pay at maturity, sometimes the maker pays the interest on the original note or includes the interest in the face value of a new note given to replace the old note. The new note is accounted for in the same manner as the old note. However, if it later becomes clear that the maker of a dishonored note will never pay, the payee should write off the account with a debit to Uncollectible Accounts Expense (or to an account with a title such as Loss on Dishonored Notes) and a credit to Accounts Receivable. The debit should be to the Allowance for Uncollectible Accounts if annual provision was made for uncollectible notes receivable.

Accruing Interest

On an interest-bearing note, interest accrues, or accumulates, on a day-to-day basis but usually is only recorded at the note's maturity date. If, however, the note is outstanding at the end of an accounting period, then the time period of the interest overlaps the end of the accounting period, and an adjusting entry is needed. Both the payee and maker of the note must make an adjusting entry to record the accrued interest so that the proper assets and revenues for the payee and the proper liabilities and expenses for the maker are reported. Failure to record accrued interest understates the payee's assets and revenues by the amount of the interest earned but not collected and understates the maker's expenses and liabilities by the interest expense incurred but not yet paid.

The paragraphs that follow show you how to record accrued interest on the payee's books and the maker's books. You will also see how to record the entry in the succeeding period when the interest is received or paid.

Payee's Books.   To illustrate how to record accrued interest on the payee's books, assume that the payee, Cooper Company (in the above example), has a fiscal year ending on October 31 instead of a December 31 year-end. On October 31, Cooper would make the following adjusting entry relating to the Price Company note:

Oct. 31 Interest Receivable	450	
Interest Revenue ($18,000 × 0.15 × 60/360) .		450
To record interest earned on Price Company note for the period September 1 through October 31.		

The **Interest Receivable account** shows the interest earned but not yet collected. Interest receivable is reported as a current asset in the balance sheet because the interest will be collected in 30 days. The interest revenue will be reported in the income statement.

When Price pays the note on November 30, Cooper makes the following entry to record the collection of the note's principal and interest:

Nov. 30 Cash	18,675	
Notes Receivable		18,000
Interest Receivable		450
Interest Revenue		225
To record collection of Price Company note and interest.		

Note that the entry credits the Interest Receivable account for the $450 accrued from September 1 through October 31, which was debited to the account in the previous entry, and credits Interest Revenue for the $225 earned in November.

Maker's Books.   Assume Price Company's accounting year also ends on October 31 instead of December 31. Price's accounting records would be incomplete unless the company makes an adjusting entry to record the liability owed for the accrued interest on the note it gave to Cooper Company. The required adjusting entry is:

Oct. 31 Interest Expense ($18,000 × 0.15 × 60/360) . . .	450	
Interest Payable		450
To record accrued interest on note to Cooper Company for the period September 1 through October 31.		

The **Interest Payable account,** which shows the interest expense incurred but not yet paid, is reported as a current liability in the balance sheet because the interest will be paid in 30 days. Interest expense will be reported in the income statement.

When the note is paid, Price will make the following entry:

Nov. 30	Notes Payable	18,000	
	Interest Payable	450	
	Interest Expense	225	
	Cash		18,675
	To record payment of principal and interest on note to Cooper Company.		

In this illustration, Cooper's financial position made it possible for the company to *carry* the Price note to the maturity date. Sometimes a company needs money immediately and must "sell" a note receivable. The next section discusses the procedure companies use to sell a note.

Discounting (Selling) Notes Receivable

Objective 4: Record the discounting of a customer's note at a bank.

When a company finds it must sell a note, the company usually takes the note to a bank or finance company. After endorsing the note, the company receives cash in return for the note. Three parties are now involved—the party that writes the note, the company that accepts the note and sells it to the bank, and the bank that buys the note. Since a note is a negotiable instrument (may be transferred legally to another party), the note must be paid regardless of who holds the note at maturity. As long as the holder obtained the note legally, the maturity value will be paid to the holder of the note.

Discounting a note receivable is the act of selling a note receivable with recourse to a bank.[1] *Discounting* means that the bank deducts the interest from the maturity value of the note immediately and gives the seller of the note only the net proceeds; and **with recourse** means that if the maker does not pay the bank at maturity, the bank can collect the maturity value from the company that discounted the note at the bank. Selling a note with recourse really changes the transaction from an outright selling transaction to a borrowing transaction. Thus, in recording the transaction, the company discounting the note records interest expense or interest revenue rather than a loss or gain on the sale. A note may be sold without recourse, but this situation is rare.

When the note is sold with recourse, the party discounting the note has a contingent liability (or is said to be "contingently liable") on the note. A **contingent liability** is a liability that may become an actual liability if a specific action does or does not occur. If the maker of the note does not pay at the maturity date, the contingent liability becomes an actual liability of the company that discounted the note.

The rate of interest the bank charges on the discounted note is called the **discount rate.** The bank may charge a different rate of interest than is stated on the note receivable. The bank uses the discount rate to compute the bank discount amount on the note's maturity value. For example, the payee of the note may have been satisfied with a 9% rate, while the bank now seeks a 10% discount rate. The bank discount will be computed using the 10% discount rate. The **cash proceeds** received by the seller are equal to the

---

[1] Actually, the term *discounting* seems to have two meanings in accounting. The first meaning is to deduct interest in advance. The second meaning is to sell a note to a bank. We will use the term *discounting* to mean the act of a company selling a note to a bank, which then deducts the interest in advance. Thus, we refer to a company discounting a note receivable in this broader sense of the term.

maturity amount of the note less the bank discount. The cash proceeds are computed as follows:

1.   Determine the maturity value of the note (face value plus interest), since this is the amount on which the bank discount is calculated.
2.   Determine the discount period. Count the exact number of days from the date of sale (discounting) to the maturity date. Exclude the date of sale, but include the maturity date in the count.
3.   Using the bank's discount rate, compute the bank discount on the maturity value for the discount period.
4.   Deduct the bank discount from the maturity value to determine the cash proceeds.

To help you understand the recording of a discounted note receivable, an example is given using a $10,000 note that Clark Company discounted at the Michigan National Bank.

Example of Recording a Discounted Note.   Assume that on May 4, 1991, Clark Company received from Kent Company a $10,000, 9%, 60-day note, dated May 4, 1991. The maturity date of the note is determined as follows:

Life of note		60 days
Days remaining in May not counting date of note (31 − 4)	27	
Total days in June	30	57
Maturity date in July		3 days

Thus, the maturity date of the note is July 3, 1991.

On May 14, 1991, Clark sold the note to Michigan National Bank, which charged a discount rate of 10%. Using the steps listed above, the discount and the cash proceeds are determined as follows:

1.   Determining maturity value:

Face value of note	$10,000.00
Add interest at 9% for 60 days:	
Face value × Interest rate on note × Life of note ÷ 360	
($10,000 × 0.09 × 60/360)	150.00
Maturity value of note	$10,150.00

2.   Determining discount period:

Days in May	31
Less date of discounting	14
Days of discount period in May	17
Days in June	30
Days of discount period in July (maturity date is July 3)	3
Total discount period	50

3.   Computing bank discount:

Maturity value × Bank discount rate of interest × Discount period ÷ 360	
($10,150 × 0.10 × 50/360)	$ 140.97

4.   Computing cash proceeds:

Maturity value	$10,150.00
Less: Bank discount	140.97
Cash proceeds	$10,009.03

The following diagram illustrates the relationship between face value, maturity value, and cash proceeds (follow the arrows):

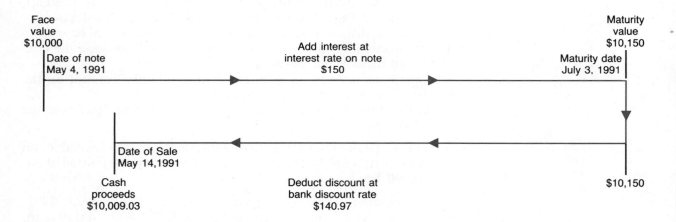

The journal entry Clark Company would make to record this transaction is:

```
May 14   Cash . . . . . . . . . . . . . . . . . . . . . . . . . . 10,009.03
                 Notes Receivable . . . . . . . . . . . . . . . .          10,000.00
                 Interest Revenue . . . . . . . . . . . . . . . .               9.03
             To record sale of notes receivable.
```

When a note is discounted, the proceeds received are rarely, if ever, exactly equal to the face value. The difference between the proceeds and face value of the note is recorded as interest expense or interest revenue. If the proceeds are less than the face value, interest expense is recorded; if the proceeds are greater than the face value, interest revenue is recorded.

Balance Sheet Presentation of Notes Receivable Discounted.   In the Clark Company example above (assume a June 30 accounting year-end), Clark should show a contingent liability of $10,000 for notes receivable discounted in its June 30, 1991, balance sheet. If we assume that the total of all Clark's notes receivable that have not been discounted is $60,000, an acceptable method of presenting this information in the balance sheet is:

Assets

Current assets:
Cash . . . . $xx,xxx
Accounts receivable . . . . . .   xx,xxx
Notes receivable (Note 1)   60,000

Notes to Financial Statements:
Note 1: At June 30, 1991, the company is contingently liable for a customer's $10,000 note receivable that it has endorsed and discounted at the local bank. This note is not included in the $60,000 of notes shown.

Discounted Notes Receivable Paid by Maker. When a discounted note receivable matures, it is usually the duty of the holder (the bank in the above illustration) to present the note to the maker for payment. If the maker pays the holder at maturity, the endorser (the company that discounted the note) is thereby relieved of its contingent liability.

Assume that in the above example, Kent Company pays the $10,000 note plus interest of $150 to Michigan National Bank on July 3, 1991, the note's maturity date. Clark Company, which discounted the note at the bank, is no longer liable for the note. No entry is necessary on Clark Company's books.

Discounted Notes Receivable Not Paid by Maker. In the above illustration, the maker paid the bank when the note matured. However, if the note is not paid at maturity and is written with recourse, the holder can collect from the endorser, who, in turn, can try to collect from the maker.

Assume that Kent Company dishonors its note. Michigan National Bank will collect the principal ($10,000), interest ($150), and a protest fee ($10) from Clark Company. Clark must make the following entry:

July 3	Accounts Receivable—Kent Company	10,160	
	Cash		10,160
	To record cash paid to bank for Kent Company's dishonored note.		

Clark, of course, will now try to collect $10,160 from Kent. However, if this is unsuccessful, the $10,160 will be removed from Accounts Receivable and treated as an uncollectible accounts expense or a loss on dishonored notes.

Short-Term Financing through Notes Payable

A company sometimes needs short-term financing. This may occur when (1) the company's cash receipts are delayed because of lenient credit terms granted customers, or (2) the company needs cash to finance the buildup of seasonal inventories, such as before Christmas. Short-term financing may be secured by issuing interest-bearing notes or by issuing noninterest-bearing notes.

Interest-Bearing Notes. To receive short-term financing from a bank, a company may issue an interest-bearing note to the bank. An interest-bearing note specifies the interest rate that will be charged on the principal borrowed. The company receives from the bank the principal borrowed; when the note matures, the company pays the bank the principal plus the interest.

Accounting for an interest-bearing note is simple. For example, assume that Needham Company issued a $10,000, 90-day, 9% note on August 18. The following entries would be made to record the loan and its payment on November 16:

Aug. 18	Cash	10,000	
	Notes Payable		10,000
	To record 90-day bank loan.		

```
Nov. 16   Notes Payable . . . . . . . . . . . . . . . . . . . . .      10,000
          Interest Expense . . . . . . . . . . . . . . . . . . .          225
             Cash . . . . . . . . . . . . . . . . . . . . . . . .                  10,225
          To record principal and interest paid on bank loan.
```

If the term of the note extended beyond a balance sheet date, an adjusting entry would be needed on that date to record the accrued interest payable.

Noninterest-Bearing Notes (Discounting Notes Payable). A company may also issue a noninterest-bearing note to receive short-term financing from a bank. A noninterest-bearing note does not have a stated interest rate applied to the face value of the note. Instead, the note is drawn for a maturity amount from which a bank discount is deducted, and the proceeds are given to the borrower. **Bank discount** is the difference between the maturity value of the note and the cash proceeds given to the borrower. The **cash proceeds,** as defined earlier, are equal to the maturity amount of a note less the bank discount. This entire process is referred to as **discounting a note payable.** The purpose of this process is to introduce interest into what appears to be a noninterest-bearing note. The meaning of *discounting* here is to deduct interest in advance.

Because interest is related to time, the bank discount is not interest on the date the loan is made; however, it becomes interest expense to the company and interest revenue to the bank as time passes. To illustrate, assume that on December 1, 1991, Needham Company presented its $10,000, 90-day, noninterest-bearing note to the bank, which discounted the note at 9%. The discount is $225 ($10,000 × 0.09 × 90/360), and the proceeds to Needham are $9,775. The entry required on the date of the note's issue is:

```
Dec. 1   Cash . . . . . . . . . . . . . . . . . . . . . . . . . .       9,775
          Discount on Notes Payable . . . . . . . . . . . . .            225
             Notes Payable . . . . . . . . . . . . . . . . . .                   10,000
          Issued 90-day note to bank.
```

Notes Payable are recorded at face value. **Discount on Notes Payable** is a contra account used to reduce Notes Payable from face value to the net amount shown on the balance sheet. The balance in the Discount on Notes Payable account is reported on the balance sheet as a deduction from the balance in the Notes Payable account.

Over time, the discount becomes interest expense. If the note in the example above was paid before the end of the fiscal year, the entire $225 of discount would be charged to Interest Expense and credited to Discount on Notes Payable when the note was paid. However, if Needham's fiscal year ended on December 31, an adjusting entry would be required as follows:

```
Dec. 31   Interest Expense . . . . . . . . . . . . . . . . . . . .         75
             Discount on Notes Payable . . . . . . . . . . .                     75
          To record interest on a note payable.
```

This entry records the interest expense incurred by Needham for the 30 days the note has been outstanding. The expense can be calculated as $10,000 × 0.09 × 30/360, or 30/90 × $225. Notice that for entries involving discounted notes payable, no separate Interest Payable account is needed. The Notes Payable account already contains the total liability that will be paid at **maturity,** $10,000. From the date the proceeds are given to the borrower to the maturity date, the liability grows by reducing the balance in the Discount on Notes Payable contra account. Thus, the current liability section of the December 31, 1991, balance sheet would show:

```
Notes payable  . . . . . . . . . . . . .  $10,000
Less: Discount on notes payable . . . .      150    $9,850
```

The $9,850 is the amount that would have to be paid to the bank if the company wishes to repay the loan on December 31 rather than at maturity date (if the interest rate has not changed). The original amount borrowed, $9,775, plus the accrued interest for 30 days, $75, equals $9,850.

When the note is paid at maturity, the entry is:

```
Mar. 1  Notes Payable . . . . . . . . . . . . . . . . . . . .   10,000
         Interest Expense . . . . . . . . . . . . . . . . . . .     150
            Cash . . . . . . . . . . . . . . . . . . . . . . .            10,000
            Discount on Notes Payable . . . . . . . . . . . .               150
         To record note payment and interest expense.
```

Long-Term Mortgage Notes Payable

When purchasing plant assets, companies sometimes give notes to finance the purchase rather than paying cash. These notes are usually long-term liabilities secured by a mortgage on the property acquired. A **mortgage** is a legal document that gives a lender possession of pledged property if the borrower does not pay the obligation as required in the terms of the agreement. Most family homes are purchased with mortgages.

Assume that a company acquired a building by giving a $100,000, 16%, 20-year mortgage note payable. The note calls for equal monthly payments, exclusive of real estate taxes and insurance. In the early years of the monthly payments, a large portion of the payment is for interest and only a limited amount for reducing principal. Mortgage payment schedule books are used that indicate how much of the monthly payment is for interest and how much for principal. On $100,000, the monthly payment for principal and interest is $1,391.26. The interest and principal for the first two months and for the last month are as follows:

	Monthly Payment	Interest	Principal	Principal Balance
Date of purchase				$100,000.00
First month	$1,391.26	$1,333.33	$ 57.93	99,942.07
Second month	1,391.26	1,332.56	58.70	99,883.37
240th month	1,391.26	18.31	1,372.95	–0–

Note that interest is calculated on the latest principal balance. For example, when the first $1,391.26 payment is made, interest for the month is calculated as follows:

$$\$100,000 \times 0.16 \times \tfrac{1}{12} = \$1,333.33$$

The entry to record the first month's mortgage payment is:

Interest Expense	1,333.33	
Mortgage Note Payable	57.93	
Cash		1,391.26

To record interest expense and reduction of mortgage
principal resulting from mortgage payment.

In the first payment, the $1,333.33 interest is subtracted from the total payment ($1,391.26), and the excess is applied against the principal ($57.93). Thus, the principal balance decreases slowly (but more rapidly each month), so that the last payment at the end of 20 years pays interest of $18.31 on the remaining principal balance of $1,372.95 and reduces the principal balance to zero.

From the study of receivables and payables, you go to the study of measuring and reporting inventories in Chapter 9. Inventories can be one of the largest assets of a company, and cost of goods sold can be a company's largest expense. For this reason, accurate accounting for inventories is most important.

■ UNDERSTANDING THE LEARNING OBJECTIVES: CHAPTER 8

1. Account for uncollectible accounts receivable.

   - Companies use two methods to account for uncollectible accounts: the allowance method, which provides in advance for uncollectible accounts; and the direct write-off method, which recognizes uncollectible accounts as an expense when judged uncollectible. The allowance method is the preferred method.
   - There are two basic methods for estimating uncollectible accounts under the allowance method—the percentage-of-sales method and the percentage-of-receivables method.
   - The percentage-of-sales method focuses attention on the income statement and the relationship of uncollectible accounts to sales. The debit to Uncollectible Accounts Expense is a certain percent of credit sales or total net sales.
   - The percentage-of-receivables method focuses on the balance sheet and the relationship of the allowance for uncollectible accounts to accounts receivable. The credit to the Allowance for Uncollectible Accounts is the amount necessary to bring that account up to a certain percentage of the Accounts Receivable balance.
   - Under the direct write-off method, Uncollectible Accounts Expense is debited only when particular accounts are identified as being uncollectible.

2. Record credit card sales and collections.

   - Credit cards are charge cards, such as VISA, that are used by customers to charge purchases of goods and services. These cards are of two types—nonbank credit cards such as American Express and bank credit cards such as VISA.

- ▪ The sale is recorded at the gross amount of the sale, and the cash or receivable is recorded at the net amount the company will receive.

3. Account for notes receivable and payable, including calculation of interest.

- ▪ A promissory note is an unconditional written promise by a borrower (maker) to pay the lender (payee) or someone else who legally acquired the note a certain sum of money on demand or at a definite time.
- ▪ Interest is the fee charged for the use of money through time. Interest = Principle × Rate of interest × Time.

4. Record the discounting of a customer's note at a bank.

- ▪ The cash proceeds are computed by determining the maturity value of the note, the discount period, and the amount of the discount charged by the bank. The bank discount is deducted from the maturity value to find the cash proceeds.

5. Define and use correctly the new terms in the glossary.

NEW TERMS INTRODUCED IN CHAPTER 8

Aging schedule   A means of classifying accounts receivable according to their age; used to determine the necessary balance in an Allowance for Uncollectible Accounts. A different uncollectibility percentage rate is used for each age category (350).

Allowance for Uncollectible Accounts   A contra-asset account to the Accounts Receivable account; it reduces accounts receivable to their net realizable value. Also called *Allowance for Doubtful Accounts* or *Allowance for Bad Debts* (346).

Bad debts expense   See Uncollectible accounts expense.

Bank discount   The difference between maturity value of a note and the actual amount—the note's proceeds—given to the borrower (364).

Cash proceeds   The maturity amount of a note less the bank discount (360).

Contingent liability   A liability that may become an actual liability if a specific action does or does not occur (360).

Credit Card Expense account   Used to record credit card agency's service charge for services rendered in processing credit card sales (354).

Credit cards   Nonbank charge cards (American Express and Diners Club) and bank charge cards (VISA and MasterCard) used by customers to charge their purchases of goods and services (353).

Direct write-off method   A way of accounting for uncollectible accounts receivable in which identified uncollectible amounts are charged directly to an expense account (352).

Discount on Notes Payable   A contra account used to reduce Notes Payable from face value to the net amount shown in the balance sheet (364).

Discount rate   The rate of interest the bank charges on a discounted note (360).

Discounting a note receivable   The act of selling a note receivable with recourse to a bank. *Discounting* means that the bank deducts the interest from the maturity value of the note immediately and gives the seller of the note only the proceeds. *With recourse* means that if the maker does not pay the bank at maturity, the bank can collect the maturity value from the company that discounted the note at the bank (360).

Dishonored note   A note that the maker failed to pay at maturity (357).

Interest The fee charged for use of money through time (I = P × R × T) (355).

Interest Payable account An account showing the interest expense incurred but not yet paid; reported as a current liability in the balance sheet (359).

Interest Receivable account An account showing the interest earned but not yet collected; reported as a current asset in the balance sheet (359).

Maker (of a note) The party who prepares a note and is responsible for paying the note at maturity (354).

Maturity date The date on which a note becomes due and must be paid (355).

Maturity value The amount that the maker must pay on the note on its maturity date (357).

Mortgage A legal document that gives a lender possession of pledged property if the borrower does not pay the obligation as required in the terms of the agreement (365).

Net realizable value The amount expected to be collected from accounts receivable (346).

Payable Any sum of money due to be paid by a company to any party for any reason (344).

Payee (of a note) The party who receives a note and will be paid cash at maturity (354).

Percentage-of-receivables method A method for determining the desired size of the Allowance for Uncollectible Accounts by basing the calculation on the Accounts Receivable balance at the end of the period (348).

Percentage-of-sales method A method of estimating the uncollectible accounts from the sales of a given period's total net sales or credit sales (347).

Principal (of a note) The face value of a note (355).

Promissory note An unconditional written promise by a borrower (maker) to pay a definite sum of money to the lender (payee) on demand or at a specific date (354).

Rate (of a note) The stated interest rate on the note (355).

Receivable Any sum of money due to be paid to a company from any party for any reason (344).

Time (of a note) The amount of time the note is to run; can be expressed in days or months (355).

Trade receivables Amounts due from customers for goods sold or services rendered on open account. Also called *accounts receivable* or *trade accounts receivable* (345).

Uncollectible accounts expense An operating expense that a business incurs when it sells on credit; also called *bad debts expense* (346).

With recourse A legal term meaning that if the maker does not pay the bank at maturity, the bank can collect the amount due from the company that sold the note to the bank (360).

DEMONSTRATION PROBLEM

Part a: Best Company estimates its uncollectible accounts expense to be 1% of sales. Sales in 1991 were $750,000.

Required: Prepare the journal entries for the following transactions:

1. The company prepared the adjusting entry for uncollectible accounts for 1991.
2. On January 15, 1992, the company decided that the account for James Ryan in the amount of $500 was uncollectible.
3. On February 12, 1992, James Ryan's check for $500 arrived.

Part b: A $15,000, 90-day, 12% note dated June 15, 1991, was received by Long Company from Short Company in payment of its account.

Required: Prepare the journal entries in the records of Long Company for each of the following:

1. Long Company received the note on June 15, 1991.
2. Long Company discounted the note on July 15, 1991, at 10% at Citizens National Bank.

3.   Short Company paid the note at maturity.
4.   Assume that Short Company did not pay the note at maturity. Citizens National Bank charged the note to Long Company and charged a protest fee of $20. Long Company decided that the note was uncollectible.

Solution to demonstration problem

Part a:

1.   1991
     Dec. 31   Uncollectible Accounts Expense   7,500
                    Allowance for Uncollectible Accounts . . .   7,500
                To record estimated uncollectible accounts
                for the year.

2.   1992
     Jan. 15   Allowance for Uncollectible Accounts   500
                    Accounts Receivable—James Ryan . . .   500
                To write off the account of James Ryan
                as uncollectible.

3.   1992
     Feb. 12   Accounts Receivable—James Ryan   500
                    Allowance for Uncollectible Accounts . . .   500
                To correct the write-off of James Ryan's
                account on January 15.

          12   Cash   500
                    Accounts Receivable—James Ryan   . . .   500
                To record the collection of James Ryan's
                account receivable.

Part b:

1.   1991
     June 15   Notes Receivable 15,000.00
                    Accounts Receivable—Short
                    Company 15,000.00
                To record receipt of a note from Short
                Company.

2.   July 15   Cash 15,192.50
                    Notes Receivable 15,000.00
                    Interest Revenue 192.50
                To record the discounting of the Short
                Company note.

                Computation of cash proceeds:
                Maturity value (Days until
                    maturity = 60) $15,450.00
                Discount = $15,450 × 10% × 60/360 . . .   257.50
                                                             $15,192.50

3.   No entry.

4. Sept. 13   Accounts Receivable—Short Company 15,470.00
                   Cash 15,470.00
                   To record the charge made against Long
                   Company account for the Short Company
                   note of $15,000, interest of $450, and
                   protest fee of $20.

        13   Allowance for Uncollectible Accounts* 15,470.00
                   Accounts Receivable—Short Company. .   15,470.00
                   To write off the Short Company note as
                   uncollectible.

        * This debit assumes that notes receivable were taken into consideration when an allow-
        ance was established. If not, the debit should be to Loss from Dishonored Notes Receivable.

QUESTIONS

1. In view of the difficulty in estimating future events, would you recommend that accountants wait until collections are made from customers before recording sales revenue? Should they wait until known accounts prove to be uncollectible before charging an expense account?

2. The credit manager of a company has established a policy of seeking to completely eliminate all losses from uncollectible accounts. Is this a desirable objective for a company? Explain.

3. What are the two major purposes to be accomplished in establishing an allowance for uncollectible accounts?

4. In view of the fact that it is impossible to estimate the exact amount of uncollectible accounts receivable for any one year in advance, what exactly does the Allowance for Uncollectible Accounts account contain after a number of years?

5. How might information in an aging schedule prove useful to management for purposes other than estimating the size of the required allowance for uncollectible accounts?

6. For a company using the allowance method of accounting for uncollectible accounts, which of the following affects its reported net income: (1) the establishment of the allowance, (2) the writing off of a specific account, or (3) the recovery of an account previously written off as uncollectible?

7. Explain why the direct write-off method of accounting for uncollectible accounts is generally unacceptable.

8. Why might a retailer agree to sell by credit card when such a substantial discount is taken by the credit card agency in paying the retailer?

9. How do a dishonored note receivable and a discounted note receivable differ? How is each reported in the balance sheet?

10. Under what circumstances does the account Discount on Notes Payable arise? How is it reported in the financial statements? Explain why.

11. For what purpose might a company issue a mortgage note payable?

EXERCISES

E-1
Prepare journal entries to record uncollectible accounts expense

The accounts of Red Robin Company as of December 31, 1990, show Accounts Receivable, $110,000; Allowance for Uncollectible Accounts, $700 (credit balance); Sales, $725,000; and Sales Returns and Allowances, $13,000. Prepare journal entries to adjust for possible uncollectible accounts under each of the following assumptions:

a. Uncollectible accounts are estimated at 1% of net sales.
b. The allowance is to be increased to 3% of accounts receivable.

E-2
Determine amount of uncollectible accounts adjusting entry

Beckler Company had a balance of $100,000 in Accounts Receivable at December 31, 1991. A decision was made to adjust the balance in the Allowance for Uncollectible Accounts to 7% of the Accounts Receivable balance. Determine the required amount of the debit to Uncollectible Accounts Expense and credit to Allowance for Uncollectible Accounts if the existing balance in the allowance is *(a)* zero, *(b)* a $500 credit, and *(c)* a $500 debit.

E-3
Record write-off and subsequent collection of account

On April 1, 1991, Victor Company, which uses the allowance method of accounting for uncollectible accounts, wrote off Bill Combs' $396 account. On December 14, 1991, the company received a check in that amount from Combs marked "in full payment of account." Prepare the necessary entries for all of the above.

E-4
Use aging schedule to estimate Allowance for Uncollectible Accounts

Compute the required balance of the Allowance for Uncollectible Accounts for the following receivables:

Accounts Receivable	Age (months)	Probability of Collection
$110,000	Less than 1	0.95
55,000	1–3	0.85
26,000	3–6	0.75
7,000	6–9	0.35
1,500	9–12	0.10

E-5
Prepare journal entries for write-off and subsequent collection of account under direct write-off method

Because its credit sales are immaterial in amount, Green Lawn Company accounts for its uncollectible accounts using the direct write-off method. During 1991, the following accounts were written off as uncollectible:

Apr. 10   J. Jones   . . . . $ 750
July 17   B. Smith   1,440
Oct. 11   L. Jackson . . .   1,020

On December 10, payment in full is received from J. Jones. Prepare journal entries for the above.

E-6
Record use of nonbank credit card

Smiley, Inc., sold $58,000 of goods in May to customers who used their Carte Blanche credit cards. Such sales are subject to a 3% discount by Carte Blanche. Prepare journal entries to record the sales and the subsequent receipt of cash from the credit card company.

E-7
Determine maturity dates on several notes

Determine the maturity date for each of the following notes:

Issue Date	Life
January 13, 1991	30 days
January 31, 1991	90 days
June 4, 1991	1 year
December 2, 1991	1 month

E-8
Prepare entries for a note

John gave a $180,000, 120-day, 12% note to Ben in exchange for merchandise. John uses periodic inventory procedure. Prepare journal entries needed to record the issuance of the note and the entries needed at maturity for both parties, assuming payment is made.

E-9
Prepare entries when maker defaults

Prepare the entries that John and Ben (Exercise E–8) would make at maturity date, assuming John defaults.

E-10
Prepare entries at date of discounting of note

On May 7, 1991, Acker Company gave a 60-day, $30,000, 12% note to Stacy Company. On June 1, Stacy Company discounted the note at 14%. Prepare the entries each company would make on the discounting date.

E-11
Prepare entries at maturity date

In Exercise E–10, prepare the entries that would be recorded on the books of each company assuming Acker Company *(a)* pays the note at maturity and *(b)* fails to pay the note at maturity (assume there is a protest fee of $10).

Determine one amount in entry for discounting note

Brandon Company received a 90-day, 12%, $10,000 note from Dixon Company on June 1, 1991. Brandon Company discounted the note at First Federal Bank, which charged a discount rate of 12%. Determine the debit to Interest Expense or credit to Interest Revenue if the note was discounted on:

a.   The date of the note.
b.   Sixty days before the maturity date.
c.   Thirty days before the maturity date.

E-13
Determine one amount in entry for discounting note

Assume the same facts as in Exercise E–12 except that the bank rate of discount is 14%. Calculate the debit to Interest Expense or credit to Interest Revenue for *(a)*, *(b)*, and *(c)*.

E-14
Prepare entries for noninterest-bearing note and interest-bearing note

Day Kreuzburg is negotiating a bank loan of $15,000 for 90 days. The bank's current interest rate is 16%. Prepare Kreuzburg's entries to record the loan under each of the following assumptions:

a.   Kreuzburg signs a note for $15,000. Interest is deducted in calculating the proceeds turned over to him.
b.   Kreuzburg signs a note for $15,000 and receives that amount. Interest is to be paid at maturity.

E-15
Prepare entries at maturity date

Prepare the entry or entries that would be made at maturity date for each of the alternatives in Exercise E–14 assuming the loan is paid before the end of the accounting period.

E-16
Prepare entry to record mortgage payment

Assume a company acquired a building by giving a $600,000, 12%, 20-year mortgage note payable. Prepare the journal entry to record the first month's mortgage payment assuming the payment is $6,606.51.

PROBLEMS, SERIES A

P8-1-A
Write off uncollectible account and record expense under alternative methods of estimation

As of December 31, 1990, Kelly Company's accounts prior to adjustment showed:

Accounts receivable . . . . $ 184,000
Allowance for uncollectible accounts (credit balance) . . .   7,000
Net sales 1,500,000

Kelly Company follows a practice of estimating uncollectible accounts at 3% of net sales.
On February 23, 1991, the account of Don Cole in the amount of $2,300 was considered uncollectible and was written off. On August 12, 1991, Cole remitted $800 and indicated that he intends to pay the balance owed as soon as possible. By December 31, 1991, no further remittance had been received from Cole, and no further remittance was expected.

Required: a.   Prepare journal entries to record uncollectible accounts expense for 1990 and to record the above transactions.
b.   Prepare the uncollectible accounts adjusting entry as of December 31, 1990, assuming Kelly estimated its uncollectible accounts at 11% of outstanding accounts receivable rather than 3% of net sales.

The following data pertain to Douglas Company which began operations in 1990:

P8-2-A
Record expense (two methods) and write-offs; record expense under direct write-off method

	1990	1991	1992
Total net sales	$120,000	$105,000	$165,000
Accounts receivable balance			
December 31	52,500	60,000	90,000
Actual accounts written off			
during the year:			
From 1990 sales	1,500	1,050	450
From 1991 sales		900	1,200
From 1992 sales			1.800

For parts *(a)*, *(b)*, and *(c)* below, assume that the company uses the allowance method and makes a year-end adjustment for uncollectible accounts. Remember that the Allowance for Uncollectible Accounts had a zero balance on January 1, 1990. Use the following format:

Account Titles	1990		1991		1992	
	Dr.	Cr.	Dr.	Cr.	Dr.	Cr.

Required:
a. Prepare the entries that were made to record the actual accounts written off in each year.
b. Prepare journal entries for 1990, 1991, and 1992 to record the uncollectible accounts expense for the year using the percentage-of-sales method with uncollectible accounts estimated at 2% of total net sales.
c. Repeat part *(b)* using the percentage-of-receivables method with the allowance adjusted to 5% of year-end receivables.
d. Prepare journal entries to record uncollectible accounts expense for 1990, 1991, and 1992 using the direct write-off method instead of the allowance method.

P8-3-A
Record use of bank and nonbank credit cards

At the close of business on a certain date, Jane's Restaurant had credit card sales of $14,400. Of this amount, $9,600 were VISA sales invoices which can be deposited in a bank for immediate credit, less a discount of 3%. The balance of $4,800 consisted of American Express charges and are subject to a discount of 5%. These invoices were mailed to American Express. Shortly thereafter, a check was received.

Required: Prepare journal entries for all of the above transactions.

P8-4-A
Account for discounted note receivable

On June 1, 1991, Bell Company received a $108,000, 90-day, 16% note from the Thomas Company dated June 1, 1991. On August 15, 1991, the note was discounted at the bank. The bank discount rate was 18%.

Required: Determine the following:

a. Maturity value of the note.
b. Number of days from the discount date to the maturity date.
c. Dollar amount of the discount.
d. Cash proceeds received by the company.
e. Entry to record the receipt of proceeds at the date of discount.

P8-5-A
Account for discounted note payable

Brent Company discounted its own $90,000, noninterest-bearing, 60-day note on November 16, 1991, at the Chautauqua County Bank at a discount rate of 12%.

Required: Prepare dated journal entries for the following:

    a.   Original discounting on November 16.
    b.   Adjustment required at the end of the company's calendar-year accounting period.
    c.   Payment at maturity.

P8-6-A
Prepare entries to record a number of note transactions, discounting of a note (customer's and own), adjusting entries for interest, and entries for payment of notes

Following are selected transactions of Green Thumb Company for 1991:

Oct. 31   Discounted its own 30-day, $12,000, noninterest-bearing note at First State Bank at 12%.

Nov. 8   Received a $8,000, 90-day, 9% note from Worst Company in settlement of an account receivable. The note is dated November 8.

     15   Purchased merchandise by issuing its own 120-day note for $8,400. The note is dated November 15 and bears interest at 10%. Green Thumb Company uses periodic inventory procedure.

     20   Discounted Worst Company note at 12% at First State Bank.

     30   First State Bank notified Green Thumb Company that it had charged the note of October 31 against the company's checking account.

All notes falling due after November 30 were paid in full on their due dates by the respective makers. (Remember that 1992 is a leap year; February has 29 days.)

Required: Prepare dated journal entries for Green Thumb Company for all of the above transactions (including the payment of the notes after November 30) and all necessary adjusting entries, assuming that the fiscal year ends on November 30.

P8-7-A
Prepare entries to record a number of note transactions, discounting of a note (customer's and own), adjusting entries for interest, and entries for payment of notes

Sunshine Company is in the chain saw manufacturing business. As of September 1, the balance in its Notes Receivable account was $210,000. One note in the amount of $144,000 had been discounted. The balance in Accounts Receivable included $90,900 (principal and interest) for Yahoo's dishonored note. A schedule of the notes (including the discounted and dishonored notes) is as follows:

Face Amount	Maker	Date	Life	Interest Rate	Comments
$120,000	A. Box Co.	6/1/91	150 days	12%	
90,000	C. Davis Co.	6/15/91	90 days	8	
144,000	Chase Co.	7/1/91	90 days	10	Discounted 8/16/91 at 9%
90,000	Yahoo Co.	7/1/91	60 days	6	Dishonored, interest $900
$444,000					

Transactions:

Sept. 5   A. Box Company note was discounted at Fulton County Bank. The discount rate was 10%.

     10   Received $42,900 from Yahoo Company as full settlement of the amount due from it. The company charges losses on notes to the Allowance for Uncollectible Accounts account.

      ?   C. Davis Company note was collected when due.

      ?   Chase Company paid its note at maturity.

      ?   A. Box Company note was not paid at maturity. The bank deducted the balance from the Sunshine Company's bank balance. A protest fee of $20 was charged.

Oct. 30   Received a new 60-day, 12% note from A. Box Company for the total balance due on the dishonored note. The note was dated as of the maturity date of the dishonored note. Sunshine Company accepted the note in good faith.

Required: Prepare dated journal entries for the 1991 transactions.

PROBLEMS, SERIES B

P8-1-B
Write-off
uncollectible
account and record
expense under
alternative methods
of estimation

Presented below are selected accounts of Sawyer Company as of December 31, 1991. Prior to closing the books, the $6,000 account of Park Company (originating from credit sales on February 12, 1991) is to be written off.

Accounts receivable	$ 315,000
Allowance for uncollectible accounts (credit balance)	4,500
Sales	3,150,000
Sales returns and allowances	75,000

Required:

a. Present the journal entries to record the above transaction and to record uncollectible accounts expense for the year, assuming the estimated expense is 1% of net sales.

b. Give the entry to record the estimated expense if the allowance is to be adjusted to 7% of outstanding receivables after the write-off of the uncollectible account instead of as in *(a)* above.

P8-2-B
Record expense
(two methods) and
write-offs; record
expense under
direct write-off
method

The following data pertain to Apex Credit Company:

	1990	1991	1992
Total net sales	$540,000	$600,000	$880,000
Accounts receivable balance,			
December 31	180,000	96,000	120,000
Actual accounts written off			
during the year:			
From 1989 sales	4,000		
From 1990 sales	6,400	7,200	
From 1991 sales		2,400	4,800
From 1992 sales			5,200

For parts *(a)*, *(b)*, and *(c)* below, the company uses the allowance method and makes a year-end adjustment for uncollectible accounts. Assume that the Allowance for Uncollectible Accounts had a credit balance of $4,400 when properly adjusted on December 31, 1989. Use the following format:

Account Titles	1990		1991		1992	
	Dr.	Cr.	Dr.	Cr.	Dr.	Cr.

Required:

a. Prepare the entries that were made to record the actual accounts written off in each year.

b. Prepare journal entries for 1990, 1991, and 1992 to record uncollectible accounts expense for the year using the percentage-of-sales method with uncollectible accounts estimated at 2% of total net sales.

c. Repeat part *(b)* using the percentage-of-receivables method with the allowance adjusted to 5% of year-end receivables.

d. Prepare journal entries to record uncollectible accounts expense for 1990, 1991, and 1992 using the direct write-off method instead of the allowance method.

P8-3-B
Record use of bank
and nonbank credit
cards

The cash register at Mickey's Place at the close of business on a certain date showed cash sales of $10,800 and credit card sales of $13,200 ($7,200 VISA and $6,000 American Express). The VISA invoices were discounted 5% when they were deposited. The American Express charges were mailed to the company and are subject to a discount of 5%. A few days later, a check was received for the net amount of the charges.

Required: Prepare journal entries to record all of the above transactions.

P8-4-B
Account for discounted note receivable

Pate Company received a note from Hill Company on July 24, 1991. The company discounted the note at the bank on August 23, 1991. A summary of the facts concerning the note follows:

Face amount	$360,000
Life of note	120 days
Date of note	7/24/91
Interest rate on note	12%
Date of discounting note at the bank . . .	8/23/91
Discount rate charged by the bank	15%

Required: Determine the following:

   a.   Maturity value of the note.
   b.   Number of days from the discount date to the maturity date.
   c.   Dollar amount of the discount.
   d.   Cash proceeds received by the company.
   e.   Entry to record the receipt of the proceeds at the date of discount.

P8-5-B
Account for discounted note payable

On November 1, 1991, Ginger Company discounted its own $180,000, 180-day, noninterest-bearing note at its bank at 18%. The note was paid on its maturity date. Ginger Company uses a calendar-year accounting period.

Required: Prepare dated entries to record *(a)* the discounting of the note, *(b)* the year-end adjustment, and *(c)* the payment of the note.

P8-6-B
Prepare entries to record a number of note transactions, discounting of a note (customer's and own), adjusting entries for interest, and entries for payment of notes

Barry Company engaged in the following transactions in 1991:

May 31   Discounted its own 30-day, $24,000, noninterest-bearing note at First National Bank at 12%.
June 8   Received a $16,000, 90-day, 9% note from Second Company in settlement of its account balance. The note is dated June 8.
    15   Issued a $16,800, 120-day, 10% note, dated today, to purchase merchandise. Barry Company uses periodic inventory procedure.
    20   Discounted Second Company note at 12% at First National Bank.
    30   The bank notified Barry Company that it had charged the note of May 31 against the company's checking account balance.

All notes falling due after June 30 were paid in full on their due dates by their respective makers.

Required: Prepared dated journal entries for Barry Company for all of the above transactions (including the payment of the notes after June 30) and all necessary adjusting entries for accrued interest, assuming that the fiscal year ends on June 30.

P8-7-B
Prepare entries to record a number of note transactions, discounting of a note (customer's and own), adjusting entries for interest, and entries for payment of notes

Taft Company has an accounting year ending on December 31. On December 1, 1991, the balances of certain ledger accounts are Notes Receivable, $40,800, and Notes Payable, $360,000. A schedule of the notes (including the discounted note) is as follows:

Face Amount	Maker	Date of Note	Life	Interest Rate	Date Discounted	Discount Rate
$108,000	Good Co.	10/15/91	60 days	14%	11/1/91	12%
12,000	Bad Co.	11/1/91	60 days	14	—	—
28,800	Rugly Co.	11/15/91	30 days	12	—	—
$148,800						

The note payable is a 60-day bank loan dated October 20, 1991. Discount on Notes Payable was debited for the discount of $3,600.

Transactions for December:

Dec. 1 Taft Company discounted its own $132,000, 90-day, noninterest-bearing note at State Bank. The discount rate was 12%, and the note was dated today.
3 Received a 20-day, 12% note, dated today, from Jones Company in settlement of an account receivable of $21,600.
6 Purchased merchandise from Hood Company, $131,400, and issued a 30-day, 12% note, dated today, for the purchase. Taft Company uses periodic inventory procedure.
8 Sold merchandise to Brass Company, $36,000. A 45-day, 8% note, dated today, was received to cover the sale.
14 The $108,000 note discounted on November 1, 1991, was paid by Good Company directly to the holder.
15 Rugly Company could only pay a part of its original note so it sent a $18,000, 30-day, 12% note, dated today, and a check to cover its note of November 15, 1991, and interest in full to this date. Taft Company agreed to this arrangement.
18 The Brass Company note of December 8 was discounted at State Bank for the remaining life of the note. The discount rate was 14%.
19 The note payable dated October 20, 1991, was paid in full.
23 Jones Company dishonored its note of December 3, due today.
26 Jones Company sent a check for the interest on the dishonored note and a new 30-day, 12% note dated December 23, 1991.
31 The Bad Company note dated November 1, 1991, was paid with interest in full.

Required: Prepare dated journal entries for the transactions and the necessary December 31 adjustments for accrued interest.

BUSINESS DECISION PROBLEM 8–1

Compare costs of maintaining own accounts receivable with costs of allowing credit cards; identify other factors to consider

Larry Lance runs an appliance store, selling items for cash and on account. During 1990, which seemed to be a typical year, some of his operating and other data were as follows:

Sales:	
For cash	$1,000,000
On credit	1,400,000
Cost of obtaining credit reports on customers	3,000
Cost incurred in paying a part-time bookkeeper to keep the accounts receivable subsidiary ledger up to date	10,000
Cost associated with preparing and mailing invoices to customers and other collection activities	16,000
Uncollectible accounts expense	44,000
The average outstanding accounts receivable balance (on which Larry estimates he could have earned 10% if it had been invested in other assets)	108,000

A national credit card agency has approached Larry and tried to convince him that instead of carrying his own accounts receivable he should only accept its credit card for sales on credit. The agency would pay Larry within two days after he submits sales charges and would deduct 4% from the amount, paying him 96%.

Required: a. Using the data given, prepare an analysis showing whether or not it would pay Larry to switch to the credit card method of selling on credit.
b. What other factors should be taken into consideration?

BUSINESS DECISION PROBLEM 8-2

Evaluate alternative means of making sales

Ken Burke operates a large garden supplies store on the outskirts of a city. In a typical year, he sells $3,000,000 of goods to regular customers. His sales are 35% for cash and 65% on credit. He carries all of the credit himself. Only after a customer has a total unpaid balance of $300 on which no payments have been made for two months does he refuse that customer credit for future purchases. His income before taxes is approximately $975,000. The total of uncollectible accounts for a given year is about 10% of credit sales, or $195,000.

You are one of Ken's regular customers. He knows that you are taking a course in accounting and has asked you to tell him your opinion of several alternatives that have been recommended to him to reduce or eliminate $195,000 of uncollectible accounts per year. The recommended alternatives are as follows:

1. Do not sell on credit.
2. Sell on credit by national credit card only.
3. Allow customers to charge only until their account balance reaches $50.
4. Allow a bill collector to "go after" uncollectible accounts. The bill collector would keep half of what he collects.
5. Require all credit customers to sign a note so that Ken can discount these at the local bank.

Required: Using your own logic and experiences plus the information in this chapter, give your opinion on these alternatives. Which alternative do you recommend he follow?

9 Measuring and Reporting Inventories

After studying this chapter, you should be able to:

1. Calculate the effects of inventory errors on certain financial statement items.
2. Indicate what costs are properly included in inventory.
3. Calculate cost of ending inventory, cost of goods sold, and effects on net income under the four major inventory cost methods.
4. Indicate the advantages and disadvantages of the four major inventory cost methods.
5. Apply the lower-of-cost-or-market method to inventory.
6. Estimate cost of ending inventory using the gross margin and retail inventory methods.
7. Record merchandise transactions under perpetual inventory procedure.
8. Define and use correctly the new terms in the glossary.

You may have been to a "pre-inventory sale" at your favorite retail store and witnessed the bargain prices designed to reduce the merchandise inventory on hand so as to minimize the time and expense of "taking the inventory." A smaller inventory enhances the probability of taking an accurate inventory since there is less merchandise to count. As you learned in Chapter 5, inventory amounts are used in determining the cost of the goods sold, which is a major expense of a merchandising company and affects the company's net income. In this chapter, you will learn how important inventories are in preparing an accurate income statement, statement of owner's equity, and balance sheet.

This chapter discusses merchandise inventory carried by merchandising companies—retailers and wholesalers. Other types of inventory carried by manufacturers are discussed in a later chapter. **Merchandise inventory** is defined as the quantity of goods held by a merchandising company for resale to customers.

The merchandise inventory figure used by accountants depends on the quantity of inventory items and the cost of the items. The quantity of inventory items is determined by a physical count. Four accepted methods of costing the items are discussed in the chapter: (1) specific identification; (2) weighted-average; (3) first-in, first-out (FIFO); and (4) last-in, first-out (LIFO). Each of these methods has its advantages and disadvantages.

In studying this chapter, you should be impressed by the importance of having accurate inventory figures and the serious consequences of using inaccurate inventory figures. Then when you read or hear that a store is closing early to "take inventory" or that employees are working late to "take inventory," you will connect this taking of inventory with the cost of goods sold figure on the store's income statement, the owner's capital account shown on the statement of owner's equity, and the inventory figure and the owner's capital amount on the store's balance sheet.

■ INVENTORIES AND COST OF GOODS SOLD

Inventory is often the largest and most important asset owned by a merchandising business. The inventory of some companies, like car dealerships or jewelry stores, may cost several times more than any other asset the company owns. As an asset, the inventory figure in the balance sheet has a direct impact on reporting the solvency of the company. As a factor in determining cost of goods sold, the inventory figure has a direct impact on reporting the profitability of the company's operations as shown in the income statement. Thus, the importance of the inventory figure should not be underestimated.

To arrive at a current inventory figure, accountants must begin with an accurate physical count of inventory items. This section first discusses taking a physical inventory. Then you will learn why it is important to correctly cost this physical inventory. The remainder of the chapter discusses the methods of costing the physical inventory, departures from the cost basis of inventory measurement, and perpetual inventory procedure.

Taking a Physical Inventory

To take a physical inventory, the physical quantities of the goods on hand must be counted, weighed, measured, or estimated. For example, the suits in a clothing store may be counted; items such as bolts, washers, and nails may be weighed; items such as wire, cloth, and gasoline in storage tanks may be measured; and quantities of lumber, coal, or other bulky materials may be estimated by experts. Throughout the taking of a physical inventory, the goal should be accuracy.

Taking a physical inventory may disrupt the normal operations of a business. Thus, the count should be administered as quickly and as efficiently as possible. The actual taking of the inventory is not considered an accounting function; however, accountants often plan and coordinate the count. Proper forms are required to record accurate counts and determine totals. Identification names or symbols must be chosen, and those who count, weigh, or measure the inventory items must know these symbols.

Several inventory-taking methods involve the use of inventory tags. These tags are consecutively numbered for control purposes. A tag usually consists of a stub and a duplicate detachable section. The duplicate section facilitates checking in case of discrepancies. The format of tags can vary, but space is usually provided for (1) a detailed description and identification of inventory items by product, class, and model; (2) location of items; (3) quantity of items on hand; and (4) initials of the counters and checkers.

After the descriptive information is entered on the tags, they may be attached to the bins, shelves, or racks that contain the goods. The counters usually work in pairs and record their counts on the detachable sections of the tags and turn them in. Discrepancies between counts of the same items by different teams are reconciled by supervisors, and the correct counts are assembled on intermediate inventory sheets. When the inventory counts are completed and checked, the final sheets are sent to the accounting department for pricing and extensions (quantity × price). The tabulated result is the dollar amount of the physical inventory. Later in the chapter, you will learn the different methods accountants use to cost an inventory.

Importance of Proper Inventory Valuation

Objective 1: Calculate the effects of inventory errors on certain financial statement items.

A merchandising company can prepare accurate income statements, statements of owner's equity, and balance sheets only if the company has correctly valued its inventory. On the income statement, inventory is used to determine the cost of goods sold. Since the cost of goods sold figure affects the company's net income, it also affects the balance of the owner's capital account shown on the statement of owner's equity. On the balance sheet, incorrect inventory amounts affect both the reported ending inventory and owner's capital. Inventories appear on the balance sheet under the heading "Current assets," which reports current assets in a descending order of liquidity. Since inventories will be consumed or converted into cash within a year or one operating cycle, whichever is longer, the order of liquidity shows inventories following cash and receivables on the balance sheet.

The cost of goods sold figure, as you will recall from Chapter 5, is determined by adding the beginning inventory to the net cost of purchases and deducting the ending inventory. In each accounting period, the appropriate costs must be matched with the revenues of that period to determine the net income. As applied to inventory, matching involves determining how much of the cost of goods available for sale during the period should be deducted from current revenues and how much should be allocated to goods on hand and thus carried forward in the balance sheet to be matched against future revenues. Cost of goods sold is determined by deducting the ending inventory from the cost of goods available for sale. As a result, a highly significant relationship exists: **net income for an accounting period depends directly on the valuation of ending inventory.** Because of this relationship, note the following.

First, it is essential that the ending inventory be properly valued. If the ending inventory is overstated, cost of goods sold will be understated, resulting in an overstatement of gross margin, net income, and owner's equity. Also, overstatement of ending inventory will cause current assets, total assets, and owner's capital to be overstated. Thus, any change in the calculation of ending inventory will be reflected, dollar for dollar (ignoring any income tax effects), in net income, current and total assets, and owner's capital.

Second, when ending inventory is misstated in the current year, that misstatement is carried forward into the next year. This misstatement occurs because the ending inventory amount of the current year is the beginning inventory amount for the next year.

Third, an error in one period's ending inventory automatically causes an error in the opposite direction in the next period. After two years, however, the undetected error will "wash out," and assets and owner's equity will be properly stated.

Illustrations 9.1 and 9.2 prove that net income for an accounting period depends directly on the valuation of the ending inventory. This is shown in both the income statements and the statements of owner's equity of Taylor Company for the years 1990 and 1991.

In Illustration 9.1, the correctly stated ending inventory for the year 1990 is $70,000. As a result, the company has a gross margin of $270,000 and net income after expenses of $100,000. The statement of owner's equity shows a beginning owner's equity of $240,000 and an ending owner's equity of $340,000. When the ending inventory is overstated by $10,000, as shown on the right, the gross margin is $280,000, and net income after expenses is $110,000. The statement of owner's equity then has an ending owner's equity of $350,000. The ending inventory overstatement of $10,000 causes a

Illustration 9.1

Effects of an Overstated Ending Inventory

		TAYLOR COMPANY		
		For Year Ended December 31, 1990		
		Ending Inventory Correctly Stated		**Ending Inventory Overstated by $10,000**
Income Statement				
Sales		$800,000		$800,000
Cost of goods available for sale	$600,000		$600,000	
Ending inventory	70,000		80,000	
Cost of goods sold		530,000		520,000
Gross margin		$270,000		$280,000
Other expenses		170,000		170,000
Net income		$100,000		$110,000
Statement of Owner's Equity				
Beginning owner's equity		$240,000		$240,000
Net income		100,000		110,000
Ending owner's equity		$340,000		$350,000

Illustration 9.2

Effects of an Overstated Beginning Inventory

	TAYLOR COMPANY	
	For Year Ended December 31, 1991	
	Beginning Inventory Correctly Stated	Beginning Inventory Overstated by $10,000
Income Statement		
Sales	$850,000	$850,000
Beginning inventory . . . . $ 70,000		$ 80,000
Purchases 580,000		580,000
Cost of goods available for sale $650,000		$660,000
Ending inventory 90,000		90,000
Cost of goods sold	560,000	570,000
Gross margin	$290,000	$280,000
Other expenses	107,000	107,000
Net income	$183,000	$173,000
Statement of Owner's Equity		
Beginning owner's equity	$340,000	$350,000
Net income	183,000	173,000
Ending owner's equity	$523,000	$523,000

$10,000 overstatement of net income, as well as a $10,000 overstatement of owner's equity. The balance sheet would show both an overstated inventory and owner's capital. Due to the error in ending inventory, both the management of the business and creditors of the business may overestimate the profitability of the business.

Illustration 9.2 is a continuation of Illustration 9.1 and gives Taylor's operations for the year ended December 31, 1991. Note that the ending inventory in Illustration 9.1 now becomes the beginning inventory of Illustration 9.2. However, the company's inventory at December 31, 1991, is now an accurate inventory of $90,000. As a result, the gross margin in the income statement with the beginning inventory correctly stated is $290,000, and the company has net income after expenses of $183,000 and an ending owner's equity of $523,000. In the income statement at the right, in which the beginning inventory is overstated by $10,000, the gross margin is $280,000, and net income after expenses is $173,000, with the ending owner's equity also at $523,000.

Thus, in contrast to an overstated ending inventory, which results in an overstatement of net income, an overstated beginning inventory results in an understatement of net income. If the cost of goods available for sale is overstated, then cost of goods sold will also be overstated. Consequently, gross margin and net income will be understated. Note, however, that when net income in the second year is closed to owner's equity, the owner's equity account will be stated at its proper amount. The overstatement of net income in the first year is offset by the understatement of net income in the second year. For the two years combined, then, the net income is correct. At the end of the second year, the balance sheet contains the correct amount for both inventory and owner's capital.

■ DETERMINING INVENTORY COST

To place the proper valuation on inventory, a business must answer the question: What costs should be included in inventory cost? Then when identical goods are purchased at different costs, a business must answer the question: Which cost should be assigned to the items sold? In this section, you will learn how accountants answer these questions.

Costs Included in Inventory Cost

*Objective 2:
Indicate what costs
are properly included
in inventory.*

Generally, inventory cost includes all necessary outlays to obtain the goods, get the goods ready to sell, and have the goods in the desired location for sale to customers. Thus, inventory cost includes:

1. Seller's gross invoice price less purchase discount.
2. Cost of insurance on the goods while in transit.
3. Transportation charges when borne by the buyer.
4. Handling costs, such as the cost of pressing clothes wrinkled during shipment.

In theory, the cost of **each** unit of inventory should include its net invoice price plus its share of other costs incurred in shipment. The 1986 Tax Reform Act requires companies to make assignments of these costs (and more) to inventory for tax purposes. For accounting purposes, these cost assignments are recommended but not required.

Practical difficulties arise in applying this rule. Assume, for example, that the freight bill on a shipment of clothes does not state separately the cost of shipping one shirt. If the freight cost is to be included as part of the inventory cost of the shirt, it would have to be **allocated** in some manner to each unit because it cannot be measured directly. As a practical matter, allocations of freight, insurance, and handling costs to the individual units of inventory purchased are often not worth the additional cost incurred to perform the allocations. Consequently, in many companies, the costs of freight, insurance, and handling are not assigned to inventory but are expensed as incurred. The effect on net income of expensing these costs is minimized when the costs are omitted from both beginning and ending inventories.

Even if a cost is derived for each unit in inventory, the inventory valuation problem is not solved. Still to be resolved are these two problems:

1. If goods were purchased at varying unit costs, how should cost of goods available for sale be allocated between the units sold and those that remain in inventory? For example, assume Storey Company purchased two identical VCRs for resale. One was purchased for $450 and the other for $400. If one recorder was sold during the period, should Storey Company assign it a cost of $450, $400, or an average cost of $425?
2. Does the fact that current market prices are less than the cost of some units in inventory have any bearing on the amount at which inventory should be carried? Using the same example as above, if

Storey Company can currently buy all VCRs at a price of $400, is it reasonable to carry some units in inventory at $450 rather than $400?

These questions are answered in the next section.

Inventory Valuation under Changing Prices

Inventories generally should be accounted for at historical cost, which is the cost at which the items were purchased. But this rule does not indicate how to assign costs to the ending inventory and to cost of goods sold when the goods have been purchased at different unit costs. For example, suppose a retailer has three units of a given product on hand. One unit was bought for $20, another for $22, and the third for $24. If the retailer sells two of the units for $30 each, what is the cost of the two units sold?

Methods of Determining Inventory Cost

Objective 3:
Calculate cost of ending inventory, cost of goods sold, and effects on net income under the four major inventory cost methods.

Four inventory costing methods have been developed to solve this type of problem. They are: (1) specific identification; (2) first-in, first-out (FIFO); (3) last-in, first-out (LIFO); and (4) weighted-average. These costing methods are explained below. The frequency of use of these methods in a sample of 600 companies for the years 1983–86 is given in Illustration 9.3. Obviously, some companies use one method for certain inventory items and another method for other inventory items.

Illustration 9.3

Frequency of Use of Inventory Methods

	Number of Companies			
	1986	**1985**	**1984**	**1983**
Methods:				
Last-in, first-out (LIFO)	393	402	400	408
First-in, first-out (FIFO)	383	381	377	366
Average cost	223	223	223	235
Other	53	48	54	52

Source: Based on American Institute of Certified Public Accountants, *Accounting Trends & Techniques* (New York: AICPA, 1987), p. 126.

Objective 4:
Indicate the advantages and disadvantages of the four major inventory cost methods.

Assuming the use of periodic inventory procedure, the data for purchases, sales, and beginning inventory given in Illustration 9.4 will be used to illustrate each of the four inventory costing methods. Total goods available for sale consist of 80 units with a total cost of $690. A physical inventory determined that 20 units are on hand at the end of the period. Sales revenue for the 60 units sold was $780. The questions to be answered are: What is the cost of the 20 units in inventory? What is the cost of the 60 units sold?

Specific Identification. The **specific identification** pricing method attaches the actual cost to an identifiable unit of product. This method is easily applied when large inventory items (such as automobiles) are purchased and sold. Under the specific identification method, each unit in inventory, unless it is unique, must be identified with a serial number plate or identification tag.

Illustration 9.4

Beginning Inventory, Purchases, and Sales

Beginning Inventory and Purchases				Sales			
Date	Units	Unit Cost	Total Cost	Date	Units	Price	Total
Beginning inventory . .	10	$8.00	$ 80	March 10	10	$12.00	$120
March 2	10	8.50	85	July 14	20	12.00	240
May 28	20	8.40	168	September 7 . . .	10	14.00	140
August 12	10	9.00	90	November 22 . . .	20	14.00	280
October 12	20	8.80	176				
December 21	10	9.10	91				
	80		$690		60		$780

Ending inventory = 20 units, determined by taking a physical inventory.

To illustrate, assume that in Illustration 9.4, the 20 units on hand at year-end can be identified as 10 units from the August 12 purchase and 10 units from the December 21 purchase. The ending inventory is computed as shown in Illustration 9.5, where the **$181 ending inventory cost is subtracted from the $690 cost of goods available for sale to get the $509 cost of goods sold.** Note that it is also possible to determine the cost of goods sold for the year by recording the cost of each unit sold. The $509 cost of goods sold is reported as an expense on the income statement, and the $181 ending inventory is a current asset on the balance sheet.

Illustration 9.5

Determining Ending Inventory under Specific Identification

	Units	Unit Cost	Total Cost
Ending inventory comprised of purchases made on:			
August 12	10	$9.00	$ 90
December 21	10	9.10	91
Ending inventory	20		$181
Cost of goods available for sale			$690
Ending inventory			181
Cost of goods sold			$509

Advantages and Disadvantages of Specific Identification. When using the specific identification method of inventory pricing, cost of goods sold and ending inventory are stated at the actual cost of specific units sold and on hand. Some accountants argue that this method provides the most precise matching of costs and revenues and is therefore the most theoretically sound method. This statement is true for some one-of-a-kind items such as automobiles or real estate, and use of any other method for these items would seem completely illogical.

Accountants criticize the specific identification method, however, because with some items it results in identical units being included in inventory at different costs. For example, when the same television sets, differing only in their serial numbers, are purchased at different prices, they will be included in inventory at different costs.

Another disadvantage of the specific identification method is that it permits the manipulation of income. For example, assume a company has three identical units of a given product that were bought at different prices. One unit cost $2,000, the second cost $2,100, and the third cost $2,200. One unit is sold for $2,800. The units are alike, so the customer does not care which of the identical units is shipped. However, the gross margin on the sale could be either $800, $700, or $600, depending on which unit is shipped.

FIFO (First-In, First-Out). Sometimes a cost flow assumption is made rather than using specific identification. For instance, the **FIFO** method of inventory pricing assumes that the costs of the first goods purchased are the first costs charged to cost of goods sold when the goods are actually sold. In other words, the company assumes that the first goods purchased are the first goods sold. In some companies, the first units "in" (bought) must be the first units "out" (sold) to avoid large losses from spoilage. Such items as fresh dairy products, fruits, and vegetables should be sold on a FIFO basis. In these cases, an assumed first-in, first-out flow corresponds with the actual physical flow of goods.

Since the older units are assumed to be the first units sold and the newer units are assumed to be still on hand, the ending inventory consists of the most recent purchases. Thus, to determine the cost of the ending inventory under the FIFO method, begin by listing the cost of the most recent purchase. If the ending inventory contains more units than acquired in the most recent purchase, it will also include units from the next-to-the-latest purchase at the unit cost incurred, and so on. These units from the latest purchases must be listed until the number of units agrees with the number of units in the ending inventory.

Illustration 9.6 shows how the cost of ending inventory is determined under the FIFO method. The 20 units in inventory are assumed to consist of 10 units purchased December 21 and 10 units purchased October 12. The total cost of the inventory is $179. Subtracting $179 from the $690 cost of goods available for sale gives $511 as the cost of goods sold to be reported on the income statement. The $179 ending inventory is reported as a current asset on the balance sheet.

Advantages and Disadvantages of FIFO. The FIFO method has several major advantages: (1) it is easy to apply, (2) the assumed flow of costs often corresponds with the normal physical flow of goods, (3) no manipulation of income is possible, and (4) the balance sheet amount for inventory is likely

Illustration 9.6

Determining FIFO Cost of Ending Inventory under Periodic Inventory Procedure

	Units	Unit Cost	Total Cost
Ending inventory comprised of purchases made on:			
December 21	10	$9.10	$ 91
October 12	10	8.80	88
Ending inventory	20		$179
Cost of goods available for sale			$690
Ending inventory			179
Cost of goods sold			$511

to approximate the current market value. All the advantages of FIFO occur because the oldest unit costs are the first costs removed from inventory when goods are sold. Income cannot be manipulated by choosing which unit to ship because the cost of a unit sold is not determined by a serial number. Instead, the cost attached to the unit sold is always the oldest cost. Thus, under FIFO, purchases made at the end of the period have no effect on cost of goods sold or income.

The disadvantages of FIFO include (1) the recognition of "paper" profits and (2) a heavier tax burden if used for tax purposes. These disadvantages are discussed later as advantages of LIFO.

LIFO (Last-In, First-Out).   The **LIFO** method of inventory pricing assumes that the costs of the most recent purchases are the first costs charged to cost of goods sold when goods are actually sold. Since the latest costs are charged to cost of goods sold, the ending inventory consists of the oldest costs. Therefore, when determining the cost of inventory under the LIFO method, the oldest units and their costs are listed first. Thus, the first units listed are those in beginning inventory, then the first purchase, and so on, until the number of units listed agrees with the number of units in ending inventory.

The use of the LIFO method is shown in Illustration 9.7. The 10 units in beginning inventory are listed first, and then the 10 units purchased on March 2, are listed. The total cost of these 20 units, $165, is the ending inventory cost; the cost of goods sold is $525.

Illustration 9.7

Determining LIFO Cost of Ending Inventory under Periodic Inventory Procedure

	Units	Unit Cost	Total Cost
Ending inventory comprised of:			
Beginning inventory	10	$8.00	$ 80
March 2 purchase	10	8.50	85
Ending inventory	20		$165
Cost of goods available for sale			$690
Ending inventory			165
Cost of goods sold			$525

Advantages and Disadvantages of LIFO.   The advantages of the LIFO method of inventory valuation are directly related to the fact that prices have risen almost constantly for decades. This upward trend in prices leads to inventory, or "paper," profits if the FIFO method is used. **Inventory, or "paper," profits** are equal to the current replacement cost to purchase a unit of inventory at time of sale minus the unit's historical cost.

For example, assume a company has three units of a product on hand, each purchased at a different cost: $12, $15, and $20 (the most recent cost). The sales price of the unit normally will rise because the unit's replacement cost is rising. Assume the company sells one unit for $30. FIFO gross margin would be $18 ($30 − $12), while LIFO would show a gross margin of $10 ($30 − $20). LIFO supporters would say that the extra $8 gross margin shown under FIFO represents inventory profit because that "profit" is merely the additional amount that must be spent over cost of goods sold to purchase another unit of inventory ($8 + $12 = $20). Thus, the profit is not real; it exists only on paper. The $8 cannot be distributed to owners but must be retained in the company if the company is to continue handling that particular product. LIFO shows the actual profits that can be distributed to the owners while still replenishing inventory.

During periods of inflation, LIFO shows the largest cost of goods sold of any of the other cost methods because the newest costs charged to cost of goods sold are also the highest costs. The larger the cost of goods sold, the smaller the net income. If LIFO is used for income tax purposes, the resulting lower income means lower income taxes. Companies may only use LIFO for tax purposes if they use it for book purposes. Many companies use LIFO for book purposes for this reason (see Illustration 9.3, page 385).

To further illustrate the appeal of LIFO, assume that Company B has one unit of product Y on hand that cost $20. The unit was sold for $30; other selling expenses totaled $7. The income tax rate is assumed to be 50%. The identical unit was purchased for $22 before the end of the accounting period. Using FIFO, net income is computed as follows:

Net sales	$30.00
Cost of goods sold	20.00
Gross margin	$10.00
Expenses	7.00
Net operating margin	$ 3.00
Federal income taxes (50% rate)	1.50
Net income	$ 1.50

According to the above schedule, the company is selling product Y at a price that is high enough to produce net income. But consider the following:

Cash secured from sale	$30.00
Expenses and taxes paid ($7.00 + $1.50)	8.50
Cash available for replacement of inventory	$21.50
Cost to replace inventory	22.00
Additional cash required to replace inventory	$ 0.50

Thus, Company B is reporting net income of $1.50, but it cannot replace its inventory unless more cash is obtained.

Note how the results differ when LIFO is used to measure inventory:

Net sales	$30.00
Cost of goods sold	22.00
Gross margin	$ 8.00
Expenses	7.00
Net operating margin	$ 1.00
Federal income taxes (50% rate)	0.50
Net income	$ 0.50
Cash secured from sale	$30.00
Expenses and taxes paid ($7.00 + $0.50)	7.50
Cash available for replacement of inventory	$22.50
Cost to replace inventory	22.00
Cash available after replacement of inventory	$ 0.50

In this case, inventory profits are $2, the difference between the original cost of the inventory ($20) and its replacement cost at the time the inventory was sold ($22). Note that the tax savings under LIFO are equal to the tax rate times the inventory profits ($0.5 \times \$2 = \$1$).

Those who favor LIFO argue that its use leads to a better matching of costs and revenues than the other methods. When LIFO is used, the income statement reports both sales revenue and cost of goods sold in current dollars. The resulting gross margin is a better indicator of management's ability to generate income than gross margin computed using FIFO, which may include substantial inventory profits.

Supporters of FIFO argue that LIFO (1) matches the cost of goods **not** sold against revenues, (2) grossly understates inventory, and (3) permits income manipulation.

The first criticism—that LIFO matches the cost of goods **not** sold against revenues—is an extension of the debate over whether the assumed flow of costs should agree with the physical flow of products. LIFO supporters contend that it makes more sense to match current costs against current revenues than to worry about matching costs to the physical flow of goods.

The second criticism—that LIFO grossly understates inventory—is valid. LIFO inventory may be reported at a fraction of its current replacement cost, especially if the historical costs included are from several decades ago. LIFO supporters contend that the increased usefulness of the income statement more than offsets the negative effect of this undervaluation of inventory on the balance sheet.

The third criticism—that LIFO permits income manipulation—is also valid; income manipulation is possible under LIFO. For example, if management wishes to reduce income, an abnormal amount of goods at current high prices could be purchased near the end of the current period with the purpose of selling the goods in the next period. Under LIFO, these higher costs will be charged to cost of goods sold in the current period, resulting in a substantial decline in reported net income. To obtain higher income, management could delay making the normal amount of purchases until the next period and thus include some of the old, lower costs in cost of goods sold.

Weighted-Average. The **weighted-average method** is a means of pricing ending inventory using a weighted-average unit cost. This average is determined by dividing the total number of units purchased plus those in beginning inventory into total cost of goods available for sale. The ending inventory is carried at this per unit cost. The weighted-average method is most often used to determine a unit cost for units that are basically the same, like identical games in a toy store or identical electrical tools in a hardware store. Since the units are alike, they can be assigned the same unit cost.

Illustration 9.8 shows how the weighted-average method is used to determine inventory costs. Weighted-average cost per unit is computed by dividing the cost of units available for sale, $690, by the total number of units available for sale, 80. Thus, the average cost per unit is $8.625, meaning that each unit sold or remaining in inventory is valued at $8.625.

Advantages and Disadvantages of Weighted-Average. When the weighted-average method is used and prices are rising, cost of goods sold is stated at an amount less than that obtained under LIFO but more than that obtained under FIFO. Inventory is not as badly understated as under LIFO, but it is

Illustration 9.8

Determining Ending Inventory under Weighted-Average Method

	Units	Unit Cost	Total Cost
Beginning inventory	10	$8.00	$ 80.00
Purchases:			
March 2	10	8.50	85.00
May 28	20	8.40	168.00
August 12	10	9.00	90.00
October 12	20	8.80	176.00
December 21	10	9.10	91.00
Total	80		$690.00

Weighted-average unit cost is $690 ÷ 80, or $8.625.
Ending inventory then is $8.625 × 20 .... 172.50
Cost of goods sold $517.50

not as up to date as under FIFO. Weighted-average costing takes a "middle-of-the-road" approach. Although income can be manipulated under the weighted-average costing method by buying or failing to buy goods near year-end, the effects of buying or not buying are lessened due to the averaging process.

The above computations for the various inventory costing methods were made assuming use of periodic inventory procedure, where merchandise inventory is determined at the end of the accounting period. Perpetual inventory procedure is discussed later in this chapter.

Differences in Cost Methods Summarized

The four inventory methods—specific identification, FIFO, LIFO, and weighted-average—involve assumptions about how costs flow through a business. In some instances, assumed cost flows may correspond with the actual physical flow of merchandise. For example, fresh meats and dairy products must flow in a FIFO manner to avoid spoilage losses. In contrast, lumber or coal stacked in a pile will be used in a LIFO manner because the newest units purchased will be unloaded on top of the pile and sold first. Gasoline held in a tank is a good example of an inventory that has an average physical flow. As the tank is refilled, the new gasoline is mixed with the old; thus, any amount used will consist of a blend of the old gas with the new.

Although physical flows are sometimes cited as support for an inventory method, accountants now recognize that an inventory method's assumed cost flows need not necessarily correspond with the actual physical flow of the goods. In fact, there are good reasons for simply ignoring physical flows and choosing an inventory method based on more significant criteria.

Illustration 9.9 uses the data from Illustration 9.4 to show the cost of goods sold, inventory cost, and gross margin for each of the four inventory cost methods. The differences shown in the illustration occurred because different prices were paid for goods purchased. No differences would occur if the purchase prices were constant. Because purchase prices are seldom constant, the inventory method used by a company affects the company's cost of goods sold, inventory cost, gross margin, and net income. There-

Illustration 9.9

Summary of Effects of Employing Different Inventory Methods with Same Basic Data

	Specific Identifi- cation	FIFO	LIFO	Weighted- Average
Sales	$780.00	$780.00	$780.00	$780.00
Cost of goods sold:				
Beginning inventory	$ 80.00	$ 80.00	$ 80.00	$ 80.00
Purchases	610.00	610.00	610.00	610.00
Cost of goods available for sale	$690.00	$690.00	$690.00	$690.00
Ending inventory	181.00	179.00	165.00	172.50
Cost of goods sold	$509.00	$511.00	$525.00	$517.50
Gross margin	$271.00	$269.00	$255.00	$262.50

fore, companies must disclose on their financial statements which inventory method(s) were used.

Which Is the "Correct" Method?   All four methods of inventory pricing are acceptable; no single method is *the* only correct method. Different methods are attractive under different conditions.

If a company wants to match sales revenue with current cost of goods sold, it would use LIFO. If a company seeks to reduce its income taxes in a period of rising prices, it would also use LIFO. On the other hand, LIFO often charges against revenues the cost of goods not actually sold, and it may allow net income to be manipulated by changing the time when additional purchases are made.

The FIFO and specific identification methods result in a more precise matching of historical cost with revenue, but specific identification can give rise to income manipulation, and FIFO can give rise to "paper" profits. The weighted-average method also allows manipulation of income. Only under FIFO is the manipulation of net income not possible.

■ DEPARTURES FROM COST BASIS OF INVENTORY MEASUREMENT

As mentioned earlier, historical cost should generally be used to value inventories and cost of goods sold. But some circumstances occur in which departures from historical cost are justified. One of these circumstances is when the utility or value of inventory items is less than the cost of the items. Such a loss of utility may be evidenced by a decline in the selling price of the goods or in its replacement cost. This section explains how accountants account for some of these departures from the cost basis of inventory measurement.

Net Realizable Value

Goods should not be carried in inventory at more than their net realizable value. **Net realizable value** is the estimated selling price of an item less the estimated costs that will be incurred in preparing the item for sale and selling it. Damaged, obsolete, or shopworn goods often have a net realizable value that is lower than their historical cost and must be written down to their net realizable value. The goods do not have to be damaged, obsolete, or shopworn for this situation to occur. Technological changes and increased competition have caused this situation to occur for products such as computers, VCRs, calculators, and microwave ovens.

To illustrate a necessary write-down in the cost of inventory, assume an automobile dealer has a demonstrator on hand. The auto was acquired at a cost of $8,000 and had an original selling price of $9,600. Since the auto was used as a demonstrator and the new models are coming in, the auto now has an estimated selling price of only $8,100. However, the dealer can get the $8,100 only if the demonstrator receives some scheduled maintenance, including a tune-up and some paint damage repairs. This work and the sales commission will cost $300. The net realizable value of the demonstrator, then, is $7,800 (selling price of $8,100 less costs of $300). For inventory purposes, the required journal entry is:

```
Loss Due to Decline in Market Value . . . . . . . . . . . . . . . . . .   200
     Inventory . . . . . . . . . . . . . . . . . . . . . . . . . . . . . . . . .          200
         To write down inventory to net realizable value ($8,000 − $7,800).
```

This entry treats the $200 inventory decline as an expense in the period in which the decline in utility occurred. Such an entry is necessary only when the net realizable value is less than cost. If net realizable value declines but still exceeds cost, the item would continue to be carried at cost.

Lower-of-Cost-or-Market Method

The **lower-of-cost-or-market (LCM) method** is an inventory pricing method that values inventory at the lower of its historical cost or its current market (replacement) cost. The term *cost* refers to historical cost of inventory as determined under the specific identification, FIFO, LIFO, or weighted-average inventory method. *Market* generally refers to a merchandise item's replacement cost in the quantity usually purchased. The basic assumption of the LCM method is that if the purchase price of an item has fallen, its selling price also has fallen or will fall. The LCM method has long been accepted in accounting.

Under LCM, inventory items are written down to market value when the market value is less than the cost of the items. For example, if the market value of the inventory is $39,600 and its cost is $40,000, a $400 loss is recorded because the inventory has lost some of its revenue-generating ability and the loss must be recognized in the period the loss occurred. On the other hand, if ending inventory has a market value of $45,000 and a cost of $40,000, this increase in value is not recognized. To do so would recognize revenue before the time of sale.

*Objective 5:
Apply the lower-of-cost-or-market method to inventory.*

LCM Applied. LCM may be applied to each inventory item (such as Trivial Pursuit), each inventory class (such as games), or total inventory. Illustration 9.10 shows an application of the method to individual items and total inventory. If LCM is applied on an item-by-item basis, ending inventory would be $5,000. The $5,000 ending inventory would be deducted from cost of goods available for sale on the income statement and would be

Illustration 9.10

Application of Lower-of-Cost-or-Market Method

Item	Quantity	Unit Cost	Unit Market	Total Cost	Total Market	LCM on Item-by-Item Basis
1	100 units	$10.00	$9.00	$1,000	$ 900	$ 900
2	200 units	8.00	8.75	1,600	1,750	1,600
3	500 units	5.00	5.00	2,500	2,500	2,500
				$5,100	$5,150	$5,000

reported in the current assets section of the balance sheet. Under the class method, LCM is applied to the total cost and total market for each class of items compared. One class might be games; another might be toys. Each class is then valued at the lower of its cost or market amount. If LCM is applied on a total inventory basis, ending inventory would be $5,100, since total cost of $5,100 is lower than total market of $5,150.

An actual example of applying LCM is contained in the annual report of Du Pont. The report stated that "substantially all inventories are valued at cost as determined by the last-in, first-out (LIFO) method; in the aggregate, such valuations are not in excess of market." The term *in the aggregate* means that LCM was applied to total inventory.

Changing Inventory Methods

Generally, companies may use the inventory method that best fits their individual circumstances. But this freedom of choice does not include changing inventory methods every year or so, especially if the goal is to report higher income. Frequent switching of methods violates the **accounting principle of consistency,** which requires the repeated use of the same accounting methods in preparing financial statements. Consistency of methods in preparing financial statements enables financial statement users to compare statements from period to period and determine trends.

A change in inventory method can sometimes be made in spite of the principle of consistency. However, such a change must be fully disclosed. Full disclosure is usually made in a footnote to the financial statements and consists of a full description of the change, the reasons why the change was made, and, if possible, the effect of the change on net income.

For example, when J. M. Tull Industries, Inc., changed from lower of average cost or market to LIFO, the following footnote appeared in its annual report:

> Note B.   Change in accounting method for inventory. Effective with the year ending December 31, 1975, the company changed its method of determining inventory cost from the lower of average cost or market method to the last-in, first-out (LIFO) method for substantially all inventory. This change was made because management believes LIFO more clearly reflects income by providing a closer matching of current cost against current revenue.

Estimating Inventory

*Objective 6:
Estimate cost of end-
ing inventory using
the gross margin and
retail inventory
methods.*

A company using periodic inventory procedure may wish to estimate its inventory for any of the following reasons:

1. To obtain an inventory cost figure for use in monthly or quarterly financial statements without taking a physical inventory. The effort of taking a physical inventory is often expensive and disrupts normal business operations; once a year is often enough.
2. To compare with physical inventories to determine whether shortages exist.
3. To determine the amount recoverable from an insurance company when inventory is destroyed by fire or is stolen.

The paragraphs that follow discuss the gross margin method and the retail inventory method.

Gross Margin Method.   The gross margin method is one method of estimating an inventory when a physical inventory is not taken. The steps in calculating ending inventory under the gross margin method are:

1. Gross margin is estimated (based on net sales) using the same gross margin rate experienced in prior accounting periods.
2. Estimated cost of goods sold is determined by deducting estimated gross margin from net sales.
3. Estimated ending inventory is determined by deducting estimated cost of goods sold from cost of goods available for sale.

Thus, the **gross margin method** estimates ending inventory by deducting estimated cost of goods sold from cost of goods available for sale.

An assumption is made that a fairly stable relationship exists between gross margin and net sales. In other words, gross margin has been a fairly constant percentage of net sales, and this relationship is assumed to have continued into the current period. If this percentage relationship has changed, the gross margin method will not yield satisfactory results.

To illustrate the gross margin method of computing inventory, assume that Field Company has for several years maintained a rate of gross margin on net sales of 30%. The following data for 1990 are available: the January 1 inventory was $40,000; net cost of purchases of merchandise was $480,000; and net sales of merchandise was $700,000. As shown in Illustration 9.11,

Illustration 9.11

***Inventory Estimation
Using Gross Margin
Method***

Inventory, January 1, 1990		$ 40,000
Net cost of purchases		480,000
Cost of goods available for sale		$520,000
Less estimated cost of goods sold:		
Net sales	$700,000	
Gross margin (30% of $700,000)	210,000	
Estimated cost of goods sold		490,000
Estimated inventory, December 31, 1990		$ 30,000

the inventory for December 31, 1990, can be estimated by deducting the estimated cost of goods sold from the actual cost of goods available for sale.

The gross margin method is not precise enough to be used for year-end financial statements. At year-end, a physical inventory must be taken and valued by the use of the specific identification, FIFO, LIFO, or weighted-average method.

Retail Inventory Method.   Retail stores frequently use the retail inventory method (hence, the name *retail inventory*) to estimate ending inventory when taking a physical inventory is too time consuming and significantly interferes with business operations. The **retail inventory method** estimates the cost of the ending inventory by applying to the ending inventory a cost/retail price ratio stated at retail prices. The advantage of this method is that companies can estimate ending inventory (at cost) without taking a physical inventory. Use of this estimate permits the preparation of interim financial statements (monthly or quarterly) without taking a physical inventory.

The retail inventory method works as follows. Accounting records must show the beginning inventory and the amount of goods purchased during the period at both cost and retail prices. The cost/retail price ratio is found by dividing the cost of goods available for sale by the retail price of the goods available for sale. Retail sales are then deducted from the retail price of the goods available for sale to determine ending inventory at retail. The cost/retail price ratio or percentage is multiplied by the inventory at retail prices to reduce it to the inventory at cost. Illustration 9.12 shows an example of the retail method.

In Illustration 9.12, the cost ($22,000) and retail ($40,000) amounts for beginning inventory are available from the preceding period's computation. The cost ($182,000) and retail ($300,000) amounts for purchases are obtained from the accounting records. The sales amount ($280,000) is obtained from the Sales account and is, of course, stated at retail (sales) prices. The difference between what was available for sale at retail prices and what was sold at retail prices (which, of course, is sales) equals what should be on hand (ending inventory of $60,000) expressed in retail prices. The retail price of the ending inventory needs to be converted into cost for use in the financial statements by multiplying it times the cost/retail price ratio. In the example, the cost/retail price ratio is 60%, which means that on the average,

Illustration 9.12

Inventory Estimation Using Retail Method

	Cost	Retail
Beginning inventory, January 1, 1990	$ 22,000	$ 40,000
Purchases, net	182,000	300,000
Goods available for sale	$204,000	$340,000
Cost/retail price ratio:		
$204,000/$340,000 = 60%		
Sales		280,000
Ending inventory at retail prices		$ 60,000
Times cost/retail price ratio		× 60%
Estimated ending inventory at cost, December 31, 1990	36,000	
Cost of goods sold	$168,000	

60 cents of each sales dollar is cost of goods sold. Ending inventory at retail ($60,000) is multiplied by 60% to find inventory at cost ($36,000). Once ending inventory has been estimated at cost ($36,000), the cost of ending inventory can be deducted from cost of goods available for sale ($204,000) to determine cost of goods sold ($168,000). Cost of goods sold can also be found by multiplying the cost/retail price ratio of 60% time sales of $280,000.

In 1991, the $36,000 and $60,000 amounts will appear on the schedule as beginning inventory at cost and retail, respectively. Purchases at cost and at retail will be added to determine goods available for sale at cost and at retail, and from these amounts a new cost/retail price ratio for 1991 will be computed.

At the end of each year, a physical inventory usually is taken at retail prices. Since the retail prices are marked on the individual items (while the cost is not), taking an inventory at retail prices is more convenient than taking the inventory at cost. The results of the physical inventory can then be compared to the calculation of inventory at retail under the retail inventory method to determine whether a shortage exists.

Both the gross margin and the retail methods can be used to detect inventory shortages. To illustrate using the example given above, assume a physical inventory taken on December 31, 1990, shows only $56,000 of retail-priced goods in the store. Comparing this to the $60,000 of goods that should be on hand, shown in Illustration 9.12, indicates a $4,000 inventory shortage at retail. The $4,000 will be converted to $2,400 of cost ($4,000 × 0.60) and reported as a "Loss from inventory shortage" in the income statement. Knowledge of such shortages may lead to management action to reduce or prevent them, such as increasing security or improving the training of employees.

■ PERPETUAL INVENTORY PROCEDURE

Emphasis thus far in this chapter has been on periodic inventory procedure. Under periodic inventory procedure, the Purchases account is debited when goods are acquired; other accounts are used for purchase-related items, and cost of goods sold is determined only at the end of the period as the difference between cost of goods available for sale and ending inventory. No records are kept of the cost of items as they are sold, and no information is provided on possible inventory shortages. Any goods not in ending inventory are assumed to have been sold.

Under perpetual inventory procedure, no purchases and purchase-related accounts·are used. All entries involving merchandise purchased for sale to customers are entered directly in the Merchandise Inventory account. Entries are also made to reduce inventory for the cost of each item sold. Therefore, at the end of the period, Merchandise Inventory will show the cost of the goods that should be on hand. Comparison of this amount with the cost obtained by taking and pricing a physical inventory will reveal any inventory shortages. Thus, perpetual inventory procedure is an important element in providing internal control over goods with a high unit cost, such as automobiles, television sets, jewelry, and cameras.

Given the recent development of inventory management computer software packages, more and more businesses that formerly used periodic inventory procedure are now using perpetual inventory procedure. The tracking of units and dollars in and out of the company is much easier with a computer than manually.

Perpetual Inventory Records

Perpetual inventory procedure can be applied manually or by use of computers. In either procedure, a record will be maintained for each item in inventory. An example of an inventory record is given in Illustration 9.13 for Entertainment World, a company that sells many different brands of television sets. Illustration 9.13 shows the information on one particular brand and model of television set carried in inventory. Other information given on the record includes the maximum and minimum number of units the company wishes to stock at any time, when and how many units were acquired and at what cost, and when and how many units were sold and what cost was assigned to cost of goods sold. The number of units on hand and their cost are readily available also.

Entertainment World is using the FIFO method of inventory costing on the record shown in Illustration 9.13. The costing method being used can be determined from the calculation of the cost of the eight units sold on July 22. Prior to this sale, 16 units were on hand—6 with a unit cost of $300 and 10 with a unit cost of $315. Cost assigned to the units sold on July 22 consists of the cost of the six oldest units and two of the more recently purchased units. Thus, costs are being removed from inventory on a FIFO basis.

Perpetual inventory procedure can also be used with the weighted-average (or moving-average) method. Illustration 9.14 shows the same information as in Illustration 9.13 except that the weighted-average method is used rather than FIFO. Note that a new weighted-average unit cost is computed after **each purchase** by dividing total cost of goods available for sale by total

Illustration 9.13

Perpetual Inventory Record (FIFO Method)

| Item | TV-96874 | Maximum | 26 |
| Location | | Minimum | 6 |

| | Purchased | | | Sold | | | Balance | | |
1990 Date	Units	Unit Cost	Total	Units	Unit Cost	Total	Units	Unit Cost	Total
July 1							8	$300	$2,400
5	10	$300	$3,000				18	$300	$5,400
7				12	$300	$3,600	6	$300	$1,800
12	10	315	3,150				6	$300	$1,800
							10	315	3,150
22				6	300	1,800			
				2	315	630	8	$315	$2,520
24	8	320	2,560				8	$315	$2,520
							8	320	2,560

Illustration 9.14

Perpetual Inventory Record (Weighted-Average Method)

1990 Date	Purchased Units	Unit Cost	Total	Sold Units	Unit Cost	Total	Balance Units	Unit Cost	Total
		Item TV-96874			Maximum 26				
		Location			Minimum 6				
July 1							8	$300.000	$2,400
5	10	$300	$3,000				18	$300.000	$5,400
7				12	$300.000	$3,600	6	$300.000	$1,800
12	10	315	3,150				10	315.000	3,150
							16	$309.375*	$4,950
22				8	309.375	2,475	8	$309.375	$2,475
24	8	320	2,560				8	320.000	2,560
							16	$314.6875†	$5,035

* $4,950/16 = $309.375.
† $5,035/16 = $314.6875.

units available for sale. Thus, the unit cost after the purchase of July 12 is $309.375 ($4,950/16). The cost of the eight units sold on July 22 is $2,475 (8 × $309.375). A new weighted-average unit cost is computed after the purchase of July 24. Under perpetual inventory procedure, the unit cost is referred to as a moving weighted-average because it changes after each purchase.

Perpetual inventories may also be maintained on a LIFO basis. Under LIFO, each sale is assumed to come from the most recent units purchased until used up, then from the next to last purchase, and so on. Thus, for the sale on July 22 in Illustration 9.15, the eight units are assumed to come out

Illustration 9.15

Perpetual Inventory Record (LIFO Method)

1990 Date	Purchased Units	Unit Cost	Total	Sold Units	Unit Cost	Total	Balance Units	Unit Cost	Total
		Item TV-96874			Maximum 26				
		Location			Minimum 6				
July 1							8	$300	$2,400
5	10	$300	$3,000				18	$300	$5,400
7				12	$300	$3,600	6	$300	$1,800
12	10	315	3,150				6	$300	$1,800
							10	315	3,150
22				8	315	2,520	6	$300	$1,800
							2	315	630
24	8	320	2,560				6	$300	$1,800
							2	315	630
							8	320	2,560

of the $315 "layer." (If 12 units had been sold, 10 would have come out of the $315 layer and 2 from the $300 layer.) The advantages of LIFO are maximized when it is applied under periodic inventory method, where only the latest purchases made during the year are charged to cost of goods sold. Thus, LIFO is not as likely to be used as the other methods on a perpetual basis.

Journal Entries under Perpetual Inventory Procedure

Objective 7:
Record merchandise transactions under perpetual inventory procedure.

Some of the data in Illustration 9.15 are used to show the entries required under perpetual inventory procedure. The purchase of 10 units on July 5 would be recorded as follows:

```
July 5   Merchandise Inventory . . . . . . . . . . . . . . . . . . . .  3,000
              Accounts Payable—Baxter Company  . . . . . . . . . .        3,000
         To record purchase on account.
```

The 10 sets purchased must also be recorded on the perpetual inventory record, as shown in Illustration 9.15. Merchandise acquisitions are best recorded at net invoice prices to avoid having to adjust the gross invoice prices on all the inventory records when purchase discounts are subsequently taken.

Assuming the 12 sets sold on July 7 had a retail price of $450, the following entries are required:

```
July 7   Accounts Receivable—Watson Company . . . . . . . . . . .  5,400
              Sales . . . . . . . . . . . . . . . . . . . . . . . . . . .        5,400
         To record 12 sets sold on account.


     7   Cost of Goods Sold . . . . . . . . . . . . . . . . . . . . . . .  3,600
              Merchandise Inventory . . . . . . . . . . . . . . . . . .        3,600
         To record cost of 12 sets sold.
```

Perpetual inventory procedure requires an entry to merchandise inventory whenever goods are purchased, returned, sold, or otherwise adjusted, so that inventory records reflect actual units on hand at all times. Thus, an entry is required to record cost of goods sold for each sale. Also, transportation costs incurred on goods purchased are debited to Merchandise Inventory.

At year-end, a physical inventory is taken and compared with perpetual records. If a shortage is discovered, an adjusting entry is required. The entry, assuming a $2,000 shortage is discovered, is:

```
Dec.
31       Loss from Inventory Shortage  . . . . . . . . . . . . . . . . .  2,000
              Merchandise Inventory . . . . . . . . . . . . . . . . . .        2,000
         To record inventory shortage.
```

At the end of the period, the Cost of Goods Sold account is closed to Income Summary. No other purchase-related accounts exist.

You should now understand the importance of taking an accurate ending inventory, as well as how to value this inventory. In Chapter 10, accounting for another important group of assets is discussed—property, plant, and equipment.

■ *UNDERSTANDING THE LEARNING OBJECTIVES: CHAPTER 9*

1. Calculate the effects of inventory errors on certain financial statement items.

    - Net income for an accounting period depends directly on the valuation of ending inventory.
    - If ending inventory is overstated, cost of goods sold will be understated, resulting in an overstatement of gross margin, net income, and owner's equity.
    - When ending inventory is misstated in the current year, that misstatement is carried forward into the next year.
    - An error in the net income of one year caused by misstated ending inventory automatically causes an error in net income in the opposite direction in the next period (e.g., misstated beginning inventory).

2. Indicate what costs are properly included in inventory.

    - Inventory cost includes all necessary outlays to obtain the goods, get the goods ready to sell, and have the goods in the desired location for sale to customers.
    - Inventory cost includes:
      1. Seller's gross invoice price less purchase discount.
      2. Cost of insurance on the goods while in transit.
      3. Transportation charges when borne by the buyer.
      4. Handling costs, such as the cost of pressing clothes wrinkled during shipment.

3. Calculate cost of ending inventory, cost of goods sold, and effects on net income under the four major inventory cost methods.

    - **Specific identification:**   Attaches actual cost of each unit of product to units in ending inventory and cost of goods sold. Specific identification creates precise matching in determining net income.
    - **FIFO (first-in, first-out):**   Ending inventory consists of the most recent purchases. FIFO assumes that the costs of the first goods purchased are the first costs charged to cost of goods sold when the goods are actually sold. FIFO usually creates higher net income since the costs charged to cost of goods sold are lower.
    - **LIFO (last-in, first-out):**   Ending inventory consists of the oldest costs. The first units listed are those in beginning inventory, then the first purchase, and so on, until the number of units listed agrees with the number of units in ending inventory. LIFO assumes that the

costs of the most recent purchases are the first costs charged to cost of goods sold. Net income is usually lower under LIFO since the costs charged to cost of goods sold are higher due to inflation.

  ■ **Weighted-average:**   Ending inventory is priced using a weighted-average unit cost. The average is determined by dividing the total number of units purchased plus those in beginning inventory into total cost of goods available for sale. In determining cost of goods sold, this average unit cost is applied to each item. Under the weighted-average method, net income is usually higher than income under LIFO and lower than income under FIFO.

4. Indicate the advantages and disadvantages of the four major inventory cost methods.

  ■ **Specific identification:**
    Advantages: (1) Cost of goods sold and ending inventory are stated at the actual cost of specific units sold and on hand, and (2) it provides the most precise matching of costs and revenues.
    Disadvantages: (1) Results in identical units being included in inventory at different costs, and (2) income manipulation is possible.

  ■ **FIFO:**
    Advantages: (1) FIFO is easy to apply, (2) the assumed flow of costs often corresponds with the normal physical flow of goods, (3) no manipulation of income is possible, and (4) the balance sheet amount for inventory is likely to approximate the current market value.
    Disadvantages: (1) The recognition of "paper" profits and (2) a heavier tax burden if used for tax purposes.

  ■ **LIFO:**
    Advantages: (1) LIFO reports both sales revenue and cost of goods sold in current dollars and (2) lower income taxes if used for tax purposes.
    Disadvantages: (1) Matches the cost of goods *not* sold against revenues, (2) grossly understates inventory, and (3) permits income manipulation.

  ■ **Weighted-average:**
    Advantages: Due to the averaging process, the effects of year-end buying or not buying are lessened.
    Disadvantages: Manipulation of income is possible.

5. Apply the lower-of-cost-or-market method to inventory.

  ■ Inventory items are written down to market value when the market value is less than the cost of the items. If market value is greater than cost, the increase in value is not recognized.

  ■ LCM may be applied to each inventory item, each inventory class, or total inventory.

6. Estimate cost of ending inventory using the gross margin and retail inventory methods.

- The steps in calculating ending inventory under the gross margin methods are:
    1. Gross margin is estimated (based on net sales) using the same gross margin rate experienced in prior accounting periods.
    2. Estimated cost of goods sold is determined by deducting estimated gross margin from net sales.
    3. Estimated ending inventory is determined by deducting estimated cost of goods sold from cost of goods available for sale.
- The retail inventory method estimates the cost of the ending inventory by applying a cost/retail price ratio to the ending inventory stated at retail prices. The cost/retail price ratio is found by dividing the cost of goods available for sale by the retail price of the goods available for sale.

7. Record merchandise transactions under perpetual inventory procedure.

- Perpetual inventory procedure requires an entry to Merchandise Inventory whenever goods are purchased, returned, sold, or otherwise adjusted, so that inventory records reflect actual units on hand at all times. Thus, an entry is required to record cost of goods sold for each sale.

8. Define and use correctly the new terms in the glossary.

NEW TERMS INTRODUCED IN CHAPTER 9

FIFO (first-in, first-out)   A method of pricing inventory that assumes the costs of the first goods purchased are the first costs charged to cost of goods sold when goods are actually sold (387).

Gross margin method   A procedure for estimating inventory cost in which estimated cost of goods sold (determined using an estimated gross margin) is deducted from the cost of goods available for sale to determine estimated ending inventory. The estimated gross margin is calculated using gross margin rates (in relation to net sales) of prior periods (395).

Inventory, or "paper," profits   Equal to the current replacement cost to purchase a unit of inventory at time of sale minus the unit's historical cost (388).

LIFO (last-in, first-out)   A method of pricing inventory that assumes the costs of the most recent purchases are the first costs charged to cost of goods sold when goods are actually sold (388).

Lower-of-cost-or-market (LCM) method   An inventory pricing method that values inventory at the lower of its historical cost or its current market (replacement) cost (393).

Merchandise inventory   The quantity of goods held by a merchandising company for resale to customers (380).

Net realizable value   Estimated selling price of an item less the estimated costs that will be incurred in preparing the item for sale and selling it (392).

Retail inventory method   A procedure for estimating the cost of the ending inventory by applying to the ending inventory a cost/retail price ratio stated at retail prices (396).

Specific identification   An inventory pricing method that attaches the actual cost to an identifiable unit of product (385).

Weighted-average method   A method of pricing ending inventory using a weighted-average unit cost; determined by dividing the total number of units purchased plus those in beginning inventory into total cost of goods available for sale. Units in the ending inventory are carried at this per unit cost (390).

DEMONSTRATION PROBLEM 9–1

Following are data related to the beginning inventory and purchases of a product of Clay Company for the year 1990:

Inventory, January 1	10,000 @	$2.00
March 15	8,000 @	2.10
May 10	14,000 @	2.25
August 12	10,000 @	2.40
November 20	6,000 @	2.60
	48,000	

During the year, 40,000 units were sold. Periodic inventory procedure is used.

Required: Compute (1) the ending inventory and (2) the cost of goods sold under each of the following methods:

a.   FIFO.
b.   LIFO.
c.   Weighted-average.

Solution to demonstration problem 9–1

1. The ending inventory consists of 8,000 units (48,000 − 40,000).
   a.   Ending inventory under FIFO:

Purchased	Units	Unit Cost	Total Cost
November 20	6,000	$2.60	$15,600
August 12	2,000	2.40	4,800
	8,000		$20,400

   b.   Ending inventory under LIFO:

	Units	Unit Cost	Total Cost
Inventory, January 1	8,000	$2.00	$16,000

   c.   Ending inventory under weighted-average:

Purchased	Units	Unit Cost	Total Cost
Inventory, January 1	10,000	$2.00	$ 20,000
March 15	8,000	2.10	16,800
May 10	14,000	2.25	31,500
August 12	10,000	2.40	24,000
November 20	6,000	2.60	15,600
	48,000		$107,900

Weighted-average unit cost is $107,900/48,000, or $2.248.
Ending inventory cost is $2.248 × 8,000 = $17,984.

2. Cost of goods sold under each method is:

    a.   Cost of goods available for sale . . . $107,900
           Ending inventory   20,400
              Cost of goods sold . . . . $ 87,500

    b.   Cost of goods available for sale . . . $107,900
           Ending inventory   16,000
              Cost of goods sold . . . . $ 91,900

    c.   Cost of goods available for sale . . . $107,900
           Ending inventory   17,984
              Cost of goods sold . . . . $ 89,916

DEMONSTRATION PROBLEM 9–2

    a.   Stripe Company reported annual net income as follows:

        1988 . . . . $34,000
        1989 35,500
        1990 30,000

    Analysis of the inventories shows that certain clerical errors were made with the following results:

	Incorrect Inventory Amount	Correct Inventory Amount
December 31, 1988	$6,000	$7,100
December 31, 1989	7,000	5,850

    What is the corrected net income for 1988, 1989, and 1990?

    b.   The records of Blake Corporation show the following account balances on the day a fire destroyed the company's inventory:

    Inventory, January 1 . . . . $ 50,000
    Purchases (to date)   250,000
    Sales (to date)   375,000
    Average rate of gross margin for the
      past five years . . . . 30% of net sales

    Compute an estimated value of the ending inventory using the gross margin method.

    c.   The records of Dodd Company show the following account balances at year-end:

	Cost	Retail
Beginning inventory, January 1	$22,000	$ 31,250
Purchases	85,000	125,000
Transportation-in	2,375	
Sales		126,250

    Compute the estimated ending inventory at cost using the retail inventory method.

Solution to demonstration problem 9–2

a.

	1988	1989	1990	Total
Net income as reported	$34,000	$ 35,500	$30,000	$99,500
Adjustments:				
(1)	1,100			
(2)		(1,100)		
		(1,150)		
(3)			1,150	
Adjusted net income	$35,100	$ 33,250	$31,150	$99,500

(1) Ending inventory understated ($7,100 − $6,000 = $1,100).
(2) Beginning inventory understated ($7,100 − $6,000 = $1,100).
    Ending inventory overstated ($7,000 − $5,850 = $1,150).
(3) Beginning inventory overstated ($7,000 − $5,850 = $1,150).

b. Computation of inventory:

Inventory, January 1	$ 50,000
Purchases	250,000
Cost of goods available for sale	$300,000
Less: Estimated cost of goods sold	
Net sales $375,000	
Gross margin ($375,000 × 0.30) 112,500	
Estimated cost of goods sold	262,500
Inventory at cost, estimated by gross	
margin method	$ 37,500

c.

	Cost	Retail
Beginning inventory, January 1	$ 22,000	$ 31,250
Purchases	85,000	125,000
Transportation-in	2,375	—
Goods available for sale	$109,375	$156,250
Cost/retail price ratio:		
$109,375/$156,250 = 70%		
Sales		126,250
Ending inventory at retail price		$ 30,000
Times cost/retail price ratio		× 70%
Ending inventory at cost, December 31	21,000	
Cost of goods sold	$ 88,375	

QUESTIONS

1. Why is proper inventory valuation so important?

2. Why does an understated ending inventory understate net income for the period by the same amount?

3. Why does an error in ending inventory affect two accounting periods?

4. What cost elements are included in inventory? What practical problems are faced by including the costs of such elements?

5. What is the meaning of "to take a physical inventory"?

6. What is the accountant's responsibility regarding the taking of a physical inventory?

7. What is the cost flow assumption? What is meant by the physical flow of goods? Is there or should there be a relationship between cost flows and the physical flow of goods?

8. Indicate how a company can manipulate its net income if it uses LIFO. Is the same opportunity available under FIFO? Why or why not?

9. What are the main advantages of using FIFO and LIFO?

10. Which inventory method is the "correct" one? Can a company change inventory methods?

11. What is net realizable value, and how is it used?

12. Why is it considered acceptable accounting practice to recognize a loss by writing down an item in inventory to market, but unacceptable to recognize a gain by writing up an inventory item?

13. Under what conditions will the gross margin method of computing an estimated inventory yield approximately correct amounts?

14. What are the main reasons for estimating ending inventory?

15. How can the retail method be used to estimate inventory?

16. Why is perpetual inventory procedure being used increasingly in business?

EXERCISES

E-1
Determine effect of inventory errors

Norris Company reported annual net income as follows:

1989 . . . . $151,400
1990 152,400
1991 128,120

Analysis of its inventories shows that the following incorrect inventory amounts were used (the correct amounts are also shown):

	Incorrect Inventory Amount	Correct Inventory Amount
December 31, 1989	$24,000	$28,000
December 31, 1990	27,000	23,000

Compute the annual net income for each of the three years assuming the correct inventories had been used.

E-2
Compute ending inventory under FIFO, LIFO, and weighted-average methods

Davis Company inventory records show:

	Units	Unit Cost	Total Cost
Beginning inventory . . .	3,000	$18.00	$54,000
February 14	900	16.80	15,120
March 18	2,400	16.50	39,600
July 21	1,800	17.40	31,320
September 27	1,800	16.80	30,240
November 27	600	17.70	10,620

The December 31 inventory was 4,200 units. Present a short schedule showing the measurement of the ending inventory using:

a. The FIFO method.
b. The LIFO method.
c. The weighted-average method.

E-3
Compute effect on net income under FIFO and LIFO and compare the results

Price Company's inventory of a certain product was 12,000 units with a cost of $64 each on January 1, 1990. During 1990, numerous units of this product were purchased and sold. Also during 1990, the purchase price of this product fell steadily until at year-end it was $48. The inventory at year-end was 18,000 units. State which of the two methods of inventory measurement, LIFO or FIFO, would have resulted in the higher reported net income, and explain briefly.

E-4
Prepare journal entries affecting inventory using periodic inventory procedure

Following are inventory data for 1990 for West Company:

1. January 1 inventory on hand, 400 units @ $12.
2. January sales were 80 units.
3. February sales totaled 120 units.
4. March 1, purchased 200 units @ $12.60.
5. Sales for March through August were 160 units.
6. September 1, purchased 40 units @ $13.80.
7. September through December sales were 180 units.

Prepare only the journal entries affecting inventory assuming use of periodic inventory procedure. A physical inventory on December 31, 1990, showed 100 units on hand. Determine the cost of the ending inventory using the weighted-average method.

E-5
Compute cost of ending inventory using FIFO, LIFO, and weighted-average

Listed below are the purchases of product A made by Greene Company in its first year of operations:

January 2	1,400 @	$2.96
March 31	1,200 @	2.80
July 5	2,400 @	3.04
November 1	1,800 @	3.20

The ending inventory of the year consisted of 2,400 units.

a.   Compute the cost of the ending inventory using each of the following methods: (1) FIFO, (2) LIFO, and (3) weighted-average.
b.   Which method would yield the highest amount of gross margin? Explain why it does.

E-6
Compute inventory profit under FIFO

A company purchased 1,000 units of a product at $10 and 2,000 units at $11. All of these units were sold at $15 each at a time when the current cost to replace the units sold was $11.50. Compute the amount of gross margin under FIFO that LIFO supporters would call inventory, or "paper," profits.

E-7
Compute value of ending inventory using LCM applied on an item-by-item basis

Your assistant has compiled the following data to assist you in determining the decline in inventory from cost to the lower-of-cost-or-market method applied on an item-by-item basis:

Item	Quantity (units)	Unit Cost	Unit Market	Total Cost	Total Market
A	300	$24	$23.00	$7,200	$6,900
B	300	12	14.00	3,600	4,200
C	900	9	9.00	8,100	8,100
D	500	5	5.50	2,500	2,750

Determine the dollar amount of the ending inventory using the lower-of-cost-or-market method, determined on an item-by-item basis, and the amount of the decline from cost to lower of cost or market.

E-8
Compute value of total inventory using LCM

Use the data in Exercise E-7 above to compute the cost of the ending inventory using the lower-of-cost-or-market method applied to ʌne total inventory.

E-9
Compute carrying cost of inventory items

Pace Motor Company owns an automobile that it has used as a demonstrator for eight months. The auto has a list or sticker price of $30,000 and cost Pace $26,000. At the end of the fiscal year, the auto is on hand and has an expected selling price of $28,000. Costs expected to be incurred to sell the auto include tune-up and maintenance costs of $800, advertising of $200, and a commission of 5% of selling price to the employee selling the auto. Compute the amount at which the auto should be carried in inventory.

E-10
Estimate ending inventory using gross margin method

Crown Company takes a physical inventory at the end of each calendar-year accounting period to establish the ending inventory amount for financial statement purposes. Its financial statements for the past few years indicate an average gross margin on net sales of 25%. On July 18, a fire destroyed the entire store building and its contents. The records were in a fireproof vault and are intact. Through July 17, these records show:

Merchandise inventory, January 1	$ 840,000
Merchandise purchases	11,760,000
Purchase returns	168,000
Transportation-in	630,000
Sales	17,920,000
Sales returns	840,000

The company was fully covered by insurance and asks you to determine the amount of its claim for loss of merchandise.

E-11
Estimate ending inventory using gross margin method

Fulton Company takes a physical inventory at the end of each calendar-year accounting period. Its financial statements for the past few years indicate an average gross margin on net sales of 30%.

On June 12, a fire destroyed the entire store building and the inventory. The records were in a fireproof vault and are intact. Through June 11, these records show:

Merchandise inventory, January 1	$ 50,000
Merchandise purchases	1,250,000
Purchase returns	15,000
Transportation-in	85,000
Sales	1,550,000

The company was fully covered by insurance and asks you to determine the amount of its claim for loss of merchandise.

E-12
Estimate ending inventory using retail inventory method

Witt Company, Inc., records show the following account balances for the year ending December 31, 1989:

	Cost	Retail
Beginning inventory	$32,800	$46,000
Purchases	20,000	30,000
Transportation-in	400	
Sales		42,000

Using the above data, compute the estimated cost of ending inventory using the retail method of inventory valuation.

E-13
Prepare journal entries for inventory under perpetual FIFO inventory procedure

The following are selected transactions and other data of the Osborne Company:

1.   Purchased 20 units @ $150 per unit on account on September 18, 1991.
2.   Sold 6 units on account for $240 per unit on September 20, 1991.
3.   At year-end, a physical inventory was taken, and a shortage of $1,100 was discovered.

Prepare journal entries for the above transactions using perpetual FIFO inventory procedure. Assume the beginning inventory consists of 20 units @ $140 per unit.

E-14

Prepare journal entries under perpetual FIFO inventory procedure

Following are selected transactions of Walton Company:

1. Purchased 100 units of merchandise at $100 each; terms 2/10, n/30.
2. Paid the invoice in transaction (1) within the discount period.
3. Sold 80 units at $160 each for cash.
4. Purchased 100 units at $150; terms 2/10, n/30.
5. Paid the invoice in transaction (4) within the discount period.
6. Sold 60 units at $230 each for cash.

Prepare journal entries for the six numbered items above. Assume goods acquired are recorded at net invoice prices, accounted for under perpetual inventory procedure, and the FIFO inventory method is used.

E-15

Compute the cost of goods sold using perpetual weighted-average and LIFO methods

Compute the cost of the goods sold in Exercise E-14 above, transaction (6), assuming perpetual inventory procedure is used, with unit costs calculated under the weighted-average method. Round decimals to three places. Then compute the cost of goods sold for the same item—transaction (6)—assuming use of the LIFO method.

E-16

Compute the impact on net income under specific identification

Tempest Motor Company manufactures trucks and identifies each truck with a unique serial plate. On December 31, a customer ordered five trucks from the company. It currently has twenty trucks in its inventory. Ten of these trucks cost $8,000 each, and the other ten cost $10,000 each. If Tempest wished to minimize its net income, which trucks would it ship? By how much is it possible to reduce net income by selecting units from one group versus the other group?

E-17

Determine the proper value of damaged inventory

Mason Stereo Shop has a stereo system it uses as a floor model. The stereo cost $1,500 and had an original selling price of $2,000. After six months, the stereo is damaged and is to be replaced by a newer model. The stereo has an estimated selling price of $1,200, but when the company performs $200 in repairs, it can be sold for $1,600. Prepare the journal entry, if any, that must be made on Mason's books to record the decline in market value.

PROBLEMS, SERIES A

P9-1-A

Determine effects of inventory errors

Grayson Company reported net income of $238,700 for 1990, $247,600 for 1991, and $217,200 for 1992, using the incorrect inventory amounts shown for December 31, 1990, and 1991. The correct inventory amounts for those dates are also given. The correct December 31, 1992, inventory amount was used in calculating 1992 net income.

	Incorrect	Correct
December 31, 1990 . . .	$48,400	$56,800
December 31, 1991 . . .	56,000	46,800

Required: Prepare a schedule that shows: (1) the reported net income for each year, (2) the amount of correction needed for each year, and (3) the correct net income for each year.

P9-2-A

Determine effects of inventory errors

An examination of the financial records of Britt Company on December 31, 1990, disclosed the following with regard to merchandise inventory for 1990 and prior years:

1. December 31, 1986, inventory was correct.
2. December 31, 1987, inventory was overstated $90,000.
3. December 31, 1988, inventory was overstated $45,000.
4. December 31, 1989, inventory was understated $99,000.
5. December 31, 1990, inventory was correct.

The reported net income for each year was:

1987 . . . . . $172,800
1988 244,800
1989 301,500
1990 380,700

Required:
a. Prepare a schedule of corrected net income for each of the four years—1987–90.
b. What error(s) would have been included in each December 31 balance sheet? Assume each year's error is independent of the other years' errors.
c. Comment on the implications of your corrected net income as contrasted with reported net income.

P9–3–A
Maximize and minimize gross margin and net income using specific identification

Zippy Company sells home computers and uses the specific identification method to account for its inventory. On November 30, 1990, the company had 23 Orange III model home computers on hand that were acquired on the following dates and at these stated costs:

July 3 . . . . 5 @ $6,400
September 10 . . . 10 @ 6,000
November 29 . . . 8 @ 7,000

Zippy sold 18 Orange III computers at $9,200 each in December. There were no purchases of this model in December.

Required:
a. Compute the gross margin on December sales of Orange III computers assuming the company shipped those units that would maximize reported gross margin.
b. Repeat part (a) assuming the company shipped those units that would minimize reported gross margin for December.
c. In view of your answers to parts (a) and (b), what would be your reaction to an assertion that the specific identification method should not be considered an acceptable method for costing inventory?

P9–4–A
Compute gross margin using LIFO and FIFO illustrating effects of end-of-year purchases

Olan Company accounts for a certain product that it handles using periodic LIFO inventory procedure. Data relative to this product for the year ended December 31, 1990, are:

Inventory, January 1, 6,000 units @ $12

Purchases		Sales	
January 5 . . . . . 12,000 @ $15.00		January 10 . . . . 8,000 @ $24	
March 31 . . . . . 36,000 @ 18.00		April 2 . . . . 30,000 @ 27	
August 12 . . . . . 24,000 @ 22.50		August 22 . . . . . 32,000 @ 30	
December 26 . . . 12,000 @ 24.00		December 24 . . . 6,000 @ 33	

Required:
a. Compute the gross margin earned on sales of this product for 1990.
b. Repeat part (a) assuming that the December 26 purchase was made in January of 1991.
c. Recompute the gross margin assuming that 20,000 rather than 12,000 units were purchased on December 26 at the same cost per unit.
d. Solve parts (a), (b), and (c) using the FIFO method.

P9–5–A
Compute ending inventory under FIFO, LIFO, and weighted-average

The purchases of a certain product for Striber Company for April 1990 are shown below. There was no inventory on April 1.

Purchases	
April 3 . . . 2,000 units @ $14.00	
April 10 . . . 1,600 units @ 14.40	
April 22 . . . 3,200 units @ 13.20	
April 28 . . . 1,800 units @ 13.60	

During the month, 5,200 units were sold. Periodic inventory procedure is used.

Required: a.   Compute the ending inventory as of April 30, 1990, under each of the following methods: (1) FIFO, (2) LIFO, and (3) weighted-average.

b.   Give the journal entries to record the purchases and the necessary month-end entries to charge Income Summary with the cost of goods sold for the month under both FIFO and LIFO.

P9-6-A
Compute ending inventory and cost of goods sold using FIFO and LIFO

Listed below are the purchases and sales of a certain product made by Mason Company during 1990 and 1991. The company had 30,000 units of this product on hand at January 1, 1990, with a cost of $5 per unit.

Purchases		Sales	
1990		**1990**	
February 20	6,000 @ $5.00	February 2	9,000 @ $7.00
April 18	15,000 @ 4.90	April 23	12,000 @ 6.00
August 28	15,000 @ 4.80	September 3	12,000 @ 5.80
December 22	12,000 @ 4.84	December 24	10,500 @ 5.90
1991		**1991**	
January 26	9,000 @ $5.00	January 7	7,500 @ $6.00
March 6	15,000 @ 5.00	March 21	12,000 @ 6.20
August 12	9,000 @ 5.20	September 8	7,500 @ 6.20
November 15	12,000 @ 5.40	December 2	13,500 @ 6.50

The company uses periodic inventory procedure.

Required: a.   Compute the cost of the ending inventory and the cost of goods sold for both years assuming the use of the FIFO method of inventory measurement.

b.   Repeat part *(a)* using LIFO.

P9-7-A
Compute difference in net income between LIFO and FIFO

Given below are the inventory amounts under FIFO and LIFO for Wilson Company:

December 31	FIFO	LIFO
1989	$120,000	$ 98,000
1990	124,000	116,000
1991	138,000	136,000

Wilson Company has used the FIFO method of inventory measurement and reported net income of $330,000 in 1990 and $340,000 in 1991.

Required: Compute the net income that would have been reported in 1990 and 1991 if Wilson Company had used the LIFO method rather than FIFO.

P9-8-A
Compute ending inventory using LCM

The accountant for Williams Company prepared the following schedule of the company's inventory at December 31, 1990, and used the lower-of-cost-or-market method applied to total inventory in determining cost of goods sold.

Item	Quantity	Unit Cost	Unit Market
Q	8,400	$3.00	$3.00
R	4,800	2.50	2.40
S	10,800	2.00	1.90
T	9,600	1.75	1.80

Required: a. State whether this is an acceptable method of inventory measurement and show the calculations used to determine the amounts.

b. Compute the amount of the ending inventory using the lower-of-cost-or-market method on an item-by-item basis.

c. State the effect on net income in 1990 if the method in *(b)* was used rather than the method referred to in *(a)*.

P9-9-A
Estimate inventory using gross margin method

As part of a loan agreement with a local bank, Sloan Company must present quarterly and cumulative income statements for the year 1990. The company uses periodic inventory procedure and marks its merchandise to sell at a price that will yield a gross margin of 30%. Selected data for the first six months of 1990 are as follows:

	First Quarter	Second Quarter
Sales	$155,000	$160,000
Purchases	100,000	115,000
Purchase returns and allowances	6,000	7,000
Purchase discounts	2,000	2,200
Sales returns and allowances	5,000	3,000
Transportation-in	5,000	5,200
Selling expenses	16,000	15,000
Administrative expenses	6,000	5,000

The cost of the physical inventory taken December 31, 1989, was $19,000.

Required: a. Indicate how income statements can be prepared without taking a physical inventory at the end of each of the first two quarters of 1990.

b. Prepare income statements for the first quarter, the second quarter, and the first six months of 1990.

P9-10-A
Estimate ending inventory using retail inventory method

Cook Company records show the following information for 1991:

	Cost	Retail
Sales	—	$292,000
Purchases	$225,000	350,000
Transportation-in	21,900	—
Inventory, January 1	10,000	14,500
Purchase returns	12,600	15,500

Required: Compute the estimated year-end inventory balance at cost using the retail method of estimating inventory.

P9-11-A
Prepare journal entries for purchases and sales using perpetual FIFO inventory procedure

The inventory records of Drew Company show the following:

Mar. 1 Beginning inventory consists of 12 units costing $20 per unit.
     3 Sold 6 units at $47 per unit.
   10 Purchased 20 units at $24 per unit.
   12 Sold 10 units at $48 per unit.
   20 Sold 9 units at $48 per unit.
   25 Purchased 20 units at $25 per unit.
   31 Sold 10 units at $48 per unit.

Assume all purchases and sales are made on credit.

Required: Using perpetual FIFO inventory procedure, prepare the appropriate journal entries for March.

P9-12-A
Compute ending inventory and cost of goods sold under FIFO, LIFO, and weighted-average

Following are data relating to the beginning inventory and purchases of a given item of product of Widner Company for the year 1991:

January 1 inventory . . . 1,400 @ $2.10
February 2 . . . . 1,000 @   2.00
April 5 . . . . 2,000 @   1.50
June 15 . . . . 1,200 @   1.25
September 30 . . . . . 1,400 @   1.20
November 28 . . . . . . 1,800 @   1.75

During the year, 6,600 units were sold. Periodic inventory procedure is used.

Required: Compute the ending inventory and cost of goods sold under each of the following methods:

a. FIFO.
b. LIFO.
c. Weighted-average.

PROBLEMS, SERIES B

P9-1-B
Determine effects of inventory errors

Drake Company reported net income of $260,000 for 1990, $270,000 for 1991, and $290,000 for 1992, using the incorrect inventory amounts shown for December 31, 1990, and 1991. The correct inventory amounts are also shown for those dates. The correct December 31, 1992, inventory amount was used in calculating 1992 net income.

	Incorrect	Correct
December 31, 1990 . . .	$80,000	$90,000
December 31, 1991 . . .	76,000	70,000

Required: Prepare a schedule that shows: (1) the reported net income for each year, (2) the amount of correction needed for each year, and (3) the correct net income for each year.

P9-2-B
Determine effects of inventory errors

An examination of the financial records of Carter Company on December 31, 1990, disclosed the following with regard to merchandise inventory for 1990 and prior years:

1. December 31, 1986, inventory was correct.
2. December 31, 1987, inventory was understated $30,000.
3. December 31, 1988, inventory was overstated $21,000.
4. December 31, 1989, inventory was understated $18,000.
5. December 31, 1990, inventory was correct.

The reported net income for each year was as follows:

1987 . . . . . . $175,500
1988   213,000
1989   229,500
1990   210,000

Required: a. Prepare a schedule of corrected net income for each of the four years—1987–90.
b. What errors would have been included in each December 31 balance sheet? Assume each year's error is independent of the other years' errors.
c. Comment on the implications of the corrected net income as contrasted with reported net income.

P9-3-B
Maximize and minimize gross margin and net income using specific identification

Sea-Surf Company sells the Ultra-Light model wind surfer and uses the specific identification method to account for its inventory. All of the Ultra-Lights are identical except for identifying serial numbers. On August 1, 1990, the company had three Ultra-Lights in its inventory that cost $11,200 each. During the month, the company purchased the following:

August 3 . . . 5 @ $10,400
August 17 . . . 6 @ 11,600
August 28 . . . 6 @ 12,000

Sea-Surf Company sold 13 Ultra-Lights in August at $16,000 each.

Required: a. Compute the gross margin earned by the company in August if it shipped the units that would maximize gross margin and net income.
b. Repeat part *(a)* assuming the company shipped the units that would minimize gross margin and net income.
c. Do you think Sea-Surf Company should be permitted to use the specific identification method of accounting for Ultra-Lights in view of the manipulation possible as shown by your calculations in *(a)* and *(b)*?

P9-4-B
Compute gross margin using FIFO and LIFO illustrating effects of end-of-year purchases

Page Company accounts for its inventory using the LIFO method under periodic inventory procedure. Data on purchases, sales, and inventory for the year ended December 31, 1990, are:

Inventory, January 1 . . .   4,000 units @ $15.00

Purchases:
    January 7 . . . . 10,000 units @ 18.00
    July 7 . . . . 20,000 units @ 21.00
    December 21 . . . . . . 12,000 units @ 24.00

During 1990, 32,000 units were sold for $960,000, leaving an inventory on December 31, 1990, of 14,000 units.

Required: a. Compute the gross margin earned on sales during 1990.
b. Compute the change in gross margin that would have resulted if the purchase of December 21 had been delayed until January 6, 1991.
c. Recompute the gross margin assuming that 18,000 units rather than 12,000 units were purchased on December 21 at the same cost per unit.
d. Solve parts *(a)*, *(b)*, and *(c)* using the FIFO method.

P9-5-B
Compute ending inventory under FIFO, LIFO, and weighted-average

Following are data for Morton Company for the year 1990:

Inventory, January 1 . . .   700 units @ $10.40

Purchases:
    February 2 . . . .   500 units @   10.00
    April 5 . . . . 1,000 units @   8.00
    June 15 . . . .   600 units @   7.00
    September 30 . . . . . .   700 units @   6.80
    November 28 . . . . . .   900 units @   9.00

During the year, 3,300 units were sold. Periodic inventory procedure is used.

Required: a. Compute the ending inventory as of December 31, 1990, under each of the following methods: (1) FIFO, (2) LIFO, and (3) weighted-average.
b. Give the journal entries to record the purchases for the year and necessary year-end entries to charge Income Summary with the cost of goods sold for the year under FIFO.

P9-6-B
*Compute cost of
goods sold and
gross margin under
FIFO and LIFO*

Goodlin Company was organized on January 1, 1988. Selected data for 1988–90 are as follows:

Year Ended December 31	Inventory		Annual Data	
	FIFO	LIFO	Purchases	Sales
1988	$ 7,680	$5,760	$34,560	$38,880
1989	9,600	6,720	28,800	45,600
1990	15,840	9,600	35,520	39,360

Required: a. Compute the cost of goods sold and gross margin for each of the three years 1988–90, using the FIFO method of inventory measurement.
b. Repeat part *(a)* using LIFO.

P9-7-B
*Compute difference
in net income
between LIFO and
FIFO*

Lark Company determined its net income for the years 1989, 1990, and 1991 as $204,000, $196,200, and $201,900, respectively, using the FIFO method of inventory measurement. Given below are ending inventories based on both the FIFO and LIFO methods:

December 31	FIFO	LIFO
1988	$45,000	$42,000
1989	51,600	47,400
1990	50,400	46,800
1991	54,900	50,100

Required: Compute the net income that would have been reported in 1989, 1990, and 1991 if Lark Company had used the LIFO method rather than FIFO.

P9-8-B
*Compute ending
inventory using LCM*

Data on the ending inventory of Meyers Company on December 31, 1990, are:

Item	Quantity	Unit Cost	Unit Market
1	8,400	$2.00	$1.95
2	16,800	1.80	1.90
3	5,600	1.75	1.80
4	14,000	2.40	2.25
5	11,200	2.25	2.30
6	2,800	1.90	1.80

Required: a. Compute the ending inventory applying the lower-of-cost-or-market method to the total inventory.
b. What would be the ending inventory applying the lower-of-cost-or-market method on an item-by-item basis?

P9-9-B
*Estimate inventory
using gross margin
method*

The sales and cost of goods sold for Charles Company for the past five years were as follows:

Year	Sales (net)	Cost of Goods Sold
1985 . . .	$4,160,400	$2,600,250
1986 . . .	4,497,600	2,811,000
1987 . . .	5,144,400	3,215,250
1988 . . .	4,969,200	3,030,000
1989 . . .	5,311,600	3,300,000

For the seven months ended July 31, 1990, the following information is available from the accounting records of the company:

Sales	$3,228,400
Purchases	1,912,000
Purchase returns	12,000
Sales returns	72,400
Inventory, January 1, 1990	395,000

To secure a loan, Charles Company has been asked to present current financial statements. But the company does not wish to take a complete physical inventory as of July 31, 1990.

Required: a.   Indicate how financial statements can be prepared without taking a complete physical inventory.

b.   From the data given, compute the estimated inventory as of July 31, 1990.

P9-10-B
Estimate ending inventory using retail inventory method

Ewing Company records disclosed the following inventory information for 1989:

	Cost	Retail
Sales	—	$350,000
Purchases	$330,000	485,000
Purchase returns	7,000	10,000
Transportation-in	9,000	
Inventory, January 1	18,000	25,000

Required: Compute the estimated year-end inventory balance at cost using the retail method of inventory valuation.

P9-11-B
Compute cost of goods sold using FIFO for both perpetual and periodic inventory procedure

The inventory records of Thomas Company show the following:

Jan.   1   Beginning inventory consists of 12 units costing $20 per unit.
     5   Purchased 15 units @ $20.80 per unit.
   10   Sold 9 units @ $45 per unit.
   12   Sold 7 units @ $45 per unit.
   20   Purchased 20 units @ $20.90 per unit.
   22   Purchased 5 units @ $20 per unit.
   30   Sold 20 units @ $46 per unit.

Assume all purchases and sales are made on account.

Required: a.   Using perpetual FIFO inventory procedure, compute cost of goods sold for January.

b.   Using perpetual FIFO inventory procedure, prepare the journal entries for January.

c.   Compute the cost of goods sold under periodic FIFO inventory procedure. Is there a difference between the amount computed using the two different methods?

P9-12-B
Compute ending inventory and cost of goods sold under FIFO, LIFO, and weighted-average

Following are data relating to the beginning inventory and purchases of a given item of product of Busch Company for the year 1991:

January 1 inventory	2,100 @ $5.25
March 10	1,500 @ 5.00
May 24	3,000 @ 3.75
July 15	1,800 @ 3.13
September 20	2,100 @ 3.00
December 1	2,700 @ 4.38

During the year, 9,900 units were sold. Periodic inventory procedure is used.

Required: Compute the ending inventory and cost of goods sold under each of the following methods:

a.   FIFO.
b.   LIFO.
c.   Weighted-average.

BUSINESS DECISION PROBLEM 9-1

Determine tax effects of FIFO, LIFO, and weighted-average

Prince Company, which began operations on January 2, 1990, sells a single product, product X. Purchases for the year were:

January 2 . . . . . 1,500 @ $8.00
February 15   . . . 2,400 @ 8.00
April 8 . . . . 3,000 @ 8.30
June 6 . . . . 1,200 @ 8.50
August 19 . . . . . 2,400 @ 8.60
October 5 . . . . . 1,800 @ 9.00
November 22 . . . 1,200 @ 9.60

    Periodic inventory procedure is used. On December 31, a physical inventory shows 2,400 units on hand.

    Mr. Prince is trying to decide which of the following inventory costing methods he should adopt for tax purposes: FIFO, LIFO, or weighted-average. Since Mr. Prince is short of cash, he wants to minimize the amount of income taxes payable.

Required: What will be the cost of goods sold and the cost of the ending inventory under each of these three inventory costing methods? Which of the three inventory costing methods will minimize Mr. Prince's net income (and income taxes)?

BUSINESS DECISION PROBLEM 9-2

Determine insurance settlement using gross margin method

Anne Ferrell owns and operates a sporting goods store. On February 2, 1990, the store suffered extensive fire damage, and all of the inventory was destroyed. Ms. Ferrell uses periodic inventory procedure and has the following information in her accounting records, which were undamaged:

Inventory, January 1 . . . $30,000

Purchases:
    January 8   12,000
    January 20   18,000
    January 30   24,000

Net sales:
    During January   90,000
    February 1 and 2   6,000

    Ms. Ferrell also knows that her gross margin rate on net sales has been 40% for the past three years. Ms. Ferrell's insurance company has offered to pay $21,000 to settle her inventory loss unless she can show that she suffered a greater loss.

Required: Should Ms. Ferrell settle for $21,000? If not, how can she show that she suffered a greater loss? What is the estimated loss?

BUSINESS DECISION PROBLEM (ETHICS) 9-3

Determine the effect of a change in ending inventory; provide justification

Jack Gardner started a small hardware store two years ago and was struggling to make it successful. The first year of operations resulted in a substantial loss, and in the second year a small net income was realized. Jack's initial cash investment was almost depleted because he had to withdraw money for living expenses. The current year of operations had looked much better. The customer base was growing and seemed to be loyal. But to increase sales,

Jack had to invest his remaining funds and the proceeds of a $50,000 bank loan into doubling the size of his inventory and purchasing some new display shelves and a new truck.

At the end of the third year, Jack's accountant asked him for his ending inventory figure and later told him that initial estimates indicated that net income (and taxable income) for the year would be approximately $100,000. Jack was delighted until he was told that the amount of federal income taxes on that income would be about $20,000. Jack told the accountant that he did not have $20,000 and could not even borrow it, since he already had an outstanding loan at the bank.

Jack asked the accountant for a copy of the income statement figures so that he could see if any items had been overlooked that might reduce his net income. He noticed that ending inventory of $200,000 had been deducted from cost of goods available for sale of $800,000 to arrive at cost of goods sold of $600,000. Net sales of $900,000 and expenses of $200,000 could not be changed. But Jack hit upon a scheme to reduce his net income. The next day he told his accountant that he had made an error in determining ending inventory and that its correct amount was $150,000. This lower inventory amount would increase cost of goods sold by $50,000 and reduce net income by that same amount. The resulting income taxes would be about $7,000. Even paying this amount of taxes would be difficult, but Jack thought it could be done.

To justify his action in his own mind, Jack used the following arguments: (1) federal taxes are too high, and the federal government seems to be taxing the "little guy" out of existence; (2) no harm is really done because when the business becomes more profitable I will use correct inventory amounts, and this "loan" from the government will be paid back; (3) since I am the only one who knows the correct ending inventory I will not get caught; and (4) I'll bet a lot of other people do this same thing.

Required: a. Do you believe that Jack's scheme will work?
              b. What would you do if you were Jack's accountant?
              c. Comment on each of Jack's points of justification.

10 Property, Plant, and Equipment

LEARNING OBJECTIVES

After studying this chapter, you should be able to:

1. Recognize the characteristics of plant assets and the initial costs of acquiring plant assets.
2. Recognize the four major factors affecting depreciation expense.
3. Understand the various methods of calculating depreciation expense.
4. Distinguish between capital and revenue expenditures for plant assets.
5. Understand the subsidiary records used to control plant assets.
6. Define and use correctly the new terms in the glossary.

In Chapter 4, you were introduced to the classified balance sheet. The asset section of that classified balance sheet was divided into (1) current assets and (2) property, plant, and equipment. Current assets were discussed in Chapters 7–9. This chapter begins a discussion of property, plant, and equipment, which are often referred to as **plant and equipment** or simply **plant assets.**

Plant assets are long-lived assets because their useful lives are expected to last for more than one year. Long-lived assets consist of tangible assets and intangible assets. **Tangible assets** have physical characteristics that we can see and touch. These tangible assets include (1) plant assets such as buildings, machinery, vehicles, and furniture, which are discussed in this chapter; and (2) natural resources such as gas and oil, which are discussed in Chapter 11. **Intangible assets** (also discussed in Chapter 11) have no physical characteristics that we can see and touch but represent exclusive privileges and rights to their owners.

You should be aware that a difference exists between the physical life of an asset and its economic life. For example, on TV you may have seen a demolition crew setting off explosives in a huge building and wondered why a decision was made to destroy what looked like a perfectly good building. The reason the building was destroyed was because the building had "lived" its economic life. The land on which the building stood, or the building site, could be put to better use, possibly by constructing a new building.

■ NATURE OF PLANT ASSETS

Objective 1: Recognize the characteristics of plant assets and the initial costs of acquiring plant assets.

To be classified as a **plant asset,** an asset must (1) be tangible, that is, capable of being seen and touched; (2) have a useful service life of more than one year; and (3) be used in business operations rather than held for resale to a customer. Common plant assets are buildings, machines, tools, and office equipment. On the balance sheet, you will find these assets included under the heading "Property, plant, and equipment."

Plant assets include all long-lived tangible assets that are used to generate the principal revenues of the business. Inventory is a tangible asset but not a plant asset because inventory is usually not long-lived and it is held for sale rather than use. What a plant asset is to one company may be inventory to another. For example, a business such as a retail appliance store may classify a delivery truck as a plant asset because the truck is used to deliver merchandise, but a business such as a truck dealership may classify the same delivery truck as inventory because the truck is held for sale. Also, land held for speculation or not yet put into service is a long-term investment rather than a plant asset because the land is not being used by the business. However, standby equipment that is used only in peak or emergency periods is classified as a plant asset because the equipment is used in the operations of the business.

Accountants view plant assets as a collection of **service potentials** that are used up or consumed over a long period of time. For example, over several years, a delivery truck may provide 100,000 miles of delivery services to an appliance business. A new building may provide 40 years of shelter, while a machine may perform a particular operation on 400,000 parts. In each instance, purchase of the plant asset actually consists of the advance payment or prepayment of expected services. Plant asset costs are an **extreme form of prepaid expense.** As was the case with short-term prepayments, the accountant must allocate the cost of these services to the accounting periods benefited.

Accounting for plant assets presents the following four challenges:

1. Record the original (acquisition) cost of the asset.
2. Record the allocation of the asset's original cost to periods of its useful life through the process of depreciation.
3. Record subsequent expenditures on the asset.
4. Account for the disposal of the asset.

These four accounting challenges are shown in Illustration 10.1. Note how the asset's life begins with its procurement and the recording of its acquisition cost, which is usually in the form of a dollar purchase; then as the asset provides services through time, accountants must record the asset's de-

Illustration 10.1

Four Challenges in Recording Life History of a Depreciable Asset

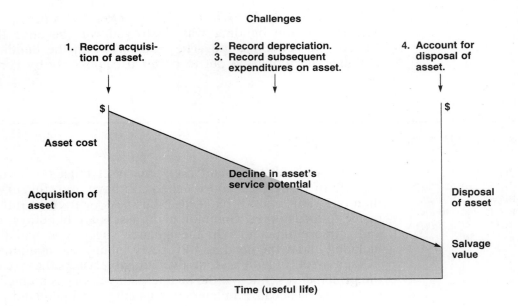

Challenges

1. Record acquisition of asset.

2. Record depreciation.
3. Record subsequent expenditures on asset.

4. Account for disposal of asset.

preciation and any subsequent expenditures on the asset; and finally, accountants must record the disposal of the asset. The first three challenges are discussed in this chapter; the disposal of an asset is discussed in Chapter 11. The last section in this chapter explains how accountants use subsidiary ledgers to control assets.

Remember that in recording the life history of an asset, accountants seek to match expenses related to the asset with the revenues generated by the asset. Since the measurement of periodic expense associated with plant assets affects net income, accounting for property, plant, and equipment is important to financial statement users.

■ INITIAL RECORDING OF PLANT ASSETS

When a company acquires a plant asset, accountants record the asset at the cost of acquisition (historical cost) because this cost is objective, verifiable, and the best measure of an asset's fair value. Even if the market value of the asset changes over time, the acquisition cost continues to be the amount reported in the asset account in subsequent accounting periods.

The acquisition cost of an asset is the amount of cash and/or cash equivalent given up to acquire a plant asset and place it in operating condition at its proper location. Thus, cost includes all normal, reasonable, and necessary expenditures to obtain the asset and get it ready for use. Acquisition cost also includes the repair and reconditioning costs for assets that were acquired in used or damaged condition. Unnecessary costs (such as traffic tickets or fines) that must be paid as a result of hauling machinery to a new plant are not part of the acquisition cost of the asset.

In this section, you will learn which costs are capitalized for (1) land and land improvements, (2) buildings, (3) machinery and other equipment, (4) self-constructed assets, (5) noncash acquisitions, and (6) gifts of plant assets.

Land and Land Improvements

The cost of land includes its purchase price and other costs such as option cost, if any; real estate commissions; title search and title transfer fees; title insurance premiums; existing mortgage note assumed; unpaid taxes (back taxes) assumed by purchaser; cost of surveying, clearing, and grading; and local assessments for sidewalks, streets, sewers, and water mains. When land purchased as a building site contains an old unusable building that must be removed, the entire purchase price should be debited to Land, including the cost of removing the old building less any cash received from the sale of salvaged items, such as crops or fruit on the land, that occur while the land is being readied for use.

To illustrate, assume that Blake Company purchased an old farm on the outskirts of San Diego, California, as a factory site. The company paid $150,000 for this property. In addition, the company agreed to pay unpaid property taxes from previous periods (called *back taxes*) of $8,000. Attorneys' fees and other legal costs relating to the purchase of the farm amounted to $1,200. The farm buildings were demolished at a cost of $12,000. Some of the structural pieces of the building were salvageable, however, and were sold for $2,000. The purpose of the demolition was to construct a new building at the factory site. Since new construction was to take place, the city assessed (charged) Blake Company $6,000 for water mains, sewers, and street paving. The cost of the land is computed as follows:

	Land
Cost of factory site	$150,000
Back taxes	8,000
Attorneys' fees and other legal costs	1,200
Demolition	12,000
Salvaged parts	(2,000)
City assessment	6,000
	$175,200

All costs relating to the farm purchase and razing of the old buildings are assignable to the Land account because the old buildings purchased with the land were not usable. The real goal was to purchase the land, but the land was not available without the buildings.

Land purchased as a building site is considered to have an unlimited life and is therefore not depreciable. However, **land improvements**, including driveways, temporary landscaping (such as bushes, gardens, and trees), parking lots, fences, lighting systems, and sprinkler systems, are attachments to the land that have limited lives and therefore are depreciable. These depreciable land improvements should be recorded in a separate account from the Land account, including a Land Improvements account. The cost of permanent landscaping, including leveling and grading, should be recorded in the Land account.

Buildings

When an existing building is purchased, its cost includes purchase price, repair and remodeling costs, unpaid taxes assumed by the purchaser, legal costs, and real estate commissions paid. When land and buildings are purchased together and both are to be used, the total cost should be divided so that separate ledger accounts may be established for land and for buildings. This division of cost is necessary to establish the proper balances in the appropriate accounts, which is especially important later because reported income will be affected by the depreciation recorded on the buildings.

Returning to our example of Blake Company, suppose one or more of the existing buildings were going to be remodeled for use by the company. Then Blake would have to determine what portion of the purchase price of the farm, back taxes, and legal fees was assignable to the buildings and what portion was assignable to the land. These costs would be assigned on the basis of appraised values of the land and the buildings. For example, assume that the land itself was appraised at $108,000 and the buildings were appraised at $72,000. The cost assignable to each of these plant assets would be determined as follows:

Asset	Appraised Value	Percent of Total Value		
Land	$108,000	60% (108/180)		
Buildings ...	72,000	40 (72/180)		
	$180,000	100%		

	Percent of Total Value	×	Purchase Price	= Cost Assigned
Land	60%	×	$159,200*	= $ 95,520
Buildings ...	40	×	159,200	= 63,680
				$159,200

* The purchase price is the sum of the cash price, back taxes, and legal fees.

The journal entry to record the purchase of the land and buildings would be:

Land	95,520	
Buildings	63,680	
Cash		159,200
To record purchase of land and buildings.		

When the city assesses the charges for the water mains, sewers, and street paving, these costs will still be debited to the Land account as they were in the previous example.

The cost of constructing new buildings is often more difficult to determine. Usually this cost includes architect's fees; building permits; payments to contractors; cost of digging the foundation; labor and materials to build the building; salaries of officers supervising construction; and insurance, taxes, and interest during the construction period. Any miscellaneous amounts earned from the building during construction reduce the cost of the building. For example, if a small completed portion of the building is rented out during construction of the remainder of the building, the rental proceeds are credited to the Buildings account.

Machinery and Other Equipment

When machinery or other equipment (such as delivery or office equipment) is purchased, its cost includes the seller's **net** invoice price (whether the discount is taken or not), transportation charges, insurance in transit, cost of installation, costs of accessories, testing and break-in costs, and other costs needed to put the machine or equipment in operating condition. **The cost of machinery does not include costs of removing and disposing of a replaced, old machine that has been used in operations.** Such costs are part of the gain or loss on disposal of the old machine, as discussed in Chapter 11.

Self-Constructed Assets

If a company builds a plant asset for its own use, the cost would include cost of materials and labor directly traceable to construction of the asset. Also included in the cost of the asset are indirect costs, such as interest costs related to the asset, and amounts paid for utilities (such as heat, light, and power) and for supplies used during construction. To determine how much of these indirect costs should be capitalized, the company compares utility and supply costs during the construction period with utility and supply costs paid in a period when there was no construction. The increase is recorded as part of the asset's cost. For example, assume a company normally incurred a $400 utility bill for June. This year a machine was constructed during June, and the utility bill was $650. The $250 increase would be recorded as part of the machine's cost.

To illustrate further, assume that Henkel Company needed a new die-casting machine and received a quote from Silkin Company for $23,000, plus $1,000 freight costs. Henkel decided to build the machine rather than buy it. The company incurred the following costs to build the machine: materials, $4,000; labor, $13,000; and indirect services of heat, power, and supplies, $3,000. The machine should be recorded at its cost of $20,000 ($4,000 + $13,000 + $3,000) rather than $24,000, the price that would have been paid if the machine had been purchased. The $20,000 is the cost of the resources actually given up to construct the machine. Also, recording the machine at $24,000 would require Henkel to recognize a gain on self-construction of assets. Accountants generally do not subscribe to the idea that a business can earn revenue, and therefore net income, by dealing with itself.

The general guidelines discussed and illustrated above can be applied to other plant assets, such as furniture and fixtures. The accounting methods are the same.

Noncash Acquisitions

When a plant asset is purchased for cash, its cost is simply the agreed cash price. However, when plant assets are acquired in exchange for other noncash assets (shares of stock, a customer's note, or tract of land) or as gifts, a cash price is more difficult to establish. Three possible asset valuation bases are discussed in this section.

Fair Market Value.   Fair market value is the normal price that would be paid for an item being sold in the normal course of business (not at a forced liquidation sale). Accountants seek to record noncash exchange transactions at fair market value.

The general rule on noncash exchanges is that **the noncash asset received is valued at its fair market value or the fair market value of what was given up, whichever is more clearly evident.** The reason for not using the book value of the old asset to value the new asset is that the asset being given up is often carried in the accounting records at an old historical cost or a depreciated book value. Neither amount may adequately represent the actual fair market value of either the old or the new asset. Therefore, if the fair market value of one of the assets is clearly evident, this amount is more representative of the value that should be recorded for the new asset in the accounting records at the time of the exchange.

Appraised Value.   Exchanges of items, neither of which has a fair market value, may be recorded at their appraised values as determined by a professional appraiser. Appraised value is an expert's opinion as to what an item's market price would be if the item were sold. Appraisals are often used to value works of art, rare books, and antiques.

Book Value.   The book value of an asset is its recorded cost less accumulated depreciation. An old asset's book value is usually not a valid indication of the new asset's economic value. The book value of an asset given up is an acceptable basis for measuring the value of the new asset received only if a better basis is not available.

Gifts of Plant Assets

Occasionally, a company will receive an asset without giving up anything for it. For example, to attract industry to an area and provide jobs for local residents, a city may give a tract of land to a company on which to build a factory. Although such a gift costs the recipient company nothing, the asset (land) is usually recorded at its fair market value. Gifts of plant assets are recorded at fair market value because accounting seeks to provide information on all assets owned by the company. Omitting some assets may make information provided misleading. These gifts are credited to Owner's Capital.

■ DEPRECIATION OF PLANT ASSETS

Depreciation is recorded on all plant assets except land. Since the amount of depreciation may be relatively large, depreciation expense is often a significant factor in determining net income. For this reason, most financial statement users are interested in the amount of, and the methods used to compute, a company's depreciation expense.

Depreciation is the amount of plant asset cost allocated to each accounting period benefiting from the asset's use and is a **process of allocation, not valuation.** Since eventually all assets except land wear out or become so inadequate or outmoded that they are sold or discarded, depreciation must be recorded on every plant asset except land. Depreciation is recorded even when the market value of a plant asset temporarily rises and is greater than its original cost, because eventually the asset will no longer be useful.

Major causes of depreciation are (1) physical deterioration, (2) inadequacy for future needs, and (3) obsolescence. **Physical deterioration** results from the use of the asset—wear and tear—and the action of the elements. For example, an automobile may have to be replaced after a time because its body rusted out. The **inadequacy** of a plant asset is its inability to produce enough products or provide enough services to meet current demands. For example, an airline cannot provide air service for 125 passengers on a flight serviced by a plane with a seating capacity of 90. The **obsolescence** of an asset is its decline in usefulness brought about by inventions and technological progress. For example, the development of the xerographic process of reproducing printed matter rendered almost all previous methods of duplication obsolete.

The use of a plant asset in business operations transforms a plant asset cost into an operating expense. Depreciation, then, is a cost of operating a business.

Because depreciation does not require a current cash outlay, it is often called a *noncash expense.* Cash was given up in the period when the asset was acquired, not during the periods when depreciation expense is recorded.

Objective 2:
Recognize the four
major factors affect-
ing depreciation
expense.

To compute depreciation expense, accountants consider four major factors:

1. Cost of the asset.
2. Estimated salvage value of the asset. **Salvage value** (or **scrap value**) is the amount of money the company expects to recover, less disposal costs, on the date a plant asset is scrapped, sold, or traded in.
3. Estimated useful life of the asset. **Useful life** refers to the length of time the company owning the asset intends to use it; useful life is not necessarily the same time period as either economic life or physical life. The economic life of a car may be seven years and its physical life may be 10 years, but if a company has a policy of trading cars every three years, the useful life for depreciation purposes is three years. Useful life may be expressed in years, months, working hours, or units of production. Obsolescence may also affect useful life. For example, a machine may be capable of producing units for 20 years,

but it is expected to be obsolete in 6 years. Thus, its estimated useful life is 6 years—not 20.

4. Depreciation method to be used in depreciating the asset. The four common depreciation methods are discussed in the next section.

Now that you know the nature of plant assets and how to initially record plant assets, including the use of subsidiary ledgers, you are ready to study the various plant asset depreciation methods accountants use. You may have read about some of these depreciation methods in the business section of your daily newspaper.

Depreciation Methods[1]

Objective 3: Understand the various methods of calculating depreciation expense.

Today, many different methods are available for calculating depreciation on assets. The most common methods—straight-line, units-of-production, and two accelerated depreciation methods (sum-of-the-years'-digits and double-declining-balance)—are discussed and illustrated below.

As is true for inventory methods, a company is normally free to adopt the method(s) of depreciation it believes most appropriate for its business operations. The theoretical guideline is to use a depreciation method that reflects most closely the actual underlying economic circumstances. Thus, companies should adopt the depreciation method that allocates plant asset cost to accounting periods according to the benefits received from the use of the asset. Illustration 10.2 shows the frequency of use of these methods for a sample of 600 companies. You can see that most companies use the straight-line method. Also, some companies use one method for certain assets and another method for other assets.

Illustration 10.2

Depreciation Methods Used

Method	Number of Companies			
	1986	1985	1984	1983
Straight-line	561	563	567	564
Declining-balance	49	53	54	57
Sum-of-the-years'-digits	14	16	15	17
Accelerated method—not specified . . .	77	73	76	74
Units-of-production	48	54	60	65
Other	12	12	13	12

Source: Based on American Institute of Certified Public Accountants, *Accounting Trends & Techniques* (New York: AICPA, 1987), p. 296.

In actual practice, the measurement of benefits from the use of a plant asset is often not possible. As a result, it is necessary for a depreciation method to meet only one standard: The depreciation method **must** allocate plant asset cost to accounting periods in a systematic and rational manner. The four methods discussed in this section meet this requirement.

Regardless of the method or methods chosen, the company must disclose its depreciation method in the footnotes to its financial statements. This

---

[1] Because depreciation expense is an estimate, calculations may be rounded to the nearest dollar.

429

information will always be included in the first footnote, which contains a summary of significant accounting policies.

The disclosure is generally straightforward: Sears, Roebuck and Co.'s Annual Report states simply that "depreciation is provided principally by the straight-line method." Corporations may use different depreciation methods for different assets. General Electric uses an accelerated method for most of its property, plant, and equipment; however, some assets are depreciated on a straight-line basis, and the company's mining properties are depreciated under the units-of-production method.

The illustrations of the four depreciation methods given below are based on the following data: On January 1, 1991, a machine was purchased for $27,000 with an estimated useful life of 10 years, or 50,000 units of output, and an estimated salvage value of $2,000.

Straight-Line Method.   The **straight-line depreciation** method has been the most widely used depreciation method in the United States for many years because it is easily applied. To apply the straight-line method, an equal amount of plant asset cost is charged to each accounting period. The formula for calculating depreciation under the straight-line method is:

$$\frac{\text{Depreciation}}{\text{per period}} = \frac{\text{Asset cost} - \text{Estimated salvage value}}{\text{Number of accounting periods in estimated useful life}}$$

Using our example of a machine purchased for $27,000, the annual depreciation charge is $2,500 [($27,000 − $2,000)/10]. Using the straight-line depreciation method, Illustration 10.3 presents a schedule of annual depreciation entries, cumulative balances in the accumulated depreciation account, and the book (or carrying) value of the $27,000 machine.

Use of the straight-line method is appropriate for assets where (1) time rather than obsolescence is the major factor limiting the asset's life and (2) relatively constant amounts of periodic services are received from the asset. Assets that possess these features include pipelines, fencing, and storage tanks.

Illustration 10.3

Straight-Line Depreciation Schedule

End of Year	Depreciation Expense Dr.; Accumulated Depreciation Cr.	Total Accumulated Depreciation	Book Value
			$27,000
1	$ 2,500	$ 2,500	24,500
2	2,500	5,000	22,000
3	2,500	7,500	19,500
4	2,500	10,000	17,000
5	2,500	12,500	14,500
6	2,500	15,000	12,000
7	2,500	17,500	9,500
8	2,500	20,000	7,000
9	2,500	22,500	4,500
10	2,500	25,000	2,000*
	$25,000		

* Estimated salvage value.

Units-of-Production (Output) Method. The **units-of-production depreciation** method assigns an equal amount of depreciation to each unit of product manufactured or service rendered by an asset. Since this method of depreciation is based on physical output, it is applied in situations where usage is the main factor leading to the demise of the asset. Under this method, first the depreciation charge per unit of output is computed; then this figure is multiplied by the number of units of goods or services produced during the accounting period to find the period's depreciation expense. The formula is:

$$\frac{\text{Depreciation}}{\text{per unit}} = \frac{\text{Asset cost} - \text{Estimated salvage value}}{\substack{\text{Estimated total units of production (or service)} \\ \text{during useful life of asset}}}$$

$$\frac{\text{Depreciation}}{\text{per period}} = \frac{\text{Depreciation}}{\text{per unit}} \times \frac{\text{Number of units of goods}}{\text{or services produced}}$$

The depreciation charge for the $27,000 machine is $0.50 per unit [($27,000 − $2,000)/50,000 units]. If the machine produced 1,000 units in 1991 and 2,500 units in 1992, depreciation expense would be $500 and $1,250, respectively.

Accelerated Depreciation Methods. **Accelerated depreciation methods** record higher amounts of depreciation during the early years of an asset's life and lower amounts in the asset's later years. A business might choose an accelerated depreciation method for the following reasons:

1. The value of the benefits received from the asset decline with age (for example, office buildings).
2. The asset is a high-technology asset subject to rapid obsolescence (for example, computers).
3. Repairs increase substantially in the asset's later years, and under this method the depreciation and repairs together remain fairly constant over the asset's life (for example, automobiles).

The two most common accelerated methods of depreciation are the sum-of-the-years'-digits (SOYD) method and the double-declining-balance (DDB) method.

Sum-of-the-Years'-Digits Method. The **sum-of-the-years'-digits (SOYD)** method is so called because the consecutive digits for each year of an asset's estimated life are added together and used as the denominator of a fraction. The numerator is the number of years of useful life remaining at the beginning of the accounting period. This fraction is then multiplied by the acquisition cost of the asset less the estimated salvage value to compute the periodic depreciation expense. The formula is:

$$\substack{\text{Periodic} \\ \text{depreciation} \\ \text{expense}} = \frac{\substack{\text{Number of years} \\ \text{of useful life} \\ \text{remaining at beginning} \\ \text{of accounting period}}}{\text{SOYD}} \times \left(\substack{\text{Asset} \\ \text{cost}} - \substack{\text{Estimated} \\ \text{salvage value}} \right)$$

The years are totaled to find SOYD. For an asset with a 10-year useful life, SOYD = 10 + 9 + 8 + 7 + 6 + 5 + 4 + 3 + 2 + 1 = 55. Alternatively, rather than adding the digits for all years together, the following formula can be used to find the SOYD for any given number of periods:

$$SOYD = \frac{n(n + 1)}{2}$$

where n is the number of periods in the asset's useful life. Thus, SOYD for an asset with a 10-year useful life is:

$$SOYD = \frac{10(10 + 1)}{2} = 55$$

The SOYD method is applied to the data given earlier for the $27,000 machine as follows. First, determine that at the beginning of year 1 (1991), the machine has 10 years of useful life remaining. Then, using the formula above, compute the first year's depreciation as 10/55 times $25,000 (the $27,000 cost less the $2,000 salvage value). The depreciation for the first year is $4,545, as shown in Illustration 10.4. Note that the fraction gets smaller every year, resulting in a declining depreciation charge for each successive year.

Illustration 10.4

Sum-of-the-Years'-Digits Depreciation Schedule

End of Year	Depreciation Expense Dr.; Accumulated Depreciation Cr.	Total Accumulated Depreciation	Book Value
			$27,000
1. $25,000* × $^{10}/_{55}$	$ 4,545	$ 4,545	22,455
2. $25,000 × $^{9}/_{55}$	4,091	8,636	18,364
3. $25,000 × $^{8}/_{55}$	3,636	12,272	14,728
4. $25,000 × $^{7}/_{55}$	3,182	15,454	11,546
5. $25,000 × $^{6}/_{55}$	2,727	18,181	8,819
6. $25,000 × $^{5}/_{55}$	2,273	20,454	6,546
7. $25,000 × $^{4}/_{55}$	1,818	22,272	4,728
8. $25,000 × $^{3}/_{55}$	1,364	23,636	3,364
9. $25,000 × $^{2}/_{55}$	909	24,545	2,455
10. $25,000 × $^{1}/_{55}$	455	25,000	2,000
	$25,000		

* $27,000 cost − $2,000 salvage value.

Double-Declining-Balance Method.   The **double-declining-balance (DDB)** method of computing periodic depreciation charges is applied by first calculating the straight-line depreciation rate. The straight-line rate is calculated by dividing 100% by the number of years of useful life of the asset. Then multiply this rate by 2. The resulting rate is applied to the declining book value of the asset. **Salvage value is ignored in making annual calculations.** However, at the point where book value is equal to the salvage value, no more depreciation is taken. The formula for DDB depreciation is:

$$\text{Depreciation expense} = (2 \times \text{Straight-line rate}) \times \left(\text{Asset cost} - \text{Accumulated depreciation}\right)$$

The calculations for the $27,000 machine using the DDB method are shown in Illustration 10.5. The straight-line rate is 10% (100%/10 years),

Illustration 10.5

Double-Declining-Balance (DDB) Depreciation Schedule

End of Year	Depreciation Expense Dr.; Accumulated Depreciation Cr.	Total Accumulated Depreciation	Book Value
			$27,000
1. (20% of $27,000)	$5,400	$ 5,400	21,600
2. (20% of $21,600)	4,320	9,720	17,280
3. (20% of $17,280)	3,456	13,176	13,824
4. (20% of $13,824)	2,765	15,941	11,059
5. (20% of $11,059)	2,212	18,153	8,847
6. (20% of $8,847)	1,769	19,922	7,078
7. (20% of $7,078)	1,416	21,338	5,662
8. (20% of $5,662)	1,132	22,470	4,530
9. (20% of $4,530)	906	23,376	3,624
10. (20% of $3,624)	725*	24,101	2,899

* This amount could be $1,624 so as to reduce the book value to the estimated salvage value of $2,000. Accumulated depreciation would be $25,000.

which, when doubled, yields a DDB rate of 20%. Since at the beginning of year 1 no accumulated depreciation has been recorded, the calculation is based on cost. In each of the following years, the calculation is based on book value at the beginning of the year.

In the 10th year, depreciation could be increased to $1,624 if the asset is to be retired and its salvage value is still $2,000. If the asset is continued in service, depreciation could be recorded until the asset's book value is equal to its estimated salvage value.

Illustration 10.6 summarizes the four depreciation methods.

Illustration 10.6

Summary of Depreciation Methods

Method	Base		Calculation
Straight-line	Asset cost −	Estimated salvage value	Base ÷ Number of accounting periods in estimated useful life
Units-of-production	Asset cost −	Estimated salvage value	(Base ÷ Estimated total units of production) × Units produced this period
Sum-of-the-years'-digits	Asset cost −	Estimated salvage value	Base × (Number of years of useful life remaining at beginning of accounting period) / SOYD
Double-declining-balance	Asset cost −	Accumulated depreciation	Base × (2 × Straight-line rate)

Illustration 10.7 compares three depreciation methods discussed above—straight-line, sum-of-the-years'-digits, and double-declining-balance—using the same example of a machine purchased on January 1, 1991, for $27,000. The machine has an estimated useful life of 10 years and an estimated salvage value of $2,000.

Illustration 10.7

Comparison of Straight-Line, Sum-of-the-Years'-Digits, and Double-Declining-Balance Depreciation Methods

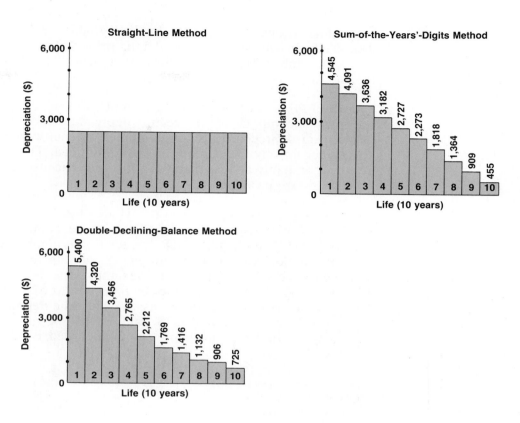

Partial-Year Depreciation

So far we have assumed that the assets were put into service at the beginning of an accounting period and have ignored the fact that assets are often put into service **during** an accounting period. When assets are acquired sometime during an accounting period, the first recording of depreciation is usually for a partial year. The depreciation for the partial year is normally calculated to the nearest full month the asset was in service. For example, an asset purchased on or before the 15th day of the month is treated as if it were purchased on the 1st day of the month; an asset purchased after the 15th of the month is treated as if it were acquired on the 1st day of the following month.

In this section, you will learn how to calculate partial-year depreciation for the four depreciation methods—straight-line, units-of-production, sum-of-the-years'-digits, and double-declining-balance. The example used is a machine purchased for $7,600 on September 1, 1991, with an estimated salvage value of $400 and an estimated useful life of five years.

Straight-Line Method. Partial-year depreciation calculations for the straight-line depreciation method are relatively easy. First, find the 12-month charge by the normal computation explained earlier. Then, multiply this annual amount by the fraction of the year for which depreciation should be recorded. For example, for the $7,600 machine purchased September 1, 1991 (estimated salvage value, $400; and estimated useful life, five years), the annual straight-line depreciation is [($7,600 − $400)/5 years] = $1,440. The machine will be used four months prior to the end of the accounting year, December 31, or one third of a year. The 1991 depreciation is ($1,440/3) = $480.

Units-of-Production Method. The units-of-production method requires no unusual computations to record depreciation for a partial year. The partial-year depreciation is still computed by multiplying the depreciation charge per unit by the number of units produced. The charge for a partial year will probably be less than for a full year because fewer units of goods or services are produced.

Sum-of-the-Years'-Digits Method. Under the SOYD method, the computation of partial-year depreciation is more complex. Problems occur because the 12 months for which depreciation is computed using the SOYD fraction do not correspond with the 12 months for which the financial statements are being prepared. For example, the depreciation recorded in 1991 on the $7,600 asset is for the last four months of 1991, which is the first one third of the first year of the asset's life. The depreciation for the four months of 1991 is computed as ($7,600 − $400) × $\frac{5}{15}$ × $\frac{1}{3}$; thus, depreciation is $800. In 1992, the depreciation recorded is $2,240, computed as follows:

For the first two thirds of the year:	($7,200 × $\frac{5}{15}$ × $\frac{2}{3}$) = $1,600
For the last one third of the year:	($7,200 × $\frac{4}{15}$ × $\frac{1}{3}$) = 640
Total depreciation expense for 1992 . . . . $2,240	

With the SOYD method, annual depreciation charges will have to be computed in this same way throughout the asset's life.

Double-Declining-Balance Method. Under the double-declining-balance method, it is relatively easy to determine depreciation for a partial year and then for subsequent full years. For the partial year, simply multiply the fixed rate times the cost of the asset times the fraction of the partial year. For example, DDB depreciation on the $7,600 asset for 1991 is ($7,600 × 0.4 × $\frac{1}{3}$) = $1,013. For subsequent years, the depreciation is computed using the regular procedure of multiplying the book value at the beginning of the period by the fixed rate. In this case, the 1992 depreciation would be [($7,600 − $1,013) × 0.4] = $2,635.

Changes in Estimates

After an asset is depreciated down to its estimated salvage value, no more depreciation is recorded on the asset even if it continues to be used. However, when the estimated useful life of an asset or its salvage value is found to be incorrect **before** the asset is depreciated down to its estimated salvage value, revised depreciation charges are computed. These revised charges do not correct **past** depreciation taken; they merely compensate for past incorrect charges through changed expense amounts in current and future periods. The new depreciation charge per period is computed by dividing the net book value less the newly estimated salvage value by the estimated periods of useful life remaining.

For example, assume that a machine cost $30,000, has an estimated salvage value of $3,000, and originally had an estimated useful life of eight years. At the end of the fourth year of the machine's life, the balance in its accumulated depreciation account (if the straight-line method was used) was $13,500. Thus, the net book value is $16,500. At the beginning of the fifth year, it is estimated that the asset will last six more years. The newly estimated salvage value is $2,700. The revised annual depreciation charge is [($16,500 − $2,700) ÷ 6] = $2,300.

Had the units-of-production method been in use, a revision of the life estimate would be in the form of units. Thus, to determine depreciation expense, a new per unit depreciation charge must be computed by dividing net book value less salvage value by the estimated remaining units of production. This per unit charge is then multiplied by the periodic production to determine depreciation expense.

Continuing the above machine example and using double-declining-balance depreciation, the book value at the beginning of year 5 would be $9,492.19 (cost of $30,000 less accumulated depreciation of $20,507.81). Depreciation expense for year 5 would be calculated as twice the new straight-line rate times book value or $2 \times \frac{1}{6} \times \$9,492.19$, or $3,164.06. Depreciation under the sum-of-the-years'-digits method would be $2,228.57. This amount is calculated as the new fraction ($\frac{6}{21}$) times [book value at the beginning of year 5 ($10,500) minus scrap ($2,700)].

Depreciation and Financial Reporting

APB Opinion No. 12 requires the amount of depreciation expense for the period to be separately disclosed in the body of the income statement or in the notes to the financial statements. The depreciation methods used must also be disclosed. Major classes of plant assets and their related accumulated depreciation amounts also are to be reported. An acceptable balance sheet presentation using some assumed data follows:

Property, plant, and equipment:		
Land		$40,000
Building	$100,000	
Less: Accumulated depreciation	60,000	40,000
Store equipment	$ 12,000	
Less: Accumulated depreciation	2,000	10,000
Total property, plant, and equipment		$90,000

The presentation of cost less accumulated depreciation in the balance sheet gives the statement user a better understanding of the percentages of a company's plant assets that have been used up than if the balance sheet presented only the book value (remaining undepreciated cost) of the assets. For example, reporting plant assets of $100,000 less $60,000 of accumulated depreciation, resulting in a net amount of $40,000, is quite different from reporting $40,000 of plant assets. In the first case, the statement user can see that the assets are about 60% used up. In the latter case, the statement user has no way of knowing whether the assets are new or old.

A Misconception.   Some financial statement users mistakenly believe that the amount of accumulated depreciation represents funds available for replacing old plant assets with new assets. But the accumulated depreciation account balance does not represent cash; accumulated depreciation shows simply how much of an asset's cost has been charged to expense. The plant asset and its contra account, accumulated depreciation, are used so that data on the total original acquisition cost and accumulated depreciation are readily available to meet reporting requirements.

Costs or Market Values in the Balance Sheet.   Plant assets are reported in the balance sheet at **original** cost less accumulated depreciation. The justification for reporting the remaining undepreciated costs of the asset rather than market values is the going-concern concept. As you recall from Chapter 1, the going-concern concept assumes that the company will remain in business indefinitely, which implies the company will use its plant assets rather than sell them. Market values generally are not considered relevant for use in the primary financial statements, although they may be reported in supplemental statements (as described in Appendix B at the end of the text).

Furthermore, an asset cannot be written up to a market value above its cost merely because its appraised value has increased. Neither can an asset be written down below its cost if future revenues from the asset are expected to exceed its cost.

■ RECORD SUBSEQUENT EXPENDITURES (CAPITAL AND REVENUE) ON ASSETS

Objective 4: Distinguish between capital and revenue expenditures for plant assets.

Companies often make current expenditures on plant assets they acquired some time ago. These expenditures are debited to (1) an asset account, (2) an accumulated depreciation account, or (3) an expense account.

Expenditures debited to an asset account or to an accumulated depreciation account are called **capital expenditures.** Capital expenditures increase the book value of plant assets. **Revenue expenditures,** on the other hand, do not qualify as capital expenditures because they help to generate the current period's revenues rather than future periods' revenues. As a result, revenue expenditures are expensed immediately and are reported in the income statement as expenses.

Expenditures Capitalized in Asset Accounts

Betterments or **improvements** to existing plant assets are capital expenditures because they increase the quality of services obtained from the asset. Because betterments or improvements add to the service-rendering ability of assets, they are charged to the asset accounts. For example, installing an air conditioner in an automobile that is not air conditioned is a betterment. Such a betterment is debited to the asset account, Automobiles.

Expenditures Capitalized as Charges to Accumulated Depreciation

Occasionally, expenditures made on plant assets extend the quantity of services **beyond the original estimate** but do not improve the quality of the services. Because these expenditures will benefit an increased number of future periods, they are capitalized rather than expensed. However, since there is no visible, tangible addition to, or improvement in, the quality of services, the expenditures are often charged to the accumulated depreciation account. Such expenditures are viewed as canceling a part of the existing accumulated depreciation and are often called **extraordinary repairs.**

To illustrate, assume that after operating a press for four years, a company spent $3,750 to recondition the press. The effect of the reconditioning is to increase the machine's life to 14 years instead of the original estimate of 10 years. The journal entry to record the major repair is:

Accumulated Depreciation—Machinery	3,750	
Cash (or Accounts Payable)		3,750
To record the cost of reconditioning a press.		

When the press was acquired, it cost $30,250. The press had an estimated useful life of 10 years with no estimated salvage value. At the end of the fourth year, the balance in its accumulated depreciation account under the straight-line method is $[(\$30{,}250 \div 10) \times 4] = \$12{,}100$. After the $3,750 spent to recondition the press is debited to the accumulated depreciation account, the balances in the asset account and its related accumulated depreciation account are as follows:

Cost of press	$30,250
Accumulated depreciation	8,350
Book value (end of four years) . . .	$21,900

Under the straight-line method, the book value of the press, $21,900, is divided equally among the 10 remaining years in amounts of $2,190 per year. The effect of the expenditure, then, is to increase the carrying amount (book value) of the asset by reducing its contra account, accumulated depreciation.

Expenditures for major repairs not extending the asset's life are also sometimes charged to accumulated depreciation to avoid distortion of net income that might result if these expenditures were expensed in the year incurred. Then a revised depreciation expense must be calculated, and the cost of major repairs is spread over a number of years.

To illustrate, assume the same facts as in the above example except that the $3,750 expenditure did not extend the life of the asset. However, because of the size of this expenditure, it is still charged to accumulated depreciation. Now the $21,900 remaining book value would be spread over the remaining six years of the life of the press. Under the straight-line method, annual depreciation would then be $(\$21{,}900 \div 6) = \$3{,}650$.

Expenditures Charged to Expense

Recurring and/or minor expenditures that neither add to the asset's quality of service-rendering abilities nor extend its quantity of services beyond the asset's original estimated useful life are treated as expenses. Thus, regular maintenance (lubricating a machine) and ordinary repairs (replacing a broken fan belt) are expensed immediately as revenue expenditures. For example, if the company mentioned previously spends $190 to repair the press after using it for some time, this amount should be debited to Maintenance Expense or Repairs Expense.

In many companies, any expenditure below an arbitrary minimum, such as $25, is charged to expense regardless of the asset's useful life. This practice is followed to avoid calculating and preparing adjusting entries for depreciation for such a nominal cost.

Errors in Classification

In an actual situation, it is often difficult to distinguish between an expenditure that should be debited to the asset account and an expenditure that should be debited to the accumulated depreciation account. For example, some expenditures seem to affect both the quality and quantity of services. Even if the wrong account is debited for the expenditure, book value of the plant asset at that point will be the same as if the correct account had been debited. A difference will arise in the carrying value of the asset for financial statement purposes for the remaining useful life of the asset. Both the asset and accumulated depreciation accounts will be misstated.

As an example of the effect of misstated asset and accumulated depreciation accounts, assume Blanchard Company had an asset that had originally cost $15,000 and had been depreciated to a book value of $6,000 at the beginning of 1991. At that time, the equipment was estimated to have a remaining useful life of two years. The company spent $4,000 in early January 1991 to install a new motor in the equipment. This motor was expected to extend the useful life of the asset four years beyond the original estimate. Since the expenditure served to extend the life, it should be capitalized by a debit to the accumulated depreciation account. The calculations for depreciation expense if the entry is made correctly and if the expenditure had been improperly charged (debited) to the asset account are shown in Illustration 10.8.

Illustration 10.8

Expenditure Extending Plant Asset Life

	December 31, 1990	After Expenditure Entry	
		Correct	Incorrect
Cost	$15,000	$15,000	$19,000
Accumulated depreciation	9,000	5,000	9,000
Book value	$ 6,000	$10,000	$10,000
Remaining life	2 years	6 years	6 years
Depreciation expense per year . . .	$ 3,000	$ 1,667	$ 1,667

If an expenditure that should be expensed is capitalized, the effects are more significant. Assume instead that $6,000 in repairs expense is incurred for a plant asset that originally cost $40,000 and had a useful life of four years and no estimated salvage value. This asset had been depreciated using the straight-line method for one year and had a book value of $30,000 ($40,000 cost − $10,000 first-year depreciation) at the beginning of 1991. The $6,000 that should have been charged to repairs expense in 1991 was capitalized instead. The charge for depreciation should have remained at $10,000 for each of the next three years. With the incorrect entry, however, depreciation increases.

Regardless of whether the repair was debited to the asset account or the accumulated depreciation account, the depreciation expense amount will be changed to $12,000 for each of the next three years ($30,000 book value + $6,000 repairs expense ÷ 3 more years of useful life). As a result, net income for the year 1991 will be overstated $4,000 due to the effects of these two errors: (1) repairs expense is understated by $6,000, causing income to be overstated by $6,000; and (2) depreciation expense is overstated by $2,000, causing income to be understated by $2,000. In 1992, depreciation will again be overstated by $2,000, causing 1992 income to be understated by $2,000.

You should remember that the $6,000 recording error affects more than just the expense accounts and net income. Plant asset and retained earnings accounts on the balance sheet will also reflect the impact of this error. Illustration 10.9 shows the effect of incorrectly capitalizing the $6,000 rather than correctly expensing it.

Illustration 10.9

Effect of Revenue Expenditure Treated as Capital Expenditure

	For 1991 under Correctly Expensing	For 1991 under Incorrectly Capitalizing
1991 depreciation expense	$10,000	$12,000
1991 repair expense	6,000	–0–
1991 net income overstated by $4,000, which affects retained earnings		
Asset cost	$40,000	$46,000
Accumulated depreciation	20,000	22,000
Book value	$20,000	$24,000

	For 1992 under Correctly Expensing	For 1992 under Incorrectly Capitalizing
1992 depreciation expense	$10,000	$12,000
1992 repair expense	–0–	–0–
1992 net income understated by $2,000, which affects retained earnings		
Asset cost	$40,000	$46,000
Accumulated depreciation	30,000	34,000
Book value	$10,000	$12,000

■ SUBSIDIARY RECORDS USED TO CONTROL PLANT ASSETS

Objective 5:
Understand the sub-
sidiary records used
to control plant
assets.

Most companies maintain formal records (ranging from handwritten documents to computer tapes) to ensure control over their plant assets. These
records include an asset account and a related accumulated depreciation
account in the general ledger for **each** major class of depreciable plant
assets, such as buildings, factory machinery, office equipment, delivery
equipment, and store equipment.

Since the general ledger account frequently cannot maintain detailed
information about each item in a major class of depreciable plant assets,
companies use subsidiary plant asset ledgers. For example, the general
ledger account for office equipment may contain entries for such items as
microcomputers, typewriters, copying machines, calculators, dictating
equipment, and filing cabinets, but it cannot contain detailed information
about these items. Subsidiary plant asset ledgers and detailed records
provide more information and make it possible for the company to maintain
better control over plant and equipment.

When subsidiary ledgers are kept for each major class of plant and
equipment, there may be a subsidiary ledger for factory machinery, office
equipment, and other classes of depreciable plant assets. Then there may be
an additional subsidiary ledger for each type of asset within each category.
For example, the subsidiary office equipment ledger may contain accounts
for microcomputers, typewriters, copying machines, calculators, and so on.
(The subsidiary ledger concept was discussed and illustrated in Chapter 6.)
Also, a detailed record will normally exist for each item represented in a
subsidiary ledger account. For example, if there is a subsidiary ledger
account for microcomputers, there may be a separate detailed record for
each microcomputer represented in the subsidiary microcomputer ledger
account. Each detailed record should include information such as the following: a description of the asset, identification or serial number, location
of the asset, date of acquisition, cost, estimated salvage value, estimated
useful life, annual depreciation, accumulated depreciation, insurance coverage, repairs, and gain or loss on final disposal of the asset. Illustration
10.10 shows how the detailed record for one particular microcomputer
might appear as of December 31, 1989.

To enhance control over plant and equipment, the identification or serial
number for each asset should be stenciled on or otherwise attached to the
asset. Periodically, a physical inventory should be taken to determine
whether all items shown in the accounting records actually exist, whether
they are where they should be, and whether they are still being used. A
company that does not use detailed records and identification numbers or
take physical inventories may find it difficult to determine whether assets
have been discarded or stolen.

The general ledger control account balance for each major class of plant
and equipment should equal the total of the amounts shown in the subsidiary ledger accounts for that class of plant and equipment. Also, the totals
shown in the detailed records for a specific subsidiary ledger account (such
as microcomputers) should equal the balance of that account. Each time a

Illustration 10.10

Detailed Record of a Specific Plant Asset

```
Item  IBM-PC, 512K                    Insurance coverage:
Id. No.  Z-43806                          United Ins. Co.
Location  Rm. 403, Adm. bldg.             Pol. No. 0052-61481-24
Date acquired  Jan. 1, 1988               Amt. $3,000
Cost  $3,000                         Repairs:
Estimated salvage value    $200        6/13/89          $140
Estimated useful life      4 yrs.
Depreciation per year      $700
Accumulated depreciation:
     12/31/88    $  700             Disposal date  _____
     12/31/89     1,400
     12/31/90   _____             Gain or loss   _____
     12/31/91   _____
```

plant asset is acquired, exchanged, or disposed of, an entry should be posted to both a general ledger control account and the appropriate subsidiary ledger account. The detailed record for the item(s) affected also should be updated.

In this chapter, you learned how to account for plant assets. The next chapter discusses how to record the disposal of plant assets and how to account for natural resources and intangible assets.

■ UNDERSTANDING THE LEARNING OBJECTIVES: CHAPTER 10

1. Recognize the characteristics of plant assets and the initial costs of acquiring plant assets.

    ■ To be classified as a plant asset, an asset must (1) be tangible, (2) have a useful service life of more than one year, and (3) be used in business operations rather than held for resale to a customer.
    ■ In accounting for plant assets, accountants must:
       1. Record the original (acquisition) cost of the asset.
       2. Record the allocation of the asset's original cost to periods of its useful life through the process of depreciation.
       3. Record subsequent expenditures on the asset.
       4. Account for the disposal of the asset.

2. Recognize the four major factors affecting depreciation expense.

    ■ Accountants consider four major factors in computing depreciation: (1) cost of the asset, (2) estimated salvage value of the asset, (3) estimated useful life of the asset, and (4) depreciation method to use in depreciating the asset.

3. Understand the various methods of calculating depreciation expense.

■ **Straight-line method:**
Assigns an equal amount of depreciation to each period. The formula for calculating straight-line depreciation is:

$$\frac{\text{Depreciation}}{\text{per period}} = \frac{\text{Asset cost} - \text{Estimated salvage value}}{\text{Number of accounting periods in estimated useful life}}$$

■ **Units-of-production method:**
Assigns an equal amount of depreciation to each unit of product manufactured by an asset. The units-of-production depreciation formulas are:

$$\frac{\text{Depreciation}}{\text{per unit}} = \frac{\text{Asset cost} - \text{Estimated salvage value}}{\text{Estimated total units of production (or service) during useful life of asset}}$$

$$\frac{\text{Depreciation}}{\text{per period}} = \frac{\text{Depreciation}}{\text{per unit}} \times \frac{\text{Number of units of goods}}{\text{or services produced}}$$

■ **Sum-of-the-years'-digits (SOYD) method:**
SOYD is an accelerated depreciation method. The SOYD depreciation formulas are:

$$\frac{\text{Periodic}}{\text{depreciation expense}} = \frac{\text{Number of years remaining at beginning of accounting period}}{\text{SOYD}} \times \left(\frac{\text{Asset}}{\text{cost}} - \frac{\text{Estimated}}{\text{salvage value}}\right)$$

$$\text{Sum-of-the-years'-digits (SOYD)} = \frac{n(n+1)}{2}$$

■ **Double-declining-balance method:**
DDB is an accelerated depreciation method. Salvage value is ignored in making annual calculations. The formula for DDB depreciation is:

$$\frac{\text{Depreciation}}{\text{expense}} = (2 \times \text{Straight-line rate}) \times \left(\frac{\text{Asset}}{\text{cost}} - \frac{\text{Accumulated}}{\text{depreciation}}\right)$$

4. Distinguish between capital and revenue expenditures for plant assets.

■ Capital expenditures are debited to an asset account or an accumulated depreciation account and increase the book value of plant assets. Expenditures that increase the quality of services or extend the quantity of services beyond the original estimate are considered to be capital expenditures.

■ Revenue expenditures are expensed immediately and reported in the income statement as expenses. Recurring and/or minor expenditures that neither add to the asset's quality of service-rendering abilities nor extend its quantity of services beyond the asset's original estimated useful life are treated as expenses.

5. Understand the subsidiary records used to control plant assets.

    ▪ Subsidiary plant asset ledgers contain detailed information about each item in a major class of depreciable plant assets that cannot be maintained in the general ledger account.

    ▪ Control over plant and equipment is enhanced by subsidiary plant asset ledgers and other detailed records. Information in a detailed record may include a description of the asset, identification or serial number, location of the asset, date of acquisition, cost, estimated salvage value, estimated useful life, annual depreciation, accumulated depreciation, insurance coverage, repairs, and gain or loss on final disposal of the asset. A periodic physical inventory should be taken to determine whether items in accounting records actually exist.

6. Define and use correctly the new terms in the glossary.

NEW TERMS INTRODUCED IN CHAPTER 10

Accelerated depreciation methods Record higher amounts of depreciation in the early years of an asset's life and lower amounts in later years (430).

Acquisition cost Amount of cash and/or cash equivalent given up to acquire a plant asset and place it in operating condition at its proper location (422).

Appraised value An expert's opinion as to what an item's market price would be if the item were sold (426).

Betterments (improvements) Capital expenditures that are properly charged to asset accounts because they add to the service-rendering ability of the assets; they increase the quality of services that can be obtained from an asset (436).

Book value As asset's recorded cost less its accumulated depreciation (426).

Capital expenditures Expenditures that are debited to an asset account or to an accumulated depreciation account (436).

Depreciation The amount of plant asset cost allocated to each period benefiting from the plant asset's use (427). The **straight-line depreciation** method charges an equal amount of plant asset cost to each period (429). The **units-of-production depreciation** method assigns an equal amount of depreciation for each unit of product manufactured or service rendered by an asset (430). The **sum-of-the-years'-digits** (SOYD) (430) and

the **double-declining-balance** (DDB) (431) methods assign decreasing amounts of depreciation to successive periods of time.

Extraordinary repairs Expenditures that are viewed as canceling a part of the existing accumulated depreciation because they increase the quantity of services expected from an asset (437).

Fair market value The normal price that would be paid for an item being sold in the normal course of business (not at a forced liquidation sale) (426).

Inadequacy The inability of a plant asset to produce enough products or provide enough services to meet current demands (427).

Land improvements Attachments to land, such as driveways, landscaping, parking lots, fences, lighting systems, and sprinkler systems, that have limited lives and therefore are depreciable (423).

Obsolescence Decline in usefulness of an asset brought about by inventions and technological progress (427).

Physical deterioration Results from use of the asset—wear and tear—and the action of the elements (427).

Plant and equipment A shorter title for property, plant, and equipment; also called *plant assets*. Included are land and manufactured or constructed assets such as buildings, machinery, vehicles, and furniture (420).

Revenue expenditures Expenditures (on a plant asset) that are immediately expensed (436).

Salvage value The amount of money the company expects to recover, less disposal costs, on the date a plant asset is scrapped, sold, or traded in. Also called *scrap or residual value* (427).

Useful life Refers to the length of time the company owning the asset intends to use it (427).

DEMONSTRATION PROBLEM 10-1

Morgan Company purchased a 2-square-mile farm under the following terms: cash paid, $405,000; mortgage note assumed, $200,000; and accrued interest on mortgage note assumed, $5,000. The company paid $46,000 for brokerage and legal services to acquire the property and secure clear title. Morgan planned to subdivide the property into residential lots and to construct homes on these lots. Clearing and leveling costs of $18,000 were paid. Crops on the land were sold for $12,000. A house on the land, to be moved by the buyer of the house, was sold for $4,200. The other buildings were torn down at a cost of $8,000, and salvaged material was sold for $8,400.

Approximately 6 acres of the land were deeded to the township for roads, and another 10 acres were deeded to the local school district as the site for a future school. After the subdivision was completed, this land would have an approximate value of $6,400 per acre. The company secured a total of 1,200 salable lots from the remaining land.

Required: Present a schedule showing in detail the composition of the cost of the 1,200 salable lots.

Solution to demonstration problem 10-1

MORGAN COMPANY
Schedule of Cost of 1,200 Residential Lots

Costs incurred:
Cash paid	$405,000	
Mortgage note assumed	200,000	
Interest accrued on mortgage note assumed	5,000	
Broker and legal services	46,000	
Clearing and leveling costs	18,000	
Tearing down costs	8,000	$682,000

Less proceeds from sale of:
Crops	$ 12,000	
House	4,200	
Salvaged materials	8,400	24,600
Net cost of land to be subdivided into 1,200 lots		$657,400

DEMONSTRATION PROBLEM 10-2

Troy Company acquired and put into use a machine on January 1, 1991, at a total cost of $41,000. The machine was estimated to have a useful life of 10 years and a scrap value of $1,000. It was also estimated that the machine would produce one million units of product during its life. The machine produced 90,000 units in 1991 and 125,000 units in 1992.

Required: Compute the amounts of depreciation to be recorded in 1991 and 1992 under each of the following:

a.   Straight-line method.
b.   Units-of-production method.
c.   Sum-of-the-years'-digits method.
d.   Double-declining-balance method.
e.   Assume 30,000 units were produced in the first quarter of 1993. Compute depreciation for this quarter under each of the four methods.

Solution to demonstration problem 10–2

a.   Straight-line method:

1990: ($41,000 − $1,000)/10 = $4,000
1991: ($41,000 − $1,000)/10 = $4,000

b.   Units-of-production method:

1990: [($41,000 − $1,000)/1,000,000] × 90,000 = $3,600
1991: [($41,000 − $1,000)/1,000,000] × 125,000 = $5,000

c.   Sum-of-the-years'-digits method:

1990: ($41,000 − $1,000) × 10/55 = $7,272.73
1991: ($41,000 − $1,000) × 9/55 = $6,545.45

d.   Double-declining-balance method:

1990: $41,000 × 20% = $8,200
1991: ($41,000 − $8,200) × 20% = $6,560

e.   Straight-line: ($41,000 − $1,000)/10 × 1/4 = $1,000
Units-of-production: (30,000 × $0.04) = $1,200
Sum-of-the-years'-digits: ($41,000 − $1,000) × 8/55 × 1/4 = $1,454.55
Double-declining-balance: ($41,000 − $8,200 − $6,560) × 0.2 × 1/4 = $1,312

QUESTIONS

1.   What is the main distinction between inventory and a plant asset?

2.   Which of the following items are properly classifiable as plant assets on the balance sheet?

   a.   Advertising to inform the public about new energy-saving programs at a manufacturing plant.
   b.   A truck acquired by a manufacturing company to be used to deliver the company's products to wholesalers.
   c.   An automobile acquired by an insurance company to be used by one of its salespersons.
   d.   Adding machines acquired by an office supply company to be resold to customers.
   e.   The cost of constructing and paving a driveway that has a useful life of 10 years.

3.   In general terms, what does the cost of a plant asset include?

4.   In any exchange of noncash assets, the accountant's task is to find the most appropriate valuation

for the asset received. What is the general rule for determining the most appropriate valuation in such a situation?

5. Why should periodic depreciation be recorded on all plant assets except land?

6. Define the terms *inadequacy* and *obsolescence* as used in accounting for plant and equipment.

7. What four factors must be known to compute depreciation on a plant asset? How *objective* is the calculation of depreciation?

8. A friend, Sara Jones, tells you her car depreciated $2,500 last year. Explain whether her concept of depreciation is the same as the accountant's concept.

9. What does the term *accelerated depreciation* mean? Give an example showing how depreciation is accelerated.

10. Provide a theoretical reason to support using an accelerated depreciation method.

11. If a machine has an estimated useful life of nine years, what will be the total digits to use in calculating depreciation under the sum-of-the-years'-digits method? How is this figure used in the depreciation calculation?

12. What does the balance in the accumulated depreciation account represent? Does this balance represent cash that can be used to replace the related plant asset when it is completely depreciated?

13. What is the justification for reporting plant assets on the balance sheet at undepreciated cost (book value) rather than market value?

14. Distinguish between *capital expenditures* and *revenue expenditures.*

15. For each of the following, state whether the expenditure made should be charged to an expense, an asset, or an accumulated depreciation account:

a. Cost of installing air-conditioning equipment in a building that was not air conditioned.
b. Painting of an owned factory building every other year.
c. Cost of replacing the roof on a 10-year-old building that was purchased new and has an estimated total life of 40 years. The expenditure did not extend the life of the asset beyond the original estimate.
d. Cost of repairing an electric motor. The expenditure extended the estimated useful life beyond the original estimate.

16. Indicate which type of account (asset, accumulated depreciation, or expense) would be debited for each of the following expenditures:

a. Painting an office building at a cost of $400. The building is painted every year.
b. Adding on a new plant wing at a cost of $10,000.
c. Expanding a paved parking lot at a cost of $60,000.
d. Replacing a stairway with an escalator at a cost of $16,000.
e. Replacing the transmission in an automobile at a cost of $600, thus extending its useful life two years beyond the original estimate.
f. Replacing a broken fan belt at a cost of $150.

17. How do subsidiary records provide control over a company's plant assets?

18. What advantages can accrue to a company that maintains subsidiary plant asset records?

EXERCISES

E-1
Determine cost of land

Brown Company paid $200,000 cash for a tract of land on which it planned to erect a new warehouse, and paid $2,500 in legal fees related to the purchase. Brown also agreed to assume responsibility for $8,000 of unpaid taxes on the property. The company incurred a cost of $9,000 to remove an old apartment building from the land.

Prepare a schedule showing the cost of the land acquired.

E-2
Determine cost of machine

Lark Company purchased a heavy machine to be used in its factory for $150,000, less a 2% cash discount. The company paid a fine of $750 because an employee hauled the machine over city streets without securing the required permits. The machine was installed at a cost of $4,500, and testing costs of $1,500 were incurred to place the machine in operation.

Prepare a schedule showing the recorded cost of the machine.

E-3
Determine cost of land and building when acquired together

Drake Company paid $350,000 cash for real property consisting of a tract of land and a building. The company intended to remodel and use the old building. To allocate the cost of the property acquired, Drake had the property appraised. The appraised values were as follows: land, $240,000; and office building, $160,000. The cost of clearing the land was $7,500. The building was remodeled at a cost of $32,000. The cost of a new identical office building was estimated to be $180,000.

Prepare a schedule showing the cost of the assets acquired.

E-4
Record cost of office equipment, depreciation, and maintenance expense

Ace Company purchased some office equipment for $6,200 cash on March 1, 1990. Cash of $100 was paid for freight costs incurred. The furniture is being depreciated over four years under the straight-line method, assuming a salvage value of $300. The company employs a calendar-year accounting period. On July 1, 1991, $40 was spent to refinish the furniture.

Prepare journal entries for the Ace Company to record all of the above data, including the annual depreciation adjustments through 1991.

E-5
Determine cost of machine of noncash acquisition

A machine is acquired in exchange for 50 shares of Jobe Corporation capital stock. The stock recently traded at $160 per share. The machine cost $12,000 three years ago. At what amount should the machine be recorded?

E-6
Compute annual depreciation for two years under each of four different methods

On January 2, 1990, a new machine was acquired for $360,000. The machine has an estimated salvage value of $30,000 and an estimated useful life of 10 years. The machine is expected to produce a total of 500,000 units of product throughout its useful life. Compute depreciation for 1990 and 1991 using each of the following methods:

a.   Straight-line.
b.   Units-of-production (assume 30,000 and 60,000 units were produced in 1990 and 1991, respectively).
c.   Sum-of-the-years'-digits.
d.   Double-declining-balance.

E-7
Compute DDB depreciation

Farmer Company purchased a machine for $400 and incurred installation costs of $100. The estimated salvage value of the machine is $25. The machine has an estimated useful life of four years.

Compute the annual depreciation charges for this machine under the double-declining-balance method.

E-8
Compute depreciation before and after revision of expected salvage value

Spring Company acquired a delivery truck on January 2, 1990, for $33,500. The truck had an estimated salvage value of $1,500 and an estimated useful life of eight years. At the beginning of 1993, a revised estimate shows that the truck has a remaining useful life of six years. The estimated salvage value changed to $500.

Compute the depreciation charge for 1990 and the revised depreciation charge for 1993 using the straight-line method.

E-9
Allocate periodic depreciation to building and to expense

Assume that the truck described in Exercise E-8 was used 40% of the time in 1991 to haul materials used in the construction of a building by Spring Company for its own use. (Remember that 1991 is before the revision was made on estimated life.) During the remaining time, the truck was used to deliver merchandise sold by Spring to its customers.

Prepare the journal entry to record straight-line depreciation on the truck for 1991.

E-10
Compute depreciation under SOYD and DDB methods

Wilson Company purchased a machine on April 1, 1990, for $30,000. The machine has an estimated useful life of five years with no expected salvage value. The company's accounting year ends on December 31.

Compute the depreciation expense for 1991 under (a) the sum-of-the-years'-digits method and (b) the double-declining-balance method.

E-11
Compute straight-line depreciation after major overhaul

On January 2, 1990, a company purchased and placed in operation a new machine at a total cost of $12,000. Depreciation was recorded on the machine for 1990 and 1991 under the straight-line method using an estimated useful life of five years and no expected salvage value. Early in 1992, the machine was overhauled at a cost of $4,000. The useful life of the machine was revised upward to a total of seven years.

Compute the depreciation expense on the machine for 1992.

E-12
Compute straight-line depreciation given reduced estimated life and salvage value

Lapp Company purchased a computer for $25,000 and placed it in operation on January 2, 1989. Depreciation was recorded for 1989 and 1990 using the straight-line method, a six-year life, and an expected salvage value of $1,000. The introduction of a new model of this computer caused the company in 1991 to revise its estimate of useful life to a total of four years and to reduce the estimated salvage value to zero.

Compute the depreciation expense on the computer for 1991.

E-13
Compute error in net income when installation and freight costs are expensed

Grant Company purchased a machine on January 3, 1990, at a cost of $30,000. Freight and installation charges of $6,000 were incurred and debited to Repairs Expense. Straight-line depreciation was recorded on the machine in 1990 and 1991 using an estimated life of 10 years and no expected salvage value.

Compute the amount of the error in net income for 1990 and 1991, and state whether net income is understated or overstated.

E-14
Determine information concerning machinery

Drake Company finds its company records are incomplete concerning a piece of machinery used in its plant. According to the company records, the machinery has a useful life of 10 years and a salvage value of $5,000. $2,500 has been depreciated each year using the straight-line method. If the Accumulated Depreciation account shows a balance of $15,000, what is the original cost of the machinery and how many years remain to be depreciated?

E-15
Determine the effect of an error in classification

Jolly Company owns a plant asset that originally cost $50,000 in 1987. The asset has been depreciated for three years assuming an 8-year useful life and no salvage value. Jolly capitalized $25,000 in repairs on the plant asset rather than expensing them. Describe the impact of this error on the asset's cost and Jolly's net income over the next five years.

PROBLEMS, SERIES A

P10-1-A
Determine cost of land

In seeking a site for its new home office building, Short Company paid a local realtor $3,000 to find the appropriate location. Short agreed to pay the owner of the site $50,000 cash, to assume responsibility for a $20,000 mortgage note on the property and $300 of accrued interest on the note, and to pay back taxes of $800 on the property. Short also paid legal fees of $400 and a $500 title insurance premium in acquiring the property. A local salvage company paid Short $9,000 for a building that it moved from the property. In addition, Short paid the city $8,000 to extend water mains and sewer lines to the property.

Required: Prepare a schedule showing the amount to be recorded as the cost of the land.

P10-2-A
Determine cost of machine

Zorn Company purchased a machine for use in its operations that had a gross invoice price of $10,000 excluding sales tax. A 4% sales tax was levied on the sale. The company estimated the total cost of hauling the machine from the dealer's warehouse to the company's plant at $700, which did not include a fine of $200 for failure to secure the necessary permits to use city streets in transporting the machine. In delivering the machine to its plant, a Zorn employee damaged the truck used; repairs cost $450. The machine was also slightly damaged with repair costs amounting to $200.

Zorn incurred installation costs of $4,000 that included the $500 cost of shoring up the floor under the machine. Testing costs amounted to $300. Safety guards were installed on the machine at a cost of $80, and the machine was placed in operation.

Required: Prepare a schedule showing the amount at which the machine should be recorded in Zorn's accounts.

P10-3-A
Determine cost of land and building

Greene Company planned to erect a new factory building and a new office building in Atlanta, Georgia. A report on a suitable site showed an appraised value of $75,000 for land and orchard and $50,000 for a building.

After considerable negotiation, the company and the owner reached the following agreement. Greene Company was to pay $90,000 in cash, assume a $37,500 mortgage note on the property, assume the interest of $800 accrued on the mortgage note, and assume unpaid property taxes of $5,500. Greene Company paid $7,500 cash for brokerage and legal services in acquiring the property.

Shortly after acquisition of the property, Greene Company sold the fruit on the trees for $1,100, remodeled the building into an office building at a cost of $16,000, and removed the trees from the land at a cost of $3,750. Construction of the factory building was to begin in a week.

Required: Prepare schedules showing the proper valuation of the assets acquired by Greene Company.

P10-4-A
Prepare entry for acquisition of machine, for depreciation under DDB, and for straight-line depreciation assuming change in estimated life

York Company acquired and placed into use a heavy factory machine on October 1, 1990. The machine had an invoice price of $288,000, but the company received a 3% cash discount by paying the bill on the date of acquisition. An employee of York Company hauled the machine down a city street without a permit. As a result, the company had to pay a $1,200 fine. Installation and testing costs totaled $28,640. The machine is estimated to have a $28,000 salvage value and a seven-year useful life. A fraction should be used for the DDB calculation rather than a decimal.

Required:
a. Prepare the journal entry to record the acquisition of the machine.
b. Prepare the journal entry to record depreciation for 1990 under the double-declining-balance method.
c. Now assume that the straight-line depreciation method is being used and that at the beginning of 1993 it is estimated the machine will last another six years. Prepare the journal entry to record depreciation for 1993. The estimated salvage value will not change.

P10-5-A
Compute cost of land, land improvements, building, and machinery; prepare entry to correct the accounts

Spartan Company has the following entries in its Building account:

			Debits	
1990				
May	5	Cost of land and building purchased		$125,000
	5	Broker fees incident to purchase of land and building		7,500
1991				
Jan.	3	Contract price of new wing added to south		52,500
	15	Cost of new machinery, estimated life 10 years		100,000
June	10	Real estate taxes for six months ended 6/30/91		2,250
Aug.	10	Cost of building parking lot for employees in back of building		3,100
Sept.	6	Replacement of windows broken in August		100
Oct.	10	Repairs due to regular usage		1,400

Credits

1990
May 24 Transfer to Land account, per allocation of purchase cost authorized in minutes of board of directors $20,000

1991
Jan. 5 Proceeds from lease of second floor for six months ended 12/31/90   5,000

The original property was acquired on May 5, 1990. Spartan Company immediately engaged a contractor to construct a new wing on the south end of the building. While the new wing was being constructed, the company leased the second floor as temporary warehouse space to Charles Company. During this period (July 1 to December 31, 1990), the company installed new machinery costing $100,000 on the first floor of the building. Regular operations began on January 2, 1991.

Required:
a. Compute the correct balance for the Building account as of December 31, 1991. The company employs a calendar-year accounting period.
b. Prepare the necessary journal entries to correct the records of Spartan Company at December 31, 1991. No depreciation entries are required.

P10-6-A
Compute depreciation for first year under each of four different methods

Noel Company acquired and placed into use equipment on January 2, 1990, at a cash cost of $748,000. Transportation charges amounted to $6,000, and installation and testing costs totaled $44,000.

The equipment was estimated to have a useful life of nine years and a salvage value of $30,000 at the end of its life. It was further estimated that the equipment would be used in the production of 1,920,000 units of product during its life. During 1990, 426,000 units of product were produced.

Required: Compute the depreciation for the year ended December 31, 1990, using:

a. Straight-line method.
b. Units-of-production method.
c. Sum-of-the-years'-digits method.
d. Double-declining-balance method.

P10-7-A
Compute depreciation for two years using three methods; partial-year depreciation used first year

Alton Company purchased a machine on October 1, 1990, for $40,000. The machine has an estimated salvage value of $12,000 and an estimated useful life of eight years.

Required: Compute the amount of depreciation to the nearest dollar Alton should record on the machine for the years ending December 31, 1990, and 1991, under each of the following methods:

a. Straight-line.
b. Sum-of-the-years'-digits.
c. Double-declining-balance.

PROBLEMS, SERIES B

P10-1-B
Determine cost of land

Ralph Company paid a local realtor $1,000 to find a suitable site for its new factory. When found, Ralph agreed to pay the owner of the site $15,000 cash, to assume responsibility for a $5,000 mortgage note on the property and $100 of accrued interest on the note, and to pay back taxes of $250 on the property. Ralph also paid legal fees of $125 and a $150 title insurance premium in acquiring the property. A local lumber yard paid Ralph $200 for some walnut trees that it removed from the property. Ralph also paid the city $1,750 to widen the street in front of the property and received $500 for a narrow strip of land deeded to the city in order to widen the street. Grading and leveling costs of $750 were also incurred by Ralph.

Required: Prepare a schedule showing the amount to be recorded as the cost of the land.

P10–2–B
Determine cost of machine

Walton Company purchased a machine for use in its operations that had a gross invoice price of $80,000 excluding sales tax. A 4% sales tax was levied on the sale. The company paid freight costs of $2,000. Special electrical connections were run to the machine at a cost of $2,800, and a special reinforced base for the machine was built at a cost of $3,600. The machine was dropped and damaged while being mounted on this base. Repairs cost $800. Raw materials with a cost of $200 were consumed in testing the machine. Safety guards were installed on the machine at a cost of $280, and the machine was placed in operation. In addition, $100 was incurred in removing an old machine.

Required: Prepare a schedule showing the amount at which the machine should be recorded in Walton Company's account.

P10–3–B
Determine cost of land

Tolbert Company purchased 2 square miles of farmland under the following terms: $605,000 cash; and liability assumed on mortgage note of $200,000 and interest accrued on mortgage note assumed, $8,000. The company paid $42,000 of legal and brokerage fees and also paid $2,000 for a title search on the property.

   The company planned to use the land as a site for a new office building and a new factory. Clearing and leveling costs of $18,000 were paid. Crops on the land were sold for $4,600, and one of the houses on the property was sold for $12,000. The other buildings were torn down at a cost of $9,000; sale of salvaged materials yielded cash proceeds of $8,500. Approximately 1% of the land acquired was deeded to the county for roads. The cost of excavating a basement for the office building amounted to $5,700.

Required: Prepare a schedule showing the amount at which the land should be carried on Tolbert Company's books.

P10–4–B
Determine cost of truck; prepare entry for depreciation under DDB and for straight-line depreciation assuming change in estimated life

Brambley Company purchased a used panel truck for $9,000 cash. The next day the company's name and business were painted on the truck at a total cost of $465. The truck was then given a minor overhaul at a cost of $60, and new tires were mounted on the truck at a cost of $600, less a trade-in allowance of $75 for the old tires. The truck was placed in service on April 1, 1990, at which time it had an estimated useful life of five years and a salvage value of $1,050.

Required: a. Prepare a schedule showing the cost to be recorded for the truck.
             b. Prepare the journal entry needed to record depreciation at the end of the calendar-year accounting period, December 31, 1990. Use the double-declining-balance method.
             c. Now assume that the straight-line depreciation method is being used and that at the beginning of 1993 it is estimated the truck will last another four years. The estimated salvage value changed to $600. Prepare the entry to record depreciation for 1993.

P10-5-B
Compute cost of land, land improvements, building, and machinery; prepare entry to correct the accounts

You are the new controller for Blake Company, which began operations on October 1, 1990, after a "start-up" period that ran from the middle of 1989. While reviewing the accounts, you find an account entitled "Fixed Assets," which contains the following items:

Cash paid to previous owner of land and old building	$ 80,000
Cash given to construction company as partial payment for the new building	30,000
Legal and title search fees	1,000
Real estate commission	6,000
Cost of demolishing old building	7,000
Cost of leveling and grading	4,000
Architect's fee (90% building and 10% improvements)	15,000
Cost of excavating basement for new building	9,000
Cash paid to construction company for new building	120,000
Repair damage done by vandals	3,000
Sprinkler system for lawn	13,000
Lighting system for parking lot	17,000
Paving of parking lot	25,000
Net invoice price of machinery	480,000
Freight cost incurred on machinery	21,000
Installation and testing of machinery	8,000
Medical bill paid for employee injured in installing machinery	1,500
Landscaping (permanent)	16,000
Repair damage to building in installation of machinery	2,000
Special assessment paid to city for water mains and sewer line	19,000
Account balance	$877,500

In addition to the above, you discover that cash receipts of $500 from selling materials salvaged from the old building were credited to Miscellaneous Revenues in 1990. Digging deeper, you find that the plant manager spent all of his time for the first nine months of 1990 supervising installation of land improvements (10%), building construction (40%), and installation of machinery (50%). The plant manager's nine-month salary of $45,000 was debited to Officers' Salaries Expense.

Required:
a. List the above items on a form containing columns for Land, Land Improvements, Building, and Machinery. Sort the items into the appropriate columns, omitting those items not properly included as an element of asset cost. Show negative amounts in parentheses. Total your columns.

b. Prepare one compound journal entry to reclassify and adjust the accounts and to eliminate the Fixed Assets account. Do not attempt to record depreciation for the partial year.

P10-6-B
Compute depreciation for first year under each of four different methods

Vincent Company acquired and put into use a machine on January 1, 1990, at a cash cost of $24,000 and immediately spent $1,000 to install it. The machine was estimated to have a useful life of eight years and a scrap value of $5,000 at the end of this time. It was further estimated that the machine would produce 500,000 units of product during its life. In the first year, the machine produced 100,000 units.

Required: Prepare journal entries to record depreciation for 1990, using:

a. Straight-line method.
b. Units-of-production method.
c. Sum-of-the-years'-digits method.
d. Double-declining-balance method.

P10-7-B
Compute depreciation for two years using three methods; partial-year depreciation used first year

Connors Company paid $24,000 for a machine on April 1, 1990, and placed it in use on that same date. The machine has an estimated life of 10 years and an estimated salvage value of $4,000.

Required:

Compute the amount of depreciation to the nearest dollar the company should record on this asset for the years ending December 31, 1990, and 1991, under each of the following methods:

a. Straight-line.
b. Sum-of-the-years'-digits.
c. Double-declining-balance.

BUSINESS DECISION PROBLEM 10-1

Compute correct cost of land, building, and land improvements; compute depreciation; prepare entry to correct the accounts

Martin Company has the following entries in its Building account:

Debits

1990			
Jan.	2	Cost of land and old buildings purchased	$450,000
	2	Legal fees incident to purchase	6,000
	2	Fee for title search	750
	12	Cost of demolishing old buildings on land	12,000
June	16	Cost of insurance during construction of new building	3,000
July	30	Payment to contractor on completion of new building	675,000
Aug.	5	Architect's fees for design of new building	30,000
Sept.	15	City assessment for sewers and sidewalks (considered permanent)	10,500
Oct.	6	Cost of landscaping (considered permanent)	6,000
Nov.	1	Cost of driveways and parking lots	37,500

Credit

Jan.	15	Proceeds received upon sale of salvaged materials from old buildings	3,000

You are in charge of auditing Martin Company's Building account. In addition to the entries in the account, you are given the following information:

1. The company began using the new building on September 1, 1990. The building is estimated to have a 40-year useful life and no salvage value.
2. The company began using the driveways and parking lots on November 1, 1990. The driveways and parking lots are estimated to have a 10-year useful life and no salvage value.
3. The straight-line depreciation method is used to depreciate all of the company's plant assets.

Required:

a. Prepare a schedule that shows separately the cost of land, buildings, and land improvements.
b. Compute the amount of depreciation expense for 1990.
c. What journal entries are required to correct the accounts at December 31, 1990? Assume that closing entries have not been made.

BUSINESS DECISION PROBLEM 10-2

Compute partial-year depreciation under each of four different methods; cite circumstances in which each of the different methods seems most appropriate

On October 1, 1991, Gordon Company acquired and placed into use new equipment costing $210,000. The equipment has a useful life of five years and an estimated salvage value of $10,000. It is estimated that the equipment will produce 2,000,000 units of product during its life. In the last quarter of 1991, the equipment produced 120,000 units of product.

Required: a.   Compute the depreciation for the last quarter of 1991, using each of the following methods:

1. Straight-line.
2. Units-of-production.
3. Sum-of-the-years'-digits.
4. Double-declining-balance.

b.   Describe the conditions in which each of the above four methods would be most appropriate.

BUSINESS DECISION PROBLEM (ETHICS) 10-3

Determine the effect of a change in depreciation methods

The Apex Steel Company has been using sum-of-the-years'-digits depreciation method for its fixed assets acquired five years ago. The resulting pattern of depreciation seemed to match well with the pattern of revenues that would result from use of the assets. The estimated useful life of the assets is 25 years. During the current year, the industry had been severely affected by foreign competition and was operating at only 60% of capacity. Prices were falling, and the company would have to start reporting losses unless some way could be found to reduce expenses. Management discovered that by switching to the straight-line method, expenses could be reduced enough to report a small profit this year and probably over the next five years. They considered this a relatively painless way of solving the problem.

Reporting income is important to management since their executive bonuses are tied to net income. As far as management could determine, the straight-line method is completely acceptable. In fact, they discovered that more companies use straight-line for book purposes than any other method.

Required: Do you see anything wrong with the company switching to the straight-line method?

11

Plant Asset Disposals, Natural Resources, and Intangible Assets

After studying this chapter, you should be able to:

1. Calculate and prepare entries for the sale, retirement, and destruction of plant assets.

2. Describe and record exchanges of dissimilar and similar plant assets.

3. Discuss the differences between accounting principles and tax rules in the treatment of gains and losses from the exchange of plant assets.

4. Determine the periodic depletion cost of a natural resource and calculate depreciation of plant assets located on extractive industry property.

5. Prepare entries for the acquisition and amortization of intangible assets.

6. Define and use correctly the new terms in the glossary.

The study of long-term assets, which includes plant assets, natural resources, and intangible assets, began in Chapter 10. Discussion in that chapter focused on determining plant asset cost, computing depreciation, and distinguishing between capital and revenue expenditures. This chapter begins by discussing the disposal of plant assets. The next topic is accounting for natural resources such as ores, minerals, oil and gas, and timber. The final topic is accounting for intangible assets such as patents, copyrights, franchises, trademarks and trade names, and leases.

Although several different long-term assets are discussed in this chapter, you will see that accounting for all long-term assets is basically the same. When a company purchases a long-term asset, the asset is recorded at cost. As the company receives benefits from the asset and the future service potential is reduced, the cost is transferred from an asset account to an expense account. Finally, the asset is sold, retired, or traded in on a new asset. Since the lives of long-term assets can extend for many years, the methods accountants use in reporting those assets can have a dramatic effect on the financial statements of many accounting periods.

■ DISPOSAL OF PLANT ASSETS

All plant assets except land eventually wear out or become inadequate or obsolete and must be sold, retired, or traded in on new assets. When a new plant asset is disposed of, both the asset's cost and accumulated depreciation must be removed from the accounts. Overall, then, all asset disposals have the following in common:

1. The asset's depreciation must be brought up to date.
2. To record the disposal, you must:
   a. Write off the asset's cost.
   b. Write off the accumulated depreciation.
   c. Record any consideration (usually cash) received or to be received.
   d. Record gain or loss on disposal.

As you study this section, remember these common procedures used by accountants to record the disposal of all plant assets. In the paragraphs that follow, we discuss accounting for the (1) sale of plant assets, (2) retirement of plant assets without sale, (3) destruction of plant assets, (4) exchange of plant assets, and (5) cost of dismantling and removing plant assets.

Sale of Plant Assets

Objective 1: Calculate and prepare entries for the sale, retirement, and destruction of plant assets.

Companies frequently dispose of plant assets by selling them. By comparing an asset's book value (cost less accumulated depreciation) with its sales price (or net amount realized if there are selling expenses), the company will show either a gain or loss. If the sales price is greater than the asset's book value, the company will show a gain. If the sales price is less than the asset's book value, the company will show a loss. Of course, if the sales price is equal to the asset's book value, there is no gain or loss.

To illustrate accounting for the sale of a plant asset, assume equipment costing $45,000 with accumulated depreciation of $14,000 is sold for $35,000. A gain of $4,000 is realized as computed below:

Equipment cost	$45,000
Accumulated depreciation	14,000
Book value	$31,000
Sales price	35,000
Gain realized	$ 4,000

The journal entry to record the sale is:

Cash	35,000	
Accumulated Depreciation—Equipment	14,000	
Equipment		45,000
Gain on Disposal of Plant Assets		4,000
To record sale of equipment at a price greater than book value.		

If on the other hand, the equipment is sold for $28,000, a loss of $3,000 ($31,000 book value − $28,000 sales price) is realized, and the journal entry to record the sale is:

Cash	28,000	
Accumulated Depreciation—Equipment	14,000	
Loss on Disposal of Plant Assets	3,000	
Equipment		45,000
To record sale of equipment at a price less than book value.		

If the equipment is sold for $31,000, there is no gain or loss; and the journal entry to record the sale is:

Cash	31,000	
Accumulated Depreciation—Equipment	14,000	
Equipment		45,000
To record sale of equipment at a price equal to book value.		

Accounting for Depreciation to Date of Disposal.   When a plant asset is sold or otherwise disposed of, it is important to record the depreciation up to the date of sale or disposal. For example, if an asset is sold on April 1 and depreciation was last recorded on December 31, depreciation for three months (January 1–April 1) should be recorded. If depreciation is not recorded for the three months, operating expenses for that period will be understated, and the gain on the sale of the asset will be understated or the loss overstated.

To illustrate, assume that on August 1, 1992, Ray Company sold a machine for $1,500. The machine cost $12,000 and was being depreciated at the straight-line rate of 10% per year. As of December 31, 1991, after closing entries were made, the machine's accumulated depreciation account had a balance of $9,600. Before a gain or loss can be determined and before an entry can be made to record the sale, the following entry must be made to record depreciation for the seven months ended July 31, 1992:

July 31	Depreciation Expense—Machinery	700	
	Accumulated Depreciation—Machinery		700
	To record depreciation for seven months		
	($12,000 × 0.10 × 7/12).		

The $200 loss on the sale is computed as shown below:

Machine cost	$12,000
Accumulated depreciation ($9,600 + $700) . . .	10,300
Book value	$ 1,700
Sales price	1,500
Loss realized	$ 200

The journal entry to record the sale is:

```
Cash . . . . . . . . . . . . . . . . . . . . . . . . . . . . . . . . .    1,500
Accumulated Depreciation—Machinery . . . . . . . . . . . . . .   10,300
Loss on Disposal of Plant Assets . . . . . . . . . . . . . . . .      200
   Machinery . . . . . . . . . . . . . . . . . . . . . . . . . . . .              12,000
      To record sale of machinery at a price less than book value.
```

Retirement of Plant Assets without Sale

When a plant asset is retired from productive service, the asset's cost and accumulated depreciation must be removed from the plant asset accounts. For example, Hayes Company would make the following journal entry when a fully depreciated machine that cost $15,000 and had no salvage value is retired:

```
Accumulated Depreciation—Machinery . . . . . . . . . . . . . .   15,000
   Machinery . . . . . . . . . . . . . . . . . . . . . . . . . . . .              15,000
      To record the retirement of a fully depreciated machine.
```

Occasionally, a plant asset is continued in use after it has been fully depreciated. In such a case, the asset's cost and accumulated depreciation should **not** be removed from the accounts until the asset is sold, traded, or retired from service. Of course, no more depreciation can be recorded on a fully depreciated asset because total depreciation expense taken on an asset may never exceed the asset's cost.

Sometimes a plant asset is retired from service or discarded before it is fully depreciated. If the asset is to be sold as scrap (even if not immediately), its cost and accumulated depreciation should be removed from the asset and accumulated depreciation accounts. In addition, its estimated salvage value should be recorded in a Salvaged Materials account, and a gain or loss on disposal should be recognized. To illustrate, assume a machine with a $10,000 original cost and $7,500 of accumulated depreciation is retired. If the machine's estimated salvage value is $500, the following entry is required:

```
Salvaged Materials . . . . . . . . . . . . . . . . . . . . . . . . .      500
Accumulated Depreciation—Machinery . . . . . . . . . . . . . .    7,500
Loss on Disposal of Plant Assets . . . . . . . . . . . . . . . .    2,000
   Machinery . . . . . . . . . . . . . . . . . . . . . . . . . . . .              10,000
      To record retirement of machinery, which will be sold for scrap at
      a later time.
```

Destruction of Plant Assets

Plant assets are sometimes wrecked in accidents or destroyed by fire, flood, storm, or other causes. Losses are normally incurred in such situations. For example, assume that an **uninsured** building costing $40,000 with accumulated depreciation of $12,000 was completely destroyed by a fire. The journal entry is:

```
Fire Loss . . . . . . . . . . . . . . . . . . . . . . . . . . . . . .   28,000
Accumulated Depreciation—Building . . . . . . . . . . . . . . .   12,000
   Building . . . . . . . . . . . . . . . . . . . . . . . . . . . . . .              40,000
      To record fire loss.
```

If the building was **insured,** only the amount of the fire loss exceeding the amount to be recovered from the insurance company would be debited to the Fire Loss account. To illustrate, assume that in the example above, the building was partially insured and that $22,000 is recoverable from the insurance company. The journal entry is:

Receivable from Insurance Company	22,000	
Fire Loss	6,000	
Accumulated Depreciation—Building	12,000	
Building		40,000

To record fire loss and amount recovered from insurance company.

Exchanges of Plant Assets (Nonmonetary Assets)

Nonmonetary assets are those items whose price may change over time, such as inventories, property, plant, and equipment. In accounting for the exchange of nonmonetary assets, ordinarily the recorded amount should be based on the fair value of the asset given up or the fair value of the asset received, whichever is more clearly evident. If a gain or loss results from the exchange, the loss is always recognized; the gain may or may not be recognized, depending on whether the asset exchanged is similar or dissimilar in nature.

Similar assets are those of the same general type, that perform the same function, or that are employed in the same line of business. Examples of the exchange of similar assets include a building for a building, a delivery truck for a delivery truck, and equipment for equipment. Conversely, the exchange of dissimilar assets includes a building for land, and equipment for inventory.

In general, losses on nonmonetary assets are always recognized, regardless of whether the assets are similar or dissimilar in nature. Gains are recognized if the assets are dissimilar in nature because the earnings process related to those assets is considered to be completed. With one exception, gains are deferred on the exchange of similar nonmonetary assets. The exception occurs when monetary consideration is received in addition to the similar asset. In this case, a partial gain may be recognized when cash is received along with an asset. Because the specific details of monetary consideration are reserved for an intermediate accounting text, assume in the examples given that cash has been paid, not received. Both gains and losses on the disposal of nonmonetary assets are computed by comparing the book value of the asset given up with the fair value of the asset given up.

The proper accounting for exchanges of dissimilar and similar plant assets is illustrated below.

Objective 2: Describe and record exchanges of dissimilar and similar plant assets.

Exchanges of Dissimilar Plant Assets. Sometimes a machine is traded for a dissimilar plant asset such as a truck. Exchanges of dissimilar plant assets are accounted for by recording the new asset at the fair market value of the asset received or the asset(s) given up, whichever is more clearly evident.[1] The cash price of the new asset may be stated; if so, the cash price

---

[1] APB, "Accounting for Nonmonetary Transactions," *APB Opinion No. 29* (New York: AICPA, May 1973), par. 16.

should be used to record the new asset. If the cash price is not stated, the fair market value of the old asset plus any cash paid is assumed to be the cash price and is used to record the new asset. Thus, the asset received would normally be recorded at either (1) the stated cash price of the new asset or (2) a known fair value of the asset given up plus any cash paid.

The book value of the old asset is removed from the accounts by debiting accumulated depreciation and crediting the old asset. The Cash account is credited for any amount paid. If the amount at which the new asset is recorded exceeds the book value of the old asset plus any cash paid, a gain is recorded to balance the journal entry. If the situation is vice versa, a loss is recorded to balance the journal entry.

To illustrate such an exchange, assume that an old factory machine is exchanged for a new delivery truck. The machine cost $45,000 and had an accumulated depreciation balance of $38,000. The truck had a $55,000 cash price and was acquired by trading in a machine with a fair value of $3,000 and paying $52,000 cash. The journal entry to record the exchange is:

Delivery Truck	55,000	
Accumulated Depreciation—Factory Machinery	38,000	
Loss on Disposal of Plant Assets	4,000	
Factory Machinery		45,000
Cash		52,000
To record loss on exchange of dissimilar plant assets.		

The $4,000 loss on the exchange can also be computed as the book value of the old asset less the fair market value of the old asset. The calculation is as follows:

Machine cost	$45,000
Accumulated depreciation	38,000
Book value	$ 7,000
Fair market value of old asset (trade-in allowance)	3,000
Loss realized	$ 4,000

To illustrate the recognition of a gain from an exchange of dissimilar plant assets, assume that the fair market value of the above machine was $9,000 instead of $3,000, and that $46,000 was paid in cash. The gain would be $2,000 ($9,000 fair market value less $7,000 book value). The journal entry to record the exchange would be:

Delivery Truck	55,000	
Accumulated Depreciation—Factory Machinery	38,000	
Factory Machinery		45,000
Cash		46,000
Gain on Disposal of Plant Assets		2,000
To record gain on exchange of dissimilar plant assets.		

Remember, both gains and losses are always recognized on exchanges of dissimilar plant assets. As shown below, gains on exchanges of similar plant assets may not be recognized.

Exchanges of Similar Plant Assets.   Plant assets such as automobiles, trucks, and office equipment are often exchanged by trading the old asset for a similar new one. When this occurs, the company usually receives a trade-in allowance for the old asset,[2] and the balance is paid in cash. The cash price of the new asset is often stated. If not, the cash price is assumed to be the fair market value of the old asset plus the cash paid.

When similar assets are exchanged, the general rule that new assets are recorded at the fair market value of what is given up or received is modified slightly. The new asset is recorded at (1) the cash price of the asset received or (2) the book value of the old asset plus the cash paid, whichever is lower. When this rule is applied to exchanges of similar assets, **losses are recognized (or recorded), but gains are not.**

To illustrate the accounting for exchanges of similar plant assets, assume $50,000 cash and delivery truck No. 1—which cost $45,000, had $38,000 accumulated depreciation, and had a $5,000 fair market value—were exchanged for delivery truck No. 2. The new truck has a cash price (fair market value) of $55,000. A loss of $2,000 is realized on the exchange.

Cost of delivery truck No. 1	$45,000
Accumulated depreciation	38,000
Book value	$ 7,000
Fair market value of old asset (trade-in allowance)	5,000
Loss on exchange of plant assets	$ 2,000

The journal entry to record the exchange is:

Delivery Trucks (cost of No. 2)	55,000	
Accumulated Depreciation—Delivery Trucks	38,000	
Loss on Disposal of Plant Assets	2,000	
Delivery Trucks (cost of No. 1)		45,000
Cash		50,000
To record loss on exchange of similar plant assets.		

Note that exchanges of similar plant assets are recorded just like exchanges of dissimilar plant assets when a *loss* occurs from the exchange.

Accounting for any gain resulting from exchanges of similar assets is handled differently than a gain resulting from exchanges of dissimilar plant assets. To illustrate, assume that in the preceding example, delivery truck No. 1 (now with a fair market value of $9,000) and $46,000 cash were given in exchange for delivery truck No. 2. A gain of $2,000 is indicated on the exchange:

Cost of delivery truck No. 1	$45,000
Accumulated depreciation	38,000
Book value	$ 7,000
Fair market value of old asset (trade-in allowance)	9,000
Gain indicated	$ 2,000

---

[2] Trade-in allowance is sometimes expressed as the difference between *list* price and cash paid, but we choose to define it as the difference between *cash* price and cash paid because this latter definition seems to agree with current practice for exchange transactions.

The journal entry to record the exchange is:

Delivery Trucks (cost of No. 2)	53,000	
Accumulated Depreciation—Delivery Trucks	38,000	
Delivery Trucks (cost of No. 1)		45,000
Cash		46,000
To record exchange of similar plant assets.		

When similar assets are exchanged, a gain is **not** recognized. The new asset is recorded at book value of the old asset ($7,000) plus cash paid ($46,000). The gain is deducted from the cost of the new asset ($55,000). Thus, the cost basis of the new delivery truck is equal to $55,000 less the $2,000 gain, or $53,000. This $53,000 cost basis is used in recording depreciation on the truck and determining any gain or loss on its disposal.

The justification used by the Accounting Principles Board for not recognizing gains on exchanges of similar plant assets is that "revenue should not be recognized merely because one productive asset is substituted for a similar productive asset but rather should be considered to flow from the production and sale of the goods or services to which the substituted productive asset is committed."[3] In effect, the gain on an exchange of similar plant assets is realized in the form of increased net income resulting from smaller depreciation charges on the newly acquired asset. In the preceding example, annual depreciation expense is less if it is based on the truck's $53,000 cost basis than if it is based on the truck's $55,000 cash price. Thus, future net income per year will be larger.

"**Material**" **gains or losses** are those that are large enough to affect the decisions of an informed user of the financial statements. When material gains or losses are recognized on the disposal of plant assets, they should be reported as a separate item on the income statement.

Objective 3: Discuss the differences between accounting principles and tax rules in the treatment of gains and losses from the exchange of plant assets.

Tax Rules and Plant Asset Exchanges.   The Internal Revenue Code does not allow recognition of **gains or losses** for income tax purposes when similar productive assets are exchanged. For income tax purposes, the cost basis of the new asset is the book value of the old asset plus any additional cash (called **boot**) paid.

Accounting principles and income tax laws agree on the treatment of gains, but they disagree on the treatment of losses. Thus, the previous example involving a $2,000 loss on the exchange of delivery trucks must be recorded as follows for income tax purposes:

Delivery Trucks (cost of No. 2) ($7,000 + $50,000)	57,000	
Accumulated Depreciation—Delivery Trucks	38,000	
Delivery Trucks (cost of No. 1)		45,000
Cash		50,000
To record exchange of similar plant assets using tax method.		

Illustration 11.1 summarizes the rules for recording exchanges of plant assets, both for accounting purposes and for income tax purposes. Studying

---

[3] *APB Opinion No. 29,* par. 16.

Illustration 11.1

Summary of Rules for Recording Exchanges of Plant Assets

	Dissimilar Assets	Similar Assets	
	For Both Accounting and Tax Purposes	**For Accounting Purposes**	**For Tax Purposes**
Recognize Gains?	Yes	No	No
Recognize Losses?	Yes	Yes	No
Record New Asset at:	Cash price of new asset **or** fair market value of old asset plus cash paid	**If loss:** Cash price of new asset **or** fair market value of old asset plus cash paid **If gain:** Book value of old asset plus cash paid	Book value of old asset plus cash paid

this illustration may help you to remember how to record these exchange transactions.

Because of differences between accounting principles and income tax laws, two sets of depreciation records must be kept if a **material** (relatively large) **loss** occurs on an exchange of similar plant assets. One set of depreciation records is based on the accounting valuation of the new asset (cash price of new asset or fair market value of old asset plus cash paid) and is used to determine net income for financial reporting purposes; the second set is based on the tax valuation of the new asset (book value of old asset plus cash paid).

The **materiality concept** allows the accountant to treat immaterial items in a theoretically incorrect manner. Thus, two sets of accounting records do not have to be kept if the loss from an exchange is immaterial. For example, assume a company that earns approximately $1,000,000 per year suffers a $25 loss on an exchange of plant assets. In relation to $1,000,000, $25 is immaterial, and the company need only keep one set of accounting records regarding the exchange and not show the loss.

Removal Costs

Removal costs are incurred to dismantle and remove a company's old plant asset. These costs are deducted from salvage proceeds to determine the asset's net salvage value. Removal costs are associated with the old asset, not a new asset acquired to replace the old asset.

The next section discusses natural resources. Again you will note the underlying accounting principle of matching expenses of an accounting period with the revenues earned in that **same** accounting period.

■ NATURAL RESOURCES

Resources supplied by nature, such as ore deposits, mineral deposits, oil reserves, gas deposits, and timber stands, are known as **natural resources** or **wasting assets.** Natural resources represent inventories of raw materials that can be consumed (exhausted) through extraction or removal from their natural setting (e.g., removing oil from the ground).

On the balance sheet, natural resources are classified as a separate group of noncurrent assets and are given headings such as "Timber stands" or "Oil reserves." Natural resources are typically recorded at their cost of acquisition plus exploration and development cost; they are reported on the balance sheet at total cost less accumulated depletion. (Accumulated depletion is similar to the accumulated depreciation used for plant assets.) When analyzing the financial condition of companies owning natural resources, caution must be exercised because the historical costs reported for the natural resources may only be a small fraction of their current value.

Depletion

Depletion is the exhaustion of a natural resource that results from the physical removal of a part of the resource. In each accounting period, the depletion recognized is an estimate of the cost of the natural resource that was removed from its natural setting during the period. Depletion is recorded by debiting a depletion account and crediting an accumulated depletion account, which is a contra asset account to the natural resource asset account.

By crediting the accumulated depletion account instead of the asset account, the original cost of the entire natural resource continues to be reported on the financial statements, and statement users can see the percentage of the resource that has been removed. This depletion cost is combined with other extraction, mining, or removal costs to determine the total cost of the resource available. This total cost is assigned to either the cost of natural resources sold or the inventory of the natural resource still on hand. Thus, it is possible that all, some, or none of the depletion and removal costs recognized in an accounting period will be expensed in that period, depending on the portion sold. If all of the resource is sold, all of the depletion and removal costs are expensed. The cost of any portion not yet sold will be part of the cost of inventory.

Objective 4: Determine the periodic depletion cost of a natural resource and calculate depreciation of plant assets located on extractive industry property.

Computing Periodic Depletion Cost.   Depletion charges usually are computed by using the units-of-production method. Total cost is divided by the estimated number of units—tons, barrels, or board feet—**that can be economically extracted** from the property. This calculation provides a per unit depletion cost. For example, assume that in 1991 a company paid $650,000 for a tract of land containing an ore deposit. The company spent $100,000 in exploration costs. The results indicated that approximately 900,000 tons of ore can be economically removed from the land, after which the land will be worth $50,000. Costs of $200,000 were incurred to develop the site, including the cost of running power lines and building roads. Total cost subject to depletion is the net cost assignable to the natural resource plus the exploration and development costs. When the property is purchased, a journal entry is made to assign the purchase price to the two assets purchased—the natural resource and the land. The entry would be:

Land	50,000	
Mineral Deposits	600,000	
Cash		650,000
To record purchase of land and mine.		

After the purchase, all other costs mentioned above are debited to the natural resource account. The entry would be:

Mineral Deposits ($100,000 + $200,000)	300,000	
Cash		300,000
To record costs of exploration and development.		

The formula for finding depletion cost per unit is:

$$\text{Depletion cost per unit} = \frac{\text{Cost of site} - \text{Residual value of land} + \text{Costs to develop site}}{\text{Number of units that can be economically extracted}}$$

In the above example, the total costs of the mineral deposits is equal to the cost of the site ($650,000) minus the residual value of land ($50,000) plus costs to develop the site ($300,000), or $900,000. The unit (per ton) depletion charge is $1 ($900,000/900,000 tons). If 100,000 tons are mined in 1991, the entry to record the depletion charge ($1 $\times$ 100,000) is:

Depletion of Mineral Deposits	100,000	
Accumulated Depletion—Mineral Deposits[4]		100,000
To record depletion for 1991.		

The depletion account contains the "in the ground" cost of the ore or natural resource mined. This cost is combined with other extractive costs to determine the total cost of the ore mined. To illustrate, assume that in addition to the $100,000 depletion cost, mining labor costs totaled $320,000, and other mining costs, such as depreciation, property taxes, power, and supplies, totaled $60,000. If 80,000 tons were sold and 20,000 remained on hand at the end of the period, the total cost of $480,000 would be allocated as follows:

Depletion cost	$100,000
Mining labor cost	320,000
Other mining costs	60,000
Total cost of 100,000 tons mined ($4.80 per ton)	$480,000
Less: Ore inventory (20,000 tons at $4.80)	96,000
Cost of ore sold	$384,000

Note that the average cost per ton to mine 100,000 tons was $4.80 ($480,000/100,000). The income statement would show cost of ore sold of $384,000. Depletion expense would not be reported separately because depletion is included in cost of ore sold. The balance sheet would show

---

[4] Instead of crediting the accumulated depletion account, the Mineral Deposits account could have been credited directly. But for reasons indicated earlier, the credit is usually to an accumulated depletion account.

inventory of ore on hand (a current asset) at $96,000 ($4.80 × 20,000). The balance sheet would also report the cost less accumulated depletion of the natural resource as follows:

Mineral deposits $900,000
Less: Accumulated depletion 100,000 $800,000

Another method of calculating depletion cost is the percentage of revenue method. This method is used only for income tax purposes and not for financial statements.

Depreciation of Plant Assets Located on Extractive Industry Property.   Depreciable plant assets erected on extractive industry property are depreciated in the same manner as other depreciable assets. If such assets will be abandoned when the natural resource is exhausted, they should be depreciated over the shorter of the (a) physical life of the asset or (b) life of the natural resource. In some cases, periodic depreciation charges are computed using the units-of-production method. Using this method matches the life of the plant asset with the life of the natural resource. This method is recommended where the **physical** life of the plant asset equals or exceeds the life of the natural resource but its **useful** life is limited to the life of the natural resource.

Assume mining property is acquired and a building on the site is purchased for exclusive use in the mining operations. Also assume the units-of-production method is used for computing building depreciation. Relevant facts are:

Building cost $310,000
Estimated physical life of building . . . .   20 years
Estimated salvage value of building (after mine exhausted) . . . $ 10,000
Capacity of mine . . . . 1,000,000 tons
Expected life of mine . . . .   10 years

Since the life of the mine (10 years or 1,000,000 tons) is shorter than the life of the building (20 years), the building should be depreciated over the life of the mine. In this case, the depreciation charge should be based on tons of ore rather than years because the mine's "life" could be longer or shorter than 10 years, depending on how rapidly the ore is removed from the mine.

Suppose that during the first year of operations, 150,000 tons of ore are extracted. Building depreciation for the first year is $45,000, computed as follows:

$$\text{Depreciation per unit} = \frac{\text{Asset cost} - \text{Estimated salvage value}}{\substack{\text{Total tons of ore in mine that} \\ \text{can be economically extracted}}}$$

$$\text{Depreciation per unit} = \frac{\$310,000 - \$10,000}{1,000,000 \text{ tons}} = \$0.30 \text{ per ton}$$

$$\text{Depreciation for year} = \text{Depreciation per unit} \times \text{Units extracted}$$

$$\text{Depreciation for year} = \$0.30 \text{ per ton} \times 150,000 \text{ tons} = \$45,000$$

Depreciation on the building would be included on the income statement as part of the cost of ore that was sold and would be carried as part of inventory cost for those tons of ore that were not sold during the period. Accumulated depreciation on the building would be reported on the balance sheet with the related asset account.

Plant assets and natural resources are tangible assets used by a company to produce revenues. A company may also acquire intangible assets to assist in producing revenues.

■ INTANGIBLE ASSETS

Intangible assets have no physical characteristics but are of value because of the advantages or exclusive privileges and rights they provide to a business. Intangible assets generally arise from two sources: (1) exclusive privileges granted by governmental authority or by legal contract, such as patents, copyrights, franchises, trademarks and trade names, and leases; and (2) superior entrepreneurial capacity or management know-how and customer loyalty, which is called *goodwill.*

All intangible assets are nonphysical, but not all nonphysical assets are classified as intangibles. For example, accounts receivable and prepaid expenses are nonphysical, but they are classified as current assets. Intangible assets are generally both nonphysical and noncurrent; they are reported in a separate long-term section of the balance sheet entitled "Intangible assets."

Acquisition of Intangible Assets

*Objective 5:
Prepare entries for
the acquisition and
amortization of intan-
gible assets.*

Like most other assets, intangible assets are recorded initially at cost. However, computing an intangible asset acquisition cost differs from computing a plant asset acquisition cost. **Only outright purchase costs are included in the acquisition cost of an intangible asset;** the acquisition cost does **not** include cost of internal development or self-creation of the asset. If an intangible asset is internally generated in its entirety, none of its costs will be capitalized. Therefore, some companies have extremely valuable assets that may not even be recorded in their asset accounts. The reasons for this practice can be understood by studying the history of accounting for research and development costs.

Research and development (R&D) costs are costs incurred in a planned search for new knowledge and in translating such knowledge into a new product or process. Prior to 1975, research and development costs were often capitalized as intangible assets when future benefits were expected from their incurrence. Since it was often difficult to determine the costs applicable to future benefits, many companies expensed all such costs as they were incurred. Other companies capitalized those costs that related to proven products and expensed the rest as incurred.

As a result of these varied accounting practices, the Financial Accounting Standards Board in *Statement No. 2* in 1974 ruled that all research and development costs, other than those directly reimbursable by government agencies and others, must be expensed when incurred. Immediate expensing is justified on the grounds that (1) the amount of costs applicable to the future cannot be measured with any high degree of precision; (2) doubt exists as to whether any future benefits will be received; and (3) even if benefits are expected, they cannot be measured. Thus, research and development costs no longer appear as intangible assets on the balance sheet.

The same line of reasoning is applied to other costs associated with internally generated intangible assets, such as costs that are related to the development of a product that is subsequently patented, to prevent them from being capitalized and reported as intangible assets.

Amortization of Intangible Assets

Amortization is the systematic write-off of the cost of an intangible asset to expense. A portion of intangible asset cost is allocated to each accounting period in the economic (useful) life of the asset. All intangible assets are subject to amortization, which is similar to plant asset depreciation. Generally, amortization is recorded by debiting Amortization Expense and crediting the intangible asset account. An accumulated amortization account could be used to record amortization. However, usually the information gained from such accounting would not be significant because intangibles do not normally account for as significant an amount of total asset dollars as do plant assets.

Intangibles should be amortized over the shorter of (1) their economic life, (2) their legal life, or (3) 40 years. The 40-year limitation was established by the Accounting Principles Board. *APB Opinion No. 17* requires an intangible asset acquired after October 31, 1970, to be amortized over a period not to exceed 40 years. Straight-line amortization must be used unless another method of amortization (such as units-of-production) can be shown to be superior. Straight-line amortization is calculated in the same way as straight-line depreciation for plant assets.

Patents

A **patent** is a right granted by the federal government giving the owner the exclusive right to manufacture, sell, lease, or otherwise benefit from an invention for a limited period of time. The real value of a patent lies in its ability to produce revenue. Patents have a legal life of 17 years. Protection for the patent owner begins at the time of patent application and lasts for 17 years from the date the patent is granted.

The purchase of a patent should be recorded in the Patents account at cost. The Patents account should also be debited for the cost of the first successful defense of the patent in lawsuits (assuming an outside law firm was hired rather than using internal legal staff). Also, the cost of any competing patents that were purchased to ensure revenue-generating capability of the purchased patent should be debited to the Patents account.

The cost of a purchased patent should be amortized over the shorter of 17 years (or remaining legal life) or its estimated useful life. If a patent cost $40,000 and has a useful life of 10 years, the journal entry to record periodic amortization is:

Patent Amortization Expense	4,000	
Patents		4,000
To record patent amortization.		

If the patent becomes worthless, the unamortized balance in the Patents account should be charged to expense.

As noted on page 467 in the discussion on research and development costs, all R&D costs incurred in the internal development of a product, process, or idea that is later patented must be expensed, rather than capitalized. In the above example, the cost of the purchased patent was amortized over its useful life of 10 years. If the patent had been the result of an internally generated product or process, its cost of $40,000 would have been expensed as incurred, in accordance with *Statement No. 2* of the Financial Accounting Standards Board.

Copyrights

A **copyright** is an exclusive right granted by the federal government giving the owner protection against the illegal reproduction by others of the owner's written works, designs, and literary productions. The copyright period is for the life of the creator plus 50 years. Since most publications have a limited life, the cost of the copyright may appropriately be charged to expense on a straight-line basis over the life of the first edition published or based on projections of the number of copies to be sold per year.

Franchises

A **franchise** is a contract between two parties granting the franchisee (the purchaser of the franchise) certain rights and privileges ranging from name identification to complete monopoly of service. In many instances, the two parties are both private businesses. For example, an individual who wishes to open a hamburger restaurant may purchase a McDonald's franchise; the two parties involved are the individual business owner and McDonald's Corporation. This franchise would allow the business owner to use the McDonald's golden arch, and would provide the owner with advertising and many other benefits.

The parties involved in a franchise arrangement are not always private businesses. A franchise may also be granted between a government agency and a private company. A city may give a franchise to a utility company, giving the utility the exclusive right to provide service to a particular area.

In addition to providing benefits, a franchise usually places certain restrictions on the franchisee. These restrictions are generally related to rates or prices charged; they may also be in regard to product quality or from whom supplies and inventory items must be purchased.

If periodic payments to the grantor of the franchise are required, they should be debited to a Franchise Expense account. If a lump-sum payment is made to obtain the franchise, the cost should be recorded in an asset account entitled Franchise and amortized over the shorter of the useful life of the franchise or 40 years.

Trademarks; Trade Names

A **trademark** is a symbol, design, or logo that is used in conjunction with a particular product or company. A **trade name** is a brand name under which a product is sold or a company does business. Many times trademarks and trade names are extremely valuable to a company, but if they have been internally developed, they will have no recorded asset cost. However, if such items are purchased by a business from an external source, they are recorded at cost and amortized over their economic life or 40 years, whichever is shorter.

Leases

A **lease** is a contract to rent property. The owner of the property is the grantor of the lease and is called the **lessor.** The person or company obtaining rights to possess and use the property is called the **lessee.** The rights granted under the lease are called a **leasehold.** The accounting for a lease depends on whether it is a capital lease or an operating lease.

Capital Leases.   In concept, a **capital lease** transfers to the lessee virtually all rewards and risks that accompany ownership of property. A lease is a capital lease if, among other provisions, it (1) transfers ownership of the leased property to the lessee at the end of the lease term or (2) contains a bargain purchase option that permits the lessee to buy the property at a price significantly below fair value at the end of the lease term.

A capital lease is a means of financing property acquisitions and has the same economic impact as a purchase made on an installment plan. Thus, the lessee in a capital lease must record the leased property as an asset and the lease obligation as a liability. Because it is an asset, the leased property is depreciated over its useful life to the lessee. A part of each lease payment is recorded as interest expense, with the balance viewed as a payment on the lease liability.

The proper accounting for capital leases for both lessees and lessors has been an extremely difficult problem. Further discussion of capital leases is left for an intermediate accounting text.

Operating Leases.   If a lease does not qualify as a capital lease, it is an **operating lease.** A one-year lease on an apartment or a week's rental of an automobile are examples of operating leases. Such leases make no attempt to transfer any of the rewards and risks of ownership to the lessee. As a result, there may be no recordable transaction when a lease is signed.

In some situations, the lease may call for an immediate cash payment that must be recorded. Assume, for example, that a business signed a lease that required the immediate payment of the annual rent of $15,000 for the first and fifth years of a five-year lease. The lessee would record the payment as follows:

Prepaid Rent	15,000	
Leasehold	15,000	
Cash		30,000
To record first and fifth years' rent on five-year lease.		

Since the Leasehold account is actually a long-term prepaid rent account for the fifth year's annual rent, it is classified as an intangible asset until the beginning of the fifth year. Then the Leasehold account is reclassified as a current asset. Accounting for the balance in the Leasehold account depends on the terms of the lease. In the above example, the $15,000 in the Leasehold account will be charged to expense over the fifth year only. The balance in Prepaid Rent will be charged to expense in the first year. Thus, assuming the lease year and fiscal year coincide, the entry for the first year is:

Rent Expense	15,000	
Prepaid Rent		15,000
To record rent expense.		

The entry in the fifth year is:

```
Rent Expense . . . . . . . . . . . . . . . . . . . . . . . . . . . . . . . . . . . . .   15,000
      Leasehold  . . . . . . . . . . . . . . . . . . . . . . . . . . . . . . . . .              15,000
      To record rent expense.
```

The accounting for the second, third, and fourth years will be the same as for the first year. The rent will be recorded in Prepaid Rent when paid in advance for the year and then expensed. The amount in the Leasehold account may be transferred to Prepaid Rent at the beginning of the fifth year by debiting Prepaid Rent and crediting Leasehold. If so, the credit in the above entry would have been to Prepaid Rent.

In some cases, when a lease is signed, a lump-sum payment is paid that does not cover a specific year's rent. If so, the payment is debited to the Leasehold account and amortized over the life of the lease. The straight-line method is required unless another method can be shown to be superior. Assume the $15,000 rent for the fifth year in the above example was, instead, a lump-sum payment on the lease in addition to the annual rent payments. An annual adjusting entry to amortize the $15,000 over five years is required. The entry would read:

```
Rent Expense . . . . . . . . . . . . . . . . . . . . . . . . . . . . . . . . . . . .   3,000
      Leasehold  . . . . . . . . . . . . . . . . . . . . . . . . . . . . . . . . .              3,000
      To amortize leasehold.
```

In this example, the annual rental expense is $18,000: $15,000 annual cash rent plus $3,000 amortization of leasehold ($15,000/5).

Periodic rent may be based on current-year sales or usage rather than being a constant amount. For example, if a lease called for rent equal to 5% of current-year sales and sales were $400,000 in 1991, the rent for 1991 would be $20,000. The rent would either be paid or adjusted to the correct amount at the end of the year.

Leasehold Improvements

A **leasehold improvement** is any physical alteration made by the lessee to the leased property in which benefits are expected beyond the current accounting period. Leasehold improvements made by a lessee usually become the property of the lessor after the lease has expired. However, since leasehold improvements are an asset of the lessee during the lease period, they should be debited to a Leasehold Improvements account. Leasehold improvements are then amortized to expense over the period of time benefited by the improvements. The amortization period for leasehold improvements should be the shorter of the life of the improvements or the life of the lease. If the lease can (and probably will) be renewed at the option of the lessee, the option period should be included in the life of the lease.

As an illustration, assume that on January 2, 1991, Wolf Company leases a building for 20 years under a nonrenewable lease at an annual rental of $20,000, payable on each December 31. Wolf immediately incurs a cost of $80,000 for improvements to the building, such as interior walls for office separation, ceiling fans, and recessed lighting. The improvements have an estimated life of 30 years. The $80,000 should be amortized over the 20-year lease period, since that period is shorter than the life of the improvements, and Wolf will not be able to use the improvements beyond the life of the lease. If only annual financial statements are prepared, the following journal entry will properly record the rental expense for the year ended December 31, 1991:

Rent Expense (or Leasehold Improvement Expense)	4,000	
Leasehold Improvements		4,000
To record leasehold improvement amortization.		
Rent Expense	20,000	
Cash		20,000
To record annual rent.		

Thus, the total cost to rent the building each year includes the $20,000 cash rent plus the amortization of the leasehold improvements.

Although leaseholds are intangible assets, leaseholds and leasehold improvements are sometimes shown in the property, plant, and equipment section of the balance sheet.

Goodwill

In accounting, goodwill is an intangible value attached to a company resulting mainly from the company's management skill or know-how and a favorable reputation with customers. A company's value may be greater than the total of the fair market value of its tangible and identifiable intangible assets. This greater value means that the company is able to generate an above-average rate of income on each dollar invested in the business. Thus, proof of the existence of goodwill for a company can be found only in its ability to generate superior earnings or income.

A Goodwill account will appear in the accounting records only if goodwill has been bought and paid for in cash or other property. Goodwill cannot be purchased by itself; an entire business or a part of a business must be purchased to obtain the accompanying intangible asset, goodwill.

To illustrate, assume that Lenox Company purchased all of Martin Company's assets for $700,000. Lenox also agrees to assume responsibility for a $350,000 mortgage note payable owed by Martin. Goodwill is determined as the difference between the amount paid for the business including the debt assumed ($700,000 + $350,000 = $1,050,000) and the **fair market value** of the assets purchased. Notice that fair market value rather than book value is used to determine the amount of goodwill. The following shows the computation for the amount of goodwill purchased by Lenox:

Cash paid		$ 700,000
Mortgage note payable assumed		350,000
Total price paid		$1,050,000
Less fair market values of individually		
identifiable assets:		
Accounts receivable	$ 95,000	
Inventories	100,000	
Land	240,000	
Buildings	275,000	
Equipment	200,000	
Patents	65,000	975,000
Goodwill		$ 75,000

The $75,000 is the amount of goodwill to be recorded as an intangible asset on the books of Lenox Company; all of the other assets will be recorded at fair market value, and the liability will be recorded at the amount due. Specific reasons for the existence of goodwill in a company might include good reputation, customer loyalty, product design, and superior human resources. Since these are not individually quantifiable, they are all grouped together and referred to as *goodwill*. The journal entry to record the above purchase is:

Accounts Receivable	95,000	
Inventories	100,000	
Land	240,000	
Buildings	275,000	
Equipment	200,000	
Patents	65,000	
Goodwill	75,000	
Cash		700,000
Mortgage Note Payable		350,000

To record the purchase of Martin Company's assets and assumption of mortgage note payble.

Goodwill, like all other intangibles, must be amortized. No limited legal life exists for goodwill, and the useful life of goodwill cannot be reasonably estimated. If, for example, the new owner made substantial changes in the method of doing business, goodwill that existed at the purchase date could rapidly disappear. Therefore, current accounting practice requires the amortization of goodwill over a period not to exceed 40 years. This requirement is necessary because the value of purchased goodwill will eventually disappear. Other goodwill may be generated in its place, but the organization cannot record its internally created goodwill any more than it can record other internally generated intangible assets.

The entry to amortize the $75,000 goodwill over a 40-year period is:

Goodwill Amortization Expense	1,875	
Goodwill		1,875

To amortize goodwill ($75,000/40 years).

Reporting Amortization

Illustration 11.2 shows the frequencies of intangible assets being amortized by a sample of 600 companies for the years 1983–86.

Illustration 11.2

Intangible Assets Held by Sample of 600 Companies

	Number of Companies			
	1986	1985	1984	1983
Goodwill	322	301	279	270
Patents	63	60	55	50
Trademarks, brand names, copyrights	39	30	26	21
Licenses, franchises, memberships	23	25	21	23
Other	45	23	13	11
Intangible assets (not otherwise described)	35	34	24	24

Source: American Institute of Certified Public Accountants, *Accounting Trends & Techniques* (New York: AICPA, 1987), p. 163.

Amortization expense for most intangible assets discussed in this chapter appears among the operating expenses on the income statement. The account titles used are all of this type: "Amortization of Goodwill (or Patents, Copyrights, Franchises, Leaseholds) Expense." Periodic amortization of leaseholds and leasehold improvements is often reported as rent expense. The amortization of goodwill is an expense in determining accounting income but is not a deductible in determining taxable income.

The amortization rules for intangible assets are summarized in Illustration 11.3.

Illustration 11.3

Rules for Amortization of Intangible Assets

Intangible Asset	Amortized over Shorter of		
	Useful Life	Legal Life	Maximum Life (years)
Patents	?	17 years	40
Copyrights	?	Life of author plus 50 years	40
Franchises	?	No limit (unless limited by contract)	40
Trademarks; trade names	?	No limit	40
Leasehold improvements	?	Life of lease	40
Goodwill	?	No limit	40

This chapter concludes your study of accounting for long-term assets. In Chapter 12, you will learn about current liabilities and payroll accounting. Current liabilities include clearly determinable, estimated, and contingent liabilities. Careful accounting for payrolls is mandatory because of the necessary federal and state income tax deductions and other payroll deductions.

■ UNDERSTANDING THE LEARNING OBJECTIVES: CHAPTER 11

1. Calculate and prepare entries for the sale, retirement, and destruction of plant assets.

   - By comparing an asset's book value (cost less accumulated depreciation) with its sales price, the company will show either a gain or a loss. If sales price is greater than book value, the company will show a gain. If sales price is less than book value, the company will show a loss.
   - When a plant asset is retired from productive service, the asset's cost and accumulated depreciation must be removed from the plant asset accounts.

- Plant assets are sometimes wrecked in accidents or destroyed by fire, flood, storm, and other causes. Losses are normally incurred in such situations. If the asset was insured, only the amount of the loss exceeding the amount to be recovered from the insurance company would be debited to the loss account.

2. Describe and record exchanges of dissimilar and similar plant assets.

- In exchanges of dissimilar assets, the asset received is recorded at either (1) a stated cash price of the new asset or (2) a known fair value of the asset given up plus any cash paid.
- In exchanges of similar assets, the new asset is recorded at (1) the cash price of the asset received or (2) the book value of the old asset plus the cash paid, whichever is lower.

3. Discuss the differences between accounting principles and tax rules in the treatment of gains and losses from the exchange of plant assets.

- When dissimilar assets are exchanged, gains and losses are recognized for both accounting and tax purposes.
- When similar assets are exchanged, losses are recognized for accounting purposes, but gains are not. For tax purposes, neither gains nor losses are recognized. Thus, for income tax purposes, the new asset is recorded at the book value of the old asset plus any cash paid.

4. Determine the periodic depletion cost of a natural resource and calculate depreciation of plant assets located on extractive industry property.

- Depletion charges usually are computed by using the units-of-production method. Total cost is divided by the estimated number of units that is economically extractable from the property. This provides a per unit depletion cost that is multiplied by the units extracted each year to obtain the depletion cost for that year.
- Depreciable assets located on extractive industry property should be depreciated over the shorter of (a) the physical life of the asset or (b) the life of the natural resource. The periodic depreciation charges usually are computed using the units-of-production method. Using this method matches the life of the plant asset with the life of the natural resource.

5. Prepare entries for the acquisition and amortization of intangible assets.

- Only outright purchase costs are included in the acquisition cost of an intangible asset. If an intangible asset is internally generated, it is immediately expensed.
- Intangibles should be amortized over the shorter of (1) their economic life, (2) their legal life, or (3) 40 years. Straight-line amortization must be used unless another method can be shown to be superior.

6. Define and use correctly the new terms in the glossary.

NEW TERMS INTRODUCED IN CHAPTER 11

Amortization The term used to describe the systematic write-off of the cost of an intangible asset to expense (468).

Boot The additional cash outlay made when one asset is exchanged for a similar one (462).

Capital lease A lease that transfers to the lessee virtually all of the rewards and risks that accompany ownership of property (470).

Copyright An exclusive right granted by the federal government giving the owner protection against the illegal reproduction by others of the owner's written works, designs, and literary productions (469).

Depletion The exhaustion of a natural resource; an estimate of the cost of the resource that was removed during the period (464).

Franchise A contract between two parties granting the franchisee (the purchaser of the franchise) certain rights and privileges ranging from name identification to complete monopoly of service (469).

Goodwill An intangible value attached to a company resulting mainly from the company's management skill or know-how and a favorable reputation with customers. Evidenced by the ability to generate an above-average rate of income on each dollar invested in the business (472).

Intangible assets Items that have no physical characteristics but are of value because of the advantages or exclusive privileges and rights they provide to a business (467).

Lease A contract to rent property. Grantor of the lease is the **lessor;** the party obtaining the rights to possess and use property is the **lessee** (470).

Leasehold The rights granted under a lease (470).

Leasehold improvement Any physical alteration made by the lessee to the leased property in which benefits are expected beyond the current accounting period (471).

"Material" gains or losses Gains or losses large enough to affect the decisions of an informed user of the financial statements (462).

Materiality concept Allows the accountant to deal with immaterial (unimportant) items in a theoretically incorrect manner (463).

Natural resources Ore deposits, mineral deposits, oil reserves, gas deposits, and timber stands supplied by nature (464).

Operating lease A lease that does not qualify as a capital lease (470).

Patent A right granted by a government giving the owner the exclusive right to manufacture, sell, lease, or otherwise benefit from an invention (468).

Research and development (R&D) costs Costs incurred in a planned search for new knowledge and in translating such knowledge into a new product or process (467).

Trademark A symbol, design, or logo that is used in conjunction with a particular product or company (469).

Trade name A brand name under which a product is sold or a company does business (469).

Wasting assets See Natural resources.

DEMONSTRATION PROBLEM 11-1

On January 2, 1991, Stephens Company purchased a machine for $30,000 cash. The machine has an estimated useful life of six years and an estimated salvage value of $1,500. The straight-line method of depreciation is being used.

Required:
a. Compute the book value of the machine as of July 1, 1994.
b. Assume the machine was disposed of on July 1, 1994. Prepare the journal entries to record the disposal of the machine under each of the following unrelated assumptions:
   1. The machine was sold for $10,000 cash.
   2. The machine was sold for $15,000 cash.

3. The machine and $20,000 cash were exchanged for a new machine that had a cash price of $32,500. Use the accounting method rather than the income tax method.
4. The machine was completely destroyed by fire. Cash of $9,000 is expected to be recovered from the insurance company.

Solution to demonstration problem 11-1

a.

STEPHENS COMPANY
Schedule to Compute Book Value
July 1, 1994

Cost	$30,000

Less accumulated depreciation:

$$\frac{\$30,000 - \$1,500}{6 \text{ years}} = \$4,750 \text{ per year}$$

$4,750 × 3½ years = $16,625	16,625
Book value	$13,375

b.

1.

Cash	10,000	
Accumulated Depreciation—Machinery	16,625	
Loss on Disposal of Plant Assets	3,375	
Machinery		30,000
To record sale of machinery at a loss.		

2.

Cash	15,000	
Accumulated Depreciation—Machinery	16,625	
Machinery		30,000
Gain on Disposal of Plant Assets		1,625
To record sale of machinery at a gain.		

3.

Machinery (new)	32,500	
Accumulated Depreciation—Machinery	16,625	
Loss on Disposal of Plant Assets	875	
Machinery (old)		30,000
Cash		20,000
To record exchange of machines.		

4.

Receivable from Insurance Company	9,000	
Accumulated Depreciation—Machinery	16,625	
Fire Loss	4,375	
Machinery		30,000
To record loss of machinery.		

DEMONSTRATION PROBLEM 11-2

Jones Company acquired on January 1, 1991, a tract of property containing timber at a cost of $10,000,000. After the timber is removed, the land will be worth about $4,000,000 and will be sold to another party. Costs of developing the site were $1,000,000. A building was erected at a cost of $200,000. The building had an estimated physical life of 20 years and will have an estimated salvage value of $100,000 when the timber is gone. It was expected that 50,000,000 board feet of timber can be economically cut. During the first year, 16,000,000 board feet were cut. The units-of-production basis is used to depreciate the building.

Required: Prepare the entries to record:

a. The acquisition of the property.
b. The development costs.
c. Depletion costs for the first year.
d. Depreciation on the building for the first year.

Solution to demonstration problem 11–2

a. Land 4,000,000
   Timber Stands 6,000,000
       Cash   10,000,000
       To record purchase of land and timber.

b. Timber Stands 1,000,000
       Cash   1,000,000
       To record costs of development of the site.

c. Depletion of Timber Stands 2,240,000
       Accumulated Depreciation—Timber Stands   2,240,000
       To record depletion for 1991:
       ($6,000,000 + $1,000,000)/50,000,000 = $0.14 per
       board foot. $0.14 × 16,000,000 = $2,240,000.

d. Depreciation Expense—Building 32,000
       Accumulated Depreciation—Building   32,000
       To record depreciation expense:
       $\frac{\$200,000 - \$100,000}{50,000,000 \text{ board feet}}$ = $0.002 per board foot.
       $0.002 × 16,000,000 = $32,000.

QUESTIONS

1. When depreciable plant assets are sold for cash, how is the gain or loss measured?

2. A plant asset that cost $15,000 and has a related accumulated depreciation account balance of $15,000 is still being used in business operations. Would it be appropriate to continue recording depreciation on this asset? Explain. When should the asset's cost and accumulated depreciation be removed from the accounting records?

3. A machine and $10,000 cash were exchanged for a delivery truck. How should the cost basis of the delivery truck be measured?

4. A plant asset was exchanged for a new asset of a similar type. How is the cost of the new asset determined for (a) accounting purposes and (b) income tax purposes?

5. a. Distinguish between depreciation, depletion, and amortization. Name two assets that are

subject to depreciation, to depletion, and to amortization.

b. Distinguish between tangible and intangible assets, and classify the above-named assets in part *(a)* accordingly.

6. A building with an estimated physical life of 40 years was constructed at the site of a coal mine. The coal mine is expected to be completely exhausted within 20 years. Over what length of time should the building be depreciated, assuming the building will be abandoned after all the coal has been extracted?

7. What are the characteristics of intangible assets? Give an example of an asset that has no physical existence but is not classified as an intangible asset.

8. What reasons justify the immediate expensing of most research and development costs?

9. Over what length of time should intangible assets be amortized?

10. Should intangible assets be amortized over their economic life or their legal life?

11. Describe the typical accounting for a patent.

12. What is a capital lease? What features may characterize a capital lease?

13. What is the difference between a leasehold (under an operating lease contract) and a leasehold improvement? Is there any difference in the accounting procedures applicable to each?

14. Brush Company leased a tract of land for 40 years at an agreed annual rental fee of $10,000. The effective date of the lease was July 1, 1990. During the last six months of 1990, Brush constructed a building on the land at a cost of $250,000. The building was placed in operation on January 2, 1991, at which time it was estimated to have a physical life of 50 years. Over what period of time should the building be depreciated? Why?

15. You note that a certain store seems to have a steady stream of regular customers, a favorable location, courteous employees, high-quality merchandise, and a reputation for fairness in dealing with customers, employees, and suppliers. Does it follow automatically that this business should have goodwill recorded as an asset? Explain.

EXERCISES

E-1
Record sale of equipment; account for removal costs

Plant equipment originally costing $9,000, on which $6,000 of depreciation has been accumulated, was sold for $2,250.

a. Prepare the journal entry to record the sale.
b. Prepare the entry to record the sale of the equipment if $25 of removal costs were incurred to allow the equipment to be moved.

E-2
Record destruction of machinery by fire—uninsured and insured asset

A machine costing $32,000, on which $24,000 of depreciation has been accumulated, was completely destroyed by fire. What journal entry should be made to record the machine's destruction and the resulting fire loss under each of the following unrelated assumptions?

a. The machine was *not* insured.
b. The machine was insured, and it is estimated that $6,000 will be recovered from the insurance company.

E-3
Record exchange of autos

Spivey Company owned an automobile acquired on January 1, 1988, at a cash cost of $18,720; at that time, the auto was estimated to have a life of four years and a $1,440 salvage value. Depreciation has been recorded through December 31, 1990, on a straight-line basis. On January 1, 1991, the auto was traded for a new auto. The old auto had a fair market value (trade-in allowance) of $3,600. Cash of $16,560 was paid.

Prepare the journal entry to record the trade-in under generally accepted accounting principles.

E-4
Record variety of cases involving sale, retirement, or exchange of equipment

Equipment costing $88,000, on which $60,000 of accumulated depreciation had been recorded, was disposed of on January 2, 1990. What journal entries are required to record the equipment's disposal under each of the following unrelated assumptions?

a.   The equipment was sold for $32,000 cash.
b.   The equipment was sold for $23,200 cash.
c.   The equipment was retired from service and hauled to the junkyard. No material was salvaged.
d.   The equipment was exchanged for similar equipment having a cash price of $120,000. A trade-in allowance of $40,000 from the cash price was received, and the balance was paid in cash.
e.   The equipment was exchanged for similar equipment having a cash price of $120,000. A trade-in allowance of $20,000 was received, and the balance was paid in cash. (Record this transaction twice—first for tax purposes, and second for financial reporting purposes.)

E-5
Update depreciation and record sale of truck

On August 31, 1990, Drew Company sold a truck for $2,300 cash. The truck was acquired on January 1, 1987, at a cost of $5,800. Depreciation of $3,600 on the truck has been recorded through December 31,1989, using the straight-line method, four-year expected life, and an expected salvage value of $1,000.

Prepare the journal entries to update the depreciation on the truck on August 31, 1990, and to record the sale of the truck.

E-6
Determine depletion cost and expense

Brown Company paid $2,000,000 for the right to extract all of the mineral-bearing ore, estimated at 5 million tons, that can be economically extracted from a certain tract of land. During the first year, Brown Company extracted 500,000 tons of the ore and sold 400,000 tons. What part of the $2,000,000 should be charged to expense during the first year?

E-7
Determine patent cost and periodic amortization

Mulkey Company purchased a patent on January 1, 1976, at a total cost of $17,000. In January 1987, the company hired an outside law firm and successfully defended the patent in a lawsuit. The legal fees amounted to $3,750. What will be the amount of patent cost amortized in 1990? (The useful life of the patent is the same as its legal life—17 years.)

E-8
Record leasehold; record rent accrued and leasehold amortization

Pratt Company leased the first three floors in a building under an operating lease contract for a 10-year period beginning January 1, 1990. The company paid $64,000 in cash (not representing a specific period's rent) and agreed to make annual payments equal to 1% of the first $400,000 of sales and 0.5% of all sales over $400,000. Sales for 1990 amounted to $1,200,000. Payment of the annual amount will be made in January 1991.

Prepare journal entries to record the cash payment of January 1, 1990, and the proper expense to be recognized for the use of the space in the leased building for 1990.

E-9
Record franchise; record accrued franchise fees and franchise amortization

Bob Martin paid Hungry Hank's Hamburgers $30,000 for the right to operate a fast-food restaurant in Gordonville under the Hungry Hank's name. Bob also agreed to pay an operating fee of 0.5% of sales for advertising and other services rendered by Hungry Hank's. Bob began operations on January 2, 1990. Sales for 1990 amounted to $300,000.

Give the entries needed to record the payment of the $30,000 and to record expenses incurred relating to the right to use the Hungry Hank's name.

E-10
Determine amount of goodwill

Lark Company purchased all of the assets of Edson Company for $500,000. Lark Company also agreed to assume responsibility for Edson Company's liabilities of $50,000. The fair market value of the assets acquired was $450,000. How much goodwill should be recorded in this transaction?

E-11
Compute periodic depletion cost per unit

College Mining Company purchased a tract of land containing ore for $350,000. After spending $50,000 in exploration costs, the company determined that 600,000 tons of ore existed on the tract but only 500,000 tons could be economically removed. No other costs were incurred. When the company finishes with the tract, it estimates the land will be worth $100,000. Determine the depletion cost per unit.

E-12

Compute depreciation charge of plant asset

The Milano Mining Company acquired a tract of land for mining purposes and erected a building on-site at a cost of $300,000 and no salvage value. Though the building has a useful life of 10 years, the mining operations are expected to last only 6 years. The company has determined that 800,000 tons of ore exist on the tract but only 600,000 tons can be economically removed. If 100,000 tons of ore are extracted in the first year of operations, what is the appropriate depreciation charge, using the units-of-production method?

PROBLEMS, SERIES A

P11-1-A

Update depreciation and record sale of truck

On July 31, 1990, Krane Company sold a truck for $3,920 cash. The truck was acquired on January 1, 1987, at a cost of $18,560; depreciation has been recorded on the truck through December 31, 1989, using the straight-line method, a four-year useful life, and $3,200 expected salvage value.

Required: Prepare all entries needed to record the above information for the year 1990.

P11-2-A

Record exchange of automobiles under GAAP

Ray Company traded in an automobile that cost $18,000 and on which $15,000 of depreciation has been recorded for a new auto with a cash price of $34,500. The company received a trade-in allowance (its fair value) for the old auto of $2,100 and paid the balance in cash.

Required:
a.   Record the exchange of the autos applying generally accepted accounting principles.
b.   Record the exchange of the autos applying federal income tax regulations.

P11-3-A

Update depreciation and record six cases of asset disposal

On January 2, 1988, Blake Company purchased a delivery truck for $105,000 cash. The truck has an estimated useful life of six years and an estimated salvage value of $9,000. The straight-line method of depreciation is being used.

Required:
a.   Prepare a schedule showing the computation of the book value of the truck on January 1, 1991.
b.   Assume the truck is to be disposed of on July 1, 1991. What journal entry is required to record depreciation for the six months ended June 30, 1991?
c.   Prepare the journal entries to record the disposal of the truck on July 1, 1991, under each of the following unrelated assumptions:
   1.   The truck was sold for $35,000 cash.
   2.   The truck was sold for $64,000 cash.
   3.   The truck was retired from service, and it is expected that $27,500 will be received from the sale of salvaged materials.
   4.   The truck and $80,000 cash were exchanged for office equipment that had a cash price of $140,000.
   5.   The truck and $90,000 cash were exchanged for a new delivery truck that had a cash price of $150,000.
   6.   The truck was completely destroyed in an accident. Cash of $34,000 is expected to be recovered from the insurance company.

P11-4-A

Update depreciation and record exchange of plant asset for similar asset

Blount Moving Company purchased a new moving van on October 1, 1990. The cash price of the new van was $27,000, and the company received a trade-in allowance from the cash price of $4,000 for a 1988 model. The balance was paid in cash. The 1988 model had been acquired on January 1, 1988, at a cost of $18,000. Depreciation had been recorded through December 31, 1989, on a straight-line basis, with three years of useful life expected and no expected salvage value.

Required: Prepare journal entries to record the exchange of the moving vans using the method required by generally accepted accounting principles.

P11-5-A

Record leasehold amortization; record depreciation and trade-in

On January 1, 1990, Morton Company had the following balances in its plant asset and accumulated depreciation accounts:

	Asset	Accumulated Depreciation
Land	$ 208,000	
Leasehold	260,000	
Buildings	1,141,920	$ 95,550
Equipment	998,400	463,320
Trucks	149,760	52,930

Additional data:

1. The leasehold covers a plot of ground leased on January 1, 1986, for a period of 20 years.
2. Building No. 1 is on the owned land and was completed on July 1, 1989, at a cost of $655,200; its life is set at 40 years with no salvage value. Building No. 2 is on the leased land and was completed on July 1, 1986, at a cost of $486,720; its life is also set at 40 years with no expected salvage value.
3. The equipment had an expected useful life of eight years with no estimated salvage value.
4. Truck A, purchased on January 1, 1988, at a cost of $49,920, had an expected life of 2½ years and a salvage value of $3,120. Truck B, purchased on July 1, 1988, at a cost of $43,680, had an expected life of two years and a salvage value of $7,280. Truck C, purchased on July 1, 1989, at a cost of $56,160, had an expected life of three years and a salvage value of $7,020.

The following transactions occurred in 1990:

Jan. 2 Rent for 1990 on leased land was paid, $29,120.
April 1 Truck B was traded in for truck D. The cash price of the new truck was $49,920. A trade-in allowance of $9,360 was granted from the cash price. The balance was paid in cash. Truck D has an expected life of 2½ years and a salvage value of $3,120. (Use GAAP method.)
   1 Truck A was sold for $9,360 cash.

Required: Prepare journal entries to record the 1990 transactions and the necessary December 31, 1990, adjusting entries, assuming a calendar-year accounting period. Use the straight-line depreciation method.

P11-6-A

Determine depletion for period and depreciation on mining equipment; compute average cost per ton of ore mined

On January 2, 1990, Mitchell Mining Company acquired land with ore deposits at a cash cost of $500,000. Exploration and development costs amounted to $50,000. The residual value of the land is expected to be $100,000. The ore deposits contain an estimated 3 million tons. Present technology will allow the economical extraction of only 85% of the total deposit. Machinery, equipment, and temporary sheds were installed at a cost of $75,000. The assets will have no further value to the company when the ore body is exhausted; they have a physical life of 12 years. In 1990, 100,000 tons of ore were extracted. The company expects the mine to be exhausted in 10 years, with sharp variations in annual production.

Required:
a. Compute the depletion charge for 1990. Round to the nearest cent.
b. Compute the depreciation charge for 1990 under the units-of-production method.
c. If all other mining costs, except depletion, amounted to $350,000, what was the average cost per ton mined in 1990?

P11-7-A
Record cost and amortization of patent

Stone Company spent $133,280 to purchase a patent on January 2, 1990. It is assumed that the patent will be useful during its full legal life. In January 1991, the company hired an outside law firm and successfully defended the patent in a lawsuit at a cost of $25,600. Also, in January 1991, the company paid $38,400 to obtain patents that could, if used by competitors, make the earlier Stone patent useless. The purchased patents will never be used.

Required: Give the entries for 1990 and 1991 to record the information relating to the patents.

P11-8-A
Record amortization expense for a variety of intangible assets

Following are selected transactions and other data relating to Floyd Company for the year ended December 31, 1990:

a.   The company rented the second floor of a building for five years on January 2, 1990, and paid the annual rent of $5,000 for the first and fifth years in advance.

b.   In 1989, the company incurred legal fees of $15,000 in applying for a patent and paid a fee of $5,000 to a former employee who conceived of a device that substantially reduced the cost of manufacturing one of the company's products. The patent on the device has a market value of $150,000 and is expected to be useful for 10 years.

c.   In 1989, the company entered into a 10-year operating lease on several floors of a building, paying $10,000 in cash immediately and agreeing to pay $5,000 at the end of each of the 10 years of life in the lease. It then incurred costs of $20,000 to install partitions, shelving, and fixtures. These items would normally last 25 years.

d.   The company spent $6,000 promoting a trademark in a manner that it believed enhanced the value of the trademark considerably. The trademark has an indefinite life.

e.   The company incurred costs amounting to $50,000 in 1989 and $65,000 in 1990 for research and development of new products that are expected to enhance the company's revenues for at least five years.

f.   The company paid $50,000 to the author of a book that the company published on July 2, 1990. Sales of the book are expected to be made over a two-year period from that date.

Required: For each of the situations described above, prepare only the journal entries to record the expense applicable to 1990.

PROBLEMS, SERIES B

P11-1-B
Update depreciation and record sale of typewriter

On January 1, 1988, Barrett Company purchased an electronic typewriter for $14,100 cash. The typewriter has a useful life of five years and an expected salvage value of $600; it is being depreciated annually under the straight-line method. The company spent $360 to clean and adjust the typewriter on February 2, 1991, and sold the typewriter on August 1, 1991, for $3,000.

Required: Prepare journal entries to record the above data for 1991, assuming Barrett Company has a calendar-year accounting period.

P11-2-B
Update depreciation and record exchange of autos under GAAP

Rice, Inc., purchased a new 1991 model automobile on December 31, 1991. The cash price of the new auto was $7,800, from which Rice received a trade-in allowance of $1,200 for a 1989 model traded in. The 1989 model had been acquired on January 1, 1989, at a cost of $5,750. Depreciation has been recorded on the 1989 model through December 31, 1990, using the straight-line method, an expected four-year useful life, and an expected salvage value of $750.

Required: a.   Record depreciation expense for 1991.

b.   Prepare the journal entries needed to record the exchange of autos using the method required under generally accepted accounting principles.

P11-3-B

Update depreciation and record six cases of asset disposal

On January 1, 1988, Kent Company purchased a truck for $24,000 cash. The truck has an estimated useful life of six years and an expected salvage value of $3,000. Depreciation on the truck was computed using the straight-line method.

Required:

a. Prepare a schedule showing the computation of the book value of the truck on December 31, 1990.

b. Prepare the journal entry to record depreciation for the six months ended June 30, 1991.

c. Prepare journal entries to record the disposal of the truck on June 30, 1991, under each of the following unrelated assumptions:

  1. The truck was sold for $2,000 cash.
  2. The truck was sold for $14,000 cash.
  3. The truck was scrapped. Used parts valued at $3,700 were salvaged.
  4. The truck (which has a fair market value of $6,000) and $18,000 of cash were exchanged for a used back hoe that did not have a known market value.
  5. The truck and $16,500 cash were exchanged for another truck that had a cash price of $28,500.
  6. The truck was stolen on July 1, and insurance proceeds of $4,200 were expected.

P11-4-B

Update depreciation and record exchange of plant asset for similar asset

Roberts Company purchased a new Model II computer on October 1, 1990. The cash price of the new computer was $66,560, and Roberts received a trade-in allowance of $24,800 from the cash price for a Model I computer. The old computer was acquired on January 1, 1988, at a cost of $61,440. Depreciation has been recorded through December 31, 1989, on a straight-line basis, with an estimated useful life of four years and $10,240 expected salvage value.

Required:

a. Prepare the journal entries needed to record the exchange using the income tax method.

b. Repeat part *(a)* applying generally accepted accounting principles.

P11-5-B

Record leasehold amortization; record depreciation and trade-in

On July 1, 1990, Rivers Company had the following balance in its plant asset and accumulated depreciation accounts:

	Asset	Accumulated Depreciation
Land	$ 560,000	
Leasehold	210,000	
Buildings	2,626,400	$308,140
Equipment	1,142,400	364,000
Trucks	198,800	59,710

Additional data:

1. The leasehold covers a plot of ground leased on July 1, 1985, for a period of 25 years under an operating lease.

2. The office building is on the leased land and was completed on July 1, 1986, at a cost of $806,400; its physical life is set at 40 years. The factory building is on the owned land and was completed on July 1, 1985, at a cost of $1,820,000; its life is also set at 40 years with no expected salvage value.

3. The equipment has a 15-year useful life with no expected salvage value.

4. The company owns three trucks—A, B, and C. Truck A, purchased on July 1, 1988, at a cost of $44,800, had an expected life of three years and a salvage value of $2,800. Truck B, purchased on January 2, 1989, at a cost of $70,000, had an expected life of four years and a salvage value of $5,600. Truck C, purchased on January 2, 1990, at a cost of $84,000, had an expected life of five years and a salvage value of $8,400.

The following transactions occurred in the fiscal year ended June 30, 1991:

1990
July 1   Rent for July 1, 1990, through June 30, 1991, on leased land was paid, $26,600.
Oct. 1   Truck A was traded in on truck D. Cash price of the new truck was $89,600. Cash of $75,600 was paid. Truck D has an expected life of four years and a salvage value of $4,900.

1991
Feb. 2   Truck B was sold for $39,200 cash.
June 1   Truck C was completely demolished in an accident. The truck was not insured.

Required: Prepare journal entries to record the above transactions and the necessary June 30, 1991, adjusting entries. Use the straight-line depreciation method.

P11–6–B
Determine depletion for period and depreciation on building and mining equipment; compute average cost per ton of ore mined

In December 1989, Tanner Company acquired a mine for $1,125,000. The mine contained an estimated 5 million tons of ore. It was also estimated that the land would have a value of $100,000 when the mine was exhausted and that only 2 million tons of ore could be economically extracted. A building was erected on the property at a cost of $150,000. The building had an estimated useful life of 35 years and no salvage value. Specialized mining equipment was installed at a cost of $206,250. This equipment had an estimated useful life of seven years and an estimated $13,750 salvage value. The company began operating on January 1, 1990, and put all of its assets into use on that date. During the year ended December 31, 1990, 200,000 tons of ore were extracted. The company decided to use the units-of-production method to record depreciation on the building and the straight-line method to record depreciation on the equipment.

Required: Prepare journal entries to record the depletion and depreciation charges for the year ended December 31, 1990. Show calculations.

P11–7–B
Record cost and amortization of patent

Houston Company purchased a patent for $90,000 on January 2, 1990. The patent was estimated to have a useful life of 10 years. The $90,000 cost was properly charged to an asset account and amortized in 1990. On January 1, 1991, the company incurred legal and court costs of $27,000 in a successful defense of the patent in a lawsuit. The legal work was performed by an outside law firm.

Required: a. Compute the patent amortization expense for 1990 and give the entry to record it.
b. Compute the patent amortization expense for 1991 and give the entry to record it.

P11–8–B
Record amortization expense for a variety of intangible assets

Given below are selected transactions and other data for Davis Company:

a. The company purchased a patent in early January 1987 for $60,000 and began amortizing it over 10 years. In 1989, the company hired an outside law firm and successfully defended the patent in an infringement suit at a cost of $16,000.
b. Research and development costs incurred in 1989 of $18,000 were expected to provide benefits over the three succeeding years.
c. On January 2, 1990, the company rented space in a warehouse for five years at an annual fee of $4,000. Rent for the first and last years was paid in advance.
d. A total of $40,000 was spent uniformly throughout 1990 by the company in promoting its lesser known trademark, which is expected to have an indefinite life.
e. In January 1988, the company purchased all of the assets and assumed all of the liabilities of another company, paying $80,000 more than the fair market value of all identifiable assets acquired, less the liabilities assumed. The company expects the benefits for which it paid the $80,000 to last 10 years.

Required: For each of the unrelated transactions given above, prepare journal entries to record only those entries required for 1990. If any of the items do not require an entry in 1990, state so.

BUSINESS DECISION PROBLEM 11-1

Record exchange of similar assets; adjust accounts for errors in accounting for depreciable assets

Paige Company acquired machine A for $50,000 on January 2, 1988. Machine A had an estimated useful life of four years and no salvage value. The machine was depreciated on the straight-line basis. On January 2, 1990, machine A was exchanged for machine B. Machine B had a cash price of $60,000. In addition to machine A, cash of $50,000 was given up in the exchange. The company recorded the exchange in accordance with income tax regulations instead of in accordance with generally accepted accounting principles. Machine B has an estimated useful life of five years and no salvage value. The machine is being depreciated using the straight-line method.

Required:
a. What journal entry did the Paige Company make when it recorded the exchange of machines? (Show computations.)
b. What journal entry should the Paige Company have made to record the exchange of machines in accordance with generally accepted accounting principles?
c. Assume the error is discovered on December 31, 1991, before adjusting journal entries have been made. What journal entries should be made to correct the accounting records? What adjusting journal entry should be made to record depreciation for 1991? (Ignore income taxes.)
d. What effect did the error have on reported net income for 1990? (Ignore income taxes.)
e. How should machine B be reported on the December 31, 1991, balance sheet?

BUSINESS DECISION PROBLEM 11-2

Record purchase of two businesses and explain differences between the two; advise client as to which company should be purchased

Jack Barkley is trying to decide whether to buy Company A or Company B. Both Company A and Company B have assets with the following book values and fair market values:

	Book Value	Fair Market Value
Accounts receivable	$120,000	$120,000
Inventories	360,000	600,000
Land	300,000	540,000
Buildings	360,000	840,000
Equipment	144,000	240,000
Patents	96,000	120,000

Liabilities that would be assumed on the purchase of either company include accounts payable, $240,000, and notes payable, $60,000.

The only difference between Company A and Company B is that Company A has net income that is about average for the industry, while Company B has net income that is greatly above average for the industry.

Required:
a. Assume Barkley can buy Company A for $2,160,000 or Company B for $2,760,000. Prepare the journal entries to record the acquisition of (1) Company A and (2) Company B. What accounts for the difference between the purchase price of the two companies?
b. Assume Barkley can buy either company for $2,160,000. Which company would you advise Barkley to buy? Why?

12 Current Liabilities and Payroll Accounting

After studying this chapter, you should be able to:

1. Define liabilities, current liabilities, and long-term liabilities.
2. Define clearly determinable, estimated, and contingent liabilities.
3. Account for clearly determinable, estimated, and contingent liabilities.
4. Describe the essential internal control features for payrolls.
5. Prepare and record a payroll.
6. Prepare an employee's earnings record.
7. Illustrate the use of a payroll checking account.
8. Prepare entries to record employer's payroll taxes and vacation pay.
9. Define and use correctly the new terms in the glossary.

Chapter 1 introduced you to the accounting equation—Assets = Liabilities + Owner's Equity—which is the framework for the entire accounting process. In Chapter 1 and subsequent chapters, we described and illustrated liabilities such as accounts payable, wages payable, unearned delivery fees, notes payable, and interest payable. You probably became aware that we focused our attention on the revenue or expense involved in the transaction rather than on the liabilities. In this chapter, we concentrate on the current liability side of the transaction. Since many current liabilities arise from payroll accounting, the chapter concludes with a detailed section on payroll accounting.

Objective 1:
Define liabilities, current liabilities, and long-term liabilities.

Liabilities result from some **past transaction** and are an obligation to pay cash, provide services, or deliver goods at some time in the **future.** Each of the liabilities discussed in previous chapters and the new liabilities presented in this chapter meet this definition. Just as every company must have assets to operate, every company incurs liabilities in conducting its operations. Corporations (IBM and General Motors), partnerships (CPA firms), and single proprietorships (corner grocery stores) all have one thing in common—they have liabilities.

On the balance sheet, the accountant divides liabilities into current liabilities and long-term liabilities. **Current liabilities** are obligations that are (1) payable within one year or one operating cycle, whichever is longer, or (2) will be paid out of current assets or result in the creation of other current liabilities. **Long-term liabilities** are obligations that do not qualify as current liabilities.

An **operating cycle** (or cash cycle) is the time it takes to begin with cash and end with cash in producing revenues. For most companies, this period is no longer than a few months. Service companies generally have the shortest operating cycle, since they do not have cash tied up in inventory. Manufacturing companies generally have the longest cycle, since their cash is tied up in several inventory accounts and then in accounts receivable before coming back as cash. But even for manufacturing companies, the cycle is generally less than one year. Thus, as a practical matter, current liabilities are those due within one year or less, and long-term liabilities are those due after one year from the present time.

The operating cycle for various types of businesses can be depicted as follows:

Type of Business	Operating Cycle
Service company selling for cash only	Instantaneous
Service company selling on credit	Cash → Accounts receivable → Cash
Merchandising company selling on credit	Cash → Inventory → Accounts receivable → Cash
Manufacturing company selling on credit (covered in Chapter 21)	Cash → Materials inventory → Work in process inventory → Finished goods inventory → Accounts receivable → Cash

This chapter focuses on current liabilities. Long-term liabilities were briefly mentioned in Chapter 8 and are discussed more thoroughly in Chapter 17.

CURRENT LIABILITIES

Current liabilities can be divided into the following three groups:

Objective 2: Define clearly determinable, estimated, and contingent liabilities.

1. **Clearly determinable liabilities.**   The existence of the liability and its amount are certain. Examples include almost all of the liabilities discussed previously, such as accounts payable, notes payable, interest payable, unearned delivery fees, and wages payable. Sales tax payable, federal excise tax payable, dividends payable, and current portions of long-term debt are other examples. Also, most of the payroll liabilities introduced in this chapter are clearly determinable liabilities.

2. **Estimated liabilities.**   The existence of the liability is certain, but its amount can only be **estimated.** Examples include estimated product warranty payable, estimated property tax payable, estimated federal income tax payable, and estimated vacation pay payable.
3. **Contingent liabilities.**   The existence of the liability is uncertain and usually the amount is uncertain because contingent liabilities depend (or are **contingent**) on some future event occurring or not occurring. Examples include liabilities arising from lawsuits, discounted notes receivable, income tax disputes, penalties that may be assessed because of some past action, and failure of another party to pay a debt that a company has guaranteed.

Clearly Determinable Liabilities

Objective 3: Account for clearly determinable, estimated, and contingent liabilities.

Companies that know they have clearly determinable liabilities also know the amount of each liability. The first 11 chapters of this text discussed many of these clearly determinable liabilities, such as accounts payable and notes payable. In this section, we discuss the following additional liabilities that are clearly determinable—sales tax payable, federal excise tax payable, dividends payable, current portions of long-term debt, and payroll liabilities.

Sales Tax Payable.   Many states have a state sales tax on items purchased by consumers. The company selling the product to the customer is responsible for collecting the sales tax from the customer. When the company collects the taxes, it debits Cash and credits Sales Tax Payable. Periodically, the sales taxes collected are paid to the state. At that time, the company debits Sales Tax Payable and credits Cash.

To illustrate, assume that a company sells merchandise in a state that has a 6% sales tax. If goods with a sales price of $1,000 are sold on credit, the following entry is made:

Accounts Receivable	1,060	
Sales		1,000
Sales Tax Payable		60
To record sales and sales tax payable.		

Assume that sales for the entire period are $100,000 and that $6,000 is in the Sales Tax Payable account when the company remits the funds to the state taxing agency. The following entry shows the payment to the state:

Sales Tax Payable	6,000	
Cash		6,000
To record the payment to the state for sales taxes collected from customers.		

When sales taxes are recorded in the same account as sales revenue, the sales tax must be separated from sales revenue at the end of the accounting period. To do this, you add the sales tax rate to 100% and divide this percentage into recorded sales revenue. For instance, assume that total recorded sales revenues for an accounting period are $10,600, and the sales tax rate is 6%. To find the sales tax, divide $10,600 by 106%. The answer of $10,000 gives sales revenue for the period. Sales tax is equal to recorded sales revenue of $10,600 less actual sales revenue of $10,000, or $600.

Federal Excise Tax Payable.   Some goods, such as alcoholic beverages, tobacco, gasoline, cosmetics, tires, automobiles, cameras, radios, television sets, and jewelry, are subject to federal excise tax. The entries a company makes when selling these goods are similar to those made for sales taxes payable. For example, assume that the Dixon Jewelry Store sells a diamond ring to a young couple for $2,000. The sale is subject to a 6% sales tax and a 10% federal excise tax. The entry to record the sale is:

Accounts Receivable	2,320	
Sales		2,000
Sales Tax Payable		120
Federal Excise Tax Payable		200
To record the sale of a diamond ring.		

The company records the remittance of the taxes to the federal taxing agency by debiting Federal Excise Tax Payable and crediting Cash.

Dividends Payable.   Corporation accounting is first discussed in Chapter 15. At that time you will learn that corporations pay dividends (usually in the form of cash) to their owners (or stockholders) just as owners of single proprietorships withdraw cash from the business. For example, assume the board of directors of a corporation declares a dividend of $400,000, but the dividend will be paid in the next accounting period. The company will list the dividend payable of $400,000 among its current liabilities on the balance sheet at the end of the current accounting period. Chapter 16 discusses in detail the entries regarding dividends.

Current Portions of Long-Term Debt.   Any portion of a long-term debt that will become due within the next year is moved to the current liability section of the balance sheet. For instance, assume a company signed a series of 10 individual notes payable for $10,000 each that come due (one each year) in the 6th year through the 15th year. Each year, beginning in the fifth year, another $10,000 would be moved from the long-term liability category to the current liability category on the balance sheet. The current portion would then be paid within one year.

Payroll Liabilities.   A number of current liabilities arise from payroll accounting. The section on payroll accounting in this chapter discusses these liabilities.

Estimated Liabilities

Companies that have estimated liabilities know they exist but can only estimate the amount. The primary accounting problem is to arrive at a reasonable estimate of the amount of the liability as of the balance sheet date. The estimated liabilities discussed below are: estimated product warranty payable, estimated property tax payable, estimated federal income taxes payable, estimated vacation pay payable, and other estimated liabilities.

Estimated Product Warranty Payable.   When companies sell merchandise and other products, such as machinery, they must often guarantee against defects by placing a warranty on their products. When defects occur, the company is obligated to reimburse the customer or repair the product. For many products, the number of defects that will occur can be predicted, based on past experience. To provide for a proper matching of revenues and expenses, the accountant estimates the amount of expense that will result from an accounting period's sales. Product Warranty Expense is debited and Estimated Product Warranty Payable is credited for that amount.

To illustrate, assume that a company sells personal computers and warrants all parts for a one-year period. The average price per computer is $1,500, and the company sells 1,000 computers in 1991. The company expects 10% of the computers to develop defective parts within one year of sale. The estimated average cost of warranty repairs per defective computer is $150. To arrive at a reasonable estimate of the amount of the entry to be made at the end of the accounting period, the accountant makes the following calculation:

Number of computers sold	1,000
Percent estimated to develop defects	× 10%
Total estimated defective computers	100
Deduct computers defective to date	40
Estimated additional number to become defective during warranty period	60
Estimated warranty repair cost per computer	×$ 150
Estimated product warranty payable	$9,000

The entry made at the end of the accounting period is:

Product Warranty Expense	9,000	
Estimated Product Warranty Payable		9,000
To record estimated product warranty expense.		

When a customer returns one of the computers purchased in 1991 for repair work (during the warranty period) in 1992, the cost of the repairs is debited to Estimated Product Warranty Payable. For instance, assume that Mr. Holman returns his computer for repairs within the warranty period. The repair cost includes parts, $40, and labor, $160. The following entry is made:

Estimated Product Warranty Payable	200	
Repair Parts Inventory		40
Wages Payable		160
To record replacement of parts under warranty.		

Estimated Property Tax Payable.   City and county governments both assess property taxes. These governments use the taxes to finance government projects that benefit all local residents, including businesses. Since the taxes are a charge for services received (road repair and other services that benefit the local economy), accountants consider these taxes as a monthly operating expense of the business.

The taxing authority usually assesses property taxes annually, and a company must prorate the taxes to each month. Quite often, governments have a fiscal year of July 1 to June 30. The property tax bill for the fiscal year usually comes several months after the beginning of the government's fiscal year and is usually payable within from one to three months. Therefore, a company must estimate the monthly property tax expense from the beginning of the government's fiscal year until the bill arrives and the actual amount of tax for that fiscal year is known.

To illustrate, assume that Dobbins Company estimated in July that its annual property tax for July 1, 1991, to June 30, 1992, would be $24,000. At the end of July, August, and September, the company made the following entry:

```
Property Tax Expense .........................   2,000
    Estimated Property Tax Payable ..............           2,000
        To record the estimated property tax expense for the month.
```

On October 1, Dobbins Company received a $24,648 property tax bill for the 1991–92 fiscal year, with payment due by November 20. The correct monthly amount of expense is ($24,648/12) = $2,054. Thus, the amount of expense recorded for July, August, and September was too low by $54 per month, or a total of 3 × $54 = $162. Since the amount of understatement is relatively small, Dobbins Company decided to charge the entire understatement to the month of October. The entry was:

```
Property Tax Expense ($2,054 + $162) ...........   2,216
    Estimated Property Tax Payable ..............           2,216
        To record property tax expense for the month.
```

After the October entry, the Estimated Property Tax Payable account had a balance of $8,216. On November 20, Dobbins Company paid the property tax bill. The entry was:

```
Estimated Property Tax Payable ................   8,216
Prepaid Property Taxes ......................   16,432
    Cash ...................................           24,648
        To record payment of the property tax bill for fiscal 1991–92.
```

At the end of each month from November 1991 through June 1992, the following entry will be made to record the monthly property tax expense:

```
Property Tax Expense .........................   2,054
    Prepaid Property Taxes ...................           2,054
        To record property tax expense for the month.
```

The Prepaid Property Taxes account will have a zero balance by the end of June 1992.

Estimated Federal Income Taxes Payable. Single proprietorships and partnerships do not pay federal income taxes. Instead, the income flows through to the individual owner(s) and appears on their personal income tax return. However, corporations are taxed as a separate entity. Although corporate taxes are based on yearly corporation income, these taxes are an operating expense that must be accrued each month if the company prepares monthly financial statements. Thus, a company must estimate its monthly income tax expense until the final tax is known.

To illustrate, assume that on January 1, Scholten Corporation estimates its federal income tax for the year at $480,000, or $40,000 per month. Each month beginning with January (assuming a December 31 year-end), Scholten would make the following entry:

```
Federal Income Tax Expense . . . . . . . . . . . . . . . . . . .   40,000
    Federal Income Tax Payable  . . . . . . . . . . . . . . . .            40,000
  To record estimated federal income tax for the month.
```

Any payments made to the Internal Revenue Service during the year would be debited to Federal Income Tax Payable and credited to Cash. At the end of the year, when the correct amount of taxable income can be determined, the accountant brings the expense and liability accounts to their correct balances.

Estimated Vacation Pay Payable. The estimated vacation pay liability results in several other payroll liabilities. Therefore, the section on payroll accounting discusses this topic.

Other Estimated Liabilities. Another estimated liability that is (unfortunately) becoming quite common relates to clean-up costs for industrial pollution. One company had the following note in its 1986 financial statements:

> In the past, the Company treated hazardous waste at its chemical facilities. Testing of the ground waters in the areas of the treatment impoundments at these facilities disclosed the presence of certain contaminants. In compliance with environmental regulations, the Company developed a plan that will prevent further contamination, provide for remedial action to remove the present contaminants and establish a monitoring program to monitor ground water conditions in the future. A similar plan has been developed for a site previously used as a metal pickling facility. Estimated future costs of $2,860,000 have been accrued in the accompanying financial statements for 1986 to complete the procedures required under these plans.

Contingent Liabilities

When liabilities are contingent, the company is not sure that the liability exists and is usually unsure about the amount. *FASB Statement No. 5* defines a contingency as "an existing condition, situation, or set of circumstances involving uncertainty as to possible gain or loss to an enterprise that will ultimately be resolved when one or more future events occur or fail to occur."[1]

According to *FASB Statement No. 5,* if the liability is probable and the amount can be reasonably estimated, contingent liabilities may be recorded in the accounts. However, since most contingent liabilities may not occur and the amount usually cannot be reasonably estimated, the accountant usually does not record them in the accounts. Instead, these contingent liabilities are disclosed in notes to the financial statements.

Many contingent liabilities arise as the result of lawsuits. In fact, 361 of the 600 companies that were included in the annual survey of accounting practices conducted by the AICPA reported contingent liabilities resulting from litigation.[2]

---

[1] FASB, "Accounting for Contingencies," *Statement of Financial Accounting Standards No. 5* (Stamford, Conn., 1975). Copyright © by Financial Accounting Standards Board, High Ridge Park, Stamford, Connecticut 06905, U.S.A.

[2] AICPA, *Accounting Trends & Techniques* (New York, 1987), p. 65.

The following two examples taken from annual reports are typical of the disclosures made in notes to the financial statements. Be aware that just because a suit is brought, the company being sued is not necessarily guilty.

As reported daily in newspapers, the past decade has seen many attempts by individuals, groups, and companies to take over corporations by acquiring a significant portion of their outstanding capital stock. Names like T. Boone Pickens and Ron Perelman are prominent in the news. Sometimes corporations buy back their shares from these "corporate raiders" at an inflated price (called "greenmail") to get rid of the threat. CPC International, Inc., was accused by some of its stockholders of paying too much to reacquire its shares from a so-called "corporate raider" to prevent a corporate takeover bid. The lawsuit brought by the stockholders resulted in the following disclosure of a contingent liability:

Litigation

Prior to November 4, 1986, entities controlled by Ronald O. Perelman (the "Perelman Group") acquired 3,680,645 shares, or approximately 7.6%, of the Company's then outstanding common stock. On November 4, 1986, the Company's investment banker, Salomon Brothers Inc. ("Salomon"), was asked to make definitive recommendations for restructuring the Company to maximize values to stockholders, and the Board of Directors authorized the repurchase of up to 10 million of the 48.7 million shares of common stock then outstanding. On November 5, 1986, Salomon purchased 4,030,645 shares of the Company's common stock, including all of the shares held by the Perelman Group, at a price of $88.50 per share (equivalent to 8,061,290 shares at a price of $44.25 per share, giving effect to the two-for-one split in January 1987). Later on November 5, 1986, the Company acquired the 4,030,645 shares from Salomon at the same price. In November and December 1986, five stockholder derivative suits and one class action were instituted in the United States District Courts for the District of Delaware, the Southern District of New York and the District of New Jersey. The defendants in the derivative suits are the Company and its directors, Salomon, Mr. Perelman and entities controlled by him. The defendants in the class action are the Company, Salomon and Mr. Perelman. The plaintiffs variously allege that the Perelman Group purchased large blocks of the common stock in an attempt to acquire control of the Company, that the Company purchased the shares which Salomon had acquired from the Perelman Group at an artificially inflated price, and that the defendant's actions constitute violations of Section 10(b) of the Securities Exchange Act of 1934 and Rule 10b-5 thereunder, breach of fiduciary duties of directors and waste of corporate assets. The plaintiffs seek unspecified damages, injunctive relief, rescission of the transactions and the return of amounts paid by the Company to the Perelman Group or to Salomon. The defendants deny all allegations of improper conduct and are defending the suits.

Another company, CSP, Inc., dismissed a former officer of the company and included the following note to disclose the contingent liability resulting from the ensuing litigation:

Litigation

In October 1986, an action was brought against the Company and its President by a former officer for an alleged wrongful termination of his employment agreement with the Company. The suit seeks $34,000,000 in damages. The Company and its President have responded by denying any wrongful termination and asserting that the former employee has been paid all amounts pursuant to the agreement. Management believes this suit is without merit and that the outcome of this matter will not materially affect the Company's financial position.

Contingent liabilities may also arise from discounted notes receivable (covered in Chapter 8), income tax disputes, penalties that may be assessed because of some past action, and failure of another party to pay a debt that a company has guaranteed.

The next section discusses payroll accounting. Most of you have had either a part-time or full-time job and have been paid weekly, semimonthly, or monthly. You probably were surprised when you received your first paycheck because the deductions were greater than expected. Payroll accounting includes the record-keeping necessary to account for employees' paychecks and deductions. Since a company's payroll costs are one of the largest expenses a company incurs, payroll accounting is an important function.

PAYROLL ACCOUNTING

In most business organizations, accounting for payroll is particularly important because (1) payrolls often represent the largest expense that a company incurs, (2) both federal and state governments require that detailed payroll records be maintained, and (3) companies must file regular payroll reports with both state and federal governments and make remittances of amounts withheld or otherwise due. Thus, the general objectives of payroll accounting are to process such data as hours worked, pay rates, and payroll deductions so that the company can:

1. Establish internal control over payroll and protect against fraud in payroll transactions.
2. Prepare and record a payroll, including gross earnings, payroll taxes and deductions, employee earnings record, and the payroll journal.
3. Pay the payroll using the payroll checking account. Also provide accurate and timely paychecks as well as an explanation of payroll data.
4. Record employer payroll taxes, including FICA (social security) taxes, federal unemployment taxes, and state unemployment taxes.
5. Remit taxes withheld, unemployment taxes, and other deductions to the proper government agency or other organization.
6. Prepare adjusting entries for end-of-period accruals, including wages, payroll taxes, and vacation pay.

This section discusses the objectives of payroll accounting and the methods of achieving these objectives. You should be aware that even though many businesses today use more efficient computerized payroll systems, the objectives and methods used to compute amounts and deductions are the same as for manual systems.

Establishing Internal Control over Payroll

Objective 4: Describe the essential internal control features for payrolls.

In small companies, the owner-manager may provide adequate internal control over payroll transactions by actually computing and preparing the payroll. Larger companies obtain internal control through application of the general principles of internal control and the more specific guides to controls over cash disbursements, as described in Chapter 7. Separation of duties is a crucial aspect of payroll internal control. Ideally, timekeeping, payroll preparation, payroll record-keeping, and payroll distribution functions should be performed by different employees.

If an employee's compensation is based on hours worked, the company must maintain an accurate record of each employee's time. In small companies, the owner may simply make notations in a notebook stating when employees report to work and leave work. Larger companies often use a time clock for hourly employees. Each day when employees report to work, every employee inserts a **time card** into the clock, which prints the date and time on the card. Employees follow the same procedure when leaving work. Companies must safeguard against one employee punching in or out for another employee; for example, the company could station someone at the time clock to supervise the check-in and check-out procedures.

In small companies, the owner usually knows the hours each employee works. The owner, or a bookkeeper, may keep the company payroll records and compute the employees' earnings and deductions, as well as prepare, sign, and distribute the paychecks. Most large companies use the following procedure to prepare paychecks: At a regular interval before payday, the payroll department collects and verifies each employee's pay rate and hours worked to compute total (gross) pay. At this point, all legally required and authorized deductions are subtracted from the total (gross) pay, individual payroll records are updated, and payroll checks are prepared. Checks are then sent to the treasurer's office for signature. Supporting documents, such as employee's earnings statements showing earnings and deductions to date, may accompany the checks. Each check should be delivered to the employee in person or deposited directly by the employer into the employee's bank account.

Payroll Fraud. Whenever cash is disbursed, the potential for fraud exists. Some payroll fraud schemes used successfully in the past are listed below.

1. A payroll department employee pays another employee more than that employee has actually earned, and then the payroll department employee receives a kickback of part of the overpayment.
2. A payroll department employee makes out a payroll check payable to a former or fictitious employee and then cashes the check.
3. A payroll department employee prepares and cashes duplicate payroll checks.

Because of these and other schemes, companies must exercise great care to ensure payroll accuracy. Separation of duties is one way to help ensure accuracy. Fraudulent transactions are difficult to arrange and cover up when one employee's work serves as a check on another's. For example, if a payroll department employee falsifies the hours worked by a plant employee in an attempt to overpay the employee, the changed hours on the payroll record will not agree with the time card record. Collusion by two payroll department employees would be required to commit such a fraud unless the same employee has access to time cards, other payroll records, and payroll checks.

Maintenance of accurate employment and payroll records is also crucial. As soon as possible, payroll department personnel must be informed of the hiring and termination of employees so that they know which employees currently work for the company. This information helps prevent the writing of fictitious checks. Also, current copies of documents authorizing payroll deductions should be on hand. Payroll fraud can be reduced by keeping accurate, detailed records for each employee. Companies must be alert to the possibility of payroll fraud and take steps to prevent it.

Preparing and Recording a Payroll

Objective 5:
Prepare and record a
payroll.

To prepare and record a payroll, you must begin by determining an employee's gross earnings. Since gross earnings are generally not the amount the employee receives, the next step is to compute the employee's payroll taxes and other payroll deductions. Using examples, the paragraphs that follow explain this phase of payroll accounting.

Computing Gross Earnings.   Although the terms *wages* and *salaries* are often used interchangeably, they are not the same. The term *wages* generally refers to gross earnings of employees who are paid by the hour for only the actual hours worked. The term *salaries,* on the other hand, usually refers to gross earnings of employees who are paid a flat amount per week or month regardless of the number of hours worked in a period.

An employee's **gross earnings** are the employee's total pay or compensation, including regular pay and overtime premium. The computation of gross earnings for wage employees and salaried employees differs. Computing gross earnings for wages usually consists of simply multiplying the number of hours the employee worked by the employee's hourly wage rate. For example, 40 hours times $10 per hour gives gross earnings of $400 for the week. Since the gross earnings for salaried employees is usually a specified yearly amount, the annual salary is divided by the number of pay periods in the year. For example, assuming an employee is paid monthly and earns $36,000 a year, you would divide $36,000 by 12 months to determine the monthly gross earnings of $3,000. In some instances, however, the calculation of gross earnings is a little more detailed due to legal or contractual requirements.

The federal **Wages and Hours Law** (also called the **Fair Labor Standards Act**) requires (1) most employees who are paid by the hour to be paid a minimum of 1½ times their normal rate for hours worked in excess of 40 per week and (2) employees to be paid at least the minimum wage. The **minimum wage** rate is set by the federal government and changes from time to time. In addition to this federal law, some union contracts also call for premium pay rates for certain hours worked, such as double time for work on Sunday. You should be aware that executive, administrative, and some professional employees are salaried and exempt from both the minimum wage and overtime pay provisions. However, lower-level, nonprofessional, salaried employees are generally subject to the minimum wage and overtime pay provisions.

The payroll department must maintain detailed time records to ensure that legal and contractual requirements are being met. In the absence of valid records, assessments for overtime pay may later be made against the employer.

Three situations follow that illustrate how to compute gross earnings that include overtime premiums.

1. Mary Kennedy's basic wage rate is $9 per hour. Her overtime premium, then, is one half of $9, or $4.50 per hour. Mary's gross pay for a week in which she worked 48 hours is $468. The $468 is computed as $(48 \times \$9) + (8 \times \$4.50)$, or ($432 + $36) = $468. (An alternative calculation is $[40 \text{ hours} \times \$9] + [8 \text{ hours} \times \$13.50] = \$468$.)

2. Grace Early's basic $18,200 annual salary is paid over 52 weeks at a guaranteed weekly minimum of $350 ($40 \times \$8.75$ per hour), even though she often only works 37.5 hours per week. She is entitled to overtime pay for hours worked in excess of 40 per week. Her gross earnings for working 42 hours in a week are computed as $350 + $(2 \times 1.5 \times \$8.75) = \$376.25$.

3. Dan Brown is paid $0.50 for each unit of product machined. In the current we k, he worked 48 hours and completed 960 units. His gross pay before overtime premium is $480 ($960 \times \$0.50$). The $480 is divided by 48 hours to get $10 as his regular hourly rate for the week. Therefore, Dan's overtime premium is $5 per hour, and his total overtime pay is $40 ($8 \times \$5$). His gross earnings for the week are $480 + $40, or $520.

Computing Payroll Taxes and Deductions.   Required **deductions from gross earnings** include withholdings for federal income taxes, state income taxes, and FICA (social security) taxes. Employees may choose to have various other deductions taken from their checks.

Federal and State Income Taxes.   Wage earners in the United States are under a pay-as-you-go federal income tax system. This means that most employees must pay federal income taxes on wages as they are earned during the year. Employers withhold **federal income tax** when the employee's earnings are paid, and the amount of **federal income tax withheld** is noted on the employee's check stub. These federal taxes are remitted (sent) periodically by the employer to federally specified banks or to the Internal Revenue Service (IRS). Companies located in states with state income taxes also must withhold **state income tax** from employees' paychecks and remit these amounts to the revenue authority in those states. Amounts paid to independent contractors, such as outside consultants, are not subject to withholding for federal income tax and FICA tax.

The amount of income tax withheld from each employee's pay depends on the (1) amount of earnings, (2) frequency of the payroll period, and (3) the number of **withholding allowances** claimed by the employee. Withholding allowances are claimed by the employee on an **Employee's Withholding Allowance Certificate (Form W-4)** filed with the employer, usually the first day on the job. Illustration 12.1 shows the W-4 form of John Hanson, who claims three withholding allowances, which usually means that he will claim three exemptions on his federal income tax return—one for himself, one for his wife, and one for his child. An exemption is a fixed amount of income ($1,950 in 1988, and $2,000 in 1989) that is not subject to taxation.

Illustration 12.1

*Employee's
Withholding
Allowance
Certificate
(Form W-4)*

------------------ Cut here and give the certificate to your employer. Keep the top portion for your records. ------------------

Form **W-4** Department of the Treasury Internal Revenue Service	**Employee's Withholding Allowance Certificate** ▶ For Privacy Act and Paperwork Reduction Act Notice, see reverse.	OMB No. 1545-0010 1988

1 Type or print your first name and middle initial	Last name	2 Your social security number
John R.	Hanson	253-13-2807

Home address (number and street or rural route) 325 St. George Drive City or town, state, and ZIP code Athens, GA 30605	3 Marital Status	☐ Single ☒ Married ☐ Married, but withhold at higher Single rate. **Note:** *If married, but legally separated, or spouse is a nonresident alien, check the Single box.*

4 Total number of allowances you are claiming (from line G above or from the Worksheets on back if they apply) . . .	**4**	3
5 Additional amount, if any, you want deducted from each pay	**5**	$

6 I claim exemption from withholding because (check boxes below that apply):

a ☐ Last year I did not owe any Federal income tax and had a right to a full refund of **ALL** income tax withheld, **AND**

b ☐ This year I do not expect to owe any Federal income tax and expect to have a right to a full refund of **ALL** income tax withheld.

c If both **a** and **b** apply and you satisfy the additional conditions outlined above under "Exemption From Withholding," enter the year effective and "EXEMPT" here. Do not complete lines 4 and 5 above . . . . . ▶   Year 19

7 Are you a full-time student? (**Note:** *Full-time students are **not** automatically exempt.*)   ☐ Yes ☒ No

Under penalties of perjury, I certify that I am entitled to the number of withholding allowances claimed on this certificate or, if claiming exemption from withholding, that I am entitled to claim the exempt status.

Employee's signature ▶   **Date** ▶   , 198

8 Employer's name and address (Employer: Complete 8, 9, and 10 only if sending to IRS) Doug's Ace Hardware 1290 Atlanta Highway, Athens, Georgia 30605	9 Office code	10 Employer identification number 15-249363

A **wage bracket withholding table** (Illustration 12.2) is a table provided by the Internal Revenue Service to help employers determine the amount of federal income tax to withhold from employees' paychecks. When the federal income tax laws are revised, the table amounts change. Tables are provided for both married and single persons for various pay periods, such as weekly, biweekly, and monthly. Note that the amount of income taxes withheld changes with the number of withholding allowances claimed.

On or before January 31, after the end of each calendar year, an employer is required to prepare for each employee a four-copy (or more) **Wage and Tax Statement (Form W-2)** for the previous calendar-year earnings. An example of a W-2 is shown in Illustration 12.3. This form provides wage and tax data needed to prepare the employee's personal federal and state income tax returns. One copy is sent by the employer to the Social Security Administration, which then transmits data contained on the form to the Internal Revenue Service. The other three copies of the W-2 are given to the employee. Of these three, one copy is filed with the employee's federal income tax return, one is filed with the state income tax return (if the employee lives in a state that has a state income tax), and one is retained by the employee as a personal record. The IRS uses data from the form to determine whether the employee has reported the proper amount of earned income and taxes withheld on the tax return.

FICA (Social Security) Taxes. The **FICA (social security) tax** was created by passage of the Federal Insurance Contributions Act in 1935. Persons who are currently working in jobs covered by the act must pay a certain percentage of their earnings (up to a maximum amount) into special trust funds. Employee contributions are matched by equal payments by employers. Money paid into the trust is used to finance retirement benefits and medical benefits (medicare) paid to persons and their families who are currently retired or disabled and who qualify for such benefits under the

Illustration 12.2

Federal Wage Bracket Withholding Table

MARRIED Persons–WEEKLY Payroll Period
(For Wages Paid After December 1987)

And the wages are–		And the number of withholding allowances claimed is–										
At least	But less than	0	1	2	3	4	5	6	7	8	9	10
		The amount of income tax to be withheld shall be–										
$0	$60	$0	$0	$0	$0	$0	$0	$0	$0	$0	$0	$0
60	65	1	0	0	0	0	0	0	0	0	0	0
65	70	1	0	0	0	0	0	0	0	0	0	0
70	75	2	0	0	0	0	0	0	0	0	0	0
75	80	3	0	0	0	0	0	0	0	0	0	0
80	85	4	0	0	0	0	0	0	0	0	0	0
85	90	4	0	0	0	0	0	0	0	0	0	0
90	95	5	0	0	0	0	0	0	0	0	0	0
95	100	6	0	0	0	0	0	0	0	0	0	0
100	105	7	1	0	0	0	0	0	0	0	0	0
105	110	7	2	0	0	0	0	0	0	0	0	0
110	115	8	2	0	0	0	0	0	0	0	0	0
115	120	9	3	0	0	0	0	0	0	0	0	0
120	125	10	4	0	0	0	0	0	0	0	0	0
125	130	10	5	0	0	0	0	0	0	0	0	0
130	135	11	5	0	0	0	0	0	0	0	0	0
135	140	12	6	1	0	0	0	0	0	0	0	0
140	145	13	7	1	0	0	0	0	0	0	0	0
145	150	13	8	2	0	0	0	0	0	0	0	0
150	155	14	8	3	0	0	0	0	0	0	0	0
155	160	15	9	4	0	0	0	0	0	0	0	0
160	165	16	10	4	0	0	0	0	0	0	0	0
165	170	16	11	5	0	0	0	0	0	0	0	0
170	175	17	11	6	0	0	0	0	0	0	0	0
175	180	18	12	7	1	0	0	0	0	0	0	0
180	185	19	13	7	2	0	0	0	0	0	0	0
185	190	19	14	8	2	0	0	0	0	0	0	0
190	195	20	14	9	3	0	0	0	0	0	0	0
195	200	21	15	10	4	0	0	0	0	0	0	0
200	210	22	16	11	5	0	0	0	0	0	0	0
210	220	23	18	12	7	1	0	0	0	0	0	0
220	230	25	19	14	8	2	0	0	0	0	0	0
230	240	26	21	15	10	4	0	0	0	0	0	0
240	250	28	22	17	11	5	0	0	0	0	0	0
250	260	29	24	18	13	7	1	0	0	0	0	0
260	270	31	25	20	14	8	3	0	0	0	0	0
270	280	32	27	21	16	10	4	0	0	0	0	0
280	290	34	28	23	17	11	6	0	0	0	0	0
290	300	35	30	24	19	13	7	2	0	0	0	0
300	310	37	31	26	20	14	9	3	0	0	0	0
310	320	38	33	27	22	16	10	5	0	0	0	0
320	330	40	34	29	23	17	12	6	1	0	0	0
330	340	41	36	30	25	19	13	8	2	0	0	0
340	350	43	37	32	26	20	15	9	4	0	0	0
350	360	44	39	33	28	22	16	11	5	0	0	0
360	370	46	40	35	29	23	18	12	7	1	0	0
370	380	47	42	36	31	25	19	14	8	2	0	0
380	390	49	43	38	32	26	21	15	10	4	0	0
390	400	50	45	39	34	28	22	17	11	5	0	0
400	410	52	46	41	35	29	24	18	13	7	1	0
410	420	53	48	42	37	31	25	20	14	8	3	0
420	430	55	49	44	38	32	27	21	16	10	4	0
430	440	56	51	45	40	34	28	23	17	11	6	0
440	450	58	52	47	41	35	30	24	19	13	7	2
450	460	59	54	48	43	37	31	26	20	14	9	3
460	470	61	55	50	44	38	33	27	22	16	10	5
470	480	62	57	51	46	40	34	29	23	17	12	6
480	490	64	58	53	47	41	36	30	25	19	13	8
490	500	65	60	54	49	43	37	32	26	20	15	9
500	510	67	61	56	50	44	39	33	28	22	16	11
510	520	68	63	57	52	46	40	35	29	23	18	12
520	530	70	64	59	53	47	42	36	31	25	19	14
530	540	71	66	60	55	49	43	38	32	26	21	15
540	550	73	67	62	56	50	45	39	34	28	22	17
550	560	74	69	63	58	52	46	41	35	29	24	18
560	570	76	70	65	59	53	48	42	37	31	25	20
570	580	77	72	66	61	55	49	44	38	32	27	21
580	590	79	73	68	62	56	51	45	40	34	28	23
590	600	80	75	69	64	58	52	47	41	35	30	24
600	610	82	76	71	65	59	54	48	43	37	31	26

act. Full retirement benefits are available to workers who reach age 65; reduced benefits can be applied for at age 62. Additional voluntary medical insurance is available to persons age 65 and over.

The amount of FICA withheld for each employee for the year 1988 was 7.51% of the first $45,000 of wages. The rates and bases scheduled to go into

Illustration 12.2
(concluded)

MARRIED Persons—**WEEKLY** Payroll Period
(For Wages Paid After December 1987)

And the wages are—		And the number of withholding allowances claimed is—										
At least	But less than	0	1	2	3	4	5	6	7	8	9	10
		The amount of income tax to be withheld shall be—										
$610	$620	$83	$78	$72	$67	$61	$55	$50	$44	$38	$33	$27
620	630	85	79	74	68	62	57	51	46	40	34	29
630	640	87	81	75	70	64	58	53	47	41	36	30
640	650	90	82	77	71	65	60	54	49	43	37	32
650	660	93	84	78	73	67	61	56	50	44	39	33
660	670	95	85	80	74	68	63	57	52	46	40	35
670	680	98	88	81	76	70	64	59	53	47	42	36
680	690	101	91	83	77	71	66	60	55	49	43	38
690	700	104	93	84	79	73	67	62	56	50	45	39
700	710	107	96	86	80	74	69	63	58	52	46	41
710	720	109	99	88	82	76	70	65	59	53	48	42
720	730	112	102	91	83	77	72	66	61	55	49	44
730	740	115	105	94	85	79	73	68	62	56	51	45
740	750	118	107	97	86	80	75	69	64	58	52	47
750	760	121	110	100	89	82	76	71	65	59	54	48
760	770	123	113	102	92	83	78	72	67	61	55	50
770	780	126	116	105	95	85	79	74	68	62	57	51
780	790	129	119	108	98	87	81	75	70	64	58	53
790	800	132	121	111	100	90	82	77	71	65	60	54
800	810	135	124	114	103	93	84	78	73	67	61	56
810	820	137	127	116	106	95	85	80	74	68	63	57
820	830	140	130	119	109	98	88	81	76	70	64	59
830	840	143	133	122	112	101	91	83	77	71	66	60
840	850	146	135	125	114	104	93	84	79	73	67	62
850	860	149	138	128	117	107	96	86	80	74	69	63
860	870	151	141	130	120	109	99	88	82	76	70	65
870	880	154	144	133	123	112	102	91	83	77	72	66
880	890	157	147	136	126	115	105	94	85	79	73	68
890	900	160	149	139	128	118	107	97	86	80	75	69
900	910	163	152	142	131	121	110	100	89	82	76	71
910	920	165	155	144	134	123	113	102	92	83	78	72
920	930	168	158	147	137	126	116	105	95	85	79	74
930	940	171	161	150	140	129	119	108	98	87	81	75
940	950	174	163	153	142	132	121	111	100	90	82	77
950	960	177	166	156	145	135	124	114	103	93	84	78
960	970	179	169	158	148	137	127	116	106	95	85	80
970	980	182	172	161	151	140	130	119	109	98	88	81
980	990	185	175	164	154	143	133	122	112	101	91	83
990	1,000	188	177	167	156	146	135	125	114	104	93	84
1,000	1,010	191	180	170	159	149	138	128	117	107	96	86
1,010	1,020	193	183	172	162	151	141	130	120	109	99	88
1,020	1,030	196	186	175	165	154	144	133	123	112	102	91
1,030	1,040	199	189	178	168	157	147	136	126	115	105	94
1,040	1,050	202	191	181	170	160	149	139	128	118	107	97
1,050	1,060	205	194	184	173	163	152	142	131	121	110	100
1,060	1,070	207	197	186	176	165	155	144	134	123	113	102
1,070	1,080	210	200	189	179	168	158	147	137	126	116	105
1,080	1,090	213	203	192	182	171	161	150	140	129	119	108
1,090	1,100	216	205	195	184	174	163	153	142	132	121	111
1,100	1,110	219	208	198	187	177	166	156	145	135	124	114
1,110	1,120	221	211	200	190	179	169	158	148	137	127	116
1,120	1,130	224	214	203	193	182	172	161	151	140	130	119
1,130	1,140	227	217	206	196	185	175	164	154	143	133	122
1,140	1,150	230	219	209	198	188	177	167	156	146	135	125
1,150	1,160	233	222	212	201	191	180	170	159	149	138	128
1,160	1,170	235	225	214	204	193	183	172	162	151	141	130
1,170	1,180	238	228	217	207	196	186	175	165	154	144	133
1,180	1,190	241	231	220	210	199	189	178	168	157	147	136
1,190	1,200	244	233	223	212	202	191	181	170	160	149	139
1,200	1,210	247	236	226	215	205	194	184	173	163	152	142
1,210	1,220	249	239	228	218	207	197	186	176	165	155	144
1,220	1,230	252	242	231	221	210	200	189	179	168	158	147
1,230	1,240	255	245	234	224	213	203	192	182	171	161	150
1,240	1,250	258	247	237	226	216	205	195	184	174	163	153
1,250	1,260	261	250	240	229	219	208	198	187	177	166	156
1,260	1,270	263	253	242	232	221	211	200	190	179	169	158

$1,270 and over   Use Table 1(b) for a **MARRIED person** on page 22. Also see the instructions on page 20.

effect for 1988–92 are shown in Illustration 12.4. The maximum tax paid by an employee will increase from $3,380 in 1988 to $4,016 in 1992 if these rates are put into effect.

Other Payroll Deductions. Besides payroll deductions for taxes, companies may make other deductions from an employee's gross earnings. Some union contracts require companies to deduct union dues from gross

Illustration 12.3 *Wage and Tax Statement (Form W-2)*

1 Control number	22222	For Paperwork Reduction Act Notice, see back of Copy D. OMB No 1545-0008	For Official Use Only ▶	
2 Employer's name, address, and ZIP code Doug's Ace Hardware 1290 Atlanta Highway Athens, GA 30605			3 Employer's identification number 15-249363	4 Employer's state I.D. number 33048
			5 Statutory employee ☐ Deceased ☐ Pension plan ☐ Legal rep ☐	942 emp ☐ Subtotal ☐ Deferred compensation ☐ Void ☐
			6 Allocated tips	7 Advance EIC payment
8 Employee's social security number 253-13-2807	9 Federal income tax withheld $1,968		10 Wages, tips, other compensation $20,000	11 Social security tax withheld $1,502
12 Employee's name (first, middle, last) John R. Hanson			13 Social security wages $20,000	14 Social security tips
			16 (See Instr for Forms W-2/W-2P)	16a Fringe benefits incl in Box 10
325 St. George Drive Athens, GA 30605			17 State income tax $296.44	18 State wages, tips, etc $20,000	19 Name of state Georgia
15 Employee's address and ZIP code			20 Local income tax	21 Local wages, tips, etc 22 Name of locality

Form **W-2 Wage and Tax Statement   1987**

Illustration 12.4

FICA (Social Security) Rates and Bases

Year	Rate	Base	Maximum
1988 . . .	7.51%	$45,000	$3,380
1989 . . .	7.51	46,800*	3,515
1990 . . .	7.65	48,600*	3,718
1991 . . .	7.65	50,400*	3,856
1992 . . .	7.65	52,500*	4,016

* These amounts are estimates based on a 4% annual wage inflation rate and computed using the automatic escalator provisions. The actual increases will represent an inflation adjustment based on the change in the average covered wage in the United States during the preceding calendar year.

pay as a convenience to employees and the union. The union then receives from the employer the dues withheld from the employees. Medical insurance and life insurance premiums may also be deducted from gross pay. These deductions are made most often when a company offers group life insurance plans to its employees. The amounts deducted are paid directly by the employer to the insurance companies. Employees may also authorize payroll deductions for loan repayments to, or savings in, the employee's credit union. Employee pledges to charities, such as the United Way Fund, are often collected through payroll deductions.

Other less common deductions are for pension or retirement plans, where the employee is obligated to pay at least a portion of the cost of the plan. Some businesses may allow payroll deductions to pay for merchandise purchased by the employee. Employees may purchase U.S. Savings Bonds through payroll deductions. The number and types of optional payroll deductions are determined by the company, the employment contract, and the employee.

Objective 6: Prepare an employee's earnings record.

Maintaining Employee Earnings Record.   Federal law requires employers to maintain an adequate payroll record for each employee. This record is called an **employee earnings record.** As shown in Illustration 12.5, an employee earnings record shows information such as name, social security number, address, phone number, date employed, date of birth, marital status, number of withholding allowances claimed, pay rate, and present job within the company. For each pay period, the record also shows the number of hours worked, gross pay, deductions, and net pay. Cumulative gross pay during the year is included to indicate when the maximum amounts have been reached for FICA tax withholdings and unemployment taxes (which will be discussed later in the chapter). The amounts shown in Illustration 12.5 for federal withholding are used for illustrative purposes.

Illustration 12.5   *Employee Earnings Record*

Name   John R. Hanson   Social Security No. 253 13 2807   Employee No. ___5___

Address   325 St. George Drive   Sex: Male (x)   Female ( )   Position ___Sales___

Athens, Ga. 30605   Single ( )   Married (x)   Hourly pay rate ___$13.00___

Date of birth   June 20, 1950   Withholding allowances ___3___   Spouse ___Susan___

Date employed March 12, 1972   Date terminated _____   Telephone No. 394-1776

1988* Period Ended	Total Hours	Earnings			Deductions					Payment		Cumulative Gross Earnings
		Regular	Overtime	Gross	Federal Income Tax	FICA Tax	State Income Tax	Medical Insurance	Other	Net Pay	Check No.	
Feb. 5	40	520.00		520.00	53.00	39.05	6.78	24.00		397.17	673	520.00
12	40	520.00		520.00	53.00	39.05	6.78	24.00		397.17	807	1,040.00
19	45	520.00	97.50	617.50	67.00	46.37	8.06	24.00		472.07	913	1,657.50

* 1988 dates are used throughout this chapter because the tables and rates used are as of 1988.

Preparing Payroll Journal.   A business may use a **payroll journal** (Illustration 12.6) to reduce the work involved in recording payroll. A payroll journal contains a debit column for each category of salary expense, such as sales, delivery, and office. Credit columns are included for withholdings made for various taxes and other deductions and Salaries Payable. These amounts all represent liabilities that must be paid either to agencies on the employee's behalf or to the employees. Note that a Check No. column is included to show which check was used to pay the Salaries Payable liability amounts. Postings can be made directly from the payroll journal to the ledger. Alternatively, a payroll register can be used merely to collect the information so a journal entry can be made in the general journal. If the payroll shown in Illustration 12.6 were recorded in the general journal, it would be as follows:

Illustration 12.6   *Payroll Journal (or Register)*

Date Week Ended 1988	Employee	Gross Pay			Deductions				Salaries Payable (Net Pay) Cr.	Check No.
		Sales Salaries Expense Dr.	Delivery Salaries Expense Dr.	Office Salaries Expense Dr.	Employees' Federal Income Taxes Payable Cr.	FICA Taxes Payable Cr.	Employees' State Income Taxes Payable Cr.	Medical Insurance Premiums Payable Cr.		
Feb. 5	John Hanson	520.00			53.00	39.05	6.78	24.00	397.17	673
	Robert Lash		510.00		68.00	38.30	4.18	10.00	389.52	674
	Mike Miller	750.00			82.00	56.33	7.29	20.00	584.38	675
	Bill Norman	640.00			77.00	48.06	5.83	15.00	494.11	676
	Allison Wheeler	590.00			69.00	44.31	5.17	15.00	456.52	677
	Cathy Yorb			520.00	64.00	39.05	4.24	10.00	402.71	678
		2,500.00	510.00	520.00	413.00	265.10	33.49	94.00	2,724.41	

```
1988
Feb. 5  Sales Salaries Expense . . . . . . . . . . . . . . . . .  2,500.00
        Delivery Salaries Expense  . . . . . . . . . . . . . .    510.00
        Office Salaries Expense . . . . . . . . . . . . . . .     520.00
              Employees' Federal Income Taxes Payable . . . .              413.00
              FICA Taxes Payable  . . . . . . . . . . . . . .               265.10
              Employees' State Income Taxes Payable  . . . . .              33.49
              Medical Insurance Premiums Payable . . . . . . .              94.00
              Salaries Payable  . . . . . . . . . . . . . . .            2,724.41
        To record the payroll for the week ending February 5.
```

All accounts credited in the February 5 entry are current liabilities and will be reported on the balance sheet if not paid prior to the preparation of financial statements. When the payroll is actually paid, the payment will be recorded in the cash disbursements journal as a debit to Salaries Payable and a credit to Cash of $2,724.41.

Paying the Payroll—Payroll Checking Account

*Objective 7:
Illustrate the use of a payroll checking account.*

The use of a **payroll checking account**—a separate checking account maintained by the business only to pay salaries and wages—is common among companies with many employees who are paid by check. In general, a payroll checking account is used as follows: The payroll checking account is established by depositing a small amount in the account and debiting Payroll Checking and crediting Cash. Before each payday, the payroll is prepared and recorded in a routine manner. One check is drawn on the company's regular checking account for the net payroll amount. This check is deposited in the payroll checking account. The accountant debits Salaries Payable and credits Cash. Payroll checks are then drawn on the payroll checking account and issued to employees. As the payroll checks are cashed by employees and clear the bank, the payroll checking account balance approaches zero.

Some companies use a payroll check register to record written payroll checks. Other companies prefer merely to list the check numbers in the payroll journal (as was shown in Illustration 12.6). Even after all the payroll checks have been cashed, a small balance may be made available in the account to cover payroll checks that might be issued between regular payroll dates for advances to employees or for employee termination pay.

Assume that the payroll checking account was opened on January 1, 1988, with a small deposit of $200 by writing a check on the general Cash account. The entry would be:

```
1988
Jan. 1   Payroll Checking Account  . . . . . . . . . . . . . . . .   200.00
            Cash   . . . . . . . . . . . . . . . . . . . . . . . . . . .            200.00
         To open the payroll checking account.
```

The following four steps illustrate how a payroll is prepared, recorded, and paid for the week ending February 5, shown in Illustration 12.6.

Step 1.   On February 5, the payroll for the week ending February 5 is prepared as shown in Illustration 12.6. Assuming postings to the general ledger are made directly from the payroll journal, column totals are posted to the ledger accounts represented in the column headings.

Step 2.   On February 5, a check for $2,724.41 is drawn on the regular business checking account and recorded as a debit to Salaries Payable and a credit to Cash. The entry would be:

```
Feb. 5   Salaries Payable  . . . . . . . . . . . . . . . . . . . . . .   2,724.41
            Cash  . . . . . . . . . . . . . . . . . . . . . . . . . . . .              2,724.41
         To record the deposit to cover the payroll checks
         for the week of February 5.
```

Step 3.   On February 8, the check is deposited in the payroll checking account. No formal journal entry is required when the check is deposited in the payroll checking account.

Step 4.   On February 8, payroll checks are issued. No formal entries are required because the payroll liability has already been debited for the check drawn and deposited in the payroll checking account. The individual paychecks could be recorded in a payroll check register. Alternatively, the payroll journal in Illustration 12.6 could serve as a check register.

The use of a payroll checking account has several advantages:

1.   A distinctive payroll check form may be used, with spaces provided on an attachment for gross earnings, various payroll deductions, and net cash paid. See Illustration 12.7.
2.   Payroll checks, identifiable as such, are easily cashed by employees.
3.   The work of reconciling the bank balances can be divided among employees. Only one check is drawn on the general bank account. The hundreds or thousands of payroll checks issued each payday are drawn on the payroll bank account. Occasionally, payroll checks will be negotiated many times or lost before clearing the bank. Including these items in the payroll reconciliation simplifies the reconciliation of the general Cash account.

Illustration 12.7

Payroll Check and Supporting Employee's Earnings Statement

Employee	Hours Worked	Rate per Hour	Regular Earnings	Extra for Overtime	Gross Earnings	Fed. Inc. Tax W/H	FICA	State Inc. Tax W/H	Hosp. Ins.	Net Pay
John R. Hanson	40	13.00	520.00	0	520.00	53.00	39.05	6.78	24.00	397.17

Retain this stub for your records – Detach before cashing check

ACE HARDWARE

DOUG'S ACE HARDWARE
1290 Atlanta Highway
ATHENS, GEORGIA 30605

673

February 8 19 88   64-1240 / 611

PAY TO THE ORDER OF   John R. Hanson $ 397.17

Three hundred ninety-seven and ¹⁷/100's ———————— DOLLARS

The CITIZENS and SOUTHERN BANK
NORTH SPRINGS OFFICE
ATLANTA, GEORGIA

FOR_____   *George C. Beacham*

⑈000673⑈ ⑆061⑈1240⑆ 038 82 131⑈

4. Only one authorization is prepared, calling for one check drawn on the general bank account; therefore, payroll checks are issued without separately prepared and signed authorizations.

5. Individual payroll checks need not be entered in the regular cash disbursements record; payroll check numbers are inserted in the payroll journal, and repetition of the entering of checks is avoided.

6. The chance of fraud is reduced in a small business. Since the monthly payroll is not likely to be large, a large bogus payroll check could not clear the bank.

Recording Employer Payroll Taxes

Objective 8: Prepare entries to record employer's payroll taxes and vacation pay.

An employer is generally obligated to pay three taxes levied on payrolls. The entry to record these taxes results in three liabilities: FICA Taxes Payable, State Unemployment Taxes Payable, and Federal Unemployment Taxes Payable.

FICA (Social Security) Taxes. An employer is required to match the amount of FICA tax withheld from each employee's pay. For example, total FICA tax in 1988 amounted to 15.02% of the first $45,000 of each employee's earnings; half (7.51%) was paid by the employee, and half (7.51%) by the employer.

Federal Unemployment Tax. The Federal Unemployment Tax Act (FUTA) requires employers to pay a federal unemployment tax based on employee salaries and wages. This tax helps finance a cooperative federal-state system of unemployment compensation. Unemployment benefits are paid to qualified unemployed persons by each of the states and territorial governments. State unemployment laws vary only in minor respects; the Federal Unemployment Tax Act sets forth certain minimum standards that must be met by each state.

The **federal unemployment tax** rate generally has varied based on the actions of Congress. In 1988, the rate was 6.2% of the first $7,000 of wages paid to each employee. This rate will be used for illustrative purposes. The Federal Unemployment Tax Act provides that employees may have a maximum credit of 5.4% against their federal unemployment tax for amounts that were paid to the state. This, in effect, makes the federal unemployment tax rate (6.2% − 5.4%) = 0.8% on the first $7,000 of individual employee wages.

State Unemployment Tax.   The **state unemployment**   generally is 5.4% of the first $7,000 of gross earnings per employee. This rate and base will be used for illustrative purposes in the text. A **merit rate** can be gained by employers to reduce the state rate to as little as 0.5% in some states and even to zero in other states. A reduced rate is earned by employers with low turnover and few layoffs. Employers with lower merit rates can still deduct a credit of 5.4% against their federal unemployment tax rate.

Payroll Tax Entry.   Employer payroll taxes are usually recorded at the same time as the payroll to which they relate. For example, the employer's payroll taxes (at 1988 rates) on the February 5 payroll in Illustration 12.6 are recorded as follows:

Feb. 5	Payroll Taxes Expense	483.96	
	FICA Taxes Payable		265.10
	State Unemployment Taxes Payable		190.62
	Federal Unemployment Taxes Payable		28.24
	To record employer's payroll taxes.		

Remember that these amounts are in addition to amounts withheld from employees. This journal entry debits Payroll Taxes Expense for the total of the employer's three payroll taxes. The credit to FICA Taxes Payable is equal to the amount deducted from the employees' gross pay. Both the employer's and employees' FICA taxes can be credited to the same liability account, since both are payable at the same time to the same agency. The credits to the state and federal unemployment accounts are for 5.4% and 0.8%, respectively, of the $3,530 of gross pay for this payroll period. It was assumed that no employee had been paid more than $7,000 in the current year. Any earnings in excess of $7,000 would have been excluded from the computation of unemployment taxes, since those taxes are levied only on the first $7,000 of annual income per employee.

Remitting Taxes Withheld, Unemployment Taxes, and Other Deductions

Generally, within one month after the end of each calendar quarter, an employer must file an **Employer's Quarterly Federal Tax Return (Form 941)** with the Internal Revenue Service. This form reports the amount of FICA and income taxes withheld for each quarter. The employer reports (1) total wages subject to withholding, (2) federal income taxes withheld, (3) total wages subject to FICA tax, (4) amount of FICA taxes due (from both employer and employees), and (5) combined amount of income tax withheld and FICA taxes due. A similar form is required by states with state income tax laws.

Taxes Withheld.   For remittance purposes, federal income taxes withheld and both the employees' and employer's FICA taxes are combined. Generally, employers are required to deposit such taxes in a Federal Reserve Bank or an authorized commercial bank called a **federal depository**

bank. When deposited, these amounts are credited by the bank to an Internal Revenue Service account. Deposit requirements are quite detailed and depend on the amount of taxes collected relative to the time elapsed since the last deposit. The more dollars of taxes that are collected, the more rapidly deposits must be made. Taxes properly deposited are considered paid.

Assuming the amount of federal income taxes withheld is $3,687 and the amount of combined FICA taxes is $2,500, the entry to record this deposit is:

```
Employees' Federal Income Taxes Payable  . . . . . . . . . . .  3,687.00
FICA Taxes Payable . . . . . . . . . . . . . . . . . . . . . . .  2,500.00
     Cash  . . . . . . . . . . . . . . . . . . . . . . . . . . . . .           6,187.00
     To record deposit of taxes withheld and employer FICA taxes.
```

State and city income taxes must be withheld by employers in most states and in many cities. The procedures for withholding and the required remittances are usually modeled after federal income tax regulations. The entry for employers to record payment of these taxes debits Employees' State (City) Income Taxes Payable and credits Cash.

Unemployment Taxes.   The amount of federal unemployment taxes to be deposited is determined quarterly. When a certain amount is reached, these taxes must be deposited in a federal depository bank. Assuming the amount of federal unemployment taxes is $400, the entry to record the deposit is:

```
Federal Unemployment Taxes Payable  . . . . . . . . . . . . .   400.00
     Cash  . . . . . . . . . . . . . . . . . . . . . . . . . . . . .            400.00
     To record deposit of federal unemployment taxes.
```

Remittance requirements for state unemployment taxes vary from state to state. Quarterly reports and payments are usually required by the end of the month following the quarter's end. The entry to record the payment is a debit to State Unemployment Taxes Payable and a credit to Cash.

Other Payroll Deductions.   The remittance of other types of payroll deductions varies based on the agency or organization to which payment is to be made. Monthly payment is likely for union dues, medical insurance premiums, charitable contributions, and pension contributions.

A summary of the various payroll taxes appears in Illustration 12.8.

Illustration 12.8

Summary of Payroll Taxes

Type of Tax	Who Pays for It	Amount of Tax
FICA (social security)	Both employer and employee pay at current rate	7.51% of first $45,000 each employee earns annually*
Income	Employee	Varies with earnings and exemptions
State unemployment	Employer (usually)	5.4% of first $7,000 each employee earns annually†
Federal unemployment	Employer	0.8% of first $7,000 each employee earns annually‡

* This rate and base are for 1988.

† Some states have a higher rate and/or base than this. Also, most states allow reduction from the basic rate to firms with low labor turnover.

‡ The federal rate varies, but in this text it is assumed to be 6.2%. An allowance of 5.4% is granted for amounts paid to the state, thus reducing the effective rate to 0.8%.

Preparing End-of-Period Accruals

Adjusting entries are usually needed at year-end to accrue wages, employer's payroll taxes, and vacation pay.

Wages and Payroll Taxes. The matching principle requires accrued wages and employer payroll taxes on these wages to be recorded at the end of every period. To illustrate, assume that Doug's Hardware Company accrues the following salaries and payroll taxes on December 31, 1988: sales salaries, $900; delivery salaries, $160; office salaries, $210; and employer's FICA tax expense, $95.38. The required entries are:

Dec. 31	Sales Salaries Expense	900.00	
	Delivery Salaries Expense	160.00	
	Office Salaries Expense	210.00	
	Salaries Payable		1,270.00
	To accrue salaries.		
31	Payroll Taxes Expense	95.38	
	FICA Taxes Payable		95.38
	To accrue payroll taxes.		

Note in the first entry that credits are not entered in separate liability accounts for payroll deductions. These deductions will be recorded when the payroll is paid since they are not actually withheld from the employees until then. The second entry recorded the employer's FICA taxes on $1,270 of salaries. The assumption was made that no employee had reached the maximum FICA limit; therefore, all accrued salaries would be subject to FICA taxation. Accrued federal and state unemployment taxes were not included in this example because by year-end all employees' earnings should have surpassed the $7,000 maximum amount subject to taxation.

Some companies do not accrue employer's payroll taxes at year-end. The following reasons are given for this violation of the matching principle: (1) no legal liability for such taxes exists until the wages are paid, (2) such taxes do not vary much in amount from year to year, and (3) the amounts of such taxes are likely to be immaterial. A policy of not accruing payroll taxes is acceptable under these circumstances.

Vacation Pay. Most employees in this country are entitled to annual vacations of from one to four weeks at full regular pay. The compensation received while on vacation is called **vacation pay.** Thus, the employer annually pays an employee for 52 weeks but receives services for a fewer number of weeks.

How to account for vacation pay raises an important question: Should vacation pay be expensed when paid, or should it be accrued over the period in which the employee works to earn the vacation? *FASB Statement No. 43,* "Accounting for Compensated Absences," requires the accrual of a liability for vacation pay if the following conditions are met:

1. The employer is obligated to pay as a result of services already received.
2. The employee's right to vacation pay does not depend on continued performance of services.
3. It is probable the vacation pay will be paid.
4. The amount of vacation pay can be reasonably estimated.

Assume Davis Company estimates that out of every 25 workdays employees will earn 1 day of vacation pay. As a result, vacation pay is to be accrued at a rate of 4% (1 day/25 days) of gross pay. The entry to accrue vacation pay on a $3,200 payroll is:

Vacation Pay Expense ($3,200 × 0.04)	128.00	
Estimated Vacation Pay Payable		128.00
To accrue vacation pay.		

Accruing vacation pay in this manner records the expense over the period in which it was earned rather than when it was paid, which results in a better matching of expenses and revenues. A liability is also recorded for the vacation pay currently owed by the employer to employees. Often employees must forfeit vacation pay earned if they leave the company before some minimum length of time, such as one year. If turnover of these employees is expected, the amount of the entry to accrue vacation pay should be reduced accordingly.

When vacation pay is paid, the estimated liability account is debited, and various accounts are credited for taxes, other deductions, and cash payment. For example, an employee earning $400 per week is to be paid for two weeks' vacation. A payroll check is drawn for the net pay due and entered in the payroll journal. Using assumed deductions, the entry in general journal form would be:

Estimated Vacation Pay Payable	800.00	
Employees' Federal Income Taxes Payable		141.00
FICA Taxes Payable		60.08
Medical Insurance Premiums Payable		50.00
Employees' State Income Taxes Payable		11.00
Salaries Payable (Cash)		537.92
To record accrued (payment) vacation pay.		

Considering More Efficient Methods of Payroll Accounting

The payroll deductions described in this chapter are used effectively by many small businesses. In larger companies with many employees, a more efficient method is desirable.

Many businesses use what is called a **pegboard system of payroll accounting** to increase efficiency. Such a system aligns the payroll check, the individual earnings record, and the payroll journal in such a way that all three are completed with one writing. Instead of having to record gross pay, deductions, and net pay three different times for each employee, it is done only once by using a pegboard system of payroll accounting. Of course, the forms must be designed so that they are compatible. Use of such a system can reduce clerical time dramatically.

Other methods of increasing efficiency include using a payroll machine to serve the same function as the pegboard system, or using a computer. As payrolls grow, the speed and efficiency of the computer make its use a virtual necessity. Many banks offer computerized payroll processing services to their customers.

By now you should know the accounting process behind the various deductions in your paychecks. Chapter 13 discusses the accounting theory you were first introduced to in Chapter 1 and also discusses international accounting.

■ *UNDERSTANDING THE LEARNING OBJECTIVES: CHAPTER 12*

1. Define liabilities, current liabilities, and long-term liabilities.

    ■ Liabilities result from some past transaction and are obligations to pay cash, provide services, or deliver goods at some time in the future.
    ■ Current liabilities are obligations that are (1) payable within one year or one operating cycle, whichever is longer, or (2) will be paid out of current assets or result in the creation of other current liabilities.
    ■ Long-term liabilities are obligations that do not qualify as current liabilities.

2. Define clearly determinable, estimated, and contingent liabilities.

    ■ Clearly determinable liabilities are those for which the existence of the liability and its amount are certain.
    ■ Estimated liabilities are those for which the existence of the liability is certain, but its amount can only be estimated.
    ■ Contingent liabilities are those for which the existence of the liability is uncertain, and the amount is usually uncertain, because they depend (or are contingent) on some future event occurring or not occurring.

3. Account for clearly determinable, estimated, and contingent liabilities.

    ■ Clearly determinable liabilities, such as accounts payable, notes payable, interest payable, unearned delivery fees, sales tax payable, and dividends payable, are relatively easy to account for because both their existence and amount are known. For instance, when sales taxes are collected, they are credited to Sales Tax Payable. When the taxes are remitted, that account is debited.
    ■ When an estimated liability exists, such as estimated product warranty payable, estimated property tax payable, estimated federal income taxes payable, or estimated vacation pay payable, the amount is unclear. Thus, the accountant estimates the amount of expense that should be matched against revenues of the accounting period. For instance, Product Warranty Expense is debited and Product Warranty Payable is credited for estimated product warranty costs. When the company makes repairs under warranty, the accountant debits Estimated Product Warranty Payable instead of an expense.
    ■ Contingent liabilities, such as those arising from lawsuits, discounted notes receivable, income tax disputes, penalties, or guaran-

tees, are recorded in the accounts only if they are likely to occur and their amount can be reasonably estimated. Very few of these liabilities meet these criteria. Therefore, most contingent liabilities are described in notes to the financial statements rather than recorded in the accounts.

4. Describe the essential internal control features for payrolls.

- Because of schemes involving payroll fraud, companies must exercise great care to ensure payroll accuracy. Separation of duties is one way to help ensure accuracy.
- In small companies the owner-manager may provide adequate internal control over payroll transactions by actually computing and preparing the payroll.
- Larger companies obtain internal control through application of the general principles of internal control and the more specific guides to controls over cash disbursements described in Chapter 7.

5. Prepare and record a payroll.

- The first step is to compute each employee's gross earnings.
- Then calculate deductions from gross earnings, including withholdings for federal income taxes, state income taxes, FICA taxes, and other deductions such as union dues, insurance, loan repayments, and pledges to charities.
- Then compute net pay by subtracting deductions from gross earnings. Net pay should be credited to Salaries Payable if not paid immediately.

6. Prepare an employee's earnings record.

- Federal laws require employers to maintain an adequate payroll record for each employee.
- An employee's earnings record shows information such as name and other personal data, number of withholding allowances claimed, pay rate, and present job within the company. The record also shows hours worked, gross pay, deductions, and net pay for each pay period. Cumulative gross pay is shown and aids in determining when to stop deducting for FICA taxes.

7. Illustrate the use of a payroll checking account.

- Use of a separate payroll checking account is common among companies with many employees who are paid by check.
- One check is drawn on the company's regular checking account for the net payroll amount and deposited in the payroll checking account.
- Payroll checks are written against the payroll checking account to avoid "clutter" in the regular checking account.

8. Prepare entries to record employer's payroll taxes and vacation pay.

- An employer is generally obligated to pay three taxes levied on payrolls: FICA (social security), federal unemployment taxes, and state unemployment taxes.

- Employer payroll taxes are usually recorded at the same time as the payroll to which they relate. The debit is to Payroll Taxes Expense. The credits are to FICA Taxes Payable, State Unemployment Taxes Payable, and Federal Unemployment Taxes Payable.
- Periodically the amounts withheld from employees and the employer's payroll taxes must be remitted to a government agency or other entity.
- Adjusting entries are usually needed at year-end to accrue wages, employer's payroll taxes, and vacation pay.

9. Define and use correctly the new terms in the glossary.

NEW TERMS INTRODUCED IN CHAPTER 12

Clearly determinable liabilities Liabilities for which both their existence and amount are certain. Examples include accounts payable, notes payable, interest payable, unearned delivery fees, wages payable, sales tax payable, federal excise tax payable, current portions of long-term debt, and various payroll liabilities (488).

Contingent liabilities Liabilities for which their existence is uncertain. Their amount is also usually uncertain. Both their existence and amount depend on some future event occurring or not occurring. Examples include liabilities arising from lawsuits, discounted notes receivable, income tax disputes, penalties that may be assessed because of some past action, and failure of another party to pay a debt that this company has guaranteed (489).

Current liabilities Obligations that (1) are payable within one year or one operating cycle, whichever is longer, or (2) will be paid out of current assets or result in the creation of other current liabilities (488).

Deductions from gross earnings Required payroll deductions, such as federal and state income taxes withheld, FICA taxes withheld, and other deductions, such as medical insurance premiums and union dues (498).

Employee earnings record A record maintained by an employer for each employee (see Illustration 12.5) showing information such as personal biographical data, hours worked, pay rate, gross pay, deductions, and net pay (503).

Employee's Withholding Allowance Certificate (Form W-4) The form (see Illustration 12.1) on which an employee indicates the number of exemptions to be used in calculating federal (and state) income tax withheld (498).

Employer's Quarterly Federal Tax Return (Form 941) A form used to report the amount of FICA and income taxes withheld for each quarter (507).

Estimated liabilities Liabilities for which their existence is certain, but their amount can only be estimated. Examples include estimated product warranty payable, estimated property tax payable, estimated federal income taxes payable, and estimated vacation pay payable (489).

Federal depository bank A bank authorized to accept deposits of taxes by employers for credit to the Internal Revenue Service (507).

Federal (state) income tax withheld The amount withheld for federal (state) income taxes deducted from employee earnings by the employer and remitted to the appropriate governmental agency under the pay-as-you-go system of government financing (498).

Federal unemployment tax A tax of 6.2% (in 1988) levied on the first $7,000 of wages paid per employee to help finance the joint federal–state system of unemployment compensation. A credit of up to 5.4% may be taken for amounts paid to a state unemployment fund, thus reducing the rate to 0.8% (506).

FICA (social security) tax The amount deducted from an employee's wages and paid into a special fund used to pay retirement and other benefits. In 1988, the rate was 7.51% on the first $45,000 of wages paid. The employer also pays a matching amount (499).

Gross earnings Total pay or compensation of an employee, including regular pay and overtime premium (497).

Liabilities Obligations that result from some past transaction and are an obligation to pay cash, perform services, or deliver goods at some time in the future (487).

Long-term liabilities   Obligations that do not qualify as current liabilities (488).

Merit rate   A reduction in the state unemployment tax rate below 5.4% as a reward for low employee turnover and few layoffs (507).

Minimum wage   Lowest hourly compensation an employer can pay an employee as required by the Wages and Hours Law (497).

Operating cycle   The time it takes to begin with cash and end with cash in producing revenues (488).

Payroll checking account   A separate checking account used only for payroll checks. Each payday, funds are transferred from the general Cash account to cover the amount of the payroll checks. One of the purposes is to keep the "clutter" of outstanding payroll checks from making more complex the reconciliation of the general Cash account (504).

Payroll journal   A formal record showing the details of each payroll, including gross pay, deductions, net pay, and check number for each employee (see Illustration 12.6). It may be used as a book of original entry (in which case postings to accounts would be made from it) or it may be only a memorandum record (503).

Pegboard system of payroll accounting   A system that aligns the payroll check, the individual earnings record, and the payroll journal in such a way that all three are completed simultaneously with one writing (510).

Social security tax   See FICA tax.

State unemployment tax   A tax of 5.4% (typically) on the first $7,000 of gross earnings per employee per year to finance unemployment benefits. A **merit rate** for not laying off employees may reduce the percent below 5.4% (507).

Time card   A form used to maintain a record of when an employee reports to and leaves work; it is used as a source document for calculating gross pay (496).

Vacation pay   Compensation received by employees while on vacation; it is actually earned by employees in the periods worked prior to the vacation (509).

Wage and Tax Statement (Form W-2)   A form that the employer must furnish to each employee after the end of the year showing gross wages, amounts withheld, and net pay (see Illustration 12.3). It is used by the employee in preparing his or her personal federal income tax return (499).

Wage bracket withholding table   A table supplied by the IRS (see Illustration 12.2) that shows the amount of federal income tax to be withheld given the wage and number of withholding allowances claimed (499).

Wages and Hours Law (Fair Labor Standards Act)   Requires that most employees be paid at least 1½ times their normal rate for hours worked in excess of 40 hours per week. It also requires that at least the minimum wage be paid (497).

Withholding allowances   A means of adjusting income taxes withheld from employee periodic earnings for exemptions that will be claimed on the income tax return (498).

DEMONSTRATION PROBLEM

Johnson Company employs four persons as salespersons (all are married) and pays them weekly salaries as shown below. The number of exemptions and weekly deductions for hospital insurance for each employee are also given.

	Weekly Salary	Exemptions	Hospital Insurance
Jenny Cain	$420	2	$20
Susan Davis . . .	500	4	25
Ellen Griffin . . .	400	3	25
David Oakes . . .	310	1	10

Each employee has 4% withheld for state income tax and 6% withheld for the retirement plan. Use the wage bracket withholding table in Illustration 12.2 to determine the federal income taxes to be withheld.

Required: *a.*   Prepare the payroll journal for the week ending January 8, 1988, using headings that will accomplish the purpose. (The check numbers are 701–4.) Use 7.51% as the rate for social security tax withheld from employees.

b.   Assuming that the payroll journal is a memorandum record only, prepare the general journal entry to record the payroll.

c.   Prepare the entry to transfer funds from general cash to the special payroll checking account.

d.   Prepare the entry to record the employer's payroll taxes using the rates given in this chapter. (In actual practice, this often is done only at the end of the month.)

e.   Prepare the entry to record the payment on January 11 of the federal income taxes and FICA taxes due to be paid to the federal government. (In actual practice, this often is done only at the end of the month or quarter, depending on the amounts involved.)

Solution to demonstration problem

a.

PAYROLL JOURNAL

| Date Week Ended 1988 | Employee | Gross Pay— Salaries Sales Expense Dr. | Deductions | | | | | Salaries Payable (Net Pay) Cr. | Check No. |
			Employees' Federal Income Taxes Payable Cr.	FICA Taxes Payable Cr.	Employees' State Income Taxes Payable Cr.	Medical Insurance Premiums Payable Cr.	Retirement Plan Premiums Payable Cr.		
Jan. 8	Jenny Cain	420.00	44.00	31.54	16.80	20.00	25.20	282.46	701
	Susan Davis	500.00	44.00	37.55	20.00	25.00	30.00	343.45	702
	Ellen Griffin	400.00	35.00	30.04	16.00	25.00	24.00	269.96	703
	David Oakes	310.00	33.00	23.28	12.40	10.00	18.60	212.72	704
		1,630.00	156.00	122.41	65.20	80.00	97.80	1,108.59	

b.

```
1988
Jan.  8  Sales Salaries Expense  . . . . . . . . . . . . . . . 1,630.00
                 Employees' Federal Income Taxes Payable  . . .          156.00
                 FICA Taxes Payable . . . . . . . . . . . . . . . .          122.41
                 Employees' State Income Taxes Payable  . . . .           65.20
                 Medical Insurance Premiums
                     Payable . . . . . . . . . . . . . . . . . . . . .           80.00
                 Retirement Plan Premiums
                     Payable . . . . . . . . . . . . . . . . . . . . .           97.80
                 Salaries Payable . . . . . . . . . . . . . . . . .        1,108.59
         To record the payroll for the week ending
         January 8.
```

c.

1988
Jan. 8 Salaries Payable 1,108.59
      Cash 1,108.59
      To record the transfer of funds to cover the
      January 8 payroll.

d.

1988
Jan. 8 Payroll Taxes Expense 223.47
      FICA Taxes Payable ($1,630 × .0751) 122.41
      State Unemployment Taxes Payable
        ($1,630 × .054) 88.02
      Federal Unemployment Taxes Payable
        ($1,630 × .008) 13.04
      To record payroll taxes on the January 8 payroll.

e.

1988
Jan. 11 Employees' Federal Income Taxes Payable 156.00
      FICA Taxes Payable 244.82
      Cash 400.82
      To record payment of federal income taxes
      payable and FICA taxes payable from the
      January 8 payroll.

QUESTIONS

1. Define liabilities, current liabilities, and long-term liabilities.

2. What is an operating cycle? Which type of company is likely to have the shortest operating cycle, and which is likely to have the longest operating cycle? Why?

3. Describe the differences between clearly determinable, estimated, and contingent liabilities. Give some examples of each type.

4. Describe some of the purposes of a payroll accounting system.

5. List the various functions regarding payroll and give a method for establishing internal control over these functions.

6. Describe how the system of internal control relating to payroll works. (Begin with the recording of time worked and end with the issuance of the paycheck.)

7. Identify some schemes involving payroll that have been used to defraud a company.

8. Why is it important to distinguish between employees and independent contractors? Give an example of each.

9. What requirements does the Wages and Hours Law place on employers? Why should accurate records be maintained as to hours worked by employees?

10. List the common deductions from gross pay.

11. What is the purpose of the Employee's Withholding Allowance Certificate (Form W-4)?

12. What purposes does the Wage and Tax Statement (Form W-2) serve?

13. Against which parties are FICA taxes levied and in what amounts?

14. What is the purpose of the Employer's Quarterly Federal Tax Return (Form 941)?

15. What are the federal and state rates for unemployment tax? What is a merit rate and what effect does it have on the credit granted by the federal government for amounts paid to the state?

16. Why should an employer maintain an individual earnings record for each employee?

17. Describe two ways in which the payroll journal might be utilized in the payroll accounting system.

18. Under what conditions would the use of a special payroll checking account be desirable? How does such an account operate?

19. What are the arguments for and against accruing employer's payroll taxes at the end of the accounting period?

20. Under what conditions should an employer accrue a liability for future vacation pay earned by employees in the current accounting period?

21. What payroll procedures might be employed that would be more efficient than the system described in the chapter? Why are these other methods not always used in a given system?

EXERCISES

E-1
Determine sales revenue and sales tax payable

The Bentley Company sells merchandise in a state that has a 5% sales tax. Rather than record sales taxes collected in a separate account, the company records both the sales revenue and the sales taxes in the Sales account. At the end of the first quarter of operations, when it is time to remit the sales taxes to the state taxing agency, the company had $236,250 in the Sales account. Determine the correct amount of sales revenue and the amount of sales tax payable.

E-2
Prepare entry for income tax

At the beginning of the year, the Westly Corporation estimated its annual federal income tax expense at $36,000. Give the entry that must be made at the end of each month to record the expense and the liability.

E-3
Answer questions regarding note in financial statements

The following note appeared in the annual report of a company:

> In 1986, two small retail customers filed separate suits against the company alleging misrepresentation, breach of contract, conspiracy to violate federal laws and state antitrust violations arising out of their purchase of retail grocery stores through the company from a third party. Damages sought range up to $45 million in each suit for actual and treble damages and punitive damages of $5 million in one suit and $45 million in the other. The company is vigorously defending the actions and management believes there will be no adverse financial effect.

What kind of liability is being reported? Why is it classified this way? Do you think it is possible to calculate a dollar amount for this obligation? How much would the company have to pay if they lost the suit and had to pay the full amount?

E-4
Determine withholding amounts for employees

Haskins Company employs four persons whose weekly wages and exemptions are as follows:

Employee	Wage	Exemptions
John Sampson	$430	4
Thomas McPherson . . .	310	2
John Lauber	380	3
Robert Conrad	540	5

Assume these employees are married. Using Illustration 12.2, determine the correct amount to withhold for federal income tax per week. Note: Unless directed otherwise, use 1988 federal income tax rates for exercises involving individuals.

E-5
Compute maximum weeks of unemployment taxes

Using the data in Exercise E-4, calculate how many weeks it would take before the employer would no longer incur federal or state unemployment taxes on each individual.

E-6
Compute FICA taxes

Using the data in Exercise E–4 and assuming a rate of 7.51% and a maximum base of $45,000, how much would the employer withhold for FICA tax from each employee for the entire year? How much would the employer's FICA tax expense be for the year?

E-7
Prepare journal entry to record payroll

The January 15, 1988, gross payroll for salaries of Krueger Corporation is $4,800. The total federal income tax withheld is $1,050. The employees' share of FICA taxes withheld is $360.48. What is the correct entry to accrue the payroll? (Ignore federal and state unemployment taxes.)

E-8
Compute difference in payroll taxes under two alternatives

Mark Mason is trying to decide whether to hire 4 workers to perform a particular job at $36,000 each per year or 12 workers to perform a particular job on a part-time basis at $12,000 each per year. Using the rates given in the chapter, calculate the difference in the employer's payroll tax expense under the two alternatives.

E-9
Prepare journal entry to record unemployment taxes

Farber Company is in a state that has a state unemployment tax rate of 5.4%. Due to a record of stable employment, the company has earned a merit rate of 4.8%. Total wages on which it incurred federal and state unemployment taxes for the month of March were $15,000. Prepare an entry to record federal and state unemployment taxes for the month.

E-10
Prepare journal entries to record accrued wages and payroll taxes

At the end of December, Greer Company had accrued wages of $1,000 ($500 for sales salaries, $300 for office salaries, and $200 for maintenance wages). The company makes the accrual for payroll taxes on accrued wages. Assume that no employee has earned over $45,000 (including the above wages) and that unemployment taxes still accrue only on the maintenance wages. Prepare the necessary adjusting entry to accrue the wages and payroll taxes.

E-11
Prepare journal entry to record unaccrued payroll taxes

Using the data in Exercise E–10, what entry would the company make if it did not follow the practice of accruing payroll taxes on accrued wages?

E-12
Prepare journal entries to accrue and pay vacation pay to employee

Gilder Company estimated its accrued vacation pay liability at the end of the year at $7,000. Frank Myers took one week of vacation in the following year for which he was paid one week's regular earnings of 40 hours at $16 per hour. Give the entry for the vacation pay accrual. Also, give the entry to record the payment of a week's vacation pay to Frank Myers. Frank is married and claims three withholding allowances. Use Illustration 12.2 to compute federal income taxes withheld. There is no state income tax.

PROBLEMS, SERIES A

P12-1-A
Prepare journal entries for sales and excise taxes

Tucker Company sells merchandise in a state that has a 6% sales tax. On July 1, 1991, goods with a sales price of $10,000 were sold on credit. Sales taxes collected are recorded in a separate account. Assume that sales for the entire month were $300,000. On July 31, 1991, the company remitted the sales taxes collected to the state taxing agency.

Required: a. Prepare the general journal entries to record the July 1 sales revenue and sales tax payable. Also prepare the entry to show the remittance of the taxes on July 31.
b. Now assume that the merchandise sold is also subject to federal excise taxes of 10% in addition to the 6% sales tax. The federal excise taxes collected are also remitted to the proper agency on July 31. Show the entries on July 1 and July 31.

P12-2-A
Prepare journal entries for product warranty

Cromley Company sells racing bicycles and warrants all parts for a one-year period. The average price per bicycle is $600, and the company sold 5,000 in 1991. The company expects 20% of the bicycles to develop defective parts within one year of sale. The estimated average cost of warranty repairs per defective bicycle is $50. By the end of the year, 700 bicycles sold that year had been returned and repaired under warranty. On January 2, 1992, a customer returned a bicycle purchased in 1991 for repairs under warranty. The repairs were made on January 3. The cost of the repairs included parts, $60, and labor, $10.

Required:
a. Calculate the amount of the estimated product warranty payable.
b. Prepare the entry to record the estimated product warranty payable on December 31, 1991.
c. Prepare the entry to record the repairs made on January 3, 1992.

P12-3-A
Prepare journal entries for property taxes

Eyler Company estimated in July that its annual property tax for July 1, 1991, to June 30, 1992, would be $36,000. On September 1, the company received a $38,880 property tax bill for the 1991–92 fiscal year, with payment due by November 15. Since the amount of understatement is relatively small, the company decided to charge the entire understatement to the month of September. On November 15, Eyler Company paid the property tax bill.

Required:
a. Prepare the journal entry to record estimated property taxes payable at the end of July and August.
b. Prepare the required entry at the end of September.
c. Show the entry to record payment of the property taxes on November 15.
d. Show the entry that would be made each month from December 1991 through June 1992.

P12-4-A
Compute FICA taxes, unemployment taxes, and total employer tax expense

Lenox Company has 18 employees and an annual payroll of $350,000; 4 employees earn $63,000 each per year; and 14 employees each earn an equal amount per year.

Required:
a. What is the annual FICA tax (1) for the employer and (2) for the employees? (Use rates shown for 1988.)
b. What are the amounts of federal and state unemployment taxes per year for this company, assuming that the federal rate is 0.8% (6.2% reduced by 5.4%) and the state rate is 5.4%?
c. Which of the preceding items would constitute expenses on the records of Lenox Company?

P12-5-A
Journalize payroll, FICA taxes, unemployment taxes, and payment of taxes

Nichols Company pays its employees once each month. The payroll data for October are as follows:

Gross payroll . . . . $41,200 (One employee is above the $7,000 limit. Prior to October, the employee's gross salary was $37,000, and the employee's gross October salary was $3,000.)
Federal income tax withheld 4,400
FICA tax . . . .   ?
State income tax . . . . 3% of gross salary

Required: Prepare entries to record:

a. The October payroll.
b. The employer's FICA tax for October (use 1988 rates).
c. The employer's federal and state unemployment taxes, assuming that the federal rate is 0.8% (6.2% reduced by 5.4%) and the state rate is 5.4%.
d. Payment of the various taxes.

P12-6-A
Prepare payroll journal, record payroll, record employer's payroll taxes, and record transfer of funds to payroll checking account

Taylor Company employs six persons in its fast-food franchise operation. The names of the employees, weekly wages, and number of exemptions are as follows:

Employee	Weekly Wage	Number of Exemptions
Bikram Garcha	$600	4
Norman Harbaugh	350	2
Fred Massey	340	3
Becky Rogers	450	1
Marc Schaefer	370	2
Paula Stephan	330	5

State income tax is withheld from employees at the rate of 5% on all wages paid. All of the employees are married.

Required:

a. Prepare a payroll journal with the following headings: Date Week Ended, Employee, Gross Pay—Salaries Expense Dr., Employees' Federal Income Taxes Payable Cr., FICA Taxes Payable Cr., Employees' State Income Taxes Payable Cr., Salaries Payable (Net Pay) Cr., and Check No.

b. Using the withholding table and rates given in the chapter (including 7.51% for FICA taxes, 0.8% [6.2% reduced by 5.4%] for federal unemployment, and 5.4% for state unemployment), enter the payroll data in the payroll journal for the week ending January 8, 1988. Check numbers used were 405–10.

c. Now assume the payroll journal is used as a memorandum record (and is therefore a payroll register). Prepare an entry as it would appear in the general journal to record the payroll.

d. Prepare the entry to record the employer's payroll taxes for FICA and unemployment.

e. Prepare the entry to record the transfer of funds to the special payroll checking account on January 8.

P12-7-A
Prepare journal entries for payroll and payroll taxes for firm using payroll checking account

The College Diner maintains a special checking account on which its payroll checks are drawn. Employees are paid on the 1st and the 15th of each month for the salaries earned in the preceding half-month. There is no state income tax. The following transactions occur in December:

1. A check for $2,400 is drawn and deposited in the payroll checking account to cover advances to employees and checks issued to employees whose services are terminated.

2. The payroll for the last half of November consists of the following:

Gross wages of employees		$100,000
Less: Federal income taxes withheld	$13,000	
FICA taxes withheld	6,540	19,540
Net payroll		$ 80,460

3. On November 30, a check is drawn in the amount of the net payroll and deposited in the payroll checking account.

4. Payroll checks equal to the amount of the net payroll are issued to employees.

5. The federal income taxes withheld and the FICA taxes of both the employees and the employer are deposited in a federal depository bank. (First, prepare the required entry to record the employer's FICA taxes.)

Required:

Assume that the company uses a payroll record to record its payroll. Prepare in general journal form the entries needed for the six numbered items above. Assume in No. 2 that an entry is to be made for the employer's FICA taxes and that the company is not subject to further unemployment taxation. Where no formal entry is needed, describe the accounting action that would be taken.

P12-8-A
Prepare journal entries to account for accrued payroll

At the end of the year (1988), Vickory Company has $30,000 of accrued wages ($15,000 sales salaries, $9,000 delivery wages, and $6,000 office salaries). Of this total, $25,000 are subject to FICA tax, and $8,000 are subject to unemployment taxes.

Required: a.   Describe the two alternatives the company may follow in making the adjusting entry and explain why these alternatives exist.
              b.   Prepare the adjusting entry under the two alternatives. (Use the 7.51% rate mentioned in the text for FICA, 0.8% [6.2% reduced by 5.4%] for federal unemployment, and 5.4% for state unemployment.)

PROBLEMS, SERIES B

P12-1-B
Prepare journal entries for sales and excise taxes

Kelly Company sells merchandise in a state that has a 5% sales tax. On January 2, 1991, goods with a sales price of $20,000 were sold on credit. Sales taxes collected are recorded in a separate account. Assume that sales for the entire month were $450,000. On January 31, 1991, the company remitted the sales taxes collected to the state taxing agency.

Required: a.   Prepare the general journal entries to record the January 2 sales revenue. Also prepare the entry to show the remittance of the taxes on January 31.
              b.   Now assume that the merchandise sold is also subject to federal excise taxes of 12%. The federal excise taxes collected are also remitted to the proper agency on January 31. Show the entries on January 1 and January 31.

P12-2-B
Prepare journal entries for product warranty

Knolls Company sells used cars and warrants all parts for a one-year period. The average price per car is $7,000, and the company sold 600 in 1991. The company expects 30% of the cars to develop defective parts within one year of sale. The estimated average cost of warranty repairs per defective car is $250. By the end of the year, 100 cars sold that year had been returned and repaired under warranty. On January 4, 1992, a customer returned a car purchased in 1991 for repairs under warranty. The repairs were made on January 8. The cost of the repairs included parts, $180, and labor, $120.

Required: a.   Calculate the amount of the estimated product warranty payable.
              b.   Prepare the entry to record the estimated product warranty payable on December 31, 1991.
              c.   Prepare the entry to record the repairs made on January 8, 1992.

P12-3-B
Prepare journal entries for property taxes

Roper Company estimated in July that its annual property tax for July 1, 1991, to June 30, 1992, would be $15,000. On November 1, the company received a $15,960 property tax bill for the 1991–92 fiscal year, with payment due by December 20. Since the amount of understatement is relatively small, the company decided to charge the entire understatement to the month of November. On December 20, Roper Company paid the property tax bill.

Required: a.   Prepare the journal entry to record estimated property taxes payable at the end of July through October.
              b.   Prepare the required entry at the end of November.
              c.   Show the entry to record payment of the property taxes on December 20.
              d.   Show the entry that would be made each month from December 1991 through June 1992.

P12-4-B
Compute FICA taxes, unemployment taxes, and total employer tax expense

Smits Company has an annual payroll of $750,000; 10 employees earn $55,000 each; and 40 part-time employees each earn an equal amount.

Required:

a. What are the total employee and employer portions of the FICA tax for the year? (Use the 7.51% rate and $45,000 maximum base.)
b. What are the amounts of federal and state unemployment taxes per year for this company, assuming that the federal rate is 0.8% (6.2% reduced by 5.4%) and the state rate is 5.4%?
c. What is the total expense incurred by the employer for these items?

P12-5-B
Journalize payroll, FICA taxes, unemployment taxes, and payment of taxes

Throughout the first quarter of the year, Jacoby Company employed seven machinists at $600 each per month and an assistant manager at $750 per month. The monthly payroll was paid on the last day of each month. On January 31, the company withheld $615 of federal income taxes from employees, along with the proper FICA tax.

Required:

Journalize:

a. The payroll for January.
b. The employer's FICA tax for January, assuming a 7.51% rate and $45,000 maximum base.
c. The employer's federal and state unemployment taxes, assuming a federal rate of 0.8% (6.2% reduced by 5.4%) and a state rate of 5.4% for this company.
d. The entry to record payment of the various taxes.

P12-6-B
Prepare payroll journal, record payroll, record transfer of funds to payroll checking account, and record employer's payroll taxes

Tasty Bakery employs five married persons. Their names, weekly wages, number of exemptions claimed, and hospital insurance premiums are as follows:

Employee	Weekly Wage	Number of Exemptions	Medical Insurance Premiums
Marge Authier . . .	$390	3	$15
Alice Cummins . . .	320	1	10
Becky Hooten	450	1	15
Betty McDowell . . .	480	2	15
Louetta Nowlin . . .	330	1	10

State income tax is withheld from employees at the rate of 5% on all wages paid.

Required:

a. Prepare a payroll journal with the following headings: Date Week Ended, Employee, Gross Pay—Salaries Expense Dr., Employees' Federal Income Taxes Payable Cr., FICA Taxes Payable Cr., Employees' State Income Taxes Payable Cr., Medical Insurance Premiums Payable Cr., Salaries Payable (Net Pay) Cr., and Check No.
b. Using the withholding table and rates given in the chapter (including the 7.51% rate for FICA taxes, 0.8% [6.2% reduced by 5.4%] for federal unemployment, and 5.4% for state unemployment), enter the payroll data in the payroll journal for the week ending May 30, 1988. Check numbers used were 210–14.
c. Prepare the general journal entry to record the transfer of funds to the special payroll checking account on May 30.
d. Prepare the general journal entry to record the employer's payroll taxes for FICA and unemployment.

P12-7-B
*Prepare journal
entries for payroll
and payroll taxes for
firm using payroll
checking account*

First Company maintains a payroll checking account with a $1,200 balance. This balance is used for payroll advances and to pay employees whose services are terminated between payroll payment dates. There is no state income tax. Following are selected transactions of the First Company during June.

June 15   Payroll department determines that the payroll and payroll deductions for the first half of the month of June are:

Office salaries	$ 60,000
Sales salaries and commissions	98,400
Sales office salaries	48,000
	$206,400

Payroll deductions:

Federal income taxes withheld	$32,304	
FICA taxes withheld	14,758	
Community Fund contributions withheld . .	7,200	54,262
Net payroll		$152,138

17   A check in the amount of the net payroll is drawn on the general checking account and deposited in the payroll checking account.
20   Payroll checks are issued.

Required: a. Assume that a payroll journal was prepared for the June 15 payroll, and prepare entries in general journal form for those transactions on June 15, 17, and 20 that require formal journal entries. For those dates that do not require a formal entry, state the accounting actions that would be taken.
b. Assume that the federal income taxes withheld and the FICA taxes owed are deposited on June 23 in a federal depository bank. Prepare the required entry to record the employer's FICA taxes, and then prepare the entry for the depositing of the taxes.

P12-8-B
*Prepare journal
entries to account
for accrued payroll*

Love Company operates an indoor tennis complex. At the end of 1988, the company has accrued wages and salaries of $36,000 ($18,000 for professional tennis staff salaries, $10,000 for administrative staff salaries, and $8,000 for maintenance personnel wages). Of these wages and salaries, $24,000 are subject to FICA taxes, and $6,000 are subject to unemployment taxes.

Required: a. Describe two alternative ways in which the company can prepare the adjusting entry. Explain why these alternatives exist.
b. Prepare the adjusting entry under the two alternatives. (Use a 7.51% rate for FICA tax, 0.8% [6.2% reduced by 5.4%] for federal unemployment, and 5.4% for state unemployment.)

BUSINESS DECISION PROBLEM 12-1

*Recommend
procedures to
strengthen internal
control over payroll*

Tom Walden operates a fine restaurant and employs 15 employees. He is interested in food preparation, supervision of servers, and customer relations. He has little aptitude for record-keeping. As a result, he hired Fred Rogers to do all of the paperwork for the business. This includes preparing the payroll, keeping payroll records, signing the payroll checks, distributing the payroll checks, and reconciling the bank account. The payroll checks are written on the general Cash account rather than on a special payroll checking account.

Business seems good, but the cash position keeps getting tighter. Wages expense seems somewhat higher than Mr. Walden believes it should be. Mr. Rogers assures Mr. Walden that all is well regarding payroll. Mr. Walden suspects something is wrong regarding the payroll function.

Required: a. What could be wrong?

b. What would you recommend to Mr. Walden to correct the situation?

BUSINESS DECISION PROBLEM 12–2

Determine which payroll system to use with alternative number of employees

Dan Hay owns and runs a motel and has 10 employees. He has one opportunity to acquire a chain of five other motels (with an additional 50 employees). A second opportunity exists to acquire a second chain of 20 other motels (with an additional 200 employees). He will only consider acquiring the second chain if he acquires the first chain.

Mr. Hay is wondering about which type of payroll system to use, given the fact that he may have 10, 60, or 260 employees. Estimated costs of three alternative payroll systems are as follows:

	Clerical Cost per Employee/Week	Cost of Forms per Employee/Week	Service Charge per Week
Manual system	$1.50	$0.20	$ 0
Pegboard system	0.50	0.30	10*
Computer Service Bureau	0.25	0.10	100

* An initial charge for pegboard equipment expressed as a weekly charge.

Required: Calculate the cost per week of using each system for 10, 60, and 260 employees, respectively. Given the different number of employees that may be hired, which payroll system would be the least costly for each number?

13 Accounting Theory and International Accounting

After studying this chapter, you should be able to:

1. Identify and discuss the basic assumptions, principles, and modifying conventions of accounting.

2. Describe the Conceptual Framework Project of the Financial Accounting Standards Board.

3. Discuss the differences in international accounting among nations (Appendix).

4. Define and use correctly the new terms in the glossary.

In the preceding chapters, you learned how accountants use the accounting process (or cycle) to account for the activities of a business. Only brief mention was made in Chapter 1 of the body of theory underlying accounting procedures. Theoretical concepts have also been mentioned in other chapters. In this chapter, accounting theory is discussed in greater depth. Now that you have learned some accounting procedures, you are better able to relate these theoretical concepts to accounting practice. **Accounting theory** is "a set of basic concepts and assumptions and related principles that explain and guide the accountant's actions in identifying, measuring, and communicating economic information."[1]

To some people, the word *theory* has the connotation of being abstract and "out of reach." In accounting, understanding the theory behind the accounting process helps you make decisions in unusual accounting situations. Accounting theory provides a logical framework for accounting practice.

---

[1] American Accounting Association, *A Statement of Basic Accounting Theory* (Sarasota, Fla., 1966), pp. 1–2.

The chapter Appendix discusses international accounting. As businesses expand their operations across international borders, accountants must become aware of the accounting challenges this presents.

■ UNDERLYING ASSUMPTIONS OR CONCEPTS

Objective 1: Identify and discuss the basic assumptions, principles, and modifying conventions of accounting.

The major underlying assumptions or concepts of accounting are (1) business entity, (2) going concern (continuity), (3) money measurement, and (4) periodicity. This section discusses the effects of these assumptions on the accounting process.

Business Entity

Data gathered in an accounting system are assumed to relate to a specific business unit or entity. The **business entity** concept assumes that each business has an existence separate from its owners, creditors, employees, customers, other interested parties, and other businesses. For each business (such as a horse stable or a fitness center), the business, not the business owner, is the accounting entity. Financial statements must be identified as belonging to a particular business entity. The content of the financial statements must be limited to reporting the activities, resources, and obligations of that entity.

A business entity may be made up of several different **legal** entities. For instance, a large business (such as General Motors Corporation) may consist of several separate corporations, each of which is a separate legal entity. But, because the corporations have a common ownership, they may be considered one business entity for reporting purposes. This concept is illustrated in Chapter 18.

Going Concern (Continuity)

Accountants record business transactions for an entity assuming the entity will continue to be a "going concern." The **going-concern (continuity) assumption** states that an entity will continue to operate indefinitely unless strong evidence indicates that the entity will terminate. An entity is terminated by ceasing business operations and selling its assets. The process of termination is called **liquidation.** If liquidation appears likely, the going-concern assumption can no longer be used.

The going-concern assumption is often cited to justify the use of historical costs rather than market values in measuring assets. Market values are thought to be of little or no significance to an entity intending to use its assets rather than sell them. On the other hand, if an entity is to be liquidated, liquidation values should be used to report assets.

The going-concern assumption permits the accountant to record certain items as assets. For example, printed advertising matter may be on hand to promote a special sale next month. This advertising material may have little, if any, value to anyone but its owner. But, because its owner is expected to continue operating long enough to benefit from it, the accountant classifies the expenditure as an asset, prepaid advertising, rather than as an expense.

Money Measurement

The economic activity of a business is normally recorded and reported in money terms. **Money measurement** is the use of a monetary unit of measurement, such as the dollar, instead of physical or other units of measurement. The use of a particular monetary unit provides accountants with a common unit of measurement to report economic activity. Without a monetary unit, it would be impossible to add such items as buildings, equipment, and inventory on a balance sheet.

The unit of measure (the dollar, in the United States) is identified in the financial statements so the statement user can make valid comparisons of values. For example, it would be difficult to compare relative asset values or profitability of a company reporting in U.S. dollars with a company reporting in Japanese yen.

Stable Dollar.   In the United States, accountants make another assumption regarding money measurement—the stable dollar assumption. Under the **stable dollar** assumption, the dollar is accepted as a **reasonably stable** unit of measurement. Thus, no adjustments are made in the primary financial statements for the changing value of the dollar.

A difficulty with following the stable dollar assumption occurs in depreciation accounting. Assume, for example, that a company acquired a building in 1961, and the 30-year depreciation on the building is computed without adjusting for any changes in the value of the dollar. Thus, the depreciation deducted in 1991 is the same as the depreciation deducted in 1961, and no adjustments are made for the difference in the values of the 1961 dollar and the 1991 dollar. Both dollars are treated as **equal monetary units** of measurement even though substantial price inflation has occurred over the 30-year period. Accountants and business executives have expressed concern over this inflation problem, especially since 1970. Inflation accounting is discussed in more detail in Appendix B at the end of the text.

Periodicity (Time Periods)

According to the **periodicity (time periods)** assumption, an entity's life can be subdivided into time periods (such as months or years) for purposes of reporting its economic activities. After subdividing an entity's life into time periods, accountants attempt to prepare accurate reports on the entity's activities for these periods—reports that will provide useful and timely financial information to investors and creditors. In fact, however, the financial reports may be inaccurate for certain of these time periods because accountants use estimates, such as depreciation expense and certain other adjusting entries.

Accounting reports cover relatively short periods of time. The time periods are usually of equal length so that valid comparisons can be made of a company's performance from period to period. The length of the accounting period must be stated in the financial statements.

Accrual Basis and Periodicity.   In Chapter 3, you learned that financial statements more accurately reflect the financial status and operations of a company when prepared under the accrual basis of accounting rather than the cash basis. Under the cash basis of accounting, revenues are recorded when cash is received, and expenses are recorded when cash is paid. Under the accrual basis, however, revenues are recorded when services are rendered or products are sold, and expenses are recorded when incurred.

The periodicity assumption makes necessary the adjusting entries prepared under the accrual basis. Without the periodicity assumption, a business would have only one time period running from the inception of the business to its termination. Then the concepts of cash basis and accrual basis accounting would be irrelevant because all revenues and all expenses would be recorded in that one time period and would not have to be assigned to artificially short time periods of one year or less.

Approximation and Judgment because of Periodicity.   To provide periodic financial information, estimates must often be made of such things as expected uncollectible accounts and useful lives of depreciable assets. Uncertainty about future events prevents precise measurement and makes estimates necessary in accounting. Estimates are often reasonably accurate when they are made by an accountant.

■ OTHER BASIC CONCEPTS

Other basic accounting concepts that affect the accounting for entities are (1) general-purpose financial statements, (2) substance over form, (3) consistency, (4) double entry, and (5) articulation. A discussion of these basic accounting concepts follows.

General-Purpose Financial Statements

As you know, results of the financial accounting process are presented in financial statements. These general-purpose financial statements are prepared at regular intervals to meet many of the general information needs of external parties and top-level internal managers. In contrast, special-purpose financial information can be gathered for a specific decision, usually on a one-time basis. For example, management may need specific information to decide whether to purchase a new computer. Because special-purpose financial information must be specific, this information is best obtained from the detailed accounting records rather than from the financial statements.

Substance over Form

In some business transactions, the economic substance of the transaction may conflict with its legal form. For example, a contract that is legally a lease may, in fact, be equivalent to a purchase. A company may have a three-year contract to lease (rent) an automobile at a stated monthly rental fee. At the end of the lease period, the company will receive title to the auto after paying a nominal sum (such as $1). The economic substance of this transaction is a purchase rather than a lease of the auto. Thus, under the substance-over-form concept, the auto is shown as an asset on the balance sheet and is depreciated instead of showing rent expense on the income statement. Accountants should record the **economic substance** of a transaction rather than be guided by the **legal form** of the transaction.

Consistency

When discussing inventories in Chapter 9, we introduced the consistency concept. **Consistency** generally requires that a company use the same accounting principles and reporting practices through time. This concept prohibits indiscriminate switching of principles or methods, such as changing inventory methods every year. However, consistency does not prohibit a change in accounting principles if the information needs of financial statement users are better served by the change. When a change in principles is made, the following disclosures are required in the financial statements—nature of the change, reasons for the change, effect of the change on current net income, if significant, and the cumulative effect of the change on past income.

Double Entry

Chapter 2 introduced the basic accounting principle of the double-entry method of recording transactions. Under the double-entry approach, every transaction has a two-sided effect on **each** company or party engaging in the transaction. Thus, to record each transaction, each company or party debits at least one account and credits at least one account. The total debits equal the total credits in each journal entry.

Articulation

When you learned how to prepare work sheets in Chapter 4, you also learned that financial statements are fundamentally related and **articulate** (interact) with each other. For example, the amount of net income is carried from the income statement to the statement of retained earnings. The ending balance on the statement of retained earnings is carried to the balance sheet to bring total assets and total equities into balance.

■ MEASUREMENT IN ACCOUNTING

In the introduction of this text, accounting was defined as "the process of identifying, measuring, and communicating economic information to permit informed judgments and decisions by the users of the information."[2] In this section, we focus on the **measurement** process of accounting.

---

[2] Ibid, p. 1.

Accountants seek to measure a business entity's assets, liabilities, and stockholders' equity and any changes that occur in them. The effects of these changes are assigned to particular time periods (periodicity) to find the net income or net loss of the accounting entity.

Measuring Assets and Liabilities

Accounting measures the various assets of a business in different ways. Cash is measured at its specified amount. Claims to cash, such as notes and accounts receivable, are measured at their expected cash inflows, taking into consideration possible uncollectibles. Inventories, prepaid expenses, plant assets, and intangibles initially are measured at their historical costs. Some items, such as inventory, are later carried at the lower-of-cost-or-market value. Plant assets and intangibles are later carried at original cost less accumulated depreciation or amortization. Liabilities are measured in terms of the cash that will be paid or the value of services that will be performed to satisfy the liabilities.

Measuring Changes in Assets and Liabilities

From the previous chapters, you have learned that some changes in assets and liabilities are easily measured by the accountant, such as the exchange of one asset for another of equal value, acquisition of an asset on credit, and payment of a liability. Other changes in assets and liabilities, such as those recorded in adjusting entries, are more difficult to measure because they often involve estimates and/or calculations. The accountant must determine when a change has taken place and the amount of the change. These decisions involve matching revenues and expenses and are guided by the principles discussed below.

■ THE MAJOR PRINCIPLES

As was mentioned in the introduction to this text, generally accepted accounting principles (GAAP) set forth standards or methods for presenting financial accounting information. A standardized presentation format enables users to compare the financial information of different companies more easily. Generally accepted accounting principles have been developed largely through accounting practice or have been established by authoritative organizations. Four major authoritative organizations that have contributed to the development of the principles are the American Institute of Certified Public Accountants (AICPA), the Financial Accounting Standards Board (FASB), the Securities and Exchange Commission (SEC), and the American Accounting Association (AAA).

In this section, you will study the following principles:

1. Exchange-price (or cost) principle.
2. Matching principle.
3. Revenue recognition principle.

4. Expense and loss recognition principle.
5. Full disclosure principle.

Exchange-Price (or Cost) Principle

When a transfer of resources takes place between two parties, such as buying merchandise on account, the accountant must follow the exchange-price (or cost) principle when presenting that information. The **exchange-price (or cost) principle** requires transfers of resources to be recorded at prices agreed on by the parties to the exchange at the time of exchange. This principle sets forth (1) what goes into the accounting system—transaction data; (2) when it is recorded—at the time of exchange; and (3) the amounts—exchange prices—at which assets, liabilities, stockholders' equity, revenues, and expenses are recorded.

As applied to most assets, this principle is often called the **cost principle,** meaning that purchased or self-constructed assets are initially recorded at historical cost. **Historical cost** is the amount paid, or the fair value of the liability incurred or other resources surrendered, to acquire an asset. The term **exchange-price principle** is preferred to **cost principle** because it seems inappropriate to refer to liabilities, stockholders' equity, and such assets as cash and accounts receivable as being measured in terms of cost.

Matching Principle

Using the **matching principle,** net income of a period is determined by associating or relating revenues earned in a period with expenses incurred to generate those revenues. The logic underlying this principle is that whenever economic resources are used, someone will want to know what was accomplished and at what cost. Every evaluation of economic activity will involve matching benefit with sacrifice. The application of the matching principle is discussed and illustrated below.

Revenue Recognition Principle

Revenue is not difficult to define or measure; it is the inflow of assets from the sale of goods and services to customers, measured by the amount of cash expected to be received from customers. But **when** revenue should be recorded (credited to a revenue account) is a crucial question for the accountant. The general answer provided under the **revenue recognition principle** is that the revenue should be **earned** and **realized** before it is recognized (recorded).

Earning of Revenue.   All economic activities undertaken by a company to create revenues are part of the earning process. The actual receipt of cash from a customer may have been preceded by many activities, including (1) placing advertisements, (2) calling on the customer several times, (3) submitting samples, (4) acquiring or manufacturing goods, and (5) selling and delivering goods. Costs are incurred by the company for these activities. Although revenue was actually being earned by these activities, in most instances accountants do not recognize revenue until the time of sale because of the requirement that revenue be **substantially** earned before it is recognized (recorded). This requirement is referred to as the **earning principle.**

Realization of Revenue.   Under the **realization principle,** the accountant does not recognize (record) revenue until the seller acquires the right to receive payment from the buyer. The seller acquires the right to receive payment from the buyer at the time of sale for merchandise transactions or when services have been performed in service transactions. Legally, a sale of merchandise occurs when title to the goods passes to the buyer. As a practical matter, accountants generally record revenue when goods are delivered.

The advantages of recognizing revenue at the time of sale are that (1) the actual transaction—delivery of goods—is an observable event; (2) revenue is easily measured; (3) risk of loss due to price decline or destruction of the goods has passed to the buyer; (4) revenue has been earned, or substantially so; and (5) because the revenue has been earned, expenses and net income can be determined. As discussed below, the disadvantage of recognizing revenue at the time of sale is that the revenue might not be recorded in the period during which most of the activity creating it occurred.

Exceptions to the Realization Principle.   The following examples illustrate instances when practical considerations may cause accountants to vary the point of revenue recognition from the time of sale. These examples illustrate the effect that the business environment has on the development of accounting principles and standards.

Cash Collection as Point of Revenue Recognition.   Some small companies record revenues and expenses at the time of cash collection and payment, which may not occur at the time of sale. This procedure is known as the **cash basis** of accounting. The cash basis is acceptable primarily in service enterprises that do not have substantial credit transactions or inventories, as is the case with doctors or dentists.

Installment Basis of Revenue Recognition.   When the selling price of goods sold is to be collected in installments (such as monthly or annually) and considerable doubt exists as to collectibility, the installment basis of accounting may be used. This kind of sale is made in spite of the doubtful collectibility of the account because the margin of profit is high and the goods can be repossessed if the payments are not received. Under the **installment basis,** the percentage of total gross margin (selling price of a good minus its cost) recognized in a period is equal to the percentage of total cash from a sale that is received in that period. In other words, the gross margin recognized in a period is equal to the amount of cash received times the gross margin percentage (gross margin divided by selling price). The formula to recognize gross profit on cash collections made on installment sales of a certain year is:

$$\boxed{\text{Cash collections}} \times \boxed{\begin{array}{c}\text{Gross margin}\\ \text{percentage}\end{array}} = \boxed{\begin{array}{c}\text{Gross margin}\\ \text{recognized}\end{array}}$$

To be a little more precise, we expand the descriptions in the formula as follows:

Cash collections this year resulting from installment sales made in a certain year	×	Gross margin percentage for the year of sale	=	Gross margin recognized this year on cash collections this year from installment sales made in a certain year

To illustrate, assume the following facts concerning the sale of a stereo set:

Date of Sale	Selling Price	Cost	Gross Margin (Selling price − Cost)	Gross Margin Percentage (Gross margin ÷ Selling price)
October 1, 1991	$500	$300	($500 − $300) = $200	($200 ÷ $500) = 40%

The buyer makes 10 equal monthly installment payments of $50 each to pay for the set (10 × $50 = $500). If three monthly payments are received in 1991, the total amount of cash received in 1991 is $150 (3 × $50).

The gross margin to recognize in **1991** is:

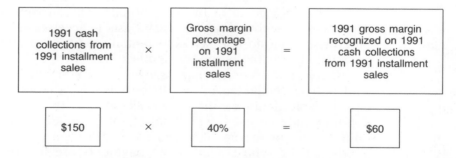

The other installments are collected when due, so that a total of $350 is received from 1991 installment sales in 1992. The gross margin to recognize in **1992** on these cash collections is shown below:

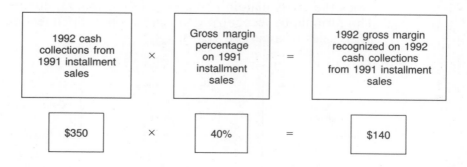

In summary, the total receipts and gross margin recognized in the two years are as follows:

Year	Total Amount of Cash Received	Gross Margin Recognized
1991	$150 (30%)	$ 60 (30%)
1992	350 (70%)	140 (70%)
Total	$500 100%	$200 100%

The installment basis of revenue recognition may be used for tax purposes only in very limited circumstances. Even for accounting purposes, since the installment basis delays revenue recognition beyond the time of sale, it is acceptable only when considerable doubt exists as to collectibility of the installments.

Revenue Recognition on Long-Term Construction Projects. Revenue from a long-term construction project can be recognized under two different methods: (1) the completed-contract method or (2) the percentage-of-completion method. The **completed-contract method** does not recognize any revenue until the period in which the project is completed. At that point, all revenue is recognized even though the contract may have required three years to complete. Thus, the **completed-contract method recognizes revenues at the time of sale,** as is true for most sales transactions. Costs incurred on the project are carried forward in an inventory account (Construction in Process) and are charged to expense in the period in which the revenue is recognized.

Some accountants argue that waiting so long to recognize any revenue is unreasonable. Revenue-producing activities have been performed during each year of construction, and revenue should be recognized in each year of construction even if estimates are needed. The **percentage-of-completion method** is a method of recognizing revenue based on the estimated stage of completion of a long-term project. The stage of completion is measured by comparing actual costs incurred in a period with the total estimated costs to be incurred on the project. The percentage-of-completion method is preferable when dependable estimates of costs can be obtained, both estimated and incurred.

To illustrate, assume that a company has a contract to build a dam for $44 million. The estimated construction cost is $40 million. Estimated gross margin is calculated as follows:

Sales Price of Dam	Estimated Costs to Construct Dam	Estimated Gross Margin (Sales price − Estimated costs)
$44 million	$40 million	($44 million − $40 million) = $4 million

This gross margin is recognized in the financial statements by recording the correct amount of revenue for the year and then deducting actual costs incurred that year.

The formula to recognize revenue is:

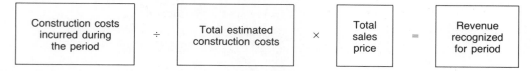

Suppose that by the end of the first year (1991), the company had incurred **actual** construction costs of $30 million. The $30 million of construction costs is 75% of the total estimated construction costs ($30 million ÷ $40 million = 75%). Under the percentage-of-completion method, the 75% figure would be used to **assign** revenue to the first year. In 1992, another $6 million of construction cost is incurred. In 1993, the final $4 million of construction cost is incurred. The amount of revenue to assign to each year is determined as follows:

Year	Ratio of Actual Construction Costs to Total Estimated Construction Costs	× Agreed Price of Dam	= Amount of Revenue to Recognize
1991	($30 million ÷ $40 million) = 75%	× $44 million =	$33 million
1992	($6 million ÷ $40 million) = 15%	× $44 million =	$6.6 million
1993	($4 million ÷ $40 million) = 10%	× $44 million =	$4.4 million

The amount of gross margin to recognize in each year is as follows:

Year	Revenues −	Construction Costs =	Gross Margin
1991	$33.0 million −	$30.0 million =	$3.0 million
1992	6.6 −	6.0 =	0.6
1993	4.4 −	4.0 =	0.4
Total	$44.0 million −	$40.0 million =	$4.0 million

Period costs, such as general and administrative expenses, would be deducted from gross margin to determine net income. For instance, assuming general and administrative expenses were $100,000 in 1992, net income would be ($600,000 − $100,000) = $500,000.

Illustration 13.1 shows the frequencies of references to the methods of accounting for long-term contracts in the financial statements of a sample of 600 companies for the years 1983–86. The percentage-of-completion method seems to be the most widely used.

Illustration 13.1

Methods of Accounting for Long-Term Contracts

	1986	1985	1984	1983
Percentage-of-completion	105	101	98	97
Completed contract	9	9	9	10
Not determinable	4	3	2	2
Referring to long-term contracts	118	113	109	109
Not referring to such contracts	482	487	491	491
Total companies	600	600	600	600

Source: American Institute of Certified Public Accountants, *Accounting Trends & Techniques* (New York: AICPA, 1987), p. 314.

Revenue Recognition at Completion of Production.   Recognizing revenue at the time of completion of production or extraction is called the **production basis.** The production basis is considered acceptable procedure when accounting for many farm products (wheat, corn, and soybeans) and for certain precious metals (gold). Accountants justify recognizing revenue prior to sale of these products because (1) the products are homogeneous in nature, (2) they can usually be sold at their market prices, and (3) unit production costs for these products are often difficult to determine.

Recognizing revenue on completion of production or extraction is accomplished by debiting inventory (an asset) and crediting a revenue account for the expected selling price of the goods. All costs incurred in the period can then be treated as expenses. For example, assume that 1,000 ounces of gold are mined at a time when gold sells for $400 per ounce. The entry to record the extraction of 1,000 ounces of gold would be:

```
Inventory of Gold . . . . . . . . . . . . . . . . . . . . . . . . . . . . . 400,000
     Revenue from Extraction of Gold . . . . . . . . . . . . . . . .          400,000
     To record extraction of 1,000 ounces of gold. Selling price
     is $400 per ounce.
```

If the gold is later sold at $400 per ounce, Cash is debited and Inventory of Gold is credited for $400,000 as follows:

```
Cash . . . . . . . . . . . . . . . . . . . . . . . . . . . . . . . . . . . . 400,000
     Inventory of Gold . . . . . . . . . . . . . . . . . . . . . . . . . .          400,000
     To record sale of 1,000 ounces of gold at $400 per ounce.
```

If expenses in producing the gold amounted to $300,000, net income on the gold mined would be $100,000.

Expense and Loss Recognition Principle

Expense and loss recognition is closely related to, and sometimes discussed as part of, the revenue recognition principle. An **expense** is the outflow or using up of assets in the generation of revenue. An expense is incurred **voluntarily** to produce a revenue. For instance, the cost of a television set delivered by a dealer to a customer in exchange for cash is an asset "consumed" to produce revenue. Similarly, the cost of such services as labor are voluntarily incurred to produce revenue.

Losses also consume assets, but they are usually involuntary and do not create revenue. An example of an involuntary loss would be a loss resulting from destruction by fire of an uninsured building. A loss on the sale of a building may be "voluntary" if management decided to sell the building even though it meant incurring a loss.

The Measurement of Expense.   Most assets used in operating a business are measured in terms of their historical costs. Therefore, expenses, such as depreciation, resulting from the consumption of those assets in producing revenues are measured in terms of the historical costs of those assets. Other expenses, such as wages, are paid for currently and are measured in terms of their current costs.

The Timing of Expense Recognition.   The matching principle implies that a relationship exists between expenses and revenues. For certain expenses, such as cost of goods sold, this relationship is easily seen. However, when a direct relationship cannot be seen, the costs of assets with limited lives may be charged to expense in the periods benefited on a systematic and rational allocation basis. Depreciation of plant assets is an example.

Product costs are costs incurred in the acquisition or manufacture of goods. Included as product costs for purchased goods are invoice, freight, and insurance-in-transit costs. For manufacturing companies, product costs include all costs of materials, labor, and factory operations necessary to produce the goods. Product costs are assumed to attach to the goods purchased or produced and are carried in inventory accounts as long as the goods are on hand. Product costs are charged to expense when the goods are sold. The result is a precise matching of cost of goods sold expense to its related revenue.

Period costs are costs that cannot be traced to specific products and are expensed in the period in which incurred. Selling and administrative costs are examples of period costs.

Full Disclosure Principle

Information important enough to influence the decisions of an informed user of the financial statements should be disclosed. Depending on its nature, this information should be disclosed either in the financial statements, in notes to the financial statements, or in supplemental statements. For instance, Appendix B at the end of this text illustrates how information regarding the effects of inflation is disclosed in supplemental financial statements. The primary financial statements continue to ignore the effects of inflation. In judging whether or not to disclose information, it is better to err on the side of too much disclosure rather than too little. Many lawsuits against CPAs and their clients have resulted from inadequate or misleading disclosure of the underlying facts.

■ MODIFYING CONVENTIONS (OR CONSTRAINTS)

In certain instances, accounting principles are not strictly applied because of modifying conventions (or constraints). **Modifying conventions** are customs emerging from accounting practice that alter the results that would be obtained from a strict application of accounting principles. Three such modifying conventions are cost-benefit, materiality, and conservatism.

Cost-Benefit.   The **cost-benefit consideration** involves deciding whether the benefits of including information in financial statements exceed the cost of providing the information. Users tend to think information is cost free since they incur none of the costs of providing the information. Preparers realize that providing information is costly. The benefits of using information should exceed the costs of providing it. The measurement of benefits is nebulous and inexact, which makes application of this modifying convention difficult in practice.

Materiality.   **Materiality** is a modifying convention that allows the accountant to deal with immaterial (unimportant) items in an expedient but theoretically incorrect manner. The fundamental question the accountant must ask in judging the materiality of an item is whether a knowledgeable user's decision would be different if the information were presented in the theoretically correct manner. If not, the item is immaterial and may be reported in a theoretically incorrect but expedient manner. For instance, since small dollar amount items like the cost of calculators often do not make a difference in a statement user's decision to invest in the company, they are considered **immaterial** (unimportant) and may be expensed when purchased. However, because large dollar amount items like the cost of mainframe computers usually do make a difference in such a decision, they are considered **material** (important) and should be recorded as an asset and depreciated. The accountant should record all material items in a theoretically correct manner. **Immaterial items may be recorded in a theoretically incorrect manner simply because it is more convenient and less expensive to do so.** For example, the purchase of a wastebasket may be debited to an expense account rather than an asset account even though the wastebasket has an expected useful life of 30 years. It simply is not worth the cost of recording depreciation expense on such a small item over its life.

Materiality involves more than the relative size of dollar amounts. Often the nature of the item may make it material. For example, it may be quite significant to know that a company is paying bribes or making illegal political contributions, even if the dollar amounts of such items are relatively small.

Conservatism.   The accountant must be aware that a fine line exists between conservative and incorrect accounting. **Conservatism** means being cautious or prudent and making sure that net assets and net income are not overstated. You have seen conservatism applied when (1) the lower-of-cost-or-market rule was used for inventory in Chapter 9 and (2) when a gain could not be recognized on a trade-in of similar assets in Chapter 11.

The next section in this chapter discusses the Conceptual Framework Project of the Financial Accounting Standards Board. The Conceptual Framework Project is designed to resolve some disagreements as to the proper theoretical foundation for accounting. Only the portions of the project relevant to this text are presented.

THE CONCEPTUAL FRAMEWORK PROJECT

Objective 2: Describe the Conceptual Framework Project of the Financial Accounting Standards Board.

The exact nature of the basic concepts and related principles composing accounting theory has been debated for years. The debate continues today even though numerous references can be found to "generally accepted accounting principles" (GAAP). To date, all attempts to present a concise statement of GAAP have received only limited acceptance.

Due to this limited success, many accountants suggest that the starting point in reaching a concise statement of GAAP is to seek agreement on the objectives of financial accounting and reporting. The belief is that if a person (1) carefully studies the environment, (2) knows what objectives are sought, (3) can identify certain qualitative traits of accounting information, and (4) can define the basic elements of financial statements, that person can discover the principles and standards that will lead to the attainment of the stated objectives. The FASB has taken the first three steps in "Objectives of Financial Reporting by Business Enterprises" and in "Qualitative Characteristics of Accounting Information."[3] The fourth step is represented by two concepts statements entitled "Elements of Financial Statements of Business Enterprises" and "Elements of Financial Statements."[4]

Objectives of Financial Reporting

Financial reporting objectives are the broad overriding goals sought by accountants engaging in financial reporting. According to the FASB, the first objective of financial reporting is to:

provide information that is useful to present and potential investors and creditors and other users in making rational investment, credit, and similar decisions. The information should be comprehensible to those who have a reasonable understanding of business and economic activities and are willing to study the information with reasonable diligence.[5]

The term *other users* is interpreted broadly and includes employees, security analysts, brokers, and lawyers. Financial reporting should provide information to all who are willing to learn to use it properly.

The second objective of financial reporting is to:

provide information to help present and potential investors and creditors and other users in assessing the amounts, timing, and uncertainty of prospective cash receipts from dividends [owner withdrawals] or interest and the proceeds from the sale, redemption, or maturity of securities or loans. Since investors' and creditors' cash

---

[3] FASB, "Objectives of Financial Reporting by Business Enterprises," *Statement of Financial Accounting Concepts No. 1* (Stamford, Conn., 1978); and "Qualitative Characteristics of Accounting Information," *Statement of Financial Accounting Concepts No. 2* (Stamford, Conn., 1980). Copyright © by the Financial Accounting Standards Board, High Ridge Park, Stamford, Connecticut 06905, U.S.A. Quoted (or excerpted) with permission. Copies of the complete documents are available from the FASB.

[4] FASB, "Elements of Financial Statements of Business Enterprises," *Statement of Financial Accounting Concepts No. 3* (Stamford, Conn., 1980); and "Elements of Financial Statements," *Statement of Financial Accounting Concepts No. 6* (Stamford, Conn., 1985). Copyright © by the Financial Accounting Standards Board, High Ridge Park, Stamford, Connecticut 06905, U.S.A. Quoted (or excerpted) with permission. Copies of the complete documents are available from the FASB.

[5] FASB, "Objectives of Financial Reporting by Business Enterprises," p. viii.

flows are related to enterprise cash flows, financial reporting should provide information to help investors, creditors, and others assess the amounts, timing, and uncertainty of prospective net cash inflows to the related enterprise.[6]

This objective ties the cash flows of investors (owners) and creditors to the cash flows of the enterprise, a tie-in that appears entirely logical. Enterprise cash inflows are the source of cash for dividends (owner withdrawals), interest, and redemption of maturing debt.

Third, financial reporting should:

> provide information about the economic resources of an enterprise, the claims to those resources (obligations of the enterprise to transfer resources to other entities and owners' equity), and the effects of transactions, events, and circumstances that change its resources and claims to those resources.[7]

A number of conclusions can be drawn from these three objectives and from a study of the environment in which financial reporting is carried out. For example, financial reporting should:

1. Provide information about an enterprise's past performance because such information is used as a basis for prediction of future enterprise performance.
2. Focus on earnings and its components, despite the emphasis in the objectives on cash flows. (Earnings computed under the accrual basis provide a better indicator of ability to generate favorable cash flows than do statements prepared under the cash basis.)

On the other hand, financial reporting does not seek to:

1. Measure the value of an enterprise but rather provides information that may be useful in determining its value.
2. Evaluate management's performance, predict earnings, assess risk, or estimate earning power but rather provides information to persons who wish to make these evaluations.

These conclusions are some of those reached in *Statement of Financial Accounting Concepts No. 1*. As the Board stated, these statements "are intended to establish the objectives and concepts that the Financial Accounting Standards Board will use in developing standards of financial accounting and reporting."[8] How successful the Board will be in the approach adopted remains to be seen.

Qualitative Characteristics

Qualitative characteristics are those characteristics that accounting information should possess to be useful in decision making. This criterion is difficult to apply. The usefulness of accounting information in a given instance depends not only on information characteristics but also on the capabilities of the decision makers and their professional advisers, if any. Accountants cannot specify who the decision makers are, their characteristics, the decisions to be made, or the methods chosen to make the

---

[6] Ibid.
[7] Ibid.
[8] Ibid., p. i.

Illustration 13.2 *A Hierarchy of Accounting Qualities*

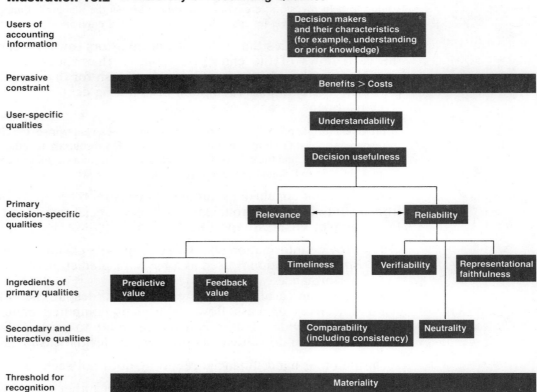

decisions; therefore, attention is directed to characteristics of accounting information. The FASB's graphic summarization of the problems faced is presented in Illustration 13.2.[9]

Relevance.   For information to have **relevance,** it must be pertinent to or affect a decision. The information must "make a difference" to someone who does not already have the information. Relevant information is capable of making a difference in a decision either by affecting user predictions of outcomes of past, present, or future events or by confirming or correcting expectations. Note that information need not be a prediction to be useful in developing, confirming, or altering expectations. Expectations are commonly based on the present or past. For example, any attempt to predict future earnings of a company would quite likely start with a review of present and past earnings. Also, information that merely confirms prior expectations may be less useful, but this information is still relevant because it reduces uncertainty.

Certain types of accounting information have been criticized because of an alleged lack of relevance. For example, some would argue that a cost of $1 million paid for a tract of land 40 years ago and reported in the current

[9] FASB, "Qualitative Characteristics of Accounting Information," p. 15.

balance sheet at that amount is irrelevant (except for possible tax implications) to users for decision making today. Such criticism has encouraged research into the types of information relevant to users. Suggestions have been made that a different valuation basis, such as current cost, be used in reporting such assets.

Predictive Value and Feedback Value.   Because actions taken now can affect only future events, information is obviously relevant when it possesses **predictive value,** or improves users' abilities to predict outcomes of events. Information that reveals the relative success of users in predicting outcomes possesses **feedback value.** Because feedback reports on past activities, it can make a difference in decision making by (1) reducing uncertainty in a situation, (2) refuting or confirming prior expectations, and (3) providing a basis for further predictions. For example, a report on the first quarter's earnings of a company reduces the uncertainty surrounding the amount of such earnings, confirms or refutes the predicted amount of such earnings, and provides a possible basis on which to predict earnings for the full year. It is important to remember that although accounting information may possess predictive value, it does not consist of predictions. Making predictions is a function performed by the decision maker, not the accountant.

Timeliness.   **Timeliness** requires accounting information to be provided at a time when it may be considered in reaching a decision. Utility of information decreases with age—to know what the net income for 1990 was in early 1991 is much more useful than to receive this information a year later. If information is to be of any value in decision making, it must be available **before** the decision is made. If not, the information is of little value. In determining what constitutes timely information, consideration must be given to the other qualitative characteristics and to the cost of gathering information. For example, a timely estimated amount for uncollectible accounts may be more valuable than a later, verified actual amount. Timeliness alone cannot make information relevant, but otherwise relevant information might be rendered irrelevant by a lack of timeliness.

Reliability.   In addition to being relevant, information must be reliable to be useful. Information has **reliability** when it faithfully depicts for users what it purports to represent. Thus, accounting information is reliable if users can depend on it to reflect the underlying economic activities of the organization. The reliability of information depends on its representational faithfulness, verifiability, and neutrality. The information must also be complete and free of bias.

Representational Faithfulness.   Insight into this quality may be gained by considering a map. A map possesses representational faithfulness when it shows roads and bridges (among other things) where roads and bridges actually exist. A correspondence exists between what is shown on the map and what is present physically. Similarly, **representational faithfulness** exists when accounting statements on economic activity correspond to the actual underlying activity. Where there is no correspondence, the cause may be (1) bias or (2) lack of completeness.

   1. *Effects of bias.*   Accounting measurements are biased if they are consistently too high or too low. Bias in accounting measurements may

exist due to the choice of measurement method or to bias introduced either deliberately or through lack of skill by the measurer.

2. *Completeness.* To be free from bias, information must be sufficiently complete to ensure that it validly represents underlying events and conditions. **Completeness** means that all significant information must be disclosed in a way that aids understanding and does not mislead. Relevance of information also may be reduced if information that would make a difference to a user is omitted. Currently, full disclosure generally requires presentation of a balance sheet, an income statement, a statement of cash flows, and necessary notes to the financial statements and supporting schedules. A statement of changes in stockholders' equity is also required in annual reports of corporations. Such statements must be complete, with items properly classified and segregated (such as reporting sales revenue separately from other revenues). Required disclosures may be made in (1) the body of the financial statements, (2) the notes to such statements, (3) special communications, and/or (4) the president's letter or other management reports in the annual report.

Another aspect of completeness is that full disclosure must be made of all changes in accounting principles and their effects.[10] Disclosure should also be made of unusual activities (loans to officers), changes in expectations (losses on inventory), depreciation expense for the period, long-term obligations entered into that are not recorded by the accountant (a 20-year lease on a building), new arrangements with certain groups (pension and profit-sharing plans for employees), and significant events that occur after the date of the statements (loss of a major customer). Accounting policies (major principles and their manner of application) followed in preparing the financial statements should also be disclosed.[11] Because of its emphasis on disclosure, this aspect of reliability is often called the *full disclosure principle*.

Verifiability. Financial information has **verifiability** when it can be substantially duplicated by independent measurers using the same measurement methods. Verifiability is directed toward eliminating measurer bias, rather than measurement method bias. The requirement that financial information be based on objective evidence is based on demonstrated needs of users for reliable, unbiased financial information. Unbiased information is especially needed when parties with opposing interests (credit seekers and credit grantors) rely on the same information. Reliability of information is enhanced if it is verifiable.

Financial information will never be free of subjective opinion and judgment; it will always possess varying degrees of verifiability. Some measurements can be supported by canceled checks and invoices. Other measurements, such as periodic depreciation charges, can never be verified because of their very nature. Thus, financial information in many instances is verifiable only in that it represents a consensus as to what would be reported if the same procedures had been followed by other accountants.

---

[10] APB, "Accounting Changes," *APB Opinion No. 20* (New York: AICPA, July 1971).

[11] APB, "Disclosure of Accounting Policies," *APB Opinion No. 22* (New York: AICPA, April 1972).

Neutrality. **Neutrality** in accounting information means that the information should be free of measurement method bias. The primary concern should be relevance and reliability of the information that results from application of the principle, not the effect that the principle may have on a particular interest. Nonneutral accounting information is designed to favor one set of interested parties over others. For example, a particular form of measurement might favor owners over creditors, or vice versa. "To be neutral, accounting information must report economic activity as faithfully as possible, without coloring the image it communicates for the purpose of influencing behavior in *some particular direction.*"[12] Accounting standards should not be developed and used like certain tax regulations that deliberately seek to foster or restrain certain types of activity. Verifiability seeks to eliminate measurer bias; neutrality seeks to eliminate measurement method bias.

Comparability (and Consistency). When **comparability** in financial information exists, reported differences and similarities in information are real and are not the result of differing accounting treatments. Comparable information will reveal relative strengths and weaknesses in a single company through time and between two or more companies at the same point in time.

Consistency requires that a company use the same accounting principles and reporting practices through time. Consistency leads to comparability of financial information for a single company through time. Comparability between companies is more difficult to achieve because the same activities may be accounted for in different ways. For example, Company B may use one method of depreciation, while Company C accounts for an identical asset in similar circumstances using another method. A high degree of intercompany comparability in accounting information will not exist unless accountants are required to account for the same activities in the same manner across companies and through time.

Pervasive Constraints. As Illustration 13.2 shows, two pervasive constraints must be considered in providing useful information. First, benefits secured from the information must be greater than the costs of providing that information. Second, only material items need be disclosed and accounted for strictly in accordance with generally accepted accounting principles (GAAP).

Cost-Benefit Analysis. Accounting information is a commodity. Like all commodities, accounting information should provide benefits greater than its cost. But unlike most commodities, accounting information has no direct cost to users since all costs are borne by the provider of the information. This fact has led users and authoritative organizations to demand ever greater amounts of financial information. The providers of this information have responded by claiming that the desired information costs more than it is worth. Such a contention was encountered frequently when the FASB proposed requiring disclosure of the impact of inflation on financial statements. Complicating the issue is the fact that accountants have no agreed

---

[12] FASB, "Qualitative Characteristics of Accounting Information," par. 100.

method of measuring benefits of information—even the measurement of cost cannot be carried out without some disagreement. Yet, in the development of accounting standards, an attempt must be made to ensure that the benefits of required disclosures exceed the costs of providing the disclosures.

Materiality.   As discussed earlier in the chapter, the basic idea inherent in materiality is that relatively large items must be accounted for in a theoretically correct manner, and relatively small, insignificant items need not be. Materiality has been defined by the FASB as "the magnitude of an omission or misstatement of accounting information that, in the light of surrounding circumstances, makes it probable that the judgement of a reasonable person relying on the information would have been changed or influenced by the omission or misstatement."[13] The term **magnitude** in this definition suggests that the materiality of an item may be assessed by looking at its **relative** size. A $10,000 error in an expense in a company with earnings of $30,000 is material. The same error in a company earning $30,000,000 may not be material.

The Basic Elements of Financial Statements

Thus far we have discussed objectives of financial reporting and qualitative characteristics of accounting information. A third important task in developing a conceptual framework for any discipline is that of identifying and defining its basic elements. The basic elements of financial statements have been identified and defined by the FASB, first in *Concepts Statement No. 3* and then as replaced in *Concepts Statement No. 6*. Most of the terms were defined earlier in this text in a less precise way to convey a general understanding of the terms. The more technical definitions follow (these items are not repeated in the glossary):

> **Assets** are probable future economic benefits obtained or controlled by a particular entity as a result of past transactions or events.
>
> **Liabilities** are probable future sacrifices of economic benefits arising from present obligations of a particular entity to transfer assets or provide services to other entities in the future as a result of past transactions or events.
>
> **Equity or net assets** is the residual interest in the assets of an entity that remains after deducting its liabilities. In a business enterprise, the equity is the ownership interest. In a not-for-profit organization, which has no ownership interest in the same sense as a business enterprise, net assets is divided into three classes based on the presence or absence of donor-imposed restrictions—permanently restricted, temporarily restricted, and unrestricted net assets.
>
> **Comprehensive income** is the change in equity of a business enterprise during a period from transactions and other events and circumstances from nonowner sources. It includes all changes in equity during a period except those resulting from investments by owners and distributions to owners.
>
> **Revenues** are inflows or other enhancements of assets of any entity or settlements of its liabilities (or a combination of both) from delivering or producing goods, rendering services, or other activities that constitute the entity's ongoing major or central operations.

---

[13] Ibid., p. xv.

Expenses are outflows or other using up of assets or incurrences of liabilities (or a combination of both) from delivering or producing goods, rendering services, or carrying out other activities that constitute the entity's ongoing major or central operations.

Gains are increases in equity (net assets) from peripheral or incidental transactions of an entity and from all other transactions and other events and circumstances affecting the entity except those that result from revenues or investments by owners.

Losses are decreases in equity (net assets) from peripheral or incidental transactions of an entity and from all other transactions and other events and circumstances affecting the entity except those that result from expenses or distributions to owners.

Investments by owners are increases in equity of a particular business enterprise resulting from transfers to it from other entities of something valuable to obtain or increase ownership interests (or equity) in it. Assets are most commonly received as investments by owners, but that which is received may also include services or satisfaction or conversion of liabilities of the enterprise.

Distributions to owners are decreases in equity of a particular business enterprise resulting from transferring assets, rendering services, or incurring liabilities by the enterprise to owners. Distributions to owners decrease ownership interest (or equity) in an enterprise.[14]

Note that the requirement that assets and liabilities be based on past transactions normally rules out the recording of contracts that are mutual promises to do something, such as entering into an employment contract with an officer. On a similar basis, the accountant refuses to record an asset and a liability when a contract is signed whereby the entity agrees to purchase a certain number of units of a product over a coming period of time.

Recognition and Measurement in Financial Statements.   In December 1984, the FASB issued *Statement of Financial Accounting Concepts No. 5,* "Recognition and Measurement in Financial Statements of Business Enterprises,"[15] describing recognition criteria and providing guidance as to the timing and nature of information to be included in financial statements. The recognition criteria established in the *Statement* are fairly consistent with those used in current practice. The *Statement* indicates, however, that when information that is more useful than currently reported information is available at a reasonable cost, it should be included in financial statements.

A slightly modified income statement format is recommended. The income statement may become a statement of earnings and comprehensive income. "Earnings" would generally be computed like income after extraordinary items (covered in Chapter 16) is presently calculated. Then, cumulative account adjustments (such as changes in accounting principle)

---

[14] FASB, "Elements of Financial Statements," *Statement of Financial Accounting Concepts No. 6* (a replacement of *FASB Concepts Statement No. 3*) (Stamford, Conn., 1985). Copyright © by the Financial Accounting Standards Board, High Ridge Park, Stamford, Connecticut 06905, U.S.A. Quoted (or excerpted) with permission. Copies of the complete document are available from the FASB.

[15] FASB, "Recognition and Measurement in Financial Statements of Business Enterprises," *Statement of Financial Accounting Concepts No. 5* (Stamford, Conn., 1984). Copyright © by the Financial Accounting Standards Board, High Ridge Park, Stamford, Connecticut 06905, U.S.A. Copies of the complete document are available from the FASB. (In case you are wondering why we do not mention *Statement of Financial Accounting Concepts No. 4,* it pertains to accounting for not-for-profit organizations and is, therefore, not relevant to this text.)

and other nonowner changes in equity would be added or deducted in arriving at "comprehensive income." The lower part of the statement would appear as follows:

```
Earnings . . . . . . . . . . . . . . . . . . . . . . . . . . . xx
+ or – Cumulative account adjustments (e.g., cumulative
        effect of changes in accounting principle) . . . . . xx
+ or – Other nonowner changes in equity (e.g., gains or
        losses on market changes in noncurrent marketable
        equity securities*) . . . . . . . . . . . . . . . . . xx
Comprehensive income . . . . . . . . . . . . . . . . . xx
```

* This item is discussed in Chapter 18.

The *Statement* also indicates that a balance sheet does not show the value of a business, but when used in combination with other information and other financial statements, the balance sheet is helpful in estimating the value of an entity. The importance of cash flow information (covered in Chapter 20) is also mentioned.

Up through Chapter 13, the single proprietorship has been used to illustrate accounting concepts. Chapter 14 discusses the partnership form of business, where there are two or more owners.

■ UNDERSTANDING THE LEARNING OBJECTIVES: CHAPTER 13

1. Identify and discuss the basic assumptions, principles, and modifying conventions of accounting.

   ■ The major underlying assumptions or concepts of accounting are (1) business entity, (2) going concern (continuity), (3) money measurement, and (4) periodicity.
   ■ Other basic accounting concepts that affect the accounting for entities are (1) general-purpose financial statements, (2) substance over form, (3) consistency, (4) double entry, and (5) articulation.
   ■ The major principles include exchange-price (or cost), matching, revenue recognition, expense and loss recognition, and full disclosure. Major exceptions to the realization principle include cash collection as point of revenue recognition, installment basis of revenue recognition, the percentage-of-completion method of recognizing revenue on long-term construction projects, and revenue recognition at completion of production.
   ■ Modifying conventions include cost-benefit, materiality, and conservatism.

2. Describe the Conceptual Framework Project of the Financial Accounting Standards Board.

   ■ The FASB has defined the objectives of financial reporting, qualitative characteristics of accounting information, and elements of financial statements.
   ■ Financial reporting objectives are the broad overriding goals sought by accountants engaged in financial reporting.

- Qualitative characteristics are those characteristics that accounting information should possess to be useful in decision making. The two primary qualitative characteristics are relevance and reliability. Another qualitative characteristic is comparability.
- Pervasive constraints include cost-benefit analysis and materiality.
- The basic elements of financial statements have been identified and defined by the FASB.
- The FASB has also described revenue recognition criteria and provided guidance as to the timing and nature of information to be included in financial statements.

3. Discuss the differences in international accounting among nations (Appendix).

   - Accounting principles differ among nations because they were developed independently.
   - There have been attempts at harmonizing accounting principles throughout the world.
   - Various differences in accounting principles that exist between nations are described.

4. Define and use correctly the new terms in the glossary.

   - See the new terms introduced following the Appendix to this chapter.

■ APPENDIX: INTERNATIONAL ACCOUNTING*

■ WHY ACCOUNTING PRINCIPLES AND PRACTICES DIFFER AMONG NATIONS

Objective 3: Discuss the differences in international accounting among nations.

In today's world, we do not find it surprising to discover a British bank in Atlanta, Coca-Cola in Paris, and French airplanes in Zaire. German auto parts are assembled in Spain and sold in the United States. Japan buys oil from Saudi Arabia and sells cameras in Italy. Soviet livestock eat American grain, and the British sip tea from Sri Lanka and China. Business has become truly international, but accounting, often described as the language of business, does not cross borders so easily. Accounting principles and reporting practices differ from country to country, and international decision making is made more difficult by the lack of a common communication system. But since business is practiced at an international level, accounting must find a way to provide its services at that level.

The problem is that accounting reflects the national economic and social environment in which it is practiced, and this environment is not the same

---

* The authors wish to express their appreciation to William P. Hauworth II, Partner, Arthur Andersen & Co., Chicago, Illinois, for updating this appendix.

in Bangkok as in Boston. Some economies, for example, are mainly agricultural. Others are based on manufacturing, trade, or service industries. Still others export natural resources, such as oil or gold, while a few derive most of their income from tourism. Accounting for inventories and natural resources, cost accounting techniques, and methods of foreign currency translation have a different orientation, emphasis, and degree of refinement in these different economies.

Other accounting differences stem from the various legal or political systems of nations. In centrally controlled economies, for instance, the state owns all or most of the property. It makes little sense to prescribe full disclosure of accounting procedures to protect investors when little or no private ownership of property exists. Some of these countries standardize their accounting methods and incorporate them into law. But in most market-oriented economies, the development of accounting principles and reporting practices is left mainly to the private sector. Where uniformity exists, it occurs more by general agreement or consensus of interested parties than by governmental decree. In countries where business firms are predominately family owned, disclosure practices usually are less complete than in countries where large, publicly held corporations dominate. The requirement in many countries that the financial statements must conform to the tax return contributes to diversity in accounting practices among countries.

The degree of development of the accounting profession and the general level of education of a country also influence accounting practices and procedures. Nations that lack a well-organized accounting profession may adopt almost wholesale the accounting methods of other countries. Commonwealth countries, for example, tend to follow British accounting standards; the former French colonies of Africa use French systems; Bermuda follows Canadian pronouncements; and the influence of the United States is widespread. At the same time, levels of expertise vary. In countries that have little knowledge or understanding of statistics, nothing is gained by advocating statistical accounting and auditing techniques. Accounting systems designed for electronic data processing are not helpful in countries where few or no businesses use computers.

Even in advanced countries, genuine differences of opinion exist regarding accounting theory and appropriate accounting methods. American standards, for example, require the periodic amortization of goodwill to expense, but British and Dutch standards do not. The lack of agreement on the objectives of financial statements and the lack of any effort in most countries to articulate objectives also contribute to diversity. Accounting methods also differ within nations. Most countries, including the United States, permit several depreciation methods and two or more inventory costing methods.

■ ATTEMPTED HARMONIZATION OF ACCOUNTING PRACTICES

The question arises as to whether financial statements that reflect the economic and social environment of, say, France can also be useful to a potential American investor. Can some of the differences between French and American accounting be eliminated or at least explained so that French and American investors will understand each other's reports and find them useful when they make decisions?

Several organizations are working to achieve greater understanding and harmonization of different accounting practices. These include the Organization for Economic Cooperation and Development (OECD), the European Economic Community (EEC), and the International Accounting Standards Committee (IASC). These organizations study the information needs and accounting and reporting practices of different nations and issue pronouncements recommending specific practices and procedures for adoption by all members.

The IASC is making a significant contribution to the development of international accounting standards. It was founded in London in 1973 by the professional accountancy bodies of nine countries: Australia, Canada, France, Germany, Japan, Mexico, the Netherlands, the United Kingdom and Ireland, and the United States. The IASC selects a topic for study from lists of problems submitted by the profession all over the world. After research and discussion by special committees, the IASC issues an exposure draft of a proposed standard for consideration by the profession and the business and financial communities. After about six months' further study of the topic in light of the comments received, the IASC issues the final international accounting standard. To date, 26 standards have been issued on topics as varied as *Disclosure of Accounting Policies* (IAS 1), *Depreciation Accounting* (IAS 4), *Statement of Changes in Financial Position* (IAS 7), and *Revenue Recognition* (IAS 18). Setting international standards is not easy. If the standards are too detailed or rigid, the flexibility needed to reflect different national environments will be lost. On the other hand, if pronouncements are vague and allow too many alternative methods, there is little point in setting international standards.

One major problem is obtaining compliance with these standards. There is no organization, nor is there likely to be, to ensure compliance with international standards. Adoption is left to national standard-setting bodies or legislatures, which may or may not adopt a recommended international standard. Generally, members commit themselves to support the objectives of the international body. The members promise to use their best endeavors to see that international standards are formally adopted by local professional accountancy bodies, by government departments or other authorities that control the securities markets, and by the industrial, business, and financial communities of their respective countries.

The American Institute of Certified Public Accountants (AICPA), for example, issued a revised statement in 1975 reaffirming its support for the implementation of international standards adopted by the IASC. The AICPA's position is that international accounting standards must be specifically adopted by the Financial Accounting Standards Board (FASB), which is not a member of the IASC, to achieve acceptance in the United States. But if no significant difference exists between an international standard and U.S. practice, compliance with U.S. generally accepted accounting principles (GAAP) constitutes compliance with the international standard. Where a significant difference exists, the AICPA publishes the IASC standard together with comments on how it differs from GAAP in the United States and undertakes to urge the FASB to give early consideration to harmonizing the differences.[16] Significant support for IASC standards has also resulted from a resolution adopted by the World Federation of Stock Exchanges in 1975. The resolution binds members to require conformance with IASC standards in securities listing agreements.[17]

Although these developments are important for international harmonization of accounting, ultimately the success of international pronouncements depends on the willingness of the members to support them. In some cases, national legislation is required and may be slow or difficult to pass. The EEC, for example, issues "Directives" that must be accepted as compulsory objectives by the 12 member states (Belgium, Denmark, France, Germany, Greece, Ireland, Italy, Luxembourg, the Netherlands, Portugal, Spain, and the United Kingdom) but are translated into national legislation at the discretion of each member state. The EEC's important *Fourth Directive* was adopted in 1978 to regulate the preparation, content, presentation, audit, and publication of the accounts and reports of companies. It applies to all limited-liability companies (corporations) registered in the EEC, except banks and insurance companies. Under the directive, member states were to introduce legislation by July 1980 so that accounts in all EEC countries would conform to the directive as of the fiscal year beginning January 1, 1982. Yet by that date, only Belgium, Denmark, and the United Kingdom had passed the necessary legislation, although most of the other member countries were planning to adopt the directive.

The general movement toward international harmonization of accounting standards is increasing in other areas of society. The accounting profession, national standard-setting bodies, universities, academic societies, and multinational corporations have all shown an increased interest in international accounting problems in recent years. The AICPA has an International Practice Division as a formal part of its line organization. The American Accounting Association officially established an International Accounting section in 1976 and has approximately one dozen international accounting organizations as Associate Members. The University of Lancaster (England) and the University of Illinois have international accounting research centers that support research studies and conduct international conferences and seminars. Georgia State University received a Touche Ross & Co. grant to internationalize its accounting curriculum. Many universities currently offer courses in international business and accounting.

All this activity helps increase the flow of information and our understanding of the accounting and reporting practices in other parts of the world. Greater understanding improves the likelihood that unnecessary differences will be eliminated and enhances the general acceptance of international standards.

The rest of this appendix gives examples of the accounting methods used in different countries and of the concepts that underlie them to illustrate the difficulty of achieving international harmonization.

---

[16] American Institute of Certified Public Accountants, *CPA Letter*, August 1975.

[17] *CA Magazine*, January 1975, p. 52.

■ FOREIGN CURRENCY TRANSLATION

Foreign currency translation is probably the most common problem in an international business environment. Foreign currency translation has two main components: accounting for transactions in a foreign currency and translating the financial statements of foreign enterprises into a different, common currency.

Accounting for Transactions in a Foreign Currency

Suppose an American automobile dealership imports vehicles from Japan and promises to pay for them in yen 90 days after receiving them. If no change in the dollar-yen exchange rate occurs between the date the goods are received and the date the invoice is paid, no problem exists. Both the purchase and the payment will be recorded at the same dollar value. But if the yen appreciates against the dollar during the 90-day period, the importer must pay more dollars for the yen needed on the settlement date.[18] Which exchange rate should the importer use to record the purchase of the vehicles—the rate in effect on the purchase date or on the payment date?

One approach to the problem is to regard the purchase of the automobiles and settlement of the invoice as two separate transactions and record them at two different exchange rates. The difference between the amount recorded in Accounts Payable on the purchase date and the amount of cash paid on the settlement date is considered an exchange gain or loss. This approach, known as the "time-of-transaction" method, was the prescribed or predominant practice in 61 of 64 countries surveyed in 1979,[19] including the United States.[20] The time-of-transaction method is also the method recommended in the IASC's Statement No. 21, *Accounting for the Effects of Changes in Foreign Exchange Rates,* issued in July 1983.

Another approach, known as the "time-of-settlement" method, regards the transaction and its settlement as a single event. If this method is used, the amount recorded on the purchase date is regarded as an estimate of the settlement amount. Any fluctuations in the exchange rate between the purchase date and the settlement date are accounted for as part of the transaction and are not treated as a separate gain or loss. Consequently, the effect on earnings is not recognized until the purchased items are sold.

Although the time-of-transaction method is widely used, the treatment of resulting exchange gains and losses is not uniform. If the gains or losses are realized (that is, if settlement is made within the same accounting period as

---

[18] This example ignores the possibility that the importer might obtain a forward exchange contract, a discussion of which is beyond the scope of this text.

[19] Price Waterhouse International *International Survey.* Data on the different methods used and on the number of countries using each method described in these examples are derived substantially from this publication.

[20] FASB, "Accounting for the Translation of Foreign Currency Transactions and Foreign Currency Financial Statements," *Statement of Financial Accounting Standards No. 8* (Stamford, Conn., 1975). The "time-of-transaction" method is also prescribed by FASB *Statement No. 52,* "Foreign Currency Translation" (Stamford, Conn., 1981), which supersedes FASB *Statement No. 8.*

the purchase), most countries recognize the gains and losses in the income statement for that period. If the **exchange gains or losses** are unrealized—that is, if they result from translating accounts payable (or accounts receivable for the vendor) at the balance sheet date—the treatment varies. Recording unrealized losses was the prescribed or predominant practice in 54 countries in 1979. But only 40 countries similarly recognized exchange gains in income, the remaining nations preferring to defer them until settlement. In the United States, under the provisions of FASB *Statement No. 52,* both realized and unrealized transaction gains and losses are recognized in earnings of the period in which the exchange rate changes.

Translating Financial Statements

Financial statements of foreign subsidiaries are translated into a single common unit of measurement, such as the dollar, for purposes of consolidation. Considerable argument has arisen in recent years regarding the correct way to do this; that is, which exchange rate should be used to translate items in the balance sheet and income statement, and what treatment is appropriate for any resulting exchange gains and losses? Items translated at the historical rate cannot result in exchange gains or losses. But items translated at the exchange rate in effect on the balance sheet date (the **current rate**) can result in exchange gains and losses if the current rate differs from the rate in effect when those items were recorded (the historical rate). If the current rate is used, a related question arises: Should the resulting exchange gains or losses be recognized immediately in income or deferred in some way?

The methods used to translate financial statements fall basically into two groups: translation of all items at the current rate and translation of some items at the current rate and others at the historical rates. The two groups are based on different concepts of both consolidation and international business.

The Current-Rate Approach.   The **current-rate** or **closing-rate approach** translates all assets and liabilities at the current rate, the exchange rate in effect on the balance sheet date. The main advantage of this method is its simplicity; it treats all items uniformly. The approach is based on the view that a foreign subsidiary is a separate unit from the domestic parent company. The subsidiary's assets are viewed as being acquired largely out of local borrowing. Multinational groups, therefore, consist of entities that operate independently but contribute to a central fund of resources. Consequently, in consolidation it is believed that stockholders of the parent company are interested primarily in the parent company's net investment in the foreign subsidiary.

The Current/Historical-Rates Approach.   The **current/historical-rates approach** regards the parent company and its foreign subsidiaries as a single business undertaking. Assets owned by a foreign subsidiary are viewed as indistinguishable from assets owned by the parent company. Foreign assets should, therefore, be reflected in consolidated statements in the same way that similar assets of the parent company are reported, that is, at historical cost in the parent company's currency.

Three translation methods are commonly used under this approach. The **current-noncurrent method** translates current assets and current liabilities at the current rate—the rate in effect on the balance sheet date—while non-current items are translated at their respective historical rates. The **historical rate** is the rate in effect when an asset or liability is originally recorded. Under the **monetary-nonmonetary method,** the current rate is used for monetary assets and liabilities—that is, for those that have a fixed, nominal value in terms of the foreign currency—while historical rates are applied to nonmonetary items. The **temporal method** is a variation of the monetary-nonmonetary method. Cash, receivables and payables, and other assets and liabilities carried at current prices (for example, marketable securities carried at current market value) are translated at the current rate of exchange. All other assets and liabilities are translated at historical rates.

Disagreement over the appropriate translation method seems likely to continue because of the different concepts of parent-subsidiary relations on which they are founded. In 1979, only six countries prescribed a single method. The temporal method was required in Austria, Canada, Bermuda, Jamaica, and the United States (under FASB *Statement No. 8*), while Uruguay required the current-rate method. Since that time the United States and Canada have changed to the current-rate method (FASB *Statement No. 52*). Apart from these 6 nations, 24 countries, including most of Europe, Japan, and Australia, predominantly followed the current-rate approach, while in 25 countries, including Germany, South Africa, and most of Central and South America, some variation of the current/historical-rates approach was common practice.

The treatment of exchange gains and losses produced by translating items at the current rate varies and is not strictly related to the translation method used. In 1979, the predominant practice in 42 nations, including much of Europe, Latin America, Japan, and the United States, was to recognize all gains and losses immediately in income. Eighteen of these countries used the current-rate translation method, and 23 followed one of the current/historical-rates methods. Alternative treatments of translation gains and losses included recording them directly in stockholders' equity (Australia), recognizing some of them immediately in income and deferring others (United Kingdom), and recognizing some in income and deferring and amortizing others over the remaining life of the items concerned (Canada and Bermuda).

Since the issuance of FASB *Statement No. 52*, the immediate recognition of translation gains and losses in income is not permitted in the United States. Instead, they are reported separately and accumulated in a separate component of stockholders' equity until the parent company's investment in the foreign subsidiary is sold or liquidated, at which time they are reported as part of the gain or loss on sale or liquidation of the investment.

■ INVENTORIES

Variations in accounting for inventories relate principally to the basis for determining cost and whether cost once determined should be increased or decreased to reflect the market value of the inventories.

Determination of Cost

Although other methods are occasionally used in some countries, this text discusses three principal bases for determining inventory cost: first-in, first-out (FIFO); last-in, first-out (LIFO); and average cost.

The most frequently used methods in 1979 were FIFO and average cost. Each of these methods was predominant in 31 countries, although no country required the use of one method to the exclusion of the other. FIFO was more common in Europe, although Austria, France, Greece, and Portugal used an average method. FIFO also predominated in Australia, Canada, South Africa, and the United States. The average method was generally followed in Latin America, Japan, and much of Africa. LIFO was the principal method in only one country—Italy—although it was a common minority method in Japan, the United States, most of Latin America, and several European countries. LIFO was considered an unacceptable method in Australia, Brazil, France, Ireland, Malawi, Norway, Peru, and the United Kingdom. IASC's Statement No. 2, *Valuation and Presentation of Inventories in the Context of the Historical Cost System,* supports the preference of the majority of countries and recommends the use of FIFO or average cost.

Market Value of Inventories

Only seven countries in 1979 did not require or predominantly follow the principle that inventories should be carried at the lower-of-cost-or-market value. Five of these countries, including Japan, used cost, even when cost exceeded market value. In the other two countries—Portugal and Switzerland—most enterprises wrote down inventories to amounts below both cost and market value, a practice permitted by law.

The main difference in the countries that did use the lower-of-cost-or-market approach was in the interpretation of "market value." Forty-eight countries equated it with net realizable value, meaning estimated selling price in the ordinary course of business less costs of completion and necessary selling expenses. This view was essentially required in 22 countries, including Australia, France, Ireland, South Africa, and the United Kingdom. IASC Statement No. 2 also requires this interpretation. Austria, Greece, Italy, and Venezuela interpreted market value as replacement cost—the current cost of replacing the inventories in their present condition and location.

The United States defines market value as replacement cost, with the stipulation that it cannot exceed net realizable value or fall below net realizable value reduced by the normal profit margin. In 1979, Chile, the Dominican Republic, Mexico, Panama, and the Philippines also used this interpretation of market value.

■ ACCOUNTING FOR THE EFFECTS OF CHANGING PRICES

The final example of international differences illustrates an opportunity for international harmonization that is almost unique. Accounting for the effects of changing prices is still in its infancy, so it may be possible to achieve a general international approach to the problem before national practices become too varied and too entrenched.

In Appendix B at the end of the text, two approaches to accounting for the effects of changing prices on business enterprises are discussed: general price-level (constant-dollar) accounting and current-cost accounting. The FASB, in *Statement No. 33,* required both methods.[21] However, *Statement No. 82* eliminated the requirements to use the first of these methods.[22] The first approach attempts to reflect the effects of changes in general purchasing power on historical-cost financial statements, while the second is concerned with the impact of specific price changes. FASB *Statement No. 89* made reporting the effects of inflation completely optional.[23]

A number of countries are concerned about the loss of relevance of historical-cost financial reporting in inflationary environments, and several have adopted one of the two standard approaches—constant dollar or current cost. Some countries, usually those with the longest history of severe inflation, have issued standards that are mandatory for all enterprises, or at least for large or publicly held entities. In other countries, the accounting profession recommends, but does not prescribe, a form of inflation-adjusted statements, usually as supplementary information. But few countries are prepared to abandon the present system based on historical cost and nominal units of currency for their primary financial statements, at least until decision makers have had sufficient experience with inflation accounting to give an opinion on its utility. Exceptions to this view are Argentina, Brazil, and Chile, which now require incorporation of general price-level accounting in the primary financial statements of all enterprises.

The United Kingdom's standard, until it was withdrawn, prescribed the provision of current-cost information either in the primary financial statements or as supplementary statements or additional information. New Zealand requires a supplementary income statement and balance sheet on a current-cost basis. Australia and South Africa recommend, but do not yet require, similar supplementary current-cost statements. Germany recommends the incorporation of current-cost information in notes to the historical-cost financial statements; while in the Netherlands, some companies prepare the primary statements on a current-cost basis, and some provide only supplementary information.

The fact that the accountancy bodies of various nations are adopting neither a uniform approach nor a uniform application of any approach, even with something as relatively new as accounting for changing prices, highlights the difficulty of achieving international harmonization of accounting standards. Adoption of different approaches to accounting for changing prices by different countries will make the preparation of consolidated financial statements by multinational corporations especially difficult, while at the same time comparability of the financial reports of companies in

---

[21] FASB, "Financial Reporting and Changing Prices," *Statement of Financial Accounting Standards No. 33,* (Stamford, Conn., 1979).

[22] FASB, "Financial Reporting and Changing Prices: Elimination of Certain Disclosures," *Statement of Financial Accounting Standards No. 82,* (Stamford, Conn., 1984).

[23] FASB, "Financial Reporting and Changing Prices," *Statement of Financial Accounting Standards No. 89,* (Stamford, Conn., 1987).

different nations will be further reduced. But even if all countries adopted a similar approach, a major barrier to comparability would still remain: the price indexes used in each country to compute adjustments for price changes are not comparable in composition, accuracy, frequency of publication, or timeliness.

Many accountants are reluctant to see current-cost-adjusted statements replace historical-cost financial statements because they believe historical cost is the most objective basis of valuation. But business entities may be more likely to favor inflation accounting, once they become accustomed to it, because of its tax implications—assuming the tax law will permit the method. Since inflation accounting generally leads to lower profit figures than those computed on the historical-cost basis, companies have a strong incentive to adopt inflation accounting in those countries where computation of the tax liability is based on reported net income. Governments, on the other hand, could then decide to prohibit the use of inflation accounting for tax purposes when a decline in tax revenues becomes apparent.

The current trend in the use of approaches to accounting for changing prices appears to be toward current-cost accounting and away from general price-level accounting. It has been suggested that, of the two approaches, governments prefer current-cost accounting, and this preference may influence the decisions of the accounting profession in some countries. As one British writer has pointed out:

> No government wants to have the effects of its currency debasement measured by anyone—certainly not by every business enterprise in the country. Much better to point the finger at all those individual prices moving around because of the machinations of big business, big labour and big aliens.[24]

Whether current-cost accounting will become common practice or whether some combination of current-cost and general price-level accounting will gain favor should depend on the usefulness to decision makers of the information provided by each approach. One thing is clear: As inflation again becomes a problem, more countries will adopt some form of inflation accounting. The opportunity to achieve a higher level of international harmonization while national standards are still at the development stage should not be missed.

We have attempted in these few pages to provide a broad and general picture of the variety of accounting principles and reporting practices that exist across the world. Articulation among countries is a challenging problem—and one that will receive increasing attention in the years to come.

---

[24] P. H. Lyons, "Farewell to Historical Costs?" *CA Magazine*, February 1976, p. 23.

■ SELECTED BIBLIOGRAPHY

Arthur Andersen & Co. (London). *European Review* nos. 1–5 (January 1981–May 1982).

Choi, Frederick D. S., and Gerhard G. Mueller, *An Introduction to Multinational Accounting.* Englewood Cliffs, N.J.: Prentice-Hall, 1978.

Hauworth, William P., II. "A Comparison of Various International Proposals on Inflation Accounting: A Practitioner's View." Monograph, 1980.

Hobson, D. "International Harmonization." *Public Finance and Accountancy* (May 1983). pp. 34–36.

Horner, Lawrence D. "Efficient Markets and Universal Standards." *Chief Executive* (Winter 1985), p. 38.

International Financial Reporting Standards: Problems and Prospects. ICRA Occasional Paper No. 13. Lancaster, England: International Centre for Research in Accounting, University of Lancaster, 1977.

Price Waterhouse International. *International Survey of Accounting Principles and Reporting Practices,* 1979.

Stamp, Edward. *The Future of Accounting and Auditing Standards. ICRA Occasional Paper No. 18.* Lancaster, England: International Centre for Research in Accounting, University of Lancaster, 1979.

Stamp, Edward, and Maurice Moonitz, "International Auditing Standards—Parts I and II." *The CPA Journal* LII, nos. 6 and 7 (June–July 1982).

NEW TERMS INTRODUCED IN CHAPTER 13

Accounting theory   "A set of basic concepts and assumptions and related principles that explain and guide the accountant's actions in identifying, measuring, and communicating economic information" (526).

Business entity   The specific unit for which accounting information is gathered. Business entities have a separate existence from owners, creditors, employees, customers, other interested parties, and other businesses (527).

Comparability   A qualitative characteristic of accounting information; when information is comparable, it reveals differences and similarities that are real and are not the result of differing accounting treatments (545).

Completed-contract method   A method of recognizing revenue on long-term projects in which no revenue is recognized until the period in which the project is completed; similar to recognizing revenue upon the completion of a sale (535).

Completeness   A qualitative characteristic of accounting information; requires disclosure of all significant information in a way that aids understanding and does not

mislead; sometimes called the *full disclosure principle* (544).

Conservatism   Being cautious or prudent and making sure that net assets and net income are not overstated (539).

Consistency   Requires a company to use the same accounting principles and reporting practices through time (530).

Cost-benefit consideration   Determining whether benefits of including information in financial statements exceed costs (539).

Cost principle   See Exchange-price principle (532).

Current/historical-rates approach   Regards the parent company and its foreign subsidiaries as a single business undertaking. All assets are shown at historical cost in the parent company's currency (554).

Current-noncurrent method   Translates current assets and current liabilities at the current rate (555).

Current rate   Exchange rate in effect on the balance sheet date (554).

Current-rate or closing-rate approach The current-rate or closing-rate method translates all assets and liabilities at current rate, the exchange rate in effect on the balance sheet date (554).

Earning principle The requirement that revenue be substantially earned before it is recognized (recorded) (533).

Exchange gains or losses (time-of-transaction method) The difference between the amount recorded in Accounts Payable on the purchase date and amount of cash paid on the settlement date (554).

Exchange-price (or cost) principle Transfers of resources are recorded at prices agreed on by the parties to the exchange at the time of the exchange (532).

Feedback value A qualitative characteristic that information has when it reveals the relative success of users in predicting outcomes (543).

Financial reporting objectives The broad overriding goals sought by accountants engaging in financial reporting (540).

Going concern (continuity) The assumption that an entity will continue to operate indefinitely unless strong evidence indicates that the entity will terminate (527).

Historical cost The amount paid, or the fair value of a liability incurred or other resources surrendered, to acquire an asset (532).

Historical rate The rate in effect when an asset or liability is originally recorded (555).

Installment basis A revenue recognition procedure in which the percentage of total gross margin recognized in a period on an installment sale is equal to the percentage of total cash from the sale that is received in that period (533).

Liquidation Terminating a business by ceasing business operations and selling off its assets (527).

Losses Asset expirations that are usually involuntary and do not create revenues (537).

Matching principle The principle that net income of a period is determined by associating or relating revenues earned in a period with expenses incurred to generate the revenues (532).

Materiality A modifying convention that allows the accountant to deal with immaterial (unimportant) items in a theoretically incorrect, expedient manner; also a qualitative characteristic specifying that financial accounting report only information significant enough to influence decisions or evaluations (539).

Modifying conventions Customs emerging from accounting practice that alter the results that would be obtained from a strict application of accounting principles; conservatism is an example (538).

Monetary-nonmonetary method The current rate is used for monetary assets and liabilities, while the historical rate is applied to nonmonetary items (555).

Money measurement Use of a monetary unit of measurement, such as the dollar, instead of physical or other units of measurement—feet, inches, grams, and so on (528).

Neutrality A qualitative characteristic that requires accounting information to be free of measurement method bias (545).

Percentage-of-completion method A method of recognizing revenue based on the estimated stage of completion of a long-term project. The stage of completion is measured by comparing actual costs incurred in a period with total estimated costs to be incurred in all periods (535).

Period costs Costs that cannot be traced to specific products and are expensed in the period in which incurred (538).

Periodicity (time periods) An assumption of the accountant that an entity's life can be subdivided into time periods for purposes of reporting its economic activities (528).

Predictive value A qualitative characteristic that information has when it improves users' abilities to predict outcomes of events (543).

Product costs Costs incurred in the acquisition or manufacture of goods. Product costs are accounted for as if they were attached to the goods, with the result that they are charged to expense when the goods are sold (538).

Production basis A method of revenue recognition used in limited circumstances that recognizes revenue at the time of completion of production or extraction (537).

Qualitative characteristics Characteristics that accounting information should possess to be useful in decision making (541).

Realization principle A principle that directs that revenue is recognized only after the seller acquires the right to receive payment from the buyer (533).

Relevance A qualitative characteristic requiring that information be pertinent to or affect a decision (542).

Reliability A qualitative characteristic requiring that information faithfully depict for users what it purports to represent (543).

Representational faithfulness A qualitative characteristic requiring that accounting statements on economic activity correspond to the actual underlying activity (543).

Revenue recognition principle The principle that revenue should be earned and realized before it is recognized (recorded) (532).

Stable dollar An assumption that the dollar is a reasonably stable unit of measurement (528).

Temporal method Cash, receivables and payables, and other assets and liabilities carried at current prices are translated at the current rate of exchange. All other assets and liabilities are translated at historical rates (555).

Timeliness A qualitative characteristic requiring that accounting information be provided at a time when it may be considered in reaching a decision (543).

Verifiability A qualitative characteristic of accounting information; information is verifiable when it can be substantially duplicated by independent measurers using the same measurement methods (544).

DEMONSTRATION PROBLEM

For each of the transactions or circumstances described below and the entries made, state which, if any, of the assumptions, concepts, principles, or modifying conventions of accounting have been violated. For each violation, give the entry to correct the improper accounting assuming the books have not been closed.

During the year, the Dorsey Company did the following:

1. Had its buildings appraised. They were found to have a market value of $410,000, although their book value was only $380,000. The accountant debited the Buildings and Accumulated Depreciation—Buildings accounts for $15,000 each and credited Owner's Capital. No separate mention was made of this action in the financial statements.
2. Purchased a number of new electric pencil sharpeners for its offices at a total cost of $60. These pencil sharpeners were recorded as assets and are being depreciated over five years.
3. Produced a number of agricultural products at a cost of $26,000. These costs were charged to expense when the products were harvested. The products were set up in inventory at their market value of $35,000, and the Farm Revenues Earned account was credited for $35,000.

Solution to demonstration problem

1. The realization principle and the modifying convention of conservatism may have been violated. Such write-ups simply are not looked on with favor in accounting. To correct the situation, the entry made needs to be reversed:

Owner's Capital	30,000	
Buildings		15,000
Accumulated Depreciation—Buildings		15,000

2. Theoretically, no violations occurred, but the cost of compiling insignificant information could be considered a violation of acceptable accounting practice. As a practical matter, the $60 could have been expensed on materiality grounds.

3. No violations occurred. The procedures followed are considered acceptable for farm products that are interchangeable and readily marketable. No correcting entry is needed, provided due allowance has been made for the costs to be incurred in delivering the products to the market.

QUESTIONS

1. Name the assumptions underlying generally accepted accounting principles. Comment on the validity of the stable unit of measurement assumption during periods of high inflation.

2. Why does the accountant assume the existence of an entity?

3. When is the going-concern assumption not to be used?

4. What is meant by the term *accrual basis of accounting*? What is its alternative?

5. What does it mean to say that accountants record substance rather than form?

6. If a company changes an accounting principle because the change better meets the information needs of users, what disclosures must be made?

7. What is the exchange-price (or cost) principle? What is the significance of adhering to this principle?

8. What two requirements generally must be met before revenue will be recognized in a period?

9. Under what circumstances, if any, is the receipt of cash an acceptable time to recognize revenue?

10. What two methods may be used in recognizing revenues on long-term construction contracts?

11. Define expense. What principles guide the recognition of expense?

12. How does an expense differ from a loss?

13. What is the full disclosure principle?

14. What role does cost-benefit play in financial reporting?

15. What is meant by the accounting term *conservatism*? How does it affect the amounts reported in the financial statements?

16. Does materiality relate only to the relative size of dollar amounts?

17. Identify the three major parts of the Conceptual Framework Project that are included in the text.

18. What are the two primary qualitative characteristics?

19. (Based on Appendix) Why do differences exist in accounting standards and practices from nation to nation?

20. (Based on Appendix) How successful have efforts at harmonization been to date?

EXERCISES

E-1
Match theory terms with definitions

Match the items in Column A with the proper descriptions in Column B.

Column A	Column B
1. Going concern (continuity).	a. An assumption relied on in the preparation of the primary financial statements that would be unreasonable when the inflation rate is high.
2. Consistency.	
3. Disclosure.	
4. Periodicity.	b. Concerned with relative dollar amounts.
5. Conservatism.	c. The usual basis for the recording of assets.
6. Stable dollar.	d. Required if the accounting treatment differs from that previously used for a particular item.
7. Matching.	
8. Materiality.	e. An assumption that would be unreasonable to use in reporting on a firm that had become insolvent.
9. Exchange-price.	
10. Entity.	f. None of these.
	g. Requires a company to use the same accounting procedures and practices through time.
	h. An assumption that the life of an entity can be subdivided into time periods for reporting purposes.
	i. Discourages undue optimism in measuring and reporting net assets and net income.
	j. Requires separation of personal activities from business activities in the recording and reporting processes.

E-2
Compute income under accrual basis and installment method

Shorter Company sells its products on an installment sales basis. Data for 1991 and 1992 follow:

	1991	1992
Installment sales	$200,000	$240,000
Cost of goods sold on installment sales . . .	140,000	180,000
Other expenses	30,000	40,000
Cash collected from 1991 sales	120,000	60,000
Cash collected from 1992 sales		160,000

a. Compute the net income for 1992 assuming use of the accrual (sales) basis of revenue recognition.

b. Compute the net income for 1992 assuming use of the installment method of recognizing gross margin.

E-3
Recognize revenue under percentage-of-completion method

A company has a contract to build a ship at a price of $500 million and an estimated cost of $400 million. In 1991, costs of $100 million were incurred. Under the percentage-of-completion method, how much revenue would be recognized in 1991?

E-4
Compute effect on financial statements of incorrectly expensing an asset

A company follows a practice of expensing the premium on its fire insurance policy when it is paid. In 1991, the company charged to expense the $5,760 premium paid on a three-year policy covering the period July 1, 1991, to June 30, 1994. In 1988, a premium of $5,280 was charged to expense on the same policy for the period July 1, 1988, to June 30, 1991.

a. State the principle of accounting that was violated by this practice.

b. Compute the effects of this violation on the financial statements for the calendar year 1991.

c. State the basis on which the company's practice might be justified.

E–5
Compute gross margin under GAAP and then comment on recognizing revenue as production is completed

Blue Ridge Company produces a product at a cost of $120 per unit that it sells for $180. The company has been successful and is able to sell all of the units that it can produce. During 1991, the company manufactured 50,000 units, but because of a transportation strike, it was able to sell and deliver only 40,000 units.

a. Compute the gross margin for 1991 following the realization principle. The cost of the units sold should be entitled "cost of goods sold" and treated as an expense.

b. Describe any circumstances under which the realization principle is ignored and revenue is recognized as production is completed.

E–6
Match accounting qualities with proper descriptions

Match the descriptions in the second column with the proper terms in the first column. Some descriptions will be used more than once.

Terms:

1. Relevance.
2. Feedback value.
3. Decision makers.
4. Representational faithfulness.
5. Reliability.
6. Comparability.
7. Benefits>costs.
8. Predictive value.
9. Timeliness.
10. Decision usefulness.
11. Verifiability.
12. Understanding.
13. Neutrality.
14. Materiality.

Descriptions:

a. Users of accounting information.
b. A pervasive constraint.
c. A user-specific quality.
d. A primary decision-specific quality.
e. An ingredient of a primary quality.
f. A secondary and interactive quality.
g. A threshold for recognition.

PROBLEMS, SERIES A

P13–1–A
Compute income assuming revenues are recognized at time of sale and then assuming installment method is used

Advent Video, Inc., sells video recorders under terms calling for a small down payment and monthly payments spread over three years. Following are data for the first three years of the company's operations:

	1991	1992	1993
Gross margin rate	30%	40%	50%
Cash collected in 1993:			
From 1991 sales			$216,000
From 1992 sales			288,000
From 1993 sales			468,000

Total sales in 1993 were $1,440,000 while general and selling expenses amounted to $432,000 in 1993.

Required: a. Compute net income for 1993 assuming that revenues are recognized at the time of sale.

b. Compute net income for 1993 using the installment method of accounting for sales and gross margin.

P13-2-A
Compute income under completed-contract and percentage-of-completion methods

The following data relate to the Goodrock Construction Company's long-term construction projects for the year 1991:

	Completed Projects	Incomplete Projects
Contract price	$18,000,000	$96,000,000
Costs incurred prior to 1991	3,700,000	16,000,000
Costs incurred in 1991	11,100,000	32,000,000
Estimated costs to complete (at 12/31/91)	–0–	32,000,000

General and administrative expenses incurred in 1991 amounted to $2,000,000, none of which is to be considered a construction cost.

Required:
a. Compute net income for 1991 under the completed-contract method.
b. Compute net income for 1991 using the percentage-of-completion method.

P13-3-A
Match principles, assumptions, or concepts with certain accounting procedures followed

For each of the numbered items listed below, state the letter or letters of the principle(s), assumption(s), or concept(s) used to justify the accounting procedure followed. The accounting procedures are all correct.

A—Entity.
B—Conservatism.
C—Earning principle of revenue recognition.
D—Going concern (continuity).
E—Exchange-price principle.
F—Matching principle.
G—Period cost (or principle of immediate recognition of expense).
H—Realization principle.
I—Stable dollar assumption.

1. The estimated liability for federal income taxes was increased by $28,000 over the amount reported on the tax return to cover possible differences found by the Internal Revenue Service in determining the amount of income taxes payable.
2. A truck purchased in January was reported at 80% of its cost even though its market value at year-end was only 70% of its cost.
3. The collection of $56,000 of cash for services to be performed next year was reported as a current liability.
4. The president's salary was treated as an expense of the year even though he spent most of his time planning the next two years' activities.
5. No entry was made to record the company's receipt of an offer of $560,000 for land carried in its accounts at $336,000.
6. A stock of printed stationery, checks, and invoices with a cost of $11,200 was treated as a current asset at year-end even though it had no value to others.
7. A tract of land acquired for $196,000 was recorded at that price even though it was appraised at $224,000, and the company would have been willing to pay that amount.
8. The company paid and charged to expense the $8,400 paid to Louis Brown for rent of a truck owned by him. Louis Brown is owner of the company.
9. $67,200 of interest collected on $560,000 of 12% bonds was recorded as interest revenue even though the general level of prices increased 16% during the year.

P13-4-A
Answer matching question regarding The Conceptual Framework Project

Match the descriptions in Column B with the proper terms in Column A.

Column A	Column B
1. Financial reporting objectives.	a. Information is free of measurement method bias.
2. Qualitative characteristics.	b. The benefits exceed the costs.
	c. Relatively large items must be accounted for in a theoretically correct way.
3. Relevance.	d. The information can be substantially duplicated by independent measurers using the same measurement methods.
4. Predictive value.	e. When information improves users' ability to predict outcomes of events.
5. Feedback value.	f. Broad overriding goals sought by accountants engaging in financial reporting.
6. Timeliness.	g. When information is pertinent or bears on a decision.
7. Reliability.	h. The characteristics that accounting information should possess to be useful in decision making.
8. Representational faithfulness.	i. Information that reveals the relative success of users in predicting outcomes.
9. Verifiability.	j. When accounting statements on economic activity correspond to the actual underlying activity.
10. Neutrality.	k. When information is provided at a time when it may be considered in decision making.
11. Comparability.	l. When information faithfully depicts for users what it purports to represent.
12. Consistency.	m. Requires a company to use the same accounting principles and reporting practices through time.
13. Cost-benefit.	n. When reported differences and similarities in information are real and not the result of differing accounting treatments.
14. Materiality.	

P13-5-A
Answer multiple-choice questions regarding international accounting (based on the Appendix)

Select the best answer to each of the following questions:

1. Methods that are used to account for transactions between companies in different nations when goods are received on one date and the invoice is paid on another date include:
   a. Time-of-transaction method.
   b. Time-of-settlement method.
   c. Current-rate method.
   d. (a) and (b) are correct.

2. Which of the following statements is **false** regarding translating financial statements of foreign subsidiaries?
   a. Under the *current-rate approach,* all assets and liabilities are translated at the exchange rate in effect on the balance sheet date.
   b. Under the *current-noncurrent method,* current assets and current liabilities are translated at the current rate, and noncurrent items are translated at their historical rates.
   c. Under the *monetary-nonmonetary method,* nonmonetary assets and liabilities are translated at their historical rate.
   d. The nations of the world now have settled on the current-rate method.

3. Variations between nations in accounting for inventories include all *except* which of the following?
   a. The basis for determining cost.
   b. Whether "cost" should be increased or decreased to reflect changes in market value.
   c. Whether inventories should be written down to an amount below both cost and market.
   d. Whether standard costs should be used.

4. In accounting for the effects of inflation, the approach that seems to be favored by most nations that have adopted an approach is:
   a. Current cost.
   b. Constant dollar (general price-level) adjusted statements.
   c. A combination of (a) and (b) in one set of financial statements.
   d. Both (a) and (b) as two sets of financial statements.

PROBLEMS, SERIES B

P13-1-B
*Compute income
assuming revenues
are recognized at
time of sale and
then assuming
installment method
is used*

The Larson Real Estate Sales Company sells lots in its development in Washed Out Canyon under terms calling for small cash down payments with monthly installment payments spread over a few years. Following are data on the company's operations for its first three years:

	1991	1992	1993
Gross margin rate	45%	48%	50%
Cash collected in 1993 from sales of lots made in	$320,000	$400,000	$480,000

The total selling price of the lots sold in 1993 was $1,600,000, while general and administrative expenses (which are not included in the costs used to determine gross margin) were $400,000.

Required:
a. Compute net income for 1993 assuming revenue is recognized upon the sale of a lot.
b. Compute net income for 1993 assuming use of the installment method of accounting for sales and gross margin.

P13-2-B
*Compute income
under completed-
contract and
percentage-of-
completion methods*

Given below are the contract prices and costs relating to all of Spring Company's long-term construction contracts (in millions of dollars):

	Contract Price	Costs Incurred Prior to 1991	Costs Incurred In 1991	Costs Yet to Be Incurred
On contracts completed in 1991	$ 92	$ 8	$72	$-0-
On incomplete contracts	288	48	96	96

General and administrative expenses for 1991 amounted to $3.6 million, none of which is to be considered a construction cost.

Required:
a. Compute net income for 1991 using the completed-contract method.
b. Compute net income for 1991 using the percentage-of-completion method.

P13-3-B
*Indicate agreement
or disagreement
with accounting
practices followed
and comment*

In each of the circumstances described below, the accounting practices followed may be questioned. You are to indicate whether you agree or disagree with the accounting practice employed and to state the assumptions, concepts, or principles that justify your position.

1. The cost of certain improvements to leased property having a life of five years was charged to expense because the improvements would revert to the lessor when the lease expires in three years.
2. The salaries paid to the top officers of the company were charged to expense in the period in which they were incurred even though the officers spent over half of their time planning next year's activities.
3. A company spent over $19.2 million in developing a new product and then spent an additional $21.6 million promoting it. All of these costs were incurred and charged to expense this year even though future years would also benefit.
4. No entry was made to record the belief that the market value of the land owned (carried in the accounts at $278,400) had increased.
5. No entry was made to record the fact that costs of $240,000 were expected to be incurred in fulfilling warranty provisions on products sold this year. The revenue from products sold was recognized this year.
6. The acquisition of a tract of land was recorded at the price paid for it of $518,400, even though the company would have been willing to pay $600,000.

7. A truck acquired at the beginning of the year was reported at year-end at 80% of its acquisition price because of the buildup of accumulated depreciation even though its market value then was only 65% of its original acquisition price.

P13-4-B
Answer multiple-choice questions regarding the Conceptual Framework Project

Select the best answer to each of the following questions:

1. In the Conceptual Framework Project, how many financial reporting objectives were identified by the FASB?
   a. One.
   b. Two.
   c. Three.
   d. Four.
2. The two primary qualitative characteristics are:
   a. Prediction value and feedback value.
   b. Timeliness and verifiability.
   c. Comparability and neutrality.
   d. Relevance and reliability.
3. A pervasive constraint of accounting information is that:
   a. Benefits must exceed costs.
   b. The information must be timely.
   c. The information must be neutral.
   d. The information must be verifiable.
4. To be reliable, information must (identify the incorrect quality):
   a. Be verifiable.
   b. Be timely.
   c. Have representational faithfulness.
   d. Be neutral.
5. The *basic elements* of financial statements consist of:
   a. Terms and their definitions.
   b. The objectives of financial reporting.
   c. The qualitative characteristics.
   d. The new income statement format.

P13-5-B
Answer fill-in-the-blank questions regarding international accounting (based on the Appendix)

Supply the missing word(s) in the following statements:

a. Accounting must reflect the national _____ and _____ environment in which it is practiced.
b. Other accounting differences among nations stem from the legal or _____ differences.
c. Commonwealth nations tend to adopt _____ accounting standards.
d. Several organizations are working to achieve greater understanding and _____ of accounting principles.
e. Ultimately, the success of international pronouncements depends on the willingness of the nations to _____ them.
f. _____ _____ translation is probably the most common problem in an international business environment.

BUSINESS DECISION PROBLEM

Evaluate correctness of accounting practices and give reasons for conclusions

Jerry Newman recently received his accounting degree from State University and went to work for a Big-Eight CPA firm. After he had been with the firm for about six months, he was sent to the Susong Clothing Company to work on the audit. He was not very confident of his knowledge at this early point in his career. But he noticed that some of the company's transactions and events were recorded in a way that might be in violation of accounting theory and generally accepted accounting principles.

Required: Study each of the following facts and see if you believe that the auditors should challenge the financial accounting practices used or the intentions of management. Give the reasoning behind your conclusions. (Some of the situations covered relate to other chapters you have studied in this text.)

1. The company recorded purchases of merchandise at the net invoice price rather than the gross invoice price.

2. Goods shipped to the company from a supplier, FOB destination, were debited to Purchases. The goods were not included in ending inventory because the goods had not yet arrived.

3. The company held the books open at the end of 1991 so they could record some early 1992 sales as 1991 revenue. The justification for this was that 1991 was not a good year in terms of profits.

4. The company counted some items twice in taking the physical inventory at the end of the year. The person taking the inventory said he had forgotten to include some items in last year's physical inventory, and this would make up for it so that net income this year would be "about correct."

5. The company switched from FIFO to LIFO in accounting for inventories. The preceding year it had switched from the weighted-average method to FIFO. The reason given for the most recent change was that federal income taxes would be lower. No indication of this switch was to appear in the financial statements.

6. Since things were pretty hectic at year-end, the accountant made no effort to reconcile the bank account. His reason was that the bank probably had not made any errors. The bank balance was lower than the book balance, so the accountant debited Miscellaneous Expense and credited Cash for the difference.

7. When a customer failed to pay the amount due, the accountant debited Uncollectible Accounts Expense and credited Accounts Receivable. The amount of accounts written off in this manner was huge. When the company later collects an account that has already been written off, Cash is debited and Miscellaneous Revenue is credited.

8. The company's buildings were appraised for insurance purposes. The appraised values were $5,000,000 higher than the book value. The accountant debited Buildings and credited Capital from Appreciation for the difference.

9. A machine was completely depreciated and was still being used. The accountant stopped recording depreciation on the machine and did not go back and correct earlier years' net income and reduce accumulated depreciation.

10. One of the senior members of management stated that the company planned to replace all of the furniture next year. He said that the cash in the Accumulated Depreciation account would be used to pay for the furniture.

11. The accountant stated that even though research and development costs incurred to develop a new product would benefit future periods, these costs must be expensed as incurred. This year $100,000 of these costs were charged to expense.

12. An old truck was traded for a new truck. Since the trade-in value of the old truck was higher than its book value, a gain was recorded on the transaction.

13. The company paid for a franchise giving it the exclusive right to operate in a given geographical area for 60 years. The accountant is amortizing the asset over 60 years.

14. The company leases a building and has a nonrenewable lease that expires in 15 years. The company made some improvements to the building. Since the improvements will last 30 years, they are being written off over 30 years.

14 Partnership Accounting

LEARNING OBJECTIVES

After studying this chapter, you should be able to:

1. Define partnerships and explain their characteristics.
2. List advantages and disadvantages of a partnership.
3. Record in entry form the formation of a partnership.
4. Know the different methods of dividing the net income (and losses) in a partnership.
5. Understand the nature and content of a partnership's financial statements.
6. Make the various entries required to account for the admissions and withdrawals of partners.
7. Understand the procedures involved in accounting for the liquidation of a partnership.
8. Define and use correctly the new terms in the glossary.

As you probably recall from Chapter 1, the three common forms of business entities in the United States are single proprietorships, partnerships, and corporations. So far in the text, we have used single proprietorships as examples. This chapter discusses accounting for partnerships, while Chapter 15 begins a discussion on accounting for corporations. Single proprietorships and partnerships are more numerous than corporations, but corporations hold more assets and generate substantially more revenues than unincorporated businesses.

The major difference between a single proprietorship and a partnership is the number of owners. The Uniform Partnership Act defines a **partnership** as "an association of two or more persons to carry on as co-owners a business for profit." This *association of persons* must establish the basis on which the partnership will operate—the partnership agreement. As an association of persons, partnerships have certain characteristics and advantages and disadvantages. However, you will note in studying this chapter that the basic accounting process and accounting principles are the same for both single proprietorships and partnerships.

■ PARTNERSHIP AGREEMENT

Objective 1:
Define partnerships and explain their characteristics.

A partnership is based on a **partnership agreement** or contract known as the **articles of copartnership.** The partnership agreement serves as a basis for the formation, operation, and liquidation of a partnership and should be in writing to avoid any misunderstandings or disagreements. Partnerships, however, can be formed without a written agreement.

A partnership agreement should specify the nature of the business, the capital contributions and duties of each partner, and the rights of each partner in the event of dissolution of the partnership. The agreement should also state the manner in which income and losses are to be divided among the partners.

When a partnership agreement is originally drawn up, it is difficult to anticipate all future events. If an issue relating to the formation, operation, and termination of a partnership arises that is not covered by the agreement, the provisions of the **Uniform Partnership Act** govern in those states that have adopted this act. Otherwise, common law as found in prior court decisions will determine the outcome of the disputed issue.

The Uniform Partnership Act has 45 sections presented in 8 major parts. Three of these major parts pertain to:

1. Relations of partners to persons dealing with the partnership.
2. Relations of partners to one another.
3. Dissolution and winding up of a partnership.

Attention will be drawn to some of these sections in the discussion that follows.

■ CHARACTERISTICS OF A PARTNERSHIP

A partnership has several unique characteristics that distinguish it from a corporation. These characteristics include voluntary association, mutual agency, limited life, and unlimited liability. Each of these characteristics is discussed below.

Voluntary Association

Any person who has the right to enter into contracts may enter into a partnership with other persons. But a person may not be forced into a partnership against that person's will. Each partner is an owner and member of management, and unless otherwise specified in the partnership agreement, each has an equal voice or vote in the partnership's activities.

Mutual Agency

Each partner is an **agent** of the partnership. The **mutual agency** of partners means each partner has the power to bind the remaining partners to any contract within the apparent scope of the partnership's business. For example, a partner could bind a partnership composed of physicians to a contract for medical supplies, but not to a contract to deliver an airplane. The individual partners must act in the best interests of the partnership and not their own personal interests when dealing in partnership matters.

Limited Life

A partnership can be terminated at any time since it is a voluntary association. The **termination (dissolution)** of a partnership may be caused by the withdrawal, retirement, insanity, death, or bankruptcy of any one of the partners. Thus, a partnership is said to have a limited life. If any of the events that may cause dissolution occur, the remaining partners may continue the business, but a new partnership entity is created. A partnership may also end because the period for which it was formed has expired or the specific purpose for which it was organized has been achieved.

Unlimited Liability

Each partner may be held liable for all debts of the partnership—a potential peril known as **unlimited liability** of each partner. If the partnership cannot pay its debts, creditors may satisfy their claims by attaching (seizing) the partners' personal assets.

Each partner's personal creditors have first claim on that partner's personal assets, but any remaining personal assets may be used to satisfy partnership creditors. For example, assume partner A has personal assets of $10,000 and personal liabilities of $8,000, and the partnership is now unable to pay its creditors. The partnership's creditors could require partner A to pay the $2,000 excess of personal assets over personal debts to satisfy their claims on the partnership. The partnership's creditors do not have to divide the debts among all partners; the creditors could seize the assets of only **one** partner to satisfy their claims. A partner who pays all of the partnership's debts acquires the right to be reimbursed by the other partners for their shares of the debts. Persons thinking of entering into a partnership agreement must carefully consider this unlimited liability feature of partnerships.

■ ADVANTAGES OF A PARTNERSHIP

Objective 2:
List advantages and
disadvantages of a
partnership.

Forming a partnership has several advantages. A partnership is (1) sufficiently flexible to permit reasonable accumulations of capital and talent, (2) easier and less expensive to organize than a corporation, (3) not required to observe as many laws and regulations as a corporation, and (4) not subject to separate corporation taxation because each partner reports his or her share of partnership income and is individually taxed. Individuals may find it advantageous to form a partnership when (1) business capital require-ments exceed the amount that may be raised by a single proprietor or (2) a variety of talent and knowledge from other persons who are willing to share the risks and rewards of ownership may result in a more profitable business.

■ DISADVANTAGES OF A PARTNERSHIP

Perhaps the greatest disadvantage of a partnership lies in the unlimited liability feature, or the fact that each partner may be held liable for all partnership debts. In this respect, corporations have an advantage over partnerships. A corporation's stockholders are not liable for the corpora-tion's debts, and stockholders' losses usually cannot exceed the amount invested.

Another disadvantage is the feature of mutual agency. Since one partner may bind the partnership to a contract, a partner who fails to exercise good judgment can cause the loss of partnership assets and, possibly, the loss of personal assets of the other partners.

As a functioning organization, the partnership generally becomes un-wieldy when there are many partners. And by virtue of the limited life feature, a partnership is subject to possible termination due to many uncon-trollable circumstances, such as the death of a partner.

Because partners are co-owners of a partnership's net assets, the transfer of ownership from one partner to another person may be difficult to accom-plish. When a partner withdraws from the partnership, the remaining part-ners will either have to purchase the withdrawing partner's interest or approve of the person to whom that interest is sold. Since a partnership is a **voluntary** association of persons, the remaining partners do not have to accept the buyer of an interest in a partnership as a partner. If a buyer acceptable as a partner cannot be found, the partners may have to terminate the partnership.

■ UNIQUE FEATURES IN PARTNERSHIP ACCOUNTING

Objective 3:
Record in entry form
the formation of a
partnership.

Because a division of interest exists in a partnership that does not exist in a single proprietorship, the accounting records for a partnership differ some-what from those presented thus far. The unique accounting features in a partnership relate specifically to the partners' capital and drawing accounts, division of business income or loss, and changes in ownership of the partnership.

Partners' Capital Accounts

A capital account is maintained for each partner. The total balance in the partner's capital account after year-end closing entries represents the part-ner's ownership equity in the business. Each partner's capital account is:

1. Credited with the original investment.
2. Credited with subsequent investments.
3. Credited with the agreed share of net income.
4. Debited with the agreed share of net loss.
5. Debited with permanent capital reductions.
6. Debited with the balance of the partner's drawing account at the end of each fiscal period.

To illustrate the use of the capital accounts, assume that James Law and Todd Hart, who have been in business as single proprietors, decide to form a partnership. The formation of the partnership creates a new accounting entity. Since assets of a business should be accounted for at fair market value when they are acquired, the assets contributed by each partner will be recorded at their current market values. These values may differ from the historical cost amounts shown on the separate accounting records of the individual proprietorships. Shown below are the assets contributed, liabilities assumed, and their fair market values:

Law		Hart	
Cash	$ 5,600	Cash	$ 6,600
Accounts receivable	6,800	Merchandise inventory	3,400
Merchandise inventory	12,000	Land	8,000
Delivery equipment	3,000	Building	20,000
Accounts payable	(3,200)	Accounts payable	(2,200)

The journal entries on January 1, 1991, to record the investment of each partner are as follows:

Cash	5,600	
Accounts Receivable	6,800	
Merchandise Inventory	12,000	
Delivery Equipment	3,000	
Accounts Payable		3,200
James Law, Capital		24,200

To record the investment of Law in the partnership of Law and Hart.

Cash	6,600	
Merchandise Inventory	3,400	
Land	8,000	
Building	20,000	
Accounts Payable		2,200
Todd Hart, Capital		35,800

To record the investment of Hart in the partnership of Law and Hart.

On August 1, 1991, the partners made the following additional cash investments that were credited to their capital accounts. The required journal entry is:

```
Cash . . . . . . . . . . . . . . . . . . . . . . . . . . . . . . . . . . . . . . .     5,800
     James Law, Capital . . . . . . . . . . . . . . . . . . . . . . . .                          2,400
     Todd Hart, Capital  . . . . . . . . . . . . . . . . . . . . . . . .                          3,400
  To record additional cash investments.
```

On December 31, 1991, before closing the books, the capital accounts of the partners would appear as follows:

		James Law, Capital				
Date		Explanation	Post. Ref.	Debit	Credit	Balance
1991 Jan.	1	Original investment			24,200	24,200
Aug.	1	Additional cash investment			2,400	26,600

		Todd Hart, Capital				
Date		Explanation	Post. Ref.	Debit	Credit	Balance
1991 Jan.	1	Original investment			35,800	35,800
Aug.	1	Additional cash investment			3,400	39,200

During the accounting period, partners sometimes withdraw cash or merchandise for personal use. A drawing account is maintained for each partner to record the partner's withdrawals. The next section discusses the withdrawals by partners.

Partners' Drawing Accounts

Partners may withdraw either cash or merchandise from the business. **Withdrawals of cash** are charged to the partner's drawing account and credited to Cash. The partnership agreement should specify whether **withdrawals of merchandise** are to be valued at **cost** or **selling price**. If merchandise is valued at cost, the withdrawal is debited to the partner's drawing account and credited to Purchases. If merchandise is valued at selling price, the withdrawal is debited to the partner's drawing account and credited to Sales.

To illustrate drawing accounts, assume that Hart and Law made withdrawals as indicated below:

James Law, Drawing					
Date	Explanation	Post. Ref.	Debit	Credit	Balance
1991					
Feb. 7	Cash		1,600		1,600
Apr. 8	Merchandise (at cost)		1,700		3,300
July 31	Cash		1,750		5,050
Dec. 1	Cash		1,650		6,700

Todd Hart, Drawing					
Date	Explanation	Post. Ref.	Debit	Credit	Balance
1991					
Mar. 1	Cash		1,900		1,900
June 7	Cash		1,700		3,600
Sept. 18	Cash		2,000		5,600
Dec. 4	Merchandise (at cost)		1,600		7,200

As a rule, partners cannot withdraw any part of their original investment without the consent of all partners. Whether partners may withdraw any part of any subsequent investments to their capital accounts depends on the partnership agreement. **Withdrawals of investments** should be debited directly to the capital account rather than to the drawing account unless stated otherwise in the agreement.

End-of-Period Entries

At the end of the fiscal period, adjusting entries are made, and all expense and revenue accounts are closed to Income Summary in the same manner as was illustrated for a single proprietorship. The Income Summary account is closed to the partners' capital accounts (like it was to the owner's capital account in a single proprietorship). The amount of net income or loss assigned to each partner is based on methods outlined in the partnership agreement. Each partner's drawing account is then closed to that partner's capital account. The drawing account is not closed to the Income Summary account because it is not an expense of the business but merely a temporary owners' equity account used to accumulate total withdrawals during a period.

To illustrate, assume that the partnership of Law and Hart has net income of $30,000 for the year ended December 31, 1991, and that the partners decide to divide income equally. The journal entry to close net income to the capital accounts is:

```
Income Summary  . . . . . . . . . . . . . . . . . . . . . . . .   30,000
     James Law, Capital . . . . . . . . . . . . . . . . . . . .            15,000
     Todd Hart, Capital  . . . . . . . . . . . . . . . . . . . .            15,000
  To close net income to the capital accounts.
```

The next step is to close the balances of the partners' drawing accounts (shown in the ledger accounts above) to their capital accounts by the following journal entries:

```
James Law, Capital  . . . . . . . . . . . . . . . . . . . . . .    6,700
     James Law, Drawing . . . . . . . . . . . . . . . . . . . .             6,700
  To close the December 31, 1991, drawing account balance.

Todd Hart, Capital  . . . . . . . . . . . . . . . . . . . . . .    7,200
     Todd Hart, Drawing . . . . . . . . . . . . . . . . . . . .             7,200
  To close the December 31, 1991, drawing account balance.
```

After the entries are posted, the drawing accounts and capital accounts of Law and Hart appear as follows:

James Law, Drawing

Date		Explanation	Post. Ref.	Debit	Credit	Balance
1991						
Feb.	7	Cash		1,600		1,600
Apr.	8	Merchandise (at cost)		1,700		3,300
July	31	Cash		1,750		5,050
Dec.	1	Cash		1,650		6,700
	31	To capital			6,700	–0–

James Law, Capital

Date		Explanation	Post. Ref.	Debit	Credit	Balance
1991						
Jan.	1	Original investment			24,200	24,200
Aug.	1	Additional cash investment			2,400	26,600
Dec.	31	Net income			15,000	41,600
	31	From drawing		6,700		34,900

Todd Hart, Drawing

Date		Explanation	Post. Ref.	Debit	Credit	Balance
1991						
Mar.	1	Cash		1,900		1,900
June	7	Cash		1,700		3,600
Sept.	18	Cash		2,000		5,600
Dec.	4	Merchandise (at cost)		1,600		7,200
	31	To capital			7,200	–0–

Todd Hart, Capital

Date		Explanation	Post. Ref.	Debit	Credit	Balance
1991						
Jan.	1	Original investment			35,800	35,800
Aug.	1	Additional cash investment			3,400	39,200
Dec.	31	Net income			15,000	54,200
	31	From drawing		7,200		47,000

■ DIVISION OF PARTNERSHIP INCOME OR LOSS

Objective 4:
Know the different methods of dividing the net income (and losses) in a partnership.

Partnership income and losses are divided in accordance with provisions in the partnership agreement. The agreed way that a partnership's income or losses are to be shared is called the **income and loss ratio (profit and loss ratio** or **earnings and loss ratio).** If the agreement is silent with respect to the division of income, income is divided equally (or 1:1, representing the fractions ½ and ½ and the percentages 50% and 50%) among the partners. If the agreement is silent as to loss distribution, losses are divided in the same manner as income. However, a partnership agreement will usually specify the means by which income and losses are to be distributed to the partners.

The method of distribution of income and losses may be based on many factors. If each of the partners invests an equal amount of assets, has approximately equal ability, devotes the same amount of time to the business, and has the same wealth at risk, then net income or net losses should probably be divided equally. If variations in the foregoing factors exist between partners, a method of income or loss distribution should be devised to reflect such differences. For example, a partner who manages the business all week may be allocated a **salary** out of net income prior to an equal distribution of the remainder to all partners. This salary is part of the income sharing agreement and is **not** an expense of the partnership in the determination of net income nor is it a cash outflow of the business.

For example, A and B have a partnership in which partner A manages the store during the week and both partners share the work load equally on the weekends. The partnership agreement states that in sharing income and losses, A is to be given credit for a salary of $10,000, and the remaining net income is to be shared equally by the two partners. Net income for the year is $50,000. When the Income Summary account is closed, A's capital account will be credited with $30,000, and B's capital account will be credited with $20,000, as shown:

	A	B	Total	Net Income to Be Distributed
Net income				$50,000
Salary to A	$10,000		$10,000	40,000
Remainder equally . . .	20,000	$20,000	40,000	–0–
Total	$30,000	$20,000	$50,000	

In some partnerships, one partner invests a larger amount of capital than another. When this occurs, the partner with the larger capital investment may insist that **interest** be allowed on capital balances in the division of income, with the remainder to be divided equally between the partners. This **interest** would simply be a means of equitable compensation to the partner with the larger investment. As in the salary example, this interest factor is **not** an expense in income determination nor is it a cash outflow.

Common methods of dividing income are listed below. Illustrations of each method follow.

1. Net income divided in a set ratio such as:
   a. Equally.
   b. Agreed ratio other than equal.
   c. Ratio of partners' capital account balances at the beginning of fiscal period.
   d. Ratio of average capital investment.
2. Net income divided by allowing interest on the capital investments, or salaries, or both, with remaining net income divided in an agreed ratio.

Examples showing the division of net income (or net loss) are given in the next section.

Illustrations of Distributions of Partnership Income

The illustrations that follow are based on data about the partnership of Anders and Budd. Net income for the year ended December 31, 1991, was $60,000. During 1991, Anders' drawings were $14,000, and Budd's drawings were $22,000. The capital account balances of the partners on December 31, 1991, before closing were Anders, $85,000, and Budd, $134,000.

Case 1. Net Income Divided in a Set Ratio. The division of income (or losses) may be based on only one factor, as is shown in each of the following situations.

a. Net Income Divided Equally. In this instance, the income and loss ratio is 1:1, or 50% and 50%. The capital accounts of Anders and Budd would each be credited with $30,000 of net income ($60,000/2).

Income Summary	60,000	
Anders, Capital		30,000
Budd, Capital		30,000
To record distribution of net income to partners.		

b.   *Net Income Divided in an Agreed Ratio Other than Equal.*   Assume that the agreed ratio is 3:2 to Anders and Budd, respectively. Sixty percent would go to Anders and 40% to Budd. Such an income and loss sharing ratio may reflect an attempt to take such factors as work load or special talent into consideration. In this example, Anders would be credited with $36,000 and Budd with $24,000 ($60,000 × 0.60 = $36,000; $60,000 × 0.40 = $24,000).

Income Summary	60,000	
Anders, Capital		36,000
Budd, Capital		24,000
To record distribution of net income to partners.		

c.   *Net Income Divided in Ratio of Partners' Capital Account Balances at the Beginning of the Fiscal Period.*   Assume that Anders' beginning capital balance on January 1, 1991, was $40,000 and Budd's was $80,000. Total capital of the partnership at the beginning of the year was $120,000. Anders had one third ($40,000/$120,000) of the total capital and Budd, two thirds ($80,000/$120,000). Net income is allocated $20,000 (one third of $60,000) to Anders and $40,000 (two thirds of $60,000) to Budd.

Income Summary	60,000	
Anders, Capital		20,000
Budd, Capital		40,000
To record distribution of net income to partners.		

d.   *Net Income Divided in Ratio of Average Capital Investment.*   In this division of net income, details must be provided showing the timing of the investment by each partner. Illustration 14.1 contains assumed data on Anders' and Budd's capital balances. The "month-dollars" amount for Anders and Budd is found by multiplying their balance times the number of months for which this balance remained unchanged. The average capital is found by dividing the total month-dollars by 12.

The ratio of average capital investment is computed by dividing each partner's average capital by the total average capital of $140,000 ($50,000 for Anders and $90,000 for Budd). This ratio is then used to compute the distribution of net income. Thus, Anders is credited with $21,429 ($50,000/$140,000 × $60,000) of net income; Budd is credited with $38,571 ($90,000/$140,000 × $60,000).

Income Summary	60,000	
Anders, Capital		21,429
Budd, Capital		38,571
To record distribution of net income to partners.		

Case 2.   Net Income Divided by Allowing Interest on Capital Investments, or Salaries, or Both, with Remaining Net Income Divided in an Agreed Ratio.   Interest and salary allocations may be specified in the partnership agreement to compensate partners for differences in investment, time spent with the business, and other factors.

Illustration 14.1

*Computation of
Average Capital*

Anders, Capital

Date	Debits	Credits	Balance	Months Unchanged	Month-Dollars (weighted equivalent)
Jan. 1			$ 40,000	6	$ 240,000
July 1		$15,000	55,000	5	275,000
Dec. 1		30,000	85,000	1	85,000
				12	$ 600,000

Average capital of Anders: $600,000 ÷ 12 = $50,000.

Budd, Capital

Date	Debits	Credits	Balance	Months Unchanged	Month-Dollars (weighted equivalent)
Jan. 1			$ 80,000	7	$ 560,000
Aug. 1		$ 4,000	84,000	3	252,000
Nov. 1		50,000	134,000	2	268,000
				12	$1,080,000

Average capital of Budd: $1,080,000 ÷ 12 = $90,000.

a. Continuing the example of Anders and Budd, assume that the partners are to be allowed 6% interest on their beginning capital balances. January 1 capital balances were Anders, $40,000; and Budd, $80,000. Salaries allowed are Anders, $16,000; and Budd, $10,000. The remainder is divided equally. The $60,000 income for the current year is distributed as follows:

	Anders	Budd	Total	Income to Be Distributed
Net income				$60,000
Interest (6% on beginning capital balances)	$ 2,400	$ 4,800	$ 7,200	52,800
Salary	16,000	10,000	26,000	26,800
Remainder	13,400	13,400	26,800	–0–
Distribution	$31,800	$28,200	$60,000	

The entry to divide net income is:

Income Summary	60,000	
Anders, Capital		31,800
Budd, Capital		28,200

To divide net income between the partners.

b. Even if the allowances for salaries or interest exceed net income, or if the period has a net loss, the partners still are given credit for their full amounts of interest and salary. For example, in the situation above, if there was a net loss of $20,000 instead of net income of $60,000 for the year, the division would be as follows:

	Anders	Budd	Total	Loss to Be Distributed
Net loss				$(20,000)
Interest (6% on beginning capital balances)	$ 2,400	$ 4,800	$ 7,200	(27,200)
Salary	16,000	10,000	26,000	(53,200)
Remainder	(26,600)	(26,600)	(53,200)	–0–
Distribution	$ (8,200)	$(11,800)	$(20,000)	

The entry to divide the net loss would be:

Anders, Capital	8,200	
Budd, Capital	11,800	
Income Summary		20,000
To divide net loss between the partners.		

c. The sharing of income may result in a credit to one partner's capital account and a debit to another partner's capital account. As a final example, assume that Anders and Budd earned $3,200 of net income for a year. The $3,200 would be shared as follows:

	Anders	Budd	Total	Income to Be Distributed
Net income				$ 3,200
Interest (6% on beginning capital balances)	$ 2,400	$ 4,800	$ 7,200	(4,000)
Salary	16,000	10,000	26,000	(30,000)
Remainder	(15,000)	(15,000)	(30,000)	–0–
Distribution	$ 3,400	$ (200)	$ 3,200	

The entry to close the Income Summary account would be:

Income Summary	3,200	
Budd, Capital	200	
Anders, Capital		3,400
To divide net income between the partners.		

Partnership Agreement Governs. This section has illustrated some factors that partners might consider when drawing up the income or sharing provisions in the partnership agreement. However, income may be shared in **any** manner the partners decide. Once the partners agree on how income is to be shared, the accountant's task is simply to apply the agreed provisions as literally as possible.

■ FINANCIAL STATEMENTS OF A PARTNERSHIP

Objective 5: Understand the nature and content of a partnership's financial statements.

Since a partnership is similar to a single proprietorship, the accounting and financial reporting for these forms of organization are basically the same. As shown above, a partnership has several capital accounts, and any income or losses must be distributed to these accounts. This section details the preparation of financial statements for a partnership.

Partnership Income Statement

A partnership's income statement may differ slightly from that of a single proprietorship. Because partners are co-owners of the business, the income statement may contain a schedule showing the distribution of the period's net income or net loss to each partner. Illustration 14.2 shows this feature for Anders and Budd using the data given in Case 2(a) on page 581.

Illustration 14.2

Partnership Income Statement

ANDERS AND BUDD
Income Statement
For Year Ended December 31, 1991

Sales			$600,000
Cost of goods sold			360,400
Gross margin			$239,600
Operating expenses:			
Selling		$100,000	
Administrative		80,000	180,000
Net operating income			$ 59,600
Nonoperating revenue: Interest			400
Net income			$ 60,000

Distribution of Net Income

	Anders	Budd	Total
Interest	$ 2,400	$ 4,800	$ 7,200
Salary	16,000	10,000	26,000
Remainder equally	13,400	13,400	26,800
Net income	$31,800	$28,200	$60,000

Statement of Partners' Capital

At the close of each period, a **statement of partners' capital** is prepared. This statement (1) is prepared from the capital accounts in the general ledger, (2) summarizes the effects of transactions on the capital account balance of each partner and in total for all partners for the period, and (3) serves the same purpose as the statement of owner's capital in a single proprietorship.

The statement of partners' capital presents details not readily shown on the balance sheet. The balance sheet contains only the final balance of each partner's capital account when it is accompanied by a statement of partners' capital.

Illustration 14.3

Statement of Partners' Capital

ANDERS AND BUDD
Statement of Partners' Capital
For the Year Ended December 31, 1991

	Anders	Budd	Total
Capital account balances, January 1, 1991	$ 40,000	$ 80,000	$120,000
Add: Additional investments	45,000	54,000	99,000
Capital account balances, December 31, 1991, before drawing charges	$ 85,000	$134,000	$219,000
Deduct: Drawings	14,000	22,000	36,000
Capital account balances before 1991 income distribution	$ 71,000	$112,000	$183,000
Net income per income statement	31,800	28,200	60,000
Capital account balances, December 31, 1991	$102,800	$140,200	$243,000

The statement of partners' capital for Anders and Budd is presented in Illustration 14.3. The statement is prepared by using the information on additional investments given in Illustration 14.1 and information on drawings given on page 579.

The statement could show net income added to the beginning capital balances before drawings are deducted, instead of after. Either format is correct.

Partnership Balance Sheet

The only distinctive feature of a partnership balance sheet is the presentation of the capital accounts in the owners' equity section, as shown in Illustration 14.4. Instead of a single capital account, the owners' equity section contains a separate capital account for each partner. However, if a partnership has many partners, the balance sheet may show only a single item and amount called *Partners' capital*. Then, each partner's name and capital balance would be reported in a supporting schedule. Accountants

Illustration 14.4

Partnership Balance Sheet

ANDERS AND BUDD
Balance Sheet
December 31, 1991

Assets		Liabilities and Owners' Equity	
Cash	$ xxx	Liabilities:	
Accounts receivable	xxx	Accounts payable	$ xxx
Merchandise inventory	xxx	Notes payable	xxx
Land	xxx	Total liabilities	$ xxx
		Owners' equity:	
		A, capital $102,800	
		B, capital 140,200	243,000
		Total liabilities and	
Total assets	$ xxx	owners' equity	$ xxx

Note: No amounts are provided for items other than owners' equity because these were not given in the illustrative data.

use supporting schedules to provide additional information that clarifies an item(s) on the primary financial statements.

Because partnerships are voluntary associations between people, the possibility of changes in ownership exists. In the next section, we discuss some of the changes in partnership personnel and how these changes are recorded in the accounts of a business.

■ CHANGES IN PARTNERSHIP PERSONNEL

A partnership is legally terminated when a new partner is admitted or an existing partner withdraws or retires. Usually, the old partnership is succeeded immediately by a new partnership, which differs from the old partnership only to the extent of the change in partners. When this occurs, the partnership termination is only technical, and the business operations and accounting continue without pause. A technical termination of a partnership, which we discuss next, differs substantially from liquidation of a partnership, which is discussed later in this chapter.

Admission of a New Partner

Objective 6: Make the various entries required to account for the admissions and withdrawals of partners.

A new partner can gain admission to a partnership either by purchasing an interest from one or more existing partners or by investing assets in the partnership. Illustration 14.5 shows each of these options.

Purchase of an Interest.   When a new partner simply purchases an interest directly from an existing partner, the partnership's assets and liabilities remain unchanged. The exchange of cash and other assets for the equity interest is a personal transaction between two individuals, occurring out-

Illustration 14.5

Options Regarding Admission of a New Partner

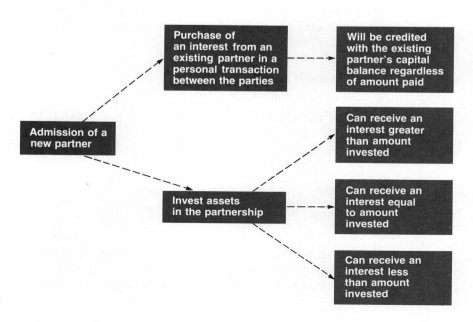

side the partnership accounting entity. **The entry on the partnership's books simply transfers a portion of the partnership capital from an existing partner to a new partner.**

To illustrate, assume that Smith and Jones are partners with capital account balances of $15,000 and $13,000, respectively. Farr purchases from Jones an $8,000 interest in the partnership capital. The journal entry on the partnership's books is:

Jones, Capital	8,000	
Farr, Capital		8,000
To transfer $8,000 of Jones' interest in the partnership assets to Farr.		

The price that Farr paid Jones might be more or less than $8,000, but this difference is not reflected on the books of the partnership. The journal entry merely reflects the transfer of the $8,000 interest in the partnership from the old partner to the new partner.

Investment in the Partnership. When a new partner acquires an interest in a partnership by investing assets (such as cash, inventory, or buildings) in the business, both partnership assets and total owners' equity increase. The journal entry for such an investment must record these increases. Three examples of a new partner's investment in the partnership follow.

Case 1. New Partner Receives an Interest Equal to Amount Invested. To illustrate, assume that the partnership of Crowe and Lang has the following assets and equities:

Assets		Equities	
Cash	$15,000	Crowe, capital	$35,000
Other assets	55,000	Lang, capital	35,000
Total assets	$70,000	Total equities	$70,000

Crowe and Lang agree to admit Potter as a partner with a one-half, or 50%, interest in the partnership on Potter's investment of $70,000 cash. The entry to record Potter's investment is:

Cash	70,000	
Potter, Capital		70,000
To record Potter's investment in the partnership.		

After the above entry is posted, the partnership has the following assets and equities:

Assets		Equities	
Cash	$ 85,000	Crowe, capital	$ 35,000
Other assets	55,000	Lang, capital	35,000
		Potter, capital	70,000
Total assets	$140,000	Total equities	$140,000

The one-half interest in the equity of the partnership credited to Potter does not automatically carry with it the right to receive one half of the future income or losses of the partnership. Income and loss distribution is a separate matter on which the three partners must agree. If the new partnership agreement does not specify how income and losses are to be shared, the law assumes that the new partners intend to share income and losses equally, which means Crowe, Lang, and Potter would each receive one third of the income or losses.

Case 2. New Partner Receives an Interest Less than Amount Invested. If an existing partnership consistently earns above-average income, the existing partners may require a new partner to pay a bonus for admission to the partnership. For example, Marsh and Will operate a partnership that has had above-average net income for the last 10 years. The partners share income and losses in a ratio of 2:1—that is, Marsh receives two thirds and Will receives one third. The partners' capital account balances show $55,000 for Marsh and $75,000 for Will. Marsh and Will agree to admit Gray as a partner with a one-fourth interest in both capital and income in exchange for $50,000. Gray's equity in the partnership is $45,000, computed as follows:

Equities of old partners ($55,000 + $75,000)	$130,000
Investment of new partner	50,000
Total equities of new partnership	$180,000
Gray's one-fourth equity ($180,000 × ¼)	$ 45,000

The entry to record Gray's investment in the partnership is:

Cash	50,000	
Gray, Capital		45,000
Marsh, Capital (⅔ of $5,000)		3,333
Will, Capital (⅓ of $5,000)		1,667
To record Gray's investment in partnership.		

Notice that Gray paid $50,000 for an equity of only $45,000. The $5,000 difference is a bonus to the old partners, which they share in their income and loss ratio of 2:1.

Case 3. New Partner Receives an Interest Greater than Amount Invested. Sometimes an incoming partner may be able to provide cash that is desperately needed, or may have extraordinary abilities or business contacts that can help increase the partnership's income. In such cases, the existing partners may be willing to give the new partner a bonus—that is, an equity in the partnership greater than the new partner's investment. For example, assume Bentz and Hahn are partners with capital balances of $100,000 and $60,000, respectively. They share income and losses in a 3:2 ratio. The partnership desperately needs cash, so the partners are willing to give Kirby a one-fourth equity interest in the partnership for an investment of only $40,000 cash. Kirby agrees, invests $40,000, and receives an equity interest computed as follows:

Equities of old partners ($100,000 + $60,000)	$160,000
Investment of new partner	40,000
Total equities of new partnership	$200,000
Kirby's one-fourth interest ($200,000 × ¼)	$ 50,000

The entry to record Kirby's investment in the partnership is:

Cash	40,000	
Bentz, Capital (⅗ of $10,000)	6,000	
Hahn, Capital (⅖ of $10,000)	4,000	
Kirby, Capital		50,000
To record Kirby's investment in partnership.		

Notice that the $10,000 bonus is contributed by the old partners in their income and loss sharing ratio of 3:2. After Kirby is admitted to the partnership, the partners should agree on new income sharing provisions.

Alternative methods could be used to record the admission of a new partner, but these methods will be left for an advanced text. Next, we consider changes in partnership ownership brought about by the retirement or withdrawal of a partner.

Retirement or Withdrawal of a Partner

When partners decide to retire, two options exist: they can sell their partnership interest, or they can withdraw assets from the partnership. Partners can sell their interest to existing partners or to a new partner. Illustration 14.6 summarizes the options available to a retiring partner. Each option requires the consent of the existing partners.

Sale of an Interest.   When a retiring partner sells his or her interest to the existing partners or to a new partner, the entry made on the partnership books transfers the retiring partner's capital balance to the purchaser(s). To illustrate, assume that Sam Harris, a partner in the Harris, Brown, and Wilson partnership, sells his $100,000 interest in the partnership to Brown and Wilson (equally) for $125,000. The entry would be:

Illustration 14.6

Options regarding Retirement of a Partner

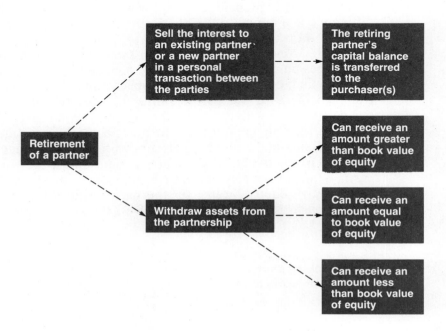

Harris, Capital	100,000	
Brown, Capital		50,000
Wilson, Capital		50,000

To transfer Harris' capital balance to Brown and Wilson.

The amount paid is not recorded on the partnership books because the transaction involved no flow of assets to or from the partnership. The transaction was between individuals.

If the interest had been sold to a new partner, Mike Roberts, for $85,000, the entry would have been as follows:

Harris, Capital	100,000	
Roberts, Capital		100,000

To transfer Harris' capital balance to Roberts.

Again, regardless of the amount exchanged between the individuals, the only entry is one transferring the retiring partner's capital balance to the purchaser.

Withdrawal of Assets from Partnership. A partnership agreement should contain the procedures to be followed when a partner retires. Specifically, these procedures should indicate how to compute the price the partnership should pay for the retiring partner's equity interest.

To compute this price, the first step is usually to audit the partnership accounts to ensure their accuracy. Then, the fair market values of the assets are determined. When the asset values are revalued at fair market values, the partners' capital accounts should reflect the gains and losses from this revaluation. This revaluation is necessary because (1) after the withdrawal of a partner, a new entity is created that should record its assets at fair values at the time of formation; and (2) the withdrawing partner will be credited or charged for a share of previously unrecorded gains or losses that must be considered in computing the retiring partner's share of the partnership's net assets at time of withdrawal. The retiring partner is typically paid an amount equal to the new balance in that partner's capital account.

Sometimes asset revaluations are not recorded when a partner retires, and the retiring partner is paid an amount that differs from the partner's capital account balance. Such asset revaluations may not be reflected because (1) too much effort might be required to change recorded book values, (2) the partners may not want to pay for an audit of the books and records, and (3) the partners may underestimate the effect that the difference between recorded book values and fair market values would have on their capital balances.

Next, we give three examples illustrating the withdrawal of assets from the partnership by a retiring partner. In these examples, the retiring partner receives (1) adjusted book value of equity, (2) more than the book value of equity, and (3) less than the book value of equity.

Case 1. Retiring Partner Receives Adjusted Book Value of Equity. Assume that Green, South, and Rock are partners sharing income and losses in a 3:1:1 ratio. Rock decides to retire when the partnership books show the following recorded values:

Assets			Equities		
Cash		$ 30,000	Green, capital		$ 50,000
Accounts receivable		10,000	South, capital		30,000
Merchandise inventory . . .		40,000	Rock, capital		20,000
Plant and equipment	$50,000				
Less: Accumulated					
depreciation	30,000	20,000			
Total assets		$100,000	Total equities		$100,000

The partnership books are audited. Certain accounts receivable, recorded at $500, are found to be uncollectible and are written off. Because of changes in replacement costs, merchandise inventory is revalued at $45,500, and plant and equipment are revalued at $54,000. Accumulated depreciation is increased to $32,000. The journal entries to record this information are:

Green, Capital	300	
South, Capital	100	
Rock, Capital	100	
Accounts Receivable		500
To write off uncollectible accounts receivable.		

Merchandise Inventory	5,500	
Green, Capital		3,300
South, Capital		1,100
Rock, Capital		1,100
To revalue inventory.		

Plant and Equipment	4,000	
Accumulated Depreciation—Plant and Equipment		2,000
Green, Capital		1,200
South, Capital		400
Rock, Capital		400
To revalue plant and equipment.		

Assuming the gains and losses computed from asset revaluations eventually would have been realized and reflected in net income, the partners would share these gains and losses in their income and loss ratio. Thus, after the above entries have been posted, the restated amounts of the partnership's assets and equities would be:

Assets			Equities		
Cash		$ 30,000	Green, capital		$ 54,200
Accounts receivable		9,500	South, capital		31,400
Merchandise inventory . . .		45,500	Rock, capital		21,400
Plant and equipment	$54,000				
Less: Accumulated					
depreciation	32,000	22,000			
Total assets		$107,000	Total equities		$107,000

With assets revalued and capital accounts adjusted, Rock has a $21,400 interest in partnership net assets. Assuming Rock is paid cash, the entry to record Rock's retirement is:

Rock, Capital	21,400	
Cash		21,400
To record Rock's withdrawal from the partnership.		

Instead of cash, Rock could have received any combination of assets (such as some inventory and a car owned by the partnership) totaling $21,400 to which the partners agreed. Or Rock could have accepted a note payable by the new partnership of Green and South. In any case, Green and South must now agree on a new income and loss sharing provision because a new partnership entity exists.

Case 2.   Retiring Partner Receives More than the Book Value of Equity. Sometimes the partners may not revalue assets or adjust the accounts when a partner withdraws. Instead, the partners may agree that the assets are undervalued and the withdrawing partner should receive assets worth **more** than the book value of that partner's equity; or the remaining partners may be so anxious for the partner to withdraw that they are willing to give up assets worth **more** than the book value of that partner's equity. In both cases, the retiring partner, in effect, withdraws assets equal to the book value of that partner's own equity plus part of the book value of the remaining partners' equities.

To illustrate, assume that North, East, and West are partners who share income and losses in a 3:2:1 ratio. East withdraws from the partnership at a time when it has the following assets and equities:

Assets		Equities	
Cash	$30,000	North, capital	$50,000
Merchandise inventory	40,000	East, capital	25,000
Equipment, net	20,000	West, capital	15,000
Total assets	$90,000	Total equities	$90,000

The partners agree that the assets are undervalued by $3,000, but they do not wish to adjust the accounts to current market values. If the accounts had been revalued, East's capital account would have been increased by $1,000, or two sixths of the $3,000 adjustment. East is therefore allowed to withdraw $26,000 cash from the partnership for his equity interest. The entry to record East's withdrawal is:

East, Capital	25,000	
North, Capital	750	
West, Capital	250	
Cash		26,000
To record East's withdrawal from partnership.		

East withdrew $1,000 more than the book value of his equity. Instead of revaluing the assets and adjusting the accounts (as shown in Case 1), the excess amount of $1,000 is charged to North's and West's capital accounts on the basis of their income and loss ratio of 3:1 ($\frac{3}{4} \times \$1,000 = \$750$ to North, and $\frac{1}{4} \times \$1,000 = \$250$ to West).

Case 3.   Retiring Partner Receives Less than the Book Value of Equity. Sometimes the partners may agree that the assets are overvalued but do not want to adjust the accounts when one partner retires. The partners may then agree that the withdrawing partner should receive assets worth **less** than the book value of the partner's equity. Or, a partner may be so anxious to withdraw from a partnership that the partner is willing to accept assets worth **less** than the book value of that partner's equity. In both cases, the undrawn equity is divided between the remaining partners in their income and loss ratio and credited to their capital accounts.

To illustrate, assume that Alda, Fonda, and Moore are partners who share income and losses in an 8:7:5 (40%, 35%, 25%) ratio. The partnership's assets and equities follow:

Assets		Equities	
Cash	$21,000	Alda, capital	$25,000
Merchandise inventory	24,000	Fonda, capital	22,000
Plant and equipment, net	20,000	Moore, capital	18,000
Total assets	$65,000	Total equities	$65,000

Moore is anxious to withdraw from the partnership and is willing to accept $16,000 in settlement of her equity. Alda and Fonda agree to the settlement. The entry to record Moore's withdrawal is:

Moore, Capital	18,000	
Cash		16,000
Alda, Capital		1,067
Fonda, Capital		933

To record Moore's withdrawal from partnership.

Moore withdrew $2,000 less than the book value of her equity. The undrawn $2,000 is credited to the capital accounts of Alda and Fonda in their income and loss sharing ratio of 8:7, that is, 8/15 × $2,000 and 7/15 × $2,000.

The illustrations above involved technical terminations or dissolutions of partnerships. One partnership was terminated but was succeeded immediately by another partnership that carried on substantially the same business operations. In the next section, attention is given to circumstances in which business operations cease and the partnership is legally terminated.

■ LIQUIDATION OF A PARTNERSHIP

Objective 7: Understand the procedures involved in accounting for the liquidation of a partnership.

The **liquidation of a partnership** means that business operations have ended, assets have been sold for cash, cash has been paid to creditors and partners, and the partnership has been legally terminated.

Partnerships may be liquidated for a number of reasons. Some common reasons for liquidation include:

1. The objective sought in forming the partnership has been achieved.
2. The time period for which the partnership was formed has expired.
3. Newly enacted legislation has made the partnership's activities illegal.
4. The partnership or one of its partners is bankrupt.

Liquidation may take place rapidly or over an extended period. If liquidation is rapid, a single cash distribution may be made to the partners after all noncash assets are sold and the liabilities are paid. If liquidation is prolonged, more than one cash distribution may be made to the partners. Only those liquidations that involve a single payment to partners are discussed below.

Partnership Liquidation Illustrated

In the following illustrations, we assume that all noncash assets are sold, the resulting gain or loss is distributed to the partners' capital accounts, all liabilities are paid, and a single distribution is made to partners to liquidate their capital accounts.

The partnership of Ring, Scott, and Terry is liquidated on August 1, 1991. The income and loss ratio is Ring, 40%; Scott, 35%; and Terry, 25%. A condensed trial balance prepared just before liquidation is shown in Illustration 14.7. The three cases that follow are based on the Ring, Scott, and Terry partnership.

Illustration 14.7

Condensed Trial Balance

RING, SCOTT, AND TERRY
Trial Balance
August 1, 1991

	Debits	Credits
Cash	$ 10,000	
Other Assets	90,000	
Liabilities		$ 10,000
Ring, Capital		30,000
Scott, Capital		30,000
Terry, Capital		30,000
	$100,000	$100,000

Case 1.   Assets Sold at a Gain.   The noncash assets are sold for $95,000, and the $5,000 gain on the sale is distributed to the partners in their income and loss ratio. The liabilities are paid in full. **The remaining cash is distributed to the partners in accordance with the balances of their capital accounts, not in the income and loss ratio.**

The journal entries to record the foregoing facts and the liquidation of the partnership on August 1, 1991, follow:

Cash	95,000	
Other Assets		90,000
Gain on Sale of Assets		5,000
To record the sale of the assets.		
Gain on Sale of Assets	5,000	
Ring, Capital ($5,000 × 0.40)		2,000
Scott, Capital ($5,000 × 0.35)		1,750
Terry, Capital ($5,000 × 0.25)		1,250
To distribute the gain on the sale of the assets.		
Liabilities	10,000	
Cash		10,000
To record the settlement of partnership liabilities.		

After the above entries are posted, the partners' capital accounts show:

Ring, Capital			Scott, Capital			Terry, Capital	
Beg. bal.	30,000		Beg. bal.	30,000		Beg. bal.	30,000
Gain from			Gain from			Gain from	
sale of			sale of			sale of	
assets	2,000		assets	1,750		assets	1,250
End. bal.	32,000		End. bal.	31,750		End. bal.	31,250

The Cash account now shows a balance of $95,000 ($10,000 + $95,000 − $10,000). The entry to record the cash distributed to the partners is:

Ring, Capital	32,000	
Scott, Capital	31,750	
Terry, Capital	31,250	
Cash		95,000

To distribute remaining cash to partners based on balances of their capital accounts.

Case 2.   Assets Sold at a Loss.   The noncash assets of Ring, Scott, and Terry are sold for $70,000, and the $20,000 loss on the sale is distributed to the partners' capital accounts in the income and loss ratio. The liabilities are paid in full. The remaining cash is distributed to the partners in accordance with the balances of their capital accounts.

The journal entries are:

Cash	70,000	
Loss on Sale of Assets	20,000	
Other Assets		90,000

To record the sale of the assets.

Ring, Capital ($20,000 × 0.40)	8,000	
Scott, Capital ($20,000 × 0.35)	7,000	
Terry, Capital ($20,000 × 0.25)	5,000	
Loss on Sale of Assets		20,000

To distribute the loss on the sale of the assets.

Liabilities	10,000	
Cash		10,000

To record the settlement of partnership liabilities.

After the above entries have been posted, the accounts show Cash, $70,000; Ring, Capital, $22,000; Scott, Capital, $23,000; and Terry, Capital, $25,000. The entry to record the cash distributed to the partners is:

Ring, Capital	22,000	
Scott, Capital	23,000	
Terry, Capital	25,000	
Cash		70,000

To distribute cash to partners.

Case 3.   Assets Sold at a Loss When One Partner's Share of the Loss Is Greater than the Balance of that Partner's Capital Account.   In Case 2, the loss charged to the capital account of each partner is smaller than that partner's capital account balance. But it is possible that a partner's portion of the loss may be greater than that partner's capital account balance. When a loss is charged to a partner and a debit balance is created in that partner's capital account, the debit balance represents an amount owed by that partner to the partnership. The cash available for distribution will be insufficient to pay the other partners in full until the partner with the debit balance pays in the amount owed. If the partner with the debit balance is unable to pay, the remaining partners must bear this loss in the income and loss ratio existing between them.

To illustrate, assume that the noncash assets of Ring, Scott, and Terry are sold for only $10,200. Entries to record the foregoing facts and the liquidation follow:

Cash	10,200	
Loss on Sale of Assets	79,800	
Other Assets		90,000
To record the sale of the assets.		

Ring, Capital ($79,800 × 0.40)	31,920	
Scott, Capital ($79,800 × 0.35)	27,930	
Terry, Capital ($79,800 × 0.25)	19,950	
Loss on Sale of Assets		79,800
To distribute the loss on the sale of the assets.		

Liabilities	10,000	
Cash		10,000
To record the settlement of partnership liabilities.		

At this stage of the liquidation, the partners' capital accounts have the following balances:

Ring, Capital		Scott, Capital		Terry, Capital	
	Beg. bal. 30,000		Beg. bal. 30,000		Beg. bal. 30,000
Loss from sale of assets 31,920		Loss from sale of assets 27,930		Loss from sale of assets 19,950	
End. bal. 1,920			End. bal. 2,070		End. bal. 10,050

Only $10,200 ($10,000 + $10,200 − $10,000) of cash is available for distribution to Scott and Terry, while the combined balance of their capital accounts is $12,120. To pay Scott and Terry the amounts owed, the partnership needs $1,920 more cash, which is the amount owed the partnership by Ring and which Ring is unable to pay. The $1,920 is thus a loss that must be shared by Scott and Terry in their income and loss sharing ratio of 35:25. Thus, Scott's share of the loss is $1,120 (35/60 × $1,920), and Terry's share is $800 (25/60 × $1,920).

The debit balance in Ring's capital account is closed and the loss absorbed by Scott and Terry, as shown in the following entry:

Scott, Capital	1,120	
Terry, Capital	800	
Ring, Capital		1,920
To charge Scott and Terry with Ring's capital deficiency.		

The only accounts left on the books now are the Cash account and Scott's and Terry's capital accounts. The remaining cash is distributed to Scott and Terry in the amounts now shown in their capital accounts:

Scott, Capital	950	
Terry, Capital	9,250	
Cash		10,200

To record final cash distribution to partners.

With this entry, all accounts of the partnership now have a zero balance, and the partnership is ended. As individuals, Scott and Terry have the legal right to collect the $1,920 Ring owes them. But the partnership is now liquidated; no further entries will be made on its books.

Suppose that in the example above, Ring was able to pay the $1,920 owed the partnership prior to closing the account. The following entries would be needed:

Cash	1,920	
Ring, Capital		1,920

To record payment of capital deficiency by Ring.

Scott, Capital	2,070	
Terry, Capital	10,050	
Cash		12,120

To distribute cash to partners in liquidation.

Notice that Ring does not receive any cash in the final settlement. He had to pay cash to the partnership to bring his capital account to a zero balance.

Assuming Ring pays the amount owed to the partnership, the analysis of the partnership liquidation may be aided by the preparation of a liquidation work sheet as shown in Illustration 14.8.

The liquidation work sheet brings together in one place all the necessary calculations and graphically illustrates the amounts involved in a partnership liquidation. This work sheet can be helpful for the accountant, the partners, and other interested parties.

Illustration 14.8

Liquidation Work Sheet

	Ring	Scott	Terry	Total
Income and Loss Ratio	40%	35%	25%	100%
Original capital account balances	$ 30,000	$ 30,000	$ 30,000	$ 90,000
Apportionment of loss on sale of assets	(31,920)	(27,930)	(19,950)	(79,800)
Capital balances after loss apportionment	$ (1,920)	$ 2,070	$ 10,050	$ 10,200
Ring's cash contribution	1,920			1,920
Ending capital account balances	$ –0–	$ 2,070	$ 10,050	$ 12,120
Liquidating distribution		(2,070)	(10,050)	(12,120)
Balances	$ –0–	$ –0–	$ –0–	$ –0–

Note: ( ) = debit.

Now that you have finished your study of partnerships, you will begin the study of corporations. Corporations are unique in that the owners are legally separate from the company. The corporate form of business makes it possible for individuals with small amounts of capital to become owners in large companies.

■ *UNDERSTANDING THE LEARNING OBJECTIVES: CHAPTER 14*

1. Define partnerships and explain their characteristics.

    - The Uniform Partnership Act defines a partnership as ''an association of two or more persons to carry on as co-owners a business for profit.''
    - Characteristics of a partnership:
      1. Voluntary association.
      2. Mutual agency.
      3. Limited life.
      4. Unlimited liability.

2. List advantages and disadvantages of a partnership.

    - Advantages of a partnership:
      1. Sufficiently flexible to permit reasonable accumulations of capital and talent.
      2. Easier and less expensive to organize than a corporation.
      3. Not required to observe as many laws and regulations as a corporation.
      4. Not subject to separate corporation taxation.
    - Disadvantages of a partnership:
      1. Unlimited liability.
      2. Mutual agency.
      3. Transfer of ownership may be difficult.

3. Record in entry form the formation of a partnership.

    - *Example:* A $10,000 cash investment each by Kaye Brice and Mike Jones.

Cash 20,000		
Kaye Brice, Capital		10,000
Mike Jones, Capital		10,000

4. Know the different methods of dividing the net income (and losses) in a partnership.

    - Net income divided in a set ratio:
      1. Equally.
      2. Agreed ratio other than equal.
      3. Ratio of partners' capital account balances at the beginning of fiscal period.
      4. Ratio of average capital investment.
    - Net income divided by allowing interest on the capital investments,

or salaries, or both, with remaining net income divided in an agreed ratio.

5. Understand the nature and content of a partnership's financial statements.

   - Income statement may contain a schedule showing the distribution of the period's net income or net loss to each partner.
   - At the close of each period, a statement of partners' capital is prepared. This statement summarizes the effects of transactions on the capital of each partner.
   - On the balance sheet, the capital accounts are shown in the owners' equity section.

6. Make the various entries required to account for the admissions and withdrawals of partners.

   - Admissions:
     1. Smith purchases $5,000 interest from Brown:

Brown, Capital	5,000	
Smith, Capital		5,000

     2. Cooper invests $20,000 cash:

Cash	20,000	
Cooper, Capital		20,000

   - Retirement and withdrawal:
     1. Jones retires and receives book value of equity:

Jones, Capital	20,000	
Cash		20,000

     2. Jones retires and receives more than book value of equity:

Jones, Capital	20,000	
Ridder, Capital	3,000	
Black, Capital	2,000	
Cash		25,000

     3. Jones retires and receives less than book value of equity:

Jones, Capital	20,000	
Cash		15,000
Ridder, Capital		3,000
Black, Capital		2,000

7. Understand the procedures involved in accounting for the liquidation of a partnership.

   - Assets are sold.
   - Distribute any gain or loss on the sale of the assets to the partners' capital accounts.
   - Liabilities are paid.
   - Single distribution is made to partners to liquidate their capital accounts.

8. Define and use correctly the new terms in the glossary.

NEW TERMS INTRODUCED IN CHAPTER 14

Agent   One who has the authority to act for another (the partnership) or in the place of another. See Mutual agency (572).

Articles of copartnership   See Partnership agreement (571).

Income and loss ratio   The agreed way that a partnership's income or losses are shared. Often called the **profit and loss ratio** or the **earnings and loss ratio** (578).

Interest (on capital invested)   A means often used in the sharing of income to give weight to the relative amounts of capital invested by the partners. The interest is sometimes based on the beginning-of-year balances in the capital accounts and sometimes on the average balances in the capital accounts. The interest is **not** an expense to be deducted in arriving at net income, nor is it a cash outflow of the business (579).

Liquidation of a partnership   Means that business operations have ended, assets have been sold for cash, cash has been paid to creditors and partners, and the partnership has been legally terminated (592).

Mutual agency   The power possessed by a partner to bind a partnership to any contract within the apparent scope of the partnership's business (572).

Partnership   "An association of two or more persons to carry on as co-owners a business for profit" (570).

Partnership agreement   Also known as articles of co-

partnership (when in written form); the conditions or provisions accepted by all of the partners to serve as the basis for the formation, operation, and liquidation of the partnership (571).

Salary (granted to partner)   A means often used in the sharing of income to reward certain partners for spending more time than other partners in running the affairs of the business. This salary is **not** an expense of the partnership in determining net income, nor is it a cash outflow of the business (578).

Statement of partners' capital   A financial statement that (1) is prepared from the capital accounts in the general ledger, (2) summarizes the effects of transactions on the capital balance of each partner and in total for all partners, and (3) serves the same purpose as the statement of owner's capital in a single proprietorship (583).

Termination (dissolution)   The legal dissolution of a partnership brought on by a change in partners (572).

Uniform Partnership Act   A written law adopted in many states that provides the general framework of law relating to the formation, operation, and termination of a partnership (571).

Unlimited liability   A characteristic of partnerships under which owners are liable for more than merely the amounts invested in the business, since their personal assets may also be taken to satisfy the claims of business creditors (572).

DEMONSTRATION PROBLEM

The Short and Long partnership had the following income and loss sharing agreement:

1. Short receives an annual salary of $24,000.
2. Short and Long each receive interest of 10% on their capital balances at the beginning of the year.
3. The remainder is divided by Short and Long in a 2:1 ratio.

On January 1, 1991, the partners' capital account balances were Short, $60,000; and Long, $80,000. On December 31, 1991, the partners' drawing account balances were Short, $20,000; and Long, $16,000. Net income for the year ended December 31, 1991, was $40,000.

Required:
    a.   Prepare a schedule showing the distribution of net income to the partners.
    b.   Prepare journal entries to close the Income Summary account and the drawing accounts.
    c.   Assume that on January 1, 1992, Short and Long admit Neil to a 25% interest in capital for an investment of $64,000 cash. Prepare the entry to admit Neil.

Solution to demonstration problem

a.

	Short	Long	Total	Amount to Be Distributed
Net income				$40,000
Salaries	$24,000	$ -0-	$24,000	16,000
Interest on beginning capital balances:				
Short (10% of $60,000)	6,000			
Long (10% of $80,000)		8,000	14,000	2,000
Remainder (2:1)	1,333	667	2,000	-0-
Distribution	$31,333	$8,667	$40,000	

b.

1991
Dec. 31

Income Summary	40,000	
Short, Capital		31,334
Long, Capital		8,666
To divide net income between the partners.		

31

Short, Capital	20,000	
Long, Capital	16,000	
Short, Drawing		20,000
Long, Drawing		16,000
To close drawing accounts.		

c.

1992
Jan. 1

Cash	64,000	
Neil, Capital		52,000
Short, Capital		8,000
Long, Capital		4,000
To record admission of Neil to the partnership.		

Computations are:

Equities of old partners on January 1, 1991	
($60,000 + $80,000)	$140,000
Net income for 1991	40,000
Drawings in 1991	(36,000)
Equities of old partners, January 1, 1992	$144,000
Capital contributed by Neil	64,000
Total capital after admission of Neil	$208,000
Neil's share ($208,000 × 25%)	$ 52,000

Bonus to the old partners:

$64,000 − $52,000 = ...	$ 12,000
Short: $12,000 × 2/3	$ 8,000
Long: $12,000 × 1/3	4,000

QUESTIONS

1. Jim Black currently is operating a small machine shop. He is considering forming a partnership with an employee, Fred Brown, whom he considers an excellent worker and supervisor and with whom he gets along well. Prepare a brief list of the advantages and disadvantages to Black of the potential partnership.

2. Many matters are covered in the typical partnership agreement. Some of them are of little significance to the accountant, while others are quite crucial. What are some of the crucial provisions as far as the accountant is concerned?

3. Jones and Smith are partners in a local grocery store. Both take home sufficient merchandise to feed their families. Would you suggest that the merchandise taken home be recorded at selling price or cost? Why?

4. Give an example of a set of circumstances in which you might be willing to enter into a partnership with another person, do all of the work needed to run the business, provide all of the capital, and yet be willing to allow the other person a substantial share of the net income.

5. Why should a partnership agreement be quite specific regarding the treatment of withdrawals by partners insofar as the sharing of income and losses is concerned?

6. What are three reasons for the formation of partnerships?

7. What is a statement of partners' capital?

8. Describe two different ways in which a new partner can be admitted to a partnership.

9. Why might a newly admitted partner's capital account balance differ from the amount actually invested?

10. Why might a withdrawing partner receive assets worth more or less than the book value of his or her equity?

11. What are three acts or conditions that will lead to the liquidation of a partnership?

12. What procedures are followed in liquidating a partnership?

EXERCISES

E-1
Compute partners' share of income

Joe, Mike, and Pam are partners. In 1990, net income of their partnership was $180,000. How much will be credited to each partner in the income distribution if:

a. Nothing is stated in the partnership agreement concerning the division of income?
b. The income and loss sharing ratio is 5:3:2, respectively?

E-2
Record income distribution and close drawing accounts

Give the entries to record the division of income in *(b)* of Exercise E-1. Also give the entries to record the closing of the drawing accounts assuming drawings were $30,000, $40,000, and $20,000, respectively.

E-3
Determine distribution of a net loss

Given an income and loss ratio of 5:3:2, how would the three partners in Exercise E-1 share a loss of 45,000? Give the journal entry.

E-4
Determine partner's share of net income

Partner C was credited with a salary of $72,000 and interest of $36,000 on her capital account. She was also charged with $6,000 as her share of the remaining negative amount to be distributed. She withdrew $84,000 during the year. What amount will she report to the Internal Revenue Service as her share of the partnership's income?

E-5
Determine each partner's share of income

The capital account balances of T and K remained at $20,000 and $75,000 throughout the entire year. T withdrew $8,000, and K withdrew $12,000. These drawings were normal withdrawals rather than withdrawals of investment.

Net income for the year was $20,000. If salaries are to be allowed to T and K in the amounts of $8,000 and $7,000 and the remainder of the income is distributed equally, what will be each partner's total share of the income for the year?

E-6
Compute average capital investment

Using the data in the following capital account, compute the average capital investment for the year:

Smith, Capital

Mar. 1	27,000	Jan. 1	144,000
Aug. 1	6,000	May 1	72,000
Dec. 1	15,000	June 1	9,000

E-7
Prepare schedule showing distribution of income

B and C are partners. They agree that each partner can withdraw $1,500 in cash at the end of each month, with such withdrawals debited to each partner's drawing account. In sharing income, 10% interest is to be allowed on the average capital investment taking into consideration withdrawals in excess of the allowed $1,500 per month. Each partner is to be credited with a salary of $18,000 per year. The remainder of the income or loss is to be shared equally by B and C.

B's capital account at January 1 was $150,000. She withdrew $7,500 on August 1, in addition to the allowed $1,500 monthly cash withdrawals.

C's capital account balance at January 1 was $225,000. She withdrew $12,000 on April 1 and $18,000 on October 1. She also withdrew the allowed $1,500 cash per month.

Prepare a short schedule showing the distribution of $112,500 net income for the current year.

E-8
Record acquisition of interest of existing partners

X, Y, and Z were partners with capital account balances of $360,000, $440,000, and $320,000, respectively. H acquired one third of X's interest and one half of Z's interest for $252,000 ($110,000 to X and $142,000 to Z) in a personal transaction between the individuals. Prepare the entry to record H's acquisition of an interest in the partnership.

E-9
Determine incoming partner's equity and record admission

Matt, Phil, and Greg are partners with capital account balances of $60,000, $90,000, and $150,000, respectively. The partners agree to admit Chris to a one-fourth interest in both capital and income for a $60,000 cash investment in the partnership. Determine Chris' equity in the new partnership, and prepare the journal entry to record the admission of Chris. (Assume that the original partners shared income and losses in the ratio of 3:3:4.)

E-10
Record asset revaluation and retirement of a partner

E, F, and G are partners with capital account balances of $450,000, $300,000, and $125,000, respectively. They share income and losses in a 4:3:2 ratio. F decides to withdraw. The partnership revalues its assets from $975,000 to $1,110,000. F then receives cash equal to the recorded amount of his equity after assets have been adjusted to current market values. These adjustments involved an increase in inventory of $75,000 and an increase in plant and equipment of $60,000. Prepare journal entries to adjust the partnership accounts and to record the withdrawal of F.

E-11
Record partner's withdrawal from the partnership

Thomas, Harden, and Payne are partners with capital account balances of $120,000, $80,000, and $40,000, respectively. They share income and losses in a 5:2:2 ratio. Payne withdraws and is paid $54,000 for his equity interest by the partnership. Give the journal entry to record the withdrawal of Payne.

E-12
Record partner's withdrawal from the partnership

Dalton, Warren, and Kessler are partners with capital accounts of $35,000, $60,000, and $45,000, respectively. They share income and losses in a 2:3:4 ratio. Although she believes the assets of the partnership are fairly valued, Kessler is so anxious to retire that she accepts $40,000 cash as payment in full for her equity. Prepare the journal entry to record Kessler's withdrawal.

E-13
Record partnership liquidation

A, B, and C are partners with capital balances of $214,500, $97,500, and $75,000, respectively. They share income and losses in a 4:4:2 ratio. The partnership has $462,000 of noncash assets, $75,000 of liabilities, and no cash. The partnership is liquidated by selling the assets for $390,000, distributing the loss to the partners' capital accounts, paying the liabilities, and distributing cash to the partners. Prepare the necessary journal entries.

E-14
Record partnership liquidation

The liability and capital accounts of the firm of Allen and Howard follow:

Accounts Payable	$ 30,000
Allen, Capital	45,000
Howard, Capital	90,000
Total	$165,000

All of the firm's noncash assets were sold for $147,000, and only that amount of cash is on hand. The entry to record sale of the assets has not been recorded. Income and losses are shared 3:2 by Allen and Howard. Prepare entries to record sale of the assets, distribution of the loss to the partners' capital accounts, and payment of the $147,000 to creditors and the partners.

E-15
Record partnership liquidation

The trial balance of the L–M partnership is as follows:

	Debits	Credits
Assets	$600,000	
Accounts Payable		$ 60,000
L, Capital		360,000
M, Capital		180,000
	$600,000	$600,000

The partners decide to liquidate. The assets are sold for $270,000, and the cash is paid out. Prepare the necessary journal entries, assuming an equal sharing of income and losses.

E-16
Close Income Summary account; record partnership liquidation

Tina, Liz, and Ann are partners. Certain data for their firm follow:

	Tina	Liz	Ann	Total
Capital account balances prior to entering effects of 1990 operations	$441,000	$123,000	$291,000	$855,000
Loss for year ended December 31, 1990				90,000
Income and loss ratio	20%	50%	30%	100%

The partners decide to liquidate. The partnership has no liabilities. All of the assets are noncash assets and are sold for $450,000.

a. Prepare the journal entry to close the Income Summary account.
b. Prepare journal entries for the sale of the assets and the distribution of cash to partners. Each partner had invested all of her personal assets in the firm prior to liquidation and will not be able to pay any deficiency in her capital account.

PROBLEMS, SERIES A

P14-1-A
Record formation of partnership from two single proprietorships

Karen Cook and Arthur Hall, who have been in business as single proprietors, decided to combine all of their business assets and liabilities in a new partnership in which they will share income and losses equally. Balance sheets of the two individuals on the date of the formation of the partnership are shown below:

KAREN COOK
Balance Sheet
September 4, 1990

Assets

Cash	$ 4,000
Accounts receivable, net	15,000
Merchandise inventory	9,000
Equipment, net	20,000
Total assets	$48,000

Liabilities and Owner's Equity

Accounts payable	$23,000
Karen Cook, capital	25,000
Total liabilities and owner's equity	$48,000

ARTHUR HALL
Balance Sheet
September 4, 1990

Assets

Cash	$14,000
Accounts receivable, net	17,000
Merchandise inventory	20,000
Total assets	$51,000

Liabilities and Owner's Equity

Accounts payable	$22,000
Arthur Hall, capital	29,000
Total liabilities and owner's equity	$51,000

An appraisal of the assets showed market values for the assets of Cook as follows: accounts receivable, $14,000; merchandise inventory, $12,000; and equipment, $15,000. A similar appraisal placed the following market values on Hall's assets: accounts receivable, $17,000; and merchandise inventory, $13,000.

Required: Prepare journal entries to record the capital contributions of Cook and Hall to their newly formed partnership.

P14-2-A
Determine and journalize division of income under alternative provisions; close drawing accounts

An analysis of the capital accounts for 1990 of Morgan and Rogers, partners, showed:

Morgan

Jan. 1	Balance	$270,000
June 1	Capital withdrawal	45,000
Nov. 1	Additional investment	67,500

Rogers

Jan. 1	Balance	$ 45,000
Aug. 1	Additional investment	90,000

The balance in the Income Summary account showed net income of $135,000 for 1990.

Required: Prepare a schedule showing the distribution of the net income under each of the following unrelated assumptions with regard to income distribution. Also prepare the entries to distribute the income and to close the drawing accounts. (Note: In each instance assume drawings were equal to salaries allowed for each partner.)

a. Morgan and Rogers are allowed annual salaries of $36,000 and $45,000, respectively; 8% interest is allowed on average capital balances; and the balance of the income is shared equally.

b. Equal annual salaries of $54,000 are allowed to each partner; interest of 10% is allowed on capital balances at the beginning of the year; and the remainder is shared in a 3:2 ratio between Morgan and Rogers.

P14-3-A
Determine division of income; prepare entries to distribute income and close drawing accounts; prepare schedule of changes in partners' capital accounts

The S and C partnership has the following agreement for the sharing of income and losses: (1) S is to be allowed interest of 10% on her capital account balance as of the beginning of the year; (2) C is to be allowed a salary of $7,200 per month; and (3) any remaining balance of income or loss is to be shared equally. The net income for 1990 was $216,000.

Required: a. Assuming that S's and C's capital account balances on January 1, 1990, were $720,000 and $180,000, respectively, prepare a schedule showing the distribution of net income and the entry required to record it.

b. Prepare the entry needed to close the drawing accounts of the partners, which had the following balances (before closing) on December 31, 1990: S, zero; and C, $86,400.

c. Present a schedule showing the changes occurring in 1990 in the capital account of each partner.

P14-4-A
Prepare schedules showing division of income under alternative provisions

The capital account balances of the T and G partnership on January 1, 1990, are $180,000 for T and $90,000 for G. These balances did not change during the year. T withdrew $18,000, and G withdrew $45,000 during the year, with all withdrawals charged to the respective drawing accounts. The net loss for the year was $18,000.

Required: Prepare schedules showing the distribution of income to each partner for the year 1990 under each of the following independent or unrelated provisions:

a. Salaries allowed are $13,500 to T and $33,750 to G. The remaining income is divided according to capital account balances at the beginning of the year.

b. Salaries allowed are $9,000 to T and $15,000 to G. Interest of 10% is allowed on capital account balances at the beginning of the year. No further provisions relating to income sharing are included in the partnership agreement.

P14–5–A
Prepare schedules showing division of income at various amounts of income and loss

Keith and Tim are partners in a retail hardware store. Their partnership agreement calls for salaries to Keith and Tim of $12,000 and $24,000, respectively, and interest of 10% on average capital for the year. Any remaining balance is to be shared equally.

During 1990, each partner withdrew his allowed salary; there were no withdrawals in excess of allowed salaries. The capital accounts of the two partners remained unchanged during the year at $60,000 for Keith and $90,000 for Tim.

Required:

Present schedules showing the distribution of net income assuming that the income statement for 1990 showed:

a. $72,000 of net income.
b. $30,000 of net income.
c.   A net loss of $12,000.

P14–6–A
Prepare adjusting and closing entries, income statement, statement of partners' capital, and balance sheet

Bass and Carr are partners operating a retail store having a fiscal year ending on June 30. Their partnership agreement calls for annual salaries of $18,000 to Bass and $24,000 to Carr, interest of 8% on average capital account balances throughout the year, and the equal sharing of the balance of the income. Their June 30, 1990, trial balance follows:

BASS AND CARR
Trial Balance
June 30, 1990

	Debits	Credits
Cash	$ 60,600	
Accounts Receivable	96,000	
Merchandise Inventory, July 1, 1989	43,200	
Accounts Payable		$ 61,200
Notes Payable		30,000
Bass, Capital		42,000
Carr, Capital		30,000
Bass, Drawing	12,000	
Carr, Drawing	15,000	
Sales		642,000
Purchases	408,000	
Purchase Returns		6,000
Employee Salaries and Wages	18,000	
Rent Expense	78,000	
Delivery Expense	25,200	
Store Expense	55,200	
	$811,200	$811,200

The $30,000 note payable is a 120-day note dated April 1, 1990, and calls for interest of 10% per year. The inventory at June 30, 1990, is $49,800. The only change in the capital accounts during the year was an additional $8,000 investment by Bass on January 1.

Required:

You are to prepare the following for the partnership:

a.   The necessary adjusting and closing entries.
b.   An income statement for the year ended June 30, 1990.
c.   A statement of partners' capital for the year ended June 30, 1990.
d.   A balance sheet for June 30, 1990.

P14–7–A
Record admission of new partner

Tony, John, and Jeff are partners who share income and losses in a 3:2:1 ratio. They decided to admit Lee to the partnership at a time when their capital account balances were:

Tony, Capital $60,000
John, Capital   30,000
Jeff, Capital 30,000

Required: Prepare journal entries to record Lee's admission to the partnership under each of the following unrelated conditions:

a. Lee acquired 40% of John's interest for $18,000 cash, paid to John personally.
b. Lee acquired all of Jeff's interest for $27,000 cash, paid to Jeff personally.
c. Lee invested $100,000 in the partnership for a one-half interest in capital.
d. Lee was admitted to a one-fifth interest in capital for an investment of $20,000 because the old partnership was badly in need of cash to pay a maturing debt.

P14–8–A
Record admission of new partner

P and Q are partners with capital account balances of $49,500 and $27,000, respectively. Income and losses are shared in a 3:2 ratio.

Required: Prepare the journal entries to record admission of R to the partnership in each of the following independent situations:

a. R paid Q $15,000 for one half of Q's interest.
b. R invested sufficient cash in the firm to acquire a one-fourth interest in capital of the new partnership.
c. R invested $28,500 for a one-fifth interest in capital.
d. R invested $19,500 for a one-fourth interest in capital.

P14–9–A
Record withdrawal of partner

On December 31, Greg Davis, a member of the partnership of Davis and Pratt, decided to retire. The partners have shared income and losses equally. On this date, their capital account credit balances were:

Greg Davis $90,000
Helen Davis 60,000
Eric Pratt 60,000

Required: Prepare entries to record the withdrawal of Greg Davis under each of the following unrelated assumptions. All payments are to be in cash, and the assets are not to be revalued.

a. Greg Davis was paid $90,000.
b. Greg Davis was paid $96,000.
c. Greg Davis was paid $80,000.

P14–10–A
Record withdrawal of partner

Dan, Frank, and Gene are partners in the DFG partnership. Ledger account balances on January 1, 1990, follow:

Cash	$ 21,000	
Accounts Receivable	36,000	
Allowance for Uncollectible Accounts		$ 3,000
Merchandise Inventory	75,000	
Equipment	18,000	
Accumulated Depreciation—Equipment		6,000
Accounts Payable		24,000
Dan, Capital		60,000
Frank, Capital		45,000
Gene, Capital		12,000
	$150,000	$150,000

The partners share income and losses in a 3:2:1 ratio.

Required: Assume that Gene retires from the partnership and receives a check for $15,000. Prepare entries to record Gene's retirement assuming:

a. The assets were not revalued.
b. Merchandise inventory was revalued at $93,000, and equipment was revalued at $18,000 with accumulated depreciation of $9,000.

P14–11–A
Record partnership liquidation

Use the data in Problem 14–10–A above, but ignore the revaluation of assets in part (b). Assume that the partners decided to liquidate instead of only Gene retiring. All of the noncash assets were sold for $45,000. After the assets were sold, the loss was charged to the partners' capital accounts, the liabilities were paid, the remaining cash was distributed to the partners, and the books were closed.

Required: Prepare journal entries to record liquidation of the partnership. Assume that none of the partners has other assets to cover possible debit balances in his capital account.

P14–12–A
Record partnership liquidation

Given below is the balance sheet of the FGH Partnership on April 30, 1990—the date the partners decided to liquidate their partnership.

FGH PARTNERSHIP
Balance Sheet
April 30, 1990

Assets

Cash	$ 20,000
Accounts receivable	40,000
Merchandise inventory	100,000
Plant and equipment	200,000
Total assets	$360,000

Liabilities and Owners' Equity

Accounts payable	$190,000
F, capital	70,000
G, capital	50,000
H, capital	50,000
Total liabilities and owner's equity	$360,000

On May 1, the noncash assets were sold for $178,000. F, G, and H share income and losses in a 5:3:2 ratio.

Required: Prepare all necessary journal entries to record the sale of the assets, the distribution of the loss to the partners' capital accounts, and the distribution of cash to creditors and partners. Assume that any partners who had debit balances in their capital accounts after loss distributions immediately paid cash to the partnership equal to the debit balances.

PROBLEMS, SERIES B

P14–1–B
Record formation of partnership from two single proprietorships

Ken Baxter and Lou Henson decided to form a partnership by combining their business assets and liabilities from their single proprietorships. Income and losses will be shared in a 2:3 ratio to Baxter and Henson, respectively. Balance sheets on November 23, 1990, the date the partnership was formed, are shown below:

```
                       KEN BAXTER
                      Balance Sheet
                   November 23, 1990
                          Assets
Cash . . . . . . . . . . . . . . . . . . .  $ 32,000
Accounts receivable, net . . . . . . . . .    92,000
Merchandise inventory . . . . . . . . . .    136,000
Total assets . . . . . . . . . . . . . .    $260,000

             Liabilities and Owner's Equity
Accounts payable . . . . . . . . . . . .    $ 88,000
Notes payable . . . . . . . . . . . . .       72,000
Ken Baxter, capital . . . . . . . . . . .    100,000
Total liabilities and owner's equity . . . .  $260,000
```

```
                       LOU HENSON
                      Balance Sheet
                   November 23, 1990
                          Assets
Cash . . . . . . . . . . . . . . . . . . .  $  8,000
Accounts receivable, net . . . . . . . . .    96,000
Merchandise inventory . . . . . . . . . .    188,000
Equipment, net . . . . . . . . . . . . .      60,000
Total assets . . . . . . . . . . . . . .    $352,000

             Liabilities and Owner's Equity
Accounts payable . . . . . . . . . . . .    $192,000
Lou Henson, capital . . . . . . . . . . .    160,000
Total liabilities and owner's equity . . . .  $352,000
```

Current market values for Baxter's assets were accounts receivable, $92,000; and merchandise inventory, $160,000. For Henson, market values were accounts receivable, $78,000; merchandise inventory, $100,000; and equipment, $72,000.

Required: Prepare journal entries to record the capital contributions by Baxter and Henson in forming their partnership.

P14-2-B
Determine and journalize division of income under alternative provisions

An analysis of Ladd's capital account for the year 1990 showed a beginning balance of $135,000, a capital withdrawal on June 1 of $45,000, and an additional investment on November 1 of $22,500. A similar analysis of partner Breeman's capital account showed a beginning balance of $22,500 and an additional investment on July 1 of $90,000. The balance in the Income Summary account showed net income for the year of $99,000.

Required: Prepare a schedule and the required journal entry to record the distribution of the net income to the partners under each of the following independent assumptions:

a.   Ladd and Breeman are allowed annual salaries of $36,000 and $45,000, respectively; 8% interest on average capital balance is to be credited to each partner, and the balance of income and losses is to be shared equally.

b.   Equal annual salaries of $45,000 and interest of 6% on beginning capital balance are allowed each partner; the remaining balance is shared in a 2:1 ratio to Ladd and Breeman.

P14-3-B
Determine division of income; prepare statement of partners' capital; journalize income distribution; close drawing accounts

The balances in the capital accounts of A and B at June 30, 1990, were $240,000 and $120,000, respectively. These balances were unchanged during the year. A drew $32,000 during the year, and B drew $36,000. Net income for the year was $160,000.

Required:

a.   Compute the income to be distributed to each partner at the end of the year under each of the following independent conditions:

1.   Salaries allowed are $24,000 to A and $40,000 to B; remaining income is to be divided in the ratio of the beginning-of-the-year capital account balances.

2.   Salaries allowed are $76,000 to A and $64,000 to B; interest of 10% is allowed on capital account balances at the beginning of the year; there were no other provisions relating to the sharing of income and losses in the partnership agreement.

b.   Assuming that income is shared as in *(a)* (1) above, prepare a statement of partners' capital for the year.

c.   Using the data in *(b),* prepare entries to distribute the income and to close the drawing accounts.

P14-4-B
Prepare schedule showing division income under alternative provisions

Chip and Mark formed a partnership on March 1, 1990, by investing $45,000 and $72,000, respectively. On July 1, Chip invested additional capital of $18,000, and Mark invested $27,000. At that time, the partners agreed that in dividing net income, interest of 10% would be allowed on average capital account balances for the period. On September 1, Chip invested another $87,000, and Mark invested another $66,000. The partnership agreement also allowed monthly drawings of $2,700 for Chip and $3,600 for Mark. Both partners withdrew the allowed amounts. Nothing further was said about the sharing of income and losses. Net income for the year ended February 28, 1991, was $120,000.

Required:

Prepare a schedule showing the distribution of income for the year ended February 28, 1991, assuming that:

a.   The allowed monthly drawings were salaries and are used in determining the distribution of income.

b.   The allowed monthly drawings were normal drawings (not salaries) and are not to be used in determining the distribution of income.

P14-5-B
Prepare schedules showing division of income for several years

Ray and Ed, as partners, have agreed to the following distribution of net income:

1.   Salaries of $48,000 to Ray and $36,000 to Ed.
2.   A bonus to Ray of 25% of net income in excess of salaries.
3.   The remainder divided equally.

Net income for 1989 and 1990 was $180,000 and $60,000, respectively; and in 1991, a $30,000 net loss occurred.

Required:

Prepare schedules showing the distribution of the income and losses to the partners for each of the years 1989, 1990, and 1991.

P14-6-B
Prepare adjusting and closing entries, income statement, statement of partners' capital, and balance sheet

The following trial balance was taken for the Black and Gold partnership on December 31, 1990.

BLACK AND GOLD
Trial Balance
December 31, 1990

	Debits	Credits
Cash	$ 30,800	
Accounts Receivable	45,000	
Allowance for Uncollectible Accounts		$ 750
Merchandise Inventory	27,750	
Equipment	52,500	
Accumulated Depreciation—Equipment		12,750
Prepaid Insurance	682	
Accounts Payable		38,250
Black, Capital		27,750
Gold, Capital		54,750
Black, Drawing	700	
Gold, Drawing	9,000	
Sales		412,500
Purchases	330,000	
Selling Expenses	30,000	
Administrative Expenses	24,750	
Other Revenue		4,432
	$551,182	$551,182

The articles of copartnership for Black and Gold provide for the distribution of income and losses in the following manner:

1. Black is allowed a salary of $22,500 and Gold a salary of $27,000 per year as a distribution of income.
2. Each partner is allowed 6% interest per year on his capital investment as of the beginning of the year.
3. The remaining income and losses are to be divided equally.

Your analysis of the books and records discloses the following data that require consideration: the ending merchandise inventory is $23,250; 1% of sales is to be added to the allowance for uncollectible accounts; and depreciation on the equipment should be recorded at 10% of cost. Black's capital account includes a credit for $3,000 invested on July 15 of the current year. Prepaid insurance at December 31, 1990, should be $60.

Required: You are to prepare the following for the partnership:

a. Adjusting and closing journal entries.
b. An income statement for the year.
c. A statement of partners' capital for the year.
d. A balance sheet for December 31, 1990.

P14–7–B
**Record admission
of new partner**

Paul and Al are partners who share income and losses in a 3:2 ratio. They decided to admit Todd as a new partner at a time when their capital account balances were $240,000 for Paul and $120,000 for Al.

Required: Prepare journal entries to record Todd's admission to the partnership in each of the following unrelated situations:

a. Todd acquired one half of Paul's interest for $125,000 cash paid to Paul personally.
b. Todd acquired one fifth of Paul's equity for $50,000 cash and one fourth of Al's equity for $31,000 cash. Both amounts were paid to the partners personally.
c. Todd invested $90,000 for a 20% interest in capital.

d. Todd invested $60,000 and was granted a 15% interest in capital because the old partnership was badly in need of cash to pay maturing debts.

e. Todd invested $210,000 for a one-third interest in capital.

P14–8–B
Record admission of new partner

T and M are partners who have capital account balances of $30,000 and $15,000, respectively, and who share income and losses in a 3:2 ratio. They negotiated the admission of K to their partnership.

Required:

Prepare journal entries to record K's admission to the partnership under each of the following unrelated situations:

a. K invested $27,000 cash and received a one-third interest in the capital of the new firm.

b. K invested $20,250 cash for a one-third interest in capital.

c. K invested sufficient cash to secure exactly a 40% interest in the new firm.

P14–9–B
Record withdrawal of partner

On July 31, 1990, John Beck, a member of the partnership Beck and Ivy, decided to retire. The partners have shared income and losses equally. On this date, their capital balances were John Beck, $80,000; Tina Beck, $100,000; and Ken Ivy, $60,000.

Prepare entries to record the withdrawal of John Beck under each of the following unrelated assumptions. All payments are made in cash, and the assets are not to be revalued.

a. John Beck was paid $80,000.

b. John Beck was paid $84,000.

c. John Beck was paid $74,000.

P14–10–B
Record withdrawal of partner

T, U, and V are partners who share income and losses in a 4:2:2 ratio. On December 31, 1990, T decided to retire. At that time, the partners' capital account balances were:

T, Capital $120,000
U, Capital 105,000
V, Capital 180,000

Required:

Prepare entries to record the retirement of T in each of the following unrelated situations:

a. The partners agreed that inventory was undervalued by $54,000 and that the books should be adjusted to reflect market values. After the books were adjusted, T received cash equal to the balance in his capital account.

b. The partners agreed that inventory was undervalued on the books by $54,000, but the books should *not* be adjusted to reflect market values. T was paid cash equal to the balance that would have been shown in his capital account if the increase to market value had been recorded.

c. The partners agreed that the amount shown for inventory was $36,000 more than its current market value, but the inventory was *not* to be adjusted to reflect market values. T was paid cash equal to the balance that would have been in his capital account if the books had been adjusted.

P14–11–B
Record partnership liquidation

The ABC partnership was liquidated on January 2, 1990. Before any of the partnership's $390,000 of assets (all noncash) were sold, the liabilities and capital account credit balances were:

Accounts Payable . . . $200,000
A, Capital   20,000
B, Capital   80,000
C, Capital   90,000

The assets were sold for $270,000. Income and losses are shared equally.

Required:

Prepare the journal entries to record the sale of the assets (credit an Assets account), distribution of the loss to the partners' capital accounts, and the distribution of the cash to creditors and partners. Assume that none of the partners has other assets to cover a debit balance in his capital account.

P14-12-B
Record partnership liquidation

The partners of the MNO Company decided to liquidate because of their creditors' demands for payment of amounts owed. The March 31, 1990, balance sheet data for the partnership follows:

Cash	$ 90,000	Accounts payable	$ 495,000
Accounts receivable	195,000	Moore, capital	225,000
Merchandise inventory	270,000	Neal, capital	270,000
Plant and equipment	795,000	Oscar, capital	360,000
	$1,350,000		$1,350,000

The noncash assets were sold on April 1, 1990, for $540,000. The partners share income and losses in a 50:25:25 ratio, respectively.

Required: Prepare journal entries to record the sale of the assets, distribution of the loss to the partners' capital accounts, and the distribution of cash to creditors and partners. Assume that partners developing debit balances in their capital accounts are not able to pay them from other assets.

BUSINESS DECISION PROBLEM 14-1

Analyze effects of proposed change in income and loss sharing provisions

Lewis Hull and Troy Davis have owned and operated a men's clothing store as a partnership. Their capital account balances as of December 31, 1990, were Hull, $320,000; and Davis, $108,000. Income and losses are shared equally after allowing salaries of $32,000 to Hull and $28,000 to Davis. Applying these provisions to the net income of $120,000 in 1990 resulted in a distribution of $62,000 to Hull and $58,000 to Davis. Hull considers this sharing to be quite unfair. He notes that he devotes full time to the store, while Davis has other interests that occupy about half of his time. Hull also notes that his equity was substantially more than Davis' in the partnership because he has not drawn all of his income. He proposes that the partnership agreement be changed to call for salaries of $40,000 and $20,000 to himself and to Davis, respectively, that interest of 10% per year be allowed on beginning of the year capital account balances, and that any remaining income be shared equally.

Davis agrees that some modification seems necessary because of changed circumstances. But before agreeing to Hull's proposed changes, he wants to know the effects of such changes.

Required: Assume that the capital account balances as of January 1, 1990, were Hull, $280,000, and Davis, $100,000.

a.   Prepare a schedule showing how the income for 1990 would have been shared if Hull's suggested provisions had been in effect for the year.
b.   Prepare a schedule showing how much each partner's share of the 1990 income would have increased or decreased if Hull's proposed revisions of the partnership agreement had been in effect in 1990.
c.   Is Davis more or less likely to accept Hull's proposals if future net income is substantially greater than or less than $120,000 per year?

BUSINESS DECISION PROBLEM 14-2

Determine proper amount for partner to receive in liquidation settlement

Joey Jones and Frank Crowe are partners sharing income and losses equally in a business that has been successful for all 25 years of its existence. The partners have been studying what they consider a tempting offer to buy their business, thus allowing the partners to retire. Shortly after receiving this offer, Jones was hospitalized as a result of an auto accident. The partners agreed that they should sell, and Crowe was authorized to negotiate the sale of the business.

Some time later, Crowe appeared at the hospital and gave Jones a check for $60,000 as his share of the cash available to the partners on liquidation of the partnership. He also gave Jones a balance sheet for the partnership as of the day before the date of the sale. Summarized, this balance sheet showed:

Cash	$ 7,500
Other assets	97,500
Total	$105,000
Liabilities	$ 22,500
Jones, capital	45,000
Crowe, capital	37,500
Total	$105,000

Crowe explained that he had sold all of the other assets and the partnership name for $135,000—a price he considered excellent. Jones agreed the price was excellent, but was unsure about whether the check Crowe gave him was in the correct amount.

Required: a.   Show the computations Crowe made to arrive at a $60,000 check for Jones.

b.   Is $60,000 the correct amount? If not, compute the correct amount.

Appendixes

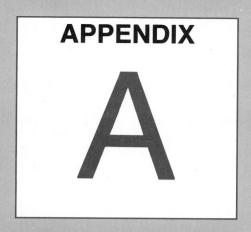

APPENDIX A

Corporate and Personal Federal Income Taxes

This appendix provides a brief introduction to corporate and personal federal income taxes. Both of these taxes have a pronounced effect on each of us. Corporations usually pass their taxes along to us in the form of higher prices. Personal income taxes affect us directly.

CORPORATE FEDERAL INCOME TAXES

Most corporations organized for profit must file a federal income tax return and pay corporate income tax on their net income. Not-for-profit organizations, specifically exempted by law, do not file an income tax return but must file an annual return of information.

■ INCOME BEFORE FEDERAL INCOME TAXES VERSUS TAXABLE INCOME

Income before federal income taxes (as shown on the income statement) and taxable income (as shown in the corporation's tax return) need not necessarily agree. Some of the reasons why they might differ are:

1. Certain items of revenue and expense included in the computation of business income are excluded from the computation of taxable income. For instance, interest earned on certain state, county, or municipal bonds is not subject to tax. The general rule is that only "ordinary" and "necessary" business expenses and "reasonable" amounts of salaries can be deducted for tax purposes. Life insurance premiums are not deductible if the corporation is the beneficiary; however, proceeds received from life insurance policies are not taxed. Costs of attempting to influence legislation are not deductible. A corporation may deduct from taxable income 80% of any dividends received from other domestic corporations. Goodwill may not be deducted for tax purposes even though it must be amortized for accounting purposes.

2. The timing of recognition of items of revenue and expense often varies for tax purposes from the timing used in determining business income. Interpretations of the tax code have generally held that revenue received in advance is taxable when received and that current expenses based on estimates of future costs (such as costs of performance under service contracts) are not deductible until actually incurred. Also, effective methods may be used for tax purposes that are different from those used for financial statements. For instance, often a corporation may use straight-line depreciation for book purposes and a different method for tax purposes.

Tax Rates

Once taxable income is determined, a tax rate is applied to find the amount of tax liability. As of this writing, the graduated tax rates applicable to corporations for the years 1988 and beyond are as shown in Illustration A.1. To illustrate, using these corporate tax rates, a corporation with taxable income of $110,000 will have a tax liability of $26,150, computed as follows:

Illustration A.1

Corporate Tax Rates

Corporate Taxable Income	Tax Rate
$0–$ 50,000	15%
$ 50,001–$ 75,000	25
$ 75,001–$100,000	34
$100,000–$335,000	39

A corporation with taxable income over $335,000 will pay a flat tax rate of 34% on all taxable income.

Tax on first $50,000 (at 15%)	$ 7,500
Tax on next $25,000 (at 25%)	6,250
Tax on next $25,000 (at 34%)	8,500
Tax on remaining $10,000 (at 39%)	3,900
	$26,150

Likewise, a corporation with taxable income of $500,000 will have a tax liability of $170,000, calculated as ($500,000 × 34%).

The tax law requires an alternative minimum tax to be calculated and paid by the corporation if the minimum tax is higher than the ordinary tax. The tax will be calculated at 20% of taxable income adjusted by adding back a number of the tax breaks allowed to arrive at taxable income and reduced, in some cases, by an exemption of up to $40,000.

Loss Carryback and Carryforward

A provision of the tax law allows corporations to carry losses incurred in the current year back 3 years and forward 15 years to offset past or future taxes. (Alternatively, the corporation may elect to only carry the loss forward for 15 years.) A loss carryback is a current loss that has been applied against taxable income of prior periods, thereby resulting in a tax refund in the current period. In applying a loss carryback, the company must apply the loss to the oldest year first, then the next oldest, and so on until the loss has been completely "used up" by offsetting it against ordinary taxable income of these years. The corporation recomputes its taxes for those previous years using the rates then in effect.

To illustrate this provision, assume the amounts of taxable income (or loss) shown below (1988 rates were used to compute taxes paid):

Year	Taxable Income (or loss)	Taxes Paid	Taxes Recovered
1988	$ 7,500	$1,125	$1,125
1989	10,000	1,500	1,500
1990	2,500	375	375
1991	(50,000)	–0–	–0–
1992	20,000	–0–	–0–
1993	5,000	–0–	–0–
1994	15,000	1,500	–0–
1995	25,000	3,750	–0–
1996	30,000	4,500	–0–

The loss of $50,000 in 1991 would first be offset against the $7,500 of taxable income in 1988, then the $10,000 in 1989, and next the $2,500 in 1990. The company would recover the taxes previously paid in these years, which total $3,000. At this point, the company would have a loss carryforward of $30,000. A **loss carryforward** is a current loss that will be applied against taxable income in future periods, thereby reducing the taxes payable of future periods. In the above example, the company would apply $20,000 of this toward taxable income in 1992 and therefore would pay no taxes in that year. This leaves $10,000 of the carryforward remaining: $5,000 of this would be used to offset taxable income in the next year (1993), and the other $5,000 would be applied against 1994 taxable income.

Accounting Methods Used for Tax Purposes

Accrual Method.   The method of accounting affects when revenues and expenses are recognized. Most corporations and large businesses use the accrual method. Under this method, revenues are generally recognized when earned. The earning of revenue normally occurs when services are rendered or when goods are delivered. When payment has been received before the revenue has been earned, an exception may require recognition of income at the time payment is received.

Expenses are generally recognized when liabilities are established for payment of the goods or services received. Costs of assets are deferred and charged to expense in the period in which the assets are used or consumed.

If inventories are a substantial factor in producing income, the company must use the accrual basis for recognizing sales, cost of goods sold, and related asset (inventory and accounts receivable) and liability (accounts payable) accounts. Accountants use several different methods to account for inventories. Each method assumes a different flow of costs and thus results in a different taxable income if used for tax purposes. In recent years many firms have adopted LIFO (last-in, first-out), in which the last goods purchased are assumed to be the first ones sold. Under this method, during periods of rising prices, the most recent **higher** costs are charged against revenues and the asset, inventory, is shown at lower earlier costs. The result is lower net income and lower taxes. The tax law generally permits a company to use the LIFO method for tax purposes only if it uses LIFO for financial statement purposes.

Modified Cash Method.   Sole proprietorships, partnerships, and certain small corporations may use a modified cash method. This method is described as a "modified" (rather than a "pure") cash method because long-term assets cannot be charged to expense when purchased, nor can all prepaid expenses (such as a three-year insurance premium) be deducted when paid. Also, revenues must be reported when constructively received even though the cash is not yet in the possession of the business. For instance, a check received at the end of the year is considered revenue even though it has not been cashed.

Depreciation Methods Used for Tax Purposes.   Tax depreciation is substantially different than depreciation used for accounting purposes. In accounting, depreciation methods are designed to match the expense of a capital investment against the revenue the investment produces. The depreciable period or useful life used for tax purposes is based on law and has no relationship to the actual useful life of the asset; thus, no attempt is made to match revenue and expenses.

Prior to 1981, several depreciation methods were available for tax purposes, including the sum-of-the-years'-digits method and the uniform-rate-on-declining-balance method. The Economic Recovery Tax Act of 1981 introduced a new depreciation system known as the **Accelerated Cost Recovery System (ACRS).** However, generally effective January 1, 1987, the Tax Reform Act of 1986 substantially modified the ACRS rules. For purposes of this appendix, we shall refer to these rules as **modified ACRS.**

The assets are grouped into one of eight different classes (see Illustration A.2). Each class has an assigned life over which costs of the assets (not reduced by salvage) are depreciated.

Assets in the 3-, 5-, 7-, and 10-year classes may be depreciated by using the 200% declining-balance method. Assets in the 15- and 20-year classes may be depreciated by using the 150% declining-balance method. Assets in the 27.5- and 31.5-year classes must be depreciated by using straight-line depreciation. The declining-balance methods result in faster write-offs in the first few years of an investment's life. Cash saved from reduced taxes in the early years of life of the assets can be invested in new productive assets or can be applied to the replacement of the old assets when they become obsolete or worn out.

Illustration A.2

Modified ACRS

Class of Investment	Kinds of Assets
3 years	Investment in some short-lived assets.
5 years	Automobiles, light-duty trucks, and machinery and equipment used in research and development.
7 years	All other machinery and equipment, such as dies, drills, or presses, furniture, and fixtures.
10 years	Some longer-lived equipment.
15 years	Sewage treatment plants and telephone distribution plants.
20 years	Sewer pipes and very long-lived equipment.
27.5 years	Residential rental property.
31.5 years	Nonresidential real estate.

Once the asset has been classified, the depreciation schedule for the life of the asset can be completed. To illustrate a depreciation schedule, assume that Bigwig Company acquired and placed in service a depreciable asset on January 1, 1988, for $10,000. The asset falls into the three-year class under the new tax law. The depreciation schedule for the asset would be as follows:

Year	Recovery Percentage* ×	Original Cost =	Depreciation Expense	Total Accumulated Depreciation	Book Value
1988	33.33%	× $10,000	$3,333	$ 3,333	$6,667
1989	44.45	× 10,000	4,445	7,778	2,222
1990	14.81	× 10,000	1,481	9,259	741
1991	7.41	× 10,000	741	10,000	0

* These cost recovery percentages are from IRS Revenue Procedure 87–57.

Tax depreciation is desirable since it decreases taxable income and hence the corporation's tax liability. However, it is sometimes beneficial for taxpayers to spread out depreciation rather than bunching it in the earlier years of asset life. For this reason, the law provides an alternative. The taxpayer may elect to use the straight-line method rather than the accelerated (table) method.

■ INCOME TAX ALLOCATION

Taxable income and income before federal income taxes (for simplicity, pre-tax income) for a corporation may differ sharply for a number of reasons. In fact, the tax return may show a loss, while the income statement shows positive pre-tax income. This difference raises a question about the amount of income taxes to be shown on the income statement. The answer lies in the nature of the items causing the difference between taxable income and pre-tax income. Some items create permanent differences, while others create temporary (or timing) differences. Both kinds of differences are discussed below.

Permanent Differences

Certain types of revenues and expenses included in the computation of net income for book purposes are excluded from the computation of taxable income. **Permanent differences** between taxable income and financial statement pre-tax income are caused by tax law provisions that exclude an item of expense, revenue, gain, or loss as an element of taxable income. For instance, interest earned on certain state, county, or municipal bonds is included in book net income but is not subject to tax and therefore is not included in determining taxable income. The same is true for life insurance proceeds received by a corporation. Other items that are expensed for book purposes are not deductible for tax purposes, such as premiums paid for officers' life insurance, costs of attempting to influence legislation, and amortization of goodwill. These are only a few of numerous items for which the tax treatment is completely different from the accounting treatment. These differences in treatment **never** change or reverse themselves. Therefore they are called **permanent differences.** Such differences cause no accounting problem—the estimated actual amount of income tax expense for the year is shown on the income statement even if this results in reporting only $1,000 of income tax expenses on $100,000 of pre-tax income.

Temporary Differences

Other items of revenue and expense are often recognized for tax purposes at times different than those for financial reporting purposes. Such temporary differences between taxable income and financial statement pre-tax income are caused by items that affect both taxable income and pre-tax income, but in different periods.

A **temporary (or timing) difference** is a difference between taxable income and financial statement pre-tax income caused by items that affect both taxable income and pre-tax income, but in different periods. For example, interpretations of the tax code generally have held that revenue received in advance is taxable when received and that current expenses based on estimates of future costs (such as costs of performance under service contracts) are not deductible until incurred. Temporary differences can also result from using accounting methods for tax purposes that are different than the ones used for financial reporting purposes. For example, a corporation may use straight-line depreciation for book purposes and modified ACRS depreciation for tax purposes. Eventually these revenues and expenses are recognized in computing both accounting income and taxable income. Therefore, these variations between taxable income and pre-tax income are called temporary differences.

On its federal tax return, a corporation must include a schedule reconciling (1) income before federal income taxes per the income statement with (2) taxable income on the tax return. Such a schedule could include a temporary difference involving depreciation and could appear as follows:

Income before federal income taxes per income statement		$74,000
Add:		
Life insurance premiums paid	$ 700	
Service revenue received in advance	5,000	
Estimated expenses under service contracts	1,000	6,700
		$80,700
Deduct:		
Interest on New York State bonds	$3,000	
Difference in depreciation for tax purposes ($8,000)		
and for book purposes ($6,000)	2,000	5,000
Taxable income		$75,700

As discussed above, temporary differences include items that will be included in both taxable income and in pre-tax income, but in different periods. The items involved thus will have a tax effect. When there are temporary differences, generally accepted accounting principles require application of tax allocation procedures. Under **interperiod income tax allocation,** the tax effect of an element of expense or revenue, or loss or gain, that will affect taxable income is allocated to the period in which the item is recognized for accounting purposes, regardless of the period in which the element is recognized for tax purposes.

In the preceding reconciliation between income before federal income taxes and taxable income, the life insurance premiums paid (for which the corporation is beneficiary of the policy) are **never deductible** for income tax purposes, and the interest on New York State bonds is **never taxable.** These are permanent differences and therefore involve no interperiod income tax allocation. The other reconciling items are temporary differences for which interperiod income tax allocation procedures are required.

Income Tax Allocation Illustrated.   To illustrate the tax allocation procedure required for temporary differences, assume that:

1. A firm acquired a depreciable asset on January 1, 1988, for $10,000 that has an estimated life of three years with no expected salvage value.
2. The firm uses the straight-line depreciation method for financial reporting purposes and the new modified ACRS method for tax purposes (the asset falls into the three-year class for which depreciation has been previously calculated).
3. Net income before depreciation and income taxes is $10,000 for each year of the asset's life.
4. No other items cause differences between pre-tax income and taxable income.
5. The tax rate is 15% (to simplify the illustration).

The tax liability for each year would be as shown in Illustration A.3.

Illustration A.3   *Calculation of Tax Liability*

	1988	1989	1990	1991	Total
Income before depreciation and federal income taxes	$10,000	$10,000	$10,000	$10,000	$40,000
Depreciation for tax purposes	3,333	4,445	1,481	741	10,000
Taxable income	$ 6,667	$ 5,555	$ 8,519	$ 9,259	$30,000
Income taxes payable (15% of taxable income)	$ 1,000	$ 833	$ 1,278	$ 1,389	$ 4,500

Income tax expense for each year for financial reporting purposes would be as shown in Illustration A.4.

Illustration A.4   *Calculation of Tax Expense*

	1988	1989	1990	1991	Total
Income before depreciation and federal income taxes	$10,000	$10,000	$10,000	$10,000	$40,000
Depreciation (straight-line method)*	3,333	3,333	3,334	–0–	10,000
Pre-tax income	$ 6,667	$ 6,667	$ 6,666	$10,000	$30,000
Federal income tax expense (15% of pre-tax income)	1,000	1,000	1,000	1,500	4,500
Net income	$ 5,667	$ 5,667	$ 5,666	$ 8,500	$25,500

* Rounded.

Note that for 1989 and 1991, tax depreciation exceeds the book expense for depreciation, but that for 1990 the opposite is true. For the entire period 1988–1991, both book and tax depreciation are the same ($10,000). The annual differences in book and tax depreciation cause annual differences in income tax expense and income taxes payable. These latter differences are recorded in the Deferred Federal Income Tax Payable account. The required entries for 1988 and 1989 to record income tax expense, income tax payable, and deferred income tax payable are:

	1988		1989	
Federal Income Tax Expense	1,000		1,000	
Federal Income Tax Payable		1,000		833
Deferred Federal Income Tax Payable		–0–		167
To record income tax expense.				

The required entries for 1990 and 1991 to record income tax expense, income tax payable, and defferred income tax payable are:

	1990		1991	
Federal Income Tax Expense	1,000		1,500	
Deferred Federal Income Tax Payable	278			111
Federal Income Tax Payable		1,278		1,389
To record income tax expense.				

Note that the amount of tax expense recognized remains constant at $1,000 even though the tax liability varies from $833 for 1989 to $1,389 for 1991. The normalizing of the tax expense for each year is accomplished by making entries in the Deferred Federal Income Tax Payable account. The tables clearly show that the tax expense for the four years is $4,500 and that the tax payments for the four years also sum to $4,500. The only difference is that the tax expense charged to each year is not the same amount as the actual liability for the year.

In this simplified example, the Deferred Federal Income Tax Payable account has a zero balance at the end of four years. But actual business experience has shown that once a Deferred Federal Income Tax Payable account is established, it is seldom decreased or reduced to zero. The reason is that most businesses acquire new depreciable assets, usually at higher prices. The result is that depreciation for tax purposes continues to be greater than depreciation for financial reporting purposes, and the balance in the Deferred Federal Income Tax Payable account also continues to grow. For this reason, many accountants seriously question the validity of tax allocation in circumstances such as those described above. Also, some accountants question whether a company can have a liability at a reporting date for income taxes for tax years that have not yet started. But discussion of these controversial issues must be left to more advanced texts. In the above example, the Deferred Federal Income Tax Payable account would be reported as a long-term liability on the balance sheet because the asset causing its existence is classified as a long-term asset.

■ THE NEED FOR TAX PLANNING

Numerous examples could be given for showing that business decisions are influenced greatly by their tax effects. With the advent of relatively high tax rates, tax planning has become an essential function of management.

The tax laws are extremely complicated and are changing constantly. Those persons who desire to stay current with the status of the law, and with the interpretations of the law made by courts, must specialize in this area.

PERSONAL FEDERAL INCOME TAXES

The remainder of this appendix gives an introductory understanding of personal income taxes. The provisions described on the tax laws went into effect in late 1988.

■ WHO MUST FILE A RETURN

In general, all U.S. citizens and resident aliens must file a federal income tax return. More specifically, the determination of who must file a return depends on filing status and income level. For 1988, the income levels at which a tax return must be filed are $4,950 for a single person; $5,700 if age 65 or older; $8,980 for a married couple filing a joint return; $8,160 if one spouse is age 65 or older; and $10,100 if both are age 65 or older.

Filing Status

Four basic filing statuses can be used in filing an income tax return. These are single, married filing jointly, married filing separately, and head of household. All of these are self-explanatory except **head of household,** which typically is an unmarried or legally separated person who maintains a residence for a person qualifying as a dependent of the taxpayer.

■ GROSS INCOME

Illustration A.5 contains a general model of the determination of taxable income. The model starts with gross (total) income. **Gross income** includes all income from whatever source derived, except income specifically exempted, such as social security benefits. Gross income includes wages, interest, dividends, tips, bonuses, gambling winnings, gains from property sales, and prizes (including noncash prizes). Even income generated illegally, such as by theft, must be included in gross income. The general rule is that every income item, unless specifically exempted by law, must be included in gross income.

Illustration A.5

Determination of Taxable Income for an Individual Taxpayer

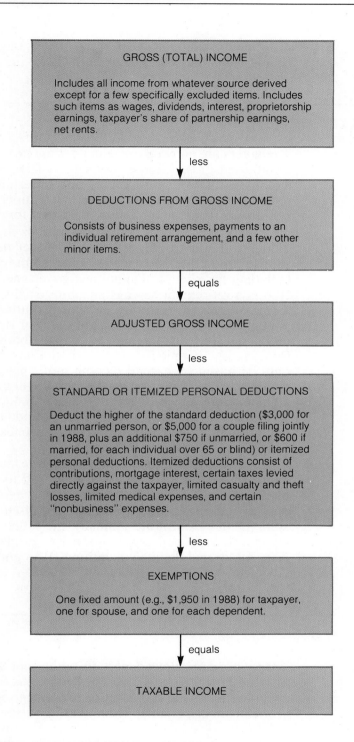

GROSS (TOTAL) INCOME

Includes all income from whatever source derived except for a few specifically excluded items. Includes such items as wages, dividends, interest, proprietorship earnings, taxpayer's share of partnership earnings, net rents.

less

DEDUCTIONS FROM GROSS INCOME

Consists of business expenses, payments to an individual retirement arrangement, and a few other minor items.

equals

ADJUSTED GROSS INCOME

less

STANDARD OR ITEMIZED PERSONAL DEDUCTIONS

Deduct the higher of the standard deduction ($3,000 for an unmarried person, or $5,000 for a couple filing jointly in 1988, plus an additional $750 if unmarried, or $600 if married, for each individual over 65 or blind) or itemized personal deductions. Itemized deductions consist of contributions, mortgage interest, certain taxes levied directly against the taxpayer, limited casualty and theft losses, limited medical expenses, and certain "nonbusiness" expenses.

less

EXEMPTIONS

One fixed amount (e.g., $1,950 in 1988) for taxpayer, one for spouse, and one for each dependent.

equals

TAXABLE INCOME

Exclusions from Gross Income

Income items specifically excluded are interest on certain state and municipal bonds, social security benefits, worker's compensation insurance benefits, and several employee "fringe" benefits, such as employer-paid health insurance premiums. Also, gifts, inheritances, certain disability benefits, scholarships, and the proceeds from life insurance policies are excluded.

■ ADJUSTED GROSS INCOME

Taxpayers are allowed to deduct certain items from gross income in arriving at **adjusted gross income. Deductions from gross income** include business expenses (only 80% of meals and entertainment), payments by certain individuals to individual retirement accounts (IRAs) or payments to Keogh retirement plans, and alimony paid to a former spouse.

Employees can also deduct from gross income contributions to an individual retirement account (IRA) if neither the taxpayer nor the taxpayer's spouse are active participants in an employer-sponsored retirement plan, including tax-sheltered annuities, government plans, and Keogh plans. An IRA is a retirement savings account usually set up in a bank, savings and loan association, insurance company, mutual fund, or brokerage firm. The annual deduction is limited to the lesser of 100% of earnings or $2,000 for an individual, $4,000 for a married couple if both spouses have jobs, and $2,250 for a married couple if only one spouse has earned income. Deductions can only be based on earned income, not "passive" income, such as interest and dividends. The maximum amount will be phased out, however, where adjusted gross income (before the IRA deduction) is over $40,000 on a joint return or $25,000 for an unmarried individual. The deduction will be eliminated when adjusted gross income reaches $50,000 on a joint return or $35,000 for an unmarried person.

Because self-employed individuals are not covered by company-established retirement plans, they are allowed to establish their own retirement plan called a Keogh plan (pronounced Key-oh). Keogh plans are available only to self-employed individuals. A self-employed individual (e.g., a consultant) may contribute annually the lesser of $30,000 or 20% of earned income to a defined contribution Keogh plan under the 1986 Tax Reform Act. Additional details concerning IRAs and Keogh plans are left to more advanced textbooks.

■ TAXABLE INCOME

Taxpayers are allowed certain additional deductions and exemptions in arriving at **taxable income.** The **deductions from adjusted gross income** are specified by law and consist of two categories: (1) standard deduction and (2) itemized or personal deductions. The **standard deduction amount** in 1988 is $3,000 for single persons and for persons filing as head of household, $5,000 for married couples filing a joint return, and $2,500 for married persons filing separate returns. The standard deduction may be increased for each individual or spouse by an additional $600 ($750 for unmarried individual) for each case of being over 65 or blind. Individuals may use either the standard deduction amount or the total of the itemized deductions, whichever is higher. A taxpayer will itemize deductions only if they exceed the standard deduction amount.

Itemized Deductions

The more common **itemized deductions** include:

1. Taxes. Real estate taxes, personal property taxes, and state and local income taxes are deductible. License fees, state sales taxes, and federal excise taxes are not deductible.

2. Interest. Interest paid on mortgages on the principal residence and the second residence is generally deductible. The interest must be attributable to loans not exceeding the original purchase price plus the cost of any home improvements (unless the excess mortgage is incurred for educational or medical expenses).

3. Charitable contributions. Gifts to educational, religious, scientific, and charitable organizations are deductible to the extent they do not exceed 50% of adjusted gross income. Donations to individuals, labor unions, and organizations that seek to influence legislation are not deductible.

4. Medical expenses. Within certain limits, unreimbursed hospital, medical, and dental expenses incurred by taxpayers and their dependents are deductible. Only that amount of medical costs that exceeds 7.5% of adjusted gross income is deductible. The entire cost of prescription drugs and insulin can be included in medical costs. The cost of other drugs and medicines cannot be included.

To clarify the treatment of medical expenses, assume that in 1987 a taxpayer with an adjusted gross income of $20,000 paid $550 of health insurance premiums, incurred other medical expenses of $700, and incurred prescription drug costs of $400. The medical deduction is:

Health insurance premiums	$ 550
Other unreimbursed medical expenses	700
Medicine costs	400
	$1,650
Less: 7.5% of adjusted gross income (0.075 × $20,000)	1,500
Medical deduction	$ 150

5. Casualty losses. Casualty losses are sudden and unexpected losses resulting from theft, accidents, storms, fires, and similar events. They are deductible to the extent that **each** casualty loss exceeds $100, **and** that the total of all unreimbursed casualty losses for the year exceeds 10% of adjusted gross income. Thus, to compute the deduction, subtract $100 from the dollar amount of **each** loss (ignore losses of less than $100) to obtain an adjusted casualty loss. Then, from the sum of the adjusted casualty losses, subtract 10% of adjusted gross income. The positive difference is the casualty loss deduction. To illustrate, assume a taxpayer had adjusted gross income of $50,000 and suffered two casualty losses during the year—a fire loss of $9,000 and a theft loss of $12,000. The casualty loss deduction is computed as follows:

Adjusted fire loss ($9,000 − $100)	$ 8,900
Adjusted theft loss ($12,000 − $100)	11,900
Total	$20,800
Less: 10% of adjusted gross income	5,000
Casualty loss deduction	$15,800

6. Other deductions.   In general, this category consists of expenses related to the taxpayer's business or profession that are not deductible from gross income. Included are the costs of professional publications and dues, union dues, safe-deposit box rentals, income tax preparer's fees, business entertainment, and job-related clothing and tools. These miscellaneous deductions are only deductible to the extent that they exceed 2% of adjusted gross income.

Exemptions

The final step to determine taxable income is to deduct exemptions. The dollar amount of exemptions is determined by multiplying the number of exemptions allowed the taxpayer by $1,950 in 1988. The exemption allowance increases to $2,000 in 1989, and will increase again in the future because of indexing for inflation. Thus, if a taxpayer has two exemptions in 1988, the dollar amount would be $3,900 ($1,950 × 2). Married persons filing jointly are both considered taxpayers and are allowed one exemption each even though only one spouse has income. An additional exemption may be taken for each dependent.

A dependent for tax purposes is a person who (1) is closely related to the taxpayer or who lived as a member of the taxpayer's family for the entire year; (2) had an income of less than $1,950; (3) received more than half of his or her support from the taxpayer; and (4) who, if married, did not file a joint return with a spouse for the taxable year. An individual eligible to be claimed as a dependent on another taxpayer's return may not deduct any amount as a personal exemption. Beginning in 1988, personal exemptions will be phased out for certain high-income taxpayers.

■ COMPUTING TAX LIABILITY

Once taxable income has been determined, the tax liability can be computed using the rates given in Illustration A.6. The tax rates in effect for 1988 will be used unless otherwise stated.

Illustration A.6 *Tax Rates for 1988 Tax Returns*

Married Filing Jointly	Head of Household	Single
$0–$29,750 . . . 15% $29,750–$71,900 . . . 28 $71,900–$149,250* . . . 33 Over $149,250 . . . 28	$0–$25,300 . . . 15% $25,300–$61,650 . . . 28 $61,650–$123,790* . . . 33 Over $123,790 . . . 28	$0–$17,850 . . . 15% $17,850–$43,150 . . . 28 $43,150–$89,560* . . . 33 Over $89,560 . . . 28

* The top figure for the 33% bracket increases by $10,920 in 1988 for each exemption.

To illustrate the use of these rates, assume Mr. and Mrs. Olson file a joint return showing taxable income of $36,280. Their tax liability is computed as follows:

$$\begin{aligned}
\$29,750 \times 0.15 &= \$4,462.50 \\
(\$36,280 - \$29,750) \times 0.28 &= \underline{1,828.40} \\
& \ \ \$6,290.90
\end{aligned}$$

Marginal and Effective Tax Rates

A quick look at the tax rate schedules in Illustration A.6 shows clearly that the rates are progressive. Progressive tax rates increase with successively higher amounts of taxable income. For example, the taxable income of a single taxpayer between $17,850 and $43,150 is taxed at a 28% rate. These percentages are called marginal tax rates. A **marginal tax rate** is the rate applied to the next dollar of taxable income or each incremental amount of income. Such rates are important in decision making because they show the marginal effect of a decision. For example, assume that Joe Hardy, a single taxpayer in the 28% tax bracket, could earn $400 on a plumbing job if he would work on Sunday. But being in the 28% bracket means that Joe would have to pay $112 ($400 × 0.28) more income taxes if he takes the job, which means that he would net only $288 from the job. Joe may decide he would rather watch a football game or go fishing. This type of analysis illustrates the correct use of the marginal tax rate.

The effective tax rate rather than the marginal rate should be used as a measure of total taxes to be paid. The **effective tax rate** is the average rate of taxation of a given amount of taxable income. For example, if Joe Hardy earns $34,600 for the year, he is in the 28% marginal tax rate bracket. But he does not pay $9,688 ($34,600 × 0.28) per year in taxes. Joe actually pays taxes at a 21.3% rate computed as follows:

$$\frac{\text{Effective}}{\text{(average) tax rate}} = \frac{\text{Total taxes paid}}{\text{Total taxable income}}$$

$$\text{Effective tax rate} = \frac{(\$17,850 \times 0.15) + [0.28 \times (\$34,600 - \$17,850)]^*}{\$34,600}$$

$$\text{Effective tax rate} = \frac{\$7,367.50}{\$34,600} = 21.3\%$$

* These rates were taken from Illustration A.6 for a single taxpayer.

■ CAPITAL GAINS AND LOSSES

Capital assets are all items of property other than inventories, receivables, copyrights, certain governmental obligations, and real and depreciable property used in a trade or business. Investments in capital stocks and bonds are examples of capital assets. A gain is an excess of selling price over cost.

Taxation of Capital Gains

Some capital gains escape taxation. For example, a taxpayer, age 55 or older, may exclude from gross income up to $125,000 ($62,500 on a separate return) of any gain on sale of the taxpayer's home.

All other capital gains are taxed at the same rates as ordinary income, but not to exceed 28%.

The tax law relative to net losses is more complex, containing certain limitations. Discussion of losses is left for a more advanced course.

■ TAX CREDITS

A tax credit is a direct deduction from the amount of taxes to be paid, resulting largely from certain expenditures made by the taxpayer. Because tax credits reduce the amount of taxes to be paid dollar for dollar, they are much more valuable to the taxpayer than deductions. A tax credit of $100 saves $100 of cash; a $100 deduction, on the other hand, is worth only $100 times the taxpayer's marginal tax rate. The maximum value, then, of any deduction in 1988 is 33% of the amount of the deduction since the highest tax rate is 33%.

Tax credits are available for persons with low earned income levels, for the elderly, for child and dependent care expenses, for income taxes paid to foreign countries, and for wages paid in work incentive programs.

■ FILING THE TAX RETURN

Personal tax returns generally must be filed on or by April 15 of the year following the tax year. Extensions may be filed, but payment of any tax liability is still due on April 15. Most taxpayers are also employees; therefore, taxes are withheld by employers under our pay-as-you-go tax system. Also, taxpayers having income above a prescribed amount that is not subject to withholding must pay an estimated tax. This estimated tax must be paid in four installments. The taxes withheld and the estimated taxes paid are entered as offsets to the total tax liability on the tax return. Any remaining unpaid taxes are paid to the Internal Revenue Service when the return is filed. In some cases, tax withholdings and estimated taxes paid may have exceeded tax liability, and the taxpayer can claim a refund.

■ COMPREHENSIVE ILLUSTRATION—PERSONAL INCOME TAXES

An actual tax return consists of a number of preprinted forms that are filled out by the taxpayer. Taxpayers normally will file either Form 1040A, often called the short form, or Form 1040, the long form. A taxpayer who intends to itemize deductions cannot file a short form, 1040A. A taxpayer who uses the long form generally must attach various schedules to it. Two common schedules included in the long form are Schedule A and Schedule B. Schedule A shows the itemized deductions, while Schedule B lists all dividends and interest income when dividend and interest income exceeds $400. As mentioned either in this chapter, one copy of the taxpayer's Form W-2 is attached to the tax return. The W-2 is issued by the employer and shows wages earned and taxes withheld during the period on these wages.

Illustration A.7 shows a brief summary schedule of the tax return items for Lee and Dora Bowman, for 1988, who are married and file a joint return. Lee is chief engineer for a manufacturing company; Dora is a full-time homemaker. Both taxpayers are under age 65; they have two dependent children, ages 13 and 15. Dora owns a number of bonds and shares of stock,

Illustration A.7

Joint Tax Return Computations

Salary		$58,000
Interest income		4,000
Dividend income		6,000
Capital gain ($10,000) less capital loss ($1,000)		9,000
Total		$77,000
Contribution to an individual retirement account		–0–
Adjusted gross income		$77,000
Itemized deductions:		
Medical expense ($5,925 − $5,775; total medical costs less 7.5% of adjusted gross income)	$ 150	
Charitable contributions	2,240	
Taxes (real estate on home, state income)	5,670	
Casualty loss ($8,250 − $7,700; total adjusted casualty losses less 10% of adjusted gross income)	550	
Miscellaneous (professional dues, subscriptions, etc.) [$1,980 − ($77,000 × 0.02)]	440	
	$ 9,050	
Standard deduction amount	3,760	
Higher of itemized versus standard deduction		9,050
		$67,950
Exemptions (4 × $1,950)		7,800
Taxable income		$60,150
Income tax (0.15 × $29,750) + (0.28 × $30,400)		$12,975
Less: Applicable tax credits		–0–
Total tax liability		$12,975
Income taxes withheld	$12,400	
Estimated taxes paid	800	13,200
Income taxes refund due		$ 225

some of which she sold during the year, realizing $10,000 of capital gains and $1,000 of capital losses. Total income taxes withheld during the year amounted to $12,400. In addition, Lee and Dora paid estimated taxes of $800. Other information needed to compute the Bowmans' tax liability and tax payment are shown in the illustration. The income tax of $12,975 is computed using the tax rate schedule in Illustration A.6.

NEW TERMS INTRODUCED IN APPENDIX A

Adjusted gross income Gross income less deductions for adjusted gross income such as business expenses, certain payments to an individual retirement account (IRA), and certain other deductions (1188).

Capital assets All items of property other than inventories, trade accounts and notes receivable, copyrights, government obligations due within one year and issued at a discount, and real or depreciable property used in a trade or business. Examples include investments in capital stocks and bonds (1192).

Deductions from adjusted gross income Specified by law; either standard deduction amount or itemized deductions (1188).

Deductions from gross income Expenses of carrying on a trade, business, or practice of a profession, certain payments to an IRA or Keogh plan, and alimony paid (1188).

Effective tax rate Average rate of taxation for a given amount of taxable income (1191).

Estimated tax A tax that must be paid in four installments by persons having amounts of income above a certain level that are not subject to withholding (1192).

Exemptions A fixed amount, $1,950 in 1988, that a taxpayer may deduct from adjusted gross income for the taxpayer, the spouse, and one more for each dependent (1190).

Gross income All items of income from whatever source derived, except for those items specifically excluded by law (1186).

Head of household Certain unmarried or legally separated persons (and those married to nonresident aliens) who maintain a residence for a relative or dependent (1186).

Interperiod income tax allocation A procedure whereby the tax effects of an element of expense or revenue, or loss or gain, that will affect taxable income is allocated to the period in which the item is recognized for accounting purposes, regardless of the period in which the element is recognized for tax purposes (1183).

Itemized deductions Deductions from adjusted gross income for items such as contributions, mortgage interest paid, taxes, casualty losses, limited medical expenses, and other employment-related expenses (1189).

Loss carryback Provision in tax law permitting corporations to apply a loss to their taxable income from three prior years and recover some or all of the taxes paid during those years (1179).

Loss carryforward Provision in tax law permitting corporations to carry any remaining, unused loss forward for up to 15 years to reduce their taxable income in future years (1180).

Marginal tax rate The tax rate that will be levied against the next dollar of taxable income (1191).

Modified ACRS A tax method of depreciation that assigns assets into particular groups that have specified lives for depreciation purposes. The 1986 Tax Reform Act modified the Accelerated Cost Recovery System (1181).

Permanent differences Differences between taxable income and financial statement pre-tax income caused by tax law provisions that exclude an item of expense, revenue, gain, or loss as an element of taxable income (1182).

Standard deduction amount An amount that can be taken in lieu of itemized deductions. For 1988 the amount is $3,000 for single persons and for persons filing as heads of households, $5,000 for married couples filing a joint return, and $2,500 for married persons filing separate returns. An additional $750 (or $600 if married) is allowed for each individual over 65 or blind (1188).

Tax credit A direct reduction from the amount of taxes to be paid, resulting largely from certain expenditures made (1192).

Taxable income Adjusted gross income less deductions and exemptions (1188).

Temporary (or timing) differences Differences between taxable income and financial statement pre-tax income caused by items that affect both taxable income and pre-tax income, but in different periods (1183).

QUESTIONS

1. What factors might cause net income on a corporation's income statement to differ from its taxable income?

2. Classified among the long-term liabilities of a corporation is an account entitled Deferred Federal Income Taxes Payable. Explain the nature of this account.

3. Define the term *adjusted gross income* as it is used for personal income tax purposes.

4. For what kinds of expenditures may personal deductions be taken on one's personal federal income tax return?

5. What are exemptions, and by how much does each one reduce taxable income?

EXERCISES

E-1
Compute corporate tax liability

a. Wexley Corporation has taxable income of $20,000, $50,000, and $70,000 in its first three years of operations. Determine the amount of federal income taxes Wexley will incur each year, assuming 1988 tax rates for all years.
b. Assume that in the fourth year of operations, Wexley Corporation suffered a loss of $95,000. How much could it recover in back taxes?

E-2
Prepare journal entry to record income tax chargeable and tax liability for year

The before-tax income reported on the income statement of R Corporation for a given year amounts to $200,000, while its taxable income is only $160,000. The difference is attributable entirely to additional modified ACRS depreciation taken for tax purposes. If the current income tax rate is assumed to be 40%, give the entry to record the income tax expense for the year and the taxes payable for the year.

E-3
Compute tax liability

John Franks has gross income of $40,000, deductions from gross income of $2,000, itemized deductions of $1,500, and six full exemptions (two personal and four dependent). He is filing a joint return with his wife, who has no income. How much is their tax liability? (Use the 1988 rates, $1,950 per exemption, and $5,000 standard deduction amount.)

PROBLEMS

PA-1
Calculate tax liability, making various assumptions about a loss carryback

Hatcher Company has the following amounts of taxable income (loss) in the years indicated:

1985	$30,000
1986	20,000
1987	60,000
1988 . . . [See parts *(a)*, *(b)*, and *(c)* below.]	
1989	40,000

1990	10,000
1991	50,000
1992	70,000
1993	80,000
1994	65,000

Assume that the rates for 1988 are in effect for all years shown above.

Required:
a. If the loss in 1988 was $110,000, how much would the company recover in back taxes if it is carried back as far as possible?
b. If the loss in 1988 was $180,000, how much would the company have to pay in taxes for the period 1989–94?
c. If the loss in 1988 was $400,000, how much would the company have to pay in taxes for the period 1989–94?
d. If there is a remaining unused carryforward at the end of 15 years, what happens to it?

PA-2
Prepare schedules showing taxable income, income taxes due, and income tax allocation; prepare year-end entries to recognize income tax expense

On January 1, 1988, of year 1, Alexis Corporation acquired an asset for $200,000 that is expected to have a four-year life and no salvage value. The company decided to use the straight-line method of depreciation for book purposes. The machine is three-year modified ACRS property. No other temporary differences exist. Net income before depreciation and income taxes is $200,000 for each of the four years.

Assume that the recovery percentages are 25%, 37.5%, 18.75%, and 18.75% for each of the four years, respectively.

Required:
a. Prepare a schedule showing taxable income and income taxes due for each of the four years (assuming a 40% tax rate for the sake of simplicity).
b. Prepare a schedule showing the income tax expense, assuming income tax allocation procedures are used.
c. Prepare the year-end adjusting entry required at the end of each of the four years to recognize federal income tax expense.
d. Show how the entries prepared in part *(c)* would be summarized in T-accounts. How would the amounts appearing in these accounts eventually be cleared from the accounts?

PA-3
Calculate taxable income and tax liability

Ellen Albee gathered together her income tax information for 1988. She is single and has no other dependents. She accumulated the following data:

Salary	$15,000
Royalties received	1,500
Interest received on savings account	600
Capital gain	7,500
Contribution to individual retirement account	
(assume not participating in employer plan)	2,000
Property taxes on residence	1,300
State income tax	1,600
Interest paid on first home mortgage	3,250
Contributions to church and other charitable organizations . . .	1,400

Required: Calculate Ellen Albee's taxable income and tax liability for 1988.

PA-4
Prepare schedule showing computation of taxable income; compute the tax liability

The records of Seek Corporation show the following for the calendar year just ended:

Sales	$375,000
Nontaxable interest earned on:	
State of New York bonds	3,000
City of Detroit bonds	1,500
Howard County, Ohio, School District No. 1 bonds	375
Cost of goods sold and other expenses	315,000

Loss on sale of asset	3,000
Gain on sale of asset acquired two years ago	7,500
Allowable extra depreciation deduction for tax purposes	4,500
Dividends declared	15,000
Revenue received in advance, considered taxable income of this year	3,000
Contribution made to influence legislation (included in the $315,000 listed above)	300

Required:
a. Present a schedule showing the computation of taxable income.
b. Compute the corporation's tax for the current year. (Use the tax rates mentioned in this appendix.)

APPENDIX

B

Inflation Accounting

■ THE IMPACT OF INFLATION ON FINANCIAL REPORTING

Until recent years, no attempt had been made to include the impact of inflation on the results of operations and financial position of the reporting company. A serious problem faced by accountants—how to account for and report financial data in periods of inflation—is discussed in this appendix.

A **period of inflation** is a time during which prices in general are rising, while a **period of deflation** occurs when prices in general are falling. Only in periods of high inflation, like in the 1970s, has the historical cost approach to recording accounting data been severely criticized. During times of inflation, the historical cost approach often reports a positive net income when the economic value of the owner's investment has not even been maintained.

There are two widely recommended accounting approaches to the problem of inflation. One approach is current cost accounting. The current cost accounting approach shows the current cost or value of items in the financial statements. The other approach is constant dollar accounting, also known as general price-level adjusted accounting. The constant dollar accounting approach shows financial statement historical cost figures as adjusted for changes in the general price level.

The Nature and Measurement of Inflation

In a period of inflation, the "real value" of the dollar—its ability to purchase goods and services—falls. In a period of deflation, the real value of the dollar rises.

Changes in the general level of prices are measured by means of a general price index, such as the consumer price index (CPI). A **price index** is a weighted average of prices for various goods and services. A base year is chosen and assigned a value of 100 for comparative purposes. If the index stands at 108 a year later, this means that prices in general rose 8% during the year. An index of 200 would mean that prices on the average doubled. Because the index is an average, prices of individual types of items may change at different rates and may, in some cases, actually decline. For example, the CPI shows that prices for a "basket" of selected consumer goods doubled in the decade of the 1970s. But during that same decade, gasoline prices quadrupled, while the price of electronic handheld calculators declined very sharply.

The real value or purchasing power of the dollar relative to that of the base year is shown by the reciprocal of the price index; the ratio is simply inverted. For example, if the index for 1991 is 200 and for 1981 is 100, the price index is 200/100, meaning that prices have doubled since 1981. Alternatively, the reciprocal of the price index is 100/200, meaning that the value of the dollar in 1991 has dropped to one half, or 50%, of its purchasing power in 1981.

Because accounting measurements consist largely of dollars of historical cost, financial reports are inadequate in periods of inflation. **Historical cost accounting** measures accounting transactions in terms of the actual dollars expended or received. Such a measurement system has worked well in periods of stable prices. But the system does not work well when the dollar, in terms of its purchasing power, is a sharply changing unit of measure.

To illustrate, assume that a tract of land was purchased for $2,000 and held several years before being sold for $2,500. While the land was held, a general price index rose from 100 to 140. Historical cost accounting would report recovery of the $2,000 cost and income of $500 as a gain on sale of the land. But if we measure this transaction in terms of dollars of constant purchasing power, a far different result is obtained. To get back the purchasing power originally invested in the land, the land would have to be sold for $2,800 ($2,000 × 140/100). Since only $2,500 was received, no real income has been earned because the cost has not been recovered. In fact, a loss of $300 of current purchasing power was incurred.

Consequences of Ignoring Effects of Inflation

As shown in the example above, transactions and, therefore, financial statements that have not been adjusted for the effects of inflation may yield misleading information. Such information may make comparisons between companies difficult. Suppose Company A acquired a tract of land for $100,000 several years ago. Now Company B acquires a virtually identical tract of land for $150,000, paying the higher price because prices in general have risen 50% since Company A bought its land. Immediately, both companies sell their land for $150,000 each. Company A would appear to have the more efficient management because it was able to earn $50,000 on the sale of the land, while Company B earned nothing. In reality, the two companies are in the same position relative to the sale of the land because they have the same number of dollars of current purchasing power. The financial statement difference is caused by recording and continuing to carry the land at its historical cost.

As another example of the consequences of ignoring the effects of inflation, assume the above land was instead a depreciable asset, such as a building. Company A and Company B earn exactly the same number of dollars of revenues and incur, except for depreciation, exactly the same number of dollars of expenses. If both companies had assumed a 10-year useful life on the asset and apply straight-line depreciation to the building, Company A will have a larger net income than Company B simply due to the fact that the historical cost of its asset and, therefore, its recorded depreciation expense is lower than for Company B.

Failure to adjust for the impact of inflation may lead to invalid conclusions. A five-year summary of sales may show that sales dollars have increased 50% over the period. If sales prices have increased 60% over the five years, physical sales volume has actually declined.

Other consequences flow from a failure to adjust financial reports for the effects of inflation. Companies are paying taxes on ''income'' when in reality, costs may not have been covered. Also, financial reports that fail to reflect the impact of inflation may be misleading to individual decision makers, causing them to make decisions that are not in their best interest.

Accounting Responses to Changing Prices

Specific price-level changes relate to changes in the price of a particular good or service, such as calculators or computers. General price-level changes relate to the changes in the economy as a whole, such as those reflected by the consumer price index. A specific price-level change may change in the same, or opposite, direction as the general price level, and at the same or a different rate. Because of this, there are two types of price changes (specific and general) and two recommended approaches to accounting for changing prices. These recommended approaches are:

1. Change the basis of measurement from historical cost to current cost or value; this approach is called **current cost accounting.**
2. Change the basis of measurement from the actual historical (nominal) dollar to a dollar of constant purchasing power; this approach is referred to as **constant dollar accounting** (or **general price-level accounting**).

An example of these two approaches is necessary before turning to a more detailed illustration. Assume the following facts regarding the purchase and resale of 1,000 units of a product:

Date	Transaction	Amount	Price-Level Index
January 1, 1991	Purchased 1,000 units	$3,000	100
December 31, 1991	Sold 1,000 units	5,000	120

The current cost of the units on December 31, 1991, was $3,900. The company incurred $800 of expenses to sell the units.

Under conventional (historical cost) accounting, income from operations for 1991 would be:

Sales		$5,000
Cost of goods sold	$3,000	
Other expenses	800	3,800
Income from continuing operations*		$1,200

* Income from continuing operations in most cases is the same as income from operations. The technical difference between these terms is covered in intermediate accounting.

The $1,200 of income results from deducting the historical cost of the goods sold as well as the other expenses from sales revenue. The company appears to be better off after the transactions because it has not only recovered the original dollar investment in the goods, together with the expenses incurred, but also has an additional $1,200. The fact that current replacement cost of the goods sold exceeds their historical cost by $900 ($3,900 − $3,000) is ignored. Also, no attention is paid to the fact that the dollars recovered do not have the same purchasing power as those originally invested.

Using the preceding example, Illustration B.1 compares income from continuing operations under historical cost and each of the two inflation accounting methods.

Illustration B.1

Alternative Reporting Approaches— Statement of Income from Continuing Operations

Statement of Income from Continuing Operations					
	Historical Cost Accounting		Current Cost Accounting		Constant Dollar Accounting
Sales		$5,000		$5,000	$5,000
Cost of goods sold	$3,000		$3,900		$3,600
Other expenses	800		800		800
Total expenses		3,800		4,700	4,400
Income from continuing operations		$1,200		$ 300	$ 600

The second set of columns in Illustration B.1 shows the income from continuing operations using the current cost method. The **current cost** of an asset is the amount that would have to be paid currently to acquire the asset. In the column headed "Current Cost Accounting," income from continuing operations is computed by deducting the current cost of replacing the goods sold and the other expenses from current revenues. No adjustments are made for **general** price-level changes. Calculating income from continuing operations in this manner is supported on the grounds that the sale of an inventory item leads directly to a further action—replenishment of the inventory—if the company is to remain a going concern. A better picture of a company's ability to compete in its markets may also be provided by comparing current revenues with current costs rather than with outdated historical costs. In addition, we can say that only the $300 represents "disposable" income. Only $300 or less can be distributed to owners without reducing the scale of operations since the remainder of the funds is necessary to replace inventory sold and to maintain productive facilities at their present level.

In Illustration B.1, in the column headed "Constant Dollar Accounting," cost of goods sold is restated in end-of-1991 dollars by use of a ratio of the current price index to the old price index: $3,000 \times 120/100 = $3,600$. The $3,600 is the amount of purchasing power invested in the goods expressed in the end-of-1991 dollars. Thus, the $3,600 is restated into the same dollars in which the sales revenue is expressed. The $800 of other expenses is assumed to be selling expenses incurred at point of sales (such as sales commissions), which are already stated in end-of-1991 dollars. All dollar amounts are now expressed in comparable terms—end-of-1991 dollars. The company is better off because it has increased its purchasing power by $600. Under constant dollar accounting, net income is a measurement of increased purchasing power—the entity's increased ability to acquire goods and services.

The next two sections illustrate the current cost and constant dollar accounting methods applied to the income statement of a hypothetical company—Carol Company.

■ CURRENT COST ACCOUNTING

In the past, inflation-adjusted statements have generally been recommended, not required, as supplementary information to conventional financial statements. In 1979, the FASB issued a standard (or Statement) that **required** certain large, publicly held corporations to present certain supplementary information about the effects of inflation.[1]

To illustrate a statement from continuing operations prepared on a current cost basis, we use the data from the historical cost income statement of Carol Company in Illustration B.2.

Management has determined that the cost of goods sold in terms of current cost is $146,000, and the current cost of the plant assets was $160,000 on December 31, 1990, and $180,000 on December 31, 1991. No additions or retirements of plant assets occurred in 1991. Carol Company depreciates its plant assets over a 20-year life, or an annual rate of 5% on a straight-line basis.

Illustration B.2

Statement of Income from Continuing Operations— Historical Cost Basis

CAROL COMPANY
Statement of Income from Continuing Operations
For the Year Ended December 31, 1991

Sales		$200,000
Cost of goods sold:		
Inventory, January 1, 1991	$ 20,000	
Purchases	160,000	
Goods available for sale	$180,000	
Inventory, December 31, 1991	40,000	
Cost of goods sold		140,000
Gross margin		$ 60,000
Depreciation	$ 4,000	
Other expenses	46,000	50,000
Income from continuing operations		$ 10,000

Current cost depreciation for 1991 can be computed by multiplying the average current cost of the plant assets for the year by the annual depreciation rate of 5%. The amount is:

$$\frac{\$160,000 + \$180,000}{2} \times 5\% = \$8,500$$

The $146,000 current cost of goods sold and $8,500 current cost depreciation are shown in the income statement prepared under current cost accounting. There is no need to adjust sales or other expenses since they are already expressed at current cost for the year.

---

[1] FASB, "Financial Reporting and Changing Prices," *Statement of Financial Accounting Standards No. 33* (Stamford, Conn., 1979). Copyright © by Financial Accounting Standards Board. High Ridge Park, Stamford, Connecticut 06905. U.S.A. Quoted (or excerpted) with permission. Copies of the complete document are available from the FASB.

Illustration B.3 shows the amounts that would be reported in the historical cost and current cost income statements shown for Carol Company.

Illustration B.3

Comparison of Historical Cost and Current Cost Income Statements

CAROL COMPANY
Statements of Income from Continuing Operations
For the Year Ended December 31, 1991

	Historical Cost	Current Cost
Sales	$200,000	$200,000
Cost of goods sold	$140,000	$146,000
Depreciation expense	4,000	8,500
Other expenses	46,000	46,000
Total	$190,000	$200,500
Income (loss) from continuing operations	$ 10,000	$ (500)

Current Cost Accounting—Pro and Con

The advantages of current cost accounting include:

1. Specific current costs incurred by a company are shown.
2. Current costs, rather than historical costs, are deducted from current revenues to calculate net income, which allows a more meaningful matching of effort and accomplishment.
3. If dividends are limited to an amount equal to or less than current cost income from continuing operations, the economic capital of the company is maintained.

The disavantages of current cost include:

1. Current costs may be subjective.
2. Current costs may be difficult and costly to determine.

■ CONSTANT DOLLAR ACCOUNTING

As already discussed briefly, historical dollar amounts in an income statement may be converted or restated into a number of constant dollars that have an equivalent amount of purchasing power. When adjusted for inflation, conventional financial statements are called constant dollar or general price-level adjusted financial statements.

To illustrate an income statement prepared on a constant dollar basis, we again refer to Illustration B.2 for Carol Company.

To convert historical dollars into constant end-of-year dollars, the formula is:

$$\text{Historical dollars} \times \frac{\text{Price index at end of current period}}{\text{Price index at date of historical transaction}} = \text{Constant dollars}$$

To convert the income statement of Carol Company, certain assumptions must be made for information provided. These data follow:

1. The general price-level index stood at 100 on December 31, 1990, and at 108 on December 31, 1991.
2. Sales, purchases, other expenses, and taxes were incurred uniformly throughout the year. This means that on the average, these items were incurred when the price index was 104.
3. Inventories are costed on a FIFO basis. The beginning inventory was acquired when the price index was 98, and the ending inventory was acquired when the index stood at 106.
4. The price index was 54 when the plant assets were acquired.

The procedure for converting the Carol Company income statement in Illustration B.2 to constant dollars is as follows. First, all revenues, purchases, and expenses were assumed to occur uniformly throughout the year; therefore, these items are converted by multiplying their historical amounts by a ratio of 108/104. Beginning inventory is converted using a ratio of 108/98, while ending inventory is converted using a 108/106 ratio. Since depreciation is calculated on the historical costs of the related assets that were acquired when the index stood at 54, depreciation expense is converted using a ratio of 108/54. Illustration B.4 shows the restated income statement for Carol Company. Purchasing power gains and losses are discussed in the next section.

Purchasing Power Gains and Losses.   Purchasing power gains and losses result from holding monetary assets and liabilities during inflation or deflation. **Monetary items** are cash and other assets and liabilities that represent fixed claims to cash, such as accounts and notes receivable and payable.

Illustration B.4

Income Statement—Constant Dollar Basis (end-of-year dollars)

CAROL COMPANY Restated Income for the Year Ended December 31, 1991 (in constant end-of-year 1991 dollars)			
	Historical Dollars	× Conversion Ratio	= Constant Dollars
Sales	$200,000 ×	108/104	= $207,692
Cost of goods sold:			
Inventory, January 1, 1991	$ 20,000 ×	108/98	= $ 22,041
Purchases	160,000 ×	108/104	= 166,154
Goods available for sale	$180,000		$188,195
Inventory, December 31, 1991	40,000 ×	108/106	= 40,755
Cost of goods sold	$140,000		$147,440
Gross margin	$ 60,000		$ 60,252
Expenses:			
Depreciation	$ 4,000 ×	108/54	= $ 8,000
Other expenses	46,000 ×	108/104	= 47,769
Total expenses	$ 50,000		$ 55,769
Income from continuing operations	$ 10,000		$ 4,483
Purchasing power gain on monetary items			2,625
Net income	$ 10,000		$ 7,108

Nonmonetary items include all items on the balance sheet other than monetary items. A **purchasing power gain** results from holding monetary liabilities during inflation or monetary assets during deflation. A **purchasing power loss** results from holding monetary assets during inflation or monetary liabilities during deflation.

Assume that Bill Allen holds $1,000 of cash during a year in which prices in general rose 25%. Even though Bill has his $1,000 at year-end, he has less purchasing power than he did at the beginning of the year. Bill needs to have $1,250, calculated as ($1,000 × 125/100), at year-end to be as well off as he was at the start of the year. Therefore, during the year, Bill has sustained a purchasing power loss of $250.

Conversely, a gain results from being in debt during inflation. Assume that Kathy Rice owes $600 during a year in which prices rise 40%. The original debt has a year-end purchasing power equivalent of $840 ($600 × 140/100). Kathy can satisfy the debt by paying $600 currently. Thus, she has experienced a purchasing power gain of $240.

Assume that Carol Company, in Illustration B.4, experienced a purchasing power gain of $2,625 during 1991. This amount would be added to income from continuing operations on the restated income statement. Carol Company has net income on a constant dollar basis of $7,108, which is nearly 30% less than the net income shown on the conventional (historical cost) income statement.

Constant Dollar Accounting—Pro and Con

The advantages of constant dollar accounting include the following:

1. Measurement of the impact of inflation on a company is objective because adjustments made to convert the statements to a constant dollar basis are based on historical cost.
2. Comparability of the financial statements between companies is improved because of the use of the same procedures and the same index numbers for each firm.
3. There is greater comparability of the financial statements of a single company through time since effects of price-level changes are removed by stating all amounts in dollars of the same purchasing power.

The disadvantages of constant dollar accounting include:

1. Benefits resulting from the use of such statements have not been shown to be in excess of the cost of preparing these statements.
2. The assumption that the impact of inflation affects all companies equally is not true.
3. Only one deficiency—the changing value of the measuring unit—is corrected; the effects of specific price changes are ignored. This is undoubtedly the most significant limitation of constant dollar accounting.

Illustration B.5 shows a comparison of all three income statements for Carol Company.

Which method of adjusting for inflation is correct? There is no simple answer. Each method is correct if one accepts the definitions of cost and

Illustration B.5

Inflation Impact Disclosures

CAROL COMPANY
Statement of Income Adjusted for Changing Prices
For the Year Ended December 31, 1991

	Historical Cost	Current Cost	Constant Dollar (end-of-year dollars)
Sales	$200,000	$200,000	$207,692
Cost of goods sold	$140,000	$146,000	$147,440
Expenses:			
Depreciation expense	4,000	8,500	8,000
Other expenses	46,000	46,000	47,769
Total	$190,000	$200,500	$203,209
Income (loss) from continuing operations	$ 10,000	$ (500)	$ 4,483
Purchasing power gain on monetary items			2,625
Net income	$ 10,000	$ (500)	$ 7,108

income assumed under the method. A much more important question is: Which method is more useful to users of the financial reports? The answer to this question has been of considerable concern to many people, including members of the FASB and the staff of the SEC.

■ THE FASB REQUIREMENTS

FASB Statement No. 33 called for disclosure by companies in their annual reports both of the impact of specific price changes and of general inflation on earnings and other selected items. The *Statement* did not require full, completely adjusted financial statements, nor did it affect the way the basic (primary) financial statements are prepared, since all required disclosures appear as supplementary information. The *Statement* applied only to publicly held companies (1) with total assets in excess of $1 billion (after deducting accumulated depreciation) or (2) having $125 million (before deducting accumulated depreciation) of inventories and property, plant, and equipment. Thus, about 1,200 to 1,400 large, publicly held companies were directly affected. The FASB also encouraged all companies to report the effects of inflation by applying the methods described in *FASB Statement No. 33*.

For fiscal years ended on or after December 25, 1979, affected companies initially had to report as supplementary information:

a. Net income on a current cost basis.
b. Net income on a constant dollar basis (historical cost adjusted for the effects of general inflation).
c. Purchasing power gain or loss on monetary items.[2]

Other disclosure requirements, including a five-year summary of selected financial data, also existed.

[2] *FASB Statement No. 33*, pars. 29–35.

Uncertainty over whether constant dollar information or current cost information is preferable caused the FASB to initially require both types. This uncertainty was shown in responses sent to the FASB by various users when the proposed statement was circulated. Some knowledgeable persons preferred current cost information, while others preferred constant dollar information.

Since *FASB Statement No. 33* was released in 1979, companies and financial statement users have had several years of experience with both approaches. In 1984, the FASB indicated its preference for current cost information over constant dollar information. In *FASB Statement No. 82,* the FASB eliminated the requirement for reporting constant dollar information in supplementary financial statements to reduce the cost incurred in preparing financial statements.[3] Under *FASB Statement No. 82,* the reporting of current cost information was still required. However, a company could substitute constant dollar information for current cost information. In 1986, the FASB issued *FASB Statement No. 89,* which *encourages,* but *does not require,* companies to disclose supplementary information on the effects of changing prices.[4]

NEW TERMS INTRODUCED IN APPENDIX B

Constant dollar accounting A recommended approach to deal with the problem of accounting for inflation by changing the unit of measure from the actual historical (nominal) dollar to a dollar of constant purchasing power (1201).

Current cost The amount that would have to be paid currently to acquire an asset (1202).

Current cost accounting A recommended approach to deal with the problem of accounting for inflation by showing current cost or value of items in the financial statements (1201).

Deflation (period of) Exists when prices in general are falling (1199).

General price-level accounting See Constant dollar accounting (1201).

Historical cost accounting Conventional accounting in which accounting measurements are in terms of the actual dollars expended or received (1199).

Inflation (period of) Exists when prices in general are rising (1199).

Monetary items Cash and other assets and liabilities that represent fixed claims to cash, such as accounts and notes receivable and payable (1205).

Nonmonetary items All items on the balance sheet other than monetary items; examples are inventories, plant assets, capital stock, and stockholders' equity (1206).

Price index A weighted average of prices for various goods and services. A base year is chosen and assigned a value of 100 for comparative purposes (1199).

Purchasing power gain The gain that results from holding monetary liabilities during inflation or monetary assets during deflation (1206).

Purchasing power loss The loss that results from holding monetary assets during inflation or monetary liabilities during deflation (1206).

---

[3] FASB, "Financial Reporting and Changing Prices: Elimination of Certain Disclosures," *Statement of Financial Accounting Standards No. 82* (Stamford, Conn., 1984). Copyright © by Financial Accounting Standards Board, High Ridge Park, Stamford, Connecticut, 06905, USA.

[4] FASB, "Financial Reporting and Changing Prices," *Statement of Financial Accounting Standards No. 89* (Stamford, Conn., 1987). Copyright © by Financial Accounting Standards Board. High Ridge Park, Stamford, Connecticut, 06905, USA.

QUESTIONS

1. How might a tax supposedly on income be really a tax on capital?

2. What two basic approaches might be used to reveal the impact of inflation on financial statements?

3. When items in a set of financial statements are all converted into constant dollars, what do they have in common?

4. If an index of the general level of prices rose 15% in a period, what is the effect on the value or real worth of the dollar?

5. How is the dollar amount for land adjusted under constant dollar accounting?

6. Explain the typical adjustment of sales and most expenses under constant dollar accounting.

7. Identify whether each of the following items is a monetary or nonmonetary item:
   a. Cash.
   b. Equipment.
   c. Notes receivable.
   d. Merchandise inventory.
   e. Accounts receivable.
   f. Patents.
   g. Common stock.
   h. Land.
   i. Accounts payable.
   j. Buildings.

8. What are purchasing power gains and losses? When do purchasing power gains occur? When do purchasing power losses occur?

9. If supplementary disclosures are made, how are the effects of inflation shown?

10. What is the major deficiency in constant dollar accounting?

EXERCISES

E-1
Compute income under historical cost accounting, current cost accounting, and constant dollar accounting

Assume the following facts regarding the purchase and sale of 100 units of a product:

Date	Transaction	Amount	Price-Level Index
January 1, 1991	Purchased 100 units	$36,000	100
December 31, 1991 . . .	Sold 100 units	60,000	110

The company incurred $7,200 of expenses to sell the units. The replacement cost of the units on December 31, 1991, was $42,000. Prepare a schedule showing income from continuing operations under historical cost accounting, current cost accounting, and constant dollar accounting.

E-2
Convert cost of goods sold section of income statement to constant dollar accounts

The cost of goods sold section of the conventional (historical cost) income statement for Thurgood Company appears below:

Cost of goods sold:
Inventory, January 1, 1991	$ 72,000
Purchases	216,000
Goods available for sale	$288,000
Inventory, December 31, 1991 . . .	36,000
Cost of goods sold	$252,000

The general price-level index was 100 on December 31, 1990, and 110 on December 31, 1991. The FIFO inventories were acquired when the index stood at 96 for the beginning inventory and 108 for the ending inventory. Purchases were incurred uniformly throughout the year. Convert the cost of goods sold section of the income statement to end-of-year constant dollar amounts.

E-3
Compute current cost depreciation

R Company's plant assets at December 31, 1990, had a historical cost of $100,000 and accumulated depreciation of $40,000 (10% annual depreciation rate). No additions or retirements occurred in 1991. The current cost of the plant assets on December 31, 1990, was $130,000 and on December 31, 1991, was $150,000. Compute the current cost depreciation for 1991.

E-4
Determine purchasing power gain or loss

In each of the situations given, determine the amount of purchasing power gain or loss:

a.   You hold cash of $20,000 during a year in which prices in general rose 10%.
b.   You are in debt $10,000 during a year in which prices in general rose 8%.

PROBLEMS

PB-1
Compute income on both current cost and constant dollar basis

A partial income statement for Ralston Company for the year ended December 31, 1991, in terms of historical dollars follows:

RALSTON COMPANY
Partial Income Statement
For the Year Ended December 31, 1991

Sales		$880,000
Cost of goods sold	$504,000	
Depreciation	48,000	
Other expenses	96,800	648,800
Income from continuing operations . . .		$231,200

The sales were made uniformly throughout the year. The cost of goods sold consisted of goods acquired when the general price index stood at 105. This same index ended the year at 120 and averaged 110 for the year. The current cost of the goods sold was $600,000.

The $48,000 of depreciation reported is on a machine that cost $240,000 when the general price index stood at 90. The machine is being depreciated over a five-year period. The machine had a current cost of $400,000 at the beginning of 1991 and a current cost of $480,000 at the end of 1991.

Required:

a.   Prepare a statement showing current cost income from continuing operations for the year ended December 31, 1991.
b.   Prepare a statement showing income from continuing operations in constant end-of-year 1991 dollars for the year ended December 31, 1991.

PB-2
Prepare income statement in constant dollars

Blake Company began business on January 2, 1991, with $384,000 of inventory and $288,000 of equipment. An index of the general level of prices stood at 100 on January 2, 1991. This index rose uniformly throughout the year, averaging 125 for the year, and ending at 150. Blake's income statement for the year in historical dollars is given below.

```
                    BLAKE COMPANY
                   Income Statement
          For the Year Ended December 31, 1991

    Sales . . . . . . . . . . .           $480,000
    Cost of goods sold  . . . .            240,000
    Gross margin  . . . . . . .           $240,000
    Depreciation . . . . . . . $48,000
    Other expenses . . . . . .  96,000    144,000
    Net income  . . . . . . . .          $ 96,000
```

In 1991, Blake sold goods out of the beginning inventory with a cost of $240,000 for $480,000 cash. Expenses in the amount of $96,000 were incurred uniformly throughout the year and were paid in cash. No new equipment was purchased during the year.

Required: Prepare an income statement for 1991 with all amounts expressed in constant end-of-year 1991 dollars. The purchasing power loss on net monetary items was $4,800.

PB-3
Compute income on both current cost and constant dollar basis

Following is a partial income statement for Drew Home Furnishings for the year ended December 31, 1991:

```
                 DREW HOME FURNISHINGS
                 Partial Income Statement
            For the Year Ended December 31, 1991

    Sales . . . . . . . . . . . . . . . . . .       $840,000
    Cost of goods sold . . . . . . . . . . . $540,800
    Depreciation . . . . . . . . . . . . . .   32,000
    Other expenses . . . . . . . . . . . .    168,000   740,800
    Income from continuing operations  . . .       $ 99,200
```

Sales were made uniformly through the year. Other expenses were also incurred rather uniformly throughout the year and largely on a cash basis. Thus, their historical cost is substantially equal to their current cost. The depreciation reported relates to a machine acquired at a cost of $320,000 that is being depreciated over a 10-year life on a straight-line basis.

The current cost of the goods sold was $600,000 at the time of sale. The current (gross) cost of the machine was $520,000 at the beginning of 1991 and $600,000 at the end of the year. An index of the general level of prices stood at 80 when the machine was acquired, stood at 100 at the beginning of 1991, averaged 105 for 1991, and ended the year at 110. The index stood at 104 when the goods sold were acquired.

Required:
a. Prepare a statement showing current cost income from continuing operations for the year ended December 31, 1991.
b. Prepare a statement showing constant dollar income from continuing operations in end-of-year dollars for the year ended December 31, 1991.

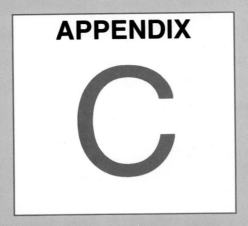

APPENDIX C

A Set of Consolidated Financial Statements and Other Financial Data for Eli Lilly and Company

Appendix C contains certain pages from the annual report of Eli Lilly and Company. Eli Lilly is a large and successful pharmaceutical company that specializes in products that have a research-based, high technology, life-sciences orientation. The following items are included from the annual report and are found on the pages indicated.

The items included relate to many of the concepts described in the text. For instance, the consolidated financial statements illustrate the coverage of that topic in Chapter 18. The consolidated statements of cash flows apply the indirect method emphasized in Chapter 20. The details contained in the financial statements and in the notes to those statements relate to many other concepts described in the text.

Review of Operations

Financial Review of 1987

For the 27th consecutive year, Eli Lilly and Company achieved increased earnings. The following pages present an in-depth review of the company's recent performance.

In December 1987, the company concluded the sale of its cosmetics segment, Elizabeth Arden, Inc. Elizabeth Arden's results have therefore been excluded from consolidated sales and expenses for all years.

In addition, both the net gain from the sale and the net operating income of Elizabeth Arden through the date of its sale are included in "income from discontinued operations" in the consolidated statements of income.

Financial Data

Return on Sales
Increased profitability reflected a higher gross-profit margin and a lower effective tax rate in 1987.

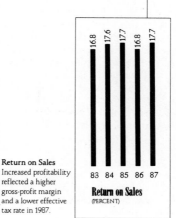

Return on Sales
(PERCENT)

Return on Shareholders' Equity
Earnings growth supported the increase in return on shareholders' equity in 1987.

Return on Shareholders' Equity (PERCENT)

Return on Assets
Continued control of both inventories and receivables strengthened the return on assets in 1987.

Return on Assets
(PERCENT)

Operating Results

Worldwide sales rose 10 percent in 1987. Three factors—higher unit volume, favorable exchange rates, and price increases—contributed equally to the sales growth.

In 1986, sales increased 14 percent. The largest factor was a 7-percent rise in unit volume, of which 1 percent came from the acquisition of Hybritech Incorporated. Favorable exchange rates and price increases contributed 4 percent and 3 percent, respectively.

Both of the company's segments reported higher sales. In addition, the company achieved sales increases both in the United States and abroad. Very strong international growth was the result of unit increases and the weaker dollar.

Sales outside the United States were $1.3 billion, a gain of 20 percent from the previous year. In 1986, the increase was 24 percent, compared with 1985.

Sales in the United States were $2.3 billion, a 5-percent increase. In 1986, U.S. sales rose 10 percent, compared with the previous year.

Sales of human health products increased 10 percent in 1987, compared with a 19-percent increase in 1986. The strong sales growth of the oral antibiotic Ceclor, now a $500 million product, offset the sales decrease of Keflex, a product in the same therapeutic class that faced strong generic competition in the United States. As a result, total sales of oral antibiotics increased 7 percent, compared with a 32-percent increase in 1986, which reflected unusually high demand. Meanwhile, sales of injectable antibiotics declined 2 percent in 1987, compared with an 11-percent increase the previous year.

During 1987, the company received permission from the U.S. Food and Drug Administration to market several new pharmaceutical products, including the antidepressant Prozac, the oral antibiotic Keftab, and the natural-sequence human growth hormone Humatrope.

Sales gains were achieved by all four medical instrument companies. Advanced Cardiovascular Systems, Inc., and Cardiac Pacemakers, Inc., both achieved excellent growth. Total sales for the Medical Instrument Systems Division were $513.4 million, a 24-percent increase. This followed an 11-percent gain the previous year.

The agriculture segment continued to adapt successfully to changing market conditions in 1987. Worldwide sales of agricultural products were $748.4 million, a 7-percent increase, compared with the previous year. This followed a 2-percent sales decline in 1986.

In 1987, sales of animal health products rose 10 percent, compared with a modest 2-percent gain in 1986. Sales of plant science products grew 5 percent in 1987, after a 5-percent decline the previous year.

Gross profits increased at a

Employees on Performance Excellence teams stress ongoing quality and productivity improvements as part of the continuing Lilly commitment to the highest standards.

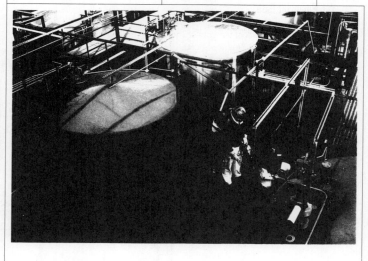

19

Review of Operations, continued

more rapid rate than sales primarily because of the company's ongoing effort to further strengthen its manufacturing operations. Manufacturing costs as a percent of sales have improved for five consecutive years, despite two percentage points added in 1986 due to the inclusion of Hybritech's manufacturing costs.

Higher marketing expenses in 1987 were largely related to the introduction of new products abroad and the negative impact of the weaker dollar on international operations. In the previous year, marketing expenses increased primarily because of the same factors that affected 1987 and the inclusion of the expenses of Hybritech, which was acquired in March 1986.

In December 1987, the company completed the sale of Elizabeth Arden, resulting in an after-tax gain of $216 million. In addition, the company approved a series of restructuring actions totaling $271.9 million. These actions are designed to strengthen the company's long-term profitability. Also included in the fourth-quarter results were special provisions of $65 million, which were included in general administrative expenses (see Note 2 to the consolidated financial statements).

Consolidated Statements of Income

ELI LILLY AND COMPANY AND SUBSIDIARIES
(Dollars in Millions, Except Per-Share Data)

Year Ended December 31	1987	1986	1985
Net sales	$3,643.8	$3,322.5	$2,918.7
Costs of products sold	1,302.8	1,224.7	1,077.6
Research and development	466.3	420.3	363.8
Marketing	656.7	570.7	501.7
General administrative (Note 2)	362.4	270.2	248.4
Restructuring (Note 2)	271.9	—	—
Other—net	(11.3)	(6.8)	(24.7)
	3,048.8	2,479.1	2,166.8
Income from continuing operations before income taxes	595.0	843.4	751.9
Income taxes (Note 8)	184.5	301.9	258.3
Income from continuing operations	410.5	541.5	493.6
Income from discontinued operations—net of taxes (Note 2)	233.2	16.7	24.0
Net income	$ 643.7	$ 558.2	$ 517.6
Earnings per share:			
Continuing operations	$ 2.83	$ 3.77	$ 3.46
Net income	4.41	3.89	3.62

See notes to consolidated financial statements.

20

Review of Operations, continued

Financial Position

The company maintained its sound financial position in 1987. The sale of Elizabeth Arden contributed significantly to cash and short-term securities, which totaled more than $1 billion at year-end. Because part of the Arden sales price was deferred, receivables increased to $281.3 million in 1987, from $88.2 million the previous year.

Included in the restructuring charges were the write-off of certain intangibles and manufacturing plant and equipment. Other liabilities include accruals for costs associated with restructuring and with other special provisions discussed in Note 2 to the consolidated financial statements.

The company has higher deductibles and lower product liability coverage than in periods prior to 1986. This reflects general trends in the industry and is not unique to the company.

The company has emphasized productivity improvements throughout its manufacturing and administrative areas under an approach called "Performance Excellence," which stresses employee involvement, product quality, never-ending improvement, and total waste elimination. In 1987, this philosophy had a positive impact on the company's levels of investment in working capital, such as inventories and receivables.

In addition, Performance Excellence resulted in expanded

Consolidated Balance Sheets

ELI LILLY AND COMPANY AND SUBSIDIARIES
(Dollars in Millions)

December 31	1987	1986
Assets		
Current Assets		
Cash and short-term securities	$1,030.9	$ 486.0
Accounts receivable, net of allowances of		
$21.1 (1987) and $31.0 (1986)	650.2	690.9
Other receivables	281.3	88.2
Inventories (Note 1)	615.5	694.6
Prepaid expenses	146.2	112.5
Total Current Assets	2,724.1	2,072.2
Other Assets		
Investments—at cost (Note 4)	286.9	274.2
Goodwill and other intangibles, net of		
allowances for amortization of $48.6 (1987)		
and $27.1 (1986)	395.7	478.8
Sundry	205.7	243.0
	888.3	996.0
Property and Equipment (Note 1)	1,642.5	1,527.6
	$5,254.9	$4,595.8

22

	December 31	1987	1986
Liabilities and Shareholders' Equity			
Current Liabilities			
Loans payable	$	238.2	$ 230.9
Accounts payable		164.5	144.6
Employee compensation		203.0	200.7
Dividends payable		80.3	69.5
Other liabilities		435.3	254.6
Income taxes payable		231.5	68.7
Deferred income taxes		95.4	145.9
Total Current Liabilities		1,448.2	1,114.9
Long-Term Debt (Note 5)		365.7	395.3
Deferred Income Taxes		297.5	298.4
Other Noncurrent Liabilities		100.9	47.6
Shareholders' Equity (Note 7)			
Common stock—par value $.62½ per share:			
Authorized shares: 400,000,000			
Issued shares: 146,012,704		91.3	91.3
Additional paid-in capital		48.2	181.8
Retained earnings		3,395.5	3,041.2
Currency translation adjustments		2.6	(89.1)
		3,537.6	3,225.2
Less cost of common shares in treasury:			
1987—6,643,983; 1986—6,957,192		495.0	485.6
		3,042.6	2,739.6
		$5,254.9	$4,595.8

See notes to consolidated financial statements.

capacity and floor space at existing facilities, enabling the company to postpone or eliminate certain capital expenditures. Nevertheless, the company expects to continue increasing its commitment to facilities expansion with significantly higher capital expenditures in 1988.

The company also continued its stock-repurchase programs. In November 1987, the Board of Directors authorized a long-term $1 billion stock-repurchase program, which would include all existing stock repurchase programs. The company spent $237.2 million in 1987 and $128.3 million in 1986 to repurchase stock and warrants.

The company's strong financial position continues to be a significant factor that contributes to its earnings growth and to its return on investment. For instance, the company's liquidity is substantial. Indicators of the company's liquidity include its ability to generate cash from operations, its low debt-to-equity ratio, its high return on equity, its substantial debt capacity, and the highest debt ratings from both Moody's and Standard & Poor's.

These factors and other financing alternatives give the company the ability and flexibility to meet its obligations and to continue to invest in growth opportunities.

Review of Operations, continued

Consolidated Statements of Cash Flows
ELI LILLY AND COMPANY AND SUBSIDIARIES
(Dollars in Millions)

Year Ended December 31	1987	1986	1985
Net Cash Flow from Operating Activities			
Income from continuing operations	$ 410.5	$541.5	$493.6
Income and depreciation from discontinued operations	26.0	23.7	30.0
Depreciation and amortization	184.3	170.7	130.2
Other noncash charges (credits) to income—net	(147.4)	35.8	55.2
	473.4	771.7	709.0
Working capital (increases) decreases:			
Receivables	(23.6)	(78.4)	(53.2)
Inventories	23.0	12.3	(61.7)
Prepaid expenses	(36.3)	41.7	(34.7)
Accounts payable and accrued liabilities	358.9	122.4	(3.8)
	322.0	98.0	(153.4)
NET CASH FLOW FROM OPERATING ACTIVITIES	795.4	869.7	555.6
Cash Flows from Investing Activities			
Additions to property and equipment	(344.1)	(283.0)	(207.1)
Disposals of property and equipment	65.5	9.8	9.7
Net assets of acquired businesses	—	(363.3)	(48.2)
Issuance of securities related to acquisitions	26.1	285.1	9.8
Decrease (increase) in other assets	128.4	(38.5)	(69.9)
Net proceeds from divestiture	561.0	—	—
Notes received in divestiture	(278.2)	—	—
Increase in other noncurrent liabilities	37.1	19.2	5.8
NET CASH PROVIDED (USED) BY INVESTING ACTIVITIES	195.8	(370.7)	(299.9)
Cash Flows from Financing Activities			
Issuances under stock plans	23.9	20.6	28.4
Purchase of common stock and warrants	(237.2)	(128.3)	(197.2)
Increase (decrease) in loans payable	7.7	(77.9)	(40.2)
Additions to long-term debt	3.8	2.5	156.9
Reductions of long-term debt	(11.7)	(4.1)	(35.4)
Cash dividends paid	(278.6)	(250.9)	(224.9)
NET CASH USED FOR FINANCING ACTIVITIES	(492.1)	(438.1)	(312.4)
Currency translation adjustments	45.8	19.0	17.5
NET INCREASE (DECREASE) IN CASH	544.9	79.9	(39.2)
Cash and short-term securities at beginning of year	486.0	406.1	445.3
CASH AND SHORT-TERM SECURITIES AT END OF YEAR	$1,030.9	$486.0	$406.1

See notes to consolidated financial statements.

24

Notes to Consolidated Financial Statements

ELI LILLY AND COMPANY AND SUBSIDIARIES
(Dollars in Millions Except Per Share Data)

Note 1: Summary of Significant Accounting Policies (DOLLARS IN MILLIONS)

Principles of Consolidation: The accounts of all wholly owned subsidiaries are included in the consolidated financial statements. With the sale of the cosmetics segment to Faberge, Incorporated, on December 22, 1987, the financial statements have been restated to reflect this disposition. Accordingly, sales of $405.5, $397.9, and $351.9 and the associated costs and expenses resulting in net income of $17.2, $16.7, and $24.0 for 1987, 1986, and 1985, respectively, are shown in discontinued operations.

Inventories: The company states all of its inventories at the lower of cost or market. The company uses the last-in, first-out (LIFO) cost method for substantially all its inventories located in the continental United States, or approximately 50 percent of its total inventories. It is not practicable to present the components of inventory on a LIFO basis. Other inventories are valued by the first-in, first-out (FIFO) method. Inventories at December 31, 1987 and 1986, consisted of the following:

	1987	1986
Finished products	$223.4	$281.8
Work in process	229.5	234.8
Raw materials and supplies	203.8	231.9
	656.7	748.5
Less reduction to LIFO cost	41.2	53.9
	$615.5	$694.6

Property and Equipment: Property and equipment is stated on the basis of cost. Provisions for depreciation of buildings and equipment are computed generally by the straight-line method at rates based on their estimated useful lives. At December 31, 1987 and 1986, property and equipment consisted of the following:

	1987	1986
Land	$ 58.3	$ 41.4
Buildings	876.3	779.1
Equipment	1,823.3	1,699.4
	2,757.9	2,519.9
Less allowances for depreciation	1,115.4	992.3
	$1,642.5	$1,527.6

Income Taxes: Federal income taxes are provided on the portion of the income of foreign subsidiaries that is expected to be remitted to the United States and be taxable. The investment tax credit is applied as a reduction of federal income taxes by the flow-through method. On December 30, 1987, the Financial Accounting Standards Board issued Statement of Financial Accounting Standards No. 96, "Accounting for Income Taxes." Companies are required to adopt the new method of accounting for income taxes no later than 1989. Its impact on the financial results of the company has not been determined.

Retirement Plans: Pension costs for 1987 and 1986 are generally computed in accordance with the provisions of Statement of Financial Accounting Standards No. 87, "Employers' Accounting for Pensions." Pension costs charged to income in 1985 generally are actuarially computed and include normal cost, interest on unfunded prior service cost, and amortization of the unfunded prior service cost over 40 years. Generally, pension costs accrued are funded.

31

Notes to Consolidated Financial Statements, continued

Earnings Per Share: Earnings per share are calculated on a fully diluted basis. They are based on the weighted average number of outstanding common shares and common share equivalents (primarily stock options and warrants) and the assumed conversion of outstanding convertible debentures. Primary earnings per share has not been presented because it does not differ significantly from the reported earnings per share computed on a fully diluted basis.

Note 2: Business Restructuring and Other Provisions

As a result of an ongoing strategic evaluation of its lines of business, the company took two major steps in 1987 to restructure its operations and concentrate its resources on businesses with a high technology and life-science orientation. On December 22, 1987, the company concluded the sale of its cosmetics business segment to Faberge, Incorporated, for cash and notes valued at $657 million. The sale resulted in an after-tax gain of $216 million (after provisions for taxes of $175 million). Also in December 1987, the company approved actions to make its agriculture segment more competitive, to streamline and modernize certain manufacturing and development facilities, and to write down certain intangible assets. These actions resulted in nonrecurring fourth-quarter charges to income of $271.9 million.

In the fourth quarter of 1987, the company made several charges to general administrative expenses, totaling $65 million. These charges relate principally to provisions for possible environmental and product liability exposures and to increased funding of charitable institutions.

Note 3: Acquisitions

On March 18, 1986, the company acquired all the outstanding shares of Hybritech Incorporated, which develops, manufactures, and markets products incorporating monoclonal antibody technology. This transaction has been accounted for as a purchase, and the financial statements include the results of operations of Hybritech from the date of purchase. The purchase price consisted of approximately $364.2 million in cash payments, convertible notes, and warrants to purchase Lilly common stock. Depending on the annual performance of Hybritech over the period ending December 31, 1995, additional cash of up to $268.5 million may be paid to holders of Contingent Payment Obligation Units, which were issued to shareholders of Hybritech in connection with the acquisition. The units are publicly traded. The excess of cost over the fair value of the assets acquired (goodwill) is being amortized over 40 years on the straight-line method. Assets acquired included patents and other intangibles, which are being amortized over 14 years on the straight-line method. The book value of these other intangibles and patents at December 31, 1987, is $151 million.

In connection with the company's acquisitions of Intec Systems, Inc. (Intec), and Advanced Cardiovascular Systems, Inc. (ACS), in 1985 and 1984, respectively, additional payments may be made and accounted for as part of the purchase price. If all performance objectives are met through 1990, an additional $67.6 million may be paid in connection with the Intec acquisition. Depending upon the annual performance of ACS over the next year, up to 417,000 additional shares of Lilly common stock may be issued in connection with the acquisition. Goodwill related to the acquisitions is being amortized over 40 years on the straight-line method.

Note 4: Investments

Investments classified as noncurrent consist primarily of interest-bearing deposits and short-term securities held in Puerto Rico in connection with tax-exemption grants. The cost of these investments approximates market value.

Note 5: Long-Term Debt

Long-term debt consists of the following:

	1987	1986
6¾-percent convertible debt (due in 1996; convertible at $66.31 per share)	$128.6	$149.8
10¼-percent Eurodollar bonds (due in 1992)	150.0	150.0
9-percent bonds sold through Swiss banks (due in 1996)	51.5	49.9
Other, including capitalized leases	35.6	45.6
	$365.7	$395.3

At December 31, 1987, unused lines of credit approximated $560 million. Compensating balances and commitment fees are not material, and there are no significant conditions under which the lines may be withdrawn. In June of 1987, the company entered into a currency swap related to the Eurodollar bonds. The effect of the swap is to lower the effective rate of interest payable on the Eurodollar bonds to 6.22 percent.

Note 6: Stock Plans and Warrants

Stock options and performance awards have been granted to officers and other executive and key employees. Stock options are granted at prices equal to 100 percent of the fair market value at the dates of grant. Stock-option activity during 1987 and 1986 is summarized below:

	Number of Shares	
	1987	1986
Unexercised at January 1	5,464,058	5,020,406
Granted	58,800	1,073,200
Assumed in acquisition	—	425,206
Exercised	(942,024)	(985,284)
Terminated	(84,532)	(69,470)
Unexercised at December 31	4,496,302	5,464,058
Exercisable at December 31	2,094,783	2,066,524

The per-share price range of unexercised options at December 31, 1987, was $16.38 to $75.19 ($1.49 to $75.19 at December 31, 1986). Options were exercised at prices ranging from $1.38 to $70.50 in 1987 ($1.49 to $47.34 in 1986). Option prices below $18.69 relate to options assumed in acquisitions.

Warrants issued in 1986 in connection with the acquisition of Hybritech Incorporated are exercisable at a price of $75.98 per Lilly share through March 31, 1991. There were 13,167,743 warrants outstanding at December 31, 1987.

At December 31, 1987, additional options, performance awards, stock appreciation rights, or restricted stock grants may be granted under the Lilly Stock Plan for not more than 3,486,052 shares (1986—3,626,235 shares).

33

Notes to Consolidated Financial Statements, continued

Note 7: Changes in Shareholders' Equity
Common Stock, Additional Paid-in Capital, and Treasury Stock

	Common Stock Issued		Additional Paid-in Capital	Common Stock in Treasury	
	Shares	Amount		Shares	Amount
Balance at January 1, 1985	76,263,067	$47.7	$128.7	4,714,643	$296.4
Purchase for treasury				2,496,600	197.2
Issuance of stock under employee stock plans			(7.4)	(697,813)	(43.4)
Stock dividend declared	69,749,637	43.6			
Other credits			2.9		
Balance at December 31, 1985	146,012,704	91.3	124.2	6,513,430	450.2
Purchase for treasury				1,877,367	123.3
Issuance of stock under employee stock plans			(42.3)	(1,271,036)	(82.7)
Acquisition of subsidiaries, including contingent payments			97.2	(162,135)	(10.2)
Other credits			2.7	(434)	—
Balance at December 31, 1986	146,012,704	91.3	181.8	6,957,192	485.6
Purchase for treasury				1,420,895	122.2
Issuance of stock under employee stock plans			(24.0)	(1,169,669)	(68.5)
Contingent payments relating to acquisition of subsidiaries			7.1	(244,894)	(15.3)
Purchase of warrants and note conversions			(122.8)	(318,888)	(29.0)
Other credits			6.1	(653)	—
Balance at December 31, 1987	146,012,704	$91.3	$ 48.2	6,643,983	$495.0

The company has 5,000,000 authorized and unissued shares of preferred stock without par value.

Retained Earnings

	1987	1986	1985
Balance at January 1	$3,041.2	$2,740.6	$2,497.0
Net income	643.7	558.2	517.6
Cash dividends declared per share: 1987—$2.075; 1986—$1.85; 1985—$1.65 .	(289.4)	(257.6)	(230.4)
Stock dividend declared	—	—	(43.6)
Balance at December 31	$3,395.5	$3,041.2	$2,740.6

Currency Translation Adjustments

Generally, the assets and liabilities of foreign operations are translated into U.S. dollars using the current exchange rate. For those operations. changes in exchange rates generally do not affect cash flows; therefore. resulting translation adjustments are made to shareholders' equity rather than to income. Following is an analysis of currency translation adjustments reflected in shareholders' equity:

	1987	1986	1985
Balance (negative amount) at January 1	$(89.1)	$(118.2)	$(155.8)
Translation adjustments and gains and losses from intercompany transactions	93.0	26.5	30.2
Allocated income taxes	(1.3)	2.6	7.4
Balance at December 31	$ 2.6	$ (89.1)	$(118.2)

Note 8: Income Taxes

Following is the composition of income taxes from continuing operations:

	1987	1986	1985
Current:			
Federal	$258.4	$204.8	$165.7
Foreign	27.6	38.8	18.2
State	45.5	21.5	19.5
Deferred:			
Accelerated depreciation	24.1	20.2	35.3
Installment sales	(21.5)	(.9)	3.9
Employee benefit plan	1.0	(32.6)	17.8
Product liability insurance	(54.2)	25.6	(1.0)
Restructuring	(56.1)	—	—
Other timing differences	(40.3)	24.5	(1.1)
Income taxes from continuing operations	$184.5	$301.9	$258.3

Unremitted earnings of foreign subsidiaries that have been, or are intended to be, permanently reinvested for continued use in foreign operations, exclusive of those amounts that if remitted would result in little or no income taxes due to relevant statutes currently in effect, aggregated approximately $445 million at December 31, 1987 ($411 million at December 31, 1986).

Following is a reconciliation of the effective income tax rate from continuing operations:

	1987	1986	1985
United States federal statutory tax rate	40.0%	46.0%	46.0%
Add (deduct):			
Tax savings from operations in Puerto Rico	(10.7)	(9.2)	(8.5)
Investment tax credit	—	(.5)	(1.3)
Research tax credit	(1.0)	(.8)	(1.2)
Effect of international operations	(3.2)	(2.4)	(2.0)
State taxes. net of federal tax benefit	4.2	2.2	2.0
Nondeductible effect of restructuring	3.6	—	—
Sundry	(1.9)	.5	(.6)
Effective rate	31.0%	35.8%	34.4%

35

Notes to Consolidated Financial Statements, continued

Following is the composition of income from continuing operations before taxes:

	1987	1986	1985
United States	$371.1	$638.7	$577.8
Foreign	227.2	208.6	176.4
Eliminations and adjustments	(3.3)	(3.9)	(2.3)
Income from continuing operations before taxes	$595.0	$843.4	$751.9

Amounts of income from continuing operations before taxes shown in the preceding table are classified based on location of the operations of the company. Amounts shown in the first table of this note are classified based on location of the taxing authority.

On May 28, 1985, the United States Tax Court rendered an opinion with regard to proposed deficiencies of income taxes for 1971 through 1973 related to subsidiary operations in Puerto Rico. The tax court reduced the $34.2 million tax deficiencies proposed by the Internal Revenue Service to approximately $14.4 million for these years. The company is appealing the results of the court's opinion.

The company has received proposed deficiencies for the years 1974 through 1981 totaling $159.6 million, primarily relating to subsidiary operations in Puerto Rico. These proposed deficiencies are being contested.

In the opinion of the company, additional taxes that may ultimately result from the tax court opinion and other proposed deficiencies and from possible proposed deficiencies related to the same issues for years subsequent to 1981 would not have a material adverse effect on the consolidated financial statements.

Note 9: Retirement Benefits

The company adopted Statement of Financial Accounting Standards No. 87, "Employers' Accounting for Pensions" (SFAS 87) with respect to its retirement plans, effective January 1, 1986. Pension costs for these plans for 1987 and 1986 including related disclosures as of December 31, 1987 and 1986, are determined under the provisions of SFAS 87. Pension costs and related disclosures for 1985 are determined under the provisions of previous accounting principles.

The company has noncontributory defined benefit retirement plans that cover substantially all United States employees and a majority of the employees in other countries. Benefits under the domestic plans are calculated by using one of several formulas. These formulas are based on a combination of the following: (1) years of service, (2) final average earnings, (3) primary social security benefit, and (4) age. The formula that yields the largest amount of retirement income is used to determine the monthly benefit. The benefits for the company's plans in countries other than the United States are based on years of service and compensation.

The company's funding policy for the domestic plans is consistent with the funding requirements of federal law and regulations. The funding policy for the plans outside the United States is consistent with local governmental and tax requirements.

Plan assets consist primarily of stocks, bonds, commingled trust funds, and cash.

Net pension expense from continuing operations for the company's retirement plans for 1987 and 1986 included the following components:

	1987	1986
Service cost—benefits earned during the year	$ 42.9	$ 32.3
Interest cost on projected benefit obligations	85.7	79.8
Return on assets—actual	(91.8)	(148.0)
deferred gain (loss)	(8.6)	59.4
	(100.4)	(88.6)
Net amortization	.7	.8
Net annual pension cost	$ 28.9	$ 24.3

Net pension expense from continuing operations was $49.3 million in 1985.

The funded status and amounts recognized in the consolidated balance sheets for the company's defined benefit retirement plans at December 31, 1987 and 1986, were as follows:

	1987	1986
Plan assets at fair value	$1,141.5	$1,018.5
Actuarial present value of benefit obligations		
Vested benefits	714.1	690.0
Nonvested benefits	70.8	78.8
Accumulated benefit obligation	784.9	768.8
Effect of projected future salary increases	231.0	261.8
Projected benefit obligation	1,015.9	1,030.6
Funded status	125.6	(12.1)
Unrecognized net (gain) loss	(74.0)	24.1
Unrecognized prior service cost	.8	—
Unrecognized net obligation at January 1, 1986	9.8	18.6
Prepaid pension cost	$ 62.2	$ 30.6

The weighted-average discount rate and rates of increase in future compensation levels used in determining the actuarial present value of the projected benefit obligation were 9.4 percent and 5.5 percent to 9.5 percent, respectively, at December 31, 1987, and 8.6 percent and 5.5 percent to 9.5 percent, respectively, at December 31, 1986. The weighted-average expected long-term rate of return on plan assets was 10.4 percent and 10.5 percent in 1987 and 1986, respectively.

The company has defined contribution plans that cover its eligible worldwide employees. The purpose of these defined contribution plans is generally to provide additional financial security during retirement by providing employees with an incentive to make regular savings. Company contributions to the plans are based on employee contributions or compensation. These company contributions totaled $28.2 million, $22.1 million, and $21.7 million for the years 1987, 1986, and 1985, respectively.

37

Notes to Consolidated Financial Statements, continued

Note 10: Leases

Total rental expense for all leases, including contingent rentals (not material), amounted to approximately $43.7 million for 1987, $35.9 million for 1986, and $28.4 million for 1985. Capital leases included in equipment in the consolidated balance sheets totaled $4.2 million at December 31, 1987, and $14.2 million at December 31, 1986. Future minimum rental commitments are not material.

Note 11: Litigation

The company is a party to product liability and various other legal actions. The product liability litigation includes numerous actions involving prescription drugs, including diethylstilbestrol and benoxaprofen. While it is not feasible to predict or determine the outcome of the actions brought against it, the company believes these actions will not ultimately result in liability that would have a material adverse effect on its consolidated financial position.

Report of Independent Accountants

Ernst & Whinney

Board of Directors and Shareholders
Eli Lilly and Company
Indianapolis, Indiana

We have examined the consolidated balance sheets of Eli Lilly and Company and subsidiaries as of December 31, 1987 and 1986, and the related consolidated statements of income and cash flows for each of the three years in the period ended December 31, 1987. Our examinations were made in accordance with generally accepted auditing standards and, accordingly, included such tests of the accounting records and such other auditing procedures as we considered necessary in the circumstances.

In our opinion, the financial statements referred to above present fairly the consolidated financial position of Eli Lilly and Company and subsidiaries at December 31, 1987 and 1986, and the consolidated results of their operations and cash flows for each of the three years in the period ended December 31, 1987, in conformity with generally accepted accounting principles applied on a consistent basis.

Ernst & Whinney

Indianapolis, Indiana
February 8, 1988

39

Responsibility for Financial Statements

The preceding consolidated financial statements, including the notes thereto, have been prepared by the company in accordance with generally accepted accounting principles and necessarily include amounts based on judgments and estimates by management. The other financial information in this annual report is consistent with that in the financial statements.

The financial statements have been audited by Ernst & Whinney, independent accountants, whose report appears above. Their responsibility is to examine the company's financial statements in accordance with generally accepted auditing standards and to express their opinion with respect to the fairness of presentation of the statements.

The company maintains internal accounting control systems that are designed to provide reasonable assurance that assets are safeguarded, that transactions are executed in accordance with management's authorization and are properly recorded, and that accounting records are adequate for preparation of financial statements and other financial information. The design, monitoring, and revision of internal accounting control systems involve, among other things, management's judgments with respect to the relative cost and expected benefits of specific control measures.

The members of the audit committee of the Board of Directors, none of whom are employees of the company, are identified on page 41 of this annual report. The audit committee recommends independent accountants for appointment by the Board of Directors, reviews the services to be performed by the independent accountants, and receives and reviews the reports submitted by them. It also determines the duties and responsibilities of the internal auditors, reviews the internal audit program, and receives and reviews reports submitted by the internal audit staff. In the exercise of its responsibilities, the audit committee meets with management, with the internal auditors, and with the independent accountants.

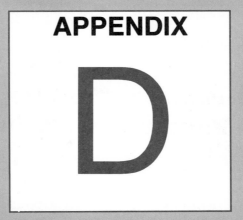

APPENDIX
D

American Institute of Certified Public Accountants Code of Professional Conduct* and National Association of Accountants Standards of Ethical Behavior for Management Accountants

Appendix D contains the codes of ethics for members of two important accounting organizations—the American Institute of Certified Public Accountants and the National Association of Accountants. By reading these codes, you can begin to understand the high standards of conduct that are expected of accountants. Being subjected to a code of ethics will not necessarily cause a dishonest person to behave honestly. An honest person will learn what behavior is expected and is likely to abide by the code.

---

* Author's note: As of this writing, the AICPA governing council and the Federal Trade Commission were negotiating an agreement that would permit the charging of contingent fees and commissions in certain circumstances (but not from audit clients; see Rule 302, page 1239).

American Institute of Certified Public Accountants
Code of Professional Conduct
as adopted January 12, 1988

Composition, Applicability, and Compliance

The Code of Professional Conduct of the American Institute of Certified Public Accountants consists of two sections—(1) the Principles and (2) the Rules. The Principles provide the framework for the Rules, which govern the performance of professional services by members. The Council of the American Institute of Certified Public Accountants is authorized to designate bodies to promulgate technical standards under the Rules, and the bylaws require adherence to those Rules and standards.

The Code of Professional Conduct was adopted by the membership to provide guidance and rules to all members—those in public practice, in industry, in government, and in education—in the performance of their professional responsibilities.

Compliance with the Code of Professional Conduct, as with all standards in an open society, depends primarily on members' understanding and voluntary actions, secondarily on reinforcement by peers and public opinion, and ultimately on disciplinary proceedings, when necessary, against members who fail to comply with the Rules.

Section I—Principles

Preamble

Membership in the American Institute of Certified Public Accountants is voluntary. By accepting membership, a certified public accountant assumes an obligation of self-discipline above and beyond the requirements of laws and regulations.

These Principles of the Code of Professional Conduct of the American Institute of Certified Public Accountants express the profession's recognition of its responsibilities to the public, to clients, and to colleagues. They guide members in the performance of their professional responsibilities and express the basic tenets of ethical and professional conduct. The Principles call for an unswerving commitment to honorable behavior, even at the sacrifice of personal advantage.

Article I

Responsibilities

In carrying out their responsibilities as professionals, members should exercise sensitive professional and moral judgments in all their activities.

As professionals, certified public accountants perform an essential role in society. Consistent with that role, members of the American Institute of Certified Public Accountants have responsibilities to all those who use their professional services. Members also have a continuing responsibility to cooperate with each other to improve the art of accounting, maintain the public's confidence, and carry out the profession's special responsibilities for self-governance. The collective efforts of all members are required to maintain and enhance the traditions of the profession.

Article II

The Public Interest

Members should accept the obligation to act in a way that will serve the public interest, honor the public trust, and demonstrate commitment to professionalism.

A distinguishing mark of a profession is acceptance of its responsibility to the public. The accounting profession's public consists of clients, credit grantors, governments, employers, investors, the business and financial community, and others who rely on the objectivity and integrity of certified public accountants to maintain the orderly functioning of commerce. This reliance imposes a public interest responsibility on certified public accountants. The public interest is defined as the collective well-being of the community of people and institutions the profession serves.

In discharging their professional responsibilities, members may encounter conflicting pressures from among each of those groups. In resolving those conflicts, members should act with integrity, guided by the precept that when members fulfill their responsibility to the public, clients' and employers' interests are best served.

Those who rely on certified public accountants expect them to discharge their responsibilities with integrity, objectivity, due professional care, and a genuine interest in serving the public. They are expected to provide quality services, enter into fee arrangements, and offer a range of services—all in a manner that demonstrates a level of professionalism consistent with these Principles of the Code of Professional Conduct.

All who accept membership in the American Institute of Certified Public Accountants commit themselves to honor the public trust. In return for the faith that the public reposes in them, members should seek continually to demonstrate their dedication to professional excellence.

Article III

Integrity

To maintain and broaden public confidence, members should perform all professional responsibilities with the highest sense of integrity.

Integrity is an element of character fundamental to professional recognition. It is the quality from which the public trust derives and the benchmark against which a member must ultimately test all decisions.

Integrity requires a member to be, among other things, honest and candid within the constraints of client confidentiality. Service and the public trust should not be subordinated to personal gain and advantage. Integrity can accommodate the inadvertent error and the honest difference of opinion; it cannot accommodate deceit or subordination of principle.

Integrity is measured in terms of what is right and just. In the absence of specific rules, standards, or guidance, or in the face of conflicting opinions, a member should test decisions and deeds by asking: "Am I doing what a person of integrity would do? Have I retained my integrity?" Integrity requires a member to observe both the form and the spirit of technical and ethical standards; circumvention of those standards constitutes subordination of judgment.

Integrity also requires a member to observe the principles of objectivity and independence and of due care.

Article IV

Objectivity and Independence

A member should maintain objectivity and be free of conflicts of interest in discharging professional responsibilities. A member in public practice should be independent in fact and appearance when providing auditing and other attestation services.

Objectivity is a state of mind, a quality that lends value to a member's services. It is a distinguishing feature of the profession. The principle of objectivity imposes the obligation to be impartial, intellectually honest. and free of conflicts of interest. Independence precludes relationships that may appear to impair a member's objectivity in rendering attestation services.

Members often serve multiple interests in many different capacities and must demonstrate their objectivity in varying circumstances. Members in public practice render attest, tax, and management advisory services. Other members prepare financial statements in the employment of others, perform internal auditing services, and serve in financial and management capacities in industry, education, and government. They also educate and train those who aspire to admission into the profession. Regardless of service or capacity, members should protect the integrity of their work, maintain objectivity, and avoid any subordination of their judgment.

For a member in public practice, the maintenance of objectivity and independence requires a continuing assessment of client relationships and public responsibility. Such a member who provides auditing and other attestation services should be independent in fact and appearance. In providing all other services, a member should maintain objectivity and avoid conflicts of interest.

Although members not in public practice cannot maintain the appearance of independence, they nevertheless have the responsibility to maintain objectivity in rendering professional services. Members employed by others to prepare financial statements or to perform auditing, tax, or consulting services are charged with the same responsibility for objectivity as members in public practice and must be scrupulous in their application of generally accepted accounting principles and candid in all their dealings with members in public practice.

Article V

Due Care

A member should observe the profession's technical and ethical standards, strive continually to improve competence and the quality of services, and discharge professional responsibility to the best of the member's ability.

The quest for excellence is the essence of due care. Due care requires a member to discharge professional responsibilities with competence and diligence. It imposes the obligation to perform professional services to the best of a member's ability with concern for the best interest of those for whom the services are performed and consistent with the profession's responsibility to the public.

Competence is derived from a synthesis of education and experience. It begins with a mastery of the common body of knowledge required for designation as a certified public accountant. The maintenance of competence requires a commitment to learning and professional improvement that must continue throughout a member's professional life. It is a member's individual responsibility. In all engagements and in all responsibilities, each member should undertake to achieve a level of competence that will assure that the quality of the member's services meets the high level of professionalism required by these Principles.

Competence represents the attainment and maintenance of a level of understanding and knowledge that enables a member to render services with facility and acumen. It also establishes the limitations of a member's capabilities by dictating that consultation or referral may be required when a professional engagement exceeds the personal competence of a member or a member's firm. Each member is responsible for assessing his or her own competence—of evaluating whether education, experience, and judgment are adequate for the responsibility to be assumed.

Members should be diligent in discharging responsibilities to clients, employers, and the public. Diligence imposes the responsibility to render services promptly and carefully, to be thorough, and to observe applicable technical and ethical standards.

Due care requires a member to plan and supervise adequately any professional activity for which he or she is responsible.

Article VI

Scope and Nature of Services

A member in public practice should observe the Principles of the Code of Professional Conduct in determining the scope and nature of services to be provided.

The public interest aspect of certified public accountants' services requires that such services be consistent with acceptable professional behavior for certified public accountants. Integrity requires that service and the public trust not be subordinated to personal gain and advantage. Objectivity and independence require that members be free from conflicts of interest in discharging professional responsibilities. Due care requires that services be provided with competence and diligence.

Each of these Principles should be considered by members in determining whether or not to provide specific services in individual circumstances. In some instances, they may represent an overall constraint on the nonaudit services that might be offered to a specific client. No hard-and-fast rules can be developed to help members reach these judgments, but they must be satisfied that they are meeting the spirit of the Principles in this regard.

In order to accomplish this, members should

- Practice in firms that have in place internal quality-control procedures to ensure that services are competently delivered and adequately supervised.
- Determine, in their individual judgments, whether the scope and nature of other services provided to an audit client would create a conflict of interest in the performance of the audit function for that client.
- Assess, in their individual judgments, whether an activity is consistent with their role as professionals (for example, Is such activity a reasonable extension or variation of existing services offered by the member or others in the profession?).

Section II—Rules

Applicability

The bylaws of the American Institute of Certified Public Accountants require that members adhere to the Rules of the Code of Professional Conduct. Members must be prepared to justify departures from these Rules.

Definitions

[*Adoption of the revised Code of Professional Conduct will require modification of some of the definitions of terms used in the Principles and Rules. The Professional Ethics Executive Committee has this project under way. Until new definitions are adopted, the definitions of terms as they appeared prior to adoption of the new Rules on January 12, 1988, are presented for reference.*]

Client.   The person(s) or entity which retains a member or his firm, engaged in the practice of public accounting, for the performance of professional services.

Council.   The Council of the American Institute of Certified Public Accountants.

Enterprise.   Any person(s) or entity, whether organized for profit or not, for which a CPA provides services.

Financial statements. Statements and footnotes related thereto that purport to show financial position which relates to a point in time or changes in financial position which relate to a period of time, and statements which use a cash or other incomplete basis of accounting. Balance sheets, statements of income, statements of retained earnings, statements of changes in financial position, and statements of changes in owners' equity are financial statements.

Incidental financial data included in management advisory services reports to support recommendations to a client and tax returns and supporting schedules do not, for this purpose, constitute financial statements; and the statement, affidavit, or signature of preparers required on tax returns neither constitutes an opinion on financial statements nor requires a disclaimer of such opinion.

Firm. A proprietorship, partnership, or professional corporation or association engaged in the practice of public accounting, including individual partners or shareholders thereof.

Institute. The American Institute of Certified Public Accountants.

Interpretations of rules of conduct. Pronouncements issued by the division of professional ethics to provide guidelines concerning the scope and application of the rules of conduct.

Member. A member, associate member, or international associate of the American Institute of Certified Public Accountants.

Practice of public accounting. Holding out to be a CPA or public accountant and at the same time performing for a client one or more types of services rendered by public accountants. The term shall not be limited by a more restrictive definition which might be found in the accountancy law under which a member practices.

Professional services. One or more types of services performed in the practice of public accounting.

Rules

Rule 101   Independence

A member in public practice shall be independent in the performance of professional services as required by standards promulgated by bodies designated by Council.

Interpretation of Rule 101

Interpretation 101-1. Independence shall be considered to be impaired if, for example, a member had any of the following transactions, interests, or relationships:

A. During the period of a professional engagement or at the time of expressing an opinion, a member or a member's firm
   1. Had or was committed to acquire any direct or material indirect financial interest in the enterprise.
   2. Was a trustee of any trust or executor or administrator of any estate if such trust or estate had or was committed to acquire any direct or material indirect financial interest in the enterprise.
   3. Had any joint, closely held business investment with the enterprise or with any officer, director, or principal stockholders thereof that was material in relation to the member's net worth or to the net worth of the member's firm.
   4. Had any loan to or from the enterprise or any officer, director, or principal stockholder of the enterprise. This proscription does not apply to the following loans from a financial institution when made under normal lending procedures, terms, and requirements:
      a. Loans obtained by a member or a member's firm that are not material in relation to the net worth of such borrower.
      b. Home mortgages.
      c. Other secured loans, except loans guaranteed by a member's firm which are otherwise unsecured.

B. During the period covered by the financial statements, during the period of the professional engagement, or at the time of expressing an opinion, a member or a member's firm
   1. Was connected with the enterprise as a promoter, underwriter or voting trustee, as a director or officer, or in any capacity equivalent to that of a member of management or of an employee.
   2. Was a trustee for any pension or profit-sharing trust of the enterprise.

The above examples are not intended to be all-inclusive.

Rule 102   Integrity and Objectivity

In the performance of any professional service, a member shall maintain objectivity and integrity, shall be free of conflicts of interest, and shall not knowingly misrepresent facts or subordinate his or her judgment to others.

Rule 201   General Standards

A member shall comply with the following standards and with any interpretations thereof by bodies designated by Council.

A. *Professional Competence.* Undertake only those professional services that the member or the member's firm can reasonably expect to be completed with professional competence.

B. *Due Professional Care.* Exercise due professional care in the performance of professional services.

C. *Planning and Supervision.* Adequately plan and supervise the performance of professional services.

D. *Sufficient Relevant Data.* Obtain sufficient relevant data to afford a reasonable basis for conclusions or recommendations in relation to any professional services performed.

Rule 202 Compliance With Standards

A member who performs auditing, review, compilation, management advisory, tax, or other professional services shall comply with standards promulgated by bodies designated by Council.

Rule 203 Accounting Principles

A member shall not (1) express an opinion or state affirmatively that the financial statements or other financial data of any entity are presented in conformity with generally accepted accounting principles or (2) state that he or she is not aware of any material modifications that should be made to such statements or data in order for them to be in conformity with generally accepted accounting principles, if such statements or data contain any departure from an accounting principle promulgated by bodies designated by Council to establish such principles that has a material effect on the statements or data taken as a whole. If, however, the statements or data contain such a departure and the member can demonstrate that due to unusual circumstances the financial statements or data would otherwise have been misleading, the member can comply with the rule by describing the departure, its approximate effects, if practicable, and the reasons why compliance with the principle would result in a misleading statement.

Rule 301 Confidential Client Information

A member in public practice shall not disclose any confidential client information without the specific consent of the client.

This rule shall not be construed (1) to relieve a member of his or her professional obligations under rules 202 and 203, (2) to affect in any way the member's obligation to comply with a validly issued and enforceable subpoena or summons, (3) to prohibit review of a member's professional practice under AICPA or state CPA society authorization, or (4) to preclude a member from initiating a complaint with or responding to any inquiry made by a recognized investigative or disciplinary body.

Members of a recognized investigative or disciplinary body and professional practice reviewers shall not use to their own advantage or disclose any member's confidential client information that comes to their attention in carrying out their official responsibilities. However, this prohibition shall not restrict the exchange of information with a recognized investigative or disciplinary body or affect, in any way, compliance with a validly issued and enforceable subpoena or summons.

Rule 302   Contingent Fees

Professional services shall not be offered or rendered under an arrangement whereby no fee will be charged unless a specified finding or result is attained, or where the fee is otherwise contingent upon the finding or results of such services. However, a member's fees may vary depending, for example, on the complexity of services rendered.

Fees are not regarded as being contingent if fixed by courts or other public authorities, or, in tax matters, if determined based on the results of judicial proceedings or the findings of governmental agencies.

Rule 401   [There are currently no rules in the 400 series.]

Rule 501   Acts Discreditable

A member shall not commit an act discreditable to the profession.

Rule 502   Advertising and Other Forms of Solicitation

A member in public practice shall not seek to obtain clients by advertising or other forms of solicitation in a manner that is false, misleading, or deceptive. Solicitation by the use of coercion, over-reaching, or harassing conduct is prohibited.

Rule 503   Commissions

The acceptance by a member in public practice of a payment for the referral of products or services of others to a client is prohibited. Such action is considered to create a conflict of interest that results in a loss of objectivity and independence.

A member shall not make a payment to obtain a client. This rule shall not prohibit payments for the purchase of an accounting practice or retirement payments to individuals formerly engaged in the practice of public accounting or payments to their heirs or estates.

Rule 504   [There is currently no rule 504.]

Rule 505   Form of Practice and Name

A member may practice public accounting only in the form of a proprietorship, a partnership, or a professional corporation whose characteristics conform to resolutions of Council.

A member shall not practice public accounting under a firm name that is misleading. Names of one or more past partners or shareholders may be included in the firm name of a successor partnership or corporation. Also, a partner or shareholder surviving the death or withdrawal of all other partners or shareholders may continue to practice under such name which includes the name of past partners or shareholders for up to two years after becoming a sole practitioner.

A firm may not designate itself as "Members of the American Institute of Certified Public Accountants" unless all of its partners or shareholders are members of the Institute.

National Association of Accountants
Standards of Ethical Conduct for Management Accountants

Management accountants have an obligation to the organizations they serve, their profession, the public, and themselves to maintain the highest standards of ethical conduct. In recognition of this obligation, the National Association of Accountants has promulgated the following standards of ethical conduct for management accountants. Adherence to these standards is integral to achieving the *Objectives of Management Accounting.*[1] Management accountants shall not commit acts contrary to these standards nor shall they condone the commission of such acts by others within their organizations.

Competence

Management accountants have a responsibility to:

- Maintain an appropriate level of professional competence by ongoing development of their knowledge and skills.

- Perform their professional duties in accordance with relevant laws, regulations, and technical standards.

- Prepare complete and clear reports and recommendations after appropriate analyses of relevant and reliable information.

Confidentiality

Management accountants have a responsibility to:

- Refrain from disclosing confidential information acquired in the course of their work except when authorized, unless legally obligated to do so.

[1] National Association of Accountants, *Statements on Management Accounting: Objectives of Management Accounting,* Statement No. 1B, New York, N.Y., June 17, 1982.

- Inform subordinates as appropriate regarding the confidentiality of information acquired in the course of their work and monitor their activities to assure the maintenance of that confidentiality.
- Refrain from using or appearing to use confidential information acquired in the course of their work for unethical or illegal advantage either personally or through third parties.

Integrity

Management accountants have a responsibility to:

- Avoid actual or apparent conflicts of interest and advise all appropriate parties of any potential conflict.
- Refrain from engaging in any activity that would prejudice their ability to carry out their duties ethically.
- Refuse any gift, favor, or hospitality that would influence or would appear to influence their actions.
- Refrain from either actively or passively subverting the attainment of the organization's legitimate and ethical objectives.
- Recognize and communicate professional limitations or other constraints that would preclude responsible judgment or successful performance of an activity.
- Communicate unfavorable as well as favorable information and professional judgments or opinions.
- Refrain from engaging in or supporting any activity that would discredit the profession.

Objectivity

Management accountants have a responsibility to:

- Communicate information fairly and objectively.
- Disclose fully all relevant information that could reasonably be expected to influence an intended user's understanding of the reports, comments, and recommendations presented. □

Resolution of Ethical Conflict

In applying the standards of ethical conduct, management accountants may encounter problems in identifying unethical behavior or in resolving an ethical conflict. When faced with significant ethical issues, management accountants should follow the established policies of the organization bearing on the resolution of such conflict. If these policies do not resolve the ethical conflict, management accountants should consider the following courses of action:

- Discuss such problems with the immediate superior except when it appears that the superior is involved, in which case the problem should be presented initially to the next higher managerial level. If satisfactory resolution cannot be achieved when the problem is initially presented, submit the issues to the next higher managerial level.

    If the immediate superior is the chief executive officer, or equivalent, the acceptable reviewing authority may be a group such as the audit committee, executive committee, board of directors, board of trustees, or owners. Contact with levels above the immediate superior should be initiated only with the superior's knowledge, assuming the superior is not involved.

- Clarify relevant concepts by confidential discussion with an objective advisor to obtain an understanding of possible courses of action.

- If the ethical conflict still exists after exhausting all levels of internal review, the management accountant may have no other recourse on significant matters than to resign from the organization and to submit an informative memorandum to an appropriate representative of the organization.

Except where legally prescribed, communication of such problems to authorities or individuals not employed or engaged by the organization is not considered appropriate.

APPENDIX

E

Compound Interest
and Annuity Tables

Table 1 *Future Value of $1 at Compound Interest: 0.5%–10%* $F_{i,n} = (1 + i)^n$

Period	.5%	1%	1.5%	2%	2.5%	3%	3.5%	4%	4.5%	5%
1	1.00500	1.01000	1.01500	1.02000	1.02500	1.03000	1.03500	1.04000	1.04500	1.05000
2	1.01003	1.02010	1.03023	1.04040	1.05063	1.06090	1.07123	1.08160	1.09203	1.10250
3	1.01508	1.03030	1.04568	1.06121	1.07689	1.09273	1.10872	1.12486	1.14117	1.15762
4	1.02015	1.04060	1.06136	1.08243	1.10381	1.12551	1.14752	1.16986	1.19252	1.21551
5	1.02525	1.05101	1.07728	1.10408	1.13141	1.15927	1.18769	1.21665	1.24618	1.27628
6	1.03038	1.06152	1.09344	1.12616	1.15969	1.19405	1.22926	1.26532	1.30226	1.34010
7	1.03553	1.07214	1.10984	1.14869	1.18869	1.22987	1.27228	1.31593	1.36086	1.40710
8	1.04071	1.08286	1.12649	1.17166	1.21840	1.26677	1.31681	1.36857	1.42210	1.47746
9	1.04591	1.09369	1.14339	1.19509	1.24886	1.30477	1.36290	1.42331	1.48610	1.55133
10	1.05114	1.10462	1.16054	1.21899	1.28008	1.34392	1.41060	1.48024	1.55297	1.62889
11	1.05640	1.11567	1.17795	1.24337	1.31209	1.38423	1.45997	1.53945	1.62285	1.71034
12	1.06168	1.12683	1.19562	1.26824	1.34489	1.42576	1.51107	1.60103	1.69588	1.79586
13	1.06699	1.13809	1.21355	1.29361	1.37851	1.46853	1.56396	1.66507	1.77220	1.88565
14	1.07232	1.14947	1.23176	1.31948	1.41297	1.51259	1.61869	1.73168	1.85194	1.97993
15	1.07768	1.16097	1.25023	1.34587	1.44830	1.55797	1.67535	1.80094	1.93528	2.07893
16	1.08307	1.17258	1.26899	1.37279	1.48451	1.60471	1.73399	1.87298	2.02237	2.18287
17	1.08849	1.18430	1.28802	1.40024	1.52162	1.65285	1.79468	1.94790	2.11338	2.29202
18	1.09393	1.19615	1.30734	1.42825	1.55966	1.70243	1.85749	2.02582	2.20848	2.40662
19	1.09940	1.20811	1.32695	1.45681	1.59865	1.75351	1.92250	2.10685	2.30786	2.52695
20	1.10490	1.22019	1.34686	1.48595	1.63862	1.80611	1.98979	2.19112	2.41171	2.65330
21	1.11042	1.23239	1.36706	1.51567	1.67958	1.86029	2.05943	2.27877	2.52024	2.78596
22	1.11597	1.24472	1.38756	1.54598	1.72157	1.91610	2.13151	2.36992	2.63365	2.92526
23	1.12155	1.25716	1.40838	1.57690	1.76461	1.97359	2.20611	2.46472	2.75217	3.07152
24	1.12716	1.26973	1.42950	1.60844	1.80873	2.03279	2.28333	2.56330	2.87601	3.22510
25	1.13280	1.28243	1.45095	1.64061	1.85394	2.09378	2.36324	2.66584	3.00543	3.38635
26	1.13846	1.29526	1.47271	1.67342	1.90029	2.15659	2.44596	2.77247	3.14068	3.55567
27	1.14415	1.30821	1.49480	1.70689	1.94780	2.22129	2.53157	2.88337	3.28201	3.73346
28	1.14987	1.32129	1.51722	1.74102	1.99650	2.28793	2.62017	2.99870	3.42970	3.92013
29	1.15562	1.33450	1.53998	1.77584	2.04641	2.35657	2.71188	3.11865	3.58404	4.11614
30	1.16140	1.34785	1.56308	1.81136	2.09757	2.42726	2.80679	3.24340	3.74532	4.32194

5.5%	6%	6.5%	7%	7.5%	8%	8.5%	9%	9.5%	10%
1.05500	1.06000	1.06500	1.07000	1.07500	1.08000	1.08500	1.09000	1.09500	1.10000
1.11303	1.12360	1.13423	1.14490	1.15563	1.16640	1.17723	1.18810	1.19903	1.21000
1.17424	1.19102	1.20795	1.22504	1.24230	1.25971	1.27729	1.29503	1.31293	1.33100
1.23882	1.26248	1.28647	1.31080	1.33547	1.36049	1.38586	1.41158	1.43766	1.46410
1.30696	1.33823	1.37009	1.40255	1.43563	1.46933	1.50366	1.53862	1.57424	1.61051
1.37884	1.41852	1.45914	1.50073	1.54330	1.58687	1.63147	1.67710	1.72379	1.77156
1.45468	1.50363	1.55399	1.60578	1.65905	1.71382	1.77014	1.82804	1.88755	1.94872
1.53469	1.59385	1.65500	1.71819	1.78348	1.85093	1.92060	1.99256	2.06687	2.14359
1.61909	1.68948	1.76257	1.83846	1.91724	1.99900	2.08386	2.17189	2.26322	2.35795
1.70814	1.79085	1.87714	1.96715	2.06103	2.15892	2.26098	2.36736	2.47823	2.59374
1.80209	1.89830	1.99915	2.10485	2.21561	2.33164	2.45317	2.58043	2.71366	2.85312
1.90121	2.01220	2.12910	2.25219	2.38178	2.51817	2.66169	2.81266	2.97146	3.13843
2.00577	2.13293	2.26749	2.40985	2.56041	2.71962	2.88793	3.06580	3.25375	3.45227
2.11609	2.26090	2.41487	2.57853	2.75244	2.93719	3.13340	3.34173	3.56285	3.79750
2.23248	2.39656	2.57184	2.75903	2.95888	3.17217	3.39974	3.64248	3.90132	4.17725
2.35526	2.54035	2.73901	2.95216	3.18079	3.42594	3.68872	3.97031	4.27195	4.59497
2.48480	2.69277	2.91705	3.15882	3.41935	3.70002	4.00226	4.32763	4.67778	5.05447
2.62147	2.85434	3.10665	3.37993	3.67580	3.99602	4.34245	4.71712	5.12217	5.55992
2.76565	3.02560	3.30859	3.61653	3.95149	4.31570	4.71156	5.14166	5.60878	6.11591
2.91776	3.20714	3.52365	3.86968	4.24785	4.66096	5.11205	5.60441	6.14161	6.72750
3.07823	3.39956	3.75268	4.14056	4.56644	5.03383	5.54657	6.10881	6.72507	7.40025
3.24754	3.60354	3.99661	4.43040	4.90892	5.43654	6.01803	6.65860	7.36395	8.14027
3.42615	3.81975	4.25639	4.74053	5.27709	5.87146	6.52956	7.25787	8.06352	8.95430
3.61459	4.04893	4.53305	5.07237	5.67287	6.34118	7.08457	7.91108	8.82956	9.84973
3.81339	4.29187	4.82770	5.42743	6.09834	6.84848	7.68676	8.62308	9.66836	10.83471
4.02313	4.54938	5.14150	5.80735	6.55572	7.39635	8.34014	9.39916	10.58686	11.91818
4.24440	4.82235	5.47570	6.21387	7.04739	7.98806	9.04905	10.24508	11.59261	13.10999
4.47784	5.11169	5.83162	6.64884	7.57595	8.62711	9.81822	11.16714	12.69391	14.42099
4.72412	5.41839	6.21067	7.11426	8.14414	9.31727	10.65277	12.17218	13.89983	15.86309
4.98395	5.74349	6.61437	7.61226	8.75496	10.06266	11.55825	13.26768	15.22031	17.44940

Table 1 *(concluded)* *Future Value of $1 at Compound Interest: 10.5%–20%*

Period	10.5%	11%	11.5%	12%	12.5%	13%	13.5%	14%	14.5%	15%
1	1.10500	1.11000	1.11500	1.12000	1.12500	1.13000	1.13500	1.14000	1.14500	1.15000
2	1.22103	1.23210	1.24323	1.25440	1.26563	1.27690	1.28822	1.29960	1.31102	1.32250
3	1.34923	1.36763	1.38620	1.40493	1.42383	1.44290	1.46214	1.48154	1.50112	1.52088
4	1.49090	1.51807	1.54561	1.57352	1.60181	1.63047	1.65952	1.68896	1.71879	1.74901
5	1.64745	1.68506	1.72335	1.76234	1.80203	1.84244	1.88356	1.92541	1.96801	2.01136
6	1.82043	1.87041	1.92154	1.97382	2.02729	2.08195	2.13784	2.19497	2.25337	2.31306
7	2.01157	2.07616	2.14252	2.21068	2.28070	2.35261	2.42645	2.50227	2.58011	2.66002
8	2.22279	2.30454	2.38891	2.47596	2.56578	2.65844	2.75402	2.85259	2.95423	3.05902
9	2.45618	2.55804	2.66363	2.77308	2.88651	3.00404	3.12581	3.25195	3.38259	3.51788
10	2.71408	2.83942	2.96995	3.10585	3.24732	3.39457	3.54780	3.70722	3.87307	4.04556
11	2.99906	3.15176	3.31149	3.47855	3.65324	3.83586	4.02675	4.22623	4.43466	4.65239
12	3.31396	3.49845	3.69231	3.89598	4.10989	4.33452	4.57036	4.81790	5.07769	5.35025
13	3.66193	3.88328	4.11693	4.36349	4.62363	4.89801	5.18736	5.49241	5.81395	6.15279
14	4.04643	4.31044	4.59037	4.88711	5.20158	5.53475	5.88765	6.26135	6.65697	7.07571
15	4.47130	4.78459	5.11827	5.47357	5.85178	6.25427	6.68248	7.13794	7.62223	8.13706
16	4.94079	5.31089	5.70687	6.13039	6.58325	7.06733	7.58462	8.13725	8.72746	9.35762
17	5.45957	5.89509	6.36316	6.86604	7.40616	7.98608	8.60854	9.27646	9.99294	10.76126
18	6.03283	6.54355	7.09492	7.68997	8.33193	9.02427	9.77070	10.57517	11.44192	12.37545
19	6.66628	7.26334	7.91084	8.61276	9.37342	10.19742	11.08974	12.05569	13.10039	14.23177
20	7.36623	8.06231	8.82058	9.64629	10.54509	11.52309	12.58686	13.74349	15.00064	16.36654
21	8.13969	8.94917	9.83495	10.80385	11.86323	13.02109	14.28608	15.66758	17.17573	18.82152
22	8.99436	9.93357	10.96597	12.10031	13.34613	14.71383	16.21470	17.86104	19.66621	21.64475
23	9.93876	11.02627	12.22706	13.55235	15.01440	16.62663	18.40369	20.36158	22.51781	24.89146
24	10.98233	12.23916	13.63317	15.17863	16.89120	18.78809	20.88818	23.21221	25.78290	28.62518
25	12.13548	13.58546	15.20098	17.00006	19.00260	21.23054	23.70809	26.46192	29.52141	32.91895
26	13.40971	15.07986	16.94910	19.04007	21.37793	23.99051	26.90868	30.16658	33.80202	37.85680
27	14.81772	16.73865	18.89824	21.32488	24.05017	27.10928	30.54135	34.38991	38.70331	43.53531
28	16.37359	18.57990	21.07154	23.88387	27.05644	30.63349	34.66443	39.20449	44.31529	50.06561
29	18.09281	20.62369	23.49477	26.74993	30.43849	34.61584	39.34413	44.69312	50.74101	57.57545
30	19.99256	22.89230	26.19667	29.95992	34.24330	39.11590	44.65559	50.95016	58.09846	66.21177

15.5%	16%	16.5%	17%	17.5%	18%	18.5%	19%	19.5%	20%
1.15500	1.16000	1.16500	1.17000	1.17500	1.18000	1.18500	1.19000	1.19500	1.20000
1.33402	1.34560	1.35722	1.36890	1.38063	1.39240	1.40422	1.41610	1.42802	1.44000
1.54080	1.56090	1.58117	1.60161	1.62223	1.64303	1.66401	1.68516	1.70649	1.72800
1.77962	1.81064	1.84206	1.87389	1.90613	1.93878	1.97185	2.00534	2.03926	2.07360
2.05546	2.10034	2.14600	2.19245	2.23970	2.28776	2.33664	2.38635	2.43691	2.48832
2.37406	2.43640	2.50009	2.56516	2.63164	2.69955	2.76892	2.83976	2.91211	2.98598
2.74204	2.82622	2.91260	3.00124	3.09218	3.18547	3.28117	3.37932	3.47997	3.58318
3.16706	3.27841	3.39318	3.51145	3.63331	3.75886	3.88818	4.02139	4.15856	4.29982
3.65795	3.80296	3.95306	4.10840	4.26914	4.43545	4.60750	4.78545	4.96948	5.15978
4.22493	4.41144	4.60531	4.80683	5.01624	5.23384	5.45989	5.69468	5.93853	6.19174
4.87980	5.11726	5.36519	5.62399	5.89409	6.17593	6.46996	6.77667	7.09654	7.43008
5.63617	5.93603	6.25045	6.58007	6.92555	7.28759	7.66691	8.06424	8.48037	8.91610
6.50977	6.88579	7.28177	7.69868	8.13752	8.59936	9.08528	9.59645	10.13404	10.69932
7.51879	7.98752	8.48326	9.00745	9.56159	10.14724	10.76606	11.41977	12.11018	12.83918
8.68420	9.26552	9.88300	10.53872	11.23487	11.97375	12.75778	13.58953	14.47167	15.40702
10.03025	10.74800	11.51370	12.33030	13.20097	14.12902	15.11797	16.17154	17.29364	18.48843
11.58494	12.46768	13.41346	14.42646	15.51114	16.67225	17.91480	19.24413	20.66590	22.18611
13.38060	14.46251	15.62668	16.87895	18.22559	19.67325	21.22904	22.90052	24.69575	26.62333
15.45460	16.77652	18.20508	19.74838	21.41507	23.21444	25.15641	27.25162	29.51143	31.94800
17.85006	19.46076	21.20892	23.10560	25.16271	27.39303	29.81035	32.42942	35.26615	38.33760
20.61682	22.57448	24.70839	27.03355	29.56618	32.32378	35.32526	38.59101	42.14305	46.00512
23.81243	26.18640	28.78527	31.62925	34.74026	38.14206	41.86043	45.92331	50.36095	55.20614
27.50335	30.37622	33.53484	37.00623	40.81981	45.00763	49.60461	54.64873	60.18134	66.24737
31.76637	35.23642	39.06809	43.29729	47.96327	53.10901	58.78147	65.03199	71.91670	79.49685
36.69016	40.87424	45.51433	50.65783	56.35684	62.66863	69.65604	77.38807	85.94045	95.39622
42.37713	47.41412	53.02419	59.26966	66.21929	73.94898	82.54240	92.09181	102.69884	114.47546
48.94559	55.00038	61.77318	69.34550	77.80767	87.25980	97.81275	109.58925	122.72511	137.37055
56.53216	63.80044	71.96576	81.13423	91.42401	102.96656	115.90811	130.41121	146.65651	164.84466
65.29464	74.00851	83.84011	94.92705	107.42321	121.50054	137.35111	155.18934	175.25453	197.81359
75.41531	85.84988	97.67373	111.06465	126.22227	143.37064	162.76106	184.67531	209.42916	237.37631

Table 2 *Future Value of an Ordinary Annuity of $1 per Period: 0.5%–10%* $F_{A_{i,n}} = \dfrac{(1 + i)^n - 1}{i}$

Period	.5%	1%	1.5%	2%	2.5%	3%	3.5%	4%	4.5%	5%
1	1.00000	1.00000	1.00000	1.00000	1.00000	1.00000	1.00000	1.00000	1.00000	1.00000
2	2.00500	2.01000	2.01500	2.02000	2.02500	2.03000	2.03500	2.04000	2.04500	2.05000
3	3.01502	3.03010	3.04522	3.06040	3.07562	3.09090	3.10622	3.12160	3.13702	3.15250
4	4.03010	4.06040	4.09090	4.12161	4.15252	4.18363	4.21494	4.24646	4.27819	4.31012
5	5.05025	5.10101	5.15227	5.20404	5.25633	5.30914	5.36247	5.41632	5.47071	5.52563
6	6.07550	6.15202	6.22955	6.30812	6.38774	6.46841	6.55015	6.63298	6.71689	6.80191
7	7.10588	7.21354	7.32299	7.43428	7.54743	7.66246	7.77941	7.89829	8.01915	8.14201
8	8.14141	8.28567	8.43284	8.58297	8.73612	8.89234	9.05169	9.21423	9.38001	9.54911
9	9.18212	9.36853	9.55933	9.75463	9.95452	10.15911	10.36850	10.58280	10.80211	11.02656
10	10.22803	10.46221	10.70272	10.94972	11.20338	11.46388	11.73139	12.00611	12.28821	12.57789
11	11.27917	11.56683	11.86326	12.16872	12.48347	12.80780	13.14199	13.48635	13.84118	14.20679
12	12.33556	12.68250	13.04121	13.41209	13.79555	14.19203	14.60196	15.02581	15.46403	15.91713
13	13.39724	13.80933	14.23683	14.68033	15.14044	15.61779	16.11303	16.62684	17.15991	17.71298
14	14.46423	14.94742	15.45038	15.97394	16.51895	17.08632	17.67699	18.29191	18.93211	19.59863
15	15.53655	16.09690	16.68214	17.29342	17.93193	18.59891	19.29568	20.02359	20.78405	21.57856
16	16.61423	17.25786	17.93237	18.63929	19.38022	20.15688	20.97103	21.82453	22.71934	23.65749
17	17.69730	18.43044	19.20136	20.01207	20.86473	21.76159	22.70502	23.69751	24.74171	25.84037
18	18.78579	19.61475	20.48938	21.41231	22.38635	23.41444	24.49969	25.64541	26.85508	28.13238
19	19.87972	20.81090	21.79672	22.84056	23.94601	25.11687	26.35718	27.67123	29.06356	30.53900
20	20.97912	22.01900	23.12367	24.29737	25.54466	26.87037	28.27968	29.77808	31.37142	33.06595
21	22.08401	23.23919	24.47052	25.78332	27.18327	28.67649	30.26947	31.96920	33.78314	35.71925
22	23.19443	24.47159	25.83758	27.29898	28.86286	30.53678	32.32890	34.24797	36.30338	38.50521
23	24.31040	25.71630	27.22514	28.84496	30.58443	32.45288	34.46041	36.61789	38.93703	41.43048
24	25.43196	26.97346	28.63352	30.42186	32.34904	34.42647	36.66653	39.08260	41.68920	44.50200
25	26.55912	28.24320	30.06302	32.03030	34.15776	36.45926	38.94986	41.64591	44.56521	47.72710
26	27.69191	29.52563	31.51397	33.67091	36.01171	38.55304	41.31310	44.31174	47.57064	51.11345
27	28.83037	30.82089	32.98668	35.34432	37.91200	40.70963	43.75906	47.08421	50.71132	54.66913
28	29.97452	32.12910	34.48148	37.05121	39.85980	42.93092	46.29063	49.96758	53.99333	58.40258
29	31.12439	33.45039	35.99870	38.79223	41.85630	45.21885	48.91080	52.96629	57.42303	62.32271
30	32.28002	34.78489	37.53868	40.56808	43.90270	47.57542	51.62268	56.08494	61.00707	66.43885

5.5%	6%	6.5%	7%	7.5%	8%	8.5%	9%	9.5%	10%
1.00000	1.00000	1.00000	1.00000	1.00000	1.00000	1.00000	1.00000	1.00000	1.00000
2.05500	2.06000	2.06500	2.07000	2.07500	2.08000	2.08500	2.09000	2.09500	2.10000
3.16802	3.18360	3.19922	3.21490	3.23062	3.24640	3.26222	3.27810	3.29402	3.31000
4.34227	4.37462	4.40717	4.43994	4.47292	4.50611	4.53951	4.57313	4.60696	4.64100
5.58109	5.63709	5.69364	5.75074	5.80839	5.86660	5.92537	5.98471	6.04462	6.10510
6.88805	6.97532	7.06373	7.15329	7.24402	7.33593	7.42903	7.52333	7.61886	7.71561
8.26689	8.39384	8.52287	8.65402	8.78732	8.92280	9.06050	9.20043	9.34265	9.48717
9.72157	9.89747	10.07686	10.25980	10.44637	10.63663	10.83064	11.02847	11.23020	11.43589
11.25626	11.49132	11.73185	11.97799	12.22985	12.48756	12.75124	13.02104	13.29707	13.57948
12.87535	13.18079	13.49442	13.81645	14.14709	14.48656	14.83510	15.19293	15.56029	15.93742
14.58350	14.97164	15.37156	15.78360	16.20812	16.64549	17.09608	17.56029	18.03852	18.53117
16.38559	16.86994	17.37071	17.88845	18.42373	18.97713	19.54925	20.14072	20.75218	21.38428
18.28680	18.88214	19.49981	20.14064	20.80551	21.49530	22.21094	22.95338	23.72363	24.52271
20.29257	21.01507	21.76730	22.55049	23.36592	24.21492	25.09887	26.01919	26.97738	27.97498
22.40866	23.27597	24.18217	25.12902	26.11836	27.15211	28.23227	29.36092	30.54023	31.77248
24.64114	25.67253	26.75401	27.88805	29.07724	30.32428	31.63201	33.00340	34.44155	35.94973
26.99640	28.21288	29.49302	30.84022	32.25804	33.75023	35.32073	36.97370	38.71350	40.54470
29.48120	30.90565	32.41007	33.99903	35.67739	37.45024	39.32300	41.30134	43.39128	45.59917
32.10267	33.75999	35.51672	37.37896	39.35319	41.44626	43.66545	46.01846	48.51345	51.15909
34.86832	36.78559	38.82531	40.99549	43.30468	45.76196	48.37701	51.16012	54.12223	57.27500
37.78608	39.99273	42.34895	44.86518	47.55253	50.42292	53.48906	56.76453	60.26384	64.00250
40.86431	43.39229	46.10164	49.00574	52.11897	55.45676	59.03563	62.87334	66.98891	71.40275
44.11185	46.99583	50.09824	53.43614	57.02790	60.89330	65.05366	69.53194	74.35286	79.54302
47.53800	50.81558	54.35463	58.17667	62.30499	66.76476	71.58322	76.78981	82.41638	88.49733
51.15259	54.86451	58.88768	63.24904	67.97786	73.10594	78.66779	84.70090	91.24593	98.34706
54.96598	59.15638	63.71538	68.67647	74.07620	79.95442	86.35455	93.32398	100.91430	109.18177
58.98911	63.70577	68.85688	74.48382	80.63192	87.35077	94.69469	102.72313	111.50116	121.09994
63.23351	68.52811	74.33257	80.69769	87.67931	95.33883	103.74374	112.96822	123.09377	134.20994
67.71135	73.63980	80.16419	87.34653	95.25526	103.96594	113.56196	124.13536	135.78767	148.63093
72.43548	79.05819	86.37486	94.46079	103.39940	113.28321	124.21473	136.30754	149.68750	164.49402

Table 2 (concluded)   *Future Value of an Ordinary Annuity of $1 per Period: 10.5%–20%*

Period	10.5%	11%	11.5%	12%	12.5%	13%	13.5%	14%	14.5%	15%
1 . . .	1.00000	1.00000	1.00000	1.00000	1.00000	1.00000	1.00000	1.00000	1.00000	1.00000
2 . . .	2.10500	2.11000	2.11500	2.12000	2.12500	2.13000	2.13500	2.14000	2.14500	2.15000
3 . . .	3.32602	3.34210	3.35822	3.37440	3.39062	3.40690	3.42322	3.43960	3.45602	3.47250
4 . . .	4.67526	4.70973	4.74442	4.77933	4.81445	4.84980	4.88536	4.92114	4.95715	4.99337
5 . . .	6.16616	6.22780	6.29003	6.35285	6.41626	6.48027	6.54488	6.61010	6.67594	6.74238
6 . . .	7.81361	7.91286	8.01338	8.11519	8.21829	8.32271	8.42844	8.53552	8.64395	8.75374
7 . . .	9.63404	9.78327	9.93492	10.08901	10.24558	10.40466	10.56628	10.73049	10.89732	11.06680
8 . . .	11.64561	11.85943	12.07744	12.29969	12.52628	12.75726	12.99273	13.23276	13.47743	13.72682
9 . . .	13.86840	14.16397	14.46634	14.77566	15.09206	15.41571	15.74675	16.08535	16.43166	16.78584
10 . . .	16.32458	16.72201	17.12997	17.54874	17.97857	18.41975	18.87256	19.33730	19.81425	20.30372
11 . . .	19.03866	19.56143	20.09992	20.65458	21.22589	21.81432	22.42036	23.04452	23.68731	24.34928
12 . . .	22.03772	22.71319	23.41141	24.13313	24.87913	25.65018	26.44711	27.27075	28.12197	29.00167
13 . . .	25.35168	26.21164	27.10372	28.02911	28.98902	29.98470	31.01746	32.08865	33.19966	34.35192
14 .:. .	29.01361	30.09492	31.22065	32.39260	33.61264	34.88271	36.20482	37.58107	39.01361	40.50471
15 . . .	33.06004	34.40536	35.81102	37.27971	38.81422	40.41746	42.09247	43.84241	45.67058	47.58041
16 . . .	37.53134	39.18995	40.92929	42.75328	44.66600	46.67173	48.77496	50.98035	53.29282	55.71747
17 . . .	42.47213	44.50084	46.63616	48.88367	51.24925	53.73906	56.35958	59.11760	62.02027	65.07509
18 . . .	47.93170	50.39594	52.99932	55.74971	58.65541	61.72514	64.96812	68.39407	72.01321	75.83636
19 . . .	53.96453	56.93949	60.09424	63.43968	66.98733	70.74941	74.73882	78.96923	83.45513	88.21181
20 . . .	60.63081	64.20283	68.00508	72.05244	76.36075	80.94683	85.82856	91.02493	96.55612	102.44358
21 . . .	67.99704	72.26514	76.82566	81.69874	86.90584	92.46992	98.41541	104.76842	111.55676	118.81012
22 . . .	76.13673	81.21431	86.66062	92.50258	98.76908	105.49101	112.70149	120.43600	128.73249	137.63164
23 . . .	85.13109	91.14788	97.62659	104.60289	112.11521	120.20484	128.91619	138.29704	148.39871	159.27638
24 . . .	95.06985	102.17415	109.85364	118.15524	127.12961	136.83147	147.31988	158.65862	170.91652	184.16784
25 . . .	106.05219	114.41331	123.48681	133.33387	144.02081	155.61956	168.20806	181.87083	196.69941	212.79302
26 . . .	118.18767	127.99877	138.68780	150.33393	163.02341	176.85010	191.91615	208.33274	226.22083	245.71197
27 . . .	131.59737	143.07864	155.63689	169.37401	184.40134	200.84061	218.82483	238.49933	260.02285	283.56877
28 . . .	146.41510	159.81729	174.53513	190.69889	208.45151	227.94989	249.36618	272.88923	298.72616	327.10408
29 . . .	162.78868	178.39719	195.60668	214.58275	235.50795	258.58338	284.03062	312.09373	343.04145	377.16969
30 . . .	180.88149	199.02088	219.10144	241.33268	265.94644	293.19922	323.37475	356.78685	393.78246	434.74515

15.5%	16%	16.5%	17%	17.5%	18%	18.5%	19%	19.5%	20%
1.00000	1.00000	1.00000	1.00000	1.00000	1.00000	1.00000	1.00000	1.00000	1.00000
2.15500	2.16000	2.16500	2.17000	2.17500	2.18000	2.18500	2.19000	2.19500	2.20000
3.48902	3.50560	3.52222	3.53890	3.55562	3.57240	3.58922	3.60610	3.62302	3.64000
5.02982	5.06650	5.10339	5.14051	5.17786	5.21543	5.25323	5.29126	5.32951	5.36800
6.80945	6.87714	6.94545	7.01440	7.08398	7.15421	7.22508	7.29660	7.36877	7.44160
8.86491	8.97748	9.09145	9.20685	9.32368	9.44197	9.56172	9.68295	9.80568	9.92992
11.23897	11.41387	11.59154	11.77201	11.95533	12.14152	12.33064	12.52271	12.71779	12.91590
13.98101	14.24009	14.50415	14.77325	15.04751	15.32700	15.61181	15.90203	16.19776	16.49908
17.14807	17.51851	17.89733	18.28471	18.68082	19.08585	19.49999	19.92341	20.35632	20.79890
20.80602	21.32147	21.85039	22.39311	22.94997	23.52131	24.10749	24.70886	25.32580	25.95868
25.03095	25.73290	26.45570	27.19994	27.96621	28.75514	29.56737	30.40355	31.26433	32.15042
29.91075	30.85017	31.82089	32.82393	33.86030	34.93107	36.03734	37.18022	38.36088	39.58050
35.54692	36.78620	38.07134	39.40399	40.78585	42.21866	43.70424	45.24446	46.84125	48.49660
42.05669	43.67199	45.35311	47.10267	48.92337	50.81802	52.78953	54.84091	56.97529	59.19592
49.57548	51.65951	53.83638	56.11013	58.48496	60.96527	63.55559	66.26068	69.08547	72.03511
58.25968	60.92503	63.71938	66.64885	69.71983	72.93901	76.31338	79.85021	83.55714	87.44213
68.28993	71.67303	75.23307	78.97915	82.92080	87.06804	91.43135	96.02175	100.85079	105.93056
79.87486	84.14072	88.64653	93.40561	98.43194	103.74028	109.34615	115.26588	121.51669	128.11667
93.25547	98.60323	104.27321	110.28456	116.65753	123.41353	130.57519	138.16640	146.21244	154.74000
108.71007	115.37975	122.47829	130.03294	138.07260	146.62797	155.73160	165.41802	175.72387	186.68800
126.56013	134.84051	143.68721	153.13854	163.23531	174.02100	185.54194	197.84744	210.99002	225.02560
147.17695	157.41499	168.39560	180.17209	192.80149	206.34479	220.86720	236.43846	253.13308	271.03072
170.98937	183.60138	197.18087	211.80134	227.54175	244.48685	262.72763	282.36176	303.49403	326.23686
198.49272	213.97761	230.71571	248.80757	268.36155	289.49448	312.33225	337.01050	363.67536	392.48424
230.25910	249.21402	269.78381	292.10486	316.32482	342.60349	371.11371	402.04249	435.59206	471.98108
266.94926	290.08827	315.29813	342.76268	372.68167	405.27211	440.76975	479.43056	521.53251	567.37730
309.32639	337.50239	368.32233	402.03234	438.90096	479.22109	523.31215	571.52237	624.23135	681.85276
358.27198	392.50277	430.09551	471.37783	516.70863	566.48089	621.12490	681.11162	746.95647	819.22331
414.80414	456.30322	502.06127	552.51207	608.13264	669.44745	737.03300	811.52283	893.61298	984.06797
480.09878	530.31173	585.90138	647.43912	715.55585	790.94799	874.38411	966.71217	1068.86751	1181.88157

Table 3 *Present Value of $1 at Compound Interest: 0.5%–7%*

$$P_{i,n} = \frac{1}{(1+i)^n}$$

Period	.5%	1%	1.5%	2%	2.5%	3%	3.5%	4%	4.5%	5%	5.5%	6%	6.5%	7%
1	0.99502	0.99010	0.98522	0.98039	0.97561	0.97087	0.96618	0.96154	0.95694	0.95238	0.94787	0.94340	0.93897	0.93458
2	0.99007	0.98030	0.97066	0.96117	0.95181	0.94260	0.93351	0.92456	0.91573	0.90703	0.89845	0.89000	0.88166	0.87344
3	0.98515	0.97059	0.95632	0.94232	0.92860	0.91514	0.90194	0.88900	0.87630	0.86384	0.85161	0.83962	0.82785	0.81630
4	0.98025	0.96098	0.94218	0.92385	0.90595	0.88849	0.87144	0.85480	0.83856	0.82270	0.80722	0.79209	0.77732	0.76290
5	0.97537	0.95147	0.92826	0.90573	0.88385	0.86261	0.84197	0.82193	0.80245	0.78353	0.76513	0.74726	0.72988	0.71299
6	0.97052	0.94205	0.91454	0.88797	0.86230	0.83748	0.81350	0.79031	0.76790	0.74622	0.72525	0.70496	0.68533	0.66634
7	0.96569	0.93272	0.90103	0.87056	0.84127	0.81309	0.78599	0.75992	0.73483	0.71068	0.68744	0.66506	0.64351	0.62275
8	0.96089	0.92348	0.88771	0.85349	0.82075	0.78941	0.75941	0.73069	0.70319	0.67684	0.65160	0.62741	0.60423	0.58201
9	0.95610	0.91434	0.87459	0.83676	0.80073	0.76642	0.73373	0.70259	0.67290	0.64461	0.61763	0.59190	0.56735	0.54393
10	0.95135	0.90529	0.86167	0.82035	0.78120	0.74409	0.70892	0.67556	0.64393	0.61391	0.58543	0.55839	0.53273	0.50835
11	0.94661	0.89632	0.84893	0.80426	0.76214	0.72242	0.68495	0.64958	0.61620	0.58468	0.55491	0.52679	0.50021	0.47509
12	0.94191	0.88745	0.83639	0.78849	0.74356	0.70138	0.66178	0.62460	0.58966	0.55684	0.52598	0.49697	0.46968	0.44401
13	0.93722	0.87866	0.82403	0.77303	0.72542	0.68095	0.63940	0.60057	0.56427	0.53032	0.49856	0.46884	0.44102	0.41496
14	0.93256	0.86996	0.81185	0.75788	0.70773	0.66112	0.61778	0.57748	0.53997	0.50507	0.47257	0.44230	0.41410	0.38782
15	0.92792	0.86135	0.79985	0.74301	0.69047	0.64186	0.59689	0.55526	0.51672	0.48102	0.44793	0.41727	0.38883	0.36245
16	0.92330	0.85282	0.78803	0.72845	0.67362	0.62317	0.57671	0.53391	0.49447	0.45811	0.42458	0.39365	0.36510	0.33873
17	0.91871	0.84438	0.77639	0.71416	0.65720	0.60502	0.55720	0.51337	0.47318	0.43630	0.40245	0.37136	0.34281	0.31657
18	0.91414	0.83602	0.76491	0.70016	0.64117	0.58739	0.53836	0.49363	0.45280	0.41552	0.38147	0.35034	0.32189	0.29586
19	0.90959	0.82774	0.75361	0.68643	0.62553	0.57029	0.52016	0.47464	0.43330	0.39573	0.36158	0.33051	0.30224	0.27651
20	0.90506	0.81954	0.74247	0.67297	0.61027	0.55368	0.50257	0.45639	0.41464	0.37689	0.34273	0.31180	0.28380	0.25842
21	0.90056	0.81143	0.73150	0.65978	0.59539	0.53755	0.48557	0.43883	0.39679	0.35894	0.32486	0.29416	0.26648	0.24151
22	0.89608	0.80340	0.72069	0.64684	0.58086	0.52189	0.46915	0.42196	0.37970	0.34185	0.30793	0.27751	0.25021	0.22571
23	0.89162	0.79544	0.71004	0.63416	0.56670	0.50669	0.45329	0.40573	0.36335	0.32557	0.29187	0.26180	0.23494	0.21095
24	0.88719	0.78757	0.69954	0.62172	0.55288	0.49193	0.43796	0.39012	0.34770	0.31007	0.27666	0.24698	0.22060	0.19715
25	0.88277	0.77977	0.68921	0.60953	0.53939	0.47761	0.42315	0.37512	0.33273	0.29530	0.26223	0.23300	0.20714	0.18425
26	0.87838	0.77205	0.67902	0.59758	0.52623	0.46369	0.40884	0.36069	0.31840	0.28124	0.24856	0.21981	0.19450	0.17220
27	0.87401	0.76440	0.66899	0.58586	0.51340	0.45019	0.39501	0.34682	0.30469	0.26785	0.23560	0.20737	0.18263	0.16093
28	0.86966	0.75684	0.65910	0.57437	0.50088	0.43708	0.38165	0.33348	0.29157	0.25509	0.22332	0.19563	0.17148	0.15040
29	0.86533	0.74934	0.64936	0.56311	0.48866	0.42435	0.36875	0.32065	0.27902	0.24295	0.21168	0.18456	0.16101	0.14056
30	0.86103	0.74192	0.63976	0.55207	0.47674	0.41199	0.35628	0.30832	0.26700	0.23138	0.20064	0.17411	0.15119	0.13137
31	0.85675	0.73458	0.63031	0.54125	0.46511	0.39999	0.34423	0.29646	0.25550	0.22036	0.19018	0.16425	0.14196	0.12277
32	0.85248	0.72730	0.62099	0.53063	0.45377	0.38834	0.33259	0.28506	0.24450	0.20987	0.18027	0.15496	0.13329	0.11474
33	0.84824	0.72010	0.61182	0.52023	0.44270	0.37703	0.32134	0.27409	0.23397	0.19987	0.17087	0.14619	0.12516	0.10723
34	0.84402	0.71297	0.60277	0.51003	0.43191	0.36604	0.31048	0.26355	0.22390	0.19035	0.16196	0.13791	0.11752	0.10022
35	0.83982	0.70591	0.59387	0.50003	0.42137	0.35538	0.29998	0.25342	0.21425	0.18129	0.15352	0.13011	0.11035	0.09366
36	0.83564	0.69892	0.58509	0.49022	0.41109	0.34503	0.28983	0.24367	0.20503	0.17266	0.14552	0.12274	0.10361	0.08754
37	0.83149	0.69200	0.57644	0.48061	0.40107	0.33498	0.28003	0.23430	0.19620	0.16444	0.13793	0.11579	0.09729	0.08181
38	0.82735	0.68515	0.56792	0.47119	0.39128	0.32523	0.27056	0.22529	0.18775	0.15661	0.13074	0.10924	0.09135	0.07646
39	0.82323	0.67837	0.55953	0.46195	0.38174	0.31575	0.26141	0.21662	0.17967	0.14915	0.12392	0.10306	0.08578	0.07146
40	0.81914	0.67165	0.55126	0.45289	0.37243	0.30656	0.25257	0.20829	0.17193	0.14205	0.11746	0.09722	0.08054	0.06678
41	0.81506	0.66500	0.54312	0.44401	0.36335	0.29763	0.24403	0.20028	0.16453	0.13528	0.11134	0.09172	0.07563	0.06241
42	0.81101	0.65842	0.53509	0.43530	0.35448	0.28896	0.23578	0.19257	0.15744	0.12884	0.10554	0.08653	0.07101	0.05833
43	0.80697	0.65190	0.52718	0.42677	0.34584	0.28054	0.22781	0.18517	0.15066	0.12270	0.10003	0.08163	0.06668	0.05451
44	0.80296	0.64545	0.51939	0.41840	0.33740	0.27237	0.22010	0.17805	0.14417	0.11686	0.09482	0.07701	0.06261	0.05095
45	0.79896	0.63905	0.51171	0.41020	0.32917	0.26444	0.21266	0.17120	0.13796	0.11130	0.08988	0.07265	0.05879	0.04761
46	0.79499	0.63273	0.50415	0.40215	0.32115	0.25674	0.20547	0.16461	0.13202	0.10600	0.08519	0.06854	0.05520	0.04450
47	0.79103	0.62646	0.49670	0.39427	0.31331	0.24926	0.19852	0.15828	0.12634	0.10095	0.08075	0.06466	0.05183	0.04159
48	0.78710	0.62026	0.48936	0.38654	0.30567	0.24200	0.19181	0.15219	0.12090	0.09614	0.07654	0.06100	0.04867	0.03887
49	0.78318	0.61412	0.48213	0.37896	0.29822	0.23495	0.18532	0.14634	0.11569	0.09156	0.07255	0.05755	0.04570	0.03632
50	0.77929	0.60804	0.47500	0.37153	0.29094	0.22811	0.17905	0.14071	0.11071	0.08720	0.06877	0.05429	0.04291	0.03395
51	0.77541	0.60202	0.46798	0.36424	0.28385	0.22146	0.17300	0.13530	0.10594	0.08305	0.06518	0.05122	0.04029	0.03173
52	0.77155	0.59606	0.46107	0.35710	0.27692	0.21501	0.16715	0.13010	0.10138	0.07910	0.06178	0.04832	0.03783	0.02965
53	0.76771	0.59016	0.45426	0.35010	0.27017	0.20875	0.16150	0.12509	0.09701	0.07533	0.05856	0.04558	0.03552	0.02771
54	0.76389	0.58431	0.44754	0.34323	0.26358	0.20267	0.15603	0.12028	0.09284	0.07174	0.05551	0.04300	0.03335	0.02590
55	0.76009	0.57853	0.44093	0.33650	0.25715	0.19677	0.15076	0.11566	0.08884	0.06833	0.05262	0.04057	0.03132	0.02420
56	0.75631	0.57280	0.43441	0.32991	0.25088	0.19104	0.14566	0.11121	0.08501	0.06507	0.04987	0.03827	0.02941	0.02262
57	0.75255	0.56713	0.42799	0.32344	0.24476	0.18547	0.14073	0.10693	0.08135	0.06197	0.04727	0.03610	0.02761	0.02114
58	0.74880	0.56151	0.42167	0.31710	0.23879	0.18007	0.13598	0.10282	0.07785	0.05902	0.04481	0.03406	0.02593	0.01976
59	0.74508	0.55595	0.41544	0.31088	0.23297	0.17483	0.13138	0.09886	0.07450	0.05621	0.04247	0.03213	0.02434	0.01847
60	0.74137	0.55045	0.40930	0.30478	0.22728	0.16973	0.12693	0.09506	0.07129	0.05354	0.04026	0.03031	0.02286	0.01726

Period	.5%	1%	1.5%	2%	2.5%	3%	3.5%	4%	4.5%	5%	5.5%	6%	6.5%	7%
61 ..	0.73768	0.54500	0.40325	0.29881	0.22174	0.16479	0.12264	0.09140	0.06822	0.05099	0.03816	0.02860	0.02146	0.01613
62 ..	0.73401	0.53960	0.39729	0.29295	0.21633	0.15999	0.11849	0.08789	0.06528	0.04856	0.03617	0.02698	0.02015	0.01507
63 ..	0.73036	0.53426	0.39142	0.28720	0.21106	0.15533	0.11449	0.08451	0.06247	0.04625	0.03428	0.02545	0.01892	0.01409
64 ..	0.72673	0.52897	0.38563	0.28157	0.20591	0.15081	0.11062	0.08126	0.05978	0.04404	0.03250	0.02401	0.01777	0.01317
65 ..	0.72311	0.52373	0.37993	0.27605	0.20089	0.14641	0.10688	0.07813	0.05721	0.04195	0.03080	0.02265	0.01668	0.01230
66 ..	0.71952	0.51855	0.37432	0.27064	0.19599	0.14215	0.10326	0.07513	0.05474	0.03995	0.02920	0.02137	0.01566	0.01150
67 ..	0.71594	0.51341	0.36879	0.26533	0.19121	0.13801	0.09977	0.07224	0.05239	0.03805	0.02767	0.02016	0.01471	0.01075
68 ..	0.71237	0.50833	0.36334	0.26013	0.18654	0.13399	0.09640	0.06946	0.05013	0.03623	0.02623	0.01902	0.01381	0.01004
69 ..	0.70883	0.50330	0.35797	0.25503	0.18199	0.13009	0.09314	0.06679	0.04797	0.03451	0.02486	0.01794	0.01297	0.00939
70 ..	0.70530	0.49831	0.35268	0.25003	0.17755	0.12630	0.08999	0.06422	0.04590	0.03287	0.02357	0.01693	0.01218	0.00877
71 ..	0.70179	0.49338	0.34746	0.24513	0.17322	0.12262	0.08694	0.06175	0.04393	0.03130	0.02234	0.01597	0.01143	0.00820
72 ..	0.69830	0.48850	0.34233	0.24032	0.16900	0.11905	0.08400	0.05937	0.04204	0.02981	0.02117	0.01507	0.01074	0.00766
73 ..	0.69483	0.48366	0.33727	0.23561	0.16488	0.11558	0.08116	0.05709	0.04023	0.02839	0.02007	0.01421	0.01008	0.00716
74 ..	0.69137	0.47887	0.33229	0.23099	0.16085	0.11221	0.07842	0.05490	0.03849	0.02704	0.01902	0.01341	0.00947	0.00669
75 ..	0.68793	0.47413	0.32738	0.22646	0.15693	0.10895	0.07577	0.05278	0.03684	0.02575	0.01803	0.01265	0.00889	0.00625
76 ..	0.68451	0.46944	0.32254	0.22202	0.15310	0.10577	0.07320	0.05075	0.03525	0.02453	0.01709	0.01193	0.00835	0.00585
77 ..	0.68110	0.46479	0.31777	0.21766	0.14937	0.10269	0.07073	0.04880	0.03373	0.02336	0.01620	0.01126	0.00784	0.00546
78 ..	0.67772	0.46019	0.31308	0.21340	0.14573	0.09970	0.06834	0.04692	0.03228	0.02225	0.01536	0.01062	0.00736	0.00511
79 ..	0.67434	0.45563	0.30845	0.20921	0.14217	0.09680	0.06603	0.04512	0.03089	0.02119	0.01456	0.01002	0.00691	0.00477
80 ..	0.67099	0.45112	0.30389	0.20511	0.13870	0.09398	0.06379	0.04338	0.02956	0.02018	0.01380	0.00945	0.00649	0.00446
81 ..	0.66765	0.44665	0.29940	0.20109	0.13532	0.09124	0.06164	0.04172	0.02829	0.01922	0.01308	0.00892	0.00609	0.00417
82 ..	0.66433	0.44223	0.29497	0.19715	0.13202	0.08858	0.05955	0.04011	0.02707	0.01830	0.01240	0.00841	0.00572	0.00390
83 ..	0.66102	0.43785	0.29062	0.19328	0.12880	0.08600	0.05754	0.03857	0.02590	0.01743	0.01175	0.00794	0.00537	0.00364
84 ..	0.65773	0.43352	0.28632	0.18949	0.12566	0.08350	0.05559	0.03709	0.02479	0.01660	0.01114	0.00749	0.00504	0.00340
85 ..	0.65446	0.42922	0.28209	0.18577	0.12259	0.08107	0.05371	0.03566	0.02372	0.01581	0.01056	0.00706	0.00473	0.00318
86 ..	0.65121	0.42497	0.27792	0.18213	0.11960	0.07870	0.05190	0.03429	0.02270	0.01506	0.01001	0.00666	0.00445	0.00297
87 ..	0.64797	0.42077	0.27381	0.17856	0.11669	0.07641	0.05014	0.03297	0.02172	0.01434	0.00948	0.00629	0.00417	0.00278
88 ..	0.64474	0.41660	0.26977	0.17506	0.11384	0.07419	0.04845	0.03170	0.02079	0.01366	0.00899	0.00593	0.00392	0.00260
89 ..	0.64154	0.41248	0.26578	0.17163	0.11106	0.07203	0.04681	0.03048	0.01989	0.01301	0.00852	0.00559	0.00368	0.00243
90 ..	0.63834	0.40839	0.26185	0.16826	0.10836	0.06993	0.04522	0.02931	0.01903	0.01239	0.00808	0.00528	0.00346	0.00227
91 ..	0.63517	0.40435	0.25798	0.16496	0.10571	0.06789	0.04369	0.02818	0.01821	0.01180	0.00766	0.00498	0.00324	0.00212
92 ..	0.63201	0.40034	0.25417	0.16173	0.10313	0.06591	0.04222	0.02710	0.01743	0.01124	0.00726	0.00470	0.00305	0.00198
93 ..	0.62886	0.39638	0.25041	0.15856	0.10062	0.06399	0.04079	0.02606	0.01668	0.01070	0.00688	0.00443	0.00286	0.00185
94 ..	0.62573	0.39246	0.24671	0.15545	0.09816	0.06213	0.03941	0.02505	0.01596	0.01019	0.00652	0.00418	0.00269	0.00173
95 ..	0.62262	0.38857	0.24307	0.15240	0.09577	0.06032	0.03808	0.02409	0.01527	0.00971	0.00618	0.00394	0.00252	0.00162
96 ..	0.61952	0.38472	0.23947	0.14941	0.09343	0.05856	0.03679	0.02316	0.01462	0.00924	0.00586	0.00372	0.00237	0.00151
97 ..	0.61644	0.38091	0.23594	0.14648	0.09116	0.05686	0.03555	0.02227	0.01399	0.00880	0.00555	0.00351	0.00222	0.00141
98 ..	0.61337	0.37714	0.23245	0.14361	0.08893	0.05520	0.03434	0.02142	0.01338	0.00838	0.00526	0.00331	0.00209	0.00132
99 ..	0.61032	0.37341	0.22901	0.14079	0.08676	0.05359	0.03318	0.02059	0.01281	0.00798	0.00499	0.00312	0.00196	0.00123
100 ..	0.60729	0.36971	0.22563	0.13803	0.08465	0.05203	0.03026	0.01980	0.01226	0.00760	0.00473	0.00295	0.00184	0.00115
101 ..	0.60427	0.36605	0.22230	0.13533	0.08258	0.05052	0.03098	0.01904	0.01173	0.00724	0.00448	0.00278	0.00173	0.00108
102 ..	0.60126	0.36243	0.21901	0.13267	0.08057	0.04905	0.02993	0.01831	0.01122	0.00690	0.00425	0.00262	0.00162	0.00101
103 ..	0.59827	0.35884	0.21577	0.13007	0.07860	0.04762	0.02892	0.01760	0.01074	0.00657	0.00403	0.00247	0.00152	0.00094
104 ..	0.59529	0.35529	0.21258	0.12752	0.07669	0.04623	0.02794	0.01693	0.01028	0.00626	0.00382	0.00233	0.00143	0.00088
105 ..	0.59233	0.35177	0.20944	0.12502	0.07482	0.04488	0.02699	0.01627	0.00984	0.00596	0.00362	0.00220	0.00134	0.00082
106 ..	0.58938	0.34828	0.20635	0.12257	0.07299	0.04358	0.02608	0.01565	0.00941	0.00567	0.00343	0.00208	0.00126	0.00077
107 ..	0.58645	0.34484	0.20330	0.12017	0.07121	0.04231	0.02520	0.01505	0.00901	0.00540	0.00325	0.00196	0.00118	0.00072
108 ..	0.58353	0.34142	0.20029	0.11781	0.06947	0.04108	0.02435	0.01447	0.00862	0.00515	0.00308	0.00185	0.00111	0.00067
109 ..	0.58063	0.33804	0.19733	0.11550	0.06778	0.03988	0.02352	0.01391	0.00825	0.00490	0.00292	0.00174	0.00104	0.00063
110 ..	0.57774	0.33469	0.19442	0.11324	0.06613	0.03872	0.02273	0.01338	0.00789	0.00467	0.00277	0.00165	0.00098	0.00059
111 ..	0.57487	0.33138	0.19154	0.11101	0.06451	0.03759	0.02196	0.01286	0.00755	0.00445	0.00262	0.00155	0.00092	0.00055
112 ..	0.57201	0.32810	0.18871	0.10884	0.06294	0.03649	0.02122	0.01237	0.00723	0.00423	0.00249	0.00146	0.00086	0.00051
113 ..	0.56916	0.32485	0.18592	0.10670	0.06140	0.03543	0.02050	0.01189	0.00692	0.00403	0.00236	0.00138	0.00081	0.00048
114 ..	0.56633	0.32164	0.18318	0.10461	0.05991	0.03440	0.01981	0.01143	0.00662	0.00384	0.00223	0.00130	0.00076	0.00045
115 ..	0.56351	0.31845	0.18047	0.10256	0.05845	0.03340	0.01914	0.01099	0.00633	0.00366	0.00212	0.00123	0.00072	0.00042
116 ..	0.56071	0.31530	0.17780	0.10055	0.05702	0.03243	0.01849	0.01057	0.00606	0.00348	0.00201	0.00116	0.00067	0.00039
117 ..	0.55792	0.31218	0.17518	0.09858	0.05563	0.03148	0.01786	0.01016	0.00580	0.00332	0.00190	0.00109	0.00063	0.00036
118 ..	0.55514	0.30908	0.17259	0.09665	0.05427	0.03056	0.01726	0.00977	0.00555	0.00316	0.00180	0.00103	0.00059	0.00034
119 ..	0.55238	0.30602	0.17004	0.09475	0.05295	0.02967	0.01668	0.00940	0.00531	0.00301	0.00171	0.00097	0.00056	0.00032
120 ..	0.54963	0.30299	0.16752	0.09289	0.05166	0.02881	0.01611	0.00904	0.00508	0.00287	0.00162	0.00092	0.00052	0.00030

Table 3 (continued)   Present Value of $1 at Compound Interest: 7.5%–14%

Period	7.5%	8%	8.5%	9%	9.5%	10%	10.5%	11%	11.5%	12%	12.5%	13%	13.5%	14%
1 ...	0.93023	0.92593	0.92166	0.91743	0.91324	0.90909	0.90498	0.90090	0.89686	0.89286	0.88889	0.88496	0.88106	0.87719
2 ...	0.86533	0.85734	0.84946	0.84168	0.83401	0.82645	0.81898	0.81162	0.80436	0.79719	0.79012	0.78315	0.77626	0.76947
3 ...	0.80496	0.79383	0.78291	0.77218	0.76165	0.75131	0.74116	0.73119	0.72140	0.71178	0.70233	0.69305	0.68393	0.67497
4 ...	0.74880	0.73503	0.72157	0.70843	0.69557	0.68301	0.67073	0.65873	0.64699	0.63553	0.62430	0.61332	0.60258	0.59208
5 ...	0.69656	0.68058	0.66505	0.64993	0.63523	0.62092	0.60700	0.59345	0.58026	0.56743	0.55493	0.54276	0.53091	0.51937
6 ...	0.64796	0.63017	0.61295	0.59627	0.58012	0.56447	0.54932	0.53464	0.52042	0.50663	0.49327	0.48032	0.46776	0.45559
7 ...	0.60275	0.58349	0.56493	0.54703	0.52979	0.51316	0.49712	0.48166	0.46674	0.45235	0.43846	0.42506	0.41213	0.39964
8 ...	0.56070	0.54027	0.52067	0.50187	0.48382	0.46651	0.44989	0.43393	0.41860	0.40388	0.38974	0.37616	0.36311	0.35056
9 ...	0.52158	0.50025	0.47988	0.46043	0.44185	0.42410	0.40714	0.39092	0.37543	0.36061	0.34644	0.33288	0.31992	0.30751
10 ...	0.48519	0.46319	0.44229	0.42241	0.40351	0.38554	0.36845	0.35218	0.33671	0.32197	0.30795	0.29459	0.28187	0.26974
11 ...	0.45134	0.42888	0.40764	0.38753	0.36851	0.35049	0.33344	0.31728	0.30198	0.28748	0.27373	0.26070	0.24834	0.23662
12 ...	0.41985	0.39711	0.37570	0.35553	0.33654	0.31863	0.30175	0.28584	0.27083	0.25668	0.24332	0.23071	0.21880	0.20756
13 ...	0.39056	0.36770	0.34627	0.32618	0.30734	0.28966	0.27308	0.25751	0.24290	0.22917	0.21628	0.20416	0.19278	0.18207
14 ...	0.36331	0.34046	0.31914	0.29925	0.28067	0.26333	0.24713	0.23199	0.21785	0.20462	0.19225	0.18068	0.16985	0.15971
15 ...	0.33797	0.31524	0.29414	0.27454	0.25632	0.23939	0.22365	0.20900	0.19538	0.18270	0.17089	0.15989	0.14964	0.14010
16 ...	0.31439	0.29189	0.27110	0.25187	0.23409	0.21763	0.20240	0.18829	0.17523	0.16312	0.15190	0.14150	0.13185	0.12289
17 ...	0.29245	0.27027	0.24986	0.23107	0.21378	0.19784	0.18316	0.16963	0.15715	0.14564	0.13502	0.12522	0.11616	0.10780
18 ...	0.27205	0.25025	0.23028	0.21199	0.19523	0.17986	0.16576	0.15282	0.14095	0.13004	0.12002	0.11081	0.10235	0.09456
19 ...	0.25307	0.23171	0.21224	0.19449	0.17829	0.16351	0.15001	0.13768	0.12641	0.11611	0.10668	0.09806	0.09017	0.08295
20 ...	0.23541	0.21455	0.19562	0.17843	0.16282	0.14864	0.13575	0.12403	0.11337	0.10367	0.09483	0.08678	0.07945	0.07276
21 ...	0.21899	0.19866	0.18029	0.16370	0.14870	0.13513	0.12285	0.11174	0.10168	0.09256	0.08429	0.07680	0.07000	0.06383
22 ...	0.20371	0.18394	0.16617	0.15018	0.13580	0.12285	0.11118	0.10067	0.09119	0.08264	0.07493	0.06796	0.06167	0.05599
23 ...	0.18950	0.17032	0.15315	0.13778	0.12402	0.11168	0.10062	0.09069	0.08179	0.07379	0.06660	0.06014	0.05434	0.04911
24 ...	0.17628	0.15770	0.14115	0.12640	0.11326	0.10153	0.09106	0.08170	0.07335	0.06588	0.05920	0.05323	0.04787	0.04308
25 ...	0.16398	0.14602	0.13009	0.11597	0.10343	0.09230	0.08240	0.07361	0.06579	0.05882	0.05262	0.04710	0.04218	0.03779
26 ...	0.15254	0.13520	0.11990	0.10639	0.09446	0.08391	0.07457	0.06631	0.05900	0.05252	0.04678	0.04168	0.03716	0.03315
27 ...	0.14190	0.12519	0.11051	0.09761	0.08626	0.07628	0.06749	0.05974	0.05291	0.04689	0.04158	0.03689	0.03274	0.02908
28 ...	0.13200	0.11591	0.10185	0.08955	0.07878	0.06934	0.06107	0.05382	0.04746	0.04187	0.03696	0.03264	0.02885	0.02551
29 ...	0.12279	0.10733	0.09387	0.08215	0.07194	0.06304	0.05527	0.04849	0.04256	0.03738	0.03285	0.02889	0.02542	0.02237
30 ...	0.11422	0.09938	0.08652	0.07537	0.06570	0.05731	0.05002	0.04368	0.03817	0.03338	0.02920	0.02557	0.02239	0.01963
31 ...	0.10625	0.09202	0.07974	0.06915	0.06000	0.05210	0.04527	0.03935	0.03424	0.02980	0.02596	0.02262	0.01973	0.01722
32 ...	0.09884	0.08520	0.07349	0.06344	0.05480	0.04736	0.04096	0.03545	0.03070	0.02661	0.02307	0.02002	0.01738	0.01510
33 ...	0.09194	0.07889	0.06774	0.05820	0.05004	0.04306	0.03707	0.03194	0.02754	0.02376	0.02051	0.01772	0.01532	0.01325
34 ...	0.08553	0.07305	0.06243	0.05339	0.04570	0.03914	0.03355	0.02878	0.02470	0.02121	0.01823	0.01568	0.01349	0.01162
35 ...	0.07956	0.06763	0.05754	0.04899	0.04174	0.03558	0.03036	0.02592	0.02215	0.01894	0.01621	0.01388	0.01189	0.01019
36 ...	0.07401	0.06262	0.05303	0.04494	0.03811	0.03235	0.02748	0.02335	0.01987	0.01691	0.01440	0.01228	0.01047	0.00894
37 ...	0.06885	0.05799	0.04888	0.04123	0.03481	0.02941	0.02487	0.02104	0.01782	0.01510	0.01280	0.01087	0.00923	0.00784
38 ...	0.06404	0.05369	0.04505	0.03783	0.03179	0.02673	0.02250	0.01896	0.01598	0.01348	0.01138	0.00962	0.00813	0.00688
39 ...	0.05958	0.04971	0.04152	0.03470	0.02903	0.02430	0.02036	0.01708	0.01433	0.01204	0.01012	0.00851	0.00716	0.00604
40 ...	0.05542	0.04603	0.03827	0.03184	0.02651	0.02209	0.01843	0.01538	0.01285	0.01075	0.00899	0.00753	0.00631	0.00529
41 ...	0.05155	0.04262	0.03527	0.02921	0.02421	0.02009	0.01668	0.01386	0.01153	0.00960	0.00799	0.00666	0.00556	0.00464
42 ...	0.04796	0.03946	0.03251	0.02680	0.02211	0.01826	0.01509	0.01249	0.01034	0.00857	0.00711	0.00590	0.00490	0.00407
43 ...	0.04461	0.03654	0.02996	0.02458	0.02019	0.01660	0.01366	0.01125	0.00927	0.00765	0.00632	0.00522	0.00432	0.00357
44 ...	0.04150	0.03383	0.02761	0.02255	0.01844	0.01509	0.01236	0.01013	0.00832	0.00683	0.00561	0.00462	0.00380	0.00313
45 ...	0.03860	0.03133	0.02545	0.02069	0.01684	0.01372	0.01119	0.00913	0.00746	0.00610	0.00499	0.00409	0.00335	0.00275
46 ...	0.03591	0.02901	0.02345	0.01898	0.01538	0.01247	0.01012	0.00823	0.00669	0.00544	0.00444	0.00362	0.00295	0.00241
47 ...	0.03340	0.02686	0.02162	0.01742	0.01405	0.01134	0.00916	0.00741	0.00600	0.00486	0.00394	0.00320	0.00260	0.00212
48 ...	0.03107	0.02487	0.01992	0.01598	0.01283	0.01031	0.00829	0.00668	0.00538	0.00434	0.00350	0.00283	0.00229	0.00186
49 ...	0.02891	0.02303	0.01836	0.01466	0.01171	0.00937	0.00750	0.00601	0.00483	0.00388	0.00312	0.00251	0.00202	0.00163
50 ...	0.02689	0.02132	0.01692	0.01345	0.01070	0.00852	0.00679	0.00542	0.00433	0.00346	0.00277	0.00222	0.00178	0.00143
51 ...	0.02501	0.01974	0.01560	0.01234	0.00977	0.00774	0.00615	0.00488	0.00388	0.00309	0.00246	0.00196	0.00157	0.00125
52 ...	0.02327	0.01828	0.01438	0.01132	0.00892	0.00704	0.00556	0.00440	0.00348	0.00276	0.00219	0.00174	0.00138	0.00110
53 ...	0.02164	0.01693	0.01325	0.01038	0.00815	0.00640	0.00503	0.00396	0.00312	0.00246	0.00194	0.00154	0.00122	0.00096
54 ...	0.02013	0.01567	0.01221	0.00953	0.00744	0.00582	0.00455	0.00357	0.00280	0.00220	0.00173	0.00136	0.00107	0.00085
55 ...	0.01873	0.01451	0.01126	0.00874	0.00680	0.00529	0.00412	0.00322	0.00251	0.00196	0.00154	0.00120	0.00094	0.00074
56 ...	0.01742	0.01344	0.01037	0.00802	0.00621	0.00481	0.00373	0.00290	0.00225	0.00175	0.00137	0.00107	0.00083	0.00065
57 ...	0.01621	0.01244	0.00956	0.00736	0.00567	0.00437	0.00338	0.00261	0.00202	0.00157	0.00121	0.00094	0.00073	0.00057
58 ...	0.01508	0.01152	0.00881	0.00675	0.00518	0.00397	0.00305	0.00235	0.00181	0.00140	0.00108	0.00083	0.00065	0.00050
59 ...	0.01402	0.01067	0.00812	0.00619	0.00473	0.00361	0.00276	0.00212	0.00162	0.00125	0.00096	0.00074	0.00057	0.00044
60 ...	0.01305	0.00988	0.00749	0.00568	0.00432	0.00328	0.00250	0.00191	0.00146	0.00111	0.00085	0.00065	0.00050	0.00039

Period	7.5%	8%	8.5%	9%	9.5%	10%	10.5%	11%	11.5%	12%	12.5%	13%	13.5%	14%
61 ..	0.01214	0.00914	0.00690	0.00521	0.00394	0.00299	0.00226	0.00172	0.00131	0.00099	0.00076	0.00058	0.00044	0.00034
62 ..	0.01129	0.00847	0.00636	0.00478	0.00360	0.00271	0.00205	0.00155	0.00117	0.00089	0.00067	0.00051	0.00039	0.00030
63 ..	0.01050	0.00784	0.00586	0.00439	0.00329	0.00247	0.00185	0.00140	0.00105	0.00079	0.00060	0.00045	0.00034	0.00026
64 ..	0.00977	0.00726	0.00540	0.00402	0.00300	0.00224	0.00168	0.00126	0.00094	0.00071	0.00053	0.00040	0.00030	0.00023
65 ..	0.00909	0.00672	0.00498	0.00369	0.00274	0.00204	0.00152	0.00113	0.00085	0.00063	0.00047	0.00035	0.00027	0.00020
66 ..	0.00845	0.00622	0.00459	0.00339	0.00250	0.00185	0.00137	0.00102	0.00076	0.00056	0.00042	0.00031	0.00023	0.00018
67 ..	0.00786	0.00576	0.00423	0.00311	0.00229	0.00169	0.00124	0.00092	0.00068	0.00050	0.00037	0.00028	0.00021	0.00015
68 ..	0.00732	0.00534	0.00390	0.00285	0.00209	0.00153	0.00113	0.00083	0.00061	0.00045	0.00033	0.00025	0.00018	0.00014
69 ..	0.00680	0.00494	0.00359	0.00262	0.00191	0.00139	0.00102	0.00075	0.00055	0.00040	0.00030	0.00022	0.00016	0.00012
70 ..	0.00633	0.00457	0.00331	0.00240	0.00174	0.00127	0.00092	0.00067	0.00049	0.00036	0.00026	0.00019	0.00014	0.00010
71 ..	0.00589	0.00424	0.00305	0.00220	0.00159	0.00115	0.00083	0.00061	0.00044	0.00032	0.00023	0.00017	0.00012	0.00009
72 ..	0.00548	0.00392	0.00281	0.00202	0.00145	0.00105	0.00075	0.00055	0.00039	0.00029	0.00021	0.00015	0.00011	0.00008
73 ..	0.00510	0.00363	0.00259	0.00185	0.00133	0.00095	0.00068	0.00049	0.00035	0.00026	0.00018	0.00013	0.00010	0.00007
74 ..	0.00474	0.00336	0.00239	0.00170	0.00121	0.00086	0.00062	0.00044	0.00032	0.00023	0.00016	0.00012	0.00009	0.00006
75 ..	0.00441	0.00311	0.00220	0.00156	0.00111	0.00079	0.00056	0.00040	0.00028	0.00020	0.00015	0.00010	0.00008	0.00005
76 ..	0.00410	0.00288	0.00203	0.00143	0.00101	0.00071	0.00051	0.00036	0.00026	0.00018	0.00013	0.00009	0.00007	0.00005
77 ..	0.00382	0.00267	0.00187	0.00131	0.00092	0.00065	0.00046	0.00032	0.00023	0.00016	0.00012	0.00008	0.00006	0.00004
78 ..	0.00355	0.00247	0.00172	0.00120	0.00084	0.00059	0.00041	0.00029	0.00021	0.00014	0.00010	0.00007	0.00005	0.00004
79 ..	0.00330	0.00229	0.00159	0.00110	0.00077	0.00054	0.00038	0.00026	0.00018	0.00013	0.00009	0.00006	0.00005	0.00003
80 ..	0.00307	0.00212	0.00146	0.00101	0.00070	0.00049	0.00034	0.00024	0.00017	0.00012	0.00008	0.00006	0.00004	0.00003
81 ..	0.00286	0.00196	0.00135	0.00093	0.00064	0.00044	0.00031	0.00021	0.00015	0.00010	0.00007	0.00005	0.00004	0.00002
82 ..	0.00266	0.00182	0.00124	0.00085	0.00059	0.00040	0.00028	0.00019	0.00013	0.00009	0.00006	0.00004	0.00003	0.00002
83 ..	0.00247	0.00168	0.00115	0.00078	0.00054	0.00037	0.00025	0.00017	0.00012	0.00008	0.00006	0.00004	0.00003	0.00002
84 ..	0.00230	0.00156	0.00106	0.00072	0.00049	0.00033	0.00023	0.00016	0.00011	0.00007	0.00005	0.00003	0.00002	0.00002
85 ..	0.00214	0.00144	0.00097	0.00066	0.00045	0.00030	0.00021	0.00014	0.00010	0.00007	0.00004	0.00003	0.00002	0.00001
86 ..	0.00199	0.00134	0.00090	0.00060	0.00041	0.00028	0.00019	0.00013	0.00009	0.00006	0.00004	0.00003	0.00002	0.00001
87 ..	0.00185	0.00124	0.00083	0.00055	0.00037	0.00025	0.00017	0.00011	0.00008	0.00005	0.00004	0.00002	0.00002	0.00001
88 ..	0.00172	0.00114	0.00076	0.00051	0.00034	0.00023	0.00015	0.00010	0.00007	0.00005	0.00003	0.00002	0.00001	0.00001
89 ..	0.00160	0.00106	0.00070	0.00047	0.00031	0.00021	0.00014	0.00009	0.00006	0.00004	0.00003	0.00002	0.00001	0.00001
90 ..	0.00149	0.00098	0.00065	0.00043	0.00028	0.00019	0.00013	0.00008	0.00006	0.00004	0.00002	0.00002	0.00001	0.00001
91 ..	0.00139	0.00091	0.00060	0.00039	0.00026	0.00017	0.00011	0.00008	0.00005	0.00003	0.00002	0.00001	0.00001	0.00001
92 ..	0.00129	0.00084	0.00055	0.00036	0.00024	0.00016	0.00010	0.00007	0.00004	0.00003	0.00002	0.00001	0.00001	0.00001
93 ..	0.00120	0.00078	0.00051	0.00033	0.00022	0.00014	0.00009	0.00006	0.00004	0.00003	0.00002	0.00001	0.00001	0.00001
94 ..	0.00112	0.00072	0.00047	0.00030	0.00020	0.00013	0.00008	0.00005	0.00004	0.00002	0.00002	0.00001	0.00001	0.00000
95 ..	0.00104	0.00067	0.00043	0.00028	0.00018	0.00012	0.00008	0.00005	0.00003	0.00002	0.00001	0.00001	0.00001	0.00000
96 ..	0.00097	0.00062	0.00040	0.00026	0.00016	0.00011	0.00007	0.00004	0.00003	0.00002	0.00001	0.00001	0.00001	0.00000
97 ..	0.00090	0.00057	0.00037	0.00023	0.00015	0.00010	0.00006	0.00004	0.00003	0.00002	0.00001	0.00001	0.00000	0.00000
98 ..	0.00084	0.00053	0.00034	0.00021	0.00014	0.00009	0.00006	0.00004	0.00002	0.00002	0.00001	0.00001	0.00000	0.00000
99 ..	0.00078	0.00049	0.00031	0.00020	0.00013	0.00008	0.00005	0.00003	0.00002	0.00001	0.00001	0.00001	0.00000	0.00000
100 ..	0.00072	0.00045	0.00029	0.00018	0.00011	0.00007	0.00005	0.00003	0.00002	0.00001	0.00001	0.00000	0.00000	0.00000
101 ..	0.00067	0.00042	0.00026	0.00017	0.00010	0.00007	0.00004	0.00003	0.00002	0.00001	0.00001	0.00000	0.00000	0.00000
102 ..	0.00063	0.00039	0.00024	0.00015	0.00009	0.00006	0.00004	0.00002	0.00002	0.00001	0.00001	0.00000	0.00000	0.00000
103 ..	0.00058	0.00036	0.00022	0.00014	0.00009	0.00005	0.00003	0.00002	0.00001	0.00001	0.00001	0.00000	0.00000	0.00000
104 ..	0.00054	0.00033	0.00021	0.00013	0.00008	0.00005	0.00003	0.00002	0.00001	0.00001	0.00000	0.00000	0.00000	0.00000
105 ..	0.00050	0.00031	0.00019	0.00012	0.00007	0.00005	0.00003	0.00002	0.00001	0.00001	0.00000	0.00000	0.00000	0.00000
106 ..	0.00047	0.00029	0.00018	0.00011	0.00007	0.00004	0.00003	0.00002	0.00001	0.00001	0.00000	0.00000	0.00000	0.00000
107 ..	0.00044	0.00027	0.00016	0.00010	0.00006	0.00004	0.00002	0.00001	0.00001	0.00001	0.00000	0.00000	0.00000	0.00000
108 ..	0.00041	0.00025	0.00015	0.00009	0.00006	0.00003	0.00002	0.00001	0.00001	0.00000	0.00000	0.00000	0.00000	0.00000
109 ..	0.00038	0.00023	0.00014	0.00008	0.00005	0.00003	0.00002	0.00001	0.00001	0.00000	0.00000	0.00000	0.00000	0.00000
110 ..	0.00035	0.00021	0.00013	0.00008	0.00005	0.00003	0.00002	0.00001	0.00001	0.00000	0.00000	0.00000	0.00000	0.00000
111 ..	0.00033	0.00019	0.00012	0.00007	0.00004	0.00003	0.00002	0.00001	0.00001	0.00000	0.00000	0.00000	0.00000	0.00000
112 ..	0.00030	0.00018	0.00011	0.00006	0.00004	0.00002	0.00001	0.00001	0.00001	0.00000	0.00000	0.00000	0.00000	0.00000
113 ..	0.00028	0.00017	0.00010	0.00006	0.00004	0.00002	0.00001	0.00001	0.00000	0.00000	0.00000	0.00000	0.00000	0.00000
114 ..	0.00026	0.00015	0.00009	0.00005	0.00003	0.00002	0.00001	0.00001	0.00000	0.00000	0.00000	0.00000	0.00000	0.00000
115 ..	0.00024	0.00014	0.00008	0.00005	0.00003	0.00002	0.00001	0.00001	0.00000	0.00000	0.00000	0.00000	0.00000	0.00000
116 ..	0.00023	0.00013	0.00008	0.00005	0.00003	0.00002	0.00001	0.00001	0.00000	0.00000	0.00000	0.00000	0.00000	0.00000
117 ..	0.00021	0.00012	0.00007	0.00004	0.00002	0.00001	0.00001	0.00000	0.00000	0.00000	0.00000	0.00000	0.00000	0.00000
118 ..	0.00020	0.00011	0.00007	0.00004	0.00002	0.00001	0.00001	0.00000	0.00000	0.00000	0.00000	0.00000	0.00000	0.00000
119 ..	0.00018	0.00011	0.00006	0.00004	0.00002	0.00001	0.00001	0.00000	0.00000	0.00000	0.00000	0.00000	0.00000	0.00000
120 ..	0.00017	0.00010	0.00006	0.00003	0.00002	0.00001	0.00001	0.00000	0.00000	0.00000	0.00000	0.00000	0.00000	0.00000

Table 3 *(concluded)* *Present Value of $1: 14.5%–20%*

Period	14.5%	15%	15.5%	16%	16.5%	17%	17.5%	18%	18.5%	19%	19.5%	20%
1	0.87336	0.86957	0.86580	0.86207	0.85837	0.85470	0.85106	0.84746	0.84388	0.84034	0.83682	0.83333
2	0.76276	0.75614	0.74961	0.74316	0.73680	0.73051	0.72431	0.71818	0.71214	0.70616	0.70027	0.69444
3	0.66617	0.65752	0.64901	0.64066	0.63244	0.62437	0.61643	0.60863	0.60096	0.59342	0.58600	0.57870
4	0.58181	0.57175	0.56192	0.55229	0.54287	0.53365	0.52462	0.51579	0.50714	0.49867	0.49038	0.48225
5	0.50813	0.49718	0.48651	0.47611	0.46598	0.45611	0.44649	0.43711	0.42796	0.41905	0.41036	0.40188
6	0.44378	0.43233	0.42122	0.41044	0.39999	0.38984	0.37999	0.37043	0.36115	0.35214	0.34339	0.33490
7	0.38758	0.37594	0.36469	0.35383	0.34334	0.33320	0.32340	0.31393	0.30477	0.29592	0.28736	0.27908
8	0.33850	0.32690	0.31575	0.30503	0.29471	0.28478	0.27523	0.26604	0.25719	0.24867	0.24047	0.23257
9	0.29563	0.28426	0.27338	0.26295	0.25297	0.24340	0.23424	0.22546	0.21704	0.20897	0.20123	0.19381
10	0.25819	0.24718	0.23669	0.22668	0.21714	0.20804	0.19935	0.19106	0.18315	0.17560	0.16839	0.16151
11	0.22550	0.21494	0.20493	0.19542	0.18639	0.17781	0.16966	0.16192	0.15456	0.14757	0.14091	0.13459
12	0.19694	0.18691	0.17743	0.16846	0.15999	0.15197	0.14439	0.13722	0.13043	0.12400	0.11792	0.11216
13	0.17200	0.16253	0.15362	0.14523	0.13733	0.12989	0.12289	0.11629	0.11007	0.10421	0.09868	0.09346
14	0.15022	0.14133	0.13300	0.12520	0.11788	0.11102	0.10459	0.09855	0.09288	0.08757	0.08258	0.07789
15	0.13120	0.12289	0.11515	0.10793	0.10118	0.09489	0.08901	0.08352	0.07838	0.07359	0.06910	0.06491
16	0.11458	0.10686	0.09970	0.09304	0.08685	0.08110	0.07575	0.07078	0.06615	0.06184	0.05782	0.05409
17	0.10007	0.09293	0.08632	0.08021	0.07455	0.06932	0.06447	0.05998	0.05582	0.05196	0.04839	0.04507
18	0.08740	0.04081	0.07474	0.06914	0.06399	0.05925	0.05487	0.05083	0.04711	0.04367	0.04049	0.03756
19	0.07633	0.07027	0.06471	0.05961	0.05493	0.05064	0.04670	0.04308	0.03975	0.03670	0.03389	0.03130
20	0.06666	0.06110	0.05602	0.05139	0.04715	0.04328	0.03974	0.03651	0.03355	0.03084	0.02836	0.02608
21	0.05822	0.05313	0.04850	0.04430	0.04047	0.03699	0.03382	0.03094	0.02831	0.02591	0.02373	0.02174
22	0.05085	0.04620	0.04199	0.03819	0.03474	0.03162	0.02879	0.02622	0.02389	0.02178	0.01986	0.01811
23	0.04441	0.04017	0.03636	0.03292	0.02982	0.02702	0.02450	0.02222	0.02016	0.01830	0.01662	0.01509
24	0.03879	0.03493	0.03148	0.02838	0.02560	0.02310	0.02085	0.01883	0.01701	0.01538	0.01390	0.01258
25	0.03387	0.03038	0.02726	0.02447	0.02197	0.01974	0.01774	0.01596	0.01436	0.01292	0.01164	0.01048
26	0.02958	0.02642	0.02360	0.02109	0.01886	0.01687	0.01510	0.01352	0.01211	0.01086	0.00974	0.00874
27	0.02584	0.02297	0.02043	0.01818	0.01619	0.01442	0.01285	0.01146	0.01022	0.00912	0.00815	0.00728
28	0.02257	0.01997	0.01769	0.01567	0.01390	0.01233	0.01094	0.00971	0.00863	0.00767	0.00682	0.00607
29	0.01971	0.01737	0.01532	0.01351	0.01193	0.01053	0.00931	0.00823	0.00728	0.00644	0.00571	0.00506
30	0.01721	0.01510	0.01326	0.01165	0.01024	0.00900	0.00792	0.00697	0.00614	0.00541	0.00477	0.00421
31	0.01503	0.01313	0.01148	0.01004	0.00879	0.00770	0.00674	0.00591	0.00518	0.00455	0.00400	0.00351
32	0.01313	0.01142	0.00994	0.00866	0.00754	0.00658	0.00574	0.00501	0.00438	0.00382	0.00334	0.00293
33	0.01147	0.00993	0.00861	0.00746	0.00648	0.00562	0.00488	0.00425	0.00369	0.00321	0.00280	0.00244
34	0.01001	0.00864	0.00745	0.00643	0.00556	0.00480	0.00416	0.00360	0.00312	0.00270	0.00234	0.00203
35	0.00875	0.00751	0.00645	0.00555	0.00477	0.00411	0.00354	0.00305	0.00263	0.00227	0.00196	0.00169
36	0.00764	0.00653	0.00559	0.00478	0.00410	0.00351	0.00301	0.00258	0.00222	0.00191	0.00164	0.00141
37	0.00667	0.00568	0.00484	0.00412	0.00352	0.00300	0.00256	0.00219	0.00187	0.00160	0.00137	0.00118
38	0.00583	0.00494	0.00419	0.00355	0.00302	0.00256	0.00218	0.00186	0.00158	0.00135	0.00115	0.00098
39	0.00509	0.00429	0.00362	0.00306	0.00259	0.00219	0.00186	0.00157	0.00133	0.00113	0.00096	0.00082
40	0.00444	0.00373	0.00314	0.00264	0.00222	0.00187	0.00158	0.00133	0.00113	0.00095	0.00080	0.00068
41	0.00388	0.00325	0.00272	0.00228	0.00191	0.00160	0.00134	0.00113	0.00095	0.00080	0.00067	0.00057
42	0.00339	0.00282	0.00235	0.00196	0.00164	0.00137	0.00114	0.00096	0.00080	0.00067	0.00056	0.00047
43	0.00296	0.00245	0.00204	0.00169	0.00141	0.00117	0.00097	0.00081	0.00068	0.00056	0.00047	0.00039
44	0.00259	0.00213	0.00176	0.00146	0.00121	0.00100	0.00083	0.00069	0.00057	0.00047	0.00039	0.00033
45	0.00226	0.00186	0.00153	0.00126	0.00104	0.00085	0.00071	0.00058	0.00048	0.00040	0.00033	0.00027
46	0.00197	0.00161	0.00132	0.00108	0.00089	0.00073	0.00060	0.00049	0.00041	0.00033	0.00028	0.00023
47	0.00172	0.00140	0.00114	0.00093	0.00076	0.00062	0.00051	0.00042	0.00034	0.00028	0.00023	0.00019
48	0.00150	0.00122	0.00099	0.00081	0.00066	0.00053	0.00043	0.00035	0.00029	0.00024	0.00019	0.00016
49	0.00131	0.00106	0.00086	0.00069	0.00056	0.00046	0.00037	0.00030	0.00024	0.00020	0.00016	0.00013
50	0.00115	0.00092	0.00074	0.00060	0.00048	0.00039	0.00031	0.00025	0.00021	0.00017	0.00014	0.00011
51	0.00100	0.00080	0.00064	0.00052	0.00041	0.00033	0.00027	0.00022	0.00017	0.00014	0.00011	0.00009
52	0.00088	0.00070	0.00056	0.00044	0.00036	0.00028	0.00023	0.00018	0.00015	0.00012	0.00009	0.00008
53	0.00076	0.00061	0.00048	0.00038	0.00031	0.00024	0.00019	0.00015	0.00012	0.00010	0.00008	0.00006
54	0.00067	0.00053	0.00042	0.00033	0.00026	0.00021	0.00017	0.00013	0.00010	0.00008	0.00007	0.00005
55	0.00058	0.00046	0.00036	0.00028	0.00022	0.00018	0.00014	0.00011	0.00009	0.00007	0.00006	0.00004
56	0.00051	0.00040	0.00031	0.00025	0.00019	0.00015	0.00012	0.00009	0.00007	0.00006	0.00005	0.00004
57	0.00044	0.00035	0.00027	0.00021	0.00017	0.00013	0.00010	0.00008	0.00006	0.00005	0.00004	0.00003
58	0.00039	0.00030	0.00023	0.00018	0.00014	0.00011	0.00009	0.00007	0.00005	0.00004	0.00003	0.00003
59	0.00034	0.00026	0.00020	0.00016	0.00012	0.00009	0.00007	0.00006	0.00004	0.00003	0.00003	0.00002
60	0.00030	0.00023	0.00018	0.00014	0.00010	0.00008	0.00006	0.00005	0.00004	0.00003	0.00002	0.00002

Period	14.5%	15%	15.5%	16%	16.5%	17%	17.5%	18%	18.5%	19%	19.5%	20%
61	0.00026	0.00020	0.00015	0.00012	0.00009	0.00007	0.00005	0.00004	0.00003	0.00002	0.00002	0.00001
62	0.00023	0.00017	0.00013	0.00010	0.00008	0.00006	0.00005	0.00003	0.00003	0.00002	0.00002	0.00001
63	0.00020	0.00015	0.00011	0.00009	0.00007	0.00005	0.00004	0.00003	0.00002	0.00002	0.00001	0.00001
64	0.00017	0.00013	0.00010	0.00007	0.00006	0.00004	0.00003	0.00003	0.00002	0.00001	0.00001	0.00001
65	0.00015	0.00011	0.00009	0.00006	0.00005	0.00004	0.00003	0.00002	0.00002	0.00001	0.00001	0.00001
66	0.00013	0.00010	0.00007	0.00006	0.00004	0.00003	0.00002	0.00002	0.00001	0.00001	0.00001	0.00001
67	0.00011	0.00009	0.00006	0.00005	0.00004	0.00003	0.00002	0.00002	0.00001	0.00001	0.00001	0.00000
68	0.00010	0.00007	0.00006	0.00004	0.00003	0.00002	0.00002	0.00001	0.00001	0.00001	0.00001	0.00000
69	0.00009	0.00006	0.00005	0.00004	0.00003	0.00002	0.00001	0.00001	0.00001	0.00001	0.00000	0.00000
70	0.00008	0.00006	0.00004	0.00003	0.00002	0.00002	0.00001	0.00001	0.00001	0.00001	0.00000	0.00000
71	0.00007	0.00005	0.00004	0.00003	0.00002	0.00001	0.00001	0.00001	0.00001	0.00000	0.00000	0.00000
72	0.00006	0.00004	0.00003	0.00002	0.00002	0.00001	0.00001	0.00001	0.00000	0.00000	0.00000	0.00000
73	0.00005	0.00004	0.00003	0.00002	0.00001	0.00001	0.00001	0.00001	0.00000	0.00000	0.00000	0.00000
74	0.00004	0.00003	0.00002	0.00002	0.00001	0.00001	0.00001	0.00000	0.00000	0.00000	0.00000	0.00000
75	0.00004	0.00003	0.00002	0.00001	0.00001	0.00001	0.00001	0.00000	0.00000	0.00000	0.00000	0.00000
76	0.00003	0.00002	0.00002	0.00001	0.00001	0.00001	0.00000	0.00000	0.00000	0.00000	0.00000	0.00000
77	0.00003	0.00002	0.00002	0.00001	0.00001	0.00001	0.00000	0.00000	0.00000	0.00000	0.00000	0.00000
78	0.00003	0.00002	0.00001	0.00001	0.00001	0.00000	0.00000	0.00000	0.00000	0.00000	0.00000	0.00000
79	0.00002	0.00002	0.00001	0.00001	0.00001	0.00000	0.00000	0.00000	0.00000	0.00000	0.00000	0.00000
80	0.00002	0.00001	0.00001	0.00001	0.00000	0.00000	0.00000	0.00000	0.00000	0.00000	0.00000	0.00000
81	0.00002	0.00001	0.00001	0.00001	0.00000	0.00000	0.00000	0.00000	0.00000	0.00000	0.00000	0.00000
82	0.00002	0.00001	0.00001	0.00001	0.00000	0.00000	0.00000	0.00000	0.00000	0.00000	0.00000	0.00000
83	0.00001	0.00001	0.00001	0.00000	0.00000	0.00000	0.00000	0.00000	0.00000	0.00000	0.00000	0.00000
84	0.00001	0.00001	0.00001	0.00000	0.00000	0.00000	0.00000	0.00000	0.00000	0.00000	0.00000	0.00000
85	0.00001	0.00001	0.00000	0.00000	0.00000	0.00000	0.00000	0.00000	0.00000	0.00000	0.00000	0.00000
86	0.00001	0.00001	0.00000	0.00000	0.00000	0.00000	0.00000	0.00000	0.00000	0.00000	0.00000	0.00000
87	0.00001	0.00001	0.00000	0.00000	0.00000	0.00000	0.00000	0.00000	0.00000	0.00000	0.00000	0.00000
88	0.00001	0.00000	0.00000	0.00000	0.00000	0.00000	0.00000	0.00000	0.00000	0.00000	0.00000	0.00000
89	0.00001	0.00000	0.00000	0.00000	0.00000	0.00000	0.00000	0.00000	0.00000	0.00000	0.00000	0.00000
90	0.00001	0.00000	0.00000	0.00000	0.00000	0.00000	0.00000	0.00000	0.00000	0.00000	0.00000	0.00000
91	0.00000	0.00000	0.00000	0.00000	0.00000	0.00000	0.00000	0.00000	0.00000	0.00000	0.00000	0.00000
92	0.00000	0.00000	0.00000	0.00000	0.00000	0.00000	0.00000	0.00000	0.00000	0.00000	0.00000	0.00000
93	0.00000	0.00000	0.00000	0.00000	0.00000	0.00000	0.00000	0.00000	0.00000	0.00000	0.00000	0.00000
94	0.00000	0.00000	0.00000	0.00000	0.00000	0.00000	0.00000	0.00000	0.00000	0.00000	0.00000	0.00000
95	0.00000	0.00000	0.00000	0.00000	0.00000	0.00000	0.00000	0.00000	0.00000	0.00000	0.00000	0.00000
96	0.00000	0.00000	0.00000	0.00000	0.00000	0.00000	0.00000	0.00000	0.00000	0.00000	0.00000	0.00000
97	0.00000	0.00000	0.00000	0.00000	0.00000	0.00000	0.00000	0.00000	0.00000	0.00000	0.00000	0.00000
98	0.00000	0.00000	0.00000	0.00000	0.00000	0.00000	0.00000	0.00000	0.00000	0.00000	0.00000	0.00000
99	0.00000	0.00000	0.00000	0.00000	0.00000	0.00000	0.00000	0.00000	0.00000	0.00000	0.00000	0.00000
100	0.00000	0.00000	0.00000	0.00000	0.00000	0.00000	0.00000	0.00000	0.00000	0.00000	0.00000	0.00000
101	0.00000	0.00000	0.00000	0.00000	0.00000	0.00000	0.00000	0.00000	0.00000	0.00000	0.00000	0.00000
102	0.00000	0.00000	0.00000	0.00000	0.00000	0.00000	0.00000	0.00000	0.00000	0.00000	0.00000	0.00000
103	0.00000	0.00000	0.00000	0.00000	0.00000	0.00000	0.00000	0.00000	0.00000	0.00000	0.00000	0.00000
104	0.00000	0.00000	0.00000	0.00000	0.00000	0.00000	0.00000	0.00000	0.00000	0.00000	0.00000	0.00000
105	0.00000	0.00000	0.00000	0.00000	0.00000	0.00000	0.00000	0.00000	0.00000	0.00000	0.00000	0.00000
106	0.00000	0.00000	0.00000	0.00000	0.00000	0.00000	0.00000	0.00000	0.00000	0.00000	0.00000	0.00000
107	0.00000	0.00000	0.00000	0.00000	0.00000	0.00000	0.00000	0.00000	0.00000	0.00000	0.00000	0.00000
108	0.00000	0.00000	0.00000	0.00000	0.00000	0.00000	0.00000	0.00000	0.00000	0.00000	0.00000	0.00000
109	0.00000	0.00000	0.00000	0.00000	0.00000	0.00000	0.00000	0.00000	0.00000	0.00000	0.00000	0.00000
110	0.00000	0.00000	0.00000	0.00000	0.00000	0.00000	0.00000	0.00000	0.00000	0.00000	0.00000	0.00000
111	0.00000	0.00000	0.00000	0.00000	0.00000	0.00000	0.00000	0.00000	0.00000	0.00000	0.00000	0.00000
112	0.00000	0.00000	0.00000	0.00000	0.00000	0.00000	0.00000	0.00000	0.00000	0.00000	0.00000	0.00000
113	0.00000	0.00000	0.00000	0.00000	0.00000	0.00000	0.00000	0.00000	0.00000	0.00000	0.00000	0.00000
114	0.00000	0.00000	0.00000	0.00000	0.00000	0.00000	0.00000	0.00000	0.00000	0.00000	0.00000	0.00000
115	0.00000	0.00000	0.00000	0.00000	0.00000	0.00000	0.00000	0.00000	0.00000	0.00000	0.00000	0.00000
116	0.00000	0.00000	0.00000	0.00000	0.00000	0.00000	0.00000	0.00000	0.00000	0.00000	0.00000	0.00000
117	0.00000	0.00000	0.00000	0.00000	0.00000	0.00000	0.00000	0.00000	0.00000	0.00000	0.00000	0.00000
118	0.00000	0.00000	0.00000	0.00000	0.00000	0.00000	0.00000	0.00000	0.00000	0.00000	0.00000	0.00000
119	0.00000	0.00000	0.00000	0.00000	0.00000	0.00000	0.00000	0.00000	0.00000	0.00000	0.00000	0.00000
120	0.00000	0.00000	0.00000	0.00000	0.00000	0.00000	0.00000	0.00000	0.00000	0.00000	0.00000	0.00000

Table 4 *Present Value of an Ordinary Annuity of $1 per Period: 0.5%-7%*

$$P_{A_{i,n}} = \frac{1 - \dfrac{1}{(1+i)^n}}{i}$$

Period	.5%	1%	1.5%	2%	2.5%	3%	3.5%	4%	4.5%	5%	5.5%	6%	6.5%	7%
1	0.99502	0.99010	0.98522	0.98039	0.97561	0.97087	0.96618	0.96154	0.95694	0.95238	0.94787	0.94340	0.93897	0.93458
2	1.98510	1.97040	1.95588	1.94156	1.92742	1.91347	1.89969	1.88609	1.87267	1.85941	1.84632	1.83339	1.82063	1.80802
3	2.97025	2.94099	2.91220	2.88388	2.85602	2.82861	2.80164	2.77509	2.74896	2.72325	2.69793	2.67301	2.64848	2.62432
4	3.95050	3.90197	3.85438	3.80773	3.76197	3.71710	3.67308	3.62990	3.58753	3.54595	3.50515	3.46511	3.42580	3.38721
5	4.92587	4.85343	4.78264	4.71346	4.64583	4.57971	4.51505	4.45182	4.38998	4.32948	4.27028	4.21236	4.15568	4.10020
6	5.89638	5.79548	5.69719	5.60143	5.50813	5.41719	5.32855	5.24214	5.15787	5.07569	4.99553	4.91732	4.84101	4.76654
7	6.86207	6.72819	6.59821	6.47199	6.34939	6.23028	6.11454	6.00205	5.89270	5.78637	5.68297	5.58238	5.48452	5.38929
8	7.82296	7.65168	7.48593	7.32548	7.17014	7.01969	6.87396	6.73274	6.59589	6.46321	6.33457	6.20979	6.08875	5.97130
9	8.77906	8.56602	8.36052	8.16224	7.97087	7.78611	7.60769	7.43533	7.26879	7.10782	6.95220	6.80169	6.65610	6.51523
10	9.73041	9.47130	9.22218	8.98259	8.75206	8.53020	8.31661	8.11090	7.91272	7.72173	7.53763	7.36009	7.18883	7.02358
11	10.67703	10.36763	10.07112	9.78685	9.51421	9.25262	9.00155	8.76048	8.52892	8.30641	8.09254	7.88687	7.68904	7.49867
12	11.61893	11.25508	10.90751	10.57534	10.25776	9.95400	9.66333	9.38507	9.11858	8.86325	8.61852	8.38384	8.15873	7.94269
13	12.55615	12.13374	11.73153	11.34837	10.98318	10.63496	10.30274	9.98565	9.68285	9.39357	9.11708	8.85268	8.59974	8.35765
14	13.48871	13.00370	12.54338	12.10625	11.69091	11.29607	10.92052	10.56312	10.22283	9.89864	9.58965	9.29498	9.01384	8.74547
15	14.41662	13.86505	13.34323	12.84926	12.38138	11.93794	11.51741	11.11839	10.73955	10.37966	10.03758	9.71225	9.40267	9.10791
16	15.33993	14.71787	14.13126	13.57771	13.05500	12.56110	12.09412	11.65230	11.23402	10.83777	10.46216	10.10590	9.76776	9.44665
17	16.25863	15.56225	14.90765	14.29187	13.71220	13.16612	12.65132	12.16567	11.70719	11.27407	10.86461	10.47726	10.11058	9.76322
18	17.17277	16.39827	15.67256	14.99203	14.35336	13.75351	13.18968	12.65930	12.15999	11.68959	11.24607	10.82760	10.43247	10.05909
19	18.08236	17.22601	16.42617	15.67846	14.97889	14.32380	13.70984	13.13394	12.59329	12.08532	11.60765	11.15812	10.73471	10.33560
20	18.98742	18.04555	17.16864	16.35143	15.58916	14.87747	14.21240	13.59033	13.00794	12.46221	11.95038	11.46992	11.01851	10.59401
21	19.88798	18.85698	17.90014	17.01121	16.18455	15.41502	14.69797	14.02916	13.40472	12.82115	12.27524	11.76408	11.28498	10.83553
22	20.78406	19.66038	18.62082	17.65805	16.76541	15.93692	15.16712	14.45112	13.78442	13.16300	12.58317	12.04158	11.53520	11.06124
23	21.67568	20.45582	19.33086	18.29220	17.33211	16.44361	15.62041	14.85684	14.14777	13.48857	12.87504	12.30338	11.77014	11.27219
24	22.56287	21.24339	20.03041	18.91393	17.88499	16.93554	16.05837	15.24696	14.49548	13.79864	13.15170	12.55036	11.99074	11.46933
25	23.44554	22.02316	20.71961	19.52346	18.42438	17.41315	16.48151	15.62208	14.82821	14.09394	13.41393	12.78336	12.19788	11.65358
26	24.32402	22.79520	21.39863	20.12104	18.95061	17.87684	16.89035	15.98277	15.14661	14.37519	13.66250	13.00317	12.39237	11.82578
27	25.19803	23.55961	22.06762	20.70690	19.46401	18.32703	17.28536	16.32959	15.45130	14.64303	13.89810	13.21053	12.57500	11.98671
28	26.06769	24.31644	22.72672	21.28127	19.96489	18.76411	17.66702	16.66306	15.74287	14.89813	14.12142	13.40616	12.74648	12.13711
29	26.93302	25.06579	23.37608	21.84438	20.45355	19.18845	18.03577	16.98371	16.02189	15.14107	14.33310	13.59072	12.90749	12.27767
30	27.79405	25.80771	24.01584	22.39646	20.93029	19.60044	18.39205	17.29203	16.28889	15.37245	14.53375	13.76483	13.05868	12.40904
31	28.65080	26.54229	24.64615	22.93770	21.39541	20.00043	18.73628	17.58849	16.54439	15.59281	14.72393	13.92909	13.20063	12.53181
32	29.50328	27.26959	25.26714	23.46833	21.84918	20.38877	19.06887	17.87355	16.78889	15.80268	14.90420	14.08404	13.33393	12.64656
33	30.35153	27.98969	25.87895	23.98856	22.29188	20.76579	19.39021	18.14765	17.02286	16.00255	15.07507	14.23023	13.45909	12.75379
34	31.19555	28.70267	26.48173	24.49859	22.72379	21.13164	19.70068	18.41120	17.24676	16.19290	15.23703	14.36814	13.57661	12.85401
35	32.03537	29.40858	27.07559	24.99862	23.14516	21.48722	20.00066	18.66461	17.46101	16.37419	15.39055	14.49825	13.68696	12.94767
36	32.87102	30.10751	27.66068	25.48884	23.55625	21.83225	20.29049	18.90828	17.66604	16.54685	15.53607	14.62099	13.79057	13.03521
37	33.70250	30.79951	28.23713	25.96945	23.95732	22.16724	20.57053	19.14258	17.86224	16.71129	15.67400	14.73678	13.88786	13.11702
38	34.52985	31.48466	28.80505	26.44064	24.34860	22.49246	20.84109	19.36786	18.04999	16.86789	15.80474	14.84602	13.97921	13.19347
39	35.35309	32.16303	29.36458	26.90259	24.73034	22.80822	21.10250	19.58448	18.22966	17.01704	15.92866	14.94907	14.06499	13.26493
40	36.17223	32.83469	29.91585	27.35548	25.10278	23.11477	21.35507	19.79277	18.40158	17.15909	16.04612	15.04630	14.14553	13.33171
41	36.98729	33.49969	30.45896	27.79949	25.46612	23.41240	21.59910	19.99305	18.56611	17.29437	16.15746	15.13802	14.22115	13.39412
42	37.79830	34.15811	30.99405	28.23479	25.82061	23.70136	21.83488	20.18563	18.72355	17.42321	16.26300	15.22454	14.29216	13.45245
43	38.60527	34.81001	31.52123	28.66156	26.16645	23.98190	22.06269	20.37079	18.87421	17.54591	16.36303	15.30617	14.35884	13.50696
44	39.40823	35.45545	32.04062	29.07996	26.50385	24.25427	22.28279	20.54884	19.01838	17.66277	16.45785	15.38318	14.42144	13.55791
45	40.20720	36.09451	32.55234	29.49016	26.83302	24.51871	22.49545	20.72004	19.15635	17.77407	16.54773	15.45583	14.48023	13.60552
46	41.00219	36.72724	33.05649	29.89231	27.15417	24.77545	22.70092	20.88465	19.28837	17.88007	16.63292	15.52437	14.53543	13.65002
47	41.79322	37.35370	33.55319	30.28658	27.46748	25.02471	22.89944	21.04294	19.41471	17.98102	16.71366	15.58903	14.58725	13.69161
48	42.58032	37.97396	34.04255	30.67312	27.77315	25.26671	23.09124	21.19513	19.53561	18.07716	16.79020	15.65003	14.63592	13.73047
49	43.36350	38.58808	34.52468	31.05208	28.07137	25.50166	23.27656	21.34147	19.65130	18.16872	16.86275	15.70757	14.68161	13.76680
50	44.14279	39.19612	34.99969	31.42361	28.36231	25.72976	23.45562	21.48218	19.76201	18.25593	16.93152	15.76186	14.72452	13.80075
51	44.91820	39.79814	35.46767	31.78785	28.64616	25.95123	23.62862	21.61749	19.86795	18.33898	16.99670	15.81308	14.76481	13.83247
52	45.68975	40.39419	35.92874	32.14495	28.92308	26.16624	23.79576	21.74758	19.96933	18.41807	17.05848	15.86139	14.80264	13.86212
53	46.45746	40.98435	36.38300	32.49505	29.19325	26.37499	23.95726	21.87267	20.06634	18.49340	17.11705	15.90697	14.83816	13.88984
54	47.22135	41.56866	36.83054	32.83828	29.45683	26.57766	24.11330	21.99296	20.15918	18.56515	17.17255	15.94998	14.87151	13.91573
55	47.98145	42.14719	37.27147	33.17479	29.71398	26.77443	24.26405	22.10861	20.24802	18.63347	17.22517	15.99054	14.90282	13.93994
56	48.73776	42.71999	37.70588	33.50469	29.96486	26.96546	24.40971	22.21982	20.33303	18.69854	17.27504	16.02881	14.93223	13.96256
57	49.49031	43.28712	38.13387	33.82813	30.20962	27.15094	24.55045	22.32675	20.41439	18.76052	17.32232	16.06492	14.95984	13.98370
58	50.23911	43.84863	38.55554	34.14523	30.44841	27.33101	24.68642	22.42957	20.49224	18.81954	17.36712	16.09898	14.98577	14.00346
59	50.98419	44.40459	38.97097	34.45610	30.68137	27.50583	24.81780	22.52843	20.56673	18.87575	17.40960	16.13111	15.01011	14.02192
60	51.72556	44.95504	39.38027	34.76089	30.90866	27.67556	24.94473	22.62349	20.63802	18.92929	17.44985	16.16143	15.03297	14.03918

Period	.5%	1%	1.5%	2%	2.5%	3%	3.5%	4%	4.5%	5%	5.5%	6%	6.5%	7%
61 ...	52.46324	45.50004	39.78352	35.05969	31.13040	27.84035	25.06738	22.71489	20.70624	18.98028	17.48801	16.19003	15.05443	14.05531
62 ...	53.19726	46.03964	40.18080	35.35264	31.34673	28.00034	25.18587	22.80278	20.77152	19.02883	17.52418	16.21701	15.07458	14.07038
63 ...	53.92762	46.57390	40.57222	35.63984	31.55778	28.15567	25.30036	22.88729	20.83399	19.07508	17.55847	16.24246	15.09350	14.08447
64 ...	54.65435	47.10287	40.95785	35.92141	31.76369	28.30648	25.41097	22.96855	20.89377	19.11912	17.59096	16.26647	15.11127	14.09764
65 ...	55.37746	47.62661	41.33779	36.19747	31.96458	28.45289	25.51785	23.04668	20.95098	19.16107	17.62177	16.28912	15.12795	14.10994
66 ...	56.09698	48.14516	41.71210	36.46810	32.16056	28.59504	25.62111	23.12181	21.00572	19.20102	17.65096	16.31049	15.14362	14.12144
67 ...	56.81291	48.65857	42.08089	36.73343	32.35177	28.73305	25.72088	23.19405	21.05811	19.23907	17.67864	16.33065	15.15833	14.13219
68 ...	57.52529	49.16690	42.44423	36.99356	32.53831	28.86704	25.81727	23.26351	21.10824	19.27530	17.70487	16.34967	15.17214	14.14223
69 ...	58.23411	49.67020	42.80219	37.24859	32.72030	28.99712	25.91041	23.33030	21.15621	19.30981	17.72974	16.36762	15.18511	14.15162
70 ...	58.93942	50.16851	43.15487	37.49862	32.89786	29.12342	26.00040	23.39451	21.20211	19.34268	17.75330	16.38454	15.19728	14.16039
71 ...	59.64121	50.66190	43.50234	37.74374	33.07108	29.24604	26.08734	23.45626	21.24604	19.37398	17.77564	16.40051	15.20872	14.16859
72 ...	60.33951	51.15039	43.84467	37.98406	33.24008	29.36509	26.17134	23.51564	21.28808	19.40379	17.79682	16.41558	15.21945	14.17625
73 ...	61.03434	51.63405	44.18194	38.21967	33.40495	29.48067	26.25251	23.57273	21.32830	19.43218	17.81689	16.42979	15.22953	14.18341
74 ...	61.72571	52.11292	44.51422	38.45066	33.56581	29.59288	26.33092	23.62762	21.36680	19.45922	17.83591	16.44320	15.23900	14.19010
75 ...	62.41365	52.58705	44.84160	38.67711	33.72274	29.70183	26.40669	23.68041	21.40363	19.48497	17.85395	16.45585	15.24788	14.19636
76 ...	63.09815	53.05649	45.16414	38.89913	33.87584	29.80760	26.47989	23.73116	21.43888	19.50950	17.87104	16.46778	15.25623	14.20220
77 ...	63.77926	53.52127	45.48191	39.11680	34.02521	29.91029	26.55062	23.77996	21.47262	19.53285	17.88724	16.47904	15.26407	14.20767
78 ...	64.45697	53.98146	45.79498	39.33019	34.17094	30.00999	26.61896	23.82689	21.50490	19.55510	17.90260	16.48966	15.27142	14.21277
79 ...	65.13132	54.43709	46.10343	39.53940	34.31311	30.10679	26.68498	23.87201	21.53579	19.57628	17.91716	16.49968	15.27833	14.21755
80 ...	65.80231	54.88821	46.40732	39.74451	34.45182	30.20076	26.74878	23.91539	21.56534	19.59646	17.93095	16.50913	15.28482	14.22201
81 ...	66.46996	55.33486	46.70672	39.94560	34.58714	30.29200	26.81041	23.95711	21.59363	19.61568	17.94403	16.51805	15.29091	14.22617
82 ...	67.13428	55.77709	47.00170	40.14275	34.71916	30.38059	26.86996	23.99722	21.62070	19.63398	17.95643	16.52646	15.29663	14.23007
83 ...	67.79531	56.21494	47.29231	40.33603	34.84796	30.46659	26.92750	24.03579	21.64660	19.65141	17.96818	16.53440	15.30200	14.23371
84 ...	68.45304	56.64845	47.57863	40.52552	34.97362	30.55009	26.98309	24.07287	21.67139	19.66801	17.97932	16.54188	15.30704	14.23711
85 ...	69.10750	57.07768	47.86072	40.71129	35.09621	30.63115	27.03680	24.10853	21.69511	19.68382	17.98987	16.54895	15.31178	14.24029
86 ...	69.75871	57.50265	48.13864	40.89342	35.21582	30.70986	27.08870	24.14282	21.71781	19.69887	17.99988	16.55561	15.31622	14.24326
87 ...	70.40668	57.92342	48.41246	41.07198	35.33251	30.78627	27.13884	24.17579	21.73953	19.71321	18.00936	16.56190	15.32040	14.24604
88 ...	71.05142	58.34002	48.68222	41.24704	35.44635	30.86045	27.18728	24.20749	21.76032	19.72687	18.01835	16.56783	15.32431	14.24864
89 ...	71.69296	58.75249	48.94800	41.41867	35.55741	30.93248	27.23409	24.23797	21.78021	19.73987	18.02688	16.57342	15.32800	14.25106
90 ...	72.33130	59.16088	49.20985	41.58693	35.66577	31.00241	27.27932	24.26728	21.79924	19.75226	18.03495	16.57870	15.33145	14.25333
91 ...	72.96647	59.56523	49.46784	41.75189	35.77148	31.07030	27.32301	24.29546	21.81746	19.76406	18.04261	16.58368	15.33470	14.25545
92 ...	73.59847	59.96557	49.72201	41.91362	35.87462	31.13621	27.36523	24.32256	21.83489	19.77529	18.04987	16.58838	15.33774	14.25743
93 ...	74.22734	60.36195	49.97242	42.07218	35.97524	31.20021	27.40602	24.34861	21.85156	19.78599	18.05675	16.59281	15.34060	14.25928
94 ...	74.85307	60.75441	50.21913	42.22762	36.07340	31.26234	27.44543	24.37367	21.86753	19.79619	18.06327	16.59699	15.34329	14.26101
95 ...	75.47569	61.14298	50.46220	42.38002	36.16917	31.32266	27.48350	24.39776	21.88280	19.80589	18.06945	16.60093	15.34581	14.26262
96 ...	76.09522	61.52770	50.70168	42.52943	36.26261	31.38122	27.52029	24.42092	21.89742	19.81513	18.07531	16.60465	15.34818	14.26413
97 ...	76.71166	61.90862	50.93761	42.67592	36.35376	31.43808	27.55584	24.44319	21.91140	19.82394	18.08086	16.60816	15.35040	14.26555
98 ...	77.32503	62.28576	51.17006	42.81953	36.44269	31.49328	27.59018	24.46461	21.92479	19.83232	18.08612	16.61147	15.35249	14.26687
99 ...	77.93536	62.65917	51.39907	42.96032	36.52946	31.54687	27.62337	24.48520	21.93760	19.84031	18.09111	16.61460	15.35445	14.26810
100-...	78.54264	63.02888	51.62470	43.09835	36.61411	31.59891	27.65543	24.50500	21.94985	19.84791	18.09584	16.61755	15.35629	14.26925
101 ...	79.14691	63.39493	51.84700	43.23368	36.69669	31.64942	27.68640	24.52404	21.96158	19.85515	18.10032	16.62033	15.35802	14.27033
102 ...	79.74817	63.75736	52.06601	43.36635	36.77726	31.69847	27.71633	24.54234	21.97281	19.86205	18.10457	16.62295	15.35964	14.27133
103 ...	80.34644	64.11619	52.28178	43.49642	36.85586	31.74609	27.74525	24.55995	21.98355	19.86862	18.10860	16.62542	15.36117	14.27228
104 ...	80.94173	64.47148	52.49437	43.62394	36.93255	31.79232	27.77318	24.57687	21.99382	19.87488	18.11241	16.62776	15.36260	14.27315
105 ...	81.53406	64.82325	52.70381	43.74896	37.00736	31.83720	27.80018	24.59315	22.00366	19.88083	18.11603	16.62996	15.36394	14.27398
106 ...	82.12344	65.17153	52.91016	43.87153	37.08035	31.88078	27.82626	24.60879	22.01307	19.88651	18.11946	16.63204	15.36521	14.27474
107 ...	82.70989	65.51637	53.11346	43.99170	37.15156	31.92308	27.85146	24.62384	22.02208	19.89191	18.12271	16.63400	15.36639	14.27546
108 ...	83.29342	65.85779	53.31375	44.10951	37.22104	31.96416	27.87581	24.63831	22.03070	19.89706	18.12579	16.63585	15.36750	14.27613
109 ...	83.87405	66.19583	53.51108	44.22501	37.28882	32.00404	27.89933	24.65222	22.03894	19.90196	18.12872	16.63759	15.36855	14.27676
110 ...	84.45180	66.53053	53.70550	44.33824	37.35494	32.04276	27.92206	24.66560	22.04684	19.90663	18.13148	16.63924	15.36953	14.27735
111 ...	85.02666	66.86191	53.89704	44.44926	37.41946	32.08035	27.94402	24.67846	22.05439	19.91108	18.13411	16.64079	15.37045	14.27789
112 ...	85.59867	67.19001	54.08576	44.55810	37.48240	32.11684	27.96523	24.69082	22.06162	19.91531	18.13659	16.64226	15.37131	14.27840
113 ...	86.16783	67.51486	54.27168	44.66480	37.54380	32.15227	27.98573	24.70272	22.06853	19.91934	18.13895	16.64364	15.37212	14.27888
114 ...	86.73416	67.83649	54.45486	44.76941	37.60371	32.18667	28.00554	24.71415	22.07515	19.92318	18.14119	16.64494	15.37289	14.27933
115 ...	87.29767	68.15494	54.63533	44.87197	37.66216	32.22007	28.02467	24.72514	22.08148	19.92684	18.14331	16.64617	15.37360	14.27975
116 ...	87.85838	68.47024	54.81313	44.97252	37.71918	32.25250	28.04316	24.73571	22.08754	19.93033	18.14531	16.64733	15.37428	14.28014
117 ...	88.41630	68.78242	54.98831	45.07110	37.77481	32.28398	28.06103	24.74588	22.09334	19.93364	18.14722	16.64843	15.37491	14.28050
118 ...	88.97144	69.09150	55.16089	45.16775	37.82908	32.31454	28.07829	24.75565	22.09889	19.93680	18.14902	16.64946	15.37550	14.28084
119 ...	89.52382	69.39753	55.33093	45.26250	37.88203	32.34421	28.09496	24.76505	22.10420	19.93981	18.15073	16.65043	15.37606	14.28116
120 ...	90.07345	69.70052	55.49845	45.35539	37.93369	32.37302	28.11108	24.77409	22.10929	19.94268	18.15235	16.65135	15.37658	14.28146

Table 4 (continued) Present Value of an Ordinary Annuity of $1 per Period: 7.5%–14%

Period	7.5%	8%	8.5%	9%	9.5%	10%	10.5%	11%	11.5%	12%	12.5%	13%	13.5%	14%
1	0.93023	0.92593	0.92166	0.91743	0.91324	0.90909	0.90498	0.90090	0.89686	0.89286	0.88889	0.88496	0.88106	0.87719
2	1.79557	1.78326	1.77111	1.75911	1.74725	1.73554	1.72396	1.71252	1.70122	1.69005	1.67901	1.66810	1.65732	1.64666
3	2.60053	2.57710	2.55402	2.53129	2.50891	2.48685	2.46512	2.44371	2.42262	2.40183	2.38134	2.36115	2.34125	2.32163
4	3.34933	3.31213	3.27560	3.23972	3.20448	3.16987	3.13586	3.10245	3.06961	3.03735	3.00564	2.97447	2.94383	2.91371
5	4.04588	3.99271	3.94064	3.88965	3.83971	3.79079	3.74286	3.69590	3.64988	3.60478	3.56057	3.51723	3.47474	3.43308
6	4.69385	4.62288	4.55359	4.48592	4.41983	4.35526	4.29218	4.23054	4.17029	4.11141	4.05384	3.99755	3.94250	3.88867
7	5.29660	5.20637	5.11851	5.03295	4.94961	4.86842	4.78930	4.71220	4.63704	4.56376	4.49230	4.42261	4.35463	4.28830
8	5.85730	5.74664	5.63918	5.53482	5.43344	5.33493	5.23919	5.14612	5.05564	4.96764	4.88205	4.79877	4.71774	4.63886
9	6.37889	6.24689	6.11906	5.99525	5.87528	5.75902	5.64632	5.53705	5.43106	5.32825	5.22848	5.13166	5.03765	4.94637
10	6.86408	6.71008	6.56135	6.41766	6.27880	6.14457	6.01477	5.88923	5.76777	5.65022	5.53643	5.42624	5.31952	5.21612
11	7.31542	7.13896	6.96898	6.80519	6.64730	6.49506	6.34821	6.20652	6.06975	5.93770	5.81016	5.68694	5.56786	5.45273
12	7.73528	7.53608	7.34469	7.16073	6.98384	6.81369	6.64996	6.49236	6.34058	6.19437	6.05348	5.91765	5.78666	5.66029
13	8.12584	7.90378	7.69095	7.48690	7.29118	7.10336	6.92304	6.74987	6.58348	6.42355	6.26976	6.12181	5.97943	5.84236
14	8.48915	8.24424	8.01010	7.78615	7.57185	7.36669	7.17018	6.98187	6.80133	6.62817	6.46201	6.30249	6.14928	6.00207
15	8.82712	8.55948	8.30424	8.06069	7.82818	7.60608	7.39382	7.19087	6.99671	6.81086	6.63289	6.46238	6.29893	6.14217
16	9.14151	8.85137	8.57533	8.31256	8.06226	7.82371	7.59622	7.37916	7.17194	6.97399	6.78479	6.60388	6.43077	6.26506
17	9.43396	9.12164	8.82519	8.54363	8.27604	8.02155	7.77939	7.54879	7.32909	7.11963	6.91982	6.72909	6.54694	6.37286
18	9.70601	9.37189	9.05548	8.75563	8.47127	8.20141	7.94515	7.70162	7.47004	7.24967	7.03984	6.83991	6.64928	6.46742
19	9.95908	9.60360	9.26772	8.95011	8.64956	8.36492	8.09515	7.83929	7.59644	7.36578	7.14652	6.93797	6.73946	6.55037
20	10.19449	9.81815	9.46334	9.12855	8.81238	8.51356	8.23091	7.96333	7.70982	7.46944	7.24135	7.02475	6.81890	6.62313
21	10.41348	10.01680	9.64363	9.29224	8.96108	8.64869	8.35376	8.07507	7.81149	7.56200	7.32565	7.10155	6.88890	6.68696
22	10.61719	10.20074	9.80980	9.44243	9.09688	8.77154	8.46494	8.17574	7.90269	7.64465	7.40058	7.16951	6.95057	6.74294
23	10.80669	10.37106	9.96295	9.58021	9.22089	8.88322	8.56556	8.26643	7.98447	7.71843	7.46718	7.22966	7.00491	6.79206
24	10.98297	10.52876	10.10410	9.70661	9.33415	8.98474	8.65662	8.34814	8.05782	7.78432	7.52638	7.28288	7.05279	6.83514
25	11.14695	10.67478	10.23419	9.82258	9.43758	9.07704	8.73902	8.42174	8.12361	7.84314	7.57901	7.32998	7.09497	6.87293
26	11.29948	10.80998	10.35409	9.92897	9.53203	9.16095	8.81359	8.48806	8.18261	7.89566	7.62578	7.37167	7.13213	6.90608
27	11.44138	10.93516	10.46460	10.02658	9.61830	9.23722	8.88108	8.54780	8.23552	7.94255	7.66736	7.40856	7.16487	6.93515
28	11.57338	11.05108	10.56645	10.11613	9.69707	9.30657	8.94215	8.60162	8.28298	7.98442	7.70432	7.44120	7.19372	6.96066
29	11.69617	11.15841	10.66033	10.19828	9.76902	9.36961	8.99742	8.65011	8.32554	8.02181	7.73717	7.47009	7.21914	6.98304
30	11.81039	11.25778	10.74684	10.27365	9.83472	9.42691	9.04744	8.69379	8.36371	8.05518	7.76638	7.49565	7.24153	7.00266
31	11.91664	11.34980	10.82658	10.34280	9.89472	9.47901	9.09271	8.73315	8.39795	8.08499	7.79234	7.51828	7.26126	7.01988
32	12.01548	11.43500	10.90008	10.40624	9.94952	9.52638	9.13367	8.76860	8.42866	8.11159	7.81541	7.53830	7.27864	7.03498
33	12.10742	11.51389	10.96781	10.46444	9.99956	9.56943	9.17074	8.80054	8.45619	8.13535	7.83592	7.55602	7.29396	7.04823
34	12.19295	11.58693	11.03024	10.51784	10.04526	9.60857	9.20429	8.82932	8.48089	8.15656	7.85415	7.57170	7.30745	7.05985
35	12.27251	11.65457	11.08778	10.56682	10.08699	9.64416	9.23465	8.85524	8.50304	8.17550	7.87036	7.58557	7.31934	7.07005
36	12.34652	11.71719	11.14081	10.61176	10.12511	9.67651	9.26213	8.87859	8.52291	8.19241	7.88476	7.59785	7.32982	7.07899
37	12.41537	11.77518	11.18969	10.65299	10.15992	9.70592	9.28700	8.89963	8.54072	8.20751	7.89757	7.60872	7.33904	7.08683
38	12.47941	11.82887	11.23474	10.69082	10.19171	9.73265	9.30950	8.91859	8.55670	8.22099	7.90895	7.61833	7.34718	7.09371
39	12.53899	11.87858	11.27625	10.72552	10.22074	9.75696	9.32986	8.93567	8.57103	8.23303	7.91906	7.62684	7.35434	7.09975
40	12.59441	11.92461	11.31452	10.75736	10.24725	9.77905	9.34829	8.95105	8.58389	8.24378	7.92806	7.63438	7.36065	7.10504
41	12.64596	11.96723	11.34979	10.78657	10.27146	9.79914	9.36497	8.96491	8.59541	8.25337	7.93605	7.64104	7.36621	7.10969
42	12.69392	12.00670	11.38229	10.81337	10.29357	9.81740	9.38006	8.97740	8.60575	8.26194	7.94316	7.64694	7.37111	7.11376
43	12.73853	12.04324	11.41225	10.83795	10.31376	9.83400	9.39372	8.98865	8.61502	8.26959	7.94947	7.65216	7.37543	7.11733
44	12.78003	12.07707	11.43986	10.86051	10.33220	9.84909	9.40608	8.99878	8.62334	8.27642	7.95509	7.65678	7.37923	7.12047
45	12.81863	12.10840	11.46531	10.88120	10.34904	9.86281	9.41727	9.00791	8.63080	8.28252	7.96008	7.66086	7.38258	7.12322
46	12.85454	12.13741	11.48877	10.90018	10.36442	9.87528	9.42739	9.01614	8.63749	8.28796	7.96451	7.66448	7.38554	7.12563
47	12.88794	12.16427	11.51038	10.91760	10.37847	9.88662	9.43656	9.02355	8.64349	8.29282	7.96846	7.66768	7.38814	7.12774
48	12.91902	12.18914	11.53031	10.93358	10.39130	9.89693	9.44485	9.03022	8.64887	8.29716	7.97196	7.67052	7.39043	7.12960
49	12.94792	12.21216	11.54867	10.94823	10.40301	9.90630	9.45235	9.03624	8.65369	8.30104	7.97508	7.67302	7.39245	7.13123
50	12.97481	12.23348	11.56560	10.96168	10.41371	9.91481	9.45914	9.04165	8.65802	8.30450	7.97785	7.67524	7.39423	7.13266
51	12.99982	12.25323	11.58119	10.97402	10.42348	9.92256	9.46529	9.04653	8.66190	8.30759	7.98031	7.67720	7.39580	7.13391
52	13.02309	12.27151	11.59557	10.98534	10.43240	9.92960	9.47085	9.05093	8.66538	8.31035	7.98250	7.67894	7.39718	7.13501
53	13.04474	12.28843	11.60882	10.99573	10.44055	9.93600	9.47588	9.05489	8.66850	8.31281	7.98444	7.68048	7.39839	7.13597
54	13.06487	12.30410	11.62103	11.00525	10.44799	9.94182	9.48043	9.05846	8.67130	8.31501	7.98617	7.68184	7.39947	7.13682
55	13.08360	12.31861	11.63229	11.01399	10.45478	9.94711	9.48456	9.06168	8.67382	8.31697	7.98771	7.68304	7.40041	7.13756
56	13.10103	12.33205	11.64266	11.02201	10.46099	9.95191	9.48829	9.06457	8.67607	8.31872	7.98907	7.68411	7.40124	7.13821
57	13.11723	12.34449	11.65222	11.02937	10.46666	9.95629	9.49166	9.06718	8.67809	8.32029	7.99029	7.68505	7.40198	7.13878
58	13.13231	12.35601	11.66104	11.03612	10.47183	9.96026	9.49472	9.06954	8.67990	8.32169	7.99137	7.68589	7.40262	7.13928
59	13.14633	12.36668	11.66916	11.04231	10.47656	9.96387	9.49748	9.07165	8.68152	8.32294	7.99232	7.68663	7.40319	7.13972
60	13.15938	12.37655	11.67664	11.04799	10.48088	9.96716	9.49998	9.07356	8.68298	8.32405	7.99318	7.68728	7.40369	7.14011

Period	7.5%	8%	8.5%	9%	9.5%	10%	10.5%	11%	11.5%	12%	12.5%	13%	13.5%	14%
61....	13.17152	12.38570	11.68354	11.05320	10.48482	9.97014	9.50225	9.07528	8.68429	8.32504	7.99394	7.68786	7.40413	7.14044
62....	13.18281	12.39416	11.68990	11.05798	10.48842	9.97286	9.50430	9.07683	8.68546	8.32593	7.99461	7.68837	7.40452	7.14074
63....	13.19331	12.40200	11.69576	11.06237	10.49171	9.97532	9.50615	9.07822	8.68651	8.32673	7.99521	7.68882	7.40487	7.14100
64....	13.20308	12.40926	11.70116	11.06640	10.49471	9.97757	9.50783	9.07948	8.68745	8.32743	7.99574	7.68922	7.40517	7.14123
65....	13.21217	12.41598	11.70614	11.07009	10.49745	9.97961	9.50935	9.08061	8.68830	8.32807	7.99621	7.68958	7.40544	7.14143
66....	13.22062	12.42221	11.71073	11.07347	10.49996	9.98146	9.51072	9.08163	8.68906	8.32863	7.99663	7.68989	7.40567	7.14160
67....	13.22848	12.42797	11.71496	11.07658	10.50224	9.98315	9.51196	9.08255	8.68974	8.32913	7.99701	7.69017	7.40588	7.14176
68....	13.23580	12.43330	11.71885	11.07943	10.50433	9.98468	9.51309	9.08338	8.69035	8.32958	7.99734	7.69042	7.40606	7.14189
69....	13.24260	12.43825	11.72245	11.08205	10.50624	9.98607	9.51411	9.08413	8.69090	8.32999	7.99764	7.69063	7.40622	7.14201
70....	13.24893	12.44282	11.72576	11.08445	10.50798	9.98734	9.51503	9.08480	8.69139	8.33034	7.99790	7.69083	7.40636	7.14211
71....	13.25482	12.44706	11.72881	11.08665	10.50957	9.98849	9.51586	9.08541	8.69183	8.33066	7.99813	7.69100	7.40648	7.14221
72....	13.26030	12.45098	11.73162	11.08867	10.51102	9.98954	9.51662	9.08595	8.69222	8.33095	7.99834	7.69115	7.40659	7.14229
73....	13.26539	12.45461	11.73421	11.09052	10.51235	9.99049	9.51730	9.08644	8.69257	8.33121	7.99852	7.69128	7.40669	7.14236
74....	13.27013	12.45797	11.73660	11.09222	10.51356	9.99135	9.51792	9.08688	8.69289	8.33143	7.99869	7.69140	7.40678	7.14242
75....	13.27454	12.46108	11.73880	11.09378	10.51467	9.99214	9.51848	9.08728	8.69318	8.33164	7.99883	7.69150	7.40685	7.14247
76....	13.27864	12.46397	11.74083	11.09521	10.51568	9.99285	9.51899	9.08764	8.69343	8.33182	7.99896	7.69160	7.40692	7.14252
77....	13.28246	12.46664	11.74270	11.09653	10.51660	9.99350	9.51945	9.08797	8.69366	8.33198	7.99908	7.69168	7.40698	7.14256
78....	13.28601	12.46911	11.74443	11.09773	10.51744	9.99409	9.51986	9.08826	8.69387	8.33213	7.99918	7.69175	7.40703	7.14260
79....	13.28931	12.47140	11.74601	11.09883	10.51821	9.99463	9.52024	9.08852	8.69405	8.33226	7.99927	7.69181	7.40707	7.14263
80....	13.29238	12.47351	11.74748	11.09985	10.51892	9.99512	9.52057	9.08876	8.69422	8.33237	7.99935	7.69187	7.40711	7.14266
81....	13.29524	12.47548	11.74883	11.10078	10.51956	9.99556	9.52088	9.08897	8.69436	8.33247	7.99942	7.69192	7.40715	7.14268
82....	13.29790	12.47729	11.75007	11.10163	10.52015	9.99597	9.52116	9.08916	8.69450	8.33257	7.99949	7.69197	7.40718	7.14270
83....	13.30037	12.47897	11.75122	11.10241	10.52068	9.99633	9.52141	9.08934	8.69462	8.33265	7.99955	7.69201	7.40721	7.14272
84....	13.30267	12.48053	11.75228	11.10313	10.52117	9.99667	9.52164	9.08949	8.69472	8.33272	7.99960	7.69204	7.40723	7.14274
85....	13.30481	12.48197	11.75325	11.10379	10.52162	9.99697	9.52185	9.08963	8.69482	8.33279	7.99964	7.69207	7.40725	7.14275
86....	13.30680	12.48331	11.75415	11.10440	10.52202	9.99724	9.52203	9.08976	8.69490	8.33285	7.99968	7.69210	7.40727	7.14277
87....	13.30865	12.48455	11.75497	11.10495	10.52240	9.99749	9.52220	9.08987	8.69498	8.33290	7.99972	7.69212	7.40728	7.14278
88....	13.31037	12.48569	11.75574	11.10546	10.52274	9.99772	9.52235	9.08998	8.69505	8.33294	7.99975	7.69214	7.40730	7.14279
89....	13.31197	12.48675	11.75644	11.10593	10.52305	9.99793	9.52249	9.09007	8.69511	8.33299	7.99978	7.69216	7.40731	7.14280
90....	13.31346	12.48773	11.75709	11.10635	10.52333	9.99812	9.52262	9.09015	8.69517	8.33302	7.99980	7.69218	7.40732	7.14280
91....	13.31485	12.48864	11.75768	11.10675	10.52359	9.99829	9.52273	9.09023	8.69522	8.33306	7.99982	7.69219	7.40733	7.14281
92....	13.31614	12.48948	11.75823	11.10711	10.52383	9.99844	9.52283	9.09029	8.69526	8.33309	7.93984	7.69221	7.40734	7.14282
93....	13.31734	12.49026	11.75874	11.10744	10.52404	9.99859	9.52293	9.09036	8.69530	8.33311	7.99986	7.69222	7.40735	7.14282
94....	13.31846	12.49098	11.75921	11.10774	10.52424	9.99871	9.52301	9.09041	8.69534	8.33314	7.99988	7.69223	7.40736	7.14283
95....	13.31949	12.49165	11.75964	11.10802	10.52442	9.99883	9.52309	9.09046	8.69537	8.33316	7.99989	7.69224	7.40736	7.14283
96....	13.32046	12.49227	11.76004	11.10827	10.52458	9.99894	9.52315	9.09050	8.69540	8.33318	7.99990	7.69225	7.40737	7.14283
97....	13.32136	12.49284	11.76040	11.10851	10.52473	9.99903	9.52322	9.09054	8.69543	8.33319	7.99991	7.69225	7.40737	7.14284
98....	13.32219	12.49337	11.76074	11.10872	10.52487	9.99912	9.52327	9.09058	8.69545	8.33321	7.99992	7.69226	7.40738	7.14284
99....	13.32297	12.49386	11.76105	11.10892	10.52500	9.99920	9.52332	9.09061	8.69547	8.33322	7.99993	7.69226	7.40738	7.14284
100....	13.32369	12.49432	11.76134	11.10910	10.52511	9.99927	9.52337	9.09064	8.69549	8.33323	7.99994	7.69227	7.40738	7.14284
101....	13.32437	12.49474	11.76160	11.10927	10.52522	9.99934	9.52341	9.09067	8.69551	8.33324	7.99995	7.69227	7.40739	7.14284
102....	13.32499	12.49513	11.76184	11.10942	10.52531	9.99940	9.52345	9.09069	8.69552	8.33325	7.99995	7.69228	7.40739	7.14285
103....	13.32557	12.49549	11.76207	11.10956	10.52540	9.99945	9.52348	9.09071	8.69553	8.33326	7.99996	7.69228	7.40739	7.14285
104....	13.32611	12.49582	11.76227	11.10969	10.52548	9.99950	9.52351	9.09073	8.69555	8.33327	7.99996	7.69228	7.40739	7.14285
105....	13.32662	12.49613	11.76246	11.10981	10.52555	9.99955	9.52354	9.09075	8.69556	8.33328	7.99997	7.69229	7.40739	7.14285
106....	13.32709	12.49642	11.76264	11.10991	10.52562	9.99959	9.52357	9.09077	8.69557	8.33328	7.99997	7.69229	7.40740	7.14285
107....	13.32752	12.49668	11.76280	11.11001	10.52568	9.99963	9.52359	9.09078	8.69558	8.33329	7.99997	7.69229	7.40740	7.14285
108....	13.32793	12.49693	11.76295	11.11010	10.52573	9.99966	9.52361	9.09079	8.69558	8.33329	7.99998	7.69229	7.40740	7.14285
109....	13.32831	12.49716	11.76309	11.11019	10.52578	9.99969	9.52363	9.09080	8.69559	8.33330	7.99998	7.69230	7.40740	7.14285
110....	13.32866	12.49737	11.76322	11.11026	10.52583	9.99972	9.52365	9.09082	8.69560	8.33330	7.99998	7.69230	7.40740	7.14285
111....	13.32898	12.49756	11.76333	11.11033	10.52587	9.99975	9.52366	9.09082	8.69560	8.33330	7.99998	7.69230	7.40740	7.14285
112....	13.32929	12.49774	11.76344	11.11040	10.52591	9.99977	9.52368	9.09083	8.69561	8.33331	7.99999	7.69230	7.40740	7.14285
113....	13.32957	12.49791	11.76354	11.11046	10.52595	9.99979	9.52369	9.09084	8.69561	8.33331	7.99999	7.69230	7.40740	7.14285
114....	13.32983	12.49807	11.76363	11.11051	10.52598	9.99981	9.52370	9.09085	8.69562	8.33331	7.99999	7.69230	7.40740	7.14285
115....	13.33008	12.49821	11.76371	11.11056	10.52601	9.99983	9.52371	9.09085	8.69562	8.33332	7.99999	7.69230	7.40740	7.14286
116....	13.33030	12.49834	11.76379	11.11060	10.52603	9.99984	9.52372	9.09086	8.69562	8.33332	7.99999	7.69230	7.40740	7.14286
117....	13.33051	12.49846	11.76386	11.11065	10.52606	9.99986	9.52373	9.09086	8.69563	8.33332	7.99999	7.69230	7.40740	7.14286
118....	13.33071	12.49858	11.76393	11.11069	10.52608	9.99987	9.52374	9.09087	8.69563	8.33332	7.99999	7.69230	7.40741	7.14286
119....	13.33089	12.49868	11.76399	11.11072	10.52610	9.99988	9.52374	9.09087	8.69563	8.33332	7.99999	7.69230	7.40741	7.14286
120....	13.33106	12.49878	11.76405	11.11075	10.52612	9.99989	9.52375	9.09088	8.69563	8.33332	7.99999	7.69230	7.40741	7.14286

Table 4 (concluded)   Present Value of an Ordinary Annuity of $1 per Period: 14.5%–20%

Period	14.5%	15%	15.5%	16%	16.5%	17%	17.5%	18%	18.5%	19%	19.5%	20%
1	0.87336	0.86957	0.86580	0.86207	0.85837	0.85470	0.85106	0.84746	0.84388	0.84034	0.83682	0.83333
2	1.63612	1.62571	1.61541	1.60523	1.59517	1.58521	1.57537	1.56564	1.55602	1.54650	1.53709	1.52778
3	2.30229	2.28323	2.26443	2.24589	2.22761	2.20958	2.19181	2.17427	2.15698	2.13992	2.12309	2.10648
4	2.88410	2.85498	2.82634	2.79818	2.77048	2.74324	2.71643	2.69006	2.66412	2.63859	2.61346	2.58873
5	3.39223	3.35216	3.31285	3.27429	3.23646	3.19935	3.16292	3.12717	3.09208	3.05763	3.02382	2.99061
6	3.83600	3.78448	3.73407	3.68474	3.63645	3.58918	3.54291	3.49760	3.45323	3.40978	3.36721	3.32551
7	4.22358	4.16042	4.09876	4.03857	3.97979	3.92238	3.86631	3.81153	3.75800	3.70570	3.65457	3.60459
8	4.56208	4.48732	4.41451	4.34359	4.27449	4.20716	4.14154	4.07757	4.01519	3.95437	3.89504	3.83716
9	4.85771	4.77158	4.68789	4.60654	4.52746	4.45057	4.37578	3.30302	4.23223	4.16333	4.09627	4.03097
10	5.11591	5.01877	4.92458	4.83323	4.74460	4.65860	4.57513	4.49409	4.41538	4.33893	4.26466	4.19247
11	5.34140	5.23371	5.12951	5.02864	4.93099	4.83641	4.74479	4.65601	4.56994	4.48650	4.40557	4.32706
12	5.53834	5.42062	5.30693	5.19711	5.09098	4.98839	4.88918	4.79322	4.70037	4.61050	4.52349	4.43922
13	5.71034	5.58315	5.46055	5.34233	5.22831	5.11828	5.01207	4.90951	4.81044	4.71471	4.62217	4.53268
14	5.86056	5.72448	5.59355	5.46753	5.34619	5.22930	5.11666	5.00806	4.90333	4.80228	4.70474	4.61057
15	5.99176	5.84737	5.70870	5.57546	5.44747	5.32419	5.20567	5.09158	4.98171	4.87586	4.77384	4.67547
16	6.10634	5.95423	5.80840	5.66850	5.53422	5.40529	5.28142	5.16235	5.04786	4.93770	4.83167	4.72956
17	6.20641	6.04716	5.89472	5.74870	5.60878	5.47461	5.34589	5.22233	5.10368	4.98966	4.88006	4.77463
18	6.29381	6.12797	5.96945	5.81785	5.67277	5.53385	5.40075	5.27316	5.15078	5.03333	4.92055	4.81219
19	6.37014	6.19823	6.03416	5.87746	5.72770	5.58449	5.44745	5.31624	5.19053	5.07003	4.95443	4.84350
20	6.43680	6.25933	6.09018	5.92884	5.77485	5.62777	5.48719	5.35275	5.22408	5.10086	4.98279	4.86958
21	6.49502	6.31246	6.13868	5.97314	5.81532	5.66476	5.52101	5.38368	5.25239	5.12677	5.00652	4.89132
22	6.54587	6.35866	6.18068	6.01133	5.85006	5.69637	5.54980	5.40990	5.27628	5.14855	5.02638	4.90943
23	6.59028	6.39884	6.21704	6.04425	5.87988	5.72340	5.57430	5.43212	5.29644	5.16685	5.04299	4.92453
24	6.62907	6.43377	6.24852	6.07263	5.90548	5.74649	5.59515	5.45095	5.31345	5.18223	5.05690	4.93710
25	6.66294	6.46415	6.27577	6.09709	5.92745	5.76623	5.61289	5.46691	5.32780	5.19515	5.06853	4.94759
26	6.69252	6.49056	6.29937	6.11818	5.94631	5.78311	5.62799	5.48043	5.33992	5.20601	5.07827	4.95632
27	6.71836	6.51353	6.31980	6.13636	5.96250	5.79753	5.64084	5.49189	5.35014	5.21513	5.08642	4.96360
28	6.74093	6.53351	6.33749	6.15204	5.97639	5.80985	5.65178	5.50160	5.35877	5.22280	5.09324	4.96967
29	6.76064	6.55088	6.35281	6.16555	5.98832	5.82039	5.66109	5.50983	5.36605	5.22924	5.09894	4.97472
30	6.77785	6.56598	6.36607	6.17720	5.99856	5.82939	5.66901	5.51681	5.37219	5.23466	5.10372	4.97894
31	6.79288	6.57911	6.37755	6.18724	6.00734	5.83709	5.67576	5.52272	5.37738	5.23921	5.10771	4.98245
32	6.80601	6.59053	6.38749	6.19590	6.01489	5.84366	5.68150	5.52773	5.38175	5.24303	5.11106	4.98537
33	6.81747	6.60046	6.39609	6.20336	6.02136	5.84928	5.68638	5.53197	5.38545	5.24625	5.11386	4.98781
34	6.82749	6.60910	6.40354	6.20979	6.02692	5.85409	5.69054	5.53557	5.38856	5.24895	5.11620	4.98984
35	6.83623	6.61661	6.40999	6.21534	6.03169	5.85820	5.69407	5.53862	5.39119	5.25122	5.11816	4.99154
36	6.84387	6.62314	6.41558	6.22012	6.03579	5.86171	5.69708	5.54120	5.39341	5.25312	5.11980	4.99295
37	6.85054	6.62881	6.42041	6.22424	6.03930	5.86471	5.69965	5.54339	5.39528	5.25472	5.12117	4.99412
38	6.85637	6.63375	6.42460	6.22779	6.04232	5.86727	5.70183	5.54525	5.39686	5.25607	5.12232	4.99510
39	6.86146	6.63805	6.42823	6.23086	6.04491	5.86946	5.70368	5.54682	5.39820	5.25720	5.12328	4.99592
40	6.86590	6.64178	6.43136	6.23350	6.04713	5.87133	5.70526	5.54815	5.39932	5.25815	5.12408	4.99660
41	6.86978	6.64502	6.43408	6.23577	6.04904	5.87294	5.70660	5.54928	5.40027	5.25895	5.12475	4.99717
42	6.87317	6.64785	6.43643	6.23774	6.05068	5.87430	5.70775	5.55024	5.40107	5.25962	5.12532	4.99764
43	6.87613	6.65030	6.43847	6.23943	6.05208	5.87547	5.70872	5.55105	5.40175	5.26019	5.12579	4.99803
44	6.87872	6.65244	6.44024	6.24089	6.05329	5.87647	5.70955	5.55174	5.40232	5.26066	5.12618	4.99836
45	6.88098	6.65429	6.44176	6.24214	6.05433	5.87733	5.71026	5.55232	5.40280	5.26106	5.12651	4.99863
46	6.88295	6.65591	6.44308	6.24323	6.05522	5.87806	5.71086	5.55281	5.40321	5.26140	5.12679	4.99886
47	6.88467	6.65731	6.44423	6.24416	6.05598	5.87868	5.71137	5.55323	5.40355	5.26168	5.12702	4.99905
48	6.88618	6.65853	6.44522	6.24497	6.05664	5.87922	5.71180	5.55359	5.40384	5.26191	5.12721	4.99921
49	6.88749	6.65959	6.44608	6.24566	6.05720	5.87967	5.71217	5.55389	5.40409	5.26211	5.12738	4.99934
50	6.88864	6.66051	6.44682	6.24626	6.05768	5.88006	5.71249	5.55414	5.40429	5.26228	5.12751	4.99945
51	6.88964	6.66132	6.44746	6.24678	6.05809	5.88039	5.71275	5.55436	5.40447	5.26242	5.12762	4.99954
52	6.89052	6.66201	6.44802	6.24722	6.05845	5.88068	5.71298	5.55454	5.40461	5.26254	5.12772	4.99962
53	6.89128	6.66262	6.44850	6.24760	6.05876	5.88092	5.71318	5.55469	5.40474	5.26264	5.12780	4.99968
54	6.89195	6.66315	6.44892	6.24793	6.05902	5.88113	5.71334	5.55483	5.40484	5.26272	5.12786	4.99974
55	6.89253	6.66361	6.44928	6.24822	6.05924	5.88131	5.71348	5.55494	5.40493	5.26279	5.12792	4.99978
56	6.89304	6.66401	6.44959	6.24846	6.05944	5.88146	5.71360	5.55503	5.40500	5.26285	5.12797	4.99982
57	6.89348	6.66435	6.44987	6.24868	6.05960	5.88159	5.71370	5.55511	5.40507	5.26290	5.12801	4.99985
58	6.89387	6.66466	6.45010	6.24886	6.05974	5.88170	5.71379	5.55518	5.40512	5.26294	5.12804	4.99987
59	6.89421	6.66492	6.45030	6.24902	6.05987	5.88180	5.71386	5.55524	5.40516	5.26297	5.12807	4.99989
60	6.89451	6.66515	6.45048	6.24915	6.05997	5.88188	5.71393	5.55529	5.40520	5.26300	5.12809	4.99991

Period	14.5%	15%	15.5%	16%	16.5%	17%	17.5%	18%	18.5%	19%	19.5%	20%
61	6.89477	6.66534	6.45063	6.24927	6.06006	5.88195	5.71398	5.55533	5.40523	5.26303	5.12811	4.99993
62	6.89499	6.66552	6.45076	6.24937	6.06014	5.88200	5.71403	5.55536	5.40526	5.26305	5.12812	4.99994
63	6.89519	6.66567	6.45088	6.24946	6.06020	5.88206	5.71406	5.55539	5.40528	5.26307	5.12814	4.99995
64	6.89536	6.66580	6.45098	6.24953	6.06026	5.88210	5.71410	5.55542	5.40530	5.26308	5.12815	4.99995
65	6.89551	6.66591	6.45106	6.24960	6.06031	5.88214	5.71413	5.55544	5.40532	5.26309	5.12816	4.99996
66	6.89565	6.66601	6.45114	6.24965	6.06035	5.88217	5.71415	5.55546	5.40533	5.26310	5.12816	4.99997
67	6.89576	6.66609	6.45120	6.24970	6.06039	5.88219	5.71417	5.55547	5.40534	5.26311	5.12817	4.99997
68	6.89586	6.66617	6.45125	6.24974	6.06042	5.88222	5.71419	5.55548	5.40535	5.26312	5.12818	4.99998
69	6.89595	6.66623	6.45130	6.24978	6.06045	5.88224	5.71420	5.55549	5.40536	5.26313	5.12818	4.99998
70	6.89602	6.66629	6.45134	6.24981	6.06047	5.88225	5.71421	5.55550	5.40537	5.26313	5.12819	4.99999
71	6.89609	6.66634	6.45138	6.24983	6.06049	5.88227	5.71422	5.55551	5.40537	5.26314	5.12819	4.99999
72	6.89615	6.66638	6.45141	6.24986	6.06050	5.88228	5.71423	5.55552	5.40538	5.26314	5.12819	4.99999
73	6.89620	6.66642	6.45144	6.24988	6.06052	5.88229	5.71424	5.55552	5.40538	5.26314	5.12819	4.99999
74	6.89624	6.66645	6.45146	6.24989	6.06053	5.88230	5.71425	5.55553	5.40539	5.26314	5.12820	4.99999
75	6.89628	6.66648	6.45148	6.24991	6.06054	5.88231	5.71425	5.55553	5.40539	5.26315	5.12820	4.99999
76	6.89632	6.66650	6.45150	6.24992	6.06055	5.88231	5.71426	5.55554	5.40539	5.26315	5.12820	5.00000
77	6.89635	6.66653	6.45151	6.24993	6.06056	5.88232	5.71426	5.55554	5.40539	5.26315	5.12820	5.00000
78	6.89637	6.66654	6.45153	6.24994	6.06057	5.88232	5.71427	5.55554	5.40540	5.26315	5.12820	5.00000
79	6.89640	6.66656	6.45154	6.24995	6.06057	5.88233	5.71427	5.55554	5.40540	5.26315	5.12820	5.00000
80	6.89642	6.66657	6.45155	6.24996	6.06058	5.88233	5.71427	5.55555	5.40540	5.26315	5.12820	5.00000
81	6.89643	6.66659	6.45156	6.24996	6.06058	5.88234	5.71427	5.55555	5.40540	5.26315	5.12820	5.00000
82	6.89645	6.66660	6.45157	6.24997	6.06058	5.88234	5.71428	5.55555	5.40540	5.26315	5.12820	5.00000
83	6.89646	6.66661	6.45157	6.24997	6.06059	5.88234	5.71428	5.55555	5.40540	5.26316	5.12820	5.00000
84	6.89647	6.66661	6.45158	6.24998	6.06059	5.88234	5.71428	5.55555	5.40540	5.26316	5.12820	5.00000
85	6.89648	6.66662	6.45158	6.24998	6.06059	5.88234	5.71428	5.55555	5.40540	5.26316	5.12820	5.00000
86	6.89649	6.66663	6.45159	6.24998	6.06059	5.88234	5.71428	5.55555	5.40540	5.26316	5.12820	5.00000
87	6.89650	6.66663	6.45159	6.24998	6.06060	5.88235	5.71428	5.55555	5.40540	5.26316	5.12820	5.00000
88	6.89651	6.66664	6.45159	6.24999	6.06060	5.88235	5.71428	5.55555	5.40540	5.26316	5.12820	5.00000
89	6.89651	6.66664	6.45160	6.24999	6.06060	5.88235	5.71428	5.55555	5.40540	5.26316	5.12820	5.00000
90	6.89652	6.66664	6.45160	6.24999	6.06060	5.88235	5.71428	5.55555	5.40540	5.26316	5.12820	5.00000
91	6.89652	6.66665	6.45160	6.24999	6.06060	5.88235	5.71428	5.55555	5.40540	5.26316	5.12820	5.00000
92	6.89652	6.66665	6.45160	6.24999	6.06060	5.88235	5.71428	5.55555	5.40540	5.26316	5.12820	5.00000
93	6.89653	6.66665	6.45160	6.24999	6.06060	5.88235	5.71428	5.55555	5.40540	5.26316	5.12820	5.00000
94	6.89653	6.66665	6.45160	6.24999	6.06060	5.88235	5.71428	5.55555	5.40540	5.26316	5.12820	5.00000
95	6.89653	6.66666	6.45161	6.25000	6.06060	5.88235	5.71428	5.55555	5.40540	5.26316	5.12820	5.00000
96	6.89654	6.66666	6.45161	6.25000	6.06060	5.88235	5.71428	5.55555	5.40540	5.26316	5.12820	5.00000
97	6.89654	6.66666	6.45161	6.25000	6.06060	5.88235	5.71428	5.55556	5.40541	5.26316	5.12820	5.00000
98	6.89654	6.66666	6.45161	6.25000	6.06060	5.88235	5.71428	5.55556	5.40541	5.26316	5.12820	5.00000
99	6.89654	6.66666	6.45161	6.25000	6.06060	5.88235	5.71429	5.55556	5.40541	5.26316	5.12821	5.00000
100	6.89654	6.66666	6.45161	6.25000	6.06060	5.88235	5.71429	5.55556	5.40541	5.26316	5.12821	5.00000
101	6.89654	6.66666	6.45161	6.25000	6.06060	5.88235	5.71429	5.55556	5.40541	5.26316	5.12821	5.00000
102	6.89654	6.66666	6.45161	6.25000	6.06061	5.88235	5.71429	5.55556	5.40541	5.26316	5.12821	5.00000
103	6.89655	6.66666	6.45161	6.25000	6.06061	5.88235	5.71429	5.55556	5.40541	5.26316	5.12821	5.00000
104	6.89655	6.66666	6.45161	6.25000	6.06061	5.88235	5.71429	5.55556	5.40541	5.26316	5.12821	5.00000
105	6.89655	6.66666	6.45161	6.25000	6.06061	5.88235	5.71429	5.55556	5.40541	5.26316	5.12821	5.00000
106	6.89655	6.66666	6.45161	6.25000	6.06061	5.88235	5.71429	5.55556	5.40541	5.26316	5.12821	5.00000
107	6.89655	6.66666	6.45161	6.25000	6.06061	5.88235	5.71429	5.55556	5.40541	5.26316	5.12821	5.00000
108	6.89655	6.66666	6.45161	6.25000	6.06061	5.88235	5.71429	5.55556	5.40541	5.26316	5.12821	5.00000
109	6.89655	6.66667	6.45161	6.25000	6.06061	5.88235	5.71429	5.55556	5.40541	5.26316	5.12821	5.00000
110	6.89655	6.66667	6.45161	6.25000	6.06061	5.88235	5.71429	5.55556	5.40541	5.26316		5.00000
111	6.89655	6.66667	6.45161	6.25000	6.06061	5.88235	5.71429	5.55556	5.40541	5.26316	5.12821	5.00000
112	6.89655	6.66667	6.45161	6.25000	6.06061	5.88235	5.71429	5.55556	5.40541	5.26316	5.12821	5.00000
113	6.89655	6.66667	6.45161	6.25000	6.06061	5.88235	5.71429	5.55556	5.40541	5.26316	5.12821	5.00000
114	6.89655	6.66667	6.45161	6.25000	6.06061	5.88235	5.71429	5.55556	5.40541	5.26316	5.12821	5.00000
115	6.89655	6.66667	6.45161	6.25000	6.06061	5.88235	5.71429	5.55556	5.40541	5.26316	5.12821	5.00000
116	6.89655	6.66667	6.45161	6.25000	6.06061	5.88235	5.71429	5.55556	5.40541	5.26316	5.12821	5.00000
117	6.89655	6.66667	6.45161	6.25000	6.06061	5.88235	5.71429	5.55556	5.40541	5.26316	5.12821	5.00000
118	6.89655	6.66667	6.45161	6.25000	6.06061	5.88235	5.71429	5.55556	5.40541	5.26316	5.12821	5.00000
119	6.89655	6.66667	6.45161	6.25000	6.06061	5.88235	5.71429	5.55556	5.40541	5.26316	5.12821	5.00000
120	6.89655	6.66667	6.45161	6.25000	6.06061	5.88235	5.71429	5.55556	5.40541	5.26316	5.12821	5.00000

Index